The Godwins
and
the Shelleys

WILLIAM ST CLAIR

The Godwins and the Shelleys

The biography of a family

W · W · NORTON & COMPANY · *NEW YORK* · *LONDON*

Library of Congress Cataloging-in-Publication Data

St. Clair, William.
　The Godwins and the Shelleys: the biography of a family / William
St. Clair.
　　p.　cm.
　Bibliography: p.
　Includes index.
　　1. Godwin, William, 1756–1836—Biography—Family.
2. Wollstonecraft, Mary, 1759–1797—Biography—Family. 3. Shelley,
Percy Bysshe, 1792–1822—Biography—Family. 4. Shelley, Mary
Wollstonecraft, 1797–1851—Biography—Family. 5. Authors.
English—18th century—Biography. 6. Authors, English—19th
century—Biography. 7. Godwin family. 8. Shelley family.
　I. Title.
PR4723.S7　1989
828'.609—dc20
　[B]　　　　　　　　　　89-32868

ISBN 0-393-02783-X

W. W. Norton & Company, Inc., 500 Fifth Avenue, New York, N.Y. 10110
W. W. Norton & Company Ltd., 37 Great Russell Street, London WC1B 3NU

1 2 3 4 5 6 7 8 9 0

Contents

CONTENTS

Illustrations

CHARTS

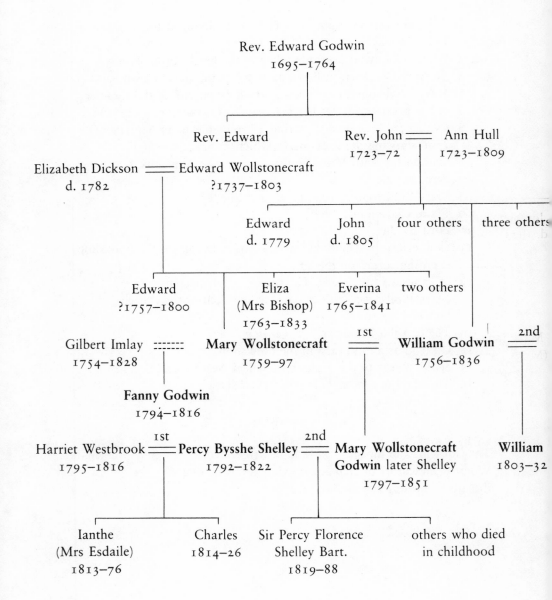

Rev. Edward Godwin
1695–1764

Rev. Edward

Rev. John ══ Ann Hull
1723–72   1723–1809

Elizabeth Dickson ══ Edward Wollstonecraft
d. 1782   ?1737–1803

Edward   John   four others   three others
d. 1779   d. 1805

Edward   Eliza   Everina   two others
?1757–1800   (Mrs Bishop) 1765–1841
                            1763–1833
                                            1st   2nd
Gilbert Imlay ┄┄┄┄┄ Mary Wollstonecraft ══ William Godwin ══
1754–1828   1759–97   1756–1836

Fanny Godwin
1794–1816

                    1st   2nd
Harriet Westbrook ══ Percy Bysshe Shelley ══ Mary Wollstonecraft   William
1795–1816   1792–1822   Godwin later Shelley   1803–32
                                                   1797–1851

Ianthe   Charles   Sir Percy Florence   others who died
(Mrs Esdaile)   1814–26   Shelley Bart.   in childhood
1813–76   1819–88

The Godwins and the Shelleys

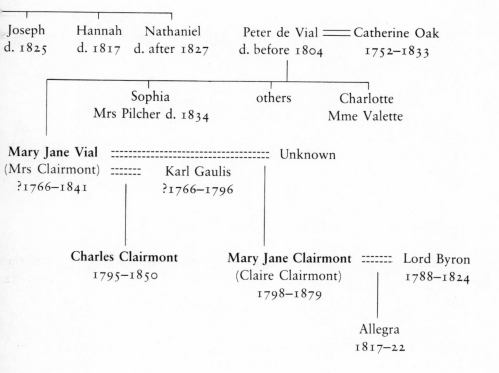

Joseph
d. 1825

Hannah
d. 1817

Nathaniel
d. after 1827

Peter de Vial ══ Catherine Oak
d. before 1804   1752–1833

Sophia
Mrs Pilcher d. 1834

others

Charlotte
Mme Valette

Mary Jane Vial
(Mrs Clairmont)
?1766–1841

Karl Gaulis
?1766–1796

Unknown

Charles Clairmont
1795–1850

Mary Jane Clairmont
(Claire Clairmont)
1798–1879

Lord Byron
1788–1824

Allegra
1817–22

Preface

Most lives follow a pattern of rise and fall. For William Godwin there was not one peak but two. At a time when his achievements had been largely forgotten and he seemed to be far down the road to final decline, the young Percy Bysshe Shelley burst into his life, claimed to be the heir to his ideas, ran off with his daughters, and tied the whole Godwin family inextricably to his own frantic career. This book is not therefore a biography of one man alone, but an account of two generations whose influence on each other was intense. Although for convenience I have called them the Godwins and the Shelleys, Mary Wollstonecraft and her daughter Mary Wollstonecraft Godwin, who took their husbands' names, are of equal importance.

Godwin's first biographer said he wished that more papers had been destroyed, and his successors know how he felt. The materials are vast, and their number continues to grow as scattered documents find their way into libraries. Fortunately a great deal is now available in print. Pollin's *Godwin Bibliography* of 1967, which lists over three thousand items, is an excellent guide, as is Janet M. Todd's *Annotated Bibliography of Mary Wollstonecraft*, 1976. Almost every sentence written by Shelley, Mary Shelley, Byron and Coleridge has been edited and printed, although I have been able to add a few items of interest which were previously unknown. The main printed books which I have used are referred to in the Notes.

The prime source for all the lives remains the Abinger archive of manuscripts now in the Bodleian Libary. This consists of Godwin's papers together with those of Wollstonecraft, Shelley, Mary Shelley and others. They passed by inheritance to Sir Percy Florence Shelley and other papers have been bought. Apart from the documents which have been edited for the collections of letters and journals they remain in an unordered state and are only partially catalogued. A microfilm copy was made in 1948 but many of the frames are illegible, and there are documents on the film which are no longer in the collection and *vice versa*. New portions of the archive are still coming to light including a substantial cache which Lord Abinger permitted me to add in 1982.

Civil servants know that the junior official who writes the first draft can set the agenda for the whole subsequent discussion. Writers who have relied on the nineteenth-century biographies as sources for documents have tended to slip into their assumptions and interpretations. In an attempt to free myself from this icy chain of custom, I have studied the whole archive anew, along with all the other manuscript evidence that I know of in libraries in this country and elsewhere. Much of what I use and quote, particularly about the earlier period, is therefore new, although I have tried to avoid exaggerating the importance of documents just because they are unpublished.

Any archive, however large, is at best only a fragment of what once existed, and it may not be representative of the lives to which it relates. With the Abinger papers a further judgement is needed. In the nineteenth century some documents were burned and others were chopped with scissors because they caused embarrassment according to the standards of the time or stood in the way of the image of the family which was then in favour. The archaeologist who sinks his trenches and sieves the soil on this site needs to remember that it has been dug before and that the chronological layers have been disturbed. He must be on special lookout for left-overs from earlier digs and other clues to what has been overlooked or destroyed. Using this approach I have been fortunate in discovering rich biographical evidence so well hidden that it escaped the eyes of earlier diggers. Other materials which predate the destruction or which strayed to safety from the main collection have been found elsewhere. To help in judging the nature and extent of the distortions I have been able to make use of the correspondence of Dowden, Rossetti, Garnett and others who took part in the first explorations and who – in Garnett's case – actively helped to spoil the site by advising on what should be destroyed and what should be kept.

In offering source references I have concentrated on the manuscript references and on explaining points which are new or which raise special problems of interpretation. At the request of the Bodleian authorities, I give the present piece numbers of the Abinger manuscripts without which it would be almost impossible to locate them. Even if the collection is later catalogued, these will still be retained as a finding guide. In a few places I refer to copies of printed books held in private collections including my own. These are books which have not been found in the major libraries and whose existence has not previously been recorded.

Most of the illustrations which appear at the head of each chapter are taken from one of M. J. Godwin and Company's books, Eliza Fenwick's *Lessons for Children, or Rudiments of Good Manners, Morals, and*

Humanity. This collection of stories was published in English and in French in a number of editions from 1809 onwards. The pictures I have used come from the 1823 edition. The name of the engraver is unfortunately not recorded.

The other chapter head illustrations are taken from the following contemporary works: Chapters 1 and 35, *A History of British Birds, the figures engraved on wood by T. Bewick, 1809*; Chapters 3, 5, 23, 26, 36, *Select Fables, with cuts, designed and engraved by Thomas and John Bewick and others*, Newcastle, 1820; Chapters 6 and 18, George Colman, *Broad Grins*, 1812, engraver unknown; Chapters 7, 9, 11, 25, William Hone, *Facetiae and Miscellanies*, 1827, which is made up from political pamphlets of earlier years, engraver George Cruikshank; Chapters 10, 12, 13, *1800 Woodcuts by Thomas Bewick and His School*, 1962; Chapters 14, 17, 24, Appendix 2 and Bibliography, *Blossoms of Morality*, 1796, engraver John Thomas Bewick; Chapter 27, *Religious Courtship or Discourses on the Choice of Husbands and Wives*, n.d., c. 1830, drawn by W. M. Craig, engraved by W. Swift; Appendix 1, *The Whole of Aristotle's Works Complete*, 1782; Appendix 3, *A Cabinet of Useful Arts and Manufactures*, 1831.

I should like to record my warm thanks to Lord Abinger for allowing me unrestricted access to the archive, for giving me permission to quote, and for much help in other ways. I am deeply grateful to the Warden and Fellows of All Souls College, Oxford, for awarding me a Visiting Fellowship which enabled me to undertake the necessary research and to HM Treasury for giving me leave of absence. A special word of thanks is also due to the Trustees of the Henry E. Huntington Library for enabling me to study their extensive collections; and to the Carl H. Pforzheimer Foundation, now part of the New York Public Library, for giving me access to a substantial proportion of their relevant holdings and for much other help.

Among the friends, colleagues, and strangers who have helped me while the book was being prepared, I should like to record my thanks to Carlene Adamson, Lawrence Airey, John Anderson, Bruce Barker-Benfield, Mary Batten, Betty Bennett, Margaret Bent, G. E. Bentley Jnr, Isaiah Berlin, Julia Briggs, Marilyn Butler, Frances Butlin, Mary Clapinson, the late Irvin Ehrenpreis, Paula Feldman, Doucet Fischer, Peter France, Ian Fraser, Kenneth Garlick, Dawn Goring, Kenneth Graham, Mihai Handrea, William Hodges, Richard Holmes, Gary Kelly, Louisa Lane Fox, Rosalie Mander, Ruth Mortimer, Eugene Murray, Rodney Needham, the late Peter Opie, Morton Paley, Mark Philp, Louise Pleydell-Bouverie, N. M.

Plumley, Dennis Porter, Donald Reiman, Anne Robinson, Deborah Rogers, David St Clair, John St Clair, Diana Scott-Kilvert, Michael Scrivener, John Simmonds, Margaret Smith, Richard Smith, Jon Stallworthy, the late David Stocking, Marion Stocking, Julia Strout, Emily Sunstein, Janet Todd, Steven Tomlinson, and the late Robert Yampolsky.

Among the institutions who have given access, supplied copies, given permission to quote or reproduce, answered questions, or helped in other ways, I should like to note my thanks to the Andover Harvard Theological Library, Bodleian Library, Boston University Library, Bristol Record Office, British Library, Brotherton Library University of Leeds, Cambridge University Library, Camden Public Library, Codrington Library, Columbia University Library, Library of Congress, Coward Trust, Dove Cottage, Duke University Library, Exeter Record Office, Folger Library, Genealogical Society, Guildhall Library, Haddington Library, Harvard University Library, Humanities Research Center University of Texas, Keats House Hampstead, Keats House Rome, Keele University Library, Knox College Library, University of Liverpool Library, London Library, University College London Library, London Record Office, Massachusetts Historical Society, Pierpoint Morgan Library, National Library of Scotland, National Portrait Gallery, New York Public Library, Newstead Abbey, Osborne Collection Toronto, Princeton University Library, Public Record Office, Royal Assurance, Royal Literary Fund, Smith College Library, Victoria and Albert Museum Library, University of Virginia Library, Walker Art Gallery, and Yale University Library.

I should like to thank my friends at Faber, Will Sulkin, Jane Robertson, and Ron Costley; the copy editor, Alison Truefitt, the proof-reader, Bryan Abraham, and the indexer Hilary Bird.

W St C
September 1988

The Godwins
and
the Shelleys

CHAPTER I

Life and Death

Like the bittern, whose dismal boom was formerly heard all over England, an older way of life persisted among the eastern wetlands long after it had died out elsewhere. Despite all human efforts, the drained fields were continually having to be abandoned back to the water, to the sedge, and to the birds. Life was a relentless struggle against the encroaching fog and damp, and there was no refuge from rheumatic illness, from depression or from despair.

In Wisbech in the remote Cambridgeshire Fens, where William Godwin was born on 3 March 1756, the mortality rate matched the worst in England. Four brothers and sisters already lay in the chapel burial ground in Deadman's Lane, and William was expected soon to follow for he was sickly throughout his infancy. A further six were to be born after him, but of a total of thirteen, only six survived into adult life and only five into middle age. During his first two years the baby was sent to a wet nurse – 'suckled by a hireling' he wrote resentfully later – and he was inclined to blame his parents for worsening their children's chances by this humiliating neglect. But there was no choice. His father, the Minister of the Wisbech Independent Chapel, took in paying pupils and the cottage was already overcrowded. His mother was so preoccupied with pregnancy that she had no strength for her babies, although by sending them away she was denied the respites which husbands and nature traditionally allowed to nursing mothers. William was brought up by a cousin of his

The Bittern, from Bewick's *British Birds*

father, Miss Godwin, who helped him through the colds and the fevers, the measles, the ringing in the ears, and the numerous unidentified illnesses which struck frequently during his childhood.

The Reverend John Godwin was himself the son of a dissenting minister, the Reverend Edward Godwin, for forty-two years pastor of the parish of Little St Helens in the City of London, a friend of Isaac Watts and Philip Doddridge. Edward Godwin had come originally from Newbury in Berkshire where his father had served as mayor, and his grandson was later to trace remoter ancestors through the baptismal records back to a phonetic Cudbert Godden of 1578. William Godwin liked to think of himself as related to the innumerable Godwins and Goodwins to be found in every period of English history since the time of Edward the Confessor. It was a name more magnificent than Caesar, de Courcis, or Plantagenet, he noted with wry amusement in a fragment of autobiography, for it was derived from the ancient northern deity Goden, otherwise known as Odin or Woden.

On his mother's side there were no eponymous heathen gods but the Hulls too, William remembered proudly, were a distinguished family, landed gentry in County Durham, rich enough to keep their own carriage. Richard Hull, his grandfather, was one of six sons, of whom the eldest was drunk for forty years and the other four died at sea. He had also been sent to sea in his youth and settled in Wisbech where he owned a number of vessels engaged in the coasting and Baltic trade. He married a local girl called Swalwell and their daughter Ann married John Godwin in 1748, the year of his appointment as minister in Wisbech. William's parents were both aged thirty-three when he was born.

For all their gentle ancestors, the family was now as poor as their neighbours, and the Christianity which they dispensed to their suffering congregation matched the joyless life of the Fens. Belief in a capricious, obdurate, wrathful God demanding abject resignation from his despised creatures provided some rationale for their miseries. Advice to concentrate on the next life offered some comfort for the hopelessness of this. But although, like the opiates which the Fenlanders also consumed in undue quantities, John Godwin's religion relieved pains and depressions only to prolong them, even in its last retreats the old tradition was slowly having to give way,

In 1758 he was involved in a dispute with his congregation, many of whom were rejecting his seventeenth-century despair and joining the modern Unitarians, and he moved with his family to a new appointment at Debenham, a market town in Suffolk. Although William was only two at the time, he was later able to remember the white rails of the coach, the family cat refusing to be held on his mother's lap, and other inconsequential details of the journey which have the ring of authenticity. But Debenham was no happier. There was again a dispute with the congregation, and two years later the Godwins moved again, this time to Guestwick, sixteen miles north of Norwich, where John Godwin was to remain with his swelling family until his death twelve years later.

The Independent meeting house at Guestwick, which was to be the centre of William Godwin's life throughout his childhood, still stands, although now ruinous and much altered in appearance. Set back from the road on the edge of the village, its studied plainness confronts and challenges the tall gothic of the parish church from which it is separated by a single field. Guestwick itself was one of the smallest villages in Norfolk – there was no street but only a handful of cottages thinly scattered – and it was surrounded by oak forest which added to the isolation. The Independents had established a congregation in this remote spot in 1652 during the period of the Commonwealth in hopes of being left to practise their simple faith undisturbed. A century later they still kept themselves conspicuously apart, heirs and custodians of a great tradition – as they saw it – of political and religious liberty. They were proud to remember Oliver Cromwell, the greatest Independent of them all, and they still debated why England's only experiment in republican liberty had ended in failure and disaster. A carved oak chair, known as Cromwell's chair, was preserved in the meeting house at Guestwick – taken, it was believed, from Irmingland Hall where the Lord Protector had stayed with his son-in-law General Fleetwood; and no doubt the young William Godwin also sat on it from time to time in a village which offered few other amusements.

The parish church across the field, like many in East Anglia, bore the mutilations inflicted by Cromwell's soldiers during their brief years of power, a perpetual reminder of puritan attempts to impose their minority beliefs by force. By the time John Godwin took up his position in 1760 the seventeenth-century enmities had receded, and he was always on good terms with his established colleague across the way. But tolerance and convergence had brought new problems. The pay for dissenting ministers was low and tenure insecure. A steady stream of despised moderates defected to the more comfortable livings of the Church of England, including one of John Godwin's recent predecessors at Guestwick.[1] On the other side the rise of the Methodists attracted away many of their natural supporters. John Godwin's elder brother, the Reverend Edward

Godwin joined the Whitefield Methodists, and for a few years he fervently proselytized in the West of England among scenes of hysteria. Uncle Edward, Godwin was told cryptically, had previously 'run a certain career of wildness and dissipation', and the minutes of his chapel mention persisting doubts among his colleagues whether Brother Godwin was 'sufficiently broken at our Saviour's feet'.[2] As the century progressed, the remaining congregations of the old tradition found themselves shrinking in numbers and torn by controversy as some opened their minds to new ideas and others sought security in ever more literal obedience to the old.

John Godwin, during his twelve years' occupancy, was credited with considerable success in keeping trouble from his parish. He spent his days on horseback visiting his scattered flock and he won respect and affection for his zeal and his care. He had, his son recalled, little taste for books or reading. His single Sunday sermon was hastily scribbled after tea on Saturday evening and he would seldom agree to preach outside his parish in the hearing of colleagues who might detect doctrinal error. He was, according to the opinion of his group, a wise and a good man, but it is hard now to recruit the historical imagination necessary to comprehend and sympathize with the view of the world to which he and his congregation clung with ever tighter tenacity.

He was, Godwin remembered, fussy over details, overconcerned about food and the appearance of his clothes, and the same qualities marked the literalism of his religion. He was a strict Calvinist, a believer in predestination, original sin, and divine retribution. Man, for him, was a spider hanging by a single thread over a fire. The Devil was everywhere, hiding in unexpected places, ready to pounce on an unwary man or child and ensure his eternal damnation. It was so easy to fall into sin. Laziness was a sin; profaning the Lord's day was a sin (William was scolded for picking up a cat on a Sunday); forgiving a sin too readily could be a sin.

His children were made to read the Bible – Godwin knew it all before he was eight – and martyrologies, books of sermons, *The Pilgrim's Progress*, and other improving literature, and with few exceptions, books on non-religious subjects were not permitted. The favourite was James Janeway's *A Token for Children, being an Exact Account of the Conversion, Holy and Exemplary Lives and Joyful Deaths of several young children*, a series of stories of children who attained grace by conforming to God's will and dying, usually of cancers and consumptions, at ages ranging from five to twelve. In the Preface Janeway warns his young readers that the Devil may catch them ('Do you dare to run up and down on the Lord's day?') and gives advice on how they can best avoid falling

4

into everlasting fire. He tells his readers to read his book one hundred times; to learn their catechisms; to pray and to weep. If they do so, they may succeed in dying like the children in the stories and 'begin everlasting sabbath' with hallelujahs on their lips. If not, they will go to the Devil; God will pour out his wrath upon them; and when they beg and pray in hellfire, He will not forgive them, but leave them to burn for ever. First published in 1676 and still being reprinted in the nineteenth century, Janeway's book was the main comfort offered to terrified dissenting children as they faced illness and death.

We may guess that the Godwin children were also encouraged to read the printed works of Uncle Edward, whose poems and sermons written especially for children included *The Death Bed, a poem containing the Joyful Death of a Believer and the Awful Death of an Unbeliever*;[3] and also the printed sermons of their grandfather Edward, including his address on the same inescapable theme.

This day, this hour, for aught you know, may be the last Opportunity of making your Peace with God . . . Make haste then out of your dangerous Estate as Lot did out of Sodom lest Fire and Brimstone overtake you . . . lay hold of the Horns of the Altar and Wrestle with your God till he gives you the Blessing . . . cry unto him with fervent Prayers and bitter Sighs and torrents of Tears.[4]

For lighter entertainment there could be reading from *The Grave* by the Scottish poet Robert Blair which also had a strong family connection. The manuscript had been sent to Godwin's grandfather by the author with a request for help in the editing and publishing.[5] It had become a best seller, and was to remain the favourite English poem on human mortality until superseded later in the century by Gray's *Elegy in a Country Churchyard* with which it was often bound up as a gift at Christmas.

At Guestwick as at Wisbech, death was always near. One brother went to sea and was duly drowned. Another brother, who was aged two at the time, was drowned in the horse pond.[6] On another occasion his brother Joseph was also believed to have drowned in the same pond but was found hiding in a garden shed. The Godwins refused on religious grounds to allow vaccination, and William was lucky to survive an attack of smallpox. 'It will be readily inferred', he wrote later in commenting on his parents' minimal precautions against accidents, 'that the persons about me were less solicitous for the health of my body than the health of my soul.' Parents often felt that they had to stiffen themselves against the inevitable loss of children and to hold back their love. Children too are said to need frightening stories and to enjoy them, and it may be that the Devil and his hellfire with which the Godwin children were unremittingly threatened were no more real or lasting in their effects than the traditional ogres of fairy tales. But it was only in the most traditional religious households that parents saw the terrorizing of their children as a solemn duty and welcomed each addition to the row of tiny burial mounds as a new release from the vale of tears.

William was a precocious child. He learned to read when he was three or four, though – another result perhaps of lack of parental interest – he could not write until he was ten. He had decided by the age of five that he too would be a dissenting minister like his father and grandfather, and he delivered sermons to his assembled family standing on his high chair in the kitchen wearing his great grandfather's legal wig. But his father disapproved and discouraged him. He feared that William's piety was motivated by a desire to show off. The boy who lay weeping and praying as Janeway recommended wanted passionately to die, but, as he himself was already aware, mainly in order to outshine in holy dying the children in the stories.

He hated to be thwarted, but was forever having to be snubbed and corrected. Whatever he did, the flames were uncomfortably near, but like any child he probably feared his parents' disapproval more. His father, he recalled, was always unkind and abrasive. His mother was warmer – she enjoyed an occasional joke and 'had an ambition to be thought the teller of a good story and an adept at hitting off a smart repartee'. But these things are relative. Some of the villagers complained that she dressed too brightly, implying that she behaved too frivolously for a minister's wife, and as the years passed, she too became increasingly engrossed in the need for a more wholehearted abasement before the God who had created her joyless and sinful world.

At the age of eight Godwin was sent with one of his brothers and another boy called Steele to the school at Hindolveston, two and a half miles from his home. As they walked each day through the woods and across the fields, he would practise his preaching. One day when he had reduced Steele to sobs of terror with his descriptions of damnation, he secretly borrowed the key of the meeting house and preached and prayed over him. Then, as he noted in a memorandum intended to record the most significant incidents of his youth, he allowed Steele to kiss him, although whether sacerdotally or sexually is not made explicit: it was an early taste of the subtle pleasures of priesthood. Akers, the Hindolveston schoolmaster, was also put in awe of his overbright and overconfident pupil. A man of limited education himself, he introduced Godwin to history and poetry which were voraciously read. He also taught him a fine, clear, uniquely distinctive handwriting which has earned him the enduring thanks of biographers.

When the boy was nine, Miss Godwin took him on a visit to Wisbech, Norwich, and King's Lynn, the first time he had been outside the wood-land villages of Guestwick and Hindolveston since he was five. Never having been in open countryside, he was astonished to see a dozen fields at once. At Wisbech they visited the cottage where he was born and met Mrs Ingrams who had nursed him as a baby – he haughtily refused to eat some raisins which she offered. At King's Lynn Miss Godwin took him to a theatre – where he saw *Venice Preserved* – and to a race meeting, both blatant acts of defiance against his father's religious views, and over the years she quietly undermined in other ways the cold Calvinism on which he was being brought up. In later life he remembered with gratitude how Mrs Sothren, as she became, had awakened his 'self-love' – meaning self-respect rather than vanity – and it was a quality he soon possessed in abundance.

Since none of the other brothers showed any sign of his intellectual ability and purposefulness of character, it was decided to educate him for the ministry. At the age of eleven he was accordingly sent to Norwich to live for three years as the sole pupil in the household of the Reverend Samuel Newton, the minister of the Old Meeting House in that town. Newton did not often take pupils but he was the best teacher in Norfolk. Godwin's father believed that a drastic remedy was needed to crush his son's arrogance – as he saw it – and instil a proper sense of religious humility, for Samuel Newton was a Sandemanian, a member of the strictest of the Calvinist sects in whose doctrines he was an acknowledged expert.

Calvin had put Christians on their guard against any delusion that good works alone could save an individual from hell. Sandeman had taken that logic a stage further by insisting that those who relied on faith were equal victims of false doctrine put about by the Devil in order to entrap them. 'God scorns to save or damn a man,' Godwin wrote in describing the Sandemanian creed, 'but according to the right or wrong judgement of his understanding.' It was important therefore, for this world and the next, that Christians should be correct in every detail of their belief, since any slippage or doubt could cause an immediate recategorization.

At Newton's house Godwin was conscientiously whipped for any suspicion of deviationism. He was subjected to incessant lectures about his stiff-necked arrogance, which he was to remember for the rest of his life. Once after a beating Newton gave him a halfpenny, an indication that even this stern indoctrinator felt occasionally that he had gone too far, but the treatment was unremitting. Newton told him that he was fortunate not to have died during one of his many childhood illnesses for he would assuredly have gone straight to hell. His teacher took a refined delight, Godwin recalled, in pointing out that most of the citizens of Norwich were Pharisees, dwelling lovingly on the details of the divine torture to which they were destined. As part of his training Godwin was assigned a servant to convert to Sandemanianism, but her chief contribution to his education was to tell him dirty stories.

On his return home to Guestwick at the age of fourteen, he worked for a while as the usher or assistant schoolmaster to Akers at his old school of Hindolveston nearby. Then in 1772 when his father fell ill, Godwin remembered being called to his bedside to hear him repeat in a quavering voice the hopeful verses of Isaac Watts, which had helped him through a hard and bitter life.

> When I can read my title clear
> To mansions in the skies,
> I'll bid farewell to every fear
> And wipe my weeping eyes.

John Godwin, his son noted with surprise, did not at the end find his faith as sustaining as he had expected, and took his leave of life with considerable reluctance. He was buried in the small cemetery beside the Guestwick meeting house where he had faithfully served for the previous twelve years.

For Mrs Godwin thirty-seven years of widowhood lay ahead but for Godwin a new life had already begun. Soon after his father's death his mother took him to London and enrolled him as a student at Dr Coward's dissenting academy of Hoxton, having tried unsuccessfully to get him into the better-known academy at Homerton. The minutes of the Coward Trust note the award to William Godwin of a bursary of £18 a year – no small amount, his father's stipend had been £60 – and on 20 September 1773, they record his arrival:

The following young persons, concerning whose Serious Disposition and Proficiency in Grammar and Learning the Trustees have received Satisfaction were admitted Divinity Students

> Nathaniel Philips
> George Smith
> James Marshall
> Willm. Godwin[7]

8

The next five years were devoted to intensive study. The academies of the dissenters, who were excluded by law from the ancient universities, easily excelled the desultory efforts of unreformed Oxford and Cambridge. Lectures started at six or seven in the morning and the work of each day was carefully prescribed. Vacations were brief and examinations tough. The emphasis of the teaching was on classics, theology, and philosophy, but Godwin appears to have acquired, besides Greek and Latin, usable quantities of French, Italian, German, and Hebrew. He read the ancient authors and many of the modern.

The tutors at Hoxton were very different men from the Reverend Samuel Newton. Far from living in the seventeenth century, they saw themselves as in the forefront looking forward to the nineteenth. Far from trying to inculcate doctrines by force and by repetition, the Reverend Abraham Rees and the Reverend Andrew Kippis encouraged debate and controversy. Godwin became known in the college for calm dedication and passionate argument. One summer he rose every day at five and went to bed at midnight, devoting every hour to exploring the great questions of theology and metaphysics. But Samuel Newton had built secure: all Godwin's studies reinforced the doctrines on which he had been brought up and he remained a convinced Sandemanian.

A few of the sermons which he delivered at the College have survived.[8] One, on the difference between foolhardiness and heroism, argues that only true religion can provide the confidence necessary for real courage, for 'how can we expect a man with no belief in an eternal world to risque his all on a single throw?' Not long afterwards he prepared a long sermon on the Christian duty of resignation, taking as his illustration the distress of Aaron whose two sons lit religious incense burners in a drunken prank and accidentally started a fire in which they both died. The comfort offered by Moses to his grieving brother is commended by the youthful preacher, 'Oh recollect the impious inexcusable inexpiable crime of blasphemy, sacrilege, and insult.' The Lord may pardon them, he advises, because it was a rash act of a moment, but Christians should never complain about poverty, disease, betrayal, deaths of children, or other disasters – since men are sinners, they have forfeited all claims to justice.

But Godwin was no bigot. An unshakeable intellectual honesty which was to persist to the end of his life was already one of his most marked and most attractive characteristics. 'Sequar veritatem ubicunque ducit,' he declared to himself with all the youthful solemnity of ungrammatical Latin, 'I will follow truth wherever she leads.' Conscious of being endowed with unusual powers, he felt a strong sense of duty to exploit them for the general benefit. When Dr Rees, the head of the College, a humane man, argued that the references to eternal sufferings in hell did not mean suffering for ever, but that ministers nevertheless had a duty to preach the erroneous view in order to maintain effective deterrents against sin, Godwin not only disputed the facts – eternal meant eternal – but condemned the dishonesty which Rees's attitude implied.

Godwin was successful at Hoxton, but not happy – 'cruelly crossed', he wrote later. A sense of loneliness, which was to grow deeper with the years and which is a pervasive theme in his novels, was already apparent. He recognized in himself a longing to be liked and a dread of being repulsed. His fellow students thought he was stiff and conceited, but shyness combined with religious earnestness often mix to give that impression. Much of his time was spent in writing, an occupation of a lonely boy. At the age of five, he wrote a poem 'The Wish', of which the first line was 'I will be a minister'. By the age of twelve, besides innumerable sermons, hymns, and religious paraphrases, he had composed a long poem called *Paradise Regained*, encompassing the whole life of Jesus, and there exist lists of titles of numerous other works completed during his teenage years, including half a dozen full-scale tragedies and comedies in verse, mainly on classical and religious themes.

Most have disappeared. However, when his daughter read the manuscripts after his death, she included some extracts among her remarks about her father's plays. There was much strength, she found, but no poetry – 'there is much of what is eloquent and much of what is puerile'. One example which she preserved was a long poem in the pastoral style written, when Godwin was nineteen, on the Age of Gold:

> No care but love the happy mortals knew,
> A love estranged to guilt and anxious fear,
> For every nymph was chaste and swain was true,
> And every heart from dark dissembling clear.[9]

In Godwin's Arcadia the shepherds and shepherdesses practised the moral standards of the Hoxton dissenting academy.

Godwin left Hoxton in May 1778 at the age of twenty-two, ready and fitted to enter the life of service for which his whole education had been a preparation. The testimonial given to him when he left praises his diligence, his proficiency, his religious temper, and his moral conduct, and recommends him as well qualified to enter the ministry.[10] He applied first to Christchurch in Hampshire and then to Ware in Hertfordshire where he spent a particularly lonely year in a temporary appointment. Then, after a brief interval in London, he was accepted for the permanent position as dissenting minister of the congregation at Stowmarket in Suffolk. During his student days he had been invited to preach at Yarmouth and at Lowestoft, and he was well known to his future colleagues in that part of the country both personally and as his father's son. He arrived at Stowmarket at the end of 1779.

The sickly child had grown into a young man of less than middle height, still somewhat frail in appearance – thin in face and body – but described as 'well-made'. His brow was high and straight and large blue eyes reinforced the immediate impression of unusual intelligence. His most striking feature was a long, large nose, which seemed almost to overhang his mouth and which added to his natural solemnity. As was the custom among dissenting ministers, his clothes were unrelieved black and he wore a large black hat; his fair hair was left long, frizzled at the sides and curled stiffly at the back.[11]

CHAPTER 2

The Young Minister

Within weeks of his arrival in Stowmarket, Godwin took a decision which was to redirect the course of his life. If Alexander the Great had not swum in the Cydnus river, he wrote later, if Shakespeare's mother had fallen from a ladder during her pregnancy, the whole subsequent history of the world would have been different. In illustrating his belief that every individual life is inescapably determined by a chain of earlier events, not necessarily important in themselves, he might equally have quoted his own experience as a young minister.

The occasion was a dispute over church doctrine. As the newly appointed minister, one of his first duties was to decide on his attitude to the ceremony of ordination on which there was at the time much controversy. Was the ancient custom of laying-on of hands, theologians debated, an essential feature of Christianity or should it be regarded rather as an unimportant accretion of purely symbolic significance? The Independents, in whose faith Godwin had been brought up, believed in general that every congregation was free to organize its worship as it wished in accordance with the presumed simplicity of the primitive church. His grandfather's friend, Isaac Watts, in a book to which a Hoxton student would naturally have turned for guidance, offered the opinion that once a minister's appointment has been approved by a congregation, he is a minister in all respects, entitled to administer the sacraments as well as to preach.

Other authorities, however, were of the belief that no minister could

Cousin James's Farmhouse, from *Lessons for Children*

legitimately administer the sacraments until he had been officially ordained, and that the right of decision lay with the other ministers in the locality who would perform the ordination ceremony. Godwin himself was sure that he had the right to celebrate communion, but he decided to follow the advice in Watts's book and to leave the final decision to the congregation. However – as appears from the earliest of his surviving letters – his diplomatic soundings threw up a difficult result.

Upon receiving the 1st invitation from the people here, I mentioned it [the wish to offer communion] cursorily to some of the principal communicants; & upon signifying my acceptance of their repeated invitation, put it to them seriously as a thing I wished to have determined. As the communicants here are very few, & chiefly of the lower class, contrary I acknowledge to my expectation, they consented.

What should he do now? Should he also consult the views of the neighbouring ministers?

I did not previously consult any of the neighbouring ministers, as . . . I took it for granted that most, particularly of the elder ones who had the most right to be consulted, but who of course would be most attached to established modes and forms, would not be forward to advise it. I was not sure that with the consent of the people I should not think it my duty to proceed (in any case); and therefore chose rather to do it without consulting them, than having consulted to be considered as flying in the face of their advice.[1]

It was a courageous act and the consequences were severe. The ministers of the county were horrified at the arrogance of their new colleague. The senior minister, the Reverend Thomas Harmer, who had been one of those who had signed the original letter of invitation, came to the conclusion after a visit that the unrepentant Godwin was far too independent in his thinking to be a satisfactory colleague. It was accordingly made clear to him that, without a change of attitude, he could not now expect to be legitimately ordained, a procedure usually regarded as a formality. If he persisted in defying the collective voice, Godwin could continue as the minister of Stowmarket, but his status would not be recognized beyond the parish boundaries. He could – and did – style himself the Reverend William Godwin but his colleagues studiously addressed him as plain Mr.

To those used to a more pragmatic view of institutions it may appear a less than vital issue on which to have forced so drastic a conclusion. But Godwin, with his knowledge of ecclesiastical history, could see a principle at stake. Who was to have the last word in such matters? The people or their paid officials? Was it not by a surrender on this point that control of the early church had been usurped by priests? To compromise would be to impugn the intellectual integrity on which – in the absence of scriptural authority – all claims to truth, he believed, ultimately had to rest. Besides, both Godwin and those who opposed him had been taught since earliest infancy that wrong choices in such matters could lead to everlasting damnation and it was important to get them right.

Godwin stayed on in isolation at Stowmarket for over two years and then in the spring of 1782 he resigned. He moved to London, probably on the advice of Andrew Kippis his tutor at Hoxton, to whom the quoted letter was addressed. One of his fellow students from Hoxton, James Marshall, who was to remain a lifelong friend, lent him money while he took stock of his position. There was talk of their both emigrating to the West Indies and Marshall paid a visit to St Vincent, but for some reason the plan was soon abandoned.[2] Godwin was still determined to enter the ministry, but besides having to overcome his failure at Stowmarket, he was now less certain of his own opinions.

When he was at Ware, his neighbouring colleague, the Reverend Joseph Fawcett had put into his hands a strange and disconcerting book, *Le Système de la Nature*, which was being secretly printed in Holland and elsewhere to escape the French authorities and surreptitiously passed from hand to hand. It was said to be by a 'M. Mirabaud' but is in fact the main work of the *philosophe* Baron d'Holbach whose famous house in the Rue Royale had offered good conversation and good dinner twice a week for three decades to the philosophers of France and of the world. D'Holbach was thought by many to be merely the hotel keeper for Diderot, Helvétius, Rousseau, Turgot, Condorcet, David Hume, Joseph Priestley, Adam Smith, Benjamin Franklin and the others who visited his salon, but in fact he himself wrote a good deal, all of it dangerously subversive of the France of King Louis.

At Hoxton Godwin had been taught to know his enemies and he learned how to answer their heretical arguments. But the author of *Le Système de la Nature* disavowed all religion. Man is a work of nature, he proclaimed, and is subject to the laws of nature. Instead of vainly looking outside the world for supernatural beings to bring him the happiness which he cannot find on earth, man should study nature, should learn her laws, and submit to her mandates. God is a meaningless term. Religion arose from men's primitive fears, which priests then exploited to enslave their minds.

To the young man who had from birth been threatened with eternal damnation by the Reverend John Godwin, the Reverend Samuel Newton and innumerable other reverends the thesis had a personal immediacy. Was the soi-disant Reverend William Godwin in danger of becoming an unwitting party to the same priestly conspiracy? Godwin studied his theology books and weighed the answers which they offered. He read other works of French philosophy including especially *De l'Esprit* by Helvétius whose publication in 1758 had led to the first attempts in France to suppress the *philosophes*. Frederick Norman, a man he met at Stowmarket, apparently possessed a small library of such books and was willing to spend long hours talking about the ideas they contained.

''Tis a sad Truth', the preacher had said at his grandfather's funeral, 'but confirmed by Scripture and Experience, that Mankind are a race of fallen, guilty, and lost Creatures, Children of Wrath, and of Disobedience, and Servants of Sin'[3] and Godwin would have agreed with him. Now, however, the Cromwellian puritan was suddenly confronted with the full blaze of the European Enlightenment.

Over the next ten years, until he reached his mid-thirties, Godwin's opinions were in turmoil as the new ideas battled with the old. By the time he reached Stowmarket he had modified the Sandemanian beliefs to which he had been educated by Samuel Newton, only to find himself wandering disconcertedly in the no man's land between the strict Christianity of his upbringing and the near agnosticism of the age of reason. At Stowmarket he became a deist, only to revert in 1782 to Socinianism, a branch of Christianity which in the eighteenth century often served as a staging post for Christians who wanted to retain some belief in divine revelation yet felt bound to reject traditional dogma.

At the end of 1782 Godwin applied for the post of minister at Beaconsfield in Buckinghamshire and he stayed there for seven months until July 1783. A year had passed since his expulsion – as he called it – from Stowmarket, and Beaconsfield was far from Suffolk; but he was again rejected. The sermons which he delivered during his unsuccessful probation contain much that would have gladdened and reassured dissenters of the old persuasion. We are all sinners, Godwin proclaims, and if I reject Christian teaching, 'I may consider my condemnation as sealed. I may say unto corruption, thou art my father, and to hell and the abyss, thou art my mother and my sister.'

But other passages would have been more worrying. Godwin treats the people of the Bible stories as fully historical figures from whose lives we can draw moral lessons, and the series is pointedly named *Sketches of History in Six Sermons*. In the printed version Jesus is not even accorded His customary initial capital, and the preacher tells his audience that their faith can be substantiated by 'calling it to the tribunal of sober reason'. To many Christians these were shocking notions verging on the blasphemous.

Calvin had ordered the burning alive of Servetus in 1553 for denying the divinity of Jesus (an example that Godwin was later to use to illustrate that morality cannot consist solely in having sincere motives irrespective of results), and two Englishmen went to the stake for the same offence as late as 1612. The abhorrence with which latter-day Calvinists of the Independent denomination, such as Godwin's father, regarded the heresy had been intensified by the recent defection of many of their members to unitarianism, 'rational dissent', and other modernizing versions allegedly based on reason. John Godwin had been obliged to move to Guestwick because his fierce unmodernized Calvinism was no longer tolerable to congregations of more liberal views. Twenty-five years later, his son's Socinianism went too far in the opposite direction for the confused dissenters of Beaconsfield.

Whatever the immediate cause of his failure, it was now clear that the young Godwin – for all his qualifications – was going to have great difficulty in finding a place in his chosen profession. He would have to look for other ways of earning his living. But, as he wrote in calm explanation to his bewildered mother, his own conscience was clear and his sense of purpose was firm:

With respect to my religious sentiments I have the firmest assurance and tranquillity. I have faithfully endeavoured to improve the faculties and opportunities God has given me, and I am perfectly easy about the consequences. No man can be sure that he is not mistaken, but I am sure that if I am so, the best of beings will forgive my error.[4]

He moved to London and began to look for literary work. He did not wholly abandon his hopes of the ministry for some years yet – he still called himself the Reverend William Godwin and gave his profession as dissenting minister in official documents – but his mind had turned to an entirely new project.

He decided to become a teacher. Having taken a lease on a large rented house in Epsom in Surrey, Godwin prepared to open a seminary for twelve pupils on 4 August 1783. A prospectus was published anonymously by Thomas Cadell, one of the leading booksellers of the time. Interested parents were invited to apply to the publisher if they wanted such basic information as the name of the proposed teacher, the level of fees or details of the curriculum, and it is unsurprising that insufficient pupils came forward. The plan had to be abandoned, with financial loss.

However, the *Account of the Seminary* as he entitled the prospectus, gives a wonderfully full indication of Godwin's opinions as he prepared to leave the ministry. More an essay on the theory of education than a practical proposal to establish a school, it illustrates how far his opinions had moved in the five years since he was first introduced to the French philosophers, and it already contains ideas which were later to feature in his more substantial works. He has already, for example, jettisoned the doctrines of original sin he was preaching at Beaconsfield a few months before. Children, he now believes, following the views of Locke, Helvétius, and Rousseau, come into the world not damned as Janeway had taught him, but pure and spotless, and it is the task of the educator to write the appropriate impressions on the clean white paper of their minds. History is the best way to teach human nature, along with literature, Greek and Latin, French and English. In careful phrases we can hear the pained memories of his own joyless, death-filled childhood now replaced by hope.

There is hardly a word about religion in the fifty-four pages. Education is the liberator of the human mind, and Godwin can already foresee the political changes that will occur when this is recognized. 'Government', he remarks, 'must always depend upon the opinion of the governed. Let the most oppressed people under heaven once change their mode of thinking and they are free.'

Deeply conscious of his unusual gifts and his great potential, he now saw his duty clearly. Brought up in one of the most backward peasant communities in England, he would become metropolitan and European. Educated in the superseded and static values of the early seventeenth century, he could share in the dynamic philosophical and scientific discoveries of the late eighteenth. Throwing off the ethics of servile abasement to a hateful God, he would teach independence and hope. Instead of theorizing about the tortures of the imaginary next world, he would do something about the present conditions in the real one from which such pessimistic doctrines drew their credibility. Rejected for the ministry of religion, Godwin would embrace the ministry of enlightenment.

CHAPTER 3

Grub Street

When Godwin arrived in London in May 1782 the area near St Paul's Cathedral was the centre of the English book trade as it had been for three hundred years and as it was to remain until the blitz of 1940. In St Paul's Churchyard and Paternoster Row successful booksellers lived in fine houses alongside their warehouses, while lesser men took lodgings above their shops or pursued their trade from stalls in the streets. Business was booming. Besides the seven or eight hundred new books produced each year – four times the number of twenty years earlier – there were several monthly periodicals and an immense output of pamphlets, broadsheets, textbooks and ephemera. Although many books were still financed by patronage or subscription the economics of the trade were altering rapidly. Entrepreneurs found that they could sell direct to a growing and increasingly literate public both at home and abroad. Already more books were published in London in a single year than in the whole century in Spain.

In the 1780s George Robinson of the Row, the biggest publisher in London, had a reputation for commercial integrity and unstinting hospitality. Across the churchyard, Joseph Johnson maintained a friendly rivalry. Newcomers, many of them Scots and many with experience of other trades, were however now setting up away from St Paul's and challenging traditional cartels and restrictive practices. Shunned by colleagues, they delighted authors by finding markets unknown to their

The Philosopher, from Bewick's *Select Fables*

old-fashioned competitors (who burned excess stocks to keep prices up). As yet there was no clear distinction betwen publisher and bookseller – the bookseller made the financial arrangements with the author, commissioned the printing, and sold the books both direct to the public and to the country booksellers.

James Lackington, who had started as a shoemaker, became rich by pricing low and denying credit even to the wealthiest nobleman. His 'Temple of the Muses' in Finsbury Square, boasting half a million books always on sale, contained a selling space round the circular counter on the ground floor so large that he arranged for the Exeter stagecoach with its four horses to be driven round on opening day. Richard Phillips brought his experience of the hosiery business to the selling of books. John Debrett of Piccadilly discovered an unfailingly profitable market supplying genealogies to the aristocracy and the gentry. John Murray, a retired lieutenant of the Royal Marines, was able to sell extensively abroad. The Hookham family, with comfortable and welcoming premises in Bond Street – convenient for Bond Street loungers – specialized in novels and light romances for town and country ladies.

The shops of the booksellers were centres of literary life. Politicians and men of fashion would call in to meet friends and pick up the latest books, pamphlets, and reviews. Authors and prospective authors were welcome to hang about in search of ideas, gossip, introductions, contracts, and invitations. Robinson's reputation as a six-bottle man referred to the amount of wine he provided on his dining table. Johnson would introduce himself to strangers with the news that he dined at four o'clock. The booksellers' shops were the unofficial forerunners of the gentlemen's clubs which were to become such a feature of London life in the following century.

Authors could make money, but for the most part they did not share in the profits. Although a few successfully negotiated contracts for royalties, the usual practice was for the bookseller to buy the copyright outright. For periodical work – which was almost invariably anonymous – authors were paid by the sheet and the rates were low. Between St Paul's and Finsbury lay the slum area of Cripplegate, a warren of old houses and narrow streets (of which the best known was Grub Street) inhabited by the less prosperous members of the profession – the fair-copyists, the translators, the indexers, the ghost-writers, the hacks, and the unrecognized geniuses. Suitably near were the debtors' prisons of Newgate and the Fleet, well known to many authors – tolerable for a short stay, comfortable if you had money, but fatal if you had to remain for any length of time.

Godwin took lodgings in Coleman Street in the poorer quarter. With his deep knowledge of the English Civil War, he probably remembered that the radicals had operated their secret printing press from there in 1642, the last resistance to the arbitrary power of the Crown. His plan was to produce a series of short biographies of famous Englishmen, an idea which was probably suggested by Andrew Kippis. For years Kippis had struggled with his own *Biographia Britannica*, an ambitious forerunner of the *Dictionary of National Biography* which gave disproportionate attention to dissenting divines, but his unwieldy project never got beyond the letter F. Godwin's first article, which took six months to write, grew to book length in the drafting. It was published anonymously in January 1783 as *History of the Life of William Pitt Earl of Chatham* by Kearsley of Fleet Street. 'This morning the late Attorney General came into his shop,' James Marshall wrote in a letter to Godwin soon after, 'Kearsley put a copy of your Chatham into his hands. The Att. Gen. opened it at Lord Chatham's *"great soul brooding over the obscurity etc"* and said *"the style is good. If his materials are equally good, it will have an extensive sale for the public has some time thirsted after such a work"*. Camden, Chatham, Shelbourne, Burke, Fox, Johnson [Dr Johnson] etc received their copies yesterday.'[1]

But although Godwin makes ambitious claims to bring Chatham before the tribunal of truth, his pleasing essay is little more than an extended eulogistic obituary notice compiled from newspaper articles. The proud 'Printed for the Author' on the title page gives off a whiff of vanity publishing. Posterity, to whose judgement he hopefully appealed in his Introduction, has shown little interest until very recent times.

The advance copy which Godwin sent to Edmund Burke bears the inscription 'Authour of the Life of Ld. Chatham, Fr. the Authour of Hist. of Ld. Chatham' and he provided an accompanying letter from which he omitted his name.

The historian of lord Chatham was once induced to flatter himself with the expectation, that his essay would have been honoured with the perusal of Mr Burke, while in manuscript. He even understands, that it was, for a moment, in his hands; but that important avocations prevented him from attending to it. The writer is indeed sensible, that one hour would have been abundantly sufficient, to have enabled Mr Burke to decide upon its merits. He however ascribes his conduct to the most amiable and honourable motive, the fear of doing a possible injustice, either to the author, or the bookseller.

At the same time, he begs leave to say, that the moment he has described, was to him a most interesting one. He is much too proud to flatter any man. The idea he had been led to entertain of the abilities and the character of Mr Burke, induced him, abstractedly considered, and long before his name was brought directly into question, to think of him, as the person, of all others, whose favour he most wished to engage, in behalf of what he has written.[2]

Godwin found it difficult to write polite letters. Keenly afraid of compromising his independence or bending the knee of flattery, he asserted the purity of his motives and thrust forward his claims to equality even in routine correspondence. In wishing to be thought fearlessly frank, he often merely sounds prickly, and his attempts to bestow justified compliments usually inclined too far in the other direction to be pleasing. Godwin frequently wrote letters which are hectoring and obsequious at the same time. Burke, who lived at Beaconsfield, would have been surprised to know that the author who sought his patronage was the candidate dissenting minister in the same town, but there is no record that they ever met.

Godwin's first book already reveals mannerisms which were to persist until the end of his life. He has, for example, a more than common fondness for double negatives, explicit or implied, and they are not wanting even in his less inconsiderable books. The hero of his most famous novel, for example, on escaping from prison, hotly pressed by pursuers, soaked to the skin and starving, found that he experienced 'no very agreeable sensations', and needed 'no common share of resolution' to walk all night in the winter frost.[3] The resulting tone of lofty imperturbability can, on occasions, be comic or irritating, but not infrequently it adds a latinate gravity which matches Godwin's own personality.

From the beginning too, Godwin conducted a personal vendetta against unnecessary consonants in proper names. Annoyed by the wasteful second l in a name like 'Cromwell', he himself always wrote 'Cromwel', and he would similarly elide the redundant k in words like Brunswick. It may have been his personal badge of modernism on the analogy of words like gothick and classick which had recently lost their last letters. He did not often apply the idiosyncrasy to monosyllabic names – no William Pit – but with longer men he was pitiless, and four of his closest friends, James Marshall, Joseph Fawcett, William Hazlitt, and Frederick Norman, were invariably cut back. Sometimes an editor insisted on printing the more normal forms, but fortunately they have often left undisturbed a surer proof of Godwinian authorship than stylistic analysis alone can usually expect. There is scarcely any work written by Godwin on any subject which does not sooner or later mention his failed hero, Oliver Cromwel.

The next book after *Chatham* was a printing under the title of *Sketches of History* of the six sermons he had delivered at Beaconsfield. Thomas Cadell, who had printed the *Account of the Seminary*, agreed to publish but only on condition that he received the manuscript and copyright outright for no fee. (Cadell incidentally never permitted his redundant l to be cut off in his own imprints.) Godwin had the satisfaction of seeing his name on a title page for the first time but Bishop Watson of Llandaff, to whom the book was dedicated, was as upset as the parishioners of Beaconsfield when he discovered its Socinian flavour.[4]

The Herald of Literature is very different. Completed in three months in the summer of 1783 and published anonymously at the end of the year, it purports to contain reviews of forthcoming books of which the author has secretly contrived to obtain advance copies. It is dedicated to the editors of the two proud literary reviews of the day, the *Monthly* and the *Critical*, whose power to influence the book-buying public was absolute. The book consists of a series of parodies of the reviews which the authors might expect, including quoted parodies of the books themselves. The *Decline and Fall of the Roman Empire* is the poorer for the lack of Gibbon's description of the early life of Mahomet, which contains a more than common superabundance of double negatives.

Having been early left an orphan by both parents, he received a hardy and robust education, not tempered by the elegancies of literature, nor much allayed by the indulgencies of natural affection. He was no sooner able to walk than he was sent naked, with the infant peasantry, to attend the cattle of the village; and was obliged to seek the refreshment of sleep, as well as pursue the occupations of the day, in the open air. He even pretended to be a stranger to the art of writing and reading. But though neglected by those who had the care of his infancy, the youth of this extraordinary personage did not pass away without some of those incidents which might afford a glimpse of the sublimity of his genius; and some of those prodigies, with which superstition is prompt to adorn the story of the founders of nations, and the conquerors of empires.

A number of modern scholars – unsurprised at reading extensive extracts from previously unknown works by Gibbon, Fanny Burney, Sterne, Burke, Sheridan, and others – have taken *The Herald of Literature* at face value, and solemnly criticized the youthful Godwin for lacking their own critical acumen.[5]

Godwin received no money for the *Herald*, but John Murray gave him a contract to undertake a translation of the memoirs of Lord Lovat, one of the highland chiefs who had sided with the Pretender in the Rebellion of 1745 and who had been publicly executed as a traitor in 1747. The manuscript, which was in French to prevent inquisitive servants from reading it, had been passed to a fellow prisoner in Edinburgh Castle shortly before Lovat's execution with a request that he should arrange publication, but it had been held back until the other principal figures had died. Godwin acted as editor as well as translator but Murray transferred the rights to another publisher, and it did not appear until 1797. The public would hardly have guessed from the title, *Memoirs of the Life of Simon Lord Lovat, Written by Himself in the French Language; and now first translated from the original language*, that it contains nothing about Lovat's part in the 'Forty-five, stopping short even before the earlier rebellion of 1715 in which Lovat had also taken part. It is a book of quite exceptional dullness.[6]

At this end of the literary business however a writer accepted the work he could get or he starved. Godwin went the round of the bookshops nearly every day and he took a wide variety of work from a wide variety of publishers. His output was huge but nevertheless, as he wrote later, 'for the most part I did not eat my dinner without previously carrying my watch or my books to the pawnbroker to enable me to eat'. He shared lodgings with Marshall and since they appear to have moved every three months – the normal letting period – we may guess that they were not satisfactory tenants. Godwin frequently provided money to bail Marshall from jail when he was arrested for debt, and Godwin was himself bailed by Robinson at least once.[7]

One sector of the market where demand was growing rapidly was fiction. The circulating libraries, a recent innovation, allowed books to be borrowed upon payment of a subscription, and many Georgian ladies softened the boredom of country life by skimming the latest gothic thrillers and high life romances rushed from London by the new mail coaches. On the whole novels were regarded as a pernicious influence, too full of sex and violence, and the circulating libraries were widely feared for disrupting family life by bringing dangerous ideas and emotions into the home. A medical doctor, Thomas Trotter, who composed a treatise on the nervous temperament, warned authoritatively that novel-reading was a form of poison which had often proved fatal to sensitive ladies.[8] In a public letter to his clergy earlier in the century, the Bishop of London drew a direct connection between novel-reading, prostitution, homosexuality, and the recent prevalence of earthquakes.[9]

In 1783 and 1784 Godwin wrote no less than three novels. *Damon and Delia* was dashed off in ten days and sold to Hookham for five guineas; *Imogen*, whose two volumes were composed in four months amongst his other work, was sold for ten pounds to William Lane; and *Italian Letters* realized twenty guineas from George Robinson. For more than a century all were lost to sight, but in recent years copies have at last been found and they turn out to be well down to the usual standard. *Italian Letters*, like the epistolary novels of Richardson, tells a story of seduction and betrayal.

And yet, my dear Ferdinand, to see the distress of the lovely Matilda, to see her bosom heave with anguish, and her eyes suffused with tears, to hear the heart-rending sighs continually bursting from her, in spite of the fancied resolution and the sweet pride that fill her soul, how callous, how void of feeling and sympathy ought the man to be, in whom objects like these can call up no relentings?

Imogen, A Pastoral Romance from the Ancient British purports to be a translation from the ancient Welsh of a work by a druid called Cadwallo. Like *The Herald of Literature* it too is a spoof – this time of the *Poems of Ossian*, itself a modern fabrication – but, fortunately for posterity, an unknown Welshman at one time took the title sufficiently seriously for a copy to have survived in a library at Aberystwyth. Godwin provided a Preface which discusses the authenticity of the manuscript, the historical background, and the literary sources and parallels. He notes knowingly that morals were looser in pre-Christian days.

But the mock-scholarly apparatus is merely intended to provide a suitably fantastical setting for another mildly arousing tale of unsuccessful rape. Bosoms are always heaving or panting, and they are invariably as white as alabaster or the driven snow. In some of Godwin's descriptions the overtones of his words could hardly have escaped even pre-Freudian readers.

Her beauties were ripened, and her attractions spread themselves in the face of day. Nor was this all. He beheld with watchful glance her slight and silent intercourse with the gallant Edwin; an intercourse which no eye but that of a lover could have penetrated. Hence his mind became pregnant with all the hateful brood of dark suspicions; he was agitated with the fury of jealousy . . . the couch of down was to him a bed of torture . . .

Historians have connected the hellfire and guilt of the dissenters with the repression of their sexuality and revulsion at its irrepressibility. Struggling to live their lives free from strong emotion and excitement, they filled their diaries with bewildered complaints and disgusted confessions. Did Godwin, one is tempted to suggest, take to writing romances in response to the same pressures? Was soft pornography a new assertion of freedom from his gloomy childhood? He knew his family would disapprove when they discovered (he seems to have deliberately kept quiet and then declined to give them the titles) and he duly received a pained scolding from Mrs Sothren.[10]

Godwin wrote many pieces of self-analysis, but for this period of his life on which there is little information any psychological explanation would be largely speculation. Most probably he wrote the novels with some shame in the style required by the publisher, in order to make money. However the rediscovery of a copy of the earliest of the three, *Damon and Delia*, known only from quotations in reviews until a unique copy was found in a Scottish castle in 1978, has now provided a little more information on which to assess Godwin's character at the outset of his literary career.[11] Despite the pastoral-sounding names, the story – of love and disappointment – is set in contemporary England and it has the lightness and charm as well as the gothic ornament and sound morals which subscribers to Hookham's library expected. The wicked Lord Martin spends his mornings writing challenges to duels – never less than a dozen – and exclaiming, 'Pox confound it,' although he never actually fights. Delia dreams of her lover Damon as a murderer reeking of blood, and like all the young ladies of Europe she sighs over *The Sorrows of Young Werther*.

What gives the book its unique interest is that one of the minor characters, Mr Godfrey, is unmistakably William Godwin himself, his story improved in a few particulars but at the same time evidently an honest self-portrait which catches many of the essential characteristics, fantasies and aspirations of the real Godwin at the age of twenty-seven. Born in a poor family, Godfrey's abilities are recognized at an early age, but he is not much liked and he 'had a stiffness and unpliableness of temper that did not easily bend to the submission that was expected of him'. He is destined for the church, and determines to overcome the stultifying obscurity of rural life by throwing himself enthusiastically into his duties. 'But there were men in the audience who loved better to criticise, than to be amended; and women, who felt more complacency in scandal, than eulogium. He displeased the one by disappointing them; it was impossible to disappoint the other.' Realizing that he is wasting his talents, he decides to leave, and after a period as a teacher, he seeks the independence of a life of writing.

Mortified, irritated, depressed, he now quitted his task half finished and threw

25

himself upon the world. 'The present age', said he, 'is not an age in which talents are overlooked, and genius depressed'. He had heard much of the affluence of writers, a Churchil, a Smollet,* and a Goldsmith . . . He saw the celebrated Dr Johnson caressed by all parties, and acknowledged to be second to no man, whatever his rank, however conspicuous his station.

At one point the rich Damon visits Godfrey 'in a wretched apartment, his hair dishevelled and his dress threadbare and neglected'. Godfrey has carried his manuscript from bookseller to bookseller but he is unknown and has no patron. Although he works hard and fast 'the time of dinner often came before the production that was to purchase it was completed, and when completed, it was frequently several days before it could find a purchaser'. But before the end Godwin and Godfrey are far away on the wings of fancy. The beautiful Delia (with 'snowy panting bosom') is seized by two agents of the wicked Lord Martin who takes her off in his carriage to a forcible marriage. On the way they meet the redoubtable Godfrey who knocks down one and scares off the other and when Lord Martin thrusts at him with his sword, Godfrey smashes it with a club, picks him up by the collar, and throws him into the road. Delia is rescued, her virtue intact. When the delighted Damon offers a reward, it turns out to be unnecessary. Godfrey has had a play accepted for the stage; and he is already rich and famous. But success has not gone (entirely) to his head:

Philosophers may tell us, that reputation, and the immortality of a name, are all but an airy shadow. Enough for me, that nature, from my earliest infancy, led me to place my first delight in these. I envy not kings their sceptres. I envy not statesmen their power. I envy not Damon his love, and his Delia. Next to the pursuits of honour and truth, my soul is conscious to but one wish, that of having my name enrolled, in however inferior a rank, with a Homer, and a Horace, a Livy and a Cicero.

When he wrote these sanctimonious words Godwin still had another nine years of hard writing before one of his literary productions again achieved even the limited immortality of having his name printed on a title page. But authors live on hope. Writing a successful play was the quickest way out of Grub Street. Among Godwin's papers is a letter dated 19 October 1784 from the manager of Covent Garden theatre firmly declining a proffered manuscript.[12] Charles Churchill's *Rosciad*, a satire on the stage, had also brought its author fame and fortune as Godfrey told Damon in the story, and Godwin evidently tried this genre too. In a list of published works compiled later, he included *The Thespiad* in

* Note the elisions.

writings of the mid-1780s, although no copy has yet been found nor even any mention in a review. Perhaps, unlike *The New Rosciad*, *The Pittiad*, *The Hastiniad*, *The Paphiad*, *The Patriad*, *The Denomiad*, *The Strolliad*, *The Aesopiad*, and *The Louisiad*, which all appeared in 1784 and 1785, it was never printed, but one day a copy may come to light.

His chief source of income in 1784 and 1785 was writing literary reviews for Murray's *English Review* at a guinea a sheet. The *English*, like its better-known rivals the *Monthly* and the *Critical*, contained, besides several long notices, a Catalogue of other new publications with briefer comment. To earn his fee for a sheet, Godwin had to provide each month the equivalent of sixteen printed pages – easily done with the main reviews which could be legitimately padded out with long quotations, but demanding work for those who merely prepared the Catalogue. Thomas Holcroft, another reviewer for the *English Review* soon to become Godwin's closest friend, complained that he often spent a whole day reading a book in order to write five lines.

Articles were anonymous or occasionally signed by a misleading initial, and it is difficult to know which can be attributed to Godwin's pen. One long article known to be written by him is initialled M. We can be fairly confident that he was responsible for reviewing a book about India by Major James Rennell for, apart from other indications, the name is unceremoniously elided to Rennel; but when we find reviews of books by Capell, Wraxall, and other double-consonant men with names intact, it is impossible to be certain, for Murray evidently objected when he noticed what was going on.

Publishers unashamedly owned and used literary reviews to puff their own books, and authors with friends could contrive to receive suitable notices, sometimes by paying money. The editor of the *Monthly* tried to prevent authors from reviewing their own books, but he was regarded as over-punctilious. Since Godwin's three novels were published anonymously by different publishers and were assigned to the Catalogue, it is likely that he himself wrote the three laudatory notices that appeared there or at least influenced what they said. The notice of *Italian Letters* for example includes a characteristically Godwinian phrase.

In these volumes there are character and incident. The morality is also to be commended, and the entertainment afforded is much beyond the common run of performances of this kind.

The essentials for a good puff are all here. Because fathers and brothers might have to order novels unseen for daughters and sisters, a reassuring comment was needed on the morals. Provided virtue triumphed in the end, however, dangerous emotions could safely occur in the earlier part of the book – indeed the more the better. *Imogen* is also recommended on all counts with other characteristic double negatives, while *Damon and Delia*, which was obviously Godwin's own favourite, was given nearly three pages of praise in the Catalogue for February 1784, the month that Godwin started writing for the *English Review*.

... the author has attempted to mix in it the two different styles, of tragic and comic writing. His tragedy, however, may be safely perused by the most tender female in the most gloomy solitude ... His smooth and well-turned periods win imperceptibly upon the man of taste, and leave him perhaps more interested and attached to the agreeable author, than the laboured sallies and studied exertions of more celebrated writers.[13]

If Godwin wrote this review, he must have derived considerable further satisfaction from being able to quote in full the story of Godfrey's disenchantment with his country parish, for it was certain to be read by the Reverend Thomas Harmer (who was himself an author and reviewer) and by the other dissenting colleagues who had turned against him at Stowmarket and Beaconsfield.

CHAPTER 4

The Political Journalist

When Godwin was five, his father took him to Norwich to see the fireworks for the Coronation of George III. But politics was never mentioned at Guestwick. John Godwin took the view that, as with religion, the best way to avoid controversy was careful silence and he was probably right. He was old enough to remember the old days and he had seen in his own lifetime the accumulating benefits of the settlement of 1688, the Glorious Revolution that had ended religious violence in Great Britain and ushered in a prolonged period of growing prosperity and unity.

The British were justifiably proud of their constitution of king, lords, and commons which gave them freedoms unknown elsewhere and which had helped transform their country from a second order European state into one of the great nations of the modern world. As the centenary year of 1788 approached, however, the defects of the famous settlement were there for all to see. The boasted liberties of Englishmen were less extensive than the propaganda of Whig grandees might suggest, and representative government was conducted through an openly corrupt and mercenary system of elections. It was easier, it was said, to determine the price of a borough than the price of a horse. Even if the British Constitution was one of the most liberal in the world, should it not be improved? Was the Revolution 'complete'? Should not the vote be extended to a wider body

Westminster, from *Lessons for Children*

of citizens? And should the groups which had been excluded from the settlement be more fully accepted into the state?

The dissenters felt a particular sense of grievance. The Act of Toleration of 1689 had given freedom to practise their religion and it had not later been reversed, but the Test Act of 1673, passed in the reign of Charles II in the royalist triumph, still stood on the Statute Book, as did the Corporation Act of 1661. These required that all holders of civil and military offices under the Crown (and all holders of offices in municipal corporations) should, besides taking an oath of allegiance, belong to the Church of England.

The law had been amended from time to time, and from 1727 onwards Parliament voted an annual indemnity. The religious tests were not in practice regularly or rigorously enforced, and there were many dissenters occupying positions of responsibility. Godwin's great grandfather who was Mayor of Newbury was one. But the humiliations and real disadvantages continued. Any man who did not belong to the established Church was legally presumed to be less than fully loyal.

However, although a minority, the dissenters exerted an influence on public questions out of proportion to their numbers. They were regarded as one of the great constituencies of the realm without whose tacit support any government would find itself in difficulties. With their superior levels of education and superior moral sense they saw themselves as intellectual leaders and progressive thinkers. In a country distrustful of modern ideas, they were the representatives of enlightenment. They dominated the media, owning several of the most widely read newspapers and reviews. Their political confidence was growing, and many believed that they were on the threshold of big new advances, the abolition of slavery, the repeal of the Test and Corporation Acts, the reform of Parliament.

Indeed, for anyone with a historical sense, it was a time of hope and optimism. As Adam Smith had recently pointed out, the gap between a European prince and his subjects was now less wide than that between a European peasant and an African king. With the growing application of science and technology to manufacturing, the way was already prepared for the greatest improvement in economic welfare since the invention of agriculture in the middle stone age. Nor were the emerging benefits wholly confined to the richer sections of the population even if they remained highly concentrated. Education was more widely available and literacy more common. Every provincial city now had its theatre and its reading rooms. Travel was easier; governments more efficient at maintaining civil peace; international relations were now conducted according to civilized codes; and even war had become less brutal as the century progressed. All these changes could be attributed to the advance of reason, and it was reasonable to expect that the methods which had proved so successful in explaining and taming the natural world would continue to yield benefits when applied to social and political questions.

It was Godwin's tutors at Hoxton who redirected his interest towards politics. In 1784 Andrew Kippis, knowing of Godwin's efforts as a literary writer, suggested to Robinson that he should be engaged as his assistant in compiling the *New Annual Register*. In that year he was accordingly employed to prepare the historical section of the volume and he performed the task so effectively that Robinson agreed to pay him an annual fee of sixty guineas for doing the same for future volumes. It was Godwin's first and – as events were to turn out – the only regular employment he ever enjoyed.

Since 1758 the *Annual Register* had provided a summary of the year's historical events; reprinted the main public documents in readily accessible form; reviewed the chief books; and in general offered a convenient reference book to be added to year by year. However, when in the late 1770s publication began to run several years late, the laws of competition took their course as elegantly as any classical economist could have wished, and in 1780 the dissenters started Robinson's *New Annual Register*, a near substitute with a near identical title page (the word 'New' printed in very inconspicuous letters) which seized a share of the market so effectively that many customers added the *New Annual Register* to their bound runs of the *Annual Register* without noticing the discontinuity. The intellectual and progressive wing of politics now had their own alternative record of contemporary events.

For the young journalist it was a wonderful political training. Godwin had to attend carefully to the news day by day and keep his own notes and chronology. He was expected to summarize the main debates in Parliament, and often attended personally to hear the speeches. To explain the background to complex questions such as Russian advances in the Crimea, Warren Hastings's activities in India, or the commercial policy of Ireland, he had to read extensively in areas to which he might not otherwise have been drawn, and all the main events of the year had to be reduced to a coherent continuous narrative of about two hundred pages in double columns. Since the history was primarily a document of record, and since the *New Annual Register* was designed to 'coalesce' with the early volumes of the *Annual Register*, there could be no extravagances of style and only the lightest comment or judgement. Balance, accuracy, comprehensiveness were the qualities the editors wanted, although with a particular duty to report the opinions of the Opposition, plus, above all, punctuality in submitting copy.

Godwin took his duties seriously. But the writing of anonymous contemporary history was frustrating work for a penniless excluded dissenter who wanted to participate not just to record, and who now had his own views on current political questions. James Marshall, who at Hoxton had predicted that his friend would one day be a member of the Cabinet, offered him direct advice on how to make the leap.

But it is no impossible flight from Grub Street to St James's. A sixpenny pamphlet may furnish wings for it. The chief thing against you is the weight of your political virtue which has hitherto and always will, if you retain it, bear you down. Could you prevail with yourself to part with one half of this ponderous quality that pervades your little frame, you would mount like a feather into the region of places and pensions and get a secure and quiet retreat from the poverty of an author, the insolence of booksellers and the claims of creditors.[1]

Marshall was not being altogether serious. But Godwin had no objection to becoming an anonymous political pamphleteer. In 1783 he wrote *A Defence of the Rockingham Party* intended to rebut the charge that Charles James Fox was a drunken old gambler who had prostituted his principles by combining with his former opponent Lord North. In 1784 he produced *Instructions to a Statesman*, a sustained piece of irony on the cynicism of politics which can still raise a smile. However, every time Godwin produced a partisan piece he knew that a few months later he would write a more balanced narrative of the same event; the journalist would become the historian, and the polemicist the philosopher. Although in his enthusiasm Godwin several times nearly lost his incubus of virtue, the *New Annual Register*, his main source of income, stood like Duty in the background, steadying any passions which threatened to surge too freely.

Andrew Kippis must have been proud when he considered the achievements of his pupil to whom he had given his first literary commission after his expulsion from Stowmarket in the spring of 1782. In three years (including seven months as candidate minister at Beaconsfield) he had produced a life of Chatham, a volume of sermons, a translation of Lord Lovat's memoirs, a pamphlet on education, three novels, a book of literary parody, two political pamphlets, digests of two years of British and foreign history for the *New Annual Register* each equivalent to a substantial volume in itself, and a quantity of reviews for the *English Review*. When therefore in the summer of 1785 Fox, Burke, and Sheridan, who had gone into opposition after the General Election of 1784, decided to establish a new political journal, the *Political Herald*, to support their cause, Kippis had no hesitation in again recommending Godwin to serve as one of the contributors.

The man chosen to be editor was Gilbert Stuart, a prolific writer of books on history and philosophy and author of an untold quantity of journalism. When a book was on the way he would disappear for weeks at a stretch, but these bursts of intensive work were invariably followed by bouts of compensatory heavy drinking. By 1785 when he took on the *Political Herald* he could still be relied on to rise the next morning to draft a long article and send it off to the printer without a correction. Stuart boasted of his desire to build a Temple of Truth, but he also boasted that he would write two articles on any public figure for a guinea each, one a panegyric and the other a libel. Some people thought he was the famous Junius whose political letters had been so sensational and influential a few years previously and whose identity had never been revealed. Godwin admired him, and the Opposition leaders and their advisers soon began to see his young assistant as a likely successor and to groom him accordingly.

In 1785 Godwin prepared a series of Junius-like letters for the *Political Herald* over the name Mucius – intended to recall the legendary Roman Mucius Scaevola who had contemptuously thrust his right hand into the fire when threatened with torture. Although they lacked the leaked inside knowledge that made Junius's letters appear so authoritative, Mucius is stylish and enjoyable, full of weighty pronouncements and classical allusions – the language of political abuse has rarely been more sonorous.

Godwin attacked all the targets of the Opposition. He became an expert on the affairs of India and like others he knew the solution to the problems of Ireland. But besides the knock-about, the *Political Herald* also claimed to offer thoughtful, honest, political analysis. The first issue of July 1785 opened with a long article, *Critique of the Administration of Mr Pitt*, which was continued in subsequent issues. The second issue offered *The Grounds of a Constitutional Opposition stated*. Readers and sponsors would have expected the most important articles to have been prepared by the editor himself, but by a happy chance that lifts the spirits of biographers, we now know they were in fact written by his assistant.[2]

In these writings we can see Godwin trying to formulate some of the general principles of political theory which were to occur later in his more substantial works. He has already adopted without question the

Newtonian model of human affairs which sees conduct as determined by scientific laws, and he is convinced that there can be no higher authority than a man's individual judgement.

In particular he has already adopted the doctrine that gratitude is a 'pernicious' emotion, a distortion of the individual's duty to decide for himself, which he had applied so courageously at Stowmarket.

... it is uniformly found in practice, that masses of intellectual individuals are guided by as regular a gravitation, and directed by as mechanical principles, as are the planets in their orbits. So long as the inequality of mankind shall subsist; so long as one shall be rich and another poor, as one shall have the power of conferring benefits and another the need of receiving them; just so long will men cohere and act together from sympathy, from gratitude, and from expectation.

As he studied day by day the operation of the political and economic process, noting how the King and the great landowners exercised their power at home and how the East India Company was inexorably extending its control over the princedoms of India, Godwin believed he had uncovered part of the explanation. Gratitude, generally considered a commendable and humane emotion, is in reality part of the insidious network of influence and patronage by which power is exercised and truth distorted. Godwin became increasingly sure that he had diagnosed one of the sources of evil in society, a 'moral error' as he called it, which had not been sufficiently recognized.

He peppered his articles and reviews with gibes at Grub Street scribblers and hackney writers who plied for hire like drivers of hackney carriages – perhaps he had to do this since he was near to being a hack himself. He craved recognition and fame, as he readily acknowledged, but his ambition was accompanied by a genuine desire to discover the truth, an urgent zeal to use his talents for the advancement of knowledge and the benefit of his fellow men.

In February 1785, after he had written a series of reviews for the *English Review* on the books and articles which had been prompted by Joseph Priestley's *History of the Corruptions of Christianity*, he used the opportunity to introduce himself to the most famous figure of the English Enlightenment. The topic was dear to his heart – how far were the customs of the modern reformed churches consistent with those of the early Christians? The Unitarians, of whom Priestley was one of the leaders, saw themselves as 'rational dissenters' who had stripped away superstitious accretions and left only the essentials. Godwin's review, a careful and conscientious appraisal of the whole controversy, ran to over thirty-eight printed pages – and even then it was not complete. His letter, assertive and apologetic by turns, replete with charmless double negatives, could not conceal the boldness which characterized the pushy young journalist.

The person who now does himself the honour to address you is the author of the article in the English Review relative to your vindication of H[istory of] C[orruptions].

I was the rather desirous of forwarding to you the pamphlet itself, as, I was apprehensive, not being, I believe, of the most general eclat, it might otherwise escape your notice. And I was willing you should be convinced, that, however illiberally some reviewers may have treated you, there were those who were disposed to do you justice.

I am myself a Socinian. Convinced of the divine origin of Christianity, and yet perfectly satisfied that it will not stand the test of philosophical examination unless stripped of its doctrinal corruptions, I should be happy by every method which providence may seem to offer to be the humble instrument of dispelling them.

I am however restrained from doing this in the most explicit manner by the character of the review [The English Review normally supported the Tory party and the Church of England] . . . But however undisguised I may be personally, and I believe, if my character should ever be thought worthy of Dr Priestley's enquiries, it will be found not to be the most impenetrable, I consider myself in the present affair, not as an individual, but the member of a corps. And I am more easy under this restriction, as the immediate business of the reviewer is not undoubtedly to make himself a party, but to represent candidly the arguments of both sides. Perhaps too if the cause of Socinianism be the cause of truth, it cannot be more effectually served than in the manner I have chalked out to myself.

I have only to add, that though I have been contented to appear openly to Dr Priestley, it is my earnest desire to remain concealed from the rest of mankind.[3]

Priestley replied politely, saying he had in fact seen the review. He commended Godwin's determination to be impartial although he offered the worrying thought that Godwin had veered too far in favour of Priestley against his opponents.

Godwin's sense of intellectual discomfort continued to grow, and the principles which he had upheld so stubbornly at Stowmarket were now put to a second test. When Gilbert Stuart fell finally ill Godwin became the acting editor of the Political Herald. When Stuart died soon afterwards, the Opposition leaders offered him the editorship, with an assured salary to be paid out of party funds. But to their astonishment he declined. In repeated interviews Sheridan urged him to change his mind. The editorship of a progressive political and philosophical journal was the prize for which the young man had been aiming since his arrival in London four years before. It was just the vehicle that, as Marshall had suggested, could carry him from the garrets of Grub Street to the drawing rooms of St James's. But Godwin stubbornly took his stand on a point not quite central to the issue of intellectual independence. While he was happy to draw a salary from the *Herald*'s revenues, he would not accept money direct from party funds. Since the journal was unprofitable this meant that no agreement was possible. Godwin remained adamant, and with his refusal, the Opposition owners allowed the *Herald* to cease publication.

Godwin's last published piece before the collapse was a sharp reply to the Earl of Buchan who had dared to hint, in a fulsome obituary of Gilbert Stuart, that his career had 'miscarried' through his becoming a writer for a party.

Why is it more disgraceful to write than to speak with a certain connection of men? Shall we decide, that every person who unites himself with the men he approves, and who generally defends the measures that must necessarily originate with such characters, is a dishonest man? The sentiment of your lordship, if it were to become universal, would inflict a deeper blow upon the liberty of the press, than any acts of parliament or legislative prohibitions that could be devised.

But such exaggerations were not persuasive even to himself. Godwin protested too much. He had no intention of becoming a second Gilbert Stuart, despite having compared him at one point to Tacitus. Godwin's defence of his old editor was his last – and most extreme – piece of paid party propaganda, and he was determined to quit. A post becoming vacant at the British Museum, he applied for sponsorship to Lord Robert Spencer – one of his political friends who knew his work for the *Political Herald* – but the agitation against the Test and Corporation Acts had highlighted the fact that the Reverend William Godwin (as he still called himself) was not a member of the Church of England and could not therefore hold this office of profit under the Crown.[4]

It was a courageous step to turn down a salaried job, and Godwin had no money except for what he earned from the *New Annual Register*. His own family were in no position to help him. Of his brothers, Hull Godwin stayed in Norfolk and became a farmer with eight children. Edward Godwin died in April 1779, still a young man. In 1772 John is described as 'of the Inner Temple' where he was probably a clerk, but he took to drink and gambling and died in 1805. Two of the other brothers, Nathaniel Godwin and Conyers Jocelyn Godwin, went to sea like their grandfather. We hear of Nat hiding unsuccessfully from the press gang in 1788, but he evidently left the Navy not long afterwards when there is mention of him failing in business and reverting to the position of journeyman servant. Conyers Jocelyn Godwin – named in honour of a family patron Sir Conyers Jocelyn with whom Godwin stayed during the vacations from Hoxton – was lost at sea in 1790. The youngest brother, Joseph Godwin, was to die in prison. Hannah, his sister, came to London to find work and was employed as a dressmaker, one of the most exploited trades open to a respectable woman.

Godwin's relations lived on the verge of poverty or beyond, and while he always seemed to have the potential to rise, they were always falling back. Over the years his mother implored him to look after his brothers and their wives, to help her grandchildren find places as apprentices, footmen, or living-in servants. It was a recurrent nightmare of her old age that her family would starve in the streets of London and she always looked to William to support the less fortunate members.[5]

His closest friends were still Marshall and Fawcett both trained at dissenting academies like himself, willing to devote hours to debating philosophical questions. Fawcett's regular Sunday night sermons at Old Jewry in London, famed for the boldness of their thinking, attracted packed congregations. Marshall spent a lifetime in the literary industry but he never found the wings to fly out of Grub Street. His most enduring work was to translate Volney's *Ruins of Empire* from the French, producing a best seller which was to be reprinted many times for a generation, but not a word of what Marshall wrote ever appeared under his own name.[6]

Godwin's career continued to advance strongly. The booksellers were happy to see the reviewer of the *English Review* at their dinner tables, and of the ten famous authors that he had parodied in *The Herald of Literature* in 1784, he knew at least six personally a few years later. The politicians of the Opposition were keen to keep the acquaintance of a man who wrote both for the *New Annual Register* and for the *Political Herald*. Always methodical, Godwin kept memoranda of prominent people he had met and others he wanted to meet, underlining the names of those he knew best.

1783

Timothy Hollis, <u>Barry</u>, Lindsey, Robinson, Cadel, Dodsley

1784

<u>Watson</u>, <u>Stuart</u>, Thomson, Grant, Moir, Disney, B Hollis

1785

Webb, <u>Priestley</u>, Jebb, Hamilton, Planta, Heywood

1786

<u>Logan</u>, <u>Holcroft</u>, <u>Shield</u>, <u>Nicholson</u>, Woodfal, Beaufoy[7]

Desiderati

Burke, <u>Fox</u>, Bentham, <u>Grey</u>, Lambton, Derby, <u>Mrs Siddons</u>, <u>Porson</u>, <u>H Tooke</u>, Cooper, <u>Williams</u>, <u>Parr</u>, Erskine, Mrs Jordan, Thurlow, <u>Inchbald</u>, Burney, Lee, Francis[8]

Fox, Burke, and Sheridan were the leaders of the Whig Opposition. Lord Grey, Lord Derby, and Sir Philip Francis were among their parliamentary supporters. The Hollis brothers, Beaufoy, Lindsey, Disney, and Heywood were prominent dissenters, active members of the Committee for the Repeal of the Test and Corporation Acts. Horne Tooke was a veteran radical politician. Robinson, Cadell, Woodfall and Dodsley were publishers; Stuart and Thompson were his colleagues on the *Political Herald*; Mrs Jordan, Mrs Inchbald and others were connected with the theatre; James Barry was a historical painter and member of the Royal Academy; Shield was a composer; Porson was a famous classical scholar; Erskine was the lawyer soon to make his reputation as a defender of reformers; Planta was at the British Museum; Burney was either Dr Burney the musicologist or more probably his daughter Fanny Burney the novelist since Lee is her less well-remembered contemporary Harriet Lee; William Nicholson was a scientist, soon to be one of Godwin's closest friends; Priestley, Bentham, David Williams, and Parr were the leading philosophers of the day.

When Godwin refused the editorship of the *Political Herald* he was already an accepted younger member of the dissenting establishment. It was in the same year, 1786, that he met Thomas Holcroft, one of the most remarkable men of the time who was to be, for many years, the most important influence in his life.[9] Eleven years older than Godwin, Holcroft was the son of a London shoemaker who made the special boots needed by the sedan chairmen. When fashions changed and business failed, the family moved to the country and Holcroft's father made a precarious living as a pedlar dealing in horses, apples, rags or spoons, and dragging the boy with him from town to town. For a time Holcroft was sent to Newmarket as a stable boy and during his few hours of leisure he contrived to educate himself. Later, after an unsuccessful attempt to be apprenticed into the shoemaking trade, he joined some strolling players, having acquired a taste for the theatre at the country fairs where his father had set up his stall. Holcroft was first prompter, then actor, then playwright until in 1780 he achieved his first success when one of his comedies, *Duplicity*, was put on at Drury Lane.

When Godwin first met him Holcroft was pursuing much the same trade as himself, with comparably wide variety and huge output. He wrote plays, he wrote reviews, he edited literary journals. He translated from the French and also from the German, including thirteen volumes of the *Posthumous Works* of Frederick the Great. In September 1784 he went to Paris specially to see Beaumarchais' *Marriage of Figaro*, which had just opened there with great success. When the proprietors would not sell him a copy of the script, he attended the performance every night for ten days and, with the help of a friend, wrote down the whole play from memory, so that his English version was able to open at Covent Garden before Christmas with Holcroft himself playing Figaro on the first night.

Holcroft disliked much of what he saw of England and of the English social system. A character in one of his plays was hissed from the stage when he declared, 'I was bred to the most useless, and often the most worthless of all professions; that of a gentleman.' But Holcroft's talents were irrepressible and many of his plays achieved success. A man of indomitable strength of character, stern in appearance and rough in manner, he seldom doubted the correctness of his opinions which he was inclined to propound with overbearing assurance. He was one of the few men of his generation to scale the high barriers that separated the poor from education and influence.

By 1788 Godwin and Holcroft were fast friends, seeing each other nearly every day. Holcroft had profound respect for Godwin's knowledge, for his vast reading, and for his clarity in argument – qualities which a self-taught shoemaker could not match. But if Godwin helped fill gaps in Holcroft, Holcroft knew things that book-learning could never supply. He had travelled all over England and visited abroad; he had consorted with an astonishing variety of men and women from the lowest labourer to the Prince Regent; he had known poverty and riches, humiliation and adulation. The two friends did however share two characteristics which had brought them each to prominence in an unsympathetic world – an unshakeable confidence in their own abilities and an absolute refusal to be thought less than the full equal of any man in the three kingdoms.

On 8 May 1788 Godwin was invited to one of the last great celebrations of the eighteenth-century spirit which he and his friends had now wholeheartedly embraced. It was a dinner given by Cadell to mark the publication of the final volume of Edward Gibbon's *Decline and Fall of the Roman Empire* and the historian made the journey from Switzerland specially to be present. Godwin was among the distinguished party who heard William Hayley (regarded *faute de mieux* as the best poet of the day) recite an ode which was later printed in the *New Annual Register*. Gibbon, who had known personally Rousseau and Helvétius and d'Holbach and many others of Godwin's intellectual heroes, may on occasions have appeared cynical, but he too shared the optimism of the age. At the end of his long description of the breakdown of ancient civilization in the West, he had given his answer to the question which everyone was asking – could it ever happen again?

Yet the experience of four thousand years should enlarge our hopes and diminish our apprehensions: we cannot determine to what height the human species may aspire in their advances towards perfection . . . we may therefore acquiesce in the pleasing conclusion that every age of the world has increased, and still increases, the real wealth, the happiness, the knowledge, and perhaps the virtue, of the human race.[10]

Godwin pestered Robinson to advance him the money to write a great work, as Gibbon had done, which would enlighten and improve the world. He proposed a *History of Literature* and apparently obtained a contract and started to write, but it was abandoned. Robinson preferred safer types of publishing – a naval history was suggested and a new translation of Livy.

In 1787 he agreed to publish anonymously Godwin's *History of the Internal Affairs of the United Provinces*, which was little more than the sections on recent Dutch history that Godwin had written for the 1786 and 1787 volumes of the *New Annual Register* plus a concluding chapter of comment. The Dutch had always been admired by the dissenters for their robust Protestantism and for having given shelter to English refugees in the seventeenth century; Godwin's grandfather, like many others, had gone to Leiden to study. Now in the 1780s the Dutch seemed set to drive out King William and estabish a democratic republic on the American model – another example of steady progress.

In later years when he had become famous Godwin had mixed feelings towards the huge quantity of undistinguished writing that he had produced during his long literary apprenticeship. 'Different things of obscure note,' he called them, 'the names of which, though innocent, and in some degree useful, I am rather inclined to suppress.'[11] He did however keep a careful record and late in life prepared guidance for the editors of his collected works – volumes which he was sure the world would demand after his death but which are still awaited without impatience.

But never once in later life did he mention the biggest book which he compiled during his last years in Grub Street, which occupied him for twelve months, almost full time, in 1788 and 1789.[12] *The English Peerage*, in three quarto volumes, the third consisting entirely of engravings of coats of arms, was printed on high quality paper from a specially designed type. The selling price of five guineas was equivalent to Godwin's gross income for a month. John Debrett had discovered that the country houses of England contained many Sir Walter Elliots who never took up any book but the *Baronetage*, and *The English Peerage* was Robinson's attempt to capture some of the market.

In the introduction, the anonymous author characteristically offered a grander justification for his work than the readers of such books generally feel in need of.

Are we accustomed to regard with admiration a Burleigh and a Sackville, a Hampden and a Vane, a Sydney and a Russel, a Shaftesbury and a Bolingbroke? In the volumes of the English Peerage we see at a glance, we see as it were associated in one illustrious society, what we must otherwise pursue through the miscellaneous page of history. We are delighted to observe virtue becoming as it were hereditary in certain families . . .

The choice of the republicans of the Commonwealth to illustrate the theme of aristocracy must have struck potential purchasers as eccentric, but the notion that virtue was becoming hereditary among the titled classes probably sounded less incredible in 1790 than at any time before or since. It was a compliment that an optimistic age conferred and accepted without surprise.

The English Peerage, the eleventh book that Godwin had launched since his arrival in London, has, like the others, long been forgotten. However it is not without its significance in the history of his intellectual development. When, a few years later, Burke and his followers were inclined to argue that the institutions of kingship and aristocracy stretched back into the mists of time, symbolized and cemented a mystical relationship with the land and with God, and represented all that was best in the nation, Godwin had expert information with which to contradict them. Most English titles he knew went no further back than the unspeakable Charles II, and over 10 per cent of the current non-royal dukes derived from that monarch's activities on the wrong side of the royal blanket.[13]

CHAPTER 5

Revolutions

In March 1787 a motion before the House of Commons for the repeal of the Test and Corporation Acts was defeated by 178 votes to 100. In the spring of 1789 the time seemed ripe to try again. Support was growing and there was a scent of success in the air. Godwin was among many reformers who attended a dinner given at Hackney – where numerous dissenters lived – for the friends of the cause assembling in London. In the House of Commons Henry Beaufoy spoke of the absurdity in modern conditions of applying religious tests to the recruitment of minor civil servants. Fox made one of his best speeches. But when the votes were counted, the motion was found to have been lost by 20 votes.

Godwin was at the House of Lords the next day reporting for the *New Annual Register* and heard the proposals opposed by the bishops of the Church of England. Dr Horsley, who had led the counterattack against Priestley, wanted fines of a shilling per omission for anyone failing to attend Sunday service. The Bishop of St Asaph also favoured strengthening the status quo: he recalled with approval the ancient Greek law which required anyone who proposed change to wear a rope round his neck. The motion was rejected.

Disappointment among the dissenters was intense. A full century had passed since the Glorious Revolution had supposedly entrenched the liberties of Englishmen – a point Fox and Sheridan rubbed home by demanding that a memorial column to commemorate the centenary should

Execution scene, from Bewick's *Select Fables*

be erected at Runnymede where King John had been forced to confirm the Magna Carta. But while eyes in England were on the parliamentary struggles, events were occurring across the Channel which soon swamped all domestic politics.

On 16 July 1789, as Godwin noted in the *New Annual Register*, 'Advice is received from Paris, of a great revolution in France, the capture of the Bastile, and the execution of the governor of that fortress, and other obnoxious persons, by the populace.' In his journal Godwin included 'Revolution in France' as an event of 27 June, the day before he finished work on *The English Peerage*.

Since 1784 he had been studying events in France in order to write the French section for the *New Annual Register*. He had watched the long ineffectual attempts of the French Government to control the public sector borrowing requirement leading to the recall of the States General for the first time in nearly two hundred years. It had been a long preamble but Godwin, like everyone else, was taken by surprise at how swiftly the ancient government of France was overthrown. Robinson scolded him for running late in submitting his history – the commercial survival of the *New Annual Register* depended on its being able to beat its better-known rival to the bookshops.

But how could any man however industrious be expected to write history fit to stand in a book of reference when every post brought new revelations and every week new explanations? The *Annual Register*, faced in earlier years with a similar problem in trying to report the American War, had chosen to publish late rather than print narrative which was liable to look silly in the light of fast-moving events. The *New Annual Register* met its deadlines by a different editorial strategy. Anyone who bought the volume for 1789 in 1790 hoping to discover about the French Revolution would have found that the history only took him to August 1787.

Godwin knew that he was observing the greatest drama of Modern Europe and he was determined to be worthy of the occasion. Prefaces to successive volumes assured readers that the history was factual and impartial, but there was soon little attempt to conceal that the 'friends of liberty' were favoured against the 'enemies of liberty'. He maintained the fiction that he was a simple chronicler but events were observed with the eye of a philosopher. If comment was needed, he offered the reported opinions of 'persons of independent and comprehensive understanding' or of 'philosophical patriots'. By this pleasing convention Godwin was able not only to offer his own commentary but to assert an identity with the philosophers of the French Enlightenment whose ideas had led to the Revolution in the first place.

On 5 November 1789 he dined with the Revolution Society at their annual dinner and was present at the committee meeting the following day. The ancient club of Whigs and dissenters traditionally met each year on the anniversary of the landing of King William at Torbay on 5 November 1688, a date which neatly coincided with that other anniversary of British liberty, Guy Fawkes Day. Many of his friends were there – Abraham Rees, the head of his college at Hoxton, Andrew Kippis, his former tutor, who had launched him on his literary career, plus Members of Parliament, and others involved in the current campaigns.

Earl Stanhope was in the chair. But before the political proceedings began, the Reverend Richard Price delivered the traditional annual sermon to the Society, at the Meeting House in Old Jewry, which he called *A Discourse on the Love of Our Country*. Like Priestley, he was a Unitarian minister, and a scholar of considerable achievement. His sermon reaffirmed a view of English history and of the English Constitution which most of his congregation shared:

We are met to thank God for that event in this country to which the name of THE REVOLUTION has been given; and for which, for more than a century, it has been usual for the friends of freedom, and more especially Protestant Dissenters, to celebrate with expressions of joy and exultation . . . By a bloodless victory, the fetters which despotism had been long preparing for us were broken; the rights of the people were asserted, a tyrant expelled, and a Sovereign of our own choice appointed in his room.

Price went on to reaffirm the ancient dissenting tradition of religious and political liberty – liberty of thought, the right to resist constituted authorities who abuse their power, the right to choose the government, to hold them to account, and to cashier them for misconduct.

It was all familiar stuff, not much different from the unremarked sermon which Andrew Kippis had delivered the previous year. What made it significant on this occasion was that in the weeks since the outbreak of the French Revolution in mid-summer, the new French Government had already conceded to Frenchmen the civic rights which the English dissenters had unsuccessfully sought by patient parliamentary means for 101 years. As Godwin noted in the *New Annual Register*, with the implicit assumption that history is progressive, in 1789 France overtook England for the first time since 1264 when Simon de Montfort beat Philip the Fair in the calling of the first Parliament.

In a burst of enthusiasm, the Revolution Society unanimously resolved to mount a third attempt to persuade Parliament to repeal the Test and Corporation Acts. By an unfortunate choice of phrase the Society called for the establishment of new societies 'upon Revolution principles' – meaning the Glorious Revolution of 1688 – and invited the chairman to send a congratulatory address to the National Assembly of France. From his seat in the hall Godwin watched and listened as his peaceful, intellectual, dissenting friends passed resolution after resolution linking the (nearly bloodless) English Revolution of 1688 with the (so far not too bloody) French Revolution of 1789.

Many of the same men sat down to another banquet on 14 July 1790, the first anniversary of the fall of the Bastille. Earl Stanhope was again in the chair and it was probably he who made a remark to Godwin on that occasion, which he noted for his journal:

We are particularly fortunate in having you among us; it is the best cause countenanced by the man by whom we most wished to see it supported.[1]

Stanhope was referring, we may guess, to Godwin's comments on the French Revolution in the *New Annual Register,* for in the volume for 1789 the annalist included a prophecy on the significance of recent events in France which the six hundred diners would have applauded.

The ideas that the intellectual heroes of France, a Rousseau, an Helvétius, and a Raynal, had conceived, that at the moment they published them they despaired to see effectually adopted, and that seemed hitherto to have remained altogether barren, were fertilised at once. From hence we are to date a long series of years, in which France and the whole human race are to enter into possession of their liberties, when the ideas of justice and truth, of intellectual independence and everlasting improvement, are no longer to remain buried in the dust and obscurity of the closet, or to be brought forth at distant intervals to be viewed with astonishment, indignation, and contempt, but to be universally received, familiar as the light of day, and general as the air we breathe.[2]

In Paris that same 14 July ceremonies were held to mark the success of the Revolution. In the Champs de Mars the King and Queen celebrated high mass in the presence, it was said, of six hundred thousand citizens and soldiers. Godwin's friend Helen Maria Williams had rushed to Paris in order to be present. 'Oh no!' she wrote of the first Bastille day ceremony, 'this was not a time in which the distinctions of country were remembered. It was the triumph of human kind; it was man asserting the noblest privilege of his nature, and it required but the common feelings of humanity to become in that moment a citizen of the world.'[3] Charles

James Fox, responding to the same excitement, described the fall of the Bastille as 'how much the greatest event . . . that ever happened in the world! and how much the best!'

But not everybody was so certain. During 1790, Fox's close friend and colleague Edmund Burke began to warn that enthusiasm for the French Revolution was misguided and dangerous. In a debate on 9 February, as Godwin reported for the *New Annual Register*, he had protested 'that the separation of a limb from his body could scarcely give him more pain than the idea of differing violently and publicly with Mr Fox in opinion'. When in March 1790 Fox introduced the third bill for the repeal of the Test and Corporation Acts, Burke again came to the House to vote against his former friends. 'Abstract principles,' he declared according to Godwin's report, 'he had never been able to bear; he detested them when a boy and he liked them no better now that he had silver hairs.'

When in November Burke published *Reflections on the French Revolution*, the most thorough and considered statement of his views, he felt no need to apologize for attacking his former friends. He took as his starting point the Revolution Society sermon of November 1789:

For my part, I looked on that sermon as the public declaration of a man much connected with literary caballers, and intriguing philosophers; with political theologians, and theological politicians, both at home and abroad . . . I almost venture to affirm, that not one in a hundred amongst us participates in the 'triumph' of the Revolution Society . . . We are not the converts of Rousseau; we are not the disciples of Voltaire; Helvétius has made no progress amongst us. Atheists are not our preachers; madmen are not our lawgivers. We know that *we* have made no discoveries; and we think that no discoveries are to be made, in morality; nor many in the great principles of government, nor in the ideas of liberty, which were understood long before we were born, altogether as well as they will be after the grave has heaped its mould upon our presumption, and the silent tomb shall have imposed its law on our pert loquacity . . . We have real hearts of flesh and blood beating in our bosoms. We fear God; we look up with awe to kings; with affection to parliaments; with duty to magistrates; with reverence to priests; and with respect to nobility.

Burke denied the Revolution Society's view of English history. In 1688 the people did not elect King William of Orange in place of the hated King James: they had no such right – the succession passed by due process of law from King James (who had abdicated) to King William and his heirs. The British Constitution, Burke insisted, conferred no right to elect governments or cashier kings. It is the duty of citizens to obey the sovereign but in doing so they are obeying not so much the person of the king as the collective wisdom handed down from ancestors from time immemorial.

Under this kind of attack the dissenters' thoughtless linking of the French Revolution with the Glorious Revolution of 1688 was soon seen to have been a disastrous mistake. The modern dissenters who claimed a right to cashier kings were the descendants of the republicans who had tried and executed King Charles on the same principles. It was remembered, too, that during the last national crisis, the American Revolution, they had largely sided with the rebellious colonists against the constituted Government. When the third bill to repeal the Test and Corporation Acts was presented in 1790, it was resoundingly defeated by a majority of 189, compared with only 20 the year before. Church bells were rung in many Anglican steeples and exultant graffiti chalked on meeting house walls reminded dissenters that 102 years after the Glorious Revolution they were still officially rebels and traitors.

Committees of landowners sprang up in the counties in defence of 'Church and King', ready to raise a mob of loyal tenants at the sounding of the Lord Lieutenant's horn. Love of foxhunting was Burkean proof enough for many that the English retained the stolid yeoman qualities of their ancestors, just as in a previous century, as Godwin later noted, gentlemen of Charles II's time took conspicuous delight in bear-baiting, bull-baiting, and cock-fighting to demonstrate their contempt for squeamish puritans.[4] One of Godwin's friends, the daughter of a dissenting minister at Hampstead, recalled that as a ten-year-old girl she was tormented because of her religion. 'I have never wondered', she wrote later, 'at the accounts of martyr children.'[5] For the first time in Godwin's life attitudes which had marked his upbringing began to be understandable. Atavistic hatreds, which his grandfather would have recognized but which had seemed absurdly anachronistic in modern times, were again stirring from their long sleep.

The reformers had long held the intellectual initiative. Now with the publication of Burke's pamphlet they suffered a counterattack which contemptuously dismissed their enlightenment clichés as based on a false notion of human nature and of human society. The debate at once moved from the limited issue with which it had started towards fundamental philosophical questions of human organization, rights and duties, so that to read Burke and his principal opponents is to participate in one of the most illuminating debates of political theory ever conducted in England. Each aspect of the question, the immediate and the long term, the theoretical and the practical, was identified and contested. Over a hundred pamphlets were published.

By far the most influential was Tom Paine's *Rights of Man*, the first part of which was prepared in February 1791.[6] The intended publisher, Joseph Johnson, apparently took fright and decided not to proceed although a few copies were printed. Holcroft was among an informal committee of sympathizers who agreed to recommend the excisions which would allow it to be published safely by another publisher, and he was evidently lent one of the first printed copies. Since Holcroft and Godwin were now friends and both had experience of the publishing world, it was natural that he should at once want to involve Godwin. As soon as he had read it, he wrote eagerly to his friend:

I have read the pamphlet once thro' and am absolutely in an extacy with the acute the profound the divine author; the friend of man and terror of Despots – I have so severe a cold that I think it prudent not to go into the night air. Should you not happen to be very poetical* and should chuse to come and sit with me an hour you would be a welcome guest – I want to consult you on the castrations – I would have the whole transcribed if I thought there were the least danger it should not be published.[7]

On 27 February Godwin himself called on Paine, but he did not meet him. On 2 March, according to his journal, he 'borrowed Paine', probably the same copy as had been lent to Holcroft and this was probably the occasion of the following letter:

Though I have as yet given only a cursory perusal to the pamphlet with a sight of which you have favoured me, I will nevertheless take the liberty to express to you the feelings excited by that perusal. I shall trespass upon your goodness by begging leave to detain it, while I give it a more careful examination. Few things indeed ever mortified me more than the recollecting, that shortly I must cease to have a copy in my possession, and that, even for the mangled remnant that is to be left, I must trust to the accidents that may attend its future publication.[8]

In the event a bolder publisher called Jordan agreed to sell the pamphlet without any excisions at all, merely adding a new title page and preface. Another ecstatic note from Holcroft giving Godwin the news is only partially comprehensible, but its general message is unmistakable.

I have got it – If this do not cure my cough it is a damned perverse mule of a cough – The Pamphlet – From the row† – But mum – We don't sell it – Oh, no – Ears and Eggs – Verbatim, except the addition of a short preface, which, as

* Godwin was then at work on a verse tragedy, *Dunstan*.
† Paternoster Row near St Paul's in the bookselling district.

you have not seen, I send you my copy – Not a single castration (Laud be unto God and J S Jordan!) can I discover – Hey for the New Jerusalem! The Milennium! And peace and eternal beatitude be unto the soul of Thomas Paine.[9]

Godwin's own view is given in a second letter to Paine, probably written soon after the Jordan version first went on sale on 13 March.

The pamphlet has exceeded my expectations, and appears to be nearly the best possible performance that can be written on the subject. It does not confine itself, as an injudicious answer would have done, to a cold refutation of Mr Burke's errors; but with equal discernment and philanthropy, embraces every opportunity of improving the purest principles of liberty upon the hearts of mankind. It is perhaps impossible to rise from perusing it, without feeling oneself both wiser and better. The seeds of revolution it contains are so vigorous in their stamina that nothing can overpower them. All that remained for the illustrious author, after having enlightened the whole Western world by the publication of Common Sense, was to do a similar service to Europe, by a production energetic as that was, and adapted with equal skill to rouse and interest the mind. The effects, it may be, of this work will not be so rapid; but if properly disseminated (and persecution cannot injure it) will be as sure.[10]

They are perceptive words to have written on the eve of publication of one of the most influential pamphlets ever written. During the American War, Paine's *Common Sense* had helped swing opinion in favour of colonists. He had been in France at the outbreak of the Revolution and brought back the key of the Bastille to be sent to George Washington as a symbol that the French doors had been unlocked in America.[11] The man who had aleady promoted two successful revolutions abroad, was now in England ready for the third.

The *Rights of Man* struck effectively and amusingly at the more obvious weaknesses of Burke's argument. The new French Constitution had made the number of representatives proportional to the number of taxable inhabitants. In England, where legitimate government still reigned, the town of Old Sarum with three houses sent two members to Parliament, while Manchester with sixty thousand sent none. Yorkshire with a population of a million sent two as did Rutland with less than ten thousand. The City of Westminster where the rich spent the winter had an electorate of nearly twenty thousand: the City of Bath where they spent the summer had just thirty-one and was not unusual. And why the uneven distribution of election charters? Because William the Conqueror had been obliged to pay the going local rate of bribery in parcelling out the country to his supporters in the eleventh century. In the face of facts like these it required imagination or stolidity beyond the ordinary to argue that the British

Constitution, with a few marginal anomalies, was the best form of government ever devised.

The *Rights of Man* was intended as a serious piece of political theory but Paine was not over-scrupulous in his choice of weapons. One of the most damaging charges was the suggestion that Burke had written the *Reflections* as the price of a political pension. He told Godwin of a conversation which interested him so much that he made a detailed note:

Paine and Burke talking together observe what a government of pensions and corruption ours is – and distributed by such a fool said Paine – I wish however, said Burke, this fool would give me one of his places. Paine communicated intelligence to B. respecting Nootka Sound – You must carry this, said B., to Grey; I cannot bring it into Parliament, I am at this moment negociating with Pitt respecting the impeachment of Hastings.[12]

To those brought up in the dissenting tradition – as both Godwin and Paine had been – the give and take of eighteenth-century aristocratic politics was deeply offensive. Although not himself near the centres of power, Godwin was now near men who were. England, he learned, was even more corrupt than an outsider would have guessed and the morals of the liberal Whigs were little better than those of the rest.

Sheridan spends the night in gambling and dissipation. Used to breakfast at Weltie's upon everything that was out of season to the amount of thirty pound per breakfast. Was arrested by Weltie and paid. His present debt to Ditto. hushed up by the Prince of Wales.[13]

Lord Lansdown says he was desired by Fox to delay entering upon the treasury two days, which was spent in granting pensions and reversions to the party, particularly to Burke's cousin and son, one of which L Lansdown negatived, 1782.

Mr Moore, private secretary of lord Holland, offers to sell a pension of £1,500 per annum on the Irish establishment – confesses that it stands in his name, but is the property of Mr Burke, granted in 1782. Mr Fox had a pension to the same amount in the same manner and at the same time.

Fox, Burke, and Sheridan had been Godwin's heroes since his first excursions into political writing in 1784. Burke had gone over to the other side but now Fox and Sheridan were also wobbling. If the summer of 1790 had marked the peak of eighteenth-century optimism, it was already clear by the summer of 1791 that confidence was tumbling. Godwin, who had proclaimed his belief as early as 1783 that a nation has only to wish to be free in order to be so, and who from his chronicler's desk had seen his opinion substantiated in America, Holland and France, looked on with horror as the process turned sharply into reverse, and the men who should have been leading the march forward hesitated and compromised. In an attempt to rally them he and Holcroft decided to send open letters both to Sheridan and to Fox – although both were probably drafted by Godwin – reminding them of their former words. Godwin signed his letter with considerable exaggeration as by 'a well-known literary character'.

Truth has gone so far that it must go farther. It cannot stop. The true principles of government are studied, reasoned upon and understood . . . And can you really think that the *new constitution of France is the most glorious fabric ever raised by human integrity since the creation of man* and yet believe that what is good there would be bad here? Does truth alter its nature by crossing the straits and become falsehood? Are men entitled to perfect equality in France and is it just to deprive them of it in England? . . . Six years only elapsed before the emancipation of America brought forth the Revolution in France . . . Will France, the most refined and considerable nation in the world remain six years without an imitator . . . [14]

As in the letter to Paine, Godwin openly advocates a revolution in Great Britain, seeing such an event not so much as a violent uprising as a swing in opinion as a result of which a more progressive political system is more or less willingly introduced. Burke's predictions of the course of the French Revolution were to prove so accurate and have applied to so many other revolutions that they now constitute the general wisdom. It is however necessary to recall how shockingly cynical they seemed in 1790. Many people believed, reasonably enough from what was known at the time, that the French Revolution was already over. The changes that were being introduced in France were carried through by due political process after high-minded debate, and many commentators besides the chronicler of the *New Annual Register* believed they detected a long-term trend towards bloodless revolution to match the long-term trend towards bloodless war.

On 14 July 1791, the second anniversary of the fall of the Bastille, Godwin and nine hundred others again assembled for a celebratory dinner at the Crown and Anchor in the Strand. Robert Merry, the Della Cruscan poet, had composed an Ode with a bold metaphor drawn from Priestley's scientific discoveries which was set to music and sung.

> Fill high the animating glass
> And let the electric ruby pass
> From hand to hand, from soul to soul:
> Who shall the energy controul

Exalted, pure, refined,
The Health of Humankind!

But despite the electric rubies – and it was usual for forty or fifty different toasts to be drunk to Liberty in her various dresses – nobody felt in the mood for celebration and at eight o'clock the chairman suggested that they should go home. Most of them had already left when an uninvited mob gathered outside and made their way along the Strand demanding that people show lights as a sign that they too were celebrating. They were soon met by another mob who insisted that they put the lights out. A few windows were broken, but decisive action by the Lord Mayor and his men quelled the trouble.

At Birmingham however they were not so fortunate. On the 14th a hostile crowd which had gathered outside the hotel where the celebration dinner was to be held hissed the guests as they arrived and broke the windows. They attacked the New Meeting House of which Priestley was the minister and set it on fire, and then tore down the Old Meeting House making a bonfire of the pews. They moved to Priestley's own house, a mile and a half from Birmingham and destroyed it along with his library, his papers, and the famous laboratory where Priestley had made some of the most significant scientific discoveries of the century. A rioter was killed by a piece of falling masonry as Priestley watched from a nearby field. Night came but the following day brought no relief. Armed with bludgeons and shouting 'Church and King' the mob systematically destroyed the houses of prosperous dissenters and all the meeting houses over a wide area. Three days later a troop of light cavalry arrived in Birmingham, but it was nearly a week before order was restored.

The Birmingham riots had been carefully orchestrated – the leaders had lists of the names and addresses of dissenters. The authorities had not been sorry in the early stages to see a show of public disapproval but had been caught off guard. But even when order was restored and the violence officially deplored, many people were inclined to agree with the King who remarked that 'I cannot but feel better pleased that Priestley is the sufferer for the doctrines that he and his party have instilled.'

In Paris too the second anniversary of the fall of the Bastille was passed in very different circumstances from the Festival described by Helen Maria Williams the previous year. On 21 June when King Louis was intercepted trying to leave Paris in disguise in hopes of staging a counter-revolution with the help of foreign powers, his credibility was destroyed, and the French Revolution took a major step down the road predicted by Burke.

Three days after Bastille Day a crowd in the Champs de Mars was fired on by the National Guard and fifty people killed. When the extreme Jacobins under the leadership of Robespierre then split from the former allies and demanded radical equalizing measures, the Governments of the European continental powers publicly threatened France with armed intervention.

Godwin had already drafted the French section of the 1790 *New Annual Register*, before the events of 14 July 1791 and the horrifying news that poured in to England from France almost continuously thereafter. On all sides matters were plainly getting worse and the level of debate about the issues was rapidly deteriorating into party abuse and physical violence. It was in an atmosphere of crisis that Godwin took the courageous decision which he described in a fragment of autobiography.

I suggested to Robinson the bookseller the idea of composing a treatise on Political Principles, and he agreed to aid me in executing it. My original conception proceeded on a feeling of the imperfections and errors of Montesquieu, and a desire of supplying a less faulty work. In the first fervour of my enthusiasm, I entertained the vain imagination of 'hewing a stone from the rock' which, by its inherent energy and weight, should overbear and annihilate all opposition and place the principles of politics on an immoveable basis. It was my first determination to tell all that I apprehended to be truth, and all that seemed to be truth, confident that from such a proceeding the best results were to be expected.[15]

To the modern reader who knows something of the history of the French Revolution and its consequences it may appear an astonishingly ambitious aim, arrogant as well as naïve. But in 1791 it was impossible to know whether recent events marked a secular turning point or were just a kink in the previous upward trend. In 1791 it was still reasonable to believe that if progress faltered, cool reason could soon retrieve the lost ground and resume its advance. If the French Revolution had been brought about by the writings of philosophers, then the writings of later philosophers should be able to steer events back on course.

Among the hundreds of authors who offered their advice at this time Godwin was better qualified than most. He was acknowledged to be a man of unusual ability and intelligence with an education second to none in England. He had studied political theory long and hard and was as familiar with the debates of the seventeenth century as with those of his own. He knew the history of Europe from ancient times and had been obliged by his work at the *New Annual Register* to study recent events with a care and impartiality not always enforced on commentators. He was an accomplished author with eight years' experience of writing in a great variety of media (history, biography, sermons, political pamphlets, humour, novels, plays, genealogy, translating, editing, reviewing) and had many friends and acquaintances, political, scholarly, artistic and literary. True, he was short of what sociologists call 'life experience' but Holcroft and the ladies of the theatre had already endured plenty of that and were happy to share. Most important of all, Godwin's integrity was unimpeachable and unshakeable. If honest thought and fearless application could solve problems, he could offer both in abundance. He proposed 'Political Principles' to Robinson on 30 June, and some kind of understanding on money was reached on 10 July. On 4 September 1791 he had finished his contribution to the New Annual Register for the eighth and last time.

One of his last acts was to slip into the British history of the 1790 volume his own opinion of why Edmund Burke had gone wrong.

Mr Burke probably conceived, as a thousand wise men had done before him, that it was his business to aim, not at all the good which his imagination suggested to him, but only at the good which in his situation appeared practicable. Men thus circumstanced soon come to soothe the fervour of their zeal by an ingenious distinction between theory and practice, between that which is eternally true, and that which, though eternally false, they conceive to be the best that can be adapted to the corruptions of mankind.[16]

Godwin was determined never to make the same mistake.

CHAPTER 6

Writing a Masterpiece

On 4 September 1791, the day he finished his last contribution to the
New Annual Register, Godwin began a new volume of his journal. He
had started on 6 April 1788 when he was thirty-two and it was to be
continued until 26 March 1836 when he had passed his eightieth birthday.
It consists of thirty-two small notebooks with marbled paper covers so
nearly identical that – were it not for the dated watermarks – you could
believe that he bought a lifetime's supply when he first decided to start.
He carefully ruled and dated each notebook, with a week to every page,
the dates being written in red.

The dissenters, like their puritan forebears, were compulsive diarists
and Godwin was no exception. At various times in his life – often at
moments of sadness or stress – he composed passages of autobiography
intended to record the events of his life for posterity. He also wrote
introspective accounts of his own character, honestly analysing his faults
(his pride, his desire for fame, his social awkwardness) and the development of his philosophical ideas. But the journal itself has none of this. It
is a document of record intended for his own eyes only and it still retains
many of its secrets.

The first three volumes are primarily an *aide-mémoire* for the chronicler
of the *New Annual Register*, noting the dates of the chief public events
which he expected to write up in the following year – opening of Parliament, changes in the Cabinet, deaths of foreign monarchs. Soon however

A Literary Conversation, from Colman's *Broad Grins*

he started to alleviate the plentiful blank spaces by including useful information about himself, such as the days worked for the *New Annual Register* (important in arguments with Robinson about missed deadlines) and occasional highlights such as meetings with famous men. By the time he gave up the *New Annual Register*, however, the journal had settled into the pattern which he was to maintain until the end. He stopped recording the public news, although he resumed later when he found that he missed it, but he noted carefully for each day the amount of writing accomplished, the books read, the names of people met, important letters sent or received, and occasional summaries of key conversations.

He devised his own abbreviations, some in Latin or French. When he dined with friends, he noted the names of all the guests including some who were 'adv.' (advenae) perhaps because they arrived unexpectedly, and he liked to record the 'invités' who had been asked but did not come. Persons called on were often 'nah' (not at home) or 'nit' (not in town). Friends sometimes called on him 'ppc' (pour prendre congé). Books which he only skipped were 'çala' (çà et là). More than with many men, social occasions included 'démêlé' the nature of which is not always clear, nor can we be confident in ascribing more than the literal meaning to 'chez elle' and 'chez moi'. The journal tantalizes with its terseness – sometimes events usually regarded as worth recording in diaries, such as his marriages, are not noted as such. But when taken with the plentiful other evidence which survives, it provides a uniquely detailed record. There are few literary figures whose lives are so fully documented.[1]

A month after finishing the *New Annual Register* he made another break with the past. His journal for 4 October 1791 noted for the first and only time 'Cut off my hair.' The man who three years before still bore the unrelieved black of a dissenting divine now shed the last outward signs of his upbringing. The Reverend had gone from his name probably in 1788, although it was said by mischievous friends that, to avoid certain duties, his official occupation continued to be dissenting minister.[2]

After the hair-cutting of October 1791 visitors were amazed at the transformation. One friend remembered his new blue coat and blue stockings with yellow breeches and matching waistcoat.[3] A lady admirer from Norwich was delighted to find him wearing a green coat with crimson waistcoat and sharp-toed red slippers, his well-powdered hair carefully parted in the middle and plaited behind. His stock or neck cloth, to judge from the portraits (Plates 2 and 3), was a little too extravagant even for those elegant days. The general effect was of a modern man-about-town, almost of a dandy.[4] Like Holcroft who dressed similarly, he wore spectacles, a custom still so unusual that short-sighted persons often preferred blurred vision to the coarse jokes which they were liable to encounter in the streets[5] – although such mockery was easier to bear than the chants of 'Damn Priestley, damn him for ever', which dissenters' black was said to provoke in Birmingham.

Godwin also shed his religion. By 1788 he had moved far from the strict Sandemanianism of his boyhood, but he was still a Christian and had been so, with the exception of one brief interlude of deism, for all his life. Characteristically when he again began to feel doubts, he approached the question with a high sense of purpose, seeing it as his right and his duty to decide the question for himself openly and honestly after full and proper consideration. Advised that Campbell's *Dissertation on Miracles* written in reply to Hume was the best defence of Christian belief, he obtained a copy and retired to Guildford with his books for several weeks' study.

It was no light step to abandon the faith of his ancestors and he was tortured with worries. Among his papers are essays and memoranda, compiled at this crisis, in which he examines the arguments that Hume and others had advanced against Christianity and then considers the Christian answers. (Why, he asks in one piece, if the resurrection was intended to be an evidential miracle, did Jesus not appear personally to more witnesses and so remove doubts? Christian answer: to promote the merits of faith.) As he wrote later, recalling his promise to pursue truth wherever she led, he viewed 'with contempt and aversion' the idea that he might be the dupe of a mistaken faith. He was afraid too, of what his family and friends would say if he lapsed, but most of all, he honestly feared the 'dreadful damnation of the gospel hanging over me, directed against them who, with advantages of Christian light and evidence, yet concluded in unbelief.'[6]

But his reason triumphed over his fear. Godwin abandoned Christianity in favour of the undemanding deism which many of the thinkers of the century, scientists and philosphers, found preferable both to revealed religion and to outright atheism which, as yet, had found no answer to the argument from design. For a year or two he still considered that acts of public worship were appropriate, but by the early 1790s he had become almost totally agnostic.

His widowed mother, once so proud of her son's decision to follow his father and his grandfather into the ministry, never lost hope that he would again be reconciled with her wrathful God. In April 1792 she sent him a copy of a sermon on the theme 'I am become a stranger unto my brethren and an alien unto my mother's children'. She prayed for him, she wrote in the accompanying letter, 'without ceasing three times a day besides the sleepless hours of the night', and her later letters too, although full of kindness and concern for her wayward children and grandchildren, consistently warn that they cannot expect to prosper or receive God's blessing 'without prayers and watchfulness against their strong enemys, Satan, ye world, and their own depraved hearts'.[7]

But it is easier to cut your hair and change your clothes than to alter the fundamental habits of thought of a lifetime, easier to change professed beliefs than escape from the traditions into which you have been born. Rationalist and agnostic though he was, Godwin's training had been as a theologian. The dissenting academies such as Hoxton were the proud heirs of the famous theologians of the seventeenth century whose methods and beliefs had been consciously readopted early in the century by Isaac Watts, Philip Doddridge, and Godwin's own grandfather.

For God, Godwin the philosopher now read Reason or Truth; and for the illumination of the Holy Spirit he read the careful and honest exercise of individual judgement; but Godwin's approach was essentially the same. To those who study hard and conscientiously with an uncorrupted mind, the truth will reveal herself proposition by proposition. If you start with incontrovertible propositions, and clamp conclusions to them by iron logic, you cannot be wrong even if the results fit uncomfortably with experience.[8]

He was determined to start with first principles. Never for a moment did he contemplate a mere reply to Burke, remarking in a lofty footnote that he was more at ease in a general consideration of Burke's views 'than in a personal attack upon this illustrious and virtuous hero of former times'.[9] The views of Tom Paine would also be considered without his being named.[10] Only if the foundations were laid securely on an immovable basis of immutable truth could he expect to bring about an enduring change of attitudes.

He began writing in September 1791 and worked continuously for sixteen months, not a long time for a work which eventually ran to 895 pages in two large quarto volumes. All aspects of his life were subordinated to the task, and he was in a state of uninterrupted high excitement. On many of the most crucial arguments he had formed his views years before and all he now had to do was write them up, but he found that the book grew in scope during the drafting and he believed that he had made important new discoveries between the beginning and the end. 'When a man writes a book of methodical investigation,' he remarked later, 'he does not write because he understands the subject, but he understands the subject because he has written.'[11] *An Enquiry Concerning Political Justice* (as 'Political Principles' was to be named) was such a work, hammered out sentence by sentence, to the demanding standards of his theologian's mind.

A list survives of nine addresses dotted over London, with the names of landladies, where Godwin lived between 1783 and 1788.[12] In that year he had taken on a teenage pupil, Thomas Cooper, a cousin whose father had died in India, who lived with him for three years before going on to a successful career on the stage. As soon as Cooper left, however, as part of the plan to devote himself unremittingly to his philosophical work Godwin moved to a small house in Chalton Street, Somers Town, in the area which now lies between Euston and St Pancras stations and which was then a village on the northern edge of London. He lived alone, apart from a servant who came in daily to clean and cook – an arrangement regarded as eccentric even for a man with little money. He was determined to have no unnecessary distraction from the great task on hand.

Soon his life settled to a pattern which he was to maintain for most of his life. He rose early and would read from the work of a Greek or Latin author before breakfast, not for its direct relevance to his studies, but to refresh himself, as he saw it, with the best literature. Like a divine of a former age, he was concerned to approach his inquiry in the right spirit of mind. The remaining morning hours until noon were devoted to writing and to reading, and it was a rare day when he wrote more than five pages. Often it was only one page or nothing. This again was a conscious decision. Writing held no terrors for a man whose output over eight years was already enormous, but throughout his life Godwin felt that he could only write at his best in short bursts when he was inspired – when the 'afflatus' was on him, he would say – like a poet, and he sustained his courage, as his ancestors had done, by writing sermons to himself.[13]

He let it be known that anyone who interrupted with a social call in the morning would be unwelcome. Reading was a vital process in the search for truth, and his first duty in the autumn of 1791 was to reread all his most important predecessors beginning with Plato and including Rousseau, Hume, Voltaire, Helvétius, d'Holbach's *Système de la Nature*, Locke, Price, Burke, Paine, Mackintosh, Bentham, Condilliac, Condorcet, Montesquieu and others. He also read an immense quantity of history, poetry, novels, and drama. For Godwin there was no artificial distinction between factual and imaginative literature. As a boy he had been worried about what he would do when he had read all the books in the world and it is easy to understand why.[14] In the course of a long life he was one of the last men to have read all the great European authors of ancient and modern times. Charles Lamb's envious gibe that he had read more books not worth reading than any man in history did not imply that he had neglected the others.[15]

But unusual as it may appear to those accustomed to modern methods of research, Godwin did not give primacy to the written word. Truth, he believed, is 'struck out . . . by the collision of mind with mind'.[16] Books are repositories of the thoughts of other minds and must be read; but you cannot argue with them. You cannot easily produce that direct clash of argument against counter argument which will throw off sparks of truth. For this you need conversation face to face, you need friends of similar outlook and dedication who will read and will argue, you need time, you need an agenda, you need occasions to meet. In the composition of *Political Justice*, the afternoons, which were devoted to social calls and to dinner, were as important as the solitary study of the mornings.

It was an age of heavy drinking. Foreigners visiting London were appalled at the number of ale houses and dram shops which offered the appealing advertisement 'Drunk for a penny, dead drunk for twopence'. The Duke of Norfolk was among many who were sometimes found asleep where they fell in the streets of London. The three Whig leaders, Fox, Sheridan and Grey all drank heavily and many of Godwin's friends did the same. Some of them also took laudanum, the mixture of wine and opium which was the prescribed medical remedy for innumerable illnesses from toothache to melancholia. The next generation were to be shocked at the personal slovenliness of Blake, Hazlitt, Coleridge and others, much of which was attributable to drink or drugs. But Godwin himself never succumbed either to excess or to teetotalism and his strong residual puritanism never overturned his moderation. Wine was served at dinner every day. Occasionally he also took spirits which still gave a tingle of guilt – or so at least we can interpret the rare mention in his journal of 'rum', coyly transliterated into Greek letters, on evenings at his sister Hannah's.

Nor, in spite of his upbringing, did Godwin succumb to the old puritan aversion to the theatre against which his mother consistently warned – 'Idleness is the mother of all Vice. Forgers, pickpockets or Players which I take to be very little better.' On the contrary, he was a devotee, attending often, sometimes more than once in a week. It was cheaper to be admitted to a part of a performance and there were many masterpieces of drama of which he saw only the first or second halves. Nor was he put off by the fact that theatres were the main venue for prostitutes and their clients, and that theatregoers were accustomed to mix their pleasures.

Besides Holcroft, his principal partner in the search for truth was William Nicholson, and the original version of the Preface (which was not printed) contained a public acknowledgement by name of the contribution of these two friends. 'It will be found by every man who has temper and advantage for the experiment', he wrote, 'that more improvement is to be derived from friendly discussion than from any other external aid.'[17] Like Holcroft and Godwin, Nicholson was a professional writer who operated in the frontier lands between journalism and literature, taking commissions from Robinson, Johnson, and others for translations, indexes, compilations, and other anonymous literary work in addition to writing a few books which appeared under his own name. His speciality was science and he produced a series of popular scientific dictionaries and encyclopedias as well as editing a *Journal of Natural Philosophy* containing digests of the latest scientific discoveries and industrial innovations.

It was to Nicholson that Godwin turned for information on the latest theories in chemistry, physics, optics, biology, and the other natural sciences, but equally important was his advice on scientific method as such. In his *Introduction to Natural Philosophy* of 1782, Nicholson had offered the three 'Rules for Philosophising':

i) No more causes of natural things ought to be admitted than are true and sufficient to explain the phenomenon;
ii) And therefore effects of the same kind are produced by the same causes;
iii) Those qualities which do not vary and are found in all bodies with which experiments can be made ought to be admitted as qualities of all bodies in general.

With these principles in mind, Godwin and his friends devoted themselves tirelessly to one of the most tantalizing of all philosophical questions, one which seemed nearer solution in the 1780s than at any previous time. Could the methods which had yielded such astonishingly rapid advances in the natural sciences be successfully applied to human psychology, to history, to politics, and to other 'social sciences'? Is it possible to discover underlying principles of human behaviour as Sir Isaac Newton discovered the laws of physics? Maybe the answers had already been found and all that remained was to collect and apply them? Among themselves the group commanded an impressive range of intellectual disciplines from theology to technology, and they were determined to succeed.

61

From Godwin's journal we can follow the process of composition of the book, with reading, drafting, and discussion with friends.

[21 September 1791] Burke on Paraguay. Write 1 page. Fawcet dines; talk of genius and virtue, and of Christianity.

[27 September 1791] Rewrite a paragraph. Tea at Nicholson's: talk of rhetoric. Dyson calls. Hume's Essays.

[30 September 1791] Write 2 pages. Tea at Nicholson's; criticise the Introduction; talk of economistes, taxation, and commerce.

[19 October 1791] Dine with Fawcet at North End: shew him letters to Fox & Sheridan: talk of property, of Helvetius and his profession. Priestley offended. Read Fred[erick the Great] on Government.

[13 May 1792] Revise: Write 1½ pages on suicide. Dine at Holcroft's, with Dyson, talk of gravitation. Sup at Nicholson's w[ith] H[olcroft]. talk of immortality, abstraction, causation, majorities, & promises. Paley 28 pages.

These are typical days. The subjects of conversation noted during the composition of *Political Justice* cover the whole field of what would now be called politics, psychology, ethics, religion, economics, and current affairs, and the number of people who participated – famous and obscure – was also great. Naturally he was particularly concerned to find opportunities to converse with the leading theorists of the day such as Priestley.

The political climate was changing fast. On 4 November 1791, 103 years from the eve of the landing of King William at Torbay, Godwin attended once more the annual commemorative dinner of the Revolution Society at the London Tavern. Two years had passed since the 1789 dinner when success in the campaign against the Test Acts had looked so near, but now everything was changed. To point the contrast, the trials began in Birmingham that day of rioters arrested after the Bastille Day riots the previous July, and over the following months the news was punctuated with reports of convictions and executions. Priestley, who was present at the dinner, remained one of the most hated men in England: his brave attempts to combine reason with Christianity and to work peaceably for reform by parliamentary means had proved worse than useless and he was shortly to leave for permanent exile in the United States. The leadership of the reformers was passing to less scrupulous men, for whom violence was not so unthinkable.

At previous Revolution Society dinners it had been usual to sing British patriotic songs, but this year French tricolours were intertwined with the British Union Jacks, and an orchestra regularly interrupted the proceedings with renderings of *Ça Ira* and other French marches. Many of the diners ostentatiously wore the French revolutionary cockade and the principal guest was Pétion, one of the revolutionary leaders, soon to be Mayor of Paris, whom Godwin had met a few days before at a private dinner at Holcroft's. When the royal toast was proposed, it was drunk in silence. Pétion's speech on Anglo-French friendship was greeted with rapturous applause. But it was Tom Paine who stole the show when he rose to propose a toast that was to echo round Europe until 1917 and beyond – 'Gentlemen, I give you the Revolution of the World.'

A few days after the dinner, Godwin met Paine at a smaller gathering at the home of one of the Revolution Society leaders. It was known that Godwin was working on a book about political principles just as Paine was working on a second part of *The Rights of Man*. The two could not properly be regarded as rivals and in seeking a meeting with the older man, Godwin's letter did not avoid the charmless tone of assertiveness to which he was habitually led by fear of insincerity and dislike of sycophancy.

I was yesterday at my own request introduced to you by Mr B. Hollis; but in the hurry and confusion of a numerous meeting, I had not had an opportunity of saying something which I have wished to say to you in person. I have wished for an occasion of expressing to you my feelings of the high obligation you have conferred upon Britain and mankind by your late publication of the Rights of Man. I believe few men have a more ardent sense of that obligation than myself; and I conceive that it is a duty incumbent upon persons so feeling to come forward with the most direct of applause of your efforts.

I regard you, Sir, as having been the unalterable champion of liberty in America, in England, and in France, from the purest views to the happiness and the virtue of mankind. I have devoted my life to these glorious purposes and I am at this moment employed upon a composition embracing the whole doctrine of politics, in which I shall endeavour to convince my countrymen of the mischiefs of monarchical government, and of certain other abuses not less injurious to society. I believe that a cordial and unreserved intercourse between men employed in the same great purposes, is of the utmost service to their own minds, and to their cause. I have therefore thought proper to break through all ceremony in thus soliciting the advantage of a personal acquaintance, and if you entertain the same opinion, you will, I am confident, favour me with an interview either at my apartments or at any other place you will please to appoint. I am, sir, already the ardent friend of your views, your principles, and your mind.[18]

Another draft written on a separate sheet may be a postscript, or an alternative version.

I should be happy in the favour of your company to dine with two or three friends on [—] if agreeable. I need not desire a man of your energy of mind to accept or slight this invitation as you shall feel inclined. I am fully certain that, while you are engaged in the great cause which I so ardently love, no mistake that you may fall into respecting me will be able to alter the esteem and veneration I entertain for you. I disdained the petty ceremonies of society in soliciting your acquaintance because I knew your merit. It was impossible you should know me so well, and I am contented to wait with patience, confident that the time will come when you will acknowledge the kindred I claim.

It is not known whether Paine replied to this invitation although among Godwin's papers are notes of an attempt to put together a suitably impressive guest list for the party. A few days later however, as his journal records, he was invited to meet Paine at the table of Joseph Johnson the publisher.

Nov. 13 Su[nday] Correct. Dyson & Dibdin call; talk of virtue and disinterest. Dine at Johnson's with Paine, Shovet & Wolstencraft; talk of monarchy, Tooke, Johnson [Dr Johnson], Voltaire, pursuits and religion. Sup at Holcrofts.

Mary Wollstonecraft, whom Godwin had not previously met, was employed by Joseph Johnson to write books and reviews but, like Godwin, although she had applied her talents to several forms of writing, none of her books had as yet raised much interest. Her recent sharp reply to Burke, *A Vindication of the Rights of Men* was abusive, emotional, and partisan, exactly the kind of political document that Godwin was determined not to follow in his own forthcoming work. He had read it and had been irritated.

The party was not a success. Godwin and Mary Wollstonecraft did not become friends, although they met one another occasionally at similar gatherings during the next months. Seven years later however when Mary was already dead, the grieving Godwin was to recall their first inauspicious meeting in an account which reveals much about his own outlook and opinions at this time.

... I had therefore little curiosity to see Mrs Wollstonecraft, and a very great curiosity to see Thomas Paine. Paine, in his general habits, is no great talker; and, though he threw in occasionally some shrewd and striking remarks, the conversation lay principally between me and Mary. I, of consequence, heard her very frequently when I wished to hear Paine. We touched on a considerable variety of topics, and particularly on the characters and habits of certain eminent men.[19]

Godwin disliked conversation which was without purpose, or which tripped unconcernedly from topic to topic. As a boy he had been made afraid by the Bible's warning that he would answer for every idle word at the day of judgement.[20] It had deeply affected him, and even when the fear lifted, the habits remained. Words were not for mere entertainment. He hated to leave a debate unresolved and he had a tendency to insist. People who admired his acuteness of observation and breadth of understanding were often at the same time disturbed by his forthright and tenacious mode of arguing. The snorting laugh, with which he would indicate disagreement, could sound sneering or triumphant. He talked too much and would not let a subject drop when the interest of the company was evidently waning. Opponents were not permitted to retreat gracefully under cover of a joke or an ambiguity but were pressed to admit defeat and to recant. To those accustomed to the conventions of a Georgian drawing room, the discourse of a dissenting academy was plain bad manners.[21]

One man who knew better was William Hazlitt whose father had been a successor to Godwin's father as dissenting minister at Wisbech and who had himself been educated at a dissenting academy. He first met Godwin in 1794 and he was, by the hard standards which both men adopted, one of Godwin's closest friends. In his essay *On Good Nature*, Hazlitt analyses 'the most selfish of all the virtues' which is usually either simple laziness or hypocritical indifference.[22] To find real concern for other people, says Hazlitt, you have to look to men whose manners are disagreeable.

They have an unfortunate attachment to a set of abstract phrases, such as *liberty*, *truth*, *justice*, *humanity*, *honour*, which are continually abused by knaves and misunderstood by fools; and they can hardly contain themselves for spleen . . . No sooner is one question set at rest than another rises up to perplex them . . . They teaze themselves to death about the morality of the Turks or the politics of the French. There are certain words that afflict their ears and things that lacerate their souls, and remain a plague-spot there for ever after. They have a fellow-feeling with all that has been done, said, or thought in the world. They have an interest in all science and in all art. They hate a lie as much as a wrong, for truth is the foundation of all justice. Truth is the first thing in their thoughts, then mankind, then their country, last themselves.

For twelve months the work continued, reading, drafting, and arguing, and the book progressed steadily paragraph by paragraph, chapter by chapter. In the early months of 1792, we find Godwin debating passivity, self love – this very frequently – free will, immortality, necessity, space and causation, property and laws, the power of the mind, war, revolution. He is reading Sophocles, Shakespeare, and Tasso as well as books of history and of political theory. His aim from the beginning had been to get the book out quickly, and he worked hard. If he was to lift the eyes of leaders from the short-term partisan considerations with which they were currently obsessed back to fundamental principles, his book would have to convince them to change their attitudes before too much damage was done.

But in the race against time, he was constantly losing ground. In the autumn of 1792, with a suddenness that took everyone by surprise, the political situation in France began to deteriorate alarmingly. As control of the Government passed to the Jacobins, increasing numbers of Frenchmen began to plan for a counter-revolution to be achieved, if necessary with the aid of outsiders. In August a crowd stormed the palace of the Tuileries in Paris amid much bloodshed. The King and Queen were arrested; and a republic was declared not long afterwards. Then in September came the first terror, during which over a thousand prisoners suspected of sympathizing with the foreign armies were summarily put to death by order of popular tribunals.

The British watched with dismay as Burke's prophecies for the course of the French Revolution were realized step by step. Was Britain, everyone now asked, destined to follow France down the same disastrous road where demands for constitutional reform led to internal disturbance, violent overthrow of government, counter-revolution, anarchy, and mass terror?

In October 1792 Godwin decided to speed up production. He agreed with Robinson that the manuscript should be sent to the printer sheet by sheet as it was written, accepting that the final version would contain internal contradictions and inelegancies. Robinson started to advertise that the book would be published early in the following January. By 5 November, the traditional date for celebrating the triumph of various alleged English liberties, the situation was already polarizing rapidly. Effigies of Tom Paine replaced the traditional Guy on many bonfires. Five hundred gentlemen attending a Revolution Society dinner the previous evening – Godwin did not go this year – sang the 'Marseillaise' and drank forty toasts of which almost half were salutes to French revolutionary and military achievements. But when a dissenting minister remarked in a traditional anniversary sermon at Exeter that he approved of the Revolution in France which he hoped had opened the eyes of the people of England, he was arrested on a charge of seditious libel and sentenced to four years' imprisonment.

Tougher measures, the Government had decided, were needed to try to stop the spread of revolutionary ideas and to give a suitable fright to anyone who might be inclining towards the wrong side in a war which now looked inevitable. When the French Government defiantly made a public offer of assistance to revolutionary movements in neighbouring countries, they acted quickly. A Royal Proclamation urged magistrates to do their duty – an effective hint in the country districts where landowning and the administration of justice were much the same thing. An 'Association for Protecting Liberty and Property against Republicans and Levellers', appealing, as the name implied, to all who feared old puritans in their new French disguises, offered cash rewards for information about seditious activities, and private spies soon came forward in large numbers to meet the demand.

On 19 December 1792, the Attorney General brought a successful action for seditious libel against Thomas Paine who had by now fled to France. Godwin, taking time off from his writing to attend the trial, heard the Attorney General make the fatuous statement that 'our glorious and incomparable constitution existed from the earliest accounts of time and was recognized by Julius Caesar'. Paine, who along with Priestley, Price, Mackintosh and a few others – mostly dissenters – had been made an honorary French citizen, was found guilty. As Godwin emerged sad and angry from the courthouse, he was met by hack booksellers offering him Paine's fictitious 'confessions'.[23]

The New Year of 1793 brought a spate of further prosecutions. A man was imprisoned for posting a notice calling for parliamentary reform. A Scottish tallow chandler who made disparaging anti-monarchical remarks about the royal guns in the armoury of the Tower of London was sentenced to three months even though he was drunk at the time and on his first sightseeing trip to London. In January and February a number of booksellers and printsellers were arrested and charged with publishing or selling seditious literature.

Most of *Political Justice* had already been sent to the printer when the crackdown started, and it required considerable courage from author and from publisher to let publication proceed. At the time when Godwin began writing there had been few inhibitions on political debate, but now the Government were giving repeated public warnings that they would proceed against anyone making what they called intemperate remarks about the Constitution, whether in speech or in writing.

Godwin had already drafted a brief Preface explaining the origin and purpose of the book and noting his thanks to Holcroft and Nicholson, but on 7 January 1793, at the moment when the extent of the Government's intentions was becoming clear, he prepared a redraft, and it was this version which was published as a carefully considered act of defiance. 'It is now twelve years since he [the author] became satisfied of the radical errors of monarchical government,' he had intended to write; the wording was now changed to '. . . became satisfied that monarchy was a species of government unavoidably corrupt'. The associations, the spies, the bounties for informers, and the Government's threats were, he now wrote dismissively 'an accident wholly unforeseen when the work was undertaken' and he was not going to be influenced by such ephemeral considerations.

Godwin's disdainful style, so irritating when employed on lesser matters, was on this occasion both wholly appropriate and wholly convincing.

Respecting the event in a personal view the author has formed his resolution. Whatever conduct his countrymen may pursue, they will not be able to shake his tranquillity. The duty he is most bound to discharge is the assisting the progress of truth; and if he suffer in any respect for such a proceeding, there is certainly no vicissitude that can befal him, that can ever bring along with it a more satisfactory consolation . . . It is the property of truth to be fearless, and to prove victorious over every adversary. It requires no great degree of fortitude, to look with indifference upon the false fire of the moment, and to foresee the calm period of reason which will succeed.

A further month was needed to correct the remaining proofs, run off the sheets and bind the book, and the fevers which he noted in his journal were of the mind as much as of the body. During this time the trial took place in Paris of King Louis who went to his death on 21 January. The following day, before the news could have reached London, Godwin called on the French Ambassador to give him an advance copy to be sent to the French Government.[24] The Ambassador was ordered to leave London three days later but he did take the book with him. France declared war on 1 February – Godwin was at the House of Commons on two successive days to hear the speeches – and the British Government responded with their own declaration three weeks later. *Political Justice* finally went on sale in London on 14 February in the twilight period between the two declarations of war.

CHAPTER 7

Political Justice

An Enquiry Concerning Political Justice and Its Influence on General Virtue and Happiness was offered to the public as an essay for consideration, not as an authoritative statement of a complete philosophy. When Godwin wrote in the Preface that he hoped to supersede the works of his predecessors, he was making not a boast but a disclaimer. Dazzled – like many of his contemporaries – by the achievements of the natural sciences, he did not question that the search for political and moral principles, 'moral philosophy', was essentially the same process as the search for the laws of nature, 'natural philosophy'. The technical vocabulary in which the two subjects were commonly debated had not yet diverged. It was reasonable too to believe that discoveries once made could not afterwards be lost, and that the follow-up work of collating and disseminating the results could be left to lesser hands.

Godwin saw his book primarily as a consolidation of the 'science' – his own word – discovered by Locke, Rousseau, Hume, Helvétius, d'Holbach, and other philosophers since the beginning of the century, and all he asked for his own findings was that they should be given a fair hearing. 'In the following work,' he wrote, 'principles will occasionally be found which it will not be just to reject without examination merely because they are new', but his prime purpose was to give an account of existing knowledge rather than to break new ground. It is not surprising therefore that a knowledgeable reader can go through the book and mark the

The Plundering of British Liberties, from Hone's *Political House that Jack Built* sources for many of the arguments. Often confirmation can be obtained by checking the journal to see what Godwin was reading when the passage was drafted. Godwin himself originally intended to note the sources of his ideas in the margin of his book but the plan was a casualty of the rush to finish.

But *Political Justice* is not a mere compilation. Apart from consolidating his predecessors' work into a coherent and consistent whole, a formidable task in itself, Godwin's approach to the subject is more ambitious. Unlike Montequieu for example, whose work he hoped to update, Godwin does not start with a comparison of existing forms of government. He inquires into the philosophical basis of government itself. He wants to discover the principles against which political questions can be judged, and only then to prescribe political systems. He quickly discovered however that he could not go far in discussing politics without being drawn into ethics and therefore into theories of the human mind and of human motivation. In the end therefore the book had to be concerned with so many prior philosophical questions that it comes near to offering an original philosophical work.

Godwin published three editions of *Political Justice*, the first in 1793, the second in 1796, and the third in 1798. The life of a thinking man, he was later to tell Shelley, is a series of retractations, and he himself was never ashamed to change his mind. Although, as he always maintained, the essentials of the argument remained unaltered, there are, as a result, considerable differences between the three editions. The order of the argument was rearranged. The title was changed. Some of his bolder speculations were dropped; others were more heavily qualified; and the ideas were put forward with more modesty and a greater sense of doubt – although Godwin never had either quality in abundance.

The third edition – the only version reprinted in recent times – is the best exposition of Godwin's mature philosophy since it reflects his consideration of comments made about the earlier editions. In its turn it was to be modified by later writings. However it was the first edition written in the hectic weeks before the outbreak of war in 1793 which established Godwin's reputation and shaped his future life. Composed in a period of sustained excitement when he saw himself as the last soldier defending the breached wall of civilization, it has a bright, forthright, visionary style which is lacking in the other editions. Many admirers continued to prefer the original despite the uncorrected flaws, seeing it as the pure milk of Godwinism which was later watered down. Opponents also found it easier – and more enjoyable – to attack and he never shook

off the ridicule which attached to certain famous passages. Godwin and
Political Justice were to prove as influential in their occasional absurdities
as in their basic strengths. In offering an account in this chapter therefore,
I try to convey some of the unusual flavour of the 1793 version while at
the same time presenting his essential arguments in as coherent and persuasive a form as appears fair.

Godwin's method of philosophical discourse reflects his theological
training. He propounds a view, lists the arguments that he has heard
advanced against it, and offers comments on each. Seldom is any question
left hanging and there is a marked absence of qualification. He is more
interested in the coherence of the total structure than in disposing of
individual difficulties or objections in detail. Logic is more important than
common sense and he is not shocked by the counter-intuitive.

Central to the whole theory is his doctrine of 'Necessity', a word in
much use at the time in theological and scientific debate. In Godwin's
sense, it can best be explained as a theory of the human mind which
attempts to resolve the problem of free will and determinism. To Godwin
– reflecting the accepted view of his times – the material universe is a
series of events each one of which derives inevitably from its predecessors.
Following the model of Newtonian physics, he sees the world as a gigantic
billiard table in which the behaviour of each billiard ball is determined
by how it is struck by the other billiard balls careering about the table.
The universe is – to use another of Godwin's favourite metaphors – a
chain in which everything is connected with everything else. If you tug
the end of a chain, there will be repercussions all along its length, the
movement of each link being at the same time both the effect of the
movement of the previous link and a cause of the movement of the next.
If we had perfect knowledge of the laws of physics, we would be able to
predict from the observed movement of the first link exactly how the last
link would behave. The operations of the mind, according to the theory,
can be regarded as a similar series of events. If there were no discoverable
general principles of human nature, history would be nothing more than
chronological tables in which no explanation is offered or expected for
the sequence of events. Without some presumption of consistency in
human nature there would be no purpose or enjoyment in literature or
in art. There must therefore be laws of mind to be discovered just like
the laws of physics.

Earlier in the century, the philosopher David Hartley had conjectured
the existence of infinitesimal 'medullary particles' in the brain which
'vibrate' in response to 'associations', a theory not much different in its

implications from the modern view that mental events are essentially to be regarded as electro-chemical pulses. Godwin follows the Hartleian model closely. But although the mind may be governed by laws of causation, this does not mean, according to Godwin, that human beings are totally pre-programmed. The key to the apparent contradiction lies in the application of perception, reason, and motive. Since all knowledge is empirical, human beings are for the most part content to apply unthinkingly what they believe to be the truth, permitting themselves to be pushed around by previous events – whether they realize it or not – as inexorably as struck billiard balls. But if they succeed in making an improved perception, that itself is a mental event as a result of which the subsequent chain of mental – and therefore physical – events is different from what it would otherwise have been. In practice, this admits a limited free will element into a generally determinist theory.

Godwin is, understandably, more lucid and more convincing on the deterministic parts of his theory than on the relationship between reason, perception, and motivation, and many obscurities remain in his account of how the chain of mental events actually works. However the general thesis is both plain and plausible. If we know a man's opinions, we can foretell how he is likely to act, and if we know enough about his upbringing, education, and subsequent experience, we are likely to be able to foretell his opinions. We are all, says Godwin, children of our environment. Our perception of the world, our beliefs about what is true and false and our resulting behaviour derive from impressions and opinions received in earlier life.

It follows that the impressions which the mind receives in childhood are particularly important for they not only determine normal opinion and therefore behaviour but provide the best opportunities at which the determinist chain can be redirected. Godwin initially shared the belief of Locke and others that, at birth, the human mind is a blank sheet on which experience then writes. He had adopted and expanded this doctrine as early as 1784 in his *Account of the Seminary*, and all his life he was to remain convinced of the overriding importance of education. But the point is not substantially weakened if, as Godwin soon came to believe from his experience of real children, we accept that at birth children are not all equal in their potentialities.

More important than education as an influence on the mind is 'government', a term which Godwin employed to describe what would now be called the entire political, social, cultural, and economic system. Men's perceptions of the world are decisively affected by the form of government under which they live, by the way they earn their living, by customs, by art and literature and by all the other ways in which opinions and values are diffused through a society. 'Government', he remarked vividly in a passage which he subsequently deleted, 'is nothing else but education on a larger scale.' Much of *Political Justice* is a discussion of how the individual mind is conditioned by false or misleading notions picked up from these influences.

Godwin is a utilitarian although he seldom uses the word. At the beginning of the book he asserts as his axioms that 'All men will grant that the happiness of the human species is the most desirable object for human science to promote; and that intellectual and moral happiness or pleasure is extremely to be preferred to those which are precarious or transitory.'[1] Godwin sees his philosophical objective as to find the political principles which, if applied, will best promote human happiness, and in the third edition he offered a list in a convenient summary at the beginning of the book. Some are in the form of factual statements about human nature or about the general tendencies of human beings; others are ethical statements or statements about desirability; some are deductions, logically derived from the others; and the initial axiomatic assertions are also included. As a philosopher of 'moral philosophy', Godwin was not unduly bothered at using the word 'principle' to cover both factual and ethical propositions. Since his axioms contained an implied ethical judgement, there was no inconsistency.

One of the principles which in 1793 he thought was too self-evident to need spelling out was the doctrine of the perfectibility of man. 'Perfectibility', he wrote, 'is one of the most unequivocal characteristics of the human species, so that the political as well as the intellectual state of man may be presumed to be in a course of progressive improvement.' It was the former dissenting minister – brought up in one of the most joyless and hopeless views of man ever devised by a suffering people – who popularized the most confident and optimistic belief of the age of enlightenment. Godwin gave currency to the English word 'perfectibility', having found the French word already coined by Condorcet, using it to mean, as he explained later, 'the progressive nature of man, in knowledge, in virtuous propensities, and in social institutions'.[2]

Early in the century Europe had debated whether ancient civilization was superior to modern, but by the time Godwin wrote, Modern Europe had so manifestly overtaken Greece and Rome that the question itself seemed hardly worth asking. Many people shared the view of Edward Gibbon that the progress of civilization was now self-sustaining and irreversible, and that with the invention of printing, it was now impossible for knowledge once acquired to be subsequently lost. Godwin, in including the perfectibility of man among his political principles, was not making a bold new claim but noting an assumption which was generally regarded as having a sound empirical foundation.

Progress occurs, according to Godwin's theory, as a result of the accumulation of improved insights, in what may be termed the intellectual economy, which lead to better decisions being taken in the moral economy. The task of the philosopher is to explain how the underlying growth rate can be stimulated and accelerated.

Godwin recommends the methods which he had employed in the writing of the book – literature, education, conversation, and the clash of mind on mind. Above all he advises a fearless sincerity, and a readiness to push every discussion to a conclusion which will ensure that the medullary particles of the mind are indeed redirected. The seventeenth-century puritans had seen it as their duty to speak freely to one another without fear and this was one feature of his religious heritage which the rationalist philosopher was able to retain unchanged. Without sincerity there can be no truth, and without truth there can be no progress.

Sincerity is such an important ingredient in the process that particular care is therefore needed to preserve it untainted. Godwin has no sympathy with those who argue that good may occasionally come from deceit (although he was to revise this view later). He is scornful of minor social hypocrisies and white lies, tracing, as an example, the accumulation of moral damage which occurs if you ask your servant to tell an unwelcome visitor that you are not at home when in fact you are. Every individual has, Godwin advises, a paramount duty to tell the truth as he sees it at all times, even to the extent of censuring friends and acquaintances. It is not necessary, when I walk down the street, to tell everybody I meet exactly what I think of him, but:

All the praise which a virtuous man and an honest action can merit, I am obliged to pay to the uttermost mite. I am obliged to give language to all the blame to which profligacy, venality, hypocrisy and circumvention are so justly entitled. I am not empowered to conceal any thing I know of myself, whether it tend to my honour or to my disgrace. I am obliged to treat every other man with equal frankness, without dreading the imputation of flattery on the one hand, without dreading his resentment and enmity on the other.[3]

It is not enough that occasional great men should discover principles which can then be prescribed for the others. Unless every individual makes his own improved perception, nothing is much altered. There can therefore be no useful division between intellectual discourse and everyday life. In his discussion of the factors which most affect minds, when Godwin lists together education, literature, and 'political justice', the third may seem out of place until we realize that by this term Godwin is embracing all the conversations and transactions which individual men and women perform in society.

Political justice is Godwin's term for the duty of every individual to treat every other individual justly in every individual transaction. This means a duty to maximize the benefit from every action. He is not much concerned with the difficult questions of how prospective good is to be measured, apparently trusting to the cumulating beneficial effects of sincerity and knowledge to improve the quality of decision-making in difficult cases. Always it is the intellectual and moral improvement in the individuals concerned on which he puts his emphasis, rather than on improvement in welfare as such. Welfare does improve with perfectibility, but it is the end of the chain not the start.

Godwin illustrated his conception of political justice by his famous fable of Archbishop Fénelon and the fire. Let us suppose that the house of the great educator is on fire and there is only time to save either Fénelon or his chambermaid. Which should it be? Undoubtedly Fénelon, says Godwin, for his life is more valuable, more 'conducive to the general good'. If I myself am the chambermaid, justice requires that I sacrifice myself. Furthermore:

Supposing the chambermaid had been my wife, my mother or my benefactor. This would not alter the truth of the proposition. The life of Fénelon would still be more valuable than that of the chambermaid; and justice, pure, unadulterated justice, would still have preferred that which was most valuable. Justice would have taught me to save the life of Fénelon at the expence of the other. What magic is there in the pronoun 'my,' to overturn the decisions of everlasting truth? My wife or my mother may be a fool or a prostitute, malicious, lying or dishonest. If they be, of what consequence is it that they are mine?[4]

Here again the rationalist philosopher is applying in starker terms an old idea of his puritan forebears − if a man loves his wife and family, is this not bound to be at the expense of his duty to love all mankind? And of his duty to love God? Godwin's friend Joseph Fawcett, who remained a fierce old-fashioned dissenting minister, condemned undue domestic affections on these grounds, and the original draft of *Political Justice* betrays the religious antecedents in Godwin's own mind. 'Father and son when they enter into the temple of virtue', he wrote in a passage subsequently much amended, 'are perfect strangers to each other. There all men are brethren.' Godwin's own Calvinist parents may have shared this view and purposely given their own children no preference over humanity at large when they dispensed their limited store of love and affection.

The individual judgement is supreme, for what other foundation can there be when belief that the scriptures contain divine revelation has been abandoned? And how can differences between individuals' opinions be brought to a conclusion except by open and sincere debate? Godwin appears to have believed initially that, in any given set of circumstances, there is only one possible action that can be regarded as right, and that any deviation from performing that single action is a derogation from political justice. If, after sincere argument, there are differences of opinion among sincere men of goodwill, that only shows that the reasoning faculty is itself in need of more perfectibility.

If follows that no respect should be paid to promises just because they are promises. If a man promises to do something which is just, then he should perform it, but because it is just, not because it is a promise. Indeed, if new facts or circumstances arise between the giving of the promise and the time for fulfilment, then it may become his duty to set the promise aside. The wise man therefore will not make promises at all if he can avoid them.

Godwin here tries to overcome the difficulty inherent in any utilitarian system dependent on rules by insisting that these must always be subject to override. It can never be just to apply a rule for its own sake. Nor can the goodness of an action lie solely in the motive, for otherwise Calvin, a sincere man, did right to order the burning of Servetus for denying the doctrine of the Trinity. The same point is illustrated more vividly by the example of pardons. If the law is just, then it cannot be right at the same time to grant pardons (only a half or a third of all condemned criminals were in Godwin's day actually executed). If the individual judgement in the individual case is always paramount, then much of the difficulty dissolves. Pardons, if exercised honestly, are only a crude form of override applied in cases where the law give a manifestly unjust result.

Godwin's rationalism is relentless. What a cold emotionless fish this philosopher must have been, the reader of *Political Justice* is liable to conclude. But Godwin's fault was not so much to ignore the emotions as to assume that other people shared the same passions – to use the eighteenth-century term – as he had always felt himself. The boy who had determined to follow truth wherever she led in the service of his fellow men and who had burst through the constraints of upbringing and religion, believed that the emotions and ambitions of other people could also be channelled with similar productive results. If the world is in disequilibrium, it is because passion and reason are pulling in opposing directions, but, with political justice, they can be made to reinforce one another. Even Caesar and Alexander, he notes, for all their murders and massacres had their virtues, and we can surely see an autobiographical reference to himself and to Holcroft in a passage in which he praises the personal arrogance, the desire for fame, the tiresome perseverance, and the abrasive manners by which the two friends demonstrated their sincere attachment to truth and justice.

A man of uncommon genius is a man of high passions and lofty design; and our passions will be found in the last analysis to have their surest foundation in a sentiment of justice. If a man be of an aspiring and ambitious temper, it is because at present he finds himself out of his place, and wishes to be in it . . . A man of quick resentment, of strong feelings, and who pertinaciously resists every thing that he regards as an unjust assumption, may be considered as having in him the seeds of eminence.[5]

As yet Godwin had in his own life faced few, if any, conflicts between duty and desire where duty was in serious danger of emerging as loser. Reason, he optimistically tended to assume, provided that it is fully informed, will always overrule passion. A man who does wrong has made a faulty analysis. Crime is only misjudgement. Vice is error.

It is only when he has established a complete – and he believed coherent – philosophical framework that Godwin discusses the various institutions of society. Religion, government, the economic system, the relations between the sexes, and numerous other institutions, customs and conventions are measured against the stern criteria of political justice, and all are found to be seriously flawed.

Religious organizations are intrinsically destructive. Built on a denial of reason and claiming a right as institutions to override individual judgement, their organized insincerity strikes at the roots of human progress. The former dissenting minister who had been refused employment for declining to subscribe to the Thirty-nine Articles, was able to land several well-aimed historical and moral blows. These articles, he noted, were orginally drafted to meet the beliefs of the Calvinists, but for the previous 150 years the clergy of the Church of England had given them the opposite interpretation.

It would perhaps be regarded as incredible, if it rested upon the evidence of history alone, that a whole body of men ... should with one consent employ themselves in a casuistry, the object of which is to prove the propriety of a man's declaring his assent to what he does not believe. These men either credit their own subterfuges, or they do not. If they do not, what can be expected from men so unprincipled and profligate? With what front can they exhort other men to virtue, with the brand of vice upon their own foreheads?[6]

Much of the book is devoted to the implications of the theory of political justice for governments and political institutions. Hereditary monarchs, even if they are intelligent and benevolent to start with, are soon corrupted by an education which cuts them off from clear perceptions and loads them with undeserved honours. They are surrounded from earliest youth by advisers who are reluctant to tell them the truth, and even if a state is fortunate enough to find itself with an enlightened despot – that favourite eighteenth-century recipe for combining security with welfare – there is no way he can ensure that justice is practised down the line.

To render despotism auspicious and benign it is necessary, not only that the sovereign should possess every human excellence, but that all his officers should be men of penetrating genius and unspotted virtue. If they fall short of this, they will, like the ministers of Elizabeth, be sometimes specious profligates, and sometimes men, who, however admirably adapted for business, consult on many occasions exclusively their private advantage, worship the rising sun, enter into vindictive cabals, and cuff down new fledged merit.[7]

But the despot can at least do something, unlike that favourite British constitutional recipe, the limited monarch. If George III ever read *Political Justice* he would not have been flattered by Godwin's accurate description of his role.

Every thing is with great parade transacted in his name ... We find him like Pharaoh's frogs 'in our houses and upon our beds, in our ovens and our kneading troughs.' Now observe the man himself to whom all this importance is annexed. To be idle is the abstract of all his duties. He is paid an immense revenue only to dance and to eat, to wear a scarlet robe and a crown. He may not choose any one of his measures. He must listen with docility to the consultations of his ministers and sanction with a ready assent whatever they determine ... He must not express to any man his opinion, for that would be a sinister and unconstitutional interference. To be absolutely perfect he must have no opinion, but be the vacant and colourless mirror by which theirs is reflected.[8]

Of all political systems, democracy is the one Godwin finds least objectionable, and since he always speaks with sympathy of the disadvantaged and is an advocate of humanitarian causes, there has been a tendency to regard him as an early socialist. But this view is seriously misleading. Godwin profoundly distrusted collective action. How can truth or justice be elucidated by the mere counting of votes? One man's opinion is not as good as another's. On the contrary it is often only the minority who are sufficiently equipped in knowledge and understanding to recognize the right course of action. Collective organizations, for Godwin, can be as harmful as aristocracy, nor has he much faith in the wisdom or disinterested behaviour of salaried public servants. In a chapter on the concept of the rights of man, he concludes that 'a most acute, original, and inestimable author' (meaning Tom Paine) has been misled, and as a result has damaged the cause of truth. For Godwin there can be no rights but only duties. Burke for once is right.

All governments usurp individual judgement. They have no interest in promoting free discussion but prefer to push the people's minds around like billiard balls on a table. Their main instrument is force.

Whips, axes and gibbets, dungeons, chains and racks are the most approved and established methods of persuading men to obedience, and impressing upon their minds the lessons of reason.[9]

Governments with money at their command exploit the persuasive potential of religion, art, and literature to glamorize their own importance and soothe the people into according them an irrational obedience. The result is that both rulers and ruled are corrupted, either by receiving flattery or by bestowing it.

Economic factors are scarcely mentioned in the first 800 pages. But the patient reader who follows Godwin's argument from his philosophical axioms through his theory of psychological necessity is not surprised at the conclusion. Personal property is another of the institutions which distorts clear perception and corrupts virtuous motive. The economic system, by reinforcing the more vicious aspects of human nature, greed, vanity, envy, and rivalry, inflicts moral damage on the minds both of the rich and the poor. A man who has a better claim to resources than I have has a right to demand them. If a beggar is starving and I have plenty of bread, I must give him some of mine. And there should be no question of requiring or offering gratitude, which is a disguised form of political dependence or deferred obligation.

Following the opinion of Adam Smith, Godwin believed that, in an equal system, there would be enough for everyone's needs with a handsome surplus and leisure for all. As things are, however, the economic system provides a mechanism whereby greater tyrants can use lesser tyrants to exercise their control. While some men starve, others are working to produce luxury goods, even the crowns, jewels, uniforms and other fripperies with which they are deceived into a false sense of respect. 'The established system of property', says Godwin in one of his many uncompromising phrases, 'may be considered as strangling a considerable portion of our children in their cradle.'[10] The rich are the 'pensioners', a needless burden on the community, not the poor on whom they smugly bestow a tiny part of their excess.

Godwin's remedy for poverty lies far from any socialist policy of compulsory redistribution. Nothing irritated him more than to be lumped with Burke's sophisters, economists, and calculators who saw economic development as the solution to social and political problems and who, by their crude materialist utilitarianism, had extinguished the glory of Europe. If societies were to become more just, the welfare of the poor would improve, but rising incomes do not make people morally better. The necessitarian chain, like a real chain, can only be pulled, it cannot be pushed.

Monopoly is a key concept. It was easy for the former chronicler of the *New Annual Register* who had followed the long unavailing parliamentary campaigns against slavery to attribute the conditions in the West Indian plantations to economic exploitation. The conspicuous abstinence from sugar which many of his dissenting friends practised had proved to be an almost entirely useless gesture. Godwin had also studied the endless wars in India caused by the rivalries of the monopoly-chartered British and French East India Companies. But monopoly for Godwin is political and intellectual as much as economic and he applies the term to any institution which deliberately limits freedom – especially freedom of thought – in the interests of a privileged minority.

For the same reasons, Godwin differs irreconcilably from socialism in his attitude to political parties. Any form of association in which an individual concedes powers to a leader to speak and act on his behalf should be treated with deep distrust. 'Man, when he consults his own understanding, is the ornament of the universe. Man, when he surrenders his reason, and becomes the blind partisan of implicit faith and passive obedience, is the most mischievous of all animals.'[11] Godwin had seen mobs in the streets shouting, 'Church and King', as they terrorized a neighbourhood, but he was thinking equally of the dinners of the Revolution Society when normally honest and sincere men allowed themselves to be turned into abject followers of doubtful propositions handed down from the top table.

Another immoral and monopolistic institution is marriage, condemned both for its affront to truth and for its connections with the worst features of property:

The habit is, for a thoughtless and romantic youth of each sex to come together, to see each other for a few times and under circumstances full of delusion, and then to vow to each other eternal attachment. What is the consequence of this? In almost every instance they find themselves deceived. They are reduced to make the best of an irretrievable mistake. They are presented with the strongest imaginable temptation to become the dupes of falsehood . . . The institution of marriage is a system of fraud; and men who carefully mislead their judgements in the daily affair of their life, must always have a crippled judgement in every other concern . . . Add to this, that marriage is an affair of property, and the worst of all properties. So long as two human beings are forbidden by positive institution to follow the dictates of their own mind, prejudice is alive and vigorous. So long as I seek to engross one woman to myself, and to prohibit my neighbour from proving his superior desert and reaping the fruits of it, I am guilty of the most odious of all monopolies.[12]

In the same inexorable style – with striking Shakespearian and Biblical allusions – Godwin marches through all the other institutions which buttress political systems; and they all turn out to have built-in corrupting features and a vested interest in hypocrisy.

If follows that if we want men to exercise their natural intelligence and benevolence, we should begin dismantling the institutions which at present blind their eyes. If we simplify and abolish property, we get rid of many of the causes of crime, and can then reduce the number of prisons and the bureaucracy of administration. Organizations such as churches which arrogantly claim a monopoly of truth can be deprivileged and will eventually wither away. Law is unnecessary, for reason and judgement should always supersede it. The same goes for marriage and other forms of non-renegotiable contract. Giving primacy to the individual does not rule out co-operation. Many desirable activities require it and even war may be an unavoidable necessity from time to time in the present state of progress. But co-operation should always be for a limited purpose and for a limited time, and the individual should be able to opt out. As things are, many decisions are taken by centralized authorities which could better be left to individual choice and the more that can be returned to individuals the better.

In the fervent final weeks of composition, as he felt his insights improving in clarity, Godwin pushed the implication of his theory to further and further extremes until some of the writing assumed a quality more often associated with the fantasies of William Blake than with the cold philosopher of rationalism. Now that the answers have been discovered, he proclaims excitedly, the speed of progress will quickly accelerate and spectacular advances towards perfectibility can be expected within a short time. In his chapter on the 'Mode of Effecting Revolutions', Godwin's solution is fully in line with his general theory. A country is changed as the views of the citizens change, and truth is eventually irresistible. Violence, as the ultimate abnegation of reason, is firmly condemned, but in 1793 it was reasonable to see the American and French Revolutions as improvements on the English Revolution of the previous century against King Charles. They were better than their predecessors because, says Godwin, truth had made progress in the intervening century through the work of Sydney, Locke, Montesquieu, and Rousseau. Perfectibility applies even to revolutions, and in the future they will be accomplished without bloodshed, violence, or even confiscation. His own book, he implies, will help to ensure that the forthcoming British revolution will be the best yet.

In another section which he is careful to mark off as detachable (a 'probable conjecture' to be distinguished from the 'irrefragable truth' of the main thesis) Godwin considers the ultimate implications of perfectibility. Since health and medicine are already progressing and the mind is learning to control the environment more effectively, the logic is inescapable – one day human beings will discover the secrets of the ageing process and learn how to halt it. If man is perfectible then man will one day become immortal.

As a practical programme for the crisis of 1793 *Political Justice* was not to be taken seriously. Even as a longer-term aspiration, Godwin's brief sketch of a society with minimal government – where everyone is kept up to the moral mark by fearless criticism from everyone else – is as unattractive as other Utopias on offer for this world or the next. This does not mean however that Godwin's theory should be dismissed as an amusing episode in the history of thought, the last wild flowering of an age of excessive optimism.

The concepts which he deploys with such confidence – truth, virtue, reason – now look infinitely more complex and slippery than they did in his day. But his theory has strengths which are often absent in more modern attempts to explain or influence the workings of society. First of all it is firmly based on empirical observation and can therefore be adapted in the light of new knowledge. It is comprehensive, linking human activities with a wider view of the nature of the physical world. It faces head-on the need to relate political and social theory to a view of the individual mind and offers a plausible approach to explaining the interaction of intellectual, ethical, and economic factors. Finally the utilitarian value judgements from which its moral recommendations are derived can be readily accepted as good provisional axioms.

A restatement might run as follows. A person's decisions derive from the insights and opinions which he brings to a situation, and the more he uses his intellectual faculties, the better informed and more insightful he is likely to be. Admittedly this does not imply that people will necessarily always choose the course of action that does most good, in preference to others, but on the whole over time they will tend to, for many damaging decisions result not so much from the lack of benevolence as from lack of information or lack of imagination. And how are these opinions determined? Mainly by upbringing, by education, and by the institutions of society, including the received values of the political and economic system, by social customs, and by the various myths and stereotypes that people pick up from the cultural environment as guides to attitude and behaviour.

If this is granted, then should not those who are in control of affairs try to use their political power to offset the socially damaging decisions which individuals take when left to follow their own imperfect opinions? No, says Godwin, this is unlikely to be effective for more than a temporary period. Society is only a convenient term for the lives of the individual human beings who compose it and we should not be misled by abstractions and generalities. Although institutional action might be helpful in some ways, it makes little impact on the innumerable decisions that men and women make in their daily transactions and which determine their opinions and lives more decisively than public policies.

If we want society to improve, the argument would then run, the emphasis must always be placed on altering and improving the opinions of individuals. This means primarily freeing them from factors which militate against honest impartial appraisal. In particular they should be freed from the temptations which arise from having an interest in a biased outcome, best done by reducing current inequalities of wealth, income, education, access to ideas, and other forms of opportunity. Enlightened men who see this will voluntarily begin the process of redistribution. They will accept a duty to be sincere in all transactions. The more this is done, the faster the general level of knowledge and wisdom will tend to rise, with the result that better decisions will be taken; and the general level of welfare will also rise.

Godwin's individual liberalism remains a robust model for all who believe they can detect progress in history and who hope to see more in the future.

CHAPTER 8

The Spirit of the Age

On 25 May 1793, some three months after publication, Godwin noted in his journal 'Prosecution of Political Justice debated this week', and although no official record has been found, we need not doubt that the Privy Council did consider taking action to suppress the book. A work which declared in the Preface that all monarchy is 'unavoidably corrupt' was an attack on the British Constitution of the kind which the Attorney General had threatened, but in the event no move was made against author or publisher. In later years Godwin liked to tell the story that William Pitt personally advised the Council that 'a three guinea book could never do much harm among those who had not three shillings to spare,'[1] and although the price was misreported or misremembered – the first edition of *Political Justice* sold for one pound sixteen shillings – the point was well made.* Compared with the *Rights of Man* which was available to farm labourers and factory workers for sixpence in every town and village *Political Justice* could not be regarded as a direct threat to social peace.

Only a small proportion of the population had access to books. Works published in quarto with large typeface, generous margins, and other comforts for candle-dependent readers were aimed at the top end of the

---

* For those too young to remember the old money, there were twelve pence in a shilling, twenty shillings in a pound. A guinea was twenty-one shillings. The average weekly wage was about ten shillings.

The Blind Girl, from *Lessons for Children*

market, and it was usual to wait until the wealthy had been satisfied before reprinting in octavo for the gentry and the middling classes. Godwin later complained that Robinson delayed too long before producing the octavo edition, but this was a grudged detail. *Political Justice*, for a book of its category, was a best seller with 3,000 copies disposed of in quarto alone. The second edition in octavo of similar numbers was published at eighteen shillings with extensive revisions in 1796, and the third with further substantial changes in 1798. The book was also pirated twice in Dublin, not because the Irish themselves were much interested in ideas of progress, but as a means of escaping British copyright law and producing cheaper reprints for sale in Great Britain. When the initial demand was at its height, Robinson bought pirated octavo sheets from the Dublin printer and sold them in London under his own imprint.

Godwin wanted his book to be influential, but he never intended to speak direct to the people. 'Literature', he wrote, 'and particularly that literature by which prejudice is superseded and the mind is sprung to a firmer tone exists only as a portion of the few. The multitude, at least in the present state of human society, cannot partake of its illuminations.' In Sheffield disaffected cutlery workers, distrustful of such elitism, contrived to club together to read the famous book, as an alarmed spy warned the Home Office,[2] and copies were reported to have been seen on sale from a baker's delivery cart in Neasden.[3] But for the most part the price was sufficient deterrent against overhasty enlightenment. Half a century later, when the price of a reprint had fallen to five shillings, a Victorian free-thinking publisher still had to offer working-class customers an arrangement to buy the book in instalments over thirty-three patient weeks.[4]

When Holcroft reviewed it for the *Monthly* he evaded the editor's request not to be too favourable by quoting lengthy extracts which spoke for themselves, and the rival *Critical*, which was openly hostile, also gave a full and fair description. But it was the subscription libraries who were mainly responsible for carrying the message of *Political Justice* to every corner of the kingdom. The subscribers would buy books collectively and draw up a rotating roster to lend them out among themselves. If the club was big enough, the volume was then retained for general use, but the smaller clubs often allowed the last man on the list to keep it. Godwin's friend John Fenwick estimated in an article in 1799 that the book was purchased by this method in 'some hundreds' of towns. 'Perhaps no work of equal bulk ever had such a number of readers,' he wrote, 'and certainly no book of such profound enquiry ever made so many proselytes in an equal space of time.'[5] Subscription libraries often doubled as philosophical and literary societies so that the book was discussed as well as read, and we hear of it having to be read aloud to the impatient subscribers before being allowed out on loan.

In the years after 1793 *Political Justice* suffused the scene, giving form and expression to many ideas that were already in the air and reinforcing them. To a nation replete and disgusted with political propaganda, it stood out as an honest attempt to take a longer view, its solid quarto volumes outclassing in intellectual weight as well as in physical bulk the ephemeral pamphlets in which the debate had been conducted since 1789. As Hazlitt remarked later, Paine was made to look flashy by comparison and Burke sophistical.[6] A modern scholar with the aid of a computer has counted 758 books and articles printed in the fifteen years after 1793 which contain extensive references to Godwin and his writings.[7]

Especially convincing to the late eighteenth-century mind was the connection which Godwin made explicit between current problems and a general theory of progress. Social and economic ills as well as political abuses were now, it had been shown, explainable by a modern theory of causation. The rotten borough, its voters limited by some forgotten charter to a handful of menial men, could now be condemned not only as an undesirable feature of the British method of government but as a corrupting influence on every individual involved in the system, whether winner or loser, and an impediment in the path of human perfectibility. The City institutions, the monopoly trading companies, the established church, the armed forces, the law, and many other organizations could now be seen as reinforcing links in a chain of necessity which kept minds in ignorance and perpetuated a cycle of degradation and deprivation.

The servile insincerity of London's teeming beggars, flaunting their sores and exaggerating their misfortunes to extract the contemptuous charity of the rich, illustrated graphically the moral corruption which inequality promoted in poor and rich alike. Prostitution too, although not mentioned in *Political Justice*, provided, in the eyes of many, a specially vivid confirmation of the same point. As an employer of female labour it was second only to domestic service, and when economic depression gripped the country, the bargaining power in both industries moved further in favour of the rich and the greedy. 'I would ask a man of feeling', wrote Robert Southey in November 1793 when urging a friend to read *Political Justice*, 'to survey the lobby and the theatres or look at the courtesans in the streets of London. Then let him say what stronger proof can be required of the wretched debasement of society . . . Sin is artificial — it is the monstrous offspring of government and property.'[8] Colquhoun's authoritative *Treatise on the Police of the Metropolis* estimated in 1797 that there were fifty thousand prostitutes in London – 9 per cent of the total female population – of whom half were 'menial servants or seduced in very early life', and two thousand were 'well educated'. It was impossible to walk out in any part of London in high life or low life without being accosted. Hereditary syphilis was rife and often led to blindness.

William Blake's 'London', first published in 1794, asserts the Godwinian connections with wonderful poetic power although there is no certain evidence that the two men knew each other personally as early as this date:

> I wander thro' each charter'd street,
> Near where the charter'd Thames does flow
> And mark in every face I meet
> Marks of weakness, marks of woe.
>
> In every cry of every Man,
> In every Infants cry of fear,
> In every voice; in every ban,
> The mind-forg'd manacles I hear.
>
> How the Chimney-sweepers cry
> Every blackning Church appalls,
> And the hapless Soldiers sigh
> Runs in blood down Palace walls.
>
> But most thro' midnight streets I hear
> How the youthful Harlots curse
> Blasts the new born Infants tear
> And blights with plagues the Marriage hearse.

In the original version of the poem, Blake had described the streets and the river as merely 'dirty' and the 'mind-forg'd manacles' were only 'german-forg'd links' – a reference not so much to the high quality of German workmanship as to the mercenary troops from Hesse with which, it was rumoured, the Hanoverian king was about to pacify his adopted country.[9]

It was easy to perceive Godwin's chains – whose original purpose was to illustrate how events are linked in a continuous sequence of causation – as manacles, fetters, and instruments of coercion. Chained gangs of convicts and prisoners of war could be seen along the banks of the Thames at low tide, ineffectively dredging with hand buckets the filthy river in which their prison hulks were moored. Rotting corpses of criminals hanged in chains reminded travellers throughout England that the statute book of their country listed over a hundred capital offences, soon to be increased to nearly two hundred. They were particularly common near Hounslow where highwaymen regularly attacked the traffic on the Bath Road. Since theft of any property worth more than twelve pence attracted the death penalty, it was unsurprising that Thomas Bewick in illustrating the carrion crow in his *British Birds* should choose a gallows as its typical habitat.

Burke, in defending traditional government, had written approvingly of the 'fetters on the passions', but according to *Political Justice* it is not emotion which government has chained but insight into the truth. Criminals are the unfortunate products of chains of wrong perceptions, but as poets regularly noted, the golden chains of office of kings, courtiers, and priests constrict the intellectual liberty of the privileged orders with similarly stultifying effects. For thirty years English literature clanks noisily with innumerable variations on the 'icy chains of custom', and the 'chains of the mind' – too often described as adamantine – became one of the clichés of the age.

It was easy too to confuse the chains of causation with that other ancient metaphor, the 'Great Chain of Being', which perceives the world as a hierarchy of all living things each linked into its proper place with man a rank below God, then the animals, fish, birds, and lesser organisms down to the pitiable insects and vegetables. This world view had traditionally been used to justify political and economic differences rather than to promote equality or liberty, but with suitable poetic ambiguity it was now successfully linked to the other chains. Some influential writers – notably those who wanted to retain a place for a God in a basically materialistic universe – contrived to employ all three chain metaphors – of causation, coercion, and hierarchy – thereby achieving literary profundity at the expense of intellectual clarity. So rich had the chain theme become by the time Shelley wrote *The Revolt of Islam* in 1817 that he was able to describe one of his favourite images, the serpent, successively as 'linked rings', and 'a chain of torment' and so to attach Godwinian connotations to the most ancient Biblical and classical myths of the origin of evil.

Equally powerful and influential were the metaphors of the mind, all of which were concerned to emphasize its passive role. Godwin compared the mind, on occasions, to a chameleon which takes its colour from its environment, to a barometer which reacts to the weather, and to a bagpipe which can only emit music in response to external pressures. As with the chains, these metaphors were not all original but Godwin's clear exposition of Hartley's theory both helped to spread it more widely and at the same time to endow it with increased respect.

The most favoured analogy of all was with the Aeolian harp, also known as the Aeolian lyre or lute, which illustrated the psychological theory of necessity with convincing vividness. More a piece of furniture than a musical instrument, the harp consisted of a simple oblong frame, loosely strung with strings, which emitted musical sounds when placed in a breeze. In France and Germany such harps were hidden in caves and ruins to augment the natural eeriness of the whistling wind, but in England they were domestic, usually fitted under an open window. Coleridge's 'Eolian Harp' composed in the summer of 1795 while listening at the window of his cottage is only the best-known example of a theme which hums and warbles through English literature from Wordsworth and Coleridge to Shelley and Keats. It was easy to imagine the human mind vibrating, like an Aeolian harp, in response to perceptions. It was easy too to see in the music-making wind a metaphor of the benevolent spirit of nature which enlightenment philosophers had substituted for the wrathful God of Jews and Christians.

But just as Godwin's chains of the mind were matched by Burke's chains of the passions, the Aeolian harp too had its direct counterpart among those whose view of human nature was less optimistic. As every classicist knew, the original Aeolus, king of the winds, kept them chained with difficulty in a cave in the Aeolian islands near Sicily from where they escaped from time to time to cause storms, shipwrecks, and havoc. The liberating breezes with whose vagaries the poets compared their own free spirits were to others the tempests, the wars, the revolutions, and the untameable destructive passions that in 1789 had temporarily escaped from their prisons in the caverns of the mind.

Published at a moment when human hopes had reason to be at their highest, *Political Justice* caught the spirit of the age. At a time when religion was increasingly recognized as an agglomeration of primeval fears and superstitions, it offered a reassuring modern scientific explanation to put in its place, many former Christians being relieved to find that the morality which it recommended differed little from superseded Christian ethics. The New Philosophy – as the ideas which Godwin collected and codified were quickly called – was firmly in the tradition of religious dissent, appealing strongly to those of an inflexible, worrying, and puritanical disposition. At the same time, it was wonderfully liberating and refreshing. If men and women are blown from perception to perception by the breezes of experience, they need feel no strong obligation to be consistent between one action and another. Provided each individual is sincere, every new situation can be judged afresh, and the practitioner is disencumbered from guilt. It may often be a clear and pleasing duty to burst out from the fetters, whether they are political obligations, economic contracts, or the more personal bonds of marriage. Indeed, a unique satisfaction attends those who know when to do so, for they are the privileged few whose improved perceptions accelerate perfectibility.

Godwin at once became a famous man. 'He blazed as a sun in the firmament,' wrote William Hazlitt, one of many admirers who first made his acquaintanceship in the mid-1790s. 'No one was more talked of, more looked up to, more sought after, and whenever liberty, truth, justice was the theme, his name was not far off.' John Taylor, father of the Victorian poet, walked from Durham for the chance to shake Godwin's hand. 'Nefas hoc nescire,' he wrote in his copy of Political Justice – 'It is a crime to be ignorant of this book.'[10] Another admirer walked from Edinburgh.[11] Letters poured in from all over the country, from the United States and occasionally from elsewhere. Everyone in London who liked to think of himself as on the progressive side wanted to meet him, and he was an object of pilgrimage for many foreign visitors.

The main pattern of his life did not change, intensive writing and reading in the mornings, calls and conversations and more reading in the afternoons and evenings. He continued to see Holcroft several times a week and to dine with him nearly every Sunday. He continued to do a little journalism, editing Paine's Common Sense for a new edition published by Jordan and writing reviews for his friends, but he preferred talking. Every day there were new opportunities to re-examine and reaffirm the political and moral discoveries to the refining of which his life was now wholeheartedly devoted.

It was a certain Major Jardine, one of that large body of anonymous writers from whose ranks Godwin had recently been released, who suggested that the conversations should be formalized and extended by the establishment of a philosophical discussion club. From Godwin's copy of a document which he circulated, it seems that Jardine drew up an outline proposal with the request that, if the potential members were interested, they should contact himself or Holcroft, who offered their names as secretaries. The club was to consist of three or four prominent individuals drawn from various professions who would meet once a week. There would be no rules, 'only to remember that truth, knowledge, mind being the chief object, no subject to be excluded from conversation'.

Among the names suggested were five medical doctors; seven mathematicians; two lawyers; a number of artists including Fuseli, Buonomi, Copley, and Dyson; the composer Clementi and the musicologist Dr Burney; and a list of 'philosophic minds in search of truth' headed by Godwin and including Holcroft, Nicholson, Priestley, Mackintosh, David Williams, Lord Stanhope, the Wedgwoods, Fox, and Sheridan.[12]

There were numerous such clubs throughout the country, which brought together men of different disciplines to discuss science, philosophy, and politics over a good dinner or a glass of wine. The Speculative Society of Edinburgh still thrives, and a few of the London West End clubs retain traces of a more intellectual past, but in Godwin's day many cities had an athenaeum, associated often with a subscription library, and even in moderate-sized provincial towns it did not seem presumptuous to believe that local professional men could make lasting discoveries from their own resources. The Lunar Society of Birmingham which met once a month when the moon was full – a sensible precaution when highwaymen lurked outside every city – was the most famous and successful, and some of the names on Jardine's list, notably the Wedgwoods and Priestley, had been associated with it. Their meetings had become infrequent after the Birmingham riots of Bastille Day 1791 when Priestley's laboratory had been destroyed and he had moved to London, and Jardine may have been consciously intending to rally the former members to start a new club in London. The Lunatics kept no records, nor unfortunately did Jardine's Select Club. However we know from Godwin's journal that in 1793 he started to attend a club called the Philomathian Society and continued doing so almost every week until 1796; and that he soon made the personal acquaintance of many of the people on Jardine's list.

The young lawyer Henry Crabb Robinson, an early disciple, recorded the questions discussed on two of the nights when he attended, 'Do the actions of men form a part of the plan of providence?' and 'The analogy between natural and moral diseases', and he wrote enthusiastically to his brother about Godwin's exposition of his theory of necessity and of the influence of motive on the mind.[13] But for the most part we only have Godwin's own notes of the topics. Original depravity versus political institution, crime, legislative power, bloodshed, treaties, a God, prostitutes versus parsons, theatres, utility of religion, fame (several times), love, marriage (several times), capital punishment, free will (many times), gratitude, suicide, self love, property, ballot, means of reform, connection of free states and despots, tribunes, soldier versus priest, Church and State, Caesar.

The list reads in places like a re-run of discussions that preceded *Political Justice*, and since Godwin and Holcroft were leading members, we may be sure that the arguments often followed the same course with new insights noted for incorporation in the future editions of the book. 'The author has always had a passion for colloquial discussion,' Godwin was later to write no doubt with the Philomaths in mind. 'There is a vivacity and . . . a richness in the hints struck out in conversation that are with difficulty attained in any other method.'[14] But the thorough and combative style of discourse practised by Godwin and Holcroft was always a minority taste. Another member, the impatient revolutionary politician John Binns, described them as 'among the most diffuse and tiresome of speakers'. The Committee, he recalled, was obliged to buy two fifteen-minute hour glasses to limit the length of set speeches but nobody ever turned them over except when Godwin or Holcroft rose to speak.[15]

The Philomaths maintained formal links with similar societies both at home and abroad, and Godwin was introduced to many eminent foreigners visiting London. All over London and in the other cities and towns of Britain other book clubs and debating societies – famous and obscure – matched the activities of the Philomaths, covering the country with a network of discussion groups. Although they contained many reformers and radicals among their members, they were not political parties. On the contrary they provided an alternative way forward, a means whereby individuals could improve their knowledge and their insights and therefore contribute more effectively to social progress in accordance with the principles of *Political Justice*.

One of the most prominent, the Moral and Political Society, met at Bunhill near the dissenters' graveyard in London. Another, which used the rooms of a reading society in Cripplegate – in the poor literary quarter – was closed when neighbours complained of excited clapping into the early hours. When debating societies spread to the artisan and working classes – one operated from a hairdresser's shop in Shoreditch – the authorities began to take fright. But when they banned the taking of money at the door, the societies met on Sunday evenings in the guise of religious discussion groups, and there was a huge increase in applications for permission to offer public preaching. (Nearly four hundred men took out licences in Clerkenwell alone in 1796/7.) An enraged Christian writing a whole book on the subject in 1800, shocked his readers with accounts of London workmen listening to talks on Paine and Godwin at Sunday evening classes without changing into their best clothes.[16]

But Godwin himself crossed and recrossed the social barriers as easily as he walked from street to street. Deeply conscious of his personal independence, he was a member of no clique or party, but a visitor at many.[17] There can have been few men of his time who enjoyed such a wide range of acquaintances. He kept his links with the dissenting community and with his former colleagues in the literary and subliterary worlds. On Sunday afternoons at Holcroft's dinners he met actors, playwrights, and musicians. He dined regularly with John King, money lender to the aristocracy, on the strict understanding that he was bestowing an honour on the bankers and merchants he met there, not putting himself under any obligation of gratitude.

He became a friend of the veteran politician John Horne Tooke whose large house at Wimbledon offered hospitality and political conversation. Tooke had played a prominent part in the Wilkes campaigns of the 1760s and 1770s – he used to say that his gout was caused by the claret he had drunk as a prophylactic against jail fever when he was imprisoned at that time. The meanings of many common words had, Tooke believed, surreptitiously altered over the centuries to help bolster the prevailing system. His favourite example, that majesty and majority were essentially the same word, may not have been well chosen, and he assumed too readily that etymology and meaning coincide, but his understanding of the pervasive power of institutions to infiltrate the nature of thought itself was an important addition and reinforcement to Godwin's theory.

Godwin was also regularly invited to the dinner table of Lord Lauderdale, one of the leaders of the small band of Whigs whose persistent opposition in Parliament helped to soften the repressive policies of Pitt's government. There he met most of the leading Whig politicians, Lord Derby, Sir Philip Francis, Adair, Courtenay, North, and William Smith. He had opportunities to talk to Charles James Fox, one of his boyhood heroes whom he had hitherto only admired from the journalists' gallery. On one occasion he even met the Prince Regent, the supreme magistrate of the nation as Godwin would have called him, but there is no record of a conversation.

It was a source of deep satisfaction to the author of *Political Justice* that he should be accorded respect by the titled, the rich, and the famous. His evident delight at this sometimes seems like snobbery and so, on occasions, it probably was. But he could be forgiven for feeling pleased. He had, he freely admitted, suffered from an intense desire for fame from an early age, and there had been many occasions during his ten years in Grub Street when it seemed that he was destined to fail. But now at last, when he was nearly forty, courage had brought its reward. Talent – or genius as he called it in the idiom of the time – had asserted its intrinsic power, and he could enjoy the twinned satisfactions of literary immortality and a sense of having benefited the human race. If he enjoyed his new distinction – one of his early tasks was to have his portrait taken – his reputation, he believed, had been fairly won. Godwin had never truckled and he never would. Indeed his new eminence was clear vindication both of his philosophical theory and of his policy of not truckling.

Letters from strangers were patiently answered with carefully thought-out advice.[18] Sometimes he sent money, but not having much himself, he was not impelled to do much sharing. Usually he prescribed courses of study and reading. Throughout his long life there was seldom a time when he did not have protégés under his care, writing to them frequently and discussing their problems. They regarded him with admiration, respect, and affection – and the gratitude which he felt bound to disown – and these robust friendships continued long after the circumstances which prompted them had passed, outliving a hundred disappointments and a dozen quarrels. By treating everyone as an equal whatever his or her age, sex, ability, character, reputation, or place in the world, Godwin somehow transmitted some of his own strength to men and women who were less stable than their mentor. Their letters complain of coldness – for he seldom allowed sympathy to detract from justice – but his apparent lack of emotion was one of the sources of his appeal. The qualities in his book which drew them to him in the first place were manifestly matched in the man.

One of his earliest pupils was Basil Montagu, an illegitimate son of the Earl of Sandwich, whose mother had been murdered outside Covent Garden. He was one of a number of law students who gave up their studies after reading *Political Justice*, although like most of the others he later resumed and eventually became a judge – it was probably he who received the advice from William Wordsworth recorded by Hazlitt, 'Throw aside your books of chemistry and read Godwin on Necessity.'[19] In the search for a scientific morality the answer had now been found, and he took lodgings at No. 15 Chalton Street in order to be near Godwin at No. 25.

Wordsworth himself, then aged twenty-five and not yet known as a poet, sought out Godwin's acquaintance when he stayed with Montagu at Chalton Street on a visit to London in 1795. Long years later, with a touch of embarrassment towards his youthful enthusiasms, he was to describe the period in his life when he too was most under the influence of *Political Justice* – one of the most powerful descriptions of the spirit of the age. It was a time, he recalled, when the speculations of philosophy

> That promised to abstract the hopes of Man
> Out of his feelings, to be fixed thenceforth
> For ever in a purer element –
> Found ready welcome. Tempting region that
> For Zeal to enter and refresh herself,
> Where passions had the privilege to work,
> And never hear the sound of their own names.
> But, speaking more in charity, the dream
> Flattered the young, pleased with extremes, nor least
> With that which makes our Reason's naked self
> The object of its fervour. What delight!
> How glorious! in self-knowledge and self-rule,
> To look through all the frailties of the world,
> And, with a resolute mastery shaking off
> Infirmities of nature, time, and place,
> Build social upon personal Liberty,
> Which, to the blind restraints of general laws
> Superior, magisterially adopts
> One guide, the light of circumstances, flashed
> Upon an independent intellect.[20]

In December 1794 Holcroft received a letter from a Robert Lovell of Bristol. It contained a practical suggestion for establishing a Godwinian community either in Great Britain or in the United States.

I would engage your thoughts to our projected plan of establishing a genuine system of property. America presents many advantages to the accomplishment of this scheme – the easy rate at which land may be purchased, is not the least important: yet we are not determined on emigration. Principle, not plan, is our object. A friend has suggested that the plan is practicable in some of the uncultivated parts of Wales . . . From the writings of William Godwin and yourself, our minds have been illuminated, we wish our actions to be guided by the same superior abilities; perhaps when together, you may bestow some thoughts to our advantage.[21]

Samuel Taylor Coleridge, who was twelve years younger than Godwin, read *Political Justice* in 1794 when he was at Cambridge. He met Robert Southey for the first time when he called at Oxford in June of that year, and they decided soon afterwards to emigrate to the United States, with Robert Lovell and others, and establish there a new community to be governed on Godwinian principles. The 'genuine system of property', mentioned in Lovell's letter, is the title of the final Book VIII of *Political Justice* which sets out the direct connections between economic equality, moral improvement, and accelerated perfectibility. The new settlement was to be called a Pantisocracy – a word invented by Coleridge to mean a society in which the government is equally in the hands of all members – and it was to practise Aspheterism – another coinage meaning the holding of all property in common. According to Southey, both words were soon well understood in the Bristol area where the main work of recruitment took place.

Initially there were to be twelve men and twelve women who would put up the capital. They would purchase a tract of land near the Susquehanna river in Pennsylvania. Following the views of Adam Smith as relayed by *Political Justice*, they believed that if everyone worked a two- or three-hour day, output would be enough to support the whole community at a modest but comfortable level. There would be no rich and no poor, and therefore no emulation and no crime. Both men had read the arguments and metaphors of *Political Justice* carefully. A successful pantisocracy, Coleridge wrote building on Godwin's chameleon metaphor of the mind, would require 'the most wakeful attentions of the most reflective minds in all moments to bring it into practice – it is not enough that we have once swallowed it – The *Heart* should have *fed* upon the *truth*, as Insects on a Leaf – till it be tinged with colour, and shew it's food in every the minutest fibre.'[22] Southey gives a more down-to-earth description of what pantisocrats would actually do all day – they would discuss metaphysics while cutting down trees, criticize poetry while hunting buffaloes, and write sonnets while following the plough.

The colonists intended that marriage would be abolished and the children brought up in common. This would not have involved sharing of wives but freedom to move from partner to partner according to their changing perceptions of each other's virtues. Here too the pantisocrats were following the precepts of *Political Justice* although they had to be circumspect in proclaiming it too openly since the new community would be subject to the laws of the United States. Southey was engaged to marry a Bristol girl, Edith Fricker, and Coleridge made the same pledge to her sister Sara. Robert Lovell married a third sister and there were two other Fricker ladies ready to go, as well as Southey's mother.

Coleridge came to London in December 1794 and, with Lovell, there were meetings with Holcroft and Godwin to discuss the pantisocracy scheme. Godwin first met him on 21 December when he noted in his journal 'dine at Holcroft's w[ith] Porson and Coleridge, talk of self-love and God', and it was clear that, from the first meeting, they were going to disagree about religion. 'There is a fierceness and *dogmatism* of conversation in Holcroft,' Coleridge had warned a few days earlier with a young man's confidence, 'for which you receive little compensation either from the variety of his information, the closeness of his Reasoning, or the splendor of his Language. He talks incessantly of Metaphysics, of which he appears to me to *know nothing* – to have *read nothing* – He is ignorant as a Scholar – and neglectful of the smaller Humanities . . . He absolutely infests you with *Atheism*.'[23]

The pantisocracy scheme was, according to Southey, approved by Gerrald,* Godwin, and Holcroft, 'the three first men in England, perhaps in the world', but recruiting officers are prone to exaggeration. Holcroft disapproved of some aspects of the organization, as well as condemning Coleridge's persistent Christianity, and both philosophers felt that their theory could be practised just as well in London as in Wild Wales or on the banks of the Susquehanna river. *Political Justice*, it had often to be explained, was not a plan for building a new society on a green field site, but a policy for improving the intellectual and moral efficiency of existing societies. The pantisocracy was never carried into execution. Southey's enthusiasm was dampened by the opposition of his family – his aunt turned him out of the house one rainy night – and there were problems in raising the money. The chances of success, if they had gone, were not high. The history of the United States was already littered with failed social experiments defeated as much by the mosquitoes as by an over-trustful view of human nature. Nevertheless, although no subsequent writer has been able to resist having his fun, pantisocracy deserves to be regarded as a serious scheme, seriously undertaken, fully within the dissenting tradition to which Coleridge and Godwin both belonged.

Godwin's admired intellectual ancestor and near-namesake, Thomas Goodwin, had, for example, been one of the group of religious independents who had gone into exile in the Netherlands during the reign of Charles I in order to be able to practise an earlier theory of perfectibility. 'Our consciences were possessed with that reverence and adoration for the fulness of the Scriptures', they wrote in the *Apologeticall Narration* on their return in 1643, 'that there is therein a complete sufficiency as to make *the man of God perfect*, so also to make the Churches of God perfect.'

---

* See pp. 112ff.

There was also the example of those other Godwinian heroes, the republican independents, Cromwell, Hampden, Pym and Haselrig who had planned to emigrate to America in 1637 shortly before the outbreak of the war with King Charles. They had actually embarked, it was said, when the King's order came to stop them, and although this part of the story has since been disproved, Cromwell and others did intend to leave England at this time to set up a new commonwealth in the new world.[24] Southey had been reading about it when the pantisocracy was proposed. The American colonies were never pantisocratic, let alone gynaecocoenic (another coinage for a society which holds the women in common) but, as Coleridge knew, the Commonwealth of Massachusetts was started by twelve men meeting at Cambridge in 1629 who pledged themselves to emigrate with their families and so began the biggest emigration yet seen from English shores. It was not unreasonable to believe that twelve men meeting in similar crisis circumstances in 1794 could do the same for the modernized perfectionist ideal.

From the beginning however, the main hope for *Political Justice* was to apply its ideas in contemporary England, and in this aim Godwin was greatly encouraged by the young Tom Wedgwood who first made his acquaintance at tea on 21 May 1793 when he was twenty-two. Coming from a rich family and due to inherit a large fortune himself, Wedgwood was deeply conscious of the responsibilities of wealth. Like his father he wanted to see the nation's resources exploited more effectively especially at a time of rising food prices, and he financed a number of important projects. His friend Dr Beddoes, another talented member of the Lunar Society, conducted research into methods of making flour from grass, suggesting that an unrelieved cereal diet might be made more appetizing by adding opium – only to discover that this was already a common practice in poorer areas. Wedgwood himself was a scientist of note, his successful attempts to produce artificial pictures by shining light on paper covered with silver nitrate earning him an honoured place among the pioneers of photography.

Fearing that his life would be short Wedgwood was determined to make use of Godwin's discoveries to speed up both the moral and the economic growth rate, and he bombarded him with questions and suggestions. One of his more interesting ideas was set out in a long letter in the summer of 1797. In addition to promoting political justice in the contemporary world, he suggested, he would use his fortune to help the next generation. The best way forward would be to improve the supply of the special types of men and women who are alone capable of significantly redirecting the chains of necessity.

My aim is high. I have been endeavouring some master stroke which should anticipate a century or two upon the lazy-paced progress of human improvement. Almost every prior step of its advance may be traced to the influence of superior character. Now it is my opinion that in the education of the greatest of these characters, not more than one hour in ten has been made to contribute to the formation of those qualities upon which this influence has depended ... What a chaos of perceptions! ... How many opposing tendencies which have negatived each other! How many great branches of knowledge have been begun at the wrong end and pursued with incredible toil in a backward direction down to the roots! how much learnt to be forgotten! how many hours, days, months have been prodigally wasted in unproductive occupation! how many false and contradictory ideas imprinted by authority! What a host of half-formed impressions and abortive conceptions blended into a mass of confusion.

Wedgwood's plan for producing an elite force of moral improvers would have appealed to Plato, and the methods proposed were equally rigorous. Intensive teaching from earliest infancy (in bare nurseries with walls painted grey to reduce distraction) was to be combined with continuous stimulation, both intellectual and physical, with the aim of forging a secure link early in life between pleasure and the exercise of reason. Traditional reward systems including frivolous 'romping, tickling, and fooling', were to be forbidden. The curriculum was to be controlled by a committee of 'such philosophers as can be induced to lend their assistance' including Godwin, Holcroft, Horne Tooke, Beddoes and others. As for the teachers, Wedgwood's candidates were two promising young men as yet only known to him by reputation.

The only persons that I know of as at all likely for this purpose, are Wordsworth and Coleridge. I never saw or had any communication with either of them. Wordsworth, I understand to have many of the requisite qualities, and from what I hear of him, he has only to be convinced that this is the most promising mode of benefiting society, to engage him to come forward with alacrity. The talents of Coleridge I suppose are considerable, and like Wordsworth, quite disengaged. I am only afraid that the former may be too much a poet and religionist to suit our view.[25]

Wedgwood's measures were, mercifully, not attempted. Perhaps, after a discussion at the Philomaths, he was persuaded that authoritarian training methods were unsuitable for the encouragement of liberal intellectual individualism. Godwin himself later produced a gentler and more effective theory of education. However, one part of the proposal was carried into practice. In accordance with the duty which requires those with a surplus to deploy it where it will promote maximum good, Tom and Josiah Wedgwood soon afterwards offered Coleridge an annuity for life of £150, with no conditions whatsoever attached. As a result the young poet was enabled to give up the career of unitarian minister which was the only paying employment available at the time to prospective philosophers. A similar arrangement would have been available to Godwin too if he had been prepared to accept it, but since at the time he had enough money for his modest purposes, he decided that he did not need it and therefore did not deserve it. (On one scolding occasion he even undertook to demonstrate to Wedgwood that his thoughtful habit of prepaying the return postage with his letters was immoral.)[26] It was reassuring to know however that if circumstances were ever to change he had only to ask and Wedgwood would see it as his duty to give. Or if not Wedgwood, then one of the other numerous rich admirers of his book.

CHAPTER 9

The Power of Mind

On the third anniversary of the French Revolution, 14 July 1792, Godwin attended no banquet, being still hard at work on *Political Justice*, and writing on that day 'one page on necessity'. His friend Joseph Fawcett, to whom he owed much of his early inspiration, had gone to Paris to witness the celebrations, and he was present at the laying of the foundation stone of a new free school on the site of the hated Bastille. His long poem composed for the occasion sets out Godwinian sentiments in some of the worst verses ever committed to print.

> Despots! ye are overcome!
> Those mighty words pronounced your doom.
> Thought ye, the marching things ye move,
> Prick'd by nor generous hate nor love,
> Could 'gainst the animated band
> of MINDS that rush to meet them stand?[1]

Godwin was eager from the beginning that his book should be read in France where, in 1793, the National Convention was drafting a new constitution, and where political progress seemed more purposefully on the march than in England. The advance copy of *Political Justice* which he had personally presented to M. Chauvelin, the departing French Ambassador, a few days before the outbreak of war was not considered by the French Government until 28 April, when the minutes duly record

The Government enslaving Truth and the Printing Press by William Hone the grateful receipt of the book, and reproduce (in translation) the accompanying letter which Godwin had written on 22 January 1793.

To the National Convention of France

Citizen Legislators

I send you the results of considerable research on the subject which is occupying you today. You invited philosophers from all parts of the world to communicate their ideas to you; and that invitation is sufficient proof of the impartiality with which you are disposed to accept them. I am one of the most eager admirers of the French Revolution; I am constantly looking at its results and have the greatest hopes. I consider it as the most notable epoch in the history of the human race . . .[2]

Godwin goes on to express the hope that he may be an instrument which can help to destroy the false notions which are still held even by men of the purest intentions, and play his part in a task to which all friends of science and humanity ought to contribute.

The book was remitted by the Convention to the Committee on Public Education but we may doubt whether it was much studied. The minds of France's new rulers, Danton and Robespierre, were already inclining towards more direct methods of destroying false notions, and the first executions of persons suspected of disloyalty or lack of revolutionary zeal took place that summer. More ominously for those who had read Burke, the French armies began to win victories – it was no longer a question of foreign armies crushing the Revolution, the French seemed set to carry their revolutionary message by force of arms all over Europe.

Another copy of *Political Justice* was sent to France by the hand of John Fenwick in the brief interval between the French declaration of war and the British counter-declaration, accompanied by a strange mandate which Godwin left unsigned.

You will remember the terms upon which the inclosed copy of my book is sent. It is to be given to General Miranda, provided you are likely to live upon terms of easy access to him; otherwise to any Frenchman of public importance and personal candour to whom you have that access: that at all events there may be an additional chance from your influence, to gain a hearing and, if possible, a translation for the work. You will please therefore to write in it To general Miranda (or as the case may happen) from the author . . . I shall be glad to hear of you. If you should choose that I should hear from you, be cautious in your expressions, that you may not bring your friend into trouble. I remain, with earnest wishes for your success, and still more for that of the cause in which you are engaged etc. etc.[3]

Fenwick was one of the circle of close friends who had helped in the preparation of the book, and it is frustrating not to know what exactly was 'the cause' which took him to see an enemy general four days after declaration of war. Was he engaged in one of the many secret last minute attempts to restore peace? Talleyrand had spent some months in London, avowedly as a private visitor, sounding out opposition groups. Before the outbreak of war many English admirers openly celebrated the French victories and subscribed money, allegedly for shoes, for the glorious French army. Whatever his main objective however, Fenwick did not succeed in securing a French translation of *Political Justice*. It emerged later that a translation was undertaken by Benjamin Constant, who described it as 'one of the masterpieces of our age',[4] but he decided to postpone publication for fear that it would provide ammunition to opponents. As a result, *Political Justice*, which was so influential in England made almost no impact in France.

In the optimism of the early days, when it still seemed unthinkable that the progressive trends of the century could ever turn downwards, it had not been over-ambitious to hope that *Political Justice* would influence the course of the French Revolution. And although after the outbreak of war, Godwin himself soon moderated his own expectations, others continued to take a different view. If, as was believed, the French Revolution had been brought about by the spread of ideas in the writings of d'Holbach, Helvétius, and the others, could it not be steered back on to a proper course by the latest work which consolidated and superseded their discoveries?

In September 1793 Major Jardine, the founder of the Philomaths, wrote to Charles James Fox to propose that William Godwin should be sent personally to France. Fox had been urging the Government, even after the outbreak of war, to send an emissary to Paris to open peace discussions with the National Convention, and Jardine's knowledge of this, together with newspaper reports of the Convention's welcome of Godwin's book may have prompted the initiative. We do not know the details, and there is no reason to suppose that it carried any weight with the British Government, but presumably Jardine believed that England's nearest equivalent to a *philosophe* would be able to negotiate more successfully with the new rulers of France than a conventional aristocratic ambassador.

Jardine deliberately did not consult Godwin before making his proposal, and he seems to have assumed that Godwin's admiration for the policies of the revolutionary Government would, by now, be ebbing as rapidly as his own. If so, Godwin's letter of indignant disapproval soon disillusioned him.

Are you the friend of liberty or the enemy? This is a problem beyond my ability to solve. You are the 'friend of peace' Aye, I grant you: so much so I fear, *ut mavis quietum servitium quam tumultuosam libertatem.** You think little of independence, of energy, of manly confidence, and manly spirit, and only wish that mankind were well asleep. Do not exclaim so bitterly upon Robespierre! I, like you, will weep over his errors; but I must still continue to regard him as an eminent benefactor of mankind. The French, you say, must again remain the prey of despotism. I answer in in the words of Agamemnon 'Prophet of plagues, for ever boding ill!' You say, you cannot long serve God and Mammon. Alas! your equivocal language is precisely calculated to hold the balance between them.[5]

Godwin's simultaneous letter to Fox in which he disowns the major's initiative is typical of his many attempts during these years to apply his principles to his own political conduct. He is determined to speak with complete candour, he says, equal to equal, courageously assuming the duty of lecturing the admired politician on the conspicuous flaws in his character. He is convinced that philosophers (including himself) have exploded earlier errors of political theory and that it is only a matter of time before the newly discovered knowledge is recognized and acted upon. The letter begins with an expression of his admiration for Fox and his determination to stay free from partisanship, and he then offers his advice:

The period in which I am now writing is a period from which the liberty and melioration of the world will take their date. Nothing can stop the dissemination of principle. No power on earth can shut the scene that has been opened. The laws of nature and of mind conspire to forward it, and it has the ardent wishes of every enlightened friend of man . . . and you may then fill the important office of mediator between the political monopolies that must gradually withdraw their pretensions, and the political justice that either by tranquil or violent means must succeed.[6]

It took time for watchers in England to discover the facts from across the Channel and to appreciate the implications. Opinion did not move along a smooth curve, but lurched gracelessly at irregular intervals. When Godwin had written the British and Foreign History year by year for the *New Annual Register*, he was able to slide unnoticed from one political stance to another without losing the confidence of readers, most of whom were themselves performing the same easy manoeuvre. During the composition of *Political Justice* its underlying assumptions had also changed as Godwin raced against history to get it out, adding and revising month by month in 1791 and 1792 as the incessant news from France suggested

---

* 'that you prefer a peaceful slavery to a troubled liberty'; quotation not identified, but it has a resemblance to the final words of Lepidus in Sallust's *Histories*, I, 55, 26.

new questions for consideration and new objections to be answered. But once published, the two quarto volumes stood petrified on the shelf, a unique monument to the unique conditions which had produced them.

In one of his more exuberant flights of hope, for example, Godwin had predicted that now that the principles had been discovered and the correct policies identified, results could confidently be expected quite soon. There would, he forecast, be 'no war, no crime, no administration of justice as it is called, and no government', and some at least of these advances would come within the lifetime of the present generation. Shelley, who preferred the first edition – the prediction was dropped in the second – was to complain to Godwin in 1812, that there ought by that time to have been more to show, for *Political Justice* had been available for twenty years. 'What has followed?' he wrote, 'have men ceased to fight, have vice and misery vanished from the earth?'[7] Shelley was not being sarcastic but there was no need to have lived through the intervening years before admitting to disappointment.

Within a few weeks of Godwin's letter to Fox, the Jacobin terror began to gather momentum, with the execution of the Queen and then of the twenty-one Girondins whose high-minded policies had done so much to stir admiration for the Revolution in earlier months. In the next three months, nearly two hundred people were put to death in Paris and the proportion of acquittals among the accused soon fell towards zero. Godwin watched with uncomprehending horror as the guillotine became the favoured instrument of determining political priorities and resolving policy differences.

Elsewhere in the book Godwin had argued that international war could be eliminated if the underlying causes of political rivalry were tackled as he suggested. Just as the French Revolution had been primarily a revolution of opinion, so too the force of opinion could prevent governments from resorting to violence. At the outbreak of the war in February 1793 he composed a long pamphlet – surviving but unpublished – on how men of good will on either side of the Channel might yet bring the two countries back from disaster.[8] However his alarmist estimate that the impending conflict would cost fifty thousand lives was to look pitiably overoptimistic within a few years as the long eighteenth-century trend towards limiting and humanizing the conduct of war went sharply into reverse. His recommendation that defending armies should unilaterally give up insincere tactics such as camouflage, deception, and ambush was not adopted, soldiers being less convinced of the usefulness of moral gestures than the philosophers who see the wider picture. His suggestion that invading armies could be successfully resisted by 'defensive' weapons – pikes were favoured both for their lack of first strike capability and for their alternative agricultural function – did not survive the French invasions of the watery Netherlands and of mountainous Switzerland. Nor did French republican soldiers, as bearers of more advanced truths, conduct military operations noticeably more philosophically than their royalist predecessors.

Conceived in the age of enlightenment, *Political Justice* was born into the age of revolution and grew up in the age of romanticism. As one by one the confident assumptions and perceptions of the eighteenth century were tested and destroyed, Godwin strove to maintain his promised integrity, surveying public events honestly and trying to revise his theories and principles, in the best empirical tradition, in accordance with new facts. Unashamed to change his opinions, but understandably bewildered by the tumble of events, the adjustment was to be long drawn out, painful, and sometimes humiliating. Within a year he had considerably modified the view of the human mind which explained and unified the general theory. The proposition in the first edition that it is enough for a man to perceive the right course of action for him to perform it, he now saw, was too simple even if 'perceive' is taken to imply comprehension of all the implications of a situation. From his journal we can plot the hours devoted to discussion of 'necessity', 'passion', 'volition', 'self-love', 'benevolence' as he and his friends strove to devise a more satisfactory account.

Godwin's grand attempt to establish timeless and immutable principles was not, however, rendered obsolete in six months as readers of some passages have been inclined to suggest. If the world is rushing to destruction the need for a sound morality is increased not lessened. There had been sharp historical downturns before, but the world had always returned eventually to the slow improvement trend which had characterized human history in modern times and which constituted the factual basis of the theory of perfectibility. In Godwinian language, since truth had always triumphed, it was the business of politics to try to mobilize and extend its power.

In England, where a few months before it had been normal to regard events in France as of little direct relevance, one lesson was clear to everyone. If radical change could be brought about with such speed in France, then the same process could be repeated in England. British reformers, having seen how easily the power of mind had overcome the power of armies, felt reassured that history was on their side, and they now had in *Political Justice* an authoritative treatise to explain the dynamics of the process. Politicians were delighted to claim alliance with the passages of the book which coincided with their own policies or which offered suitable material for propaganda. Quotable extracts, such as the remarks on kings, were frequently reprinted in the popular anti-Government press, along with similar stuff from *The Rights of Man*. Because much was similar, it was easy to assume that there was one cause on which all forward-looking men including Godwin were united, and this mistake has often been repeated.

In fact there were severe and ultimately irreconcilable differences between the policies which Godwin recommended and those of the politicians of the day who made use of his prestige. As long ago as 1785, in his first theoretical essay in the *Political Herald*, he had written scornfully of those who create a political hurricane in hopes of riding the whirlwind and directing the storm.[9] Politics based on party, he wrote then, are bound by their very nature to encourage exaggeration and distortion. 'The people will never be able to see objects as they are,' he advised in a famous phrase which he was soon to make particularly his own. 'You must either permit them to amplify them into the gigantic and the marvellous, or you may be morally assured they will degrade them into objects of derision and abhorrence.' Just as you cannot reform a criminal by loading him with chains so too it is pointless (however worthy the objective) to organize bodies of men into slogan-shouting political parties if they have no true individual perception of the choices.

It is one thing for honest men to come together to discuss issues: it is quite another to organize mass protests, to inflame passions by appeals to sectional self-interests, and to hint at violence. Political propaganda is not only morally wrong but ultimately ineffective, for truth and success cannot for long be kept separate. A good latinist, Godwin was always sharply aware of the cognate meanings of 'party' and 'partial'. Party politics can offer only a part of the truth. 'Impartial' was his favourite term of praise.

For a while the differences between Godwin's individual liberalism and the policies of reforming politicians were masked by a greater unity. If for him the Government's attempts to suppress political discussion were striking at the roots of perfectibility, the right of free speech was also of importance to old-fashioned Whigs and others whose commitment to individual liberty was even more modest. While waiting for the last sheets of *Political Justice* to be printed, Godwin had written four long open letters about the recent trials for seditious libel which were published soon afterwards in the *Morning Chronicle*.[10] Signed 'Mucius', the pseudonym that he had used when writing for the *Political Herald* seven years before, the tone is angry. What is the boasted English constitution, Mucius demands, if it does not include the ancient English liberty of freedom of speech? With the regretful patience of Jehovah seeking just men in the cities of the Plain, he returns to one of the central tenets of his theory of progress, the power of honest truth, calmly affirmed, to win the argument eventually even in unfavourable circumstances. All that was needed was one brave juryman.

Let us figure this man to ourselves, contending with the prejudices and passions of his colleagues. Let us figure his mildness and equanimity in the midst of their impatience, and perhaps their scurrility. Let us figure to ourselves that clear, simple, unornamented understanding, which furnishes him with a plain and undeniable answer to all their objections. Let us suppose truth by his instrumentality victorious, not merely over the passions, but over the understanding of united numbers . . . Is there no such man? Oh, for a man like this, to suspend the torrent of absolute power, and prove that I am not fallen upon an age of savage barbarism and ignorance! Oh, for a man like this, to inscribe his name upon the page of history, and eclipse with its lustre the renown of Hampden and Russel!

There were many such jurymen. Time and again, to the anger of judges, juries insisted on acquitting booksellers accused of publishing seditious libel or on bringing in an irregular verdict of 'guilty of publishing but without criminal intent'. But many reasonable people were drawing a political lesson from recent events in France entirely different from that of the believers in the power of truth. If in France reform had begun with moderate men and moderate measures, that had not prevented one group after another finding itself outflanked and then destroyed by more extreme and more ruthless colleagues. As the news from France told of ever more radical changes, normally pragmatic British Tories concluded that their only hope was to defend and sustain every absurd corrupt feature of the existing order with every means in their power.

In Scotland, where the political system was even more corrupt and unrepresentative than in England – Edinburgh had thirty-three voters on its electoral roll – the judges not only claimed wider powers of interpreting and extending the law, but virtually selected their own juries. It was therefore a good place at which to mount a counterattack on the reformers. In the summer of 1793 Thomas Muir, an Edinburgh advocate, and Thomas Palmer, a Unitarian minister in Perth, were charged with sedition in Scottish courts, and after unfair trials, were sentenced to transportation to Botany Bay for fourteen years and seven years respectively. As convicted felons, they were taken by sea to Woolwich to await their passage to Australia, and kept fettered in the hulks with thieves and murderers except when taken ashore for hard labour in chain-gangs on the riverbank.

On 7 December 1793 Godwin walked to Woolwich to visit them.[11] On the 17th he went again and stayed overnight and then again on 17 January to say goodbye. He presented Muir with a copy of *Political Justice*, but the captain of the hulks denied him the comfort. On 3 March, when there was some parliamentary and popular interest in the case, Godwin wrote a letter to the *Morning Chronicle* signing himself 'Valerius', whose tone, in contrast to that of Mucius, is this time one of studied reasonableness. Admitting that the men should not have appeared to encourage or condone violence, his main argument concerns the senselessness of the punitive sentences. How can we condemn the French, he asks, and at the same time imitate them in their atrocities?[12]

The political argument in the country was now shifting ground. No longer was the debate about how far it is right for a government to limit freedom of speech when social stability is under threat, but about the circumstances in which a good man can reasonably abandon attempts at persuasion and offer physical resistance. In England those found guilty of seditious libel were thought harshly treated to be fined or imprisoned for a few weeks. In Scotland the judges had deliberately magnified the seriousness of the offence, coming down especially vindictively because the accused were educated men and leaders of opinion. Transportation, it was correctly assumed, was tantamount to a death sentence for men not already inured to prison life.

As if to illustrate Godwin's point a group of his friends were dining under the chairmanship of Horne Tooke on the very afternoon that he visited the prisoners at Woolwich. The Society for Constitutional Information, normally one of the most moderate of the reforming associations, angrily passed resolution after resolution which in their exasperation came near to advocating violent resistance.

Resolved, That law ceases to be an object of obedience whenever it becomes an instrument of oppression. Resolved, That we recall to mind, with the deepest satisfaction, the merited fate of the infamous Jeffreys, once lord chief justice of England, who at the era of the glorious revolution, for the many iniquitous sentences which he had passed, was torn to pieces by a brave and injured people. Resolved, That those who imitate his example deserve his fate . . .

A few days later the popular politicians in London held a mass open-air meeting at which other defiant challenges were thrown out. For the first time for over a century there now seemed a real possibility of civil war. Politicians and philosophers suddenly found themselves personally confronting the most difficult of all political questions.

It was an issue which Godwin honestly faced. Unlike some optimists who are inclined to argue evasively that dilemmas are escapable if only their own policies are adopted, he acknowledged from the beginning that if his theory was to be complete, it must give an account of how, in practice, the power of mind prevails against those who are prepared to resort to lies and to violence. And, as befitted the philosopher of individual liberty, his answer lay properly in his theory of the individual human mind. If the mind receives a sufficiently strong moral shock, he argued, it can be jerked out of its previously determined mode of thinking. Seeing the mind as usual primarily in terms of the physical operation of the brain, Godwin imagined a powerful shock which rearranges the 'medullary particles', and by causing them to interact with one another in a new way, redirects the chain of perception, opinion, and behaviour. On 13 December 1791, he had read in Sallust the story of Marius who turned away a man sent to kill him with a stern look and an intrepid retort, 'Wretch, have you the temerity to kill Marius,' and he included it in *Political Justice* to illustrate how an 'energetic idea compressed in the mind' can make its way with irresistible force to the mind of another person and convince him. 'Who shall say', he wrote, 'how far the whole species might be improved were they accustomed to despise force in others and refuse to employ it for themselves?' Shelley was later to use Godwin's story to make the same point in the *Revolt of Islam*.[13]

It is an attractive theory and there are better examples of its success in practice than the tough talk of the unadmirable Marius. Like so many of Godwin's ideas, however, it too was more plausible at the time it was first written than when Shelley readopted it a generation later (let alone in the late twentieth century) although even in 1794 an intrepid manner did not save many Frenchmen from their ride in the tumbrils. It is not a theory of martyrdom as such. The longer-term effects on other people are brought into the argument as a back-up, to explain and justify cases where the psychological shock has plainly failed by itself to produce the improvement. 'Men will see the progressive advancement of virtue and good', Godwin wrote in *Political Justice*, 'and feel that, if things occasionally happen contrary to their hopes, the miscarriage itself was a necessary part of that progress. They will know that they are members of the chain, and each has his several utility and they will not feel indifferent to that utility.' As the years passed, the weight of the argument tended to shift, with more emphasis being placed on the longer-term effects and less on the immediate efficacy. But in 1793 and 1794 it was not absurd to believe that the educated and public-spirited noblemen and gentlemen who composed the judiciary of England and Scotland, the consummation of thousands of years of human progress, could be successfully influenced by the energy of mind.

Among those present at the dinner on 17 January 1794 at which the defiant resolutions were proposed was Joseph Gerrald, one of the acknowledged leaders of the radical reformers. Rich and brilliant, he had devoted his life to the cause, despised by those who disliked his politics as a traitor to his upbringing. At the time of the dinner, he and another wealthy radical called Charles Sinclair were on bail from a court in Edinburgh where they had been arrested at the end of 1793 with other prominent delegates while attending the 'British Convention'. They had been permitted to return to London to tidy up their affairs having given their parole to return to stand trial in March.

On 10 January two of the other accused, Margarot and Skirving, were tried in Edinburgh, found guilty and, like Muir, sentenced to fourteen years' transportation for their part in promoting 'a determined and systematic plan to subvert the limited monarchy and free constitution of Britain and substitute in its place, by intimidation, force, and violence, a republic or democracy'. It is uncertain how far they had, in fact, advocated or planned violence but the news of the sentences, arriving a few days before the dinner, contributed to the mounting revolutionary fervour. A chain of necessity whereby fear of violence was causing acts of violence, which in their turn were causing counter-violence, could be clearly discerned.

Godwin saw Gerrald frequently during his time on bail and debated the issues with him. On 14 January Gerrald attended a supper at the Philomaths at which they considered strategies for breaking into the downward spiral without either violent revolution or surrender of moral principle. The immediate question was whether Gerrald and Sinclair should return to Edinburgh to face trial, with the risk that they too would be sentenced to transportation like Muir, Palmer, Margarot and Skirving, or whether they could justifiably break their bail and flee the country as a contribution to a longer-term greater good. Horne Tooke, an experienced politician, advised them to make their escape and offered to pay the bail money out of his own pocket. Others were worried that if they did that – as Tom Paine had done – they would give the propaganda victory to the Government and forgo an opportunity for truth to reveal her inexorable power. It would also be a breach of their word of honour, a consideration that weighed heavily in Gerrald's mind, although *Political Justice* advised that no promise need be kept if greater good can be accomplished by breaking it.

Gerrald decided to return. He knew the risks and he was prepared to accept the martyrdom if he failed. But he also believed that a Godwinian response to coercion might give him the victory. On 23 January, following a day in which Godwin met him twice, the philosopher wrote a long letter of advice, beginning with sentiments which might have strained the credibility of anyone with a less secure reputation for sincerity.

I cannot recollect the situation in which you are in a few days to be placed without emotions of respect, I had almost said of envy. For myself I will never adopt any conduct for the express purpose of being put upon my trial, but if I be ever so put, I will consider that as a day of triumph.

As a scientist Godwin was pleased that such a good opportunity had arisen to put his theory to an experimental test. He advised Gerrald to avoid boastful talk and personal abuse – much needed advice for Gerrald was arrogant – to concentrate on establishing the lawfulness of the Convention, and to emphasize that his reforming efforts were aimed at preventing violence. But the main argument was the power of truth to change the human mind.

What an event would it be for England and mankind if you could gain an acquittal! Is not such an event worth striving for? It is in man, I am sure it is, to effect that event. Gerrald, you are that man. Fertile in genius, strong in moral feeling, prepared with every accomplishment that literature and reflection can give. Stand up to the situation – be wholly yourself ... It is in the nature of the human mind to be great in proportion as it is acted upon by great incitements. Remember this. Now is your day. Never, perhaps never, in the revolution of human affairs, will your mind be the same illustrious and irresistible mind as it will be on this day ... [14]

The trials at Edinburgh were a fiasco. After a few brief appearances Charles Sinclair was unexpectedly dismissed on technical legal grounds which were obscure to everyone who had followed his case. It was widely believed that his uncle, Sir John Sinclair the important Scottish landowner, had corruptly secured the acquittal. At his own trial Gerrald attempted a calm, reasoned defence, connecting his theory of political progress, as Godwin had done, with the theory of the individual mind.[15] But the court was brusquely impatient. The judge constantly interrupted, making little attempt to conceal the contempt he felt both for the prisoner and for his philosophy. Gerrald was duly found guilty of sedition and sentenced to fourteen years' transportation. He was brought to Newgate Prison in London where Godwin and his other friends visited him often during the following months. A hint from the Government that he would be pardoned if he renounced his views and agreed to keep out of politics was indignantly rejected. Gerrald never complained of his role in the failed experiment, but calmly awaited the arrival of a prison ship and of the longer-term benefits.

At the beginning of April came news from France of the downfall of Danton, and the guillotining for excessive moderation of the leaders who a few months before had seemed more extreme than the wildest imaginings could have feared. Pétion, whom Godwin had met, was among the victims. At home when an open-air meeting passed resolutions implying that they favoured violence the Government decided that severer action was necessary to avert a catastrophe. The papers of the London Corresponding Society were seized, and on the basis of the information found there the House of Commons voted a suspension of Habeas Corpus on 17 May, removing the ancient safeguard against imprisonment without trial. Arrests followed soon after. The power of mind which had swept away the prisons of King Louis less than five years before had failed to prevent the creation of Bastilles in Great Britain.

CHAPTER 10

Things As They Are

Like Regulus who returned to Carthage, like Curtius who plunged into the fiery gulf, Joseph Gerrald was frequently compared with the heroes of ancient Rome. Those plain, proud, incorruptible republicans, so different from the sophisticated, aristocratic courtiers of modern governments, attracted profound respect and much of the philosophical effort of the eighteenth century was devoted to considering how the Roman civic virtues could be re-grafted back on to modern European nation states.

Godwin wrote his political articles under the name of Mucius (who contemptuously thrust his hand into the fire when threatened with torture) and of Valerius (who permitted the plebs to share in the government of Rome). The identity of Junius, the famous political letter-writer of an earlier generation remained unknown, although Horne Tooke told Godwin that he knew the author. Junius, he explained, had also used the pseudonyms Lucius and Brutus to give the full name of the just Roman who had conscientiously ordered his two sons to be beaten with rods and then executed before his eyes.

It was entirely in keeping that Godwin should propose to Robinson, shortly after *Political Justice* was published, that his next project should be a history of the Roman Republic in three volumes quarto, an enterprise which he estimated would take three years to complete.[1] History, for Godwin, was always as important as philosophy. If there are general

The Chained Prisoner by Bewick

truths about human psychology, it is by studying the experience of the men and women of the past that they will be found. History had been the most important topic in the curriculum for his proposed seminary at Epsom in 1783, and when young people asked for help on improving their education, he always put it at the top of his prescribed list. A history of Rome would allow him to discuss the virtues and the errors of the greatest characters, he told Robinson, and would also cover the 'contention at home between aristocracy and democracy' – a hint that he had in mind to discuss present day politics in the guise of Roman history. But, perhaps for that reason, Robinson declined the proposal, and although the journal records a *démêlé*, he refused to change his mind.

Godwin also considered writing a play. Ever since Mr Godfrey had sprung from poverty to instant riches in the fictional pages of *Damon and Delia* in 1784, he nourished a hope that life would copy literature and that he himself would write a successful tragedy that would transform his reputation. He had written many plays in his younger years, and it was an obvious medium for a philosopher who had a message to diffuse. In 1790, before embarking on *Political Justice*, he composed a tragedy in five acts, in blank verse, which he called *Dunstan*. He revised and updated it from time to time, and as late as 1795, he was still contemplating bringing it forward for possible production or publication. A fair copy was prepared in his neatest handwriting and submitted to a friend – probably Holcroft – for comment, but it was never accepted or printed. His daughter read it, without enthusiasm, after Godwin's death, and in the summer of 1982, the manuscript itself again came to light.

Although the drama is allegedly set in Anglo-Saxon England, Godwin's purpose is to comment on the French Revolution debate, the attempts to claim religious authority for particular forms of political institution, and the exploiting of passions by political parties for their own purposes. The reader of *Political Justice* would have recognized the sentiments:

> There is no enemy to the human mind
> So fell as superstition. All that dignifies our nature,
> The seeds of wisdom, virtue, truth and honour,
> Are sprung from liberty, the man that acts
> Fearless and confident the dictates of
> His mind, the man whose firm intrepid judgement
> Pursues the useful and the just through all their mazes,
> Gives lustre to the universe.[2]

It was Holcroft who convinced him that the novel was the best instrument for influencing opinion. Both men during their days in Grub Street had written reviews, commenting, as was the custom, not only on the literary qualities but on the moral tendencies of novels and plays. If novels could spread immorality – as most people believed – then they could also be enlightening and improving. Holcroft's first long novel *Anna St. Ives* was being composed at the time when Godwin was drafting *Political Justice* and the two men discussed it in draft with the same candour as they applied to all their dealings. 'I declare myself', wrote Godwin introducing two pages of unsympathetic criticisms, 'with all my heart and from the bottom of my soul, the utter and irreconcilable enemy of this fourth volume. I feared as much. I said at the end of the third volume. No. Mortal man cannot support it . . . There are two objections, both insuperable.' It is wrong, he complains, to allow the seducer Clifton to overcome Anna's scruples by a deployment of Godwinian arguments about the evils of marriage. That is to give victory to hypocrisy and bring their philosophical principles into disrepute – even if in the novel the couple are mercifully disturbed by the maid when Clifton is 'in the very act of fastening on her'. Secondly, Godwin notes, Holcroft has failed to show convincingly that the culmination of the story, the persuasion of Anna, is a necessary consequence of the characters of the people and the logic of the situation.[3]

Godwin was right. Holcroft's chosen medium – seven volumes of panting bosoms, attempted rapes, confinements in madhouses, rescues from highwaymen, and other clichés of the eighteenth-century epistolary novel – was not well suited to his purpose. *Anna St. Ives* is deservedly well known as the first English 'Jacobin' novel, but few readers are likely to have found the chain of their moral opinions redirected when they finally closed the pages. It is too like a priggish version of the standard fiction of the day to stir the imagination of any but the already-converted.

Soon afterwards Holcroft embarked on a second attempt to use a fictional form to promote Godwinian ideas, and Godwin again read and criticized the manuscript. For *Hugh Trevor*, Holcroft chose that other well-favoured eighteenth-century medium, the picaresque, and his hero like Gil Blas or Peregrine Pickle learns wisdom and maturity as he adventures from one corrupt institution to another, an Oxford college, a church living, a lawyer's office, a gambling den, and others. Holcroft's purpose, as he explained in the Preface, was not to expose the hypocrisies and injustices of contemporary England – a superfluous task – but to explain the perfectibility of man. 'What profession', he asks, 'should a man of principle, who is anxiously desirous to promote individual and general happiness, choose for his son?' It is not however clear what the correct answer is since the only unsullied occupation Holcroft is able to find is that of improving novelist.

It was Godwin himself who triumphantly overcame the literary problem which he had correctly identified and which Holcroft had failed to solve. *Things As They Are, or the Adventures of Caleb Williams* which was published in May 1794, on the same day as *Hugh Trevor*, is a near-masterpiece, the finest work of fiction to appear in the long and prolific interval between the age of Richardson and the emergence of Jane Austen and Walter Scott. For Hazlitt it was 'unquestionably the best modern novel'.[4] If it has never quite been accepted as a classic, it has always had its champions, a book to be read with pleasure in its own right even by those unfamiliar with the circumstances in which it was produced. When he was an old man and his novels were chosen to be reprinted with other contemporary classics, Godwin admitted with his usual lack of false modesty that his aims had been high. 'I will write a tale', he recalled saying to himself during the composition, 'that shall constitute an epoch in the mind of the reader, that no one, after he has read it, shall ever be exactly the same man that he was before.'[5]

Abandoning the literary models which Holcroft had tried to adapt, he chose a story of mystery and pursuit which can be read simply as a thriller. Novels were usually sent to the press, volume by volume, as they were written, so that many are diffuse and shapeless, but Godwin carefully worked out his whole plot in advance, beginning at the end. As with *Political Justice* he wrote only a few pages each day in the mornings, and as with *Political Justice* he fed his imagination with an immense amount of related reading, including especially Fielding, Sterne, and Swift.

The work progressed steadily from the spring of 1793 until the end of the year. Then from 2 January 1794 until 1 April, although he had written most of the book, he found that he could make no progress, his ideas thrown into turmoil by the sedition trials. When he was able to start again, the book took on a more immediately political flavour than had been in his mind at the beginning. *Things As They Are, or the Adventures of Caleb Williams* described aspects of England that readers of romance were seldom asked to consider, but which the author had himself witnessed in Newgate.

Our dungeons were cells, 7½ feet by 6½, below the surface of the ground, damp, without window, light, or air, except from a few holes worked for that purpose in the door. In some of these miserable receptacles three persons were put to sleep together. I was fortunate enough to have one to myself. It was now the approach of winter. We were not allowed to have candles; and, as I have already said, were thrust in here at sun set and not liberated till the returning day. This was our situation for fourteen or fifteen hours out of the four and twenty . . . Thank God, exclaims the Englishman, we have no Bastille! Thank God, with us no man can be punished without a crime! Unthinking wretch! Is that a country of liberty where thousands languish in dungeons and fetters? Go, go, ignorant fool! and visit the scenes of our prisons! witness their unwholesomeness, their filth, the tyranny of their governors, the misery of their inmates! After that show me the man shameless enough to triumph, and say, England has no Bastille![6]

Godwin described how easy and common it was for an unscrupulous landowner to manipulate the law to dominate and oppress his tenants, explaining the links in the mechanisms whereby greater tyrants use economic power (and the associated ties of gratitude and obligation) to create a structure of lesser tyrants obedient to their will. But the novel would not have achieved its purpose if it had been merely a propaganda tale of the wicked rich exploiting innocent victims. By choosing the novel as his medium, he was, he claimed, enabled to do 'the thing in which my imagination revelled the most freely . . . the analysis of the private and internal operations of the mind, employing my metaphysical dissecting knife in tracing and laying bare the involutions of motive, and recording the gradually accumulating impulses'. As in *Political Justice* Godwin united his criticisms of political institutions with the psychology of the individuals who are influenced by them.

The phrase 'Things As They Are' firmly linked the book to the tradition of protest. Richard Price, in the already famous Revolution Society sermon of 4 November 1789 had urged every man present to 'think of all things as they are, and not suffer any partial affections to bind his understanding'. *Political Justice* in its turn advised that 'the wise and virtuous man ought to see things precisely as they are, and judge of the actual constitution of his country with the same impartiality as if he had simply read of it in the remotest page of history. Wilful refusal to face facts cuts the vital links between true perception and right conduct. If you cannot see things as they are, you see a part only and since you cannot therefore be impartial, your understanding is certain to be imperfect.

Things-as-they-are clusters readily in Godwin's writings with the dual meaning of 'partial' with the Aeolian harp, and with the rich and varied metaphors of the chains of the mind. And like them, it too had its counterpart meaning when used by Burke and his supporters – to the extent that the phrase could not be uttered on either side without irony or scorn. As Godwin himself wrote elsewhere in *Political Justice*:

There is no mistake more thoroughly to be deplored on this subject than that of persons, sitting at their ease and surrounded with all the conveniences of life, who are apt to exclaim, 'We find things very well as they are;' and to inveigh bitterly against all projects of reform, as 'the romances of visionary men, and the declamations of those who are never to be satisfied.' Is it well, that so large a part of the community should be kept in abject penury, rendered stupid with ignorance and disgustful with vice, perpetuated in nakedness and hunger, goaded to the commission of crimes, and made victims to the merciless laws which the rich have instituted to oppress them?[7]

Godwin's purpose, which he avowed from the beginning, was to repeat the lessons of *Political Justice*. He wanted to describe how men who are intrinsically good and benevolent can be vitiated by false notions picked up from the political, economic, and institutional environment. Falkland who pursues Caleb relentlessly through the story is an admirable English gentleman – his name recalls Viscount Falkland, the overchivalrous secretary of state in Charles II's reign – but his moral standard is honour not justice and he prefers the reputation of virtue to the reality. Forrester, his cousin, is also a man whose inherent goodness is spoiled – in his case by excessive respect for partial laws and his determination to apply them to the letter. Caleb Williams could have used his great talents productively for the good of his fellow men if economic circumstances had not forced him into an unsuitable employment where they had no suitable outlet. The brutal Grimes is also a prisoner of his environment for 'without an atom of intentional malice, he was fitted by the mere coarseness of his perceptions for the greatest injuries'. The band of thieves with whom Caleb stays practise their own form of justice, but all that distinguishes them from the greater thieves from whom they steal is that they do not have the permission of the formal law.

Despite occasional abruptnesses and infelicities, Godwin is more successful than Holcroft in linking the incidents of the story to the developing characters of the participants, and thus infiltrating his message into the minds of readers. A story of pursuit in which the roles of pursuer and pursued can unexpectedly be reversed offered wonderfully good opportunities for exploring the mixed motives that bind differing personalities in mutual hatred. The more truthful Caleb Williams is in telling his story, the more evil he appears to his listeners, yet Falkland, who had set up the clever net of deceit which tightens more strongly the more the victim struggles, soon comes to depend on Caleb. They share a wicked secret and their personalities are complements rather than opposites.

By the end Godwin's main point is well made. Caleb Williams and Falkland are both destroyed. That is the inevitable consequence of things as they are. But what has happened to the omnipotence of truth? Is Caleb Williams doomed to go to his grave unbelieved? Will the truth only come out if his prison manuscript is – against all probability – allowed to survive? If so then Godwin would have written a convincing story of things as they are, but made no new converts to political justice. Such an outcome would have been as damaging to his philosophical principles as Holcroft's tale of the silver-tongued deceiver.

Godwin evidently thought hard about the resolution of his novel. As originally drafted the story marches inexorably to an entirely credible end with Caleb Williams and Falkland both broken, but with Falkland's crimes and lies still triumphant. Godwin laid down his pen on 30 April 1794, having completed the story according to the plan which he had worked out in February of the previous year. Then, as his journal records between 4 and 8 May, he wrote a 'new catastrophe' and it was this version which was printed when the book was published shortly afterwards.[8]

The revised ending also flows credibly from the characters even though there is a sudden and dramatic reversal. The dying Falkland when confronted with the truth fearlessly presented face to face admits his guilt although he has denied it hitherto, but Caleb finds to his surprise that, far from rejoicing at his vindication, he himself is overcome with remorse at having forced the downfall of an intrinsically admirable man. Truth has triumphed. Moral insight has triumphed. The chain of events has been successfully redirected, and despite the destructive consequences of things as they are, the world has moved a small step forward towards perfection.

The book was completed with the drafting of a Preface on 12 May 1794 setting out the author's hopes and aims:

The following narrative is intended to answer a purpose more general and important than immediately appears upon the face of it. The question now afloat in the world respecting THINGS AS THEY ARE, is the most interesting that can be presented to the human mind. While one party pleads for reformation and change, the other extols in the warmest terms the existing constitution of society . . . What is now presented to the public is no refined and abstract speculation; it is a study and delineation of things passing in the moral world. It is but of late that the inestimable importance of political principles has been adequately apprehended. It is now known to philosophers that the spirit and character of the government intrudes itself into every rank of society. But this is a truth highly worthy to be communicated to persons whom books of philosophy and science are never likely to reach. Accordingly it was proposed in the invention of the following work, to comprehend, as far as the progressive nature of a single story would allow, a general review of the modes of domestic and unrecorded despotism, by which man becomes the destroyer of man.

On that same day warrants were going out for the arrest of Hardy, Thelwall, Horne Tooke, and other reformers, and the first moves were made to suspend Habeas Corpus. *Caleb Williams*'s entry into the world, like that of its great predecessor, coincided with a major crisis of free speech. Crosby, the publisher, felt that he could not take the risk of publishing the Preface and it was not printed. By the time the book was put on sale on 26 May, several of Godwin's friends were in jail. One of the first copies off the press was taken by Godwin to Newgate to be presented to Joseph Gerrald whose case had been high in his mind during the writing and whose experience provided some of the incidents of the story.

In the event the Government, while clamping down even more severely on overtly political publications, made no move against novels, and *Caleb Williams*, like its predecessor, became an immediate success. It was reprinted thirteen times before the end of the century and twenty-six times in Godwin's lifetime, in England, Ireland, the United States, France, Germany and Switzerland. Godwin's fame was redoubled, and if the readers of *Political Justice* were different from the readers of *Caleb Williams*, as on the whole they probably were, everyone was amazed that two such different and original works of literature should appear from the same pen in just over a year.

Two years after publication, the novel was adapted for the stage (without permission) by George Colman the Younger, and the first performance of *The Iron Chest*[9] took place at Drury Lane on 12 March 1796 with Godwin in the audience. Kemble, who played the leading role, had a heavy cold which became steadily worse as the hours passed, not helped by the opium pills which he had been taking since before the curtain rose. Colman later accused him of having deliberately sabotaged the play by not bothering to rehearse, but a reporter who was there on the first night claimed implausibly that the audience 'with one voice cried out, "No, no, Kemble, it is not your fault." ' The piece was then drastically revised, with cuts equivalent to one and a half hours and it soon became a favourite of the repertory of the Haymarket Theatre, performed nearly every year well into the nineteenth century.

But although dramatization was a good method of carrying the novel to a wider audience, just as the novel reached a readership unlikely to comprehend philosophy direct, Godwin's message was largely lost in the dilution. All the names were changed. Falkland became Sir Edward Mortimer, Caleb Williams became Wilford. The action was rescheduled to the politically safer days of James I. The plot was reduced to Wilford's inquisitive peep into the mysterious iron chest, and an eventual denouement when it is opened. The prudent Colman carefully excluded the politics with which, he complained, *Caleb Williams* teemed. Things-as-they-are degenerated into Crime-does-not-Pay. The central thesis relies on a single remark by a robber, 'My story is a chain. Take all together. 'Twill not unlink,' but hundreds of playgoers who never read *Political Justice* or *Caleb Williams* heard the Burkean Sir Edward Mortimer incessantly proclaim that his fault was to prefer the reputation to the reality of virtue.

CHAPTER 11

Impartial Politics

In the spring of 1795, as part of a series of measures to reduce public borrowing, the Government introduced a tax on hair powder. Anyone wishing to apply powder to his own head or to those of his family or footmen was required to obtain a licence costing one guinea. Officers in the armed forces, Church of England clergymen, and dissenting ministers were exempted provided they earned less than £100 per year, and there was abatement for gentlemen with two or more daughters unmarried. When a few years later the custom died out there were few regrets even in the Treasury. Hair powder was basically flour, and the nation at war could not afford to waste food on unhygienic extravagances, although the simultaneous tax on dogs was not viewed in the same light.

The Frenchmen who took control of their country in 1789 had been proud to wear their hair long and unpowdered to differentiate themselves from the royalists and aristocrats whom they displaced, and their English admirers adopted the fashion long before the Government added an economic motive. Earl Stanhope who had taken the chair at celebratory dinners which Godwin attended in 1789 and 1790 was among the first to flaunt his French sympathies in this way and others soon followed. The greater the loyalty to the existing order, the curlier and grizzlier the hair, and among the opposition a short crop was regarded as more radical than long and lanky. By 1794 the parties – calling themselves 'aristocrats'

The Forces of the Law by Hone

and 'democrats' – were as readily distinguishable as the cavaliers and roundheads of whose attitudes they were the inheritors.

John Horne Tooke, although one of the keenest of the radicals, remained a mid-eighteenth-century man and refused to change his appearance, but he was deliberately contrary in this as in much else. Joseph Gerrald added to his difficulties by appearing before the Scottish judges with long hair and open-necked shirt, seeing the gesture as part of the fearless avowal of principle on which he took his stand. Godwin changed his style in 1794 although the date when the enlightenment gentleman was snipped into the radical intellectual is not recorded in his journal. In September Amelia Alderson noted that he was 'bien poudré' but to judge from portraits made the following year, he probably changed not long afterwards. Like Holcroft he now wore his hair neatly parted, neck length, and unpowdered. The two friends retained their clean clothes and fresh appearance, seeing no necessary connection between political egalitarianism and slovenliness of dress. Connoisseurs of fashion would not have been able to tell that their liberal opinions differed in important respects from those of the revolutionary politicians with whom they consorted.

In France the Revolution continued with new ferocity, and the congratulatory fraternal good wishes which the British reformers, including Godwin, had proudly sent to the National Convention were now taken by many people as further confirmation that English Jacobins were no more benign than the French on whom they had foolishly lavished their admiration. In June, the Great Terror began and upwards of thirty-five thousand men and women were put to death in the name of the people. Many of the British radicals and reformers who had rushed to Paris to be in at the birth of the new society found themselves unceremoniously thrust into prison, and Tom Paine was lucky to escape the guillotine.

When Lord Howe defeated the French at sea on the Glorious First of June, Great Britain was reckoned to be safe from invasion for the time being. Three days of victory illuminations were ordered, and loyal mobs armed with sticks roamed the streets smashing any unlit windows which betrayed lack of patriotic enthusiasm. An organized party attacked Citizen Stanhope's house and set it on fire several times, while an unknown 'aristocrat' drove up and down outside in a carriage distributing money and advice. In August three days of rioting in London destroyed the 'crimping houses' where prostitutes enticed men inside for forcible recruitment to the army.

The papers seized in the raid on the London Corresponding Society apparently confirmed the existence of a nationwide organized opposition movement although there was little direct evidence of preparations for violence. But what more could the authorities do? The laws on seditious libel had proved ineffective, and unofficial methods (such as counter-propaganda and intimidation) only intensified anti-Government feeling. Although convictions had been obtained in Scotland for 'sedition', no such crime was known to the law of England. There was only the ultimate weapon in the armoury, the law against treason, but it was inconceivable to most people that a modern government would resort to such extreme and archaic measures against unarmed agitators.

Under the Act of 1351 (which is still in force) it is high treason when 'a man doth compass or imagine the death of our lord the king or our lady his queen, or of their eldest son and heir; or if a man do violate the king's companion or the king's eldest daughter unmarried, or the wife of the king's eldest son and heir, or if a man do levy war against our lord the king in his realm . . .' The same statute goes on to deal with low treason, servants disloyal to masters, wives disobeying husbands, and other socially disruptive practices, most of which have long since either been legalized or renamed. Whatever its merits as a deterrent to armed medieval family feuds and usurpations, this ancient Norman French law – with its evocations of medieval witchcraft and murder by long-range magic – was not an obviously suitable instrument for quelling public demands for parliamentary reform.

That summer Godwin took a holiday. With the success of *Political Justice* and then of *Caleb Williams*, he was financially comfortable for the first time in his life. He could reasonably believe that his days in Grub Street were finally over and that he could henceforth expect to earn an adequate income by his pen. It was twelve years since he had been home, and in June he set off on an extended visit to his native East Anglia. He began by visiting Stowmarket, the scene of his liberation from religion fourteen years before, and he discussed 'God, industry, drinking, and swearing' with Frederick Norman who had first introduced him to the works of the French philosophers. At Norwich dinners were arranged in his honour and he talked to the Reverend Samuel Newton who had whipped him into Sandemanianism during his teenage years. He went on to Dalling where his mother lived near his brother Hull Godwin and his family, and Mrs Sothren came to breakfast.

By the time he arrived back in London in early July, the political crisis had deepened with the continuing arrest of prominent reformers and three days of rioting. Godwin made repeated visits to Gerrald in Newgate, sometimes accompanied by Charles Sinclair the man who had been unaccountably acquitted. Knowing that he himself was likely to be under surveillance by the authorities, he scrupulously avoided any action which might be construed as incriminating, carefully leaving his letters unsigned. A year after the publication of *Political Justice* Godwin was now an active political figure, trying to put into practice his theory of impartial individual liberalism.

However, as can be seen from a letter sent on 18 September to John Thelwall, arrested and imprisoned in the Tower of London, the principles of maximizing utility could make strange reading when applied to an actual case.

The line of conduct I have chalked out to myself is as follows; it remains to be seen whether I shall have the virtue to act up to it: – Upon all occasions to carry my life in my hand; not to indulge a particle of selfish retrospect to life or its pleasures, or the fear of pain and death; but – to expend this treasure, which does not belong to me, but to the public, with all the wisdom I am able: therefore, to risk it freely in matters of solid and palpable benefit, but not in matters of mere gratification. Now, I believe the visit I proposed is rather a matter of gratification to me, and not less to you, than of indispensable utility. I cannot therefore reconcile myself for the sake of it to submit to the terms proposed. These persons fixed on a day and hour when I was to attend them if I pleased. Now I cannot lie: I abhor duplicity and suppression of every sort; and I have no inclination unnecessarily to expose myself to the caprice of persons who by Act of Parliament have abolished all law and seized a despotical power into their hands. What business have I, then, with the sittings of these conspirators?

Having taken up the pen, I have one or two other things to add. I am sorry to see in your letter a spirit of resentment and asperity against your persecutors. I was in hopes that the solitude of a prison might have taught you to reflect on this error and amend it. How senseless and idiot-like it is to be angry with what we know to be a mere passive instrument, moved according to certain regular principles, and in no degree responsible for its operations![1]

Godwin went on to set out his theory of the power of mind at extended length. On a scrap of paper which he kept for the guidance of biographers, he asked them to note:

a The Lords of the Privy Council
b Man: the argument proceeds upon the idea of the necessary and irresistible influence of motives on the mind.[2]

He knew that the letter would be intercepted by the authorities – perhaps read personally by William Pitt and the Privy Council. It was therefore a good opportunity to explain how his theory should be translated into conduct.

He knew too that Thelwall was careless, unable to resist a good joke or a good debating point and was liable to bring friends into trouble for no adequate benefit. When drinking beer after a rally, Thelwall had scooped off the froth with his knife, remarking to the assembled company, spies as well as friends, that he wished he could do the same with the heads of tyrants. Was this 'imagining the death of the king' under the terms of the old statute? Nevertheless a man shortly to go on trial for a capital offence might be excused if he found Godwin's advice somewhat self-regarding and heartless. As yet his philosophy had no place for the softer virtues – tact, consideration, sympathy – derogations all from absolute truth and absolute virtue.

On 5 October he set off on his second journey of the year. He had been invited by Dr Samuel Parr to visit him at his home in Hatton near Coventry where he was the parson, and a series of dinners was arranged at which Godwin met the intellectuals of the district. Parr was at the time one of England's most eminent philosophers – a judgement posterity has not endorsed – and he was a combative man. There was scarcely a friend with whom he did not quarrel at some time and he published his tedious controversies on the minutiae of classical literature with unattractive relish for the unimportant. Until stopped by the bishop he liked to relieve his aggressive instincts by personally butchering the cattle at the local slaughter house with an axe.

One evening at a friend's house Godwin and Parr argued so fiercely and so late that they had to be invited to stay overnight – it would not be safe, Parr remarked, to let such opponents go out together on a dark night. It was the kind of discussion which Godwin enjoyed and at which he excelled, the clash of mind on mind, striking out truth spark by spark. Then suddenly, in the midst of a protracted debate about impartiality on 9 October, the discussions took on a new immediacy. In the *Morning Chronicle* of 7 October just arrived from London, it was reported that a grand jury had found 'true bills' against twelve of the arrested reformers on a capital charge of high treason under the 1351 Act, and that the name of Thomas Holcroft had been added to the list of those charged. Holcroft, it was reported, was already in custody in Newgate Prison. After the prosecution's unexpected success in the preliminary hearings – 'true bills' – it now looked probable that the accused would all be found guilty in the forthcoming trials, and that Godwin's dearest friend would be judicially put to death.

It was the beginning of the most intensive month in Godwin's life. The unsigned letter which he immediately sent to Holcroft's daughter, like the letter to Thelwall, tries calmly to assess the comparative benefit of the various courses of action, but this time the emotion cannot be kept back.

I see by the Chronicle just received that Mr Holcroft is in custody. I am of course unwilling to quit Hatton without some prospect of usefulness, and there seems to be an uncertainty as to the admission of friends to visit them. At the same time I will make any sacrifice with chearfulness to his smallest benefit or consolation. This letter will arrive time enough for an answer by Friday post, which I shall receive on Saturday.

For God's sake inform me whether I can have admission to him, or be of consolation to his family. I will set off at an hour's notice. Deliver the inclosed [an official request for admission to Newgate] yourself in person, unless Mr Erskine [defence counsel] should direct otherwise, and let me have the precise answer. At all events state to Mr Erskine that I am Mr Holcroft's principal friend, upon whom he chiefly depends, and that I prefer his happiness to every earthly consideration.

Let me hear satisfactorily or unsatisfactorily by return of post; but perhaps you should not summon me to town without the possibility of some small benefit.[3]

The following day Holcroft sent a shaming reply from Newgate. He himself had no need of his friend's consolation in prison, he remarked sarcastically – and he had surrendered voluntarily without waiting to be arrested – but Godwin's reasoning surprised him:

By exercising your understanding, weighing the circumstances as they occur, helping me to search for that mass of facts which have motivated my conduct, aiding me in arrangement and in deeply considering a case that may be productive of so much general good; are not these sufficient to incite you? or is the sacrifice you mention in any respect adequate to the benefit that may result? I do not wish to stimulate you to think of me, my consolation, or my advantage, not because I would not accept most willingly any good great or small that you could do me; but because there is a nobler purpose at which we both should aim. Nothing but your letter could have induced me to write thus to you. It appears like wishing to swell the sea by laving water with a tea cup.[4]

On Monday, 12 October, as soon as Holcroft's letter arrived, Godwin walked the seven miles to Hockley, took the stage coach to Oxford and then the mail coach to London arriving in time to visit his friend next morning in Newgate Prison. The trial of the first of the accused was due to begin before a special court on 25 October. Now, for the first time, Godwin realized the full gravity and urgency of the situation. Reading the long and complex charge delivered by Lord Chief Justice Eyre to the grand jury on 2 October, he learned that it was being argued that the crime of high treason took so many possible forms that its full extent had never been established in law, but since the king was indisputably the centre of the entire British constitution, 'all traitorous attempts upon any part of it are instantly communicated to that Centre, and felt there'. Anyone who sought to establish a republican form of administration in Great Britain was, therefore, according to this interpretation of the law, trying to remove the king and was therefore guilty of high treason. Terrified that English Jacobins were about to seize power as their namesakes had done in France, the Government was determined to get its retaliation in first and was looking for a death sentence.[5]

On Thursday the 16th Godwin called on Joseph Ritson, a medieval scholar and antiquarian to whom he had been introduced earlier in the year, and the next day, we note in his journal 'Read with Ritson'. Then, for the remainder of the day and over the weekend, he shut himself up with his books, seeing nobody but Marshall and Dyson, composing by dictation, with Marshall acting as amanuensis. His text was then rushed to James Perry, editor of the *Morning Chronicle*, another man whom Godwin knew well personally, where it appeared anonymously in the issue of 21 October under the title *Cursory Strictures on the Charge delivered by Lord Chief Justice Eyre to the Grand Jury*.[6] It began on the first page and occupied over half of the entire printed space in that day's newspaper. At the same time James Kearsley, the bookseller who had published Godwin's first book in 1783, put the article on sale as a separate pamphlet, and it was immediately reprinted or summarized as a news item by other newspapers.

Drawing on his deep knowledge of the history of the English Constitution, which he had studied from the days of the campaign against the Test Acts, Godwin was able to attack the Lord Chief Justice's arguments on his own legal ground. The Treason Act of Edward III, he argued, far from being vague, was narrow and precise. It was one of the safeguards of the English Constitution, deliberately limiting the definition of treason to the waging of war against the state and direct attempts on the king's life. Godwin gave a brief history of unsuccessful moves over the centuries to extend its coverage, quoting the views of respected commentators such as Blackstone. The law, he insisted, was clear, and if the courts now extended its scope beyond the current understanding of its meaning, that was equivalent to *ex post facto* legislation. The tone was indignant but respectful, avoiding any temptation to score propaganda points or smear his opponent.

As soon as the trial opened, it was obvious that the prosecution's case had suffered a serious blow. Nobody who had read the article could now believe that a political demand for parliamentary reform was equivalent to a plot to assassinate the king. As for any words that might have been uttered by the accused men in favour of violent revolution, that offence at most amounted to seditious libel – for which other laws were available – provided that no physical preparations for rebellion had actually been made. The article had cut through the legal obfuscation with which the prosecution had sought to conceal the issues. It was, admittedly, an attempt to influence the court while the case was *sub judice*, but so was the Lord Chief Justice's intervention.

More than an hour of the first day's proceedings was taken up with discussion of Godwin's arguments and a horrified Government hurried to hit back. On the day the pamphlet went on sale, Kearsley was officially warned that he would be prosecuted if he sold another copy, and he withdrew the pamphlet from sale. But Godwin was able to arrange immediate republication by another publisher, Daniel Eaton, who proclaimed boldly in his edition that he was not prepared to regard a Government warning as the law of the land.

In an attempt to counter its impact, an *Answer to Cursory Strictures* was hurriedly prepared and put on sale. The author (thought to be the judge Sir Francis Buller famed for his ruling that a husband may legally beat his wife provided the stick is no thicker than his thumb) called for Godwin to be prosecuted, describing him as impudent, malignant, detestable, stupidly ignorant, wilfully mistaken, an officious and unprincipled scribbler, and a most dangerous villain. But the abusive language simply drew attention to the very different tone of the original pamphlet. On 31 October, when the trial was in its sixth day, Godwin drafted a *Reply to an Answer to Cursory Strictures* and Daniel Eaton put this too on sale immediately, the *Morning Chronicle* having declined to do so after Perry had received a warning from the Government. In the end, after a month of hearings, all the accused were either acquitted or had the charges dropped. Godwin attended every day.

It was a famous victory, and we can now see how near a panicked Government had come to a pre-emptive terror against their opponents. Recently discovered secret papers record the Attorney General's assurance to ministerial colleagues that if the jury found a true bill against Horne Tooke, he would 'undertake to hang him'. It was said that two hundred arrest warrants were already signed, to be issued the moment the first guilty verdict was obtained, and we can be sure that Godwin would have been included in any round-up of suspects.[7] When the Attorney General announced to the court that proceedings against Holcroft were being dropped, the prisoner rose from his place in the dock, crossed the court-room, and took his seat alongside Godwin. The two men sat together during the remainder of the trials, aware that events were moving in their favour, but aware too that a verdict of guilty against any of the remaining accused would immediately reverse the whole situation. Sir Thomas Law-rence's sketch of the two men, taken on the spot, vividly catches the spirit of earnest defiance with which they faced the greatest crisis in their lives. [See Plate 1.]

John Horne Tooke, whose trial came last, used to remark later that it was to *Cursory Strictures* that he owed his life. At a party at his home in Wimbledon on 21 May 1795, when the immediate dangers had passed, Godwin was persuaded to admit that he was the author. Tooke immedi-ately led him to the head of the table and ceremonially kissed his hand, declaring to his guest's intense embarrassment that nothing less was due to the hand that had written *Cursory Strictures*. But the secret of Godwin's authorship was well kept, and as late as 1818 the editor of *State Trials*, who reprinted the pamphlet in full, attributed it to Felix Vaughan, one of the defence counsel.

While Godwin's intervention may not have been the only deciding factor, it is understandable that both he and Holcroft should have seen the verdicts not only as a victory for liberty but as a vindication of the discoveries set out in *Political Justice*. As in *Caleb Williams* the calm, courageous, impartial and individual voice of truth had carried the day against apparently superior forces. But Godwin declined to attend the round of political dinners which were eaten to celebrate the acquittals. More than ever he was now convinced of the damage which they caused by whipping up party spirit, and he was determined never again to risk compromising his independence in that way. *Cursory Strictures* had shown that individual action could be an effective method of political change and he determined to continue his campaign for a non-partisan politics.

We do not know how Lord Chief Justice Eyre reacted when he received a polite (but unsigned) appraisal of his recent performance.

The writer of this letter is the person who took upon himself to answer through the medium of the press your Charge to the Grand Jury at the Sessions House at Clerkenwel.

I should be ashamed not to be equally ready to give praise where praise is due, as to bestow censure where I thought it incurred. To this sentiment you are indebted for the trouble I now give you.

I listened with great pleasure to your summing up of the evidence in the trial of Mr Horne Tooke. I thought it for the most part fair and manly, candid both to the prosecutor and the prisoner, and such as was worthy of an English Judge. There were parts undoubtedly from which I differed widely in sentiment, but, supposing them blameable, what human composition is without its defects? I thought it upon the whole noble and admirable. I still however feel in their full extent my objections to your exposition of the law of treason.

As to the pamphlet I published, I cannot repent of it. I conceive that it was fair to bring forward one publication on the favourable side, after the infinite pains that had been taken in every form to excite prejudice against the accused for six months together. I think I had as much right to publish my pamphlet pending the trials as you had to publish yours . . .

But, though I do not repent of the publication, I did not altogether approve at the time, and still less approve now, the warmth of some of the expressions. I cannot believe that truth will ever be injured by a sober and benevolent style. Entertaining this opinion, I should certainly have made my style less offensive, if I had had more opportunity for leisure and reflection. Add to this, that my mind was inexpressibly affected with a sense of the deep iniquity that would have attended the conviction of the prisoners, and the tremendous consequences that would have grown out of it. After all, I am persuaded that the language by no means exceeds in severity that which ordinarily falls to the share of the most temperate controversial writings.

I have no wish upon the subject but that, as you have in the late instance, justly earned my appreciation, you may go on to deserve the applause and esteem of an impartial honest man.[8]

Holcroft too attempted to follow up the success in the same way. When, after the acquittal of Hardy, he foresaw that the case against him might be dropped, he wrote to Godwin from Newgate urging him to gather information from the witnesses, and some of this later appeared in *A Letter to the Rt Hon William Windham* published early in 1795.[9] 'I do not charge you', he wrote in his open letter to the Home Secretary, 'with intentional guilt. It is a thing indeed with which I believe no man can be truly charged: and in your case, I find abundant proofs that your intentions have been virtuous. It is your ignorance, your errors, your passions only that are wicked and destructive.'

The same impartiality could be shown in matters of more direct concern. Charles Sinclair, who had been readmitted to the confidence of the reformers after his trial, was bearded at a meeting at Horne Tooke's on 24 November 1794 – two days after his host had been acquitted on a capital charge – and confronted with a mass of evidence that he had all along been a spy. While protesting his eagerness to die for the cause, he had hung about Daniel Eaton's bookshop picking up gossip about the reformers.[10] Furthermore he had, it was now clear, deliberately tried to entrap Horne Tooke into making a written endorsement of violence in order to assist the prosecution's attempt to hang him. The careful letter, scrupulous in its doubts and its qualifications which Godwin wrote immediately after the meeting, is a magnificent example of political justice at its unrealistic best.

Mr Godwin is extremely ready to afford Mr Sinclair the means, as far as he is able, of wiping off any unjust suspicions that may have been fixed upon his character. For that purpose he is willing to recollect the tenour of the conversation that passed at Mr Tooke's on Monday the 24 of November, being persuaded that Mr Tooke is no less willing than he that justice should be done and truth be ascertained.

Mr Godwin has heard Mr Tooke upon several occasions early in the present year vindicate Mr Sinclair from the suspicions of others. He had heard that Mr Tooke during his imprisonment had changed his opinion upon that subject; and what passed at Wimbledon on the above mentioned day confirmed this report. Mr Tooke read, or repeated from memory (Mr Godwin believes read) the contents of a letter from Mr Sinclair to him, dated Edinburgh, desiring advice as to the conduct he should pursue. Mr Tooke observed that such a letter from a young man who had gone to Scotland without his advice and contrary to his expostulations had an extraordinary appearance. He then read the answer he returned, and remarked that it was a guarded and a short answer such as the most determined foe could make nothing of, at the same time that it contained the best advice the circumstances would admit. The general impression of the conversation upon Mr Godwin was that Mr Tooke had now scarcely doubt upon his mind that Mr Sinclair acted in a double character.[11]

There followed a list of seven other lengthy pieces of evidence against Sinclair, each one of which might have been regarded as sufficient proof by a less scrupulous inquisitor. Sinclair retired into a despised obscurity – but the men whom he had helped to convict were not so fortunate. Skirving died in Botany Bay in March 1796. Muir escaped and eventually reached France, to be greeted as a hero, and he died there in 1799. Palmer, after serving seven years, set out on the voyage home but the ship was seized at Guam and he died there in 1802 from dysentery first contracted in the hulks at Woolwich. Margarot, the only one of the transported reformers to see his native land again, returned in 1809, penniless and broken in health.

Joseph Gerrald remained in prison in London during the treason trials, visited frequently by Godwin and other friends, and reassured that the power of truth had proved stronger in England than in Scotland. He continued to hope for a French victory and a French invasion that would remove Mr Guelph – as he called George III – from his position of authority. He wrote in a farewell letter to Godwin from Newgate:

Friend and Citizen

From some circumstances I am induced to think (however erroneously perhaps) that my residence in this Temple of British Freedom will not be of much longer duration. I must, therefore, request that you will remember your engagement to dine with me tomorrow; and though Tooke accuses you with laying it down as a position that to *make* a promise is criminal, and to *keep* it still more, I beg that upon this occasion you will suspend the rigour of your morality and be *guilty* of the performance of it.[12]

Gerrald believed he was destined for Sierra Leone and he had an appropriate quotation from Horace to describe his prospective tropical exile. Hopes revived after the English acquittals that he might be reprieved or the sentence moderated, but in May 1795 he too was sent to Botany Bay, where he died within the year.

The radical movement as a whole did not however follow the example of Godwin and Holcroft or draw the same conclusions as they did from the success in the trials. Freed from fear of the treason law, they became bolder in their demands, more strident in their tone, more partisan in their organization and increasingly intimidatory in their tactics. John Thelwall, now the undoubted leader, who owed his life to *Cursory Strictures*, filled his newspapers and pamphlets with Godwinian sentiments but at the same time organized mass outdoor meetings which he addressed with fervent speeches that stopped just short of exhortation to violence. Three meetings in London in 1795, each of which was said to have attracted a hundred thousand participants, were bound to be seen as a growing threat to civil peace. When on 29 October 1795 the King's carriage was attacked by a crowd at the opening of Parliament, with the fatal injuring of a footman and the narrow escape of the King, the Government rushed in two emergency bills seeking drastic powers to suppress political meetings and seditious publications. Having failed with the clumsy treason law, they decided this time to proceed with scrupulous regard for constitutional and parliamentary propriety.

Once more Godwin took up his pen and in a few days of intensive work in November 1795 he wrote an eighty-six page pamphlet called *Considerations on Lord Grenville's and Mr Pitt's Bills* which was published anonymously by Joseph Johnson, Robinson having refused to run the risks. It was his second direct intervention in politics in just over a year, a further attempt to see if an individual impartial voice could win the day against organized opposition. Like its predecessor, the *Considerations* is a closely argued legal, historical, and philosophical defence of freedom of speech, but on this occasion the pamphlet is addressed as much to the reformers who were now abusing freedom of speech as to the Government which wished to curtail it. Calling himself on the title page 'A Lover of Order', a sentiment more often associated with conservative than with reforming politics, he pointedly compared the tactics of the British radicals with those of the French Jacobins. The debating clubs and lecture societies, he noted, were ceasing to be honest attempts to improve individual perception of issues, becoming instead opportunities for stirring up emotion, for misrepresenting opponents, and for implicitly encouraging partisanship, hatred, and violence. In a direct reference to the political methods of Thelwall, Godwin noted 'saving clauses that are, from time to time, introduced into the discourse, to persuade men to unbounded and universal benevolence'. This was, he remarked, 'Iago adjuring Othello not to dishonour himself by giving harbour to a thought of jealousy'.

The Godwinians and the politicians might be united against the Government, united in favour of free speech, parliamentary reform, abolition of slavery, and on innumerable other issues. They might all extol the ancient Roman virtues, wear their hair unpowdered, and dine at the same tables. But their differences were at last out in the open. With Godwin now a political figure, his scolding of his former allies was bound to cause a stir. Amelia Alderson teased that the radical movement would now be comparing him to turncoat Burke – 'd—n him, the dog is pensioned by G—d'.[13] Eliza Fenwick wrote confessionally that reading the *Considerations* had made her realize how far her cool reason had been heated by hatred and revenge. 'Godwin bruises his friends but he slays his enemies.'[14] When John Thelwall wrote indignantly to demand if Godwin was the 'Lover of Order' he received a characteristically robust reply.

I am most assuredly the author of the pamphlet you mention, and I am fully persuaded that it contains the sentiments of an honest man. There is not one word in it respecting you that I have not pressed upon your personal attention again and again with earnest anxiety. My favourable sentiments of you are not in the smallest degree altered, though I confess the undistinguishing fury of the letter before me is more than I can reconcile with these sentiments.

I do not conceive that my frankness in acknowledging the pamphlet entitles you to the public use of my name. I would not advise anyone who has a respect for morality to enter upon a public discussion in the angry temper in which your letter is written. But you will, of course, do as you think fit, and contribute perhaps, as far as your power may extend, to consign me also to the lamp-post.[15]

Neither man came out well from the exchanges, but when they met during Godwin's visit to Norwich, they were reconciled although they were never friends. As Godwin used to explain later when accused of deserting the progressive cause, it was the politicians who had changed, not he. It was they who, having drawn intellectual justification from *Political Justice*, had ignored its individual liberalism in favour of political partisanship. It was they who had converted calm Philomathic discussions into emotional hostility and who were now refusing to modify their opinions in the light of actual experience since 1789.

But if the collectivist policies of Paine and Thelwall had failed, Godwin's alternative of individual liberalism had done no better and he could not deny it. It was a more modest Godwin who addressed his fellow countrymen in 1796 and 1797 than the optimist of *Political Justice*. He himself had misjudged the French Revolution, he now freely admitted. The 'friends of innovation' had been 'somewhat too imperious in their tone'. In their enthusiasm they had been impatient and impetuous and 'there was something in their sternness that savoured of barbarism'. In their desire for improvement, reformers should not risk losing the gains which civilization had already made. They must take account of the historical circumstances of the time, and not imagine that human nature can be altered by destroying society and rebuilding.

He even occasionally began to doubt whether his eighteenth-century approach to the discovery of truth, by propounding general axioms and then considering their implications, could ever be expected to succeed. The method of *Political Justice*, he wrote in 1797, 'though there be nothing that it involves too high for our pride, it is perhaps a method of investigation incommensurate to our powers'. Perhaps it would be better to postpone the search for a general theory, and concentrate instead on building up isolated pieces of empirical knowledge. Since everything is connected with everything else, he confessed ruefully in his favourite chain metaphor, a general theory can be badly weakened by a single mistake in a single link.[16]

The two bills against which he had written his *Considerations* were presented to Parliament in November and December 1795 with Godwin attending to hear the debates. It appears from an entry in his journal that he also drafted a petition, one of many, against the bills. But with the double threat of invasion and civil war hanging over the country, arguments for unrestricted freedom of speech were not as convincing, even to Whigs, as they once were, and the bills were quickly passed into law. The Government obtained powers more extensive than at any time since the Glorious Revolution, backed by penalties of transportation and death.

Dr Parr suggested that Godwin would be well advised to seek a legal opinion before publishing the second edition of *Political Justice* – it was already at the proof stage – but the advice was indignantly rejected and the book came out without mishap on 24 November, less than a month before the bills received royal assent on 18 December.[17] In the Preface Godwin confessed that the first edition had been 'a crude and unequal performance'. Some of the passages which now seemed too speculative – such as the remarks on immortality – were dropped or revised, and much care was devoted to revising the chapter on 'resistance' which was now of far more immediate application than it had been in 1791–3. On this point the essential message was however unchanged – although in some extreme circumstances violent resistance is justifiable, the nature of oppressive regimes can in the end only be changed by changing perceptions.

It was already only an academic question. By the middle of 1796 traditional politics had virtually ceased and the small band of Whigs who maintained an opposition to the Government were – with one brief interval – out of office for a generation. The Two Acts of 1796, The 'Gagging Acts' as they came to be called, were entirely effective. Few publishers would risk the publication of words which might be interpreted as inflammatory or treasonable, and the law against unlicensed assemblies killed off the debating clubs which had done so much to spread the doctrines of *Political Justice* a few years before. When Thelwall tried to circumvent the restrictions on political lecturing by giving talks on Roman history, his meetings were forcibly suppressed. Even the Philomaths, who were careful to avoid dangerous topics, were disbanded after a ballot in 1796. The only radical politics that survived were revolutionary and underground.

Three years after the first publication of *Political Justice*, Godwin could nevertheless reflect with satisfaction that patient persistence had found some reward. Both *Political Justice* and *Caleb Williams* were selling well. Letters of admiration were still pouring in from all over the English-speaking world and he was surrounded by numerous admirers and disciples, including some of the most talented men of the day. Ladies were now vying for his attention – a new and gratifying experience – and he had an impressive array of wealthy and influential admirers, many of them near the centre of national life. His portrait had been painted and there was scarcely a literary or political publication in which his name was not frequently mentioned. William Godwin's immortality was already secure.

His plans for future books were firm, a third edition of *Political Justice* with further revisions, a *Dissertation on Religion*, *Observations on the French Revolution*, a *Life of Alexander the Great*, his tragedy *Dunstan*, which he again looked over and revised, and three tales to be called *The Coward*, *The Lover*, and *The Adept*.[18] Most immediate was a series of essays on unconnected subjects, many of them derived from conversations, published in 1797 under the title *The Enquirer*.

On 3 March 1796, Godwin reached his fortieth birthday, an occasion when men often reflect on their past lives, their prospects, and their ambitions. Signs of encroaching middle age were already plain – the receding hairline, the occasional overwhelming need for sleep which caused embarrassment whenever he dined late, the painful minor ailments connected with a low fibre diet. Godwin's youth was behind him, but never having had the opportunity to enjoy that allegedly happy time of life, he had nothing to regret. On the contrary, or so it seemed, his most productive years were yet to come.

But was a literary life now enough? Change, Thelwall had sneered, could never be achieved by writing quartos of philosphy. And could books be expected to improve the individual perceptions without the clashes of mind and mind, which he had found essential to the process? Maybe he should enlarge his ambitions and attempt to redirect the chain of history by a more direct intervention? In a fragment of self-analysis, Godwin contemplated joining the most important Philomathic club of them all:

I ought to be in parliament
My principles of gradual improvement are particularly congenial to such a situation. It is probable that in the course of the next six years circumstances may occur, in which my talents, such as they are, might be of use. I am now forty years of age: the next six years will be six of the most vigorous years of my life
I would be no unfrequent speaker
I would adhere to no party
I would vote for no proposition that I did not wish to see carried
I would be an author of motions; thus endeavouring to call public attention to salutary ideas
I ought to be brought in without expense
The present moment is a crisis, greatly tending to determine whether my destination shall be for active or contemplative life. This is a situation that would

excite envy and satire; it would be incumbent by splendour and activity of talent to dispense the cloud.

If I were elected into parliament, this would be at first a source of humiliation; I should then be the last of the gentlemen who am now one of the first of plebians; it must be the task of great energies to enable me look erect in this situation.

It is better, in a personal view, that the man should always appear greater than the situation, rather than that the situation should appear greater than the man.[19]

To those who only know Godwin's later life it may be hard to regard his suggestion as anything more than a midlife birthday fancy. But in 1796 it was not unrealistic to believe that rich and powerful friends and admirers – Wedgwood, King, Lansdowne, or Sheridan – might be willing to finance him into Parliament if he so wished. Although his theory demanded the progressive dismantling of political institutions, consultative assemblies would still be needed so no inconsistency of attitude was implied.

But, as he later acknowledged in looking back on this period of his life, his character was not suited to active politics. In the five or six years after the first appearance of *Political Justice*, he found in himself 'a boldness and an eloquence more than was natural'. Since he was a 'star' – his own word – he tended to be surrounded too much by people who agreed with his views. He talked too much. Since he lacked charm, he was not as persuasive as the strength of his arguments deserved, and his uncomfortable debating methods were aimed at a more absolute truth than is normally attainable in politics. A few years later when he drew up lists of the eminent men and women whom he had known, to match the lists of '*desiderati*' whose acquaintanceship he had sought in his early days, most of the politicians, Whig or radical, had to be sadly consigned either to his lists of '*amis perdus*' or to the '*teneurs à distance*'. Godwin's brief period of direct influence was already near its end.[20]

CHAPTER 12

Women

The word love does not occur in *Political Justice*. There are discussions of the moral and social problems of marriage, of cohabitation, and of divorce, but Godwin assumed when he first wrote his book that the choice of a partner was little different from any other decision, to be weighed in terms of comparative virtue and comparative benefit. The 'propensity to intercourse of the sexes' was listed along with hunger among the unfortunate passions, but with the progress of perfectibility, interest in sex for its own sake would soon become obsolete.

I shall assiduously cultivate the intercourse of that woman whose accomplishments shall strike me in the most powerful manner. 'But it may happen that other men will feel for her the same preference that I do.' This will create no difficulty. We may all enjoy her conversation; and we shall all be wise enough to consider the sensual intercourse as a very trivial object . . . Reasonable men now eat and drink, not from the love of pleasure, but because eating and drinking are essential to our healthful existence. Reasonable men then will propagate their species, not because a certain sensible pleasure is annexed to this action, but because it is right the species should be propagated; and the manner in which they exercise this function will be regulated by the dictates of reason and duty.[1]

The subject was not given much attention, but there was no need. A few months before, *Vindication of the Rights of Woman with Strictures on Political and Moral Subjects* by Mary Wollstonecraft had been published,

A Visit to the Bookshop by Bewick

which although entirely different in style, is based on the same philosophical axioms – Reason leads to Virtue; Man (including Woman) is perfectible; and current vices are mainly environmental in origin. Women, according to Wollstonecraft, are among the victims of the unnatural institutional distinctions in society; their characters are corrupted by chains of association started in their minds at an early age by female education; women are taught by the false traditions of chivalry to prefer reputation to virtue; and the feminine virtues which males most value are in reality imposed errors. *Political Justice* and *Vindication of the Rights of Woman* stand together on the shelf like a colossal Pharaoh and his consort, enduring monuments of the spirit of their age.

As the law stood at the end of the eighteenth century, a married woman could not hold property or make a contract. Husband and wife were one entity, and – as Blackstone had pointed out in his *Commentaries on the Laws of England* – the legal existence of a woman was in suspense during the period of her marriage. Marriage transferred the responsibility of protection from the father to the husband, but the security thus conferred was unreliable. If the husband squandered his wife's money or ran off with it there was no redress, but even happy marriages carried heavy risks for the wife. In mid-century the chances of dying in childbirth were one in ten, given the average of six or seven pregnancies per marriage, and most married women were pregnant more often than not throughout their child-bearing years.[2]

Because of the high mortality rate among mothers, there were widowers glad to have an unmarried sister in their household, but most spinsters lived on in the parental home, sewing now more than spinning, to await a lonely old age. If they had education or a skill such as music, they could become teachers or governesses – although the pay was very low – or they might be able to join the workers of the literary industry where it was even lower. Further down the social scale, hat-making and glove-making were respectable occupations, but with growing unemployment many traditional female occupations were being encroached on by men. There was domestic service and there was prostitution.

Dissenters, including Mary Wollstonecraft who had attended the same meeting house as Dr Price in her youth, were inclined to blame Charles II for women's degradation as for much else. It was his reactionary Government, they believed, which had destroyed the previous balance of responsibility between men and women that had characterized the tradition of the Middle Ages and Renaissance. In Charles's reign whores had been accepted into society and into the royal bed, and the ladies of the court had publicly bared their nipples for the first and only time in the history of English fashion. The men who had treacherously imposed the Test and Corporation Acts had also reduced women to the status of sex objects. A recent traveller in Lesbos reported in a learned paper to the Royal Irish Academy that in that island property inheritance was on the female side, the women wore trousers, and told the men – who wore skirts – what to do. While few feminists wanted to go as far as the Amazons to whom they were frequently compared, it was reassuring to know that alternative societies were practicable.[3]

Meanwhile the instruments by which custom and opinion reinforced unequal and partial laws could be seen piled high in any bookshop or circulating library. Ladies' advice books, for which there was an exploding market, commended the traditional feminine virtues of prudence, humility and obedience.* Novels and romances implied that a woman's first duty was to be pleasing to men, flirtatious before marriage, submissive afterwards. Well-bred ladies were expected to display weakness and tears at all minor crises, to be vulnerable to cold draughts and wet feet, and to faint away at the mention of anything shocking. Delicate health was as desirable a sexual characteristic as a pretty face.

In the years when *Political Justice* was the talk of the literary and philosophical societies the subjection of women was a favourite topic, and Godwin took part in several discussions at the Philomaths and elsewhere. Not all his friends were convinced that the equality advocated by Wollstonecraft and her friends was either deserved or desirable. Porson robustly argued that women are 'by nature and by necessity' inferior.[4] Fawcett published a sermon comparing sexual love with foxhunting – the pleasure is in the chase not the attainment.[5] Captain Gawler, a friend of Horne Tooke, was prepared to defend the superior pleasure of masturbation.[6] Godwin himself all his life continued to use 'manly' as a term of praise and 'feminine' as a reproof whether referring to a man or to a woman. Rousseau, who had done so much to spread the enlightenment of naturalism in other aspects of life, had believed that women are by nature inferior, dependent, coquettish and cunning.

The difficulty was to know what was natural and what was the result of necessitarian chains. Mary Wollstonecraft believed that monogamous marriage was natural. Others thought that women had a natural interest in fine clothes and bright ornaments. In the south seas, societies of happy, beautiful, scantily dressed, noble savages had recently been found who, it

* For the evidence which these books provide about the debate on women see Appendix 2.

was reported, practised sex without social restriction, individual feelings of guilt, or even worries about pregnancy. Which was the more natural, the stern morals of the Roman republican matrons or the free love of Tahiti?

The same metaphors did service as in the wider debate. Is the passion of love, literary societies wondered, to be regarded as a tempest that has escaped temporarily from its underground cavern or as a snatch of divine music vibrating on the Aeolian harp of the mind? Mary Wollstonecraft herself referred to the 'adamantine chains of destiny' and to the 'silken fetters' which had enslaved women's own view of themselves. Such fetters could be seen in the uncomfortable tight-fitting clothes, stiffened with whalebone stays, by which they were physically as well as mentally subdued, and the passages in the *Vindication* about the need for lighter clothing, fresh air, and regular exercise were as important as anything in the theory. One of Godwin's feminist friends gave public lectures on the damage to the lungs caused by wearing stays, illustrating her thesis by cutting up dead rabbits on the lecture room table.[7] Major Jardine suggested that women should give up their heavy ankle-length skirts in favour of short dresses provided that they took to wearing drawers underneath.[8]

On the other side of the question 'staysmaker' was a gibe thrown by traditionalists at the reformers, in commemoration of the fact that Tom Paine had been trained in that ignoble profession. In Paris women of all classes were reported to be making plentiful use of the sexual freedom won by the sansculottes. In the debate about petticoat power, images of underclothing were never far from the surface of men's minds.

During his first ten years in London Godwin found no difficulty in applying his own principles to the women he met, mainly friends of his sister. While having no objection to other adults entering into relationships if they chose, he assumed that he would live his own life a bachelor. The periods when he had shared lodgings with Cooper, Marshall, and Holcroft had revealed the strain caused by having too many opportunities for mutual sincerity, and he also believed, with a touch of residual priestly dedication, that no man could be a great writer or great benefactor if distracted by domesticity.

After he became famous it was natural that he should continue to practise his normal impartiality undistracted by society's artificial distinctions. An unknown lady from Blackburn, writing under the name of R. A. C. Prescott sent him long letters – in which she described him as 'the legislator of our island's morals' and 'the first chymist to chrystalize our morals to make virtue and ourselves akin and mend the manners of a polluted hemisphere' – before coming to the main point: what would he recommend in the case of an unhappily married couple where the husband met a former admirer and 'a development ensued'? In his reply Godwin, while reaffirming his view that the official institution of marriage was 'unfounded and injurious' and that he could see 'no reason in nature or morality' to regard it as indissoluble, was as cautious as any agony columnist. He offered help in the method of calculating the costs and benefits of the alternative courses of action, giving a low weighting to the interests of the former admirer, and we may doubt whether Miss Prescott, who was probably herself the lady in question, welcomed what she read.[9]

Unfortunately we do not have his reply to a letter from R. M., a Liverpool lady, who asked to be known as 'Miss Lexington'.

Hitherto I have never suffered my actions to be shackled by the tyranny of *custom* – the consequence is, I have but *one* friend, *few* acquaintances and *no* lover – men in general prefer tameness in a woman (which they dignify, or rather *burlesque* with the name of sensibility) to the noble sentiment of *independence* – you – *you* are different – therefore naturally enthusiastic and warm – where I *admire* I cannot debar myself the pleasure of telling you so – I heard you spoken of in a certain company as too free in disseminating your opinions – I felt my heart bound, and the moment I went home, sent for all I could collect of your writings – now dissolved in tears of *extasy* – now lost in admiration, now elevated with *enthusiasm* – now transported by the *intensity* of my feelings, I read and, paused, and read again – I languished to *converse* with the immortal author – to gaze at him *unseen* – but to identify him in the passing world – my recourse was only in a feeble pen as incapable of surprising my *ideas*, as *your* portrait would express your *mind* – another strong inducement to my addressing you, was – that leagued as I am with minds *dissimilar* – never beholding (as it were) a creature of my *species* – never conversing in the warm language of my heart – no congeniality of *soul* no *vibration* of *sentiment* – no sublimity of intellect to draw forth my powers of *reflection* or edify my *mind* – I am lost buried, in more than immense a darkness – take pity on me then – *write* – let me be edified – correspond morally – tho' *physically* unknown – refuse me not.[10]

The letter proceeds in similar vein for several pages.

After the departure of Mary Wollstonecraft for France in 1792, the leadership of the women's movement passed to her friend Mary Hays, whose *Appeal to the Men of Great Britain in Behalf of Women*, drafted before the *Vindication* but published later, enjoys the small fame given to those who come second. The preamble to her first letter to Godwin is typical of many received during his years of fame, admirers normally seeing it as a point of honour to disregard the petty formalities (such as the need for a personal introduction) which separate man from man and man from woman.

Perhaps no apology could be equally proper for a stranger addressing Mr Godwin, and presuming to solicit a favor, as a plain statement of the truth! Disgusted with the present constitutions of civil society ... the writer of this has been roused from a depression of spirits, at once melancholy and indignant, by an attention to the 'few puissant and heavenly endowed spirits, that are capable of guiding, enlightening and leading the human race onward to felicity!' Among these, fame has given a distinguished place to the Author of 'Political Justice.'[11]

Mary Hays frankly explained that her purpose was to borrow a copy of *Political Justice* which was not available at the circulating library, but as often happened, the letter was intended to lead to a visit. Soon she became a regular caller, and took to writing further long letters, seeking his opinion both on the philosophical basis of feminism and on her own emotional problems. For a time she was one of Godwin's most enthusiastic disciples, 'possessed', as she told him, 'with an inexpressible passion for the acquisition of knowledge, an ardor approaching the limits of pain'. She hoped he would join her in condemning Rousseau, Voltaire, Fielding, Smollett and other authors who encouraged men to see women as objects, but he – recalling perhaps his own contributions to the panting bosoms school of novel writing – felt unable to agree that literary value should be judged solely by soundness on this one question.

For a time he patiently wrote out his replies but later he suggested that she should ask her questions by letter, while he would answer them orally. On one cold March day he called on her unexpectedly in the morning – himself despising the etiquette that required such visits to be made by appointment – and found her dressing in front of the sitting room fire. But, as she explained later in a mortified letter of apology, though she disdained convention she was not French enough in her manners to admit him while still undressed.

Mary Hays was then writing a novel, *Memoirs of Emma Courtney*, which she invited Godwin to read in manuscript and which was published shortly afterwards.[12] It tells an unhappy story of unrequited love in which the distressed heroine – who is really Mary Hays – is strengthened by the philosophical advice of 'Mr Francis', who is Godwin. Since the novel was in epistolary form, Mary Hays was able to use Godwin's actual letters to her as models, so that, buried in her forgotten book, there is preserved

Godwin's own view on this matter, a fusion of *Political Justice* and the *Rights of Woman*. The customs of society have enslaved, enervated, and degraded the female sex, Mr Francis acknowledges, but even if things cannot be changed quickly, progress will come. Do not indulge yourself with your extreme feelings, he recommends to the distraught girl who admits to reading over ten novels a week, but try to reconstruct the events of the past which have formed your present character. The roots of her depression lay in her childhood and in the 'indissoluble chain of sentiment and habit', but this did not mean that nothing could be done. Even unrequited love – which she had suffered three times in quick succession – was susceptible to analysis.

Mary Hays, Godwin believed, for all her intellectualism was an extreme example of the traditional image of femininity, weak, emotional, and unpredictable, unduly concerned about her appearance – and easily upset by small annoyances. After a while her attempts to link the science of *Political Justice* with the sensibility of popular contemporary romances became rather tiring.

Another lady who received Godwin's impartial advice was Amelia Alderson, the daughter of Dr Alderson of Norwich, whom Godwin first met at her father's house during his visit there in the summer of 1794. Norwich was one of the main provincial centres of the reform movement with its own thriving Revolution Society and radical philosophical periodical, *The Cabinet*, both of which ceased after the Two Acts. Dr Alderson was famous for looking after the sick poor of the town at no charge, carrying into practice, year in and year out, the principles of voluntary redistribution of the dissenting Godwinian tradition. Godwin noted Amelia's presence at a dinner party given by her father in his honour on 29 June 1794 when the subject of discussion – shortly before the treason trials – was the topical 'punishment of kings'. Miss Alderson, who was then aged twenty-five, had all the traditional feminine qualities, beauty, amiability, a talent for singing, a talent for poetry, but as a true daughter of rational dissent, she also took a keen interest in the political and philosophical questions of the day and was eager to be improved.

A few weeks after meeting Godwin, she made a visit to London, staying with relatives at the village of Southgate outside, and it was natural that she should renew the acquaintanceship. Her description of a visit to Chalton Street, in a letter home, is a good example of how fearlessness and charmlessness tended to coincide.

He received me very kindly, but wondered I should think of being out of London;

147

– could I be either amused or *instructed* at Southgate? How did I pass my time? What were my pursuits? and a great deal more, which frightened my protector, and tried me, till at last I told him I had not yet outlived my affections, and that they bound me to the family at Southgate. But was I to acknowledge any other dominion than that of reason? – 'but are you sure that my affections in this case are not the result of reason?' He shrugged disbelief, and after debating some time, he told me I was more of the *woman* than when he saw me last. Rarely did we agree, and little did he gain on me by his mode of attack, but he seemed alarmed lest he should have offended me, and apologised several times, with much feeling, for the harshness of his expressions. In short, he convinced me that his theory has not yet gotten entire ascendancy over his practice.[13]

A few days later, on 8 September, Godwin followed up his homily with a long reproving letter

I cannot forget your remark when I last saw you, that in your present visit you was [sic] governed by your affections. If you meant what is most usually meant by that phrase, I must contemplate your situation with a melancholy regret. To be governed by our affections, in the company we keep, or the conduct we pursue, most usually means, to discard our understanding, and bind with our own hands the fillet over our eyes . . . [14]

He repeated that it was foolish to waste her time in Southgate when she could have more useful conversations in London. 'If you would excel in the degree you are capable of doing,' he wrote, 'you must not shut your eyes, but exercise a penetrating scrutiny, into the persons you see and the principles you adopt.' Mr Morgan, her friend at Southgate, he assured her was not suitable. Since he was a dissenting minister from Norwich, Godwin may have recognized some of his own early failings in the young man. 'The sentiments I have just written,' he concluded, 'however uncouthly expressed, prove not only the interest I feel in your well doing, but the uncommon esteem I have conceived for your merits.'

Despite this unpromising start, the friendship grew. Godwin took Amelia with him when he visited Joseph Gerrald in prison, sometimes with the yet unmasked spy Charles Sinclair as one of the party, and Amelia sat proudly through every day of the trials, giving Horne Tooke a much publicized kiss when he was acquitted. Unwilling to surrender her own beliefs, she nevertheless contrived to treat Godwin with seriousness, respect, and good humour. 'Do not *chill* me,' she wrote when sending a play for his comments, 'I am sooner depressed, than encouraged, and by that Truth which you worship, I *swear* to you that I always feel more doubtful of than *confident* of my talents in every respect.'[15]

Determined on a career in the theatre as actress or playwright, she offered to put herself under his instruction as well as that of Holcroft. 'I can no longer withhold from you the general information', a surprised Godwin wrote, with his habitual dampening double negatives, in returning her manuscript, 'that your comedy has, in my opinion, no inconsiderable merit.'[16] He recommended her to improve her dramatic sense by cultivating the art of conversation, advice which, from her experience of Godwin's own conversational methods, she wisely discounted.

Not all women were prepared to be deferential. Elizabeth Inchbald, three years his senior and brought up like him in a remote village in East Anglia, had run away to London at an early age. Resisting immediate offers to become an upmarket prostitute, she was driven to marry an elderly actor after six weeks and so began a career on the stage. Godwin first met her through his friendship with Holcroft, and in 1791 she asked him to read over the manuscript of her novel *A Simple Story*, which was published, with great success, soon afterwards. In her turn she offered her criticisms of *Caleb Williams* and, as a result, amendments were made in the second edition. 'I have no patience', she wrote to Godwin on that occasion, 'that anything so near perfection should not be perfection'[17] – it was one of her favourite words and Mary Wollstonecraft was later to tease Godwin about his association with 'Mrs Perfection'. In 1793 her play *Everyone Has His Fault*, which Godwin reviewed in the *European Magazine*, confirmed her reputation as one of the most talented women of her day, competing with her friend Sarah Siddons in the literary press for the title of the Tenth Muse. Mary Shelley, reporting some of her father's remarks, called Mrs Inchbald a flirt, but her reputation, unlike those of many actresses, was, it was said, unimpeached. She demanded attention and admiration wherever she went, 'a piquante mixture', Godwin said, 'between a lady and a milkmaid'.[18] He often accused women of being flirts and coquettes, drawing as much on his reading of Rousseau as on real experience, and another of his favourite epithets, 'womanish', carried the same connotations.

In his late thirties and early forties Godwin was an attractive, slim and fine-featured man. According to Mary Hays's description, his eye was piercing, his manner impressive, and his glance seemed to search the soul. Men with long noses, women had believed since time immemorial, enjoyed corresponding sexual potency.[19] Godwin was famous, even fashionable, a regular diner-out at the tables of the Whig aristocracy, and moving freely in theatrical and literary circles. He had written the most profound work of philosophy of the day – and was the acclaimed author of an original and perceptive work of fiction which explored aspects of human psychology seldom previously touched. He was approachable, patient, fair – as innumerable instances of help to strangers continually proved – if at the same time unaccommodating and overbearing in his opinions. If he lacked tact or good humour, this was manifestly the result of single-minded adherence to the greater virtues of truth and justice.

Women found him puzzling. How was it possible for such a clever man to be so absurdly simple? Surely there must be a way to pierce the punctilious and unrelenting high-mindedness and earnestness which he brought to every trivial transaction of daily life, and to engage direct with the warm sympathetic human being whom they believed they could perceive inside. Between 1794 and 1797 Godwin underwent a belated intensive education in the complexities of human nature unknown to the author of *Political Justice* and *Caleb Williams*.

After the tour in June 1794 in which he first met Amelia Alderson, he had gone to Warwickshire in October to visit Dr Parr and here again, as at Dr Alderson's, he attracted the attention of one of the daughters of the house, the twenty-two-year-old Sarah Anne Parr. Her father at this time still managed to reconcile a belief in the essential truth of Godwin's philosophy with staunch support for his employer, the Church of England, and there were hard-fought arguments not only with Parr but with his wife, in which Miss Parr was a fascinated participant. The 'altercation de m^c. de coena dom.' noted in Godwin's journal for 6 October 1794, fortunately followed by an 'explication avec m^c.' on the 12th, referred to some discussion with Madame or Mademoiselle about the nature of the Christian communion service. An anonymous letter postmarked 21 April 1795 at a time when the Parr family was visiting London is in the handwriting of Sarah Anne Parr. Signed *L'Amie des Philosophes*, it was the second she sent to him using a coffee house in Fleet Street as a secret address.

Most ungrateful of mankind

Did I not send you a most pastoral and pathetic Epistle from the rural bower ycleped Nando's Coffee House, written under the immediate inspiration of those sylvan deities who delight to revel in the shades of Fleet Street? did I not give it to one of those Fauns or Dryads who sport about the aforesaid Bower, in the similitude of Waiters, with orders to send it by that mercenary Mercury the Penny postman? . . .

And what return have you made me for all this? does not your reply begin with sounds as *un*arcadian as your quarto of philosophy? do you not shock my eyes and ears by accusations in prose, and declarations in verse enough to kill all the Cloes that ever existed?

Oh thou ungrateful, unfeeling, cruel, insulting, barbarous man, or to sum up thy iniquities in one word, thou Philosopher – art thou not ashamed, that is to say as much as one of thy sect can be ashamed, of conduct so atrocious? I am so angry that I could marry thee in downright spite, if I did not hold sacred the oath I swore six years ago never to marry – a wise man.[20]

Such a game needs willing players, and if one side does not reciprocate, the other feels humiliated. Godwin later described Miss Parr as 'a seducer', although without implying that he himself had ever been at risk. She had, he told Mary Wollstonecraft, 'an uncommon understanding and an exquisite sensibility which glows in her complexion and flashes from her eyes', but women were less sure.[21] The determination never to marry a wise man was not a joke. Dr Parr's wife, who did not enjoy being married to a famous philosopher, had consistently advised her daughter that 'the wisest thing a young woman of sense could do was to marry a fool', and she was on the lookout for a suitable candidate.

Another exasperated letter from Sarah Parr dated 23 March 1796 again conceals the name of the writer.

One miracle deserves another, and since you have to my infinite surprise been civil enough to call upon me, I am resolved to amase you in return by writing a note to thank you for this extraordinary effort of politeness – I am sorry I was not at home, but perhaps if we had met we should have been less civil to each other, for I have even an increased antipathy to truth and precision because I daily find fresh reason to believe them mere cloaks for rudeness and affectation –

Is not this a shocking declaration, and do you not wonder at my stupidity in confounding the principles with the practice – Well, you may be shocked and surprised at your leisure, but I am obstinately resolved not to yield one solitary prejudice to your eloquence, I defy truth and precision and all their Apostles to convert me from my darling errors, and as I have energy enough to avow and even defend my system, I desire you will not pretend to a monopoly of this excellent quality on your side of the question ... I leave Town on Saturday morning owing to an absurd prejudice I have of obeying my Father's orders. I am, with every possible prejudice against you, and in falsehood, Anne[22]

It was daring even among practitioners of the New Philosophy for a lady to be on first name terms with a man outside her immediate family circle, but Miss Parr enjoyed the intimacy of conspiracy, and it was for the same reason no doubt that she had adopted her middle name Anne, although to family and friends she was always Sarah. The occasion for her annoyance this time seems to have been Godwin's failure to keep an appointment – he had gone instead to the first performance of the *Iron Chest* relying upon her seeing in the newspapers that the date had been changed. The same evening Godwin tried to make his peace, as his journal records ('Sup chez Mrs Mackintosh w S. P. explanation'), and soon afterwards she left for the country.

Godwin was bewildered at the attitude of such women. Why did everything have to be turned into a game or into a joke? Why could they not discuss issues sensibly and seriously like Holcroft, Nicholson, Fawcett and his other male friends? He knew he was not naturally a humorous man – as he could have explained, he had been brought up to regard frivolity as sin by a father literal-minded to the point of superstition – but he was prepared to learn. Comedy and humour, he told Amelia Alderson, are 'among the most autumnal fruits of the human understanding', as distinct from tragedy which any teenager could comprehend. But the more he accused his friends of lack of seriousness, the more frivolous they became. Women of talent and intelligence who had reached positions of respect in a man's world, friends of Mary Wollstonecraft and believers in the principles of her *Vindication*, were driven back to traditional feminine responses which, in theory, they despised. They teased, they cajoled, they wheedled, they conspired, they flirted.

Soon Godwin gave up trying. If women could not bear the manly frankness which is the mark of equals, he would play along; he would quash their mannered expostulations with courtly compliments; he would unilaterally return to the age of chivalry when women had been treated with respect. Soon, he was a knight surrounded by helpless ladies, with the word 'love' never off his lips. 'Seriously, madam,' he wrote typically at the end of a letter to a lady whom he hardly knew, 'I have received two letters from you in all, and both of them uncommonly excellent. I am determined therefore to love and admire you, take it as you will; you may repel my advances, but you shall never erase from my mind the sentiments with which the strength and richness of yours have impressed it?'[23] Amelia Alderson, in a letter of June 1795 gives us a very different Godwin from the man who had scolded her the previous September.

Godwin drank tea and supt here last night; a leave-taking visit, as he goes tomorrow to spend a fortnight at Dr. Parr's. It would have entertained you highly to have seen him bid me farewell. He wished to salute* me, but his courage failed him. 'While oft he looked back, and was loth to depart.' 'Will you give me nothing to keep for your sake, and console me during my absence,' murmured out the

---

* Meaning kiss on the cheek.

philosopher, 'not even your slipper? I had it in my possession once, and need not have returned it!' This was true; my shoe had come off, and he had put it in his pocket for some time. You have no idea how gallant he is become; but indeed, he is much more amiable than ever he was. Mrs Inchbald says, the report of the world is that Mr Holcroft is in love with her, *she* with Mr Godwin, Mr Godwin with *me*, and I am in love with Mr Holcroft! A pretty story indeed! This report Godwin brings to me, and he says Mrs I. always tells him that when she praises *him* I praise Holcroft. This is not fair in Mrs I. She appears to me jealous of G's attention to me, so she makes him believe I prefer H to him. She often says to me, 'Now you are come, Mr Godwin does not come near me.' Is not this very womanish?[24]

The last sentence is a dig at Godwin's habit of regarding all show of femininity as flirtatious.

Just before Christmas 1794, Mrs Inchbald sent him a mysterious letter.

I have received a Note this moment from a very Beautiful Lady requiring I would direct it to you as she does not know your address. I am afraid to send it by the Post for fear it should fall into the hands of the Privy Council who might not set a proper value upon it – I trust you will for I assure you it contains her real sentiments and I think you will own with me that she has made choices of one word in particular to express those sentiments which is so very characteristick of *herself* that no one will ever suspect the note a forgery, or that she did not speak with sincerity.

this is Monday I shall be at home all tomorrow except in the evening – you shall have it either by attending on me personally, or by despatching a proper personage to whom I may with safety deliver it. EI.[25]

Is this too part of some game of gallantry? Which Beautiful Lady would ask Mrs Inchbald to act as intermediary for a letter too secret to be entrusted to the post, and at the same time leave it open to be read and commented on? Is Mrs Inchbald archly passing on an innocuous Christmas greeting from Amelia Alderson or even from herself?

Godwin for all his emphasis on sincerity was a secretive man. Fearful not so much of the Privy Council – although there were times when seizure of his papers was a risk – as of prying servants, friends, and family, he usually confined his memoranda and journal entries to a few key words (often in his idiosyncratic mixture of French or Latin) enough to reconnect the chain of memory in his mind. The modern researcher is, as a result, often as baffled as contemporary peepers must have been, although paradoxically – as with Sarah Parr's letters – it is only because they are obscure that some revealing documents have been permitted to survive at all, their significance unappreciated by those who weeded Godwin's papers after his death.

Two, apparently unimportant, scraps of memoranda which escaped the fire and scissors tell more than appears at first sight. The first is written on the back of a list of his early addresses in London:

Born	Mar. 1770
Married	April 1788
ditto	Nov. —
Henry	Jan. 1789
Connoissance	Sep. 21 1793
Greenwich	Jan. 9 1795
Letter to Hatton	June 30 —
Negociation	Nov 10 or 17 1797
– ended	Feb 18 1798[26]

The other is jotted on the back of a letter:

nature of habit

Born Mar 1770

Reveley's confidence
Her repeated consultation
Lapse of three years

Sep. 21 1793
Jan. 23 1795 – 16 mths.
Nov. 17 1797 – 34 mths
June 30 1795

July 27, Oct 15, Dec 5, 7, Italy Mar 16

maintenance while separated[27]

Maria James had been born in Constantinople in March 1770 the daughter of a British merchant, and at the age of eighteen while living in Rome she married William Reveley. He was studying to be an architect – he later engraved for *The Antiquities of Athens* – and she was learning to paint under the direction of Angelica Kauffman. In 1790 the couple were back in London with two babies (including the Henry of the first note who was later to become a friend of Shelley) and Reveley was active in radical politics. The double marriage mentioned in the first note is not necessarily significant – it was often regarded as prudent to confirm a foreign marriage with a second ceremony in England.

The young Mrs Reveley evidently had a weakness for philosophers. When she was fifteen Jeremy Bentham stayed at her father's house in Constantinople, and in 1790, probably on the strength of the acquaintanceship, he engaged William Reveley in London to help him with the architectural designs for his Panopticon prison, and he started to visit the

Reveleys' house every morning in time for breakfast. Bentham was irritated by Reveley's jokes, Maria recalled later, but she noticed that the great moral classifier was incapable of keeping his papers in order, and when she became his filing clerk the three worked happily together. As a reward Bentham designed her a more efficient teapot said to stop the first cup being too strong and the last cup too weak.[28]

Godwin first met Maria Reveley on 21 September 1793, when his journal records a routine day of reading and calls, ending with 'tea Reveley's, with Jardine, Sinclair and Mrs Jennings'. Thereafter he apparently saw both Reveley and Mrs Reveley frequently. The Reveleys led separate lives in the modern fashion, Mrs Reveley dining out often without her husband. Before long she had developed an enormous admiration for the famous philosopher which he accepted at face value with habitual lack of false modesty.

However from the dates in the two notes it is evident that a turning point occurred betwen 9 and 23 January 1795, and this is confirmed by entries in his journal for that time. On 9 January he noted 'call on Inchbald: dine at Foulkes's' and added in the next line the single word 'Greenwich'. On the 12th, he records 'sup at Reveley's, courir dehors'; on the 15th a unique X; on the 19th 'sup at Reveley's l'eternel'; on the 21st 'Le Mondain'; and on the 24th 'tea Reveley's, t. à t. [tête à tête], l'imposteur.'

These enigmatic events can be matched with Mrs Inchbald's teasing letter of 22 December. Men seldom understand the solidarity which women maintain even when they are competitors, and it seems likely that Mrs Inchbald was relaying an overture from Mrs Reveley. The journal notes that Godwin called on Mrs Inchbald on 29 December, the first opportunity at which he could have picked up the letter if he had decided not to trust a messenger, and later the same day, he noted 'sup at Reveley's t. à t. [tête à tête]'. He saw her again on 5 January, a few days before 'Greenwich'.

It would be rash to speculate too imaginatively about the meaning of these scattered clues, but it seems certain that on 9 January Godwin went with Mrs Reveley on a secret trip to Greenwich, a favourite outing for those liable to be recognized in central London.* The X was presumably an overstepping of the rules followed shortly afterwards by a row in

---

* Mary Hays, writing to a prospective lover shortly before a day trip to Greenwich Park, described the proper feelings on such occasions. 'Thursday approaches! How my heart flutters at the idea! Its emotions do not proceed from want of confidence in you, nor from any false delicacy, or female pride, but from a native diffidence, a bashfulness which I cannot overcome. Meet me with composure, with the tranquil tenderness of friendship; let the shades, the solitude, the silence of the Park, diffuse a soft serenity over our minds, and calm the turbulence of passion.'[29]

which Godwin, who had previously been called l'éternel, was now le mondain and l'imposteur.

It was evidently Mrs Reveley who took the initiative, and Mrs Reveley who was rebuffed. In writing to her years later about the absurdity of obeying irrational social conventions, Godwin recalled the incident when he had resisted the inclination of his feeling:

Esteeming me probably more than you ever esteemed any other man, you, with a resolution that does you the highest honour, preserved my acquaintance often in spite of Mr Reveley, once in spite of myself. Again and again when he was unwilling to receive my visits, by your perseverance you conquered his inflexibility; at another time when I was no longer willing to pay them to him, you conquered me.[30]

For a while after the events of January 1795 Godwin continued to see her frequently, but there was evidently another turning point in June when she wrote to him at Hatton where he was staying with the Parrs, a fact he noted unusually in his journal as well as in his confidential notes. No copy of the letter survives, but from clues in their later correspondence, it seems that William Reveley took the opportunity of Godwin's absence to ask his wife to stop seeing him and she reluctantly agreed. Godwin called on her immediately the day he returned to London, but if he pressed her to change her decision, he had no success, and it was six weeks before he saw her again.

Thereafter for the next few months he saw her every few weeks, and as is the way in such matters, Mrs Reveley's admiration for her philosophical hero became, if anything, more intense. In his turn Godwin was only vaguely aware that, for the first time in his life, he had been touched by powerful emotions which did not easily match his understanding of his own character.

CHAPTER 13

Mary Wollstonecraft

It was Mary Hays who suggested that Godwin might like to meet again the author of the *Vindication of the Rights of Woman*, who had recently returned to England from France and whom he had not seen since 1792. Mary Hays had mentioned her friend in a number of enthusiastic recent letters, but as Godwin's reply shows, he accepted the invitation with some suspicion, and he could not even spell the name properly.

I will do myself the pleasure of waiting on you on Friday, and shall be happy to meet Mrs Wolstencraft, of whom I know not that I ever said a word of harm, and who has frequently amused herself with depreciating me. But I trust you acknowledge in me the reality of habit upon which I pique myself, that I speak of the qualities of others uninfluenced by personal considerations, and am as prompt to do justice to an enemy as to a friend.[1]

Godwin's journal duly records tea with Miss Hays on 8 January along with Holcroft and Wollstonecraft and it was evidently a success. 'I was glad to see her so lively,' Mary Hays wrote a few days later with a touch of compliment, 'though I knew the gaiety to be very superficial.'[2] Godwin met Wollstonecraft again at a dinner party on the 14th at which she was among the guests. But it was nearly a month later before he responded politely if not eagerly with a social call. On 13 February he called at the Christies' home where she was staying only to find her 'nah' (not at

The Author by Bewick

home). It should have been his other abbreviation 'nit' (not in town) for she had already left London to spend some weeks in the country.

Mary Wollstonecraft was a very different woman from the strident feminist radical who had hogged the conversation at Godwin's meeting with Tom Paine on 13 November 1791 when they had first met. At that time neither *Political Justice* nor the *Vindication* had been published, but Mary had been sure of her opinions to a degree unusual even in those confident days. She had gone to France in December 1792 with a tricolour in her bonnet and her head full of New Philosophy. The Revolution was, she wrote in the first volume of her aptly named *Historical and Moral View of the French Revolution*, a 'natural consequence of intellectual improvement gradually proceeding to perfection', a time when 'man may contemplate with benevolent pride the approaching reign of reason and peace', with 'knowledge rapidly advancing to perfectibility'.[3] For some of her factual information she drew on the narratives in the *New Annual Register*, without knowing that they had been written by the author of *Political Justice*, and her own book in its turn was regarded as primary evidence by Godwin's successors at the *Register*. Like other English radicals who remembered the English uprising against King Charles I, she was prepared to regard the execution of King Louis as an unavoidable, if regrettable, demonstration that no public official is above the law, although when she watched from her window as the carriage took him to his trial she could not restrain the tears of sensibility.

For a time she was a prominent member of a group of exiles and expatriates, mainly British and American, who had come to witness and report the birth of the new order. Helen Maria Williams, whose volumes of published letters describing the exuberant days of 1790 had found their way into Godwin's *New Annual Register* narratives (thus completing another closed and self-reinforcing circle) kept open salon in the appropriately renamed Rue Helvétius where foreigners could meet the French leaders. Modern scholars pondering how the poetess could support such an establishment have conjectured that she was subsidized by British secret service funds and they may be right. True to her principles, Miss Williams lived openly with John Hurford Stone, a writer who was not her husband and was probably paid by the French Government to report on the English in Paris.

At the house of Tom Paine, now a citizen of France and member of the National Assembly, Mary Wollstonecraft met Roland, Madame Roland, Isnard, and other leading Girondins. She lived for a while with the family of Thomas Christie, later a member of the Philomaths, the first volume of whose *Letters on the Revolution of France* published in 1791 had described the Revolution as 'the greatest and most glorious event that ever took place in the history of the world . . . the only revolution that has *completely* respected the rights of mankind'.[4] The American writer Joel Barlow and his wife Ruth Baldwin were other close friends. A corresponding member of the Philomaths, Barlow was famous for his long poem, *The Vision of Columbus* known for a time as the *Columbiad*, a bold attempt to do for the United States what Virgil had done for Ancient Rome. He too had recently written his own reply to Burke, *Advice to the Privileged Orders*. Indeed anyone visiting Helen Maria Williams's salon who had *not* written an ecstatic book in defence of the French Revolution had not paid his or her subscription.

It was at the Barlows where Mary met Gilbert Imlay and fell in love with him. Captain Imlay – as he called himself – was European agent of the Scioto Land Company of Ohio and with Barlow was marketing the attractions of the new world to the distressed, disappointed, and dispossessed of the old. Aged forty-one when Mary met him in 1793, he was an exotic and mysterious figure. He had fought as an officer in the American War of Independence and was full of stories of his past life. Mary probably knew that he was now advising the French on their plans for an armed seizure of the Mississippi valley, perhaps as a secret agent of the United States Government. Europe swarmed with American real-estate salesmen – one of whom fast-talked Coleridge into pantisocracy over a few drinks in the Cat and Salutation in August 1794 – but few were as literary as Imlay. In his *Topographical Description of the Western Territory of North America* published in 1792, he described in the language of New Philosophy a simple rustic way of life still free from the fetters which priestcraft had forged for the human mind. In a novel called *The Emigrants* he told a pleasing tale of a financially ruined English lady living in accordance with nature in the wilds near Pittsburgh. Rescued from the Indians by Captain Arlington, Caroline T—n wears her panting bosom half-uncovered like a revolutionary heroine of Delacroix, and eventually the couple move to Ohio, no doubt on land made available by the Scioto Corporation. If Roman virtue could coexist with the ethics of Tahiti, the United States was the obvious place to make the attempt.

For several months Mary's affair with Imlay thrived. With the downfall of the Girondin party however everything changed. Many of Mary's French friends went to the guillotine, and Danton and Robespierre were contemptuous of the liberal foreigner sympathizers in Paris. Tom Paine, Helen Maria Williams, and other members of the group were thrown into prison and were fortunate to escape being guillotined as spies or counter-revolutionaries. Others scuttled gratefully back to the safety of England, trying to forget their public predictions of imminent perfectibility. Seldom have so many two-volume works come to an abrupt end with volume one.

As a citizen of the United States, a country with which France was not at war, Gilbert Imlay was exempt from the new restrictions. He turned to business, arranging deals to import British goods in defiance of the naval blockade. In order that Mary could stay with him in France he registered her name with the American Consul in Paris as 'Mrs Imlay' in a marriage document of uncertain legal status. In 1794 Mary Wollstonecraft gave birth to a daughter whom they named Frances, or Fanny, and they decided to emigrate to the United States as soon as they could, like the characters in Imlay's novel.

Travelling constantly in France and beyond, however, Imlay seemed increasingly reluctant to be with her. In the summer of 1795 Mary herself made an enterprising visit to Scandinavia with her baby and a servant girl called Marguerite in an attempt to help him in his business, but when they returned to meet him in London in the autumn it was plain that he no longer wished to live with her. Mary found herself alone and penniless with her baby.

For a time she sank into a deep depression. Mary Hays told Godwin that many of Mary Wollstonecraft's former friends in England had decided that they could no longer associate with an unmarried mother. In October, having written a suicide note with instructions about Fanny, she walked up and down in the rain to weigh down her clothes and then threw herself off Putney Bridge. But she was picked up by boatmen and revived. It was her second unsuccessful suicide attempt within a few months.

The meeting with Godwin at Mary Hays's was followed by several weeks staying with a friend called Mrs Cotton in rural Berkshire to recover her health. On returning to London in March she met Imlay one day as he was riding along the street now known as Euston Road. He dismounted and they walked together for a time in what was to be their last meeting. To her relief Mary found that she was able to keep calm, and she reconciled herself soon afterwards to the life which she had abandoned five years before. On 14 April, in a characteristic gesture of social defiance, she boldly called alone on William Godwin at Chalton Street to return his call of 13 February. He called on her the next day for tea; she responded a few days later; and before long they were seeing each other regularly.

Mary Wollstonecraft at thirty-six was beyond the customary marriageable age, but her attractiveness was undiminished. Stories of her confessed passion for the Swiss painter Fuseli whom she had offered to share with his wife in the days before she left for France (keeping her own relationship with him platonic) convinced many wives that she was a dangerous seducer, but aroused pleasing mixtures of excited shock, admiration, and envy in their husbands. Her recent unhappy experiences with Imlay – whom she had also offered to share with another woman without any such limits – added to her fascination. The slight cast in one of her eyes which gave a look both alluring and demonic fitted her emerging reputation, and Godwin thought that she had picked up habits of cynicism from the diabolical painter of the subconscious. But those whose view of the hyena in petticoats derived solely from reading the *Vindication* were now delightedly surprised to read the *Letters Written during a Short Residence in Sweden, Norway, and Denmark*, which Johnson published late in 1795, based on letters purportedly sent to Imlay on her recent journey.[5] Modest, warm, good-humoured, and hopeful, the book matched the new character of the author, and on the final page Mary acknowledged the conclusion that Godwin and other honest observers had already admitted.

An ardent affection for the human race makes enthusiastic characters eager to produce alteration in laws and governments prematurely. To render them useful and permanent, they must be the growth of each particular soil, and the gradual fruit of the ripening understanding of the nation, matured by time, not forced by an unnatural fermentation.

Godwin obtained one of the first copies and read it between meeting Mary in January and her return from the country in March. 'If ever there was a book calculated to make a man in love with its author, this appears to me to be the book,' he wrote later. 'She speaks of her sorrows in a way that fills us with melancholy and dissolves us in tenderness, at the same time that she displays a genius which commands our admiration.'[6] Others felt the same. Several young men addressed poems to her including John Stoddart, a law student who was one of Godwin's most eager disciples at the time.[7] Robert Southey in the dedication of his next volume of verses compared her with cumulative inappropriateness to Joan of Arc, Madame Roland and Charlotte Corday (the latter-day female Brutus who murdered Marat in his bath). In 'The Triumph of Woman', he came near to suggesting that women are a superior species who, if given a political chance, could turn aside the aggressiveness of males and bring about international peace and disarmament.[8]

A love poem to 'Eliza', the name of the wise sister in *The Emigrants*, has survived among Godwin's papers along with an accompanying unsigned love letter, postmarked 2 January 1796, addressed to Mrs Imlay. 'You and I ought to do that which will most increase and secure our happiness,' the unknown admirer begins, with a good Godwinian argument. 'It will be increased and secured in proportion to our utility.' But as he warms, the writer admits openly to his desire for

the woman of reason all day, the philosopher . . . [who] . . . in the evening becomes the playful and passionate child of love . . . in whose arms I should encounter all that playful luxuriance, those warm balmy kisses, and that soft yet eager and extatic assaulting and yielding known only to beings that seem purely etherial.

From other remarks it emerges that the writer is not a young man and he is concerned that he may not be considered suitable. He does not wish to be unjust to Gilbert Imlay (whom he only knows from Mary's affectionate descriptions) but he asks her to consider his proposal well and 'bid me once more come and try if this Lovers' Millenium may not yet be ours'.

The writer's identity has not been established beyond doubt but there is a sufficiently strong resemblance in the unusual handwriting and evidence of other kinds – such as his invocation of the millennium and misspelling of ecstasy – to suggest that Mary's admirer was none other than Thomas Holcroft who was at that time a widower on the lookout for a wife.[9] If he was indeed the writer, Mary took no offence, even if she did not respond, for she continued to see Holcroft socially although she disliked going to his Sunday dinners and avoided him when she could. Nor did Godwin, if he knew of the incident, yet permit it to affect his relationship with his oldest friend at whose table he had dined every Sunday afternoon, year in and year out since 1788 with scarcely a week missed. *Political Justice* had always envisaged that preferences among men and women would alter with perceptions, and there could be no monopolistic restrictions on the proffering of love.

On 22 April Godwin gave a dinner party at Chalton Street at which Mary was introduced or reintroduced to a dozen of his friends including Holcroft, Dr Parr and Sarah Anne, Mackintosh, and Mrs Inchbald, and over the next few months, there was hardly a day when he was not present at some distinguished literary or artistic gathering, often in her company. The author of the *Vindication* (she disdained the prissy overtones of 'authoress') and the author of *Political Justice* were the two acknowledged leaders of the New Philosophy. They had much to say to each other and soon had many friends in common and many admirers. Godwin became a personal friend of James Northcote the portraitist – he painted Godwin in 1801 – and was introduced to more of the other leading artists of the day including Fuseli and, on 26 May 1796, William Blake who had illustrated one of Mary Wollstonecraft's children's books. John Opie, then at the height of his celebrity (the equal it was being said of Caravaggio and Velasquez combined) called on Mary so often that it was rumoured at the Royal Academy that he intended to marry her. Francis Twiss, who had compiled a concordance to Shakespeare, was another regular caller, and he brought them the friendship of his sister Mrs Siddons, and of the Kemble family. Mary dined at the Twiss's every third Sunday.

From the first Mary was attracted to Godwin. As Basil Montagu, Thomas Wedgwood and innumerable others had discovered, he offered a source of strength from which friends could draw without limit, and to the confused and the depressed his uncompromising advice was often more sustaining than the vaguer sympathy of more tactful friends. In the *Wrongs of Woman*, the projected sequel to the *Rights*, Mary teased him by introducing as a minor character 'an advocate for unequivocal sincerity' who sends the heroine a long essay on the energy of mind with advice on how to mobilize it. But her appreciation was genuine. When she had been soaring high she had failed to notice him, but now that she had a wing down, she valued the steadiness and imperturbability which she herself lacked. When she decided to find permanent lodgings of her own in London (instead of going abroad as she had intended) she chose Judd Place not far from Somers Town so as to be near Godwin.[10]

Gradually, as Godwin described later, friendship melted into love. In his journal for Saturday 21 May 1796, one of many occasions of 'tea Wolstencraft's'* he noted mysteriously 'la b.p.' evidently code for something important which happened on that day – perhaps the first stirrings of *'la belle passion'* – and he himself did not realize fully what was happening. Their attachment grew, he noted later in some astonishment, 'with equal advances in the mind of each. It would have been impossible for the most minute observer to have said who was before, and who was after. One sex did not take the priority which long-established custom has awarded it, nor the other overstep that delicacy which is so severely

---

* Godwin called her Wollstonecraft in the privacy of his journal, still misspelled, but his letters were addressed on the outside to 'Mrs Imlay'.

imposed.' It was not until his visit to Norfolk in July 1796 however that he discovered how much he missed her.

Godwin's first letter, sent from Norwich in discharge of a promise to write, is heavy, embarrassed, and mannered, replete with the mock gallantry and forced humour without which at this time he was unable to address any woman. Mary was disappointed especially as he did not call on her immediately on the day of his return, but as she wrote at once showing him how to contrive honesty with charm, 'Now I am out of humour I mean to bottle up my kindness, unless something in your countenance, when I do see you, should make the cork fly out – whether I will or not.' There are many such clues to suggest that the equal advances were in reality tactful initiatives by Mary.

On 10 July, three days before the first letter, Godwin had noted in his journal 'Propose to Alderson', as a result of which earlier biographers of Godwin and Wollstonecraft have believed, with insufficient surprise, that he made the journey to Norwich in order to propose marriage to Amelia Alderson. In fact, Godwin's proposal was addressed to her father – Amelia was not in Norwich at the time – and concerned a plan to buy off the creditors of Robert Merry (the Della Cruscan poet who had composed the odes at Revolution Society dinners) who had been arrested for debt in Norwich two days before and who wanted now to emigrate to the United States.[11]

Far from contemplating marriage for himself, Godwin could be relied upon at this time to give any questioner a detailed exposition of the moral destructiveness of the institution. But Mary enjoyed teasing him, not without a touch of jealousy, about his association with Mrs Reveley, Mrs Inchbald ('Mrs Perfection') and also with Miss Alderson, and on 6 August she sent a note addressed 'To William Godwin Philosopher. Not to be opened till the Philosopher has been an hour at least in Miss Alderson's company, cheek by jowl.'

Miss Alderson was wondering, this morning whether you *ever* kissed a maiden fair – As you do not like to solve problems, *on paper*, TELL her *before* you part – She will tell *me* next – year –

The answer was provided direct by Miss Alderson a few weeks later in a conspiratorial letter to Mary Wollstonecraft whom she had recently met. When she had known her only as the author of the *Vindication*, she explained, she had regarded her with cold awe, but this had all changed when she read the *Letters from Sweden*. Only two experiences in her life had lived up to expectations, Mary Wollstonecraft and the Lakes of

Cumberland. As for her expectations of Godwin, she was frankly disappointed.

I found him indeed eloquent, entertaining, and luminous in argument even beyond my conception of his abilities, but my fancy had so long delighted to picture him a man *after his own heart* that I shrunk back almost displeased from a man after the *present state of things* – The fault was in *me* I know, and I have made ample amends since – every day pass'd with him, has indeared him to me more strongly – and made me cease to regret he was not what I expected to find him – viz one whose 'nay was nay and his yea yea' – I am reconciled even to *flattery*, *Horne Tookian flattery* from his lips, and in ye words of a charming song–

'I fear him less, but love him more'

(Do you know the next lines? Do not *laugh* if I transcribe them –

'When with licentious boldness fired
I dared to *clasp* what I admired,
Dared round thy neck my arms to twine
And *press thy balmy lips to mine,*
Then thro' my soul sharp poison ran,
Twas then my *keenest* pangs began
For by the dangerous bliss half slain
I drag a life of ceaseless pain –

apropos – I am glad the philosopher revenged my quarrel, but I hope you are not *half slain* in consequence of it . . . [12]

Mary evidently showed the letter to Godwin and teased him with it later, for in the intervening fortnight, a new conspiracy superseding the old, Mary had become Godwin's lover in the fullest sense of the word. Nothing, Mary had written as early as 1787 in *Thoughts on the Education of Daughters,* is so destructive of peace of mind as platonic friendships, but Godwin was still a virgin, keenly aware of his ignorance and fearful of humiliation.

On a scrap of paper recording the critical events of those heady days, he later noted Saturday 13 August 1796 as 'Explication', meaning explanation. This was the evening at her lodgings, when, as he wrote later, for both of them, 'the sentiment which trembled upon the tongue burst from the lips'. The next day, to Mary's deep disappointment, Godwin did not call but went instead to dine as usual with Holcroft and Ritson. Having taken one bold step, he found himself wavering and confused and took his refuge in familiar things. He had been rereading *Political Justice,* in the spirit, we may guess, of a doubting priest who clutches his bible, but the New Philosophy offered no explanation of the feelings with which he now found himself gripped. Not far beneath the bold enlightenment thinker still lurked the puritan dissenting minister to whom strong feeling was as frightening as strong drink.

On Monday 15 August, two days after Saturday's explanation, the journal notes 'chez moi', the first time Godwin uses this expression to record one of Mary's visits. Early the following morning, Mary sent him a playful affectionate note, the maid taking it round to his house accompanied by the two-year-old Fanny:

I send you the newspaper before the hour, because I suppose you will go out earlier than usual today. Give Churchill [a book] to Fanny if you can spare him, and you may kiss her, if you please.

Entre nous – did you feel very lonely last night?

But before this letter could be read, Godwin had sent his own note, an alarmed, defiant, and embarrassed reaction to what had probably been a gesture of intimacy gracelessly repelled.

I have been very unwell all night. You did not consider me enough in that way yesterday, & therefore unintentionally impressed upon me a mortifying sensation. When you see me next; will you condescend to take me for better for worse, that is, be prepared to find me, as it shall happen, full of gaiety & life, or a puny valetudinarian? Farewel, remember our agreement!

That afternoon Godwin attended a dinner party with Clementi the musician, Bonnycastle the mathematician, and others, and when for a second time he defensively did not call on her afterwards Mary characteristically presented herself at Chalton Street. This time however it was her turn to be mortified, for having, it would seem, again offered physical affection, all she received was a lecture on the nature of feelings, a topic on which she rightly regarded her own expertise as superior. The following morning, deeply hurt, she sent a careful letter, scolding but still affectionate, in which she announced her decision to follow the example of her admired Rousseau, the 'solitary walker', and make her way in the world alone.

Sincerely intended – insofar as lovers' threats are ever sincere – the letter changed Godwin's life more decisively than any message he had received in twenty years. At one o'clock he sent his reply, one of the best and most revealing he ever wrote.

. . . You do not know how honest I am. I swear to you that I told you nothing but the strict and literal truth, when I described to you the manner in which you set my imagination on fire on Saturday. For six and thirty hours I could think of nothing else. I longed inexpressibly to have you in my arms. Why did not I come to you? I am a fool. I feared still that I might be deceiving myself as to your feelings, and that I was feeding my mind with groundless presumptions. I determined to suffer the point to arrive at its own denouement. I was not aware that the fervour of my imagination was exhausting itself. Yet this, I believe, is no uncommon case.

Like any other man, I can speak only of what I know. But this I can boldly affirm, that nothing that I have seen in you would in the slightest degree authorise the opinion, that, *in despising the false delicacy, you have lost sight of the true.* I see nothing in you but what I respect and adore.

I know the acuteness of your feelings, and there is perhaps nothing upon earth that would give me so pungent a remorse, as to add to your unhappiness. Do not hate me. Indeed I do not deserve it. Do not cast me off. Do not become again a *solitary walker*. Be just to me, and then, though you will discover in me much that is foolish and censurable, yet a woman of your understanding will still regard me with some partiality.

Upon consideration I find in you one fault, and but one. You have the feelings of nature, and you have the honesty to avow them. In all this you do well. I am sure you do. But do not let them tyrannise over you. Estimate every thing at its just value. It is best that we should be friends in every sense of the word;* but in the mean time let us be friends.

Suffer me to see you. Let us leave every thing else to its own course. My imagination is not dead, I suppose, though it sleeps. But, be it as it will, I will torment you no more. I will be your friend, the friend of your mind, the admirer of your excellencies. All else I commit to the disposition of futurity, glad, if completely happy; passive and silent in this respect, while I am not so.

Be happy. Resolve to be happy. You deserve to be so. Every thing that interferes with it, is weakness and wandering; and a woman, like you, can, must, shall, shake it off. Afford, for instance, no food for the morbid madness, & no triumph to the misanthropical gloom, of your afternoon visitor [Mary Hays]. Call up, with firmness, the energies, which, I am sure, you so eminently possess.

Send me word that I may call on you in a day or two. Do you not see, while I exhort you to be a philosopher, how painfully acute are my own feelings? I need some soothing, though I cannot ask it from you.

Mary saw at once that it was a love letter, the genuineness of his feelings surging over his defensive double negatives and softening even his determination to proffer advice. It was a vindication of his principle of total honesty and of the power of concentrated mind, and the chain of history was duly redirected. No less than four letters passed between the pair that Wednesday, three of them carried personally, between Chalton Street and Judd Place. Confused and bewildered, the lovers found it easier to communicate by letter than face to face.

---

* In the idiom of the day 'friend' often meant 'lover'.

In the afternoon, the first letter having already been delivered, it suddenly struck Godwin for the first time what Mary had been offering and scarcely able to believe the extent of his own crassness, he hurriedly wrote another letter of abject apology, totally shorn now of the protective moralizing to which he had instinctively resorted. But before he had time to deliver it the wise Mary had already arrived on his doorstep with her own letter, dated two o'clock, which she had written in reply to his first. This time there was no talk of leaving him. Mary was calm, tender, forgiving, and motherly. 'Now will you not be a good boy and smile upon me,' she wrote, inviting him to have dinner with her at half past four. 'You say you want soothing,' she remarked archly with the ironic humour which he was only beginning to understand, 'will it sooth you to tell the truth? . . . I cannot withhold my friendship from you, and will try to merit yours, that *necessity* may bind you to me.' Godwin was at home when she called with the letter, the two met, and the crisis was over. Mary had found the way to deal with him, and he accepted her leadership with relief.

The dinner had to be shared with Mary Hays and the following day, Thursday, was no better since Mary's servant Marguerite was in the next room of the thin-walled house. On the Friday they did not see each other. Mary sent a teasing letter with a story of a sycamore tree which buds hopefully in the spring and is shrivelled by the frost, but Godwin crushed with fear could only repeat plaintively that he needed soothing. Saturday evening was again spent 'chez elle', and then on Sunday, with 'chez moi toute', the final barrier of false delicacy was at last passed and they made love for the first time.

'I am sometimes painfully humble,' Mary wrote the next day. 'Write me but a line just to assure me, that you have been thinking of me with affection, now and then – Since we parted –' But Godwin was already relapsing. 'Humble!' the now soothed philosopher wrote back immediately, 'for heaven's sake, be proud, be arrogant! You are – but I cannot tell what you are, I cannot yet find the circumstance about you that allies you to the frailty of our nature. I will hunt it out.' In the weeks that followed, there were to be many instances of misunderstanding and impatience, of coolness and withdrawal followed by warm reconciliations. Mary, afraid of being hurt, sometimes repelled the love which she craved. The inexperienced Godwin, struggling to maintain equilibrium in the face of volatility, too often retreated into pomposity and dogmatism. As in a Godwinian novel, the ambiguous roles of pursuer and pursued were reversed and reversed again.

Godwin was hard at work, revising *Political Justice* for a new edition and compiling a series of new essays to be published as *The Enquirer*. Besides reading *The Rights of Woman* again he was persuaded to study Mary's favourite, Rousseau, the 'Prometheus of Sentiment' as she called him, the first writer to give an adequate account of the irrational forces by which she knew her own life had been governed and which he too was beginning to understand. Mary was at work on her novel, *The Wrongs of Woman*, in which, with *Caleb Williams* as a model, she was attempting to develop the ideas of *The Rights* for a wider audience. Like Godwin, she wanted to demonstrate that oppression is not a prerogative of the traditional oppressing classes, but – with things as they are – permeates all unequal relationships. Her picture of the exploited woman confined in a madhouse has become one of the most vivid and enduring images of the feminist movement.

During the day they led separate lives, writing, reading, and seeing friends. Occasionally when they met in company or at the theatre there would be knowing looks or a squeeze of the hand, but the affair was a well-kept secret. The notes which they exchanged during the day are like overheard conversations. Totally free from the literary self-awareness that infiltrates the letters of famous writers when they are aware of posterity looking over their shoulder, they are wonderfully revealing of the characters of the lovers. The bewildered Godwin strove to maintain his accustomed equanimity, conscious that Mary depended on his imperturbability and admired him for it. Mary in her turn gave him a dazzling display of all the qualities he himself lacked. Godwin, always fearful of peepers, was inclined to retreat into schoolboy French for his endearments. Some of Mary's are as full of humour, charm, and love as any man has ever received.

On 15 September they went away together for a day in the country – staying overnight at Ilford – but for the most part they met in the evening. After dinner in the afternoon Mary would steal across to Chalton Street or Godwin would slip unnoticed into Judd Place. Godwin noted all their meetings in his journal, devising a simple code to record the occasions on which they made love, and it has now proved possible to trace the course of their relationship in unusual detail.* They were happy.

With the coming of winter however there was a crisis. Johnson, Mary's publisher, who had financed her since she had been an anonymous hack writer, seems to have demanded that she settle some of her debt, and

---

* See Appendix 1 and Plate 6.

although she was sure that he had made money from the *Vindication* and the *Letters from Sweden*, he evidently told her that she could have no more credit. At about the same time she realized that she was pregnant. Every morning she was sick with 'the inelegant complaint' as she explained wryly to Godwin, 'which no novelist has yet ventured to mention as one of the consequences of sentimental distress' and she plunged again into depression. She had already often tasted the humiliations of an unmarried mother described graphically in *The Wrongs of Woman* although many friends now politely maintained the fiction that Mrs Imlay had been legally married to the American who had deserted her. But there was no such fiction available to explain away a second pregnancy. When the second child was born, Mary Imlay would be a social outcast, a woman whom men could visit but certain to be shunned by all women, married or unmarried, who valued their reputations.

Johnson had a solution to propose. Several of Mary's friends had already become the kept companions of dull elderly men, traditional superannuation for a successful career in theatre or *demi-monde*. Johnson knew someone who was rich, willing to marry her, and so able to confer respectability on all her past irregularities. Whoever he was, he was told sharply through an intermediary that Mary was insulted by the suggestion and could not 'for a moment think of prostituting her person' by such a marriage. Instead, as she told Johnson, she preferred to turn to the 'source of perfection who perhaps never disregarded an almost broken heart, especially when a respect, a practical respect for virtue, sharpened the wounds of adversity.'[13]

Whether or not it is Godwin who is meant by the 'source of perfection', it was he who resolved Mary's money crisis and so pulled her back from the edge. On 28 February 1797 he wrote to Thomas Wedgwood asking for an immediate loan of £50 on behalf of a friend.[14] For fear of unduly influencing Wedgwood's judgement he did not explain the circumstances nor give the name of the friend, simply assuring Wedgwood that in his own view the money would do good. The £50 was sent immediately, a spectacular example of impartial political justice, a problem solved without compromise, without loss of principle, and without creating the corrupting bonds of mutual obligation normally inseparable from financial transactions.

By comparison, Godwin's next act was a shameful and squalid compromise. He decided to marry her. For months she had liked to tease him about her wifely role in helping with the shopping and the laundry. She had asked for a key to the Chalton Street house as much as a symbol as for practical convenience. On 1 January when all doubts about the reality of the pregnancy had passed, the two philosophers had a long conversation about marriage and children, during which she urged him to marry her. They partook of the ceremony at the nearest church, St Pancras, on 29 March 1797 with Marshall in attendance but none of their other friends. In his journal for a busy day, Godwin cryptically noted 'Panc.'.

Many of their friends had by now guessed that they were lovers. Mary Hays, who had brought them together in the first place, could not conceal her disappointment; and others felt that it was somehow regrettable that the leaders of the New Philosophy should be so human as to fall in love. The ladies of the theatre had looked on with disdained amusement, and there is a hint in one of Mary's letters that she expected Mrs Perfection – whom Godwin continued to see often – to make a trial of her own charms. But love is one thing, marriage another. Of the many changes of opinion that Godwin was obliged to account for in the course of a long life, his famous description of the 'most odious of all monopolies' was the most indigestible, and he showed acute discomfort from the first.

For a few days he went about his usual life seeing friends without telling them anything. On the day of the ceremony he dined with a group of politicians and journalists at the house of Debrett the publisher. On the following Sunday he dined with Holcroft and took tea with a large group of friends connected with theatre. On the Wednesday he was at Johnson's with William Blake but still nothing was said. Maria Reveley was the first to be told. Since the secret day together in Greenwich in January 1795, Godwin and she had continued to see each other and recently the earlier warmth had returned. She is said to have shed tears at the news, but she liked Mary Wollstonecraft and contrived to remain friends, arranging for her children to play with Fanny.

Mrs Inchbald is also said to have shed tears. She had long been one of Godwin's closest friends but refused to meet Mary Wollstonecraft socially. There had been an occasion when Mary had seen Godwin and Elizabeth Inchbald together in a box at the theatre when she herself sat humiliated in another seat at the back.[15] They had made an arrangement to go to the theatre again together on 19 April which was shortly after the news broke. 'I most sincerely wish you and Mrs Godwin joy,' she wrote bitterly. 'But, assured that your joyfulness would obliterate from your memory every trifling engagement, I have entreated another person to supply your place . . . If I have done wrong, when you next marry, I will act differently.'[16] It was a challenge which could not be ignored and Godwin and Mary boldly presented themselves at the theatre on the day to meet not only Mrs Inchbald but Mrs Reveley, Amelia Alderson, the Fenwicks, and other friends. What exactly happened is not recorded, but Mrs Inchbald made a joke which Godwin regarded as 'base, cruel, and insulting' that was heard by everyone present.[17] Although there were social calls in the months that followed, their friendship never fully recovered.

In leaking the news slowly as if it were either a shameful secret or a matter of no importance, Godwin gracelessly multiplied his difficulties. In a letter to Mary Hays, he tried to cover embarrassment with heavy-handed frivolity, the equivalent of his former mock gallantry.[18] His letter to Holcroft was probably also jocular, omitting even the name of his wife, and Holcroft's reply probably represents the puzzled feelings of many of his friends.

From my very heart and soul I give you joy. I think you the most extraordinary married pair in existence. May your happiness be as pure as I firmly persuade myself it must be. I hope and expect to see you both, and very soon. If you show coldness or refuse me, you will do injustice to a heart which, since it has really known you, never for a moment felt cold to you.

I cannot be mistaken concerning the woman you have married. It is Mrs W. Your secrecy a little pains me. It tells me you do not yet know me.[19]

With everyone enjoying jokes about his marriage, Godwin felt the embarrassment deeply, and in several letters he defended himself vigorously against the easy accusation that he had contravened his own principles. First of all, he declared, after reminding one questioner (whom he had never met) that he was only answering his impertinent letter in a spirit of helpfulness, he rejected the suggestion that he had ever laid down dogmatic rules of behaviour on marriage or indeed on anything else. Had not *Political Justice* been purposely called *An Enquiry*? And his latest book *The Enquirer*? Godwin reserved the right to change his own views as he hoped others would change theirs.

But, as it happened, as far as marriage was concerned, he did not want to alter his opinion. As practised in Europe the institution was primarily an affair of property whereby the woman irrevocably surrendered her independence to the man. He still wanted to see it abolished. It was true, he admitted, that by marrying her had submitted to an abhorrent institution, but every day of life he was obliged to comply with institutions and customs about which he felt the same. Morality – political justice he might have said – consists in striking a balance between evils, social and personal, and in judging the respective utility of compliance and non-compliance. 'I find the prejudice of the world in arms against the woman who practically opposes herself to the European institution of marriage,' he concluded. 'I found that the comfort and peace of a woman for whose comfort and peace I interest myself would be much injured if I could have prevailed on her to defy those prejudices.'[20] Compared with this, he gave little weight to a mere ceremony, confident that his behaviour would not be altered in the slightest way as a result of having submitted to it.

The last point was an important one. Godwin assured his wife that he would not live with her one day longer as a result of undergoing the ceremony than he would if it had never taken place, and she no doubt solemnly reciprocated the vow – with the proviso of course that the promise should be set aside if greater justice would result. In explaining to Wedgwood about the £50 to settle Mary's debt, he remarked that in entering into 'a new mode of living which will probably be permanent, I find a further supply of fifty pounds will be necessary to enable us to start fair,'[21] and this too was promptly provided. Most importantly, as a means of moderating the damaging monopoly aspects of traditional marriage in which partners engross minds as well as bodies, it was agreed that they should continue to live part of their lives separately. They moved to a newly built house in Somers Town, 29 The Polygon, on 30 March, and Godwin rented a room nearby to which he retired to work every morning.[22]

They continued to see their friends separately as well as together. Mary's admirers including Opie and Southey were invited to dine. Maria Reveley was a frequent visitor unaccompanied by her husband. The Godwins, it was universally admitted, were a most unusual couple. As he worked in his lodgings in the mornings Mary still had to send him little notes, one moment scolding him for not telling the landlord to mend the drains, at another cautioning him after a tiff that total sincerity within a marriage was incompatible with the present state of reason. 'A husband is a convenient part of the furniture of a house,' she assured him when he went away for a few days, 'unless he be a clumsy fixture. I wish you, from my soul, to be rivetted in my heart; but I do not desire to have you always at my elbow.' As confirmation that they had chosen well, the peace of The Polygon was regularly interrupted by thuds and screams from an adjoining house where a more traditional husband frequently exercised his legal right to beat his wife.[23]

But in deciding as a matter of expediency to submit to the icy chains of custom, they underestimated their complexity. If Mary Wollstonecraft was now legitimately married to William Godwin, then it was no longer possible to pretend that she had been legitimately married to Gilbert

Imlay. Mrs Godwin, it seemed, was even more of a threat to female virtue than Mrs Wollstonecraft or Mrs Imlay. Sarah Siddons, with a delicacy unusual in her profession, felt that her theatrical career would be damaged if she were seen consorting with immorality and abruptly broke off acquaintanceship. Others, fearing the loss of friends whom they valued more highly, prudently did the same. By contrast a certain Miss Pinkerton, taking Godwin's protestations at face value, continued with her attempts to demonstrate her own superior claims despite his changed legal status, until an affronted Mary peremptorily forbade her from the matrimonial home.

Other friends drifted away. Amelia Alderson accepted a proposal of marriage not long afterwards from the painter John Opie whose rough country manners provided a challenging contrast to the sweet chivalry she had received from Godwin. Opie painted Mary's portrait in 1797 when her pregnancy bulge was already visible,* but his friendship did not long survive the change, and the Opies soon had to be added to the list of Godwin's 'amis perdus'. For all her admiration for Mary Wollstonecraft and for her writings, it was always the puritan element in the New Philosophy that had attracted Amelia. She remained a Christian and she could not approve of women being liberated from the Bastille of marriage. A few years later, after Opie's early death, she returned finally to Norwich where she led a plain life of such conspicuous virtue that it was written up in a religious tract.[24] Perhaps only Godwin's mother approved fully. 'Your broken resolution in regard to matrimony', she wrote in reply to a letter in which he had warned her against jumping to wrong conclusions, 'incourages me to hope that you will ere long embrace the Gospel, that sure word of promise to all believers . . . you are certainly transformed in a moral sense, why is it impossible in a spiritual sense which last will make you shine with the radiance of the sun for ever.'

The most remarkable reaction came from Sarah Anne Parr who promised Godwin the roasting of his life when he should next visit Hatton. In June he arranged to visit Tom Wedgwood at Etruria in company with Basil Montagu (the by now heavily pregnant Mary being left at home) and Hatton was on the route. At Oxford they were entertained by an admirer, John Horseman, who declared that Godwin and Wollstonecraft were 'the two greatest men in the world,'[25] and Godwin was expecting to participate in one of Dr Parr's famous argumentative dinners the following evening. But when the carriage reached Stratford, they were surprised to

* See Plate 5.

meet the doctor himself who had ridden ahead to meet them. During the night, Sarah had eloped to Gretna Green with the eighteen-year-old son of a neighbouring landowner described by Godwin as a 'raw country booby',[26] inarticulate, slovenly, slouching, and boorish. The *Amie des Philosophes* had taken her mother's advice and seduced a fool. A few days later on their return from Scotland the married Godwin was introduced to the married Sarah and her husband.

It was a bold stroke of theatre, but Sarah Parr's defiant attempt to uphold the traditional values was not a success. With its unending arguments, disputes over money, quarrels about the children, lawsuits, separations and patched-up reconciliations, violence, and final breakdown, Sarah's marriage was destined to match the most lurid descriptions of *The Wrongs of Woman*. After a few years, her health and spirit broken, she escaped back to her father's house where she died at the age of thirty-seven. Dr Parr commissioned a painting of her as she lay in her coffin, and as the years passed, he spent increasing hours gazing at this macabre reminder of his beloved daughter, gradually ceasing to speak to the wife whose antipathy to philosophers had contributed to the catastrophe.

Godwin's own views soon began to change. After his marriage it no longer seemed so self-evident that family ties – 'domestic affections' – are bonds of gratitude which link the oppressed to their oppressors. In the second edition of *Political Justice*, revised during the months with Mary, Godwin toned down the now famous story in which the reader was invited to rescue Fénelon from the burning house in preference to the chambermaid even if she was the reader's mother. The sex of the servant was changed to valet, to avoid any suspicion that Godwin regarded women as intrinsically of less value than men, but he still had to yield preference to Fénelon even if he were the reader's father or brother. Since Mary Wollstonecraft had a large Fénelonian potential for improving the moral economy the dilemma would have been acute if she had been the valet, and for a time Godwin believed that it was for Mary's moral worth that he loved her, but to his credit he was too honest to rely for long on that over-neat resolution. Soon he realized that he had abandoned his belief in impartiality. 'I have singularly the propensity without affectation or the desire of paradox to overlook or reject the most obvious truths,' he wrote with admirable detachment in 1800.[27] He regretted bitterly the long loveless childhood which had blinded him to the role of the emotions in human psychology. 'My writings hitherto,' he wrote in a distressed autobiographical fragment, '. . . have exhibited a view of only half the human mind.' Nevertheless nothing was wasted. His own experience, he began to perceive, was not only an illustration of the necessitarian influence of early environment on opinion and behaviour, but a triumphant vindication of the eventual power of truth.

The baby which had precipitated the marriage was due at the end of August and much of the summer was devoted to excited preparations for the arrival of 'William'. Mary, as befitted the world's leading feminist, was much interested by pregnancy, childbirth, breast-feeding, and infant care, seeing in the conventional treatment of these matters further examples of society's unthinking masculine bias.

While a governess in Ireland Mary had been a close friend of one of the daughters of the household, Lady Mountcashell, who later, after successfully rearing a large family, was to set out their theories in a book unequalled until the time of Dr Spock.[28] The *Advice to Young Mothers* can be regarded as a practical companion volume to *The Rights of Woman*, and if its admirable recommendations on clothing, fresh air, cleanliness, diet, and painted toys had been adopted, generations of women and children would have been spared considerable misery. The genteel English habit of staying in the bedroom for a month after a confinement was, Mary believed, an example of the false sensibility imposed on women by men. She would be up for dinner the next day, she declared, as she had been after Fanny was born. Nor would she need a doctor, preferring instead to be attended only by an experienced midwife. Godwin was less sure but he allowed himself to be overruled. On 21 August, the nineteen-year-old William Hazlitt called, and in the only eye-witness comment on the pair together which is known, he confirms the picture which emerges from the letters. 'She seemed to me', he told Coleridge, 'to turn off Godwin's objections to something he advanced with quite a playful easy air.'[29]

Four days later Mary began to feel the initial contractions in the morning. The midwife was sent for.[30] Mary went upstairs to bed at two o'clock, and after a long labour, a baby girl was born at twenty past eleven at night. Shortly afterwards Godwin went into the bedroom and in a simple gesture which touched him deeply, the mother presented the child to the father. The description in one of his later novels is obviously drawn from his own experience.

This, she seemed to say, is the joint result of our common affection. It partakes equally of both, and is the shrine in which our sympathies and our life have been poured together, never to be separated. Let other lovers testify their engagements by presents and tokens; we record and stamp our attachment in this precious creature, a creature of that species which is more admirable than anything else the world has to boast, a creature susceptible of pleasure and pain, of affection and love, of sentiment and fancy, of wisdom and virtue. This creature will daily stand in need of an aid we shall delight to afford; will require our meditations and exertions to forward its improvement, and confirm its merits and its worth. We shall each blend our exertions for that purpose, and our union, confirmed by this common object of our labour and affection, will every day become more sacred and indissoluble.[31]

Six years after *Political Justice* had recommended that children should be brought up in common, Godwin's intense feelings towards love, marriage, and parenthood now demanded the imagery of religion.

At two o'clock however, less than three hours after the birth, the midwife suddenly warned Godwin that his joy was premature. Mary was not yet safe. As Lady Mountcashell was to explain later in her book, probably with Mary Wollstonecraft's case in mind, there was much misunderstanding:

Another great source of evil, is the prejudice common amongst women, that they must be in great danger as long as the after-birth remains in the womb; and, for this reason, the expulsion is seldom left to nature, which in most cases would require no artificial aid to bring away either the child, or its appendages. The common expression, 'is she safe yet?' to demand whether the after-birth has been expelled, clearly shows the vulgar opinion on this subject; i.e. that the woman is in danger of dying while it is retained . . . To one woman it may be natural to expel the after-birth in five minutes, to another in five hours, after the birth of the child; and the premature extraction, even when not attended with danger, is usually followed by severe afterpains and unnecessary loss of blood.[32]

Godwin was later to torture himself with the thought that if he had only been more firm at the beginning and insisted on having a doctor, the tragedy might have been averted. Once the alarm was raised however he set off immediately, probably in a waiting carriage, and within an hour Dr Poignand, described as 'physician and man-midwife' at the Westminster Lying-In Hospital, arrived at Somers Town. The doctor proceeded immediately to surgery, removing the placenta piece by piece, and probably causing severe damage in the process. Infection and fever set in soon afterwards.

Poignand was highly regarded in his profession, being one of only nine physicians of the Royal College of Physicians specially qualified with a licentiate in midwifery. George Fordyce, the Godwins' family doctor and a personal friend who arrived soon afterwards, fully approved of the action that had been taken, and he believed for several days that he saw hopeful signs of recovery. Anthony Carlisle (later Sir Anthony), another personal friend, who had been appointed surgeon at Westminster Hospital at the age of twenty-five fourteen years before, also made regular visits at Godwin's request and during the crisis did not leave the house for several days. Godwin himself when the news first worsened rushed round London calling on friends with medical knowledge, but it was Fordyce who brought in Dr John Clarke whose *Practical Essays on the Management of Pregnancy and Labour and on the Inflammatory and Febrile Diseases of Lying-in Women* published by Johnson in 1793 had established him as the leading authority. It was on his advice – approved also by Carlisle – that Mary was given as much wine as her stomach would tolerate, along with quinine and 'other cordials'.

The risks had been reduced dramatically since the days when Godwin's mother had borne thirteen children. Deaths of mothers admitted to the lying-in hospitals in London fell from 1 in 42 in 1749–59 to 1 in 288 in 1789–98. Mary was given the most modern care available. But there was no cure for infection. Certain religious writers were later to imply that it was not unfitting that Mary Wollstonecraft should die in childbirth, a suitably primitive punishment for one who presumed to challenge the ordained place of women in society.[33] But it was the philosopher who had proclaimed that man would become immortal who was the Promethean figure in the tragedy. If Mary's childbirth had been left to nature, if Godwin had been less concerned, less efficient, less well-connected, or less speedy in fetching the doctors, then she might have lived. But with the heaped ironies which the gods enjoy on such occasions, the more the victims struggled the more certain was their fate. During Mary's dying days Godwin spent anguished hours forcing her to drink the wine, vaguely aware that he was partaking in a superstitious ritual of substituting red wine for her lost red blood. At intervals Mary was made to give suck to the puppies employed to draw off her excess milk. The day before she died there was a disturbance outside the house when the man upstairs threatened to throw his shrieking wife over the balcony into the street.

Important conversations before Mary became too ill to speak were dutifully noted in the journal, 'Idea of death: solemn conversation', 'Talk to her of Fanny and Mary', and then on 10 September the plain words '20 minutes before 8'. Mary was cheerful and courteous to the end.

CHAPTER 14

The Memoirs

Godwin was too distressed to attend the funeral which took place in St Pancras Churchyard on 15 September 1797. Marshall made the arrangements and Mrs Fenwick and Mrs Nicholson looked after the children in turns. A wet nurse was engaged for the infant Mary Wollstonecraft Godwin (who was not expected to survive) and Mrs Reveley's practical help was unfailing. It was not long however before Godwin showed his usual resilience. Putting into practice the advice which he had offered to others, he decided to redirect his thoughts. Life had to go on. Letters had to be written to give the news to Mary's family and friends. Her complex financial affairs had to be settled, and the manuscripts, letters, and other documents which she had left had to be gone through, sorted out, destroyed, returned, or kept.

Grief was mixed with other emotions as the survivors struggled to come to terms with the shock. One of Mary's friends, George Tuthill, who had sat patiently downstairs at The Polygon during the final days ready to be sent on errands, caused unnecessary offence by ostentatiously refusing to attend the religious funeral ceremony, implying that the non-believers who did so were compromising their integrity.[1] Another of Mary's oldest friends, the Reverend John Hewlett, pleaded an alternative engagement perhaps as a result of similar scruples.[2] Mrs Inchbald used the occasion to explain how she had never liked Mary Wollstonecraft and to justify her insulting behaviour at the theatre in April 1797.[3] Mary Hays rushed

The Conversation, from *Blossoms of Morality*

into print with a fulsome obituary of her beloved leader, quoting without permission information she had received in a private letter from Godwin.[4] Before long came further confirmation that marriage is indeed an affair of property, as a succession of creditors approached the widower for settlement of his dead wife's debts.

Godwin moved into Mary's study, hanging Opie's portrait above the fireplace as an inspiration, a comfort, and a challenge. 'I hope to be made wise and more human by the contemplation of the memory of a beloved object,' he wrote nine days after her death. 'I find a pleasure, difficult to be described, in the cultivation of melancholy. It weakens indeed my stoicism in the ordinary awareness of life, but it refines and raises my sensibility.'[5] Without hesitation he decided to adopt the three-year-old Fanny, Mary's daughter by Imlay, and bring her up as his own. She was taught to call herself Fanny Godwin and Godwin waited until she was nearly twelve before telling her that he was not her natural father.[6] A friend of his sister, Louisa Jones, agreed to be housekeeper and foster mother, and came to live in The Polygon. Baby Mary grew to love her, but never Fanny.[7]

Within a week of the funeral Godwin was again hard at work. He never expected to be happy again, he told his friends; Mary had been the most remarkable woman of her time, perhaps in the whole history of the world.[8] It was his duty to prepare for publication the works which she had left unfinished at her death, and to write a memoir of her life. Johnson agreed to pay off Mary's creditors in return for the copyright and within days Godwin was deep in his research.

Convinced that all human beings are the product of the impressions they have received, he had always been interested in learning about Mary's earlier life and on one occasion he had compiled a note of the principal dates and events, which survives among his papers.[9] As in everything, he wanted to know the complete truth. He reread her printed works; he talked to her friends and wrote to others;[10] and he studied his journal for the times they had been together. With the scrupulousness of an archivist, he dated and numbered the 160 letters which he had exchanged with her, establishing a detailed record of how they fell in love.

Within four months the two books were ready, *Posthumous Works of the Author of a Vindication of the Rights of Woman* and *Memoirs of the Author of a Vindication of the Rights of Woman*. So famous had Mary Wollstonecraft become in the seven years since the publication of her book that it was unnecessary to mention her name. On the plain square tombstone which was erected over her grave in St Pancras Churchyard she was proudly commemorated in the modern fashion as Mary Wollstonecraft Godwin.

The *Posthumous Works*, which are in four volumes, consist of the incomplete *Wrongs of Woman*, some notes for the second part of *The Rights of Woman* which was never written, an incomplete tale called *The Cave of Fancy*, and various practical hints relating to the upbringing of children which were also sold separately for sixpence. In addition to these writings which had always been intended for publication, Godwin filled most of two volumes with transcripts of Mary's letters to Gilbert Imlay, boldly proclaimed in the Preface to contain 'the finest examples of the language of sentiment and passion ever presented to the world', superior to those in Goethe's *Sorrows of Young Werther*, and 'the offspring of a glowing imagination and a heart penetrated with the passion it essays to describe'. The letters covered Mary's first meetings with Imlay, their love affair, the birth of Fanny, Mary's threatened suicides, and the long painful breakdown of their relationship.[11]

The grieving widower printed his dead wife's letters to her former lover without a suspicion of jealousy. Finding no difficulty in applying the impartiality which he regularly urged on others, it never occurred to him that his revelations might strike others as disrespectful. To the philosopher of man looking into his own nature with the detachment of a professional, Mary's letters were documents of inestimable value, revealing psychological truths to which he had himself been blind for forty years, and which it was now his duty to bring to the world's attention.

And certainly, if the literary *Letters from Sweden* had made strong men fall in love with her from afar, the real-life letters which Mary Wollstonecraft wrote in France confirmed again that there is no contradiction between reason and passion, between femininity and intelligence. As Mary had herself teasingly explained to Imlay in a typical letter:

With ninety nine men out of a hundred, a very sufficient dash of folly is necessary to render a woman *piquante*, a soft word for desirable; and, beyond these casual ebullitions of sympathy, few look for enjoyment by fostering a passion in their hearts. One reason, in short, why I wish my whole sex to become wiser, is, that the foolish ones may not, by their pretty folly, rob those whose sensibility keeps down their vanity, of the few roses that afford them some solace in the thorny road of life.[12]

The charm of the letters has won as many converts to the cause of women as the indignation of the *Rights* and the gloom of the *Wrongs*. Godwin edited his book carefully, and there are plentiful dashes where he omitted passages which he considered unsuitable for publication, but he made few concessions to conventional reticence. He did not conceal or apologize for the sexual aspects of Mary's love, and he explained in a scholarly footnote that Fanny was called the 'barrier child' because she had been conceived at the toll gate barrier between Paris and Neuilly. The lovers had arranged uncomfortable assignations there during the time when Imlay was forbidden to leave the city limits.

In the same month, as a companion volume, Godwin published the brief biography which he entitled *Memoirs of the Author of a Vindication of the Rights of Woman*, an even more frank account. As he wrote in the Preface:

I cannot easily prevail on myself to doubt, that the more fully we are presented with the picture and story of such persons as the subject of the following narrative, the more generally shall we feel in ourselves an attachment to their fate and a sympathy in their excellencies. There are not many individuals with whose character the public welfare and improvement are more intimately connected than the author of a Vindication of the Rights of Woman.

Boldly reversing the conventions of contemporary biography – which normally sought to demonstrate how admirable qualities lead to admirable achievements, the book is a vindication of Mary Wollstonecraft, a vindication of the principles of the *Vindication*, and an open celebration of characteristics which writers on women usually mentioned only to deplore.

Godwin omitted nothing which seemed relevant to an understanding. He commented by name on living people who had been closely connected with her during her lifetime (and who, in some cases, now preferred to forget). Unconscious of taboo, he told of her father's violence,[13] he described her love for Fuseli and for Imlay, the birth of Fanny, her suicide attempts, and the gynaecological details of the circumstances of her death. At the end, instead of the conventional scene of resurgent Christianity, Godwin noted that her religion was 'not calculated to be a torment of a sick bed' and that no word of religion was spoken during her final illness.

Many people knew that Mary had been in love with Henry Fuseli, and that her decision to go to France had been prompted by disappointment. Having accepted without question the Enlightenment presumption that passion can be controlled by reason, she was surprised to find herself unable to keep her feelings under control. Simple physical sexual frustration was not only causing her intense discomfort but interfering with her rational judgement and behaviour. On her return to England, as Godwin discovered when he looked over her papers, she had asked for the return of her letters, but Fuseli kept them.[14] When Godwin asked to see them after her death, the artist is said to have opened a drawer to give him a glimpse, and then, with his cruel humour, shut it sharply.

Godwin's trust matched that of his dead wife. Johnson tried to warn him against being too explicit, suggesting a number of changes when the book was in proof, but Godwin was not prepared to yield to another's judgement in a matter where he believed he had made a new insight.

With respect to Mr Fuseli, I am sincerely sorry not to have pleased you ... As to his cynical cast, his impatience of contradiction, and his propensity to satire, I have carefully observed them, and I protest in the sincerity of my judgement that the resemblance between Mary's traits of this kind to his was so great as clearly to demonstrate that the one was copied from the other.[15]

In the *Memoirs* he described sadly and tenderly the ambiguous feelings which followed the 'explication' with himself of 13 August 1796.

Mary rested her head upon the shoulder of her lover, hoping to find a heart with which she might safely treasure her world of affection; fearing to commit a mistake, yet, in spite of her melancholy experience, fraught with that generous confidence, which, in a great soul, is never extinguished. I had never loved till now; or at least, had never nourished a passion to the same growth or met with an object so consummately worthy.

It is typical of his scrupulous honesty that he should have remembered his earlier passion for Maria Reveley as he wrote these words and carefully qualified the literary exaggeration to which his pen was leading him. It is also typical that he should slip into sexual metaphors in the passage which follows without apparently realizing the full significance of his words:

We did not marry. It is difficult to recommend any thing to indiscriminate adoption, contrary to the established rules and prejudices of mankind; but certainly nothing can be so ridiculous upon the face of it, or so contrary to the genuine march of sentiment, as to require the overflowing of the soul to wait upon a ceremony, and that at which, wherever delicacy and imagination exist, is of all things most sacredly private, to blow a trumpet before it, and to record the moment when it has arrived at its climax.[16]

The *Memoirs of the Author of a Vindication of the Rights of Woman* marks an important step in the development of the art of biography. Published just before the turn of the century, it has more in common with the poets and novelists of the future than with the moral philosophers and classifiers of the past. For Mary Wollstonecraft sentiment had neither reinforced reason nor militated against it. In the *Memoirs* the long tradition of rationalism from Locke and Hartley through Hume and the French *philosophes* to its culmination in *Political Justice* is implicitly acknowledged to have rested on an incomplete understanding.

As it happened, a better model was ready to hand. If it was Mary Wollstonecraft who brought the fire of love to Godwin's heart, it was her Prometheus of sentiment who enabled him to capture the experience in literary terms. In December 1789 while still writing for the *New Annual Register* Godwin had contracted to translate the second volume of Rousseau's *Confessions*, and although he never did the work – or transferred the contract to Elizabeth Inchbald – he read the book when Robinson published it in 1790. With Mary's encouragement he was to read much more Rousseau and his papers include notes on the *Confessions*. Godwin's memoir, consciously or unconsciously, is written in the confessional mode. It seeks to tell all and explain all in a spirit of discovery. The author's love and admiration are seldom far below the surface. Readers who do not readily sympathize with the assumptions behind *Political Justice* or *Caleb Williams* are often delightfully surprised at its refreshing modernity. It is the most readable book that Godwin ever wrote.

But it is the mark of pioneers to be misunderstood and their reward to be feared. The *Memoirs* shocked Godwin's contemporaries more than any of his other writings. Protected by the isolation that surrounds the bereaved, he could not see that his sense of high moral purpose would not be obvious to others. Through a study of her papers he had contrived to prolong his life with Mary Wollstonecraft for a few months, and he rashly assumed that others would share his wonderment. Mary's sisters, Everina, who was unmarried, and Eliza Bishop, who had been induced by Mary to leave her husband, were horrified. They had been against Godwin's writing the book and their worst fears were underestimated.[17] Neither had fully shared their sister's views nor could they afford to. Having attempted with only mixed success to earn their living as governesses or school teachers, the *Memoirs* was a direct assault on their livelihood, and when parents withdrew their children from the Wollstonecraft contamination, it was small consolation that the theme of the newly published *Wrongs of Woman* was the unfair penalty that society extracts from the innocent associates of reformers. Everina considered emigrating to the United States and Eliza brought up her sons to dread the name of their infamous aunt.

The same reviews that had helped to promulgate the spirit of 1793 now reflected and reinforced the changed national mood. With scarcely an exception they were hostile, contemptuous, and bursting with shock and outrage. 'Shameless' was the most charitable description; 'lascivious' and 'disgusting' were more common. Godwin, it was frequently noted, had flaunted his dead wife's immorality. His careful, loving, and sympathetic passages of descriptions were coarsely summarized in the uncompromising language of sneer, innuendo, and moral indignation.[18] Even Godwin's former friends on the *New Annual Register* felt obliged to condemn.

The index to the recently established *Anti-Jacobin Review*, whose circulation of 3,500 already made it one of the most influential periodicals, summarizes a long article that was only slightly more extreme than those of its longer-established competitors.

Godwin edits the Posthumous Works of his wife, 91 – inculcates the promiscuous intercourse of the sexes, ib. – reprobates marriage, 93 – considers Mary Godwin as a model for female imitation, 94 – certifies his wife's constitution to have been amorous, 96 – memoirs of her, ib. – account of his wife's adventures as a kept mistress, 97 – celebrates her happiness while the concubine of Imlay, ib. – informs the public that she was concubine to himself before she was his wife, 98 – . . . her passions inflamed by celibacy, 96 – falls in love with a married man, ib. – on the breaking out of the war betakes herself to our enemies, ib. – intimate with the French leaders under Robespierre, 97 – with Thomas Paine, ib. – taken by Imlay into keeping, ib. – her husband declares that her soul had panted for that connection . . . [19]

At the end of the entry for 'Mary Wollstonecraft' the reader is cross-referred to 'Prostitution', but the single entry under that heading is '*see* Mary Wollstonecraft'. A wife who was a prostitute was not to be preferred to Fénelon in the hypothetical fire at Cambrai, the first edition of *Political Justice* had recommended, but should be left to burn by a just husband while he gave priority to the educator.

A second 'corrected' edition of the *Memoirs*, which altered the passages that attracted most criticism, was hurriedly prepared and put on sale in the summer of 1798, but the more that Godwin protested, with his tortuous double negatives, that 'a sound morality requires that nothing human should be regarded by us with indifference', the easier it was to accuse him of commercializing his dead wife's sordid reputation.[20] Like Lord Byron in 1816, Godwin suddenly found himself the astonished victim of one of the British public's ridiculous fits of morality.

A flood of books reaffirmed the former conventions.*[21] 'Wives, submit

* See Appendix 2.

yourselves in all things unto your husbands as unto the Lord,' advised the author of *An Enquiry into the Duties of the Female Sex*, skilfully combining old-fashioned religious authoritarianism with the apparent philosophical modernity of a volume calling itself an inquiry. Hannah More's *Strictures on Female Education* cautioned women against any 'impious discontent with the post to which God has assigned them in this world'. The aptly named *Ladies' Monitor* redirected its ladies back to religion, clothes, cookery and other traditional outlets for feminine excellence. Part-time employment was permissible, a moderate suggested in an attempt to hold the middle ground – toy shops and perfume shops were recommended. One writer suggested a tax on women who wore bare arms in public.[22] A distraught mother writing in the agony column of the *Ladies Monthly Museum*, complained that her four daughters had all been corrupted by reading the *Vindication* – one had taken up horse racing, fox hunting, and betting; another had her head in Greek and Latin books; a third dissected her pet animals in the cause of science; and the fourth was so determined to be like the men that she was challenging them to duels. It was not long before an evangelist lady was declaring that Eve was the Original Sinner, the serpent having correctly perceived her intrinsic inferiority to Adam.

The Reverend Richard Polwhele, concerned to demonstrate that Mary Wollstonecraft had advocated something he called priapism, helped spread the story that she encouraged children to 'speak of the organs of generation as freely as we mention our eyes or our hands' although this unguarded example of her dislike of false delicacy occurs in one of her earliest and least read works.[23] In her own life, it was suggested elsewhere, Mary Wollstonecraft had enjoyed an improper relationship with Lord Kingsborough when she was a governess in Ireland, and had actively encouraged one of her girl pupils to seduce her cousin. The stereotype of the importunate male whom Mary Wollstonecraft had described from personal experience in Lisbon, was now matched by that of the insatiable virago.

It became fashionable to ridicule the theories of Godwin and Wollstonecraft in the same story. Isaac d'Israeli's anonymous *Vaurien or Sketches of the Times*, which appeared during 1797 while Mary was still alive, shows signs of incorporating genuine gossip. Mr Subtile is 'the coldest blooded metaphysician of the age' who after spending ten years in a garret learned to reason but forgot to feel. Miss Million, a modern lady, defends sex outside marriage provided that it is a result of genuine emotion, declaring that 'the conjugal couch we consider polluted when two congenial spirits meet – but meet too late'.[24]

Several novels, drawing on the revelations of the *Memoirs*, concern the fate of ladies seduced after reading *A Vindication of the Rights of Woman*.[25] In George Walker's *The Vagabond*, the hero stands before a burning house in which the girl he has made pregnant is trapped along with her father, but both are burned to death before he can calculate the comparative utility of his options.[26] If Alexander the Great had not burned down the Palace of Persepolis, Mr Myope declares at tea time in Elizabeth Hamilton's *Memoirs of Modern Philosophers*, the tarts they are eating would not taste so sweet. The reading of the modern lady, Bridgetina Botherim, is confined to metaphysics (for her intellect) and to novels (for her passions). When someone breaks an arm, he is recommended to try the energy of mind to make it better, and anyone who says thank you is reminded that nothing is so immoral as gratitude. Mr Myope repeats Godwin's famous remark on the higher obligation to impartiality, 'What magic is there in the word *my* to overturn the decision of everlasting truth?'[27] But in the frightened and outraged mood of the time, humour was rare. The anti-Jacobin writings of the late 1790s and 1800s are as serious in tone as the Jacobin novels whose influence they sought to counter.[28]

More interesting is *Adeline Mowbray* which Amelia Alderson published under her married name of Amelia Opie in 1805, for it contains authentic details about Godwin and Wollstonecraft picked up from the days when the author had (nearly) shared their views. Frederic Glenmurray is a famous author who engages the affections of the innocent Adeline, and 'by a train of reasoning, captivating though sophistical, and plausible though absurd, made her a delighted convert to his opinions, and prepared her young and impassioned heart for the practice of vice'. Glenmurray wants to marry Adeline but she plays back the arguments in his book about odious monopoly and insists on living with him unfettered. He tries gallantry and a version of the real-life incident of the slipper is included, but to no avail. The result is a cold-shouldering such as Mary Wollstonecraft had experienced, followed by a series of disasters which mirror those described in *The Wrongs of Woman*. Mrs Opie's intention was to warn against the New Philosophy, but her limping attempt to celebrate conventional marriage makes freedom seem so much more attractive that a disconcerted critic in the 1980s has concluded that *Adeline Mowbray* must be an ironic bluff.[29]

Perhaps the most influential of all the anti-Jacobin writings was *The*

Progress of the Pilgrim Good-Intent in Jacobinical Times first published in 1799 and still being reprinted in 1814.[30] Written by a lady, it earnestly updates the famous story by John Bunyan which had been accorded near-biblical status by generations of dissenters. The house where Mr Christian once lived has now been taken over by such interlopers as Mr Hate-Controul, Mr False-Reasoning, and Mr Credulity. Other people to be avoided are Mr Philosophy, one of whose pupils is looking for the elixir of immortality; Mr Mental-Energy, who strikes out so many sparks that he causes a loss of the critical faculties; and Mrs Sensibility who, when not lying idly on a sofa is unshackling her free nature and throwing herself at men.

The battle of the books reflected the battles of life and the result was the same. The cause of women's equality like the cause of reform was decisively lost, and Godwin's simple honest memoir contributed heavily to the defeat. Women had been unusually prominent in the French Revolution, and if violent revolution was the consequence of earlier well-meaning political concessions, Mary Wollstonecraft's life was an equally frightening warning against easing any of the constraints of virginity and of marriage. For years after 1798 there was scarcely an unwanted pregnancy anywhere in England for which Mary Wollstonecraft did not take a share of the blame.

CHAPTER 15

The Jacobin Monster

Gradually Godwin's life settled back into a previous pattern. Louisa Jones the housekeeper looked after Fanny and baby Mary for most of the day while Godwin pursued his studies. After an hour with a major author before breakfast, he would devote the rest of the morning to uninterrupted writing and reading. In the afternoons he called on friends or received them for tea and spent time with the children. Dinner was at four or five o'clock and the evening was spent in conversation and more reading. Most weeks he went to the theatre on at least one evening.

Every second Sunday he dined with Holcroft and a few of his cronies of the older generation, Nicholson, Barry, Ritson, or Porson, as he had done – previously it had been every week – for more than ten years. In the intervening Sunday his sister Hannah would often dine at The Polygon along with James Marshall, and other family friends. Marshall, a married man, was suspected of taking too close an interest both in Miss Godwin and in Louisa Jones who in her turn was believed to be setting her cap at her employer, but Godwin despising false delicacy was either oblivious or tolerant.

Nearly every week he went to dinner at Joseph Johnson's in St Paul's Churchyard where Fuseli and Bonnycastle were invariably also among the guests. When in February 1798 Johnson was sentenced to six months' imprisonment for publishing a seditious pamphlet, the dinners continued for the duration at their new venue in Newgate Prison, where Johnson

The Bad Family, from *Lessons for Children*

was able – according to the prison rules of the day – to hire comfortable rooms. These dinners were to become one of the fixed points of his life for ten years, but he and Fuseli were never friends. Fuseli never made a secret of his view that Godwin's powers had been overrated and that he was not the genius that admirers believed, while Godwin in his turn regarded Fuseli as 'the most frankly ingenuous and conceited man' he ever knew, who could not bear to be eclipsed by true brilliance such as his own.[1] Bound by their shared memories of the woman they had both loved, the philosopher of reason and the painter of dreams were as irreconcilable and as inseparable as Falkland and Caleb Williams.

Occasionally he would take the long walk to Edgware to visit Joseph Fawcett, still practising as a dissenting minister, with whom he had first read the *Système de la Nature* in 1778. Fawcett was now in poor health, said to have been brought about by disappointment at the course of the French Revolution, and although we may be sceptical of relating his personal difficulties too directly to public events, those whose hopes had been highest now had the furthest to fall. Fawcett, who appears to have suffered a nervous breakdown, died not long afterwards. Occasionally too Godwin and Holcroft would dine at Horne Tooke's where a small band of radical politicians defiantly awaited a change in their fortunes.

Holcroft was in constant pain as a result of a severe illness. Often referred to as a traitor who had unfairly escaped the gallows in 1794, he found it difficult to continue his career in the theatre, and the other enterprises to which he turned his hand – such as dealing in old paintings and trying to commercialize a polygraphic writing machine – were financially unsuccessful. In 1799, to Godwin's sorrow, his old friend decided to leave England in hopes of finding better luck in Germany. It was Holcroft who had suggested some of the most optimistic sections in *Political Justice*, including the theory (removed in the second edition) that perfectibility would eventually lead to immortality. Doubting friends had teased him that the progress of mind would not have prevented the public executioner from breaking his neck if the verdict had gone the other way in 1794, nor stopped him from being crushed to death if he were struck by a falling tree. They were mistaken, the perfectibilian would reply. Men will come to see the moral error of judicial homicide and will gradually become more skilful at anticipating accidents. Recommended after his illness to bathe his feet in hot water mixed with sulphuric acid, he was holding the acid bottle over the bath when the steam caused it to shatter. His face was horribly scarred, his wrists were burned to the bone, and it was two days before he learned that his eyes had survived, saved by the spectacles which in earlier days had caused jeering in the streets. Holcroft's calm acceptance of his heaped misfortunes as he slipped back towards poverty earned widespread admiration, and it was evident that energy and courage had indeed prolonged his life.

Godwin's own health seemed robust enough. But the philosopher who had vauntingly proclaimed that Mind would soon conquer Sleep – before confronting his more formidable brother Death – was also to be mocked by the insulted gods. Frequently he found himself falling fast asleep at unexpected moments, usually shortly after a meal. Whatever the company, he invariably lost consciousness during Joseph Johnson's Monday dinners, sometimes for only a fraction of a minute but occasionally for as long as an hour. 'William Godwin sleeps in St Paul's Churchyard,' his friends teased, but they were unfair to attribute his impoliteness to arrogance or to boredom. The sleeping, as can now be recognized, was an early manifestation of a disturbance to the brain mechanism known as narco-lepsy whose victims are attacked by a craving which is compulsive and irresistible.[2]

Although by itself the sleeping was an inconvenience rather than an illness, it was connected with the slow development of a more serious condition which was to grow more insistent over the years. In cataplexy the sudden onset of sleep is like a fit. The victim loses all control of his muscles, his jaw drops, and his legs crumble. If he is standing near a fire, the results can be disastrous even if he is not directly hurt by the force of the fall. The first fit struck on 6 February 1800, a month before his forty-fourth birthday: it lasted a full minute. He was struck again on 25 July and again on the 28th, after which he was unable to sleep for forty-eight hours. Thereafter the fits occurred irregularly every few months. Fortunately Godwin, like other sufferers, usually had some notice of imminent attacks and was sometimes able to lie down before the attack came.

From the notes in his journal, he was later able to give Sir Anthony Carlisle and his other medical advisers a detailed history of his illness – a succession of fits over a period of weeks when he was twenty-seven, occasional asthma, perfect recovery without recurrence until an attack of vertigo in 1792, the start of the uncontrollable sleeping bouts in 1795, and the onset of the fits in 1800. Like Holcroft, Godwin had only one answer to his problem, the power of mind over matter. If the medullary particles were disarranged the remedy was to redirect them by thought into their proper equilibrium. The advice which in earlier years he had offered to Montagu, Wedgwood, and innumerable other young men and women with psychological problems had now to be applied to his own case.

In the years after 1797 he was given plentiful opportunities for practice. At the moment of his deepest grief Godwin found himself one of the most hated men in the country, deserted by friends, and spat at in the streets. The spirit of 1793 had now been superseded by something entirely different. By 1797 French armies were victorious all over Europe, and one by one Britain's allies either capitulated or made peace. The British exchequer was in huge deficit and was at risk, like the hated French, of repudiating its debt. A mutiny in the Navy at Spithead was only ended when the mutineers' demands were conceded, and in the other fleet at the Nore the red flag of the Floating Republic flew for several weeks. A story that armed marines were marching towards London turned out to be exaggerated but it was reasonable to fear that the rank and file of the British forces might choose this moment to throw off their fetters.

In many European countries the French had been welcomed in by a sizeable proportion of the population. Even after the experience of Jacobin rule in France, the ideals of liberty, equality, and fraternity retained their power to inspire, and many nations did not reverse the French changes after the French armies had left. Was Britain, it was again being asked, destined to be the next nation to be revolutionized, republicanized and secularized, its laws modernized, its taxation more evenly spread, its priests deprivileged, and its hereditary landowners treated more equally with other citizens? Napoleon Bonaparte himself believed that the moment a French army landed in Britain, the people would rise up against the hereditary oligarchy.

Ever since Burke's warnings the British conservatives had been gathering their strength. In 1798, with panic in the air, they were able to press their counterattack to a victory so complete and so decisive that it became dangerous to raise even the faintest protest. The Two Acts of 1796 gave plentiful powers to suppress virtually all political activity outside Parliament, but if the French Revolution had been caused by ideas, then those ideas themselves had to be rolled back. The *Anti-Jacobin Review*, founded in July 1798 with the help of a secret government subsidy, announced as its aim to expose and destroy the Jacobin conspiracy which it saw at work in the country. A separate publication, the *Anti-Jacobin*, commented on the daily political news from abroad. Not long after came the *Anti-Gallican*, which aimed at promoting national unity against the French enemy by giving currency to French atrocities and British heroism.

The anti-Jacobin reaction was content to be negative. Its leaders, including the Government, were more clear about what they were against than about what they were for. It was hard, as Burke himself had found, to mount a positive defence of the system of social and economic privilege which even its admirers called the Old Corruption, but they were determined to preserve it down to the last rotten charter. Innumerable sermons, pamphlets, histories, poems, novels, and cartoons offered their support and, with the nation in danger, they caught and encouraged a new national mood.

Godwin's friends were surprised that it was five years after the first publication of *Political Justice* before replies began to appear. Writing in 1800, John Fenwick attributed the silence to the persuasive power of his friend's arguments.[3] The fundamental axiom of *Political Justice*, that virtue consists in producing the happiness of society, was, he suggested, difficult to confront face on. Yet the anti-Jacobins knew in their hearts that it struck at the roots of everything they wished to preserve.

By offering a purely human aim for human life, the New Philosophy broke the link between religion and ethics. By removing the social purpose of God, Godwin not only brought into question the monopolistic privileges of the churches, but struck at the apex of the whole existing moral economy. A man brought up as Godwin himself had been needed no reminding that one of the chief duties of God is to punish. It was a point on which virtually all eighteenth-century Christians agreed whether established or dissenting. Even at Hoxton, the home of sincerity, Dr Rees had explained to Godwin that – whatever the truth of the matter or whatever was said in Scripture – he was duty-bound to maintain the credibility of hell as a deterrent to earthly crime. To abolish religion was to weaken the police.

Equally worrying to anti-Jacobins was the modern notion that human nature is benevolent and only needs to be freed from its institutional environment for the benevolence to shine through. That too struck at the roots of the existing political and social order. What was the blood lust of the French revolutionaries but a throwing off of the fetters that previously kept nature in check? Was not the sex lust of women like Mary Wollstonecraft due to the same error? In 1800 a bill was introduced to strengthen the financial penalties for adultery, eternal damnation having recently proved an inadequate deterrent, as one bishop pointed out.[4]

The notion that honour is a reward for virtue was equally frightening. If that idea were ever to gain currency, what future for a hereditary system of government? As the news of every French victory confirmed, opening careers to the talents was not only more just but more efficient. Anti-

Jacobins clung to the view that honour is a personal heritable property which they were entitled to defend with violence just as they defended their rabbits and their pheasants. More duels were fought in anti-Jacobin England than for many years past.

The New Philosophy suggestion that there was a connection between disturbances in the moral economy – envy, greed, competition and crime – and disparities in the economic economy was personally threatening. Burke had defended a hereditary wealth-owning class as an essential curb on human passions. With a logic which did not flatter, he argued that the privileges of aristocrats needed to be constantly reinforced by positive discrimination to prevent them becoming more 'sluggish, inert, and timid' and to keep out newcomers of superior ability. St Augustine had argued that private property had been instituted by God as an act of revenge for sin, although his corollary that wealth in the right hands provided a partial relief for the results of that sin was given more attention. For those who preferred a more modern validation, there was Adam Smith's invisible hand which allegedly ensured that a cumulation of individual acts of selfishness was ultimately beneficial to society as a whole.

One by one the fundamental propositions of the New Philosophy – 'discoveries' as admirers called them – were turned on their heads. The *Anti-Jacobin Review* adopted as its motto the 'power of truth' and in the cartoon prepared for its first number showed concentrated truth extirpating error with a beam of light. It was an image that Godwin and others had used to explain the concentrated power of mind. 'Enlightened' became a term of contempt carefully printed in italics in issue after issue to ensure that readers could not mistake the sarcasm. The anti-Jacobin opposite of perfectibility was not deterioration but 'institutions', and this false antithesis was batted to and fro in innumerable slogans. When in 1794 Robinson rushed out a two-volume history of recent events in France, it was natural that he should call it *An Impartial History of the French Revolution*. Anti-Jacobins however had no hesitation in ostentatiously glorying in their 'partiality' for Christianity, monarchy, and strong institutions.

If there was one word that summed up everything the anti-Jacobins feared, it was 'philosophy'. And if there was one philosopher who exemplified all the hated ideas in his books and in his life, it was the author of *Political Justice*, and of the *Memoirs of the Author of a Vindication of the Rights of Woman*. Godwin was the best-known philosopher in England. From the *Life of Chatham* in 1783, he had applied the word freely both to himself as an author and to the readers whom he hoped to convince. In the *New Annual Register* the chronicler had offered himself as the philosophic eye observing the world with impartiality. In *Political Justice* the philosophical enquirer endeavoured to further the work of his French and English predecessors who had written on the philosophy of man. Even in *Caleb Williams* the Preface proclaimed the author's aspiration to diffuse the discoveries of moral philosophy to a wider audience. It was a proud title, and if Godwin was frequently teased for over-using it, there was no alternative. The search for a general theory of man and the universe embraced all lesser branches of knowledge, and the more that was discovered in science, history, political theory, and psychology, the more imperative was the need for a unifying discipline.

Burke had dismissed as 'petulant, assuming, short-sighted coxcombs of philosophy' the men who dared to suggest a reform of the English political system and the anti-Jacobins soon dropped the qualification. In 1792 in an official *démarche* to the Government of the Netherlands the British Ambassador referred to the French Revolutionary Government as 'some wretches assuming the title of philosophers . . . with a dream of vanity'.[5] The organized mobs who burned down Priestley's library are said to have shouted 'No philosophers.' William Playfair's *History of Jacobinism* carried a secondary title *An Inquiry into the Manner of Disseminating, Under the Appearance of Philosophy and Virtue, Principles which are equally subversive of Order, Virtue, Religion, Liberty, and Happiness*, a formulation which would have reminded many readers of that earlier philosophical *Enquiry* which on its title page attributed General Virtue and Happiness to Political Justice. Professor Robison's huge *Proofs of a Conspiracy* purported to demonstrate that the international Jacobin conspiracy operated in England through philosophical subscription libraries and literary societies.[6]

For a time an attempt was made to distinguish reputable philosophy from the pernicious new variety, and philosophists and philosophisters made a brief appearance in the language peddling their philosophisms. But the new words made little headway against their more pronounceable predecessors, and all discrimination was soon abandoned. A word seldom uttered without a sneer of contempt or a snort of defiance, 'Philosophy' meant William Godwin and Mary Wollstonecraft, atheism, treason, economic redistribution, and sexual immorality.

The main weapons of the anti-Jacobins were fear and ridicule. Only in the sermons of a few clergymen can genuine heartfelt hatred be found. The anti-Jacobins had a near monopoly of propaganda, enforced by the sedition laws, and there was no need for other methods. But just as the French Jacobins had resorted to the guillotine when propaganda failed, everyone knew that the British Government had plentiful legal instruments for breaking necks if this should prove necessary. If a French invasion had ever seemed a real prospect, the lives of Godwin, Holcroft, Horne Tooke, and many others would have again been at risk. Meanwhile they were themselves presented as favouring assassination and violent revolution. Godwin was parodied in the *Anti-Jacobin Review* as 'Mr Higgins of St Mary Axe', a reference to his eagerness to introduce the guillotine to England.

But the event which turned anti-Jacobin fears into serious crisis was the outbreak of the rebellion in Ireland in 1798. The British Government knew through their intelligence agents that the United Irishmen were in close touch with the French and had been asked to penetrate the British radical movement as a condition of armed support. Mary Wollstonecraft, whose mother was Irish, had been friendly with Hamilton Rowan in Paris, and before the rebellion Godwin had met many of the Irish nationalists at Horne Tooke's and elsewhere. His journal contains a number of references to his meeting 'Morris', the pseudonym adopted by Arthur O'Connor, the most prominent of the Irish rebels.[7] If the immediate prospect of being hanged concentrates the mind, Godwin himself was never under that stimulus. But he had regularly dined with the men who had not been hanged in 1794, Holcroft, Horne Tooke, Hardy, Thelwall, Joyce, Bonney, and sat at the same table with Despard and Emmet and others who were hanged in 1803.

By the turn of the century the men and women who had dominated the intellectual scene in the early years of the decade were widely perceived and portrayed as a conspiracy of disloyal dissenters of the type who had killed King Charles, international atheists and liberals who admired every country but their own, fast-talking theorists intent on tearing down every social institution, agitators who made the poor discontented, sexually loose media people, ambitious fifth columnists awaiting their opportunity, and Irish rebels subsidized by the country's external enemies. William Godwin qualified under six of the seven categories.

He was at first genuinely surprised at the virulence of the abuse. He knew that as far as he personally was concerned, the attacks were unfair. He had suddenly become – to use a contemporary metaphor which was becoming as common as mental chains and Aeolian harps – like the gigantic upas tree of the East Indies which was said to poison every living creature that came under its shadow.[8] It was not the least of the ironies that some of the fiercest attacks should concentrate on a point on which he had already altered his position.

W. C. Proby's *Modern Philosophy and Barbarism, or a Comparison between the Theory of Godwin and the Practice of Lycurgus* pointed out in 1798 that Godwin's theory, by denying weight to natural affections, would be little different from the system of ancient Sparta whereby children were brought up with no commitment except to the state. Thomas Green's *Examination of the Leading Principle of the New System of Morals as that Principle is Stated and Applied in Mr Godwin's Enquiry* also attacked the question that Godwin had argued interminably with Parr, Fawcett, Dyson, Holcroft, and the others: how to reconcile political justice (which imposes a duty to maximize utility irrespective of recipient) with the normal human wish to give some preference to nearest and dearest. The story of Fénelon and the chambermaid had survived into the third edition of *Political Justice* where, although much altered, it continued, as present-day philosophers say, to be counter-intuitive, affronting common sense and common feelings. The duty to be impartial in the interests of the general good now had an uncomfortable resemblance to the arguments used by Robespierre to justify state terror.

In fact Godwin's view had already changed before the rebuttals started to appear. Although published in early 1798, the revision of the third edition of *Political Justice* had been completed in the early part of 1797 before Mary Wollstonecraft had worked her magic. The Preface is dated July 1797. Anyone reading the *Memoirs* would have seen that Godwin's whole outlook had altered, but few thought of taking that sympathetic little book as a corrigendum to the main theory.

Many of the attacks were scarcely worthy of a reply. Whatever their titles they were not genuine 'inquiries' but propaganda for things-as-they-are. In June 1798 however, before the reaction reached its height, Johnson published an anonymous and modest book in a small edition which was a serious attempt to address the ideas of the New Philosophy. *An Essay on the Principle of Population as it affects the Future Improvement of Society, with remarks on the speculations of Mr Godwin, M. Condorcet and other writers*, was written by Thomas Robert Malthus, a man ten years younger than Godwin. This was his first book. Born into a household whose respect for philosophers was unlimited, Malthus had been admired as a baby both by David Hume and by Jean-Jacques Rousseau who had been brought together by his father in 1766. But whereas Godwin moved from religion to enlightenment, Malthus passed him in the other direction. He became a clergyman of the Church of England and devoted his life to denying the beliefs of his upbringing.

His book begins with an eloquent passage which might have come from

Political Justice itself. Man, Malthus declares, stands at a critical juncture. The great question of the hour is whether he will progress with accelerated velocity towards improvement or be condemned instead to the perpetual cycles of misery which have marked previous history. Unfortunately, Malthus notes, the thinkers who should be examining the evidence impartially have shown little but contempt for their intellectual opponents and in such a contest the chief sufferer is the cause of truth.

The *Essay on Population* is for the most part written in the admirable spirit which the author commends. The plentiful references to Godwin – several chapters are devoted almost exclusively to his theories – are respectful and fair. He wishes he could find grounds for accepting more, but a theory of man should rest on more solid empirical foundations. His biggest difficulty, he explains, is that the historical evidence for moral perfectibility is not convincing. A writer may say that man will ultimately become an ostrich, but before he can expect any reasonable person to believe him, he should be able to show that human necks are growing longer, lips are becoming harder, shapes are changing, and that hair is turning into feathers.

Malthus then develops his own theory which has fascinated and terrified the world ever since. Like Godwin, he begins with axioms, and he chooses two apparently uncontentious propositions:

First, that food is necessary to the existence of man. Secondly, that the passion between the sexes is necessary and will remain nearly in its present state.

These two principles, says the mathematician, cannot be reconciled. The supply of food can be increased, at best, only in an arithmetic progression: 1, 2, 3, 4, 5, 6, etc. Population however, if unchecked, expands in a geometric progression: 1, 2, 4, 8, 16, 32, 64, etc. In China and India, a teeming population scraped a bare subsistence, with every corner of productive land under intensive cultivation. In the only case known to history where land and food resources were once unlimited, the settlement of North America, the population had doubled every twenty-five years. Normally, Malthus concludes lugubriously, equilibrium is only restored by famine, disease, and war, which periodically reduce the population to a level commensurate with the food supply.

Godwin, who read the *Essay* as soon as it was published, was introduced to Malthus shortly afterwards at a dinner at Johnson's on 14 August 1798, and they met on several other occasions at this time. It was the beginning of an argument which was to run for many years. The shortage of resources, Godwin suggested at once, was not an absolute shortage. If property were more equally divided and if everyone worked a fair day's labour, there would be enough for everyone to live on at a moderate but comfortable level. Malthus, in his reply, while conceding that redistribution could increase output, was doubtful whether demand could be successfully stabilized. People would always want more than they had, whatever the absolute level of their standard of living, and there would be a continuing tendency to depress wages.

In 1798, however, Malthus's second axiom was a much more dangerous topic than any question about food supply, and it was probably because he dared to discuss the 'passion between the sexes' that the *Essay* was published anonymously. Handicapped in speech and disfigured in appearance by a cleft palate, hereditary in his family since Cromwell's time, Malthus was a shy, polite, and modest man. Sex was not a subject on which an unmarried priest was expected to have either experience or opinions. Furthermore it was not easy to discuss population questions sensibly without being drawn towards topics which even Mary Wollstonecraft had treated with great reserve.

Malthus argued as an economist from observed aggregate data. Godwin remained an individual moralist, convinced that improved perceptions could lead to alterations in sexual activity just as they can affect more obviously rational aspects of human behaviour. Sex, Godwin contended, is not like food. People cannot live without food, but celibacy is common among certain groups, even regarded as healthful. Sexual desire, far from being an irresistible urge, can be turned off by a sore finger. The answer to the population problem, Godwin advised, was late marriage and moral restraint.

It was an uncomfortable coincidence that at the time his dispute with Malthus began, Godwin was widely believed to have advocated sexual promiscuity, no-strings divorce, abortion, and infanticide, and to have shamelessly revealed the bedroom secrets of his dead wife in an attempt to persuade others to his opinions. The picture was unfair, but there was a truer paradox. The philosopher who had once looked forward wishfully to the withering of desire and the bringing up of children in common was behaving by 1798 as if he was the first man in the world to have discovered the joys of married love.

Soon after Mary Wollstonecraft's death, when Godwin decided that justice to the children required him to find a suitable companion who would help with their upbringing, it was natural that he should turn to the woman who had been one of his closest friends – perhaps in love with him – since 1795 and who, unlike others, had admired Mary Woll-

stonecraft and continued to see them both after the marriage. The 'negoci-
ation' with Maria Reveley which began on 17 November 1797, was
probably a proposal that she should become housekeeper and foster-
mother to the children. Since she took three full months to say no, the
implied affront to her continuing married status was evidently not at that
time regarded as decisive. However after the publication of the *Memoirs*
and the anti-Jacobin outburst which coincided with it, even the boldest
of Mary Wollstonecraft's followers was obliged to think again.

When William Reveley died in 1799 after a short illness, releasing his
estranged wife from her legal fetters, Mrs Reveley ostentatiously refused
even to meet Godwin alone until a decent period of mourning had elapsed.
'How my whole soul disdains and tramples upon these cowardly
ceremonies!' he wrote bitterly. 'Is woman always to be a slave? Is she so
wretched an animal that every breath can destroy her, and every temptation, or more properly every possibility of an offence, is to be supposed
to subdue her?'[9] When Godwin proposed marriage, she firmly declined,
half suspecting, we may guess, that his pressing need for a housekeeper
caused him to give more weight to the practical obligations of marriage
than his theories should have permitted. When she said that she was sorry,
but could 'not live without a passion' he protested sulkily that her attitude
was selfishly consigning him to a bitter solitude. He protested his great
virtues, his public fame, and the benefits he could bring her, but facts are
powerless against failing courage and failing love.

Lacking the lightness of touch of Mary Wollstonecraft, Maria Reveley
brought out the self-assertive aspects of Godwin's character. When faced
with feminine unreasonableness, he retreated into sermonizing and his
former pupil answered in his own terms. When she finally said no, and
refused to see him again, she exasperatingly sent word by Mrs Fenwick
that she felt herself unworthy of a man of such profound understanding.
It was so unfair. 'I disdain compassion,' Godwin wrote to complain, 'but
wrote to root out from your mind the idea, if it ever has been there, that
I am a philosopher and cannot be a lover.'[10] But the word which had
drawn her to Godwin (and to Bentham) in the first place now gave all
the wrong signals. 'Lover' was scarcely less terrifying. 'How singularly
perverse and painful is my fate,' he declared in another letter. 'When all
obstacles interposed between us, when I had a wife, when you had a
husband, you said you loved me, for years loved me! Could you for years
be deceived?'[11] The next time he met her – several months later – she
was in the company of John Gisborne, a man not unlike himself (with
immense knowledge, an earnest manner, and a large nose) whom she

married shortly afterwards. In 1800 the Gisbornes emigrated to Italy, the normal place of exile for couples with a past to cover, and Godwin was not to see her for twenty years.

It was his second rebuff within a year. Since 1794 he had made a point of taking a holiday outside London, and in March 1798, six months after Mary Wollstonecraft's death, he spent a few days in Bath where he met Sophia and Harriet Lee. Both sisters were established authors. Sophia's comedy, *Chapter of Accidents*, had been performed with some success in 1780 and Harriet's *New Peerage* in 1787, and in the years that followed both ladies also wrote a number of novels and tales as well as further plays which were published by Robinson. Godwin attended the performance of Sophia's *Almeyda* at Drury Lane in April 1796 and, as a compliment from a famous author to a promising newcomer, he had written to give his comments. The sisters had established a school for ladies in Bath, but they frequently visited London and had many friends in theatrical and literary circles whom Godwin shared. The name 'Lee' occurs alongside that of Burney in one of his lists of people he wanted to meet as early as 1786, but he does not seem actually to have met Harriet until he arrived at Bath in March 1798.

The previous year the sisters had achieved their greatest literary success with the publication of the *Canterbury Tales*, a series of modern stories to which both contributed. Godwin had read the book on the coach in the summer of 1797 when he had visited Parr and Wedgwood, and he was eager to meet the two authoresses. He was enchanted with Harriet from the first. The topic of conversation at one of her supper parties was whether it is possible to attend to trifles while engaged on a serious enterprise. While she listened carefully, she also gave lively and sensible answers; and if he thought at first that she was too pert, that had been his initial reaction to every woman he had ever met who was unashamed of her femininity.

Bath was the national marriage mart for the gentry and professional classes, one of the few places outside his immediate circle in London where he might expect to meet ladies of education, and Godwin decided at once that Harriet Lee would be a suitable successor to Mary Wollstonecraft. On his return to London he wrote her an honest letter.

... Allow me to believe that I have the probability of seeing you in no long time here in the metropolis. You said, if I recollect right, that this was rather the less likely as the friend with whom you used to reside in London had lately removed to some other place. Why should not I venture to suggest the practicability of your substituting my house, instead of the accommodation you have lost? I do not perceive that there could be any impropriety in it. A sister of the Miss Jones, with whom I resided at Bath, lives at my house upon the footing of an acquaintance, and is so obliging as to superintend my family and to take care of the children. I am sure she would be happy to do everything to accommodate you . . .[12]

Harriet said later that she had never received the letter, but she was probably preferring politeness to sincerity. A maiden lady of forty unblemished years could not stay in the same house as an unmarried man. Mary Wollstonecraft had been daringly unconventional in calling alone at Godwin's house on 14 April 1796 during the afternoon, trampling on the rules which, as Godwin proclaimed in the *Memoirs*, 'are built on the assumption of the imbecility of her sex',[13] but everyone now knew the long catalogue of depravity and disaster which resulted from that first false step. If Harriet Lee had accepted Godwin's invitation, it would have meant the instant ruin both of her reputation and of her school, as Mary Wollstonecraft's sisters with a less direct connection were at that moment experiencing.

When nearly two months passed without a reply Godwin wrote again. He had heard that Harriet had been in London in the meantime and had made no effort to contact him, and he decided that he would go again to Bath and try to meet her there. Among his papers are three full drafts of a long letter in which he struggled to strike the right balance between friendliness and honesty. He considered at first sending a brief announcement of his intended visit but that sounded too cold. He then drafted an alternative in which he set out his feelings.

You haunt me; I see nothing else; I think of nothing else; I can bear any thing rather than the uncertainty in which you plunge me. I recollect our conversations: there every thing was soothing; every thing spoke pleasure to my heart. I found, or thought I found, a responsive chord, the vibrations of which suggested to me emotions, too pure, too full of meaning, for mere words to explain . . .

Do not conclude from the incoherence of what I write that I am not influenced by the maturest deliberation . . . I am not a boy; and my proposal, though the result of sentiment, is authorised in my mind by the conclusion of reason and the inferences of experience.[14]

Tact was not a quality he yet understood or valued, seeing it – as it often is – as a cowardly dereliction from sincerity. In the version eventually sent, however, he bent so far as to imply that his visit to Bath was a short detour from a visit to Bristol which he had to make anyway, and he reverted to the courtly style from which Mary Wollstonecraft had almost cured him by the time of her death, but which seemed again to offer a retreat to the overbold:

... silence is so ambiguous a thing, and admits of so many interpretations, that with the admiration I had conceived for you, I could not sit down tranquilly under its discipline. It might mean simply that I had not been long enough your knight, to entitle me to such a distinction. But it might mean disapprobation, displeasure, or offence, when my heart prompted me to demand cordiality and friendship ...

Harriet in reply sent a brief formal note agreeing that he might call on her. At the same time, however, she returned Godwin's letter, marked up with snubbing third person comments:

The tone of this letter appears to me to betray vanity disappointed by the scantiness of the homage it has received, rather than mortified by any apprehension of discouragement. If any offence was given by the former letter, this is calculated to renew and increase it ...

She noted the unattractive mixture of humility and assurance which Godwin did not always avoid, and scolded him for his sole attempt at tact:

... this journey to Bristol has no reference to me: as far as that is concerned, he visits me simply as an acquaintance: but his title to be received as such has been lost by his forwardness to employ the privileges and claim the rights of a more endeared relation.[15]

A meeting took place at Bath on 5 June 1798 at which Godwin evidently proposed marriage and the lady, while admitting regard and esteem, refused. But Godwin knew enough of the female heart to realize that no often means yes, and over the next few months he sent her a series of letters arguing his case and trying to rebut her objections. He deployed again his Aeolian harp metaphor, picturing their two minds vibrating happily in response to the stimulus each would provide. He replayed arguments about the Promethean fire, which Mary Wollstonecraft had used, sounding on occasions as if love was his personal discovery, and he commended marriage with the conviction of a convert.

Do not go out of life without having ever known what life is. Celibacy contracts and palsies the mind, and shuts us out from the most valuable topics of experience ... [16]

When she said she was worried that God would punish her in the next world if she embraced an atheist in this, he wrote her a long explanation of the origins of Christianity, and elucidated the chains of causation which had led to her present erroneous views. He showered her with letters, all prepared with great care and a few constituting substantial ethical essays in their own right.

Gradually they took their effect. Whether it was the energy of mind concentrating the power of truth, or whether she simply tired of hearing his arguments, Harriet began to yield and even to encourage him. At the end of June he noted a few hopeful conferences alone with her 'chez elle' in London, but there was probably never any real prospect of moving to the ' – .' which Mary Wollstonecraft had encouraged at a similar stage. Only one thing prevented Harriet from saying yes, she finally told him with a candour which he ought to have commended, a fear of what people would say. That was however decisive. Harriet Lee, as Mary Shelley remarked when she read her father's correpondence after his death, was a lover of etiquette and of provincial life.

Godwin's note for one of his last letters written when he was seeing her in London in January 1799 is probably fair to both parties:

The world is of importance to you now; is so at Bath.
My character in the world: the talk of an old woman has shaken you.
We are formed for each other; you know it;
I am your choice, the object of your judgement and your feelings.
Few such men.
What will you be?[17]

They met occasionally later, but Harriet's determination did not soften nor did the world's view. The man who had been surrounded by female admirers in 1796 and 1797 now found nothing but humiliation wherever he turned. The letters he received now tended to be abusive rather than admiring, and he was begged by an anonymous 'Lancashire Woman' who had read the *Memoirs* to shield his children from their mother's disgrace.[18]

Stopped boldly in the street by an attractive young lady whom he did not know well, he was surprised by the frightened defensiveness of his own reactions, and when he got home, he sent an immediate apology for his temporary relapse into false values.

My dear Miss Kinsman,

As I did not say to you the things that I ought when I saw you, I feel myself prompted to say them to you on paper. You overstepped the dull rules of old fashioned etiquette and ceremony by the action which gave me the pleasure of conversing with you, I therefore make no apology for the liberty I take in addressing you . . . In reality for some time I was in doubt whether you had not

accosted me from the mere unflattering curiosity with which you might have gone
to see a wild beast or a child with two heads. The ingenuousness of your countenance and manners ought instantly to have banished that conception from my
mind. There was a noble and honest animation about you that could only flow
from a love of improvement and virtue. I have often seen something like it in
persons of your age . . . [19]

Godwin always scrupulously varied his method of address according to
the warmth which he intended to convey, and intimate friends were used
to moving up and down a scale ranging from 'My dear Holcroft', through
'Dear Holcroft', 'Dear Sir', 'Sir', to the cold rebuff of an unaddressed
third person note. To write so warmly to Miss Kinsman on first meeting
was a presumptuous disregard of her modesty and he never saw her again.

On 1 August 1798 shortly after the second visit to Bath, the *Anti-
Jacobin Review* published the most famous cartoon of the year, prompted
by the efforts of the French Government to de-Christianize public worship.
It shows the British radicals leading a monstrous Leviathan to St Paul's
Cathedral where three whores posing as Justice, Philanthropy, and Sensibility trample down old-fashioned values such as love of country and
family ties. A Cornucopia of Ignorance pours out the hated books of the
day including *Political Justice*, *The Enquirer*, *The Wrongs of Woman*,
and the works of Paine, Priestley, Holcroft, Wakefield, Thelwall, Coleridge, and others. In a corner are the heaped bibles and mitres, which the
reformers have discarded. A unilateral disarmer in uniform proudly hands
over his sword to the smirking French enemy. The Whig politicians led
by Fox ride cynically on the back of the monster waving red caps to cheer
on the mob. The newspapers print news of rebellion, blasphemy and
sedition. Paine is a weeping crocodile, Godwin is a pig. The cartoon was
accompanied by a long sarcastic poem 'The New Morality' by George
Canning, a future prime minister, who had once been among Godwin's
admirers.

Many, including Godwin himself, were willing to draw lessons from
events since 1794. But it was distressing to find that people whom he
regarded as his closest friends and allies should suddenly swing to the
opposite extreme. In January 1799 James Mackintosh offered a series of
lectures in London on 'The Law of Nature and of Nations' which Godwin
attended personally at Lincoln's Inn. Mackintosh had been one of the
most effective advocates of the French Revolution in its early days. His
Vindiciae Gallicae of 1791 written in reply to Burke hailed the French
Constitution as the first in the history of the world (with the then unimportant exception of that of the United States) to be deliberately designed

to benefit from the discoveries of philosophy, in contrast to the muddled political agglomerations of other nations. He became a friend of Mary Wollstonecraft and had been present at Godwin's dinner party in 1796 when she was reintroduced to her London friends after her depressive illness. Godwin regarded him as one of his most valued supporters.

When however Mackintosh's view of the French Revolution changed, so did his opinion of the writers whose writings had made it possible and of their supporters in England. After the first lecture was published Godwin wrote his old friend a pained letter.

. . . Will you give me leave to enquire (I hope you will not impute to an impertinence of disposition, a question I should scarcely have deigned to address to a less man than yourself) who are the speculators whom you designate by the following epithets? – 'Superficial and most mischievous sciolists, p. 24 – mooters of fatal controversies, p. 30 – men who, in pursuit of a transient popularity, have exerted their art to disguise the most miserable common places in the shape of paradox, p. 32 – promulgators of absurd and monstrous systems, p. 35 – of abominable and pestilential paradoxes, p. 36 – shallow metaphysicians – sophists swelled with insolent conceit, p. 26 – savage desolators, p. 38.[20]

Mackintosh's reply was superficially in the same spirit. He denied any intention to be disrespectful to Godwin personally, and reciprocated the hope that they would 'continue to exhibit the example, which is but too rare, of men who are literary antagonists but personal friends'. He promised that in future lectures he would carefully distinguish between his comments on individuals and comments on their ideas.[21] Unfortunately he found difficulty, in practice, in adhering to his intentions, until Godwin stopped attending in disgust, but one of Godwin's friends – probably Hazlitt or Stoddart – carefully reported his remarks. 'Gentlemen,' he is said to have declared on one occasion, 'you may be assured that if these self-called philosophers once came to have power in their hands . . . they would be found as ferocious, as blood-thirsty, and full of personal ambition, as the worst of those men who sheltered themselves under similar pretensions in a neighbouring country.'[22] Never once in several months of lectures did he mention these dangerous men by name.

Soon Godwin began to suspect that other friends were laughing at him behind his back. When he heard a (false) rumour from Holcroft's daughter that Basil Montagu was planning to become a priest of the Church of England and write an answer to *Political Justice*, he felt betrayed.[23] When he heard that Tom Wedgwood, another of his earliest admirers, had been in London and made no effort to see him, he wrote bitterly to ask what crime he had committed since the days of 1794 when Wedgwood had been so eager to make his acquaintance.[24] Even Holcroft seemed to have cooled. Offended at the lack of confidence which Godwin had shown when he secretly married Mary Wollstonecraft and then again at some incident after her death, he insisted on being fearlessly frank about Godwin's feelings at the very moment when he most needed help and reassurance.

Some of the cries of 1799 would be laughable if they were not at the same time symptoms of his deep mortification and pain, made more intense by the inflexibility to which the earnest are temperamentally condemned. A surprised letter from Sophia Lee, whom he had always suspected of turning Harriet against him, is a reply to a letter of complaint which he had written to Harriet on 1 June 1799 about one of the stories in the *Canterbury Tales*.

In a scene like that I have attempted ludicrously to depict, there must be some opposition of character, and certainly I never supposed when terming an opinionated Valet 'a philosopher of the new school' I should be suspected of an impertinence to a Man of Genius and Merit from whose conversation I had derived pleasure, and from whom I have never heard a syllable that I had either right or reason to question. I live so entirely out of the literary world even when in London, that I was not apprized of the designation your Friends give you, or I should from delicacy have chosen some other way to contrast my characters.[25]

But if Sophia Lee's letter is pathetic evidence of how far Godwin's suspicions were becoming morbidly obsessive, it was also disingenuous. Everyone knew the name of the famous writer whose weighty book had given respectability to the New Philosophy in its expanding years and who could now be conveniently blamed for the whole unfortunate movement.

Another lady novelist called Sophia whom Godwin knew, Sophia King, wrote two anti-Jacobin novels *Waldorf or the Dangers of Philosophy* in 1798 and *Cordelia or A Romance of Real Life* in 1800. In the first the philosopher who advocates atheism, revolution, and free love is not named, but the mention of Caleb Williams left no room for doubt. Godwin wrote twice to complain but Miss King was unrepentant. She went on to write other lurid works which connected the perils of atheism and the delights of sex even more intimately.[26]

A man can only truly be dishonoured, Godwin knew, if he himself commits a dishonourable action and he knew he had not done so. But it was difficult to be philosophical. Shocked with grief and humiliated by rejection, the more he struggled the more unattractive he appeared, and the more alone. In a long fragment of self-analysis begun on 26 September 1798 he made a just assessment of his own character:

... I am tormented about the opinions others may entertain of me; fearful of intruding myself, and of cooperating in my own humiliation ... and by my fear producing the thing I fear. I am bold and adventurous in opinions, not in life; it is impossible that a man with my diffidence and embarrassment should be. This, and perhaps only this, renders me often cold, uninviting, and unconciliating in society ...

My nervous character ... often deprives me of self possession, when I would repel injury or correct what I disapprove. Experience of this renders me, in the first case a frightened fool, and in the last a passionate ass.

He knew that his manners were often unintentionally hurtful, and he was intensely shy of strangers.

I am unfit to be alone in a crowd, in a circle of strangers, in an inn, almost in a shop ... I carry feelers before me, and am often hindered from giving an opinion by the man who spoke before giving one wholly adverse to mine.[27]

Easily excited, he was easily thrown off balance. He would feel his heart begin to palpitate, he noted, and his limbs to tremble, and the words would tumble out, confused and often wounding despite his best endeavours. It was an unrecognized prelude to the cataplectic fits.

Among friends the effect on the medullary particles was different. Then, 'my temper is one of the soundest and most commendable I ever knew'. William Austin, a young American who called at The Polygon after having been introduced at one of Johnson's dinners, has left a pleasing description of the quiet philosopher sitting in his study surrounded by his books with the portrait of Mary Wollstonecraft over the fireplace.

Imagine to yourself a man of short stature, who has just past the prime of life, whose broad high forehead is fast retreating to baldness, but whose ruddy, thoughtful, yet open countenance discovers both the temperature of health and philosophy: of manners remarkably mild, unassuming, rather reserved; in conversation cautious, argumentative, frequently doubtful, yet modestly courting reply, more from a desire of truth, than a love of contending; in his family, affectionate, cordial, accommodating; to his friends, confidential, ready to make any sacrifice; to his enemies – you would never know from Mr Godwin that he had an enemy.[28]

Another young American, Joseph Carrington Cabell, who also met him at one of Johnson's dinners, confirms the picture of Godwin in placid mood.

An unaffected smile indicative of good temper is generally playing on his countenance. His voice is well modulated, a circumstance in which he differs with most Englishmen whom I have conversed with. He never interrupts others. When he opposes in reply what has been said, it is done indirectly and very respectfully. He makes no little personal attacks, and bears them from his friends with much good nature, discovering no symptom of irritation and never losing the serenity of his temper.[29]

The real Godwin was hardly recognizable as the Jacobin monster of the anti-Jacobin press.

CHAPTER 16

The Philosopher's Stone

Godwin's response to the assault was to mount a counterattack. For a time after the publication of the third edition of *Political Justice*, he made notes for a new work, provisionally called *First Principles of Morals* which he intended would supersede the earlier work and consolidate his most recent discoveries.[1] At the end of 1797, he was already drafting for a book referred to immodestly in his journal as 'Opus Magnum' which he interrupted to write the *Memoirs* and the *Posthumous Works*. But then the plan was laid aside to await more propitious times. Even if two revised editions of *Political Justice* had escaped prosecution, an entirely new philosophical work which affronted religion and government might not be so fortunate. In any case the world was disgusted with philosophy and publishers were not interested. If Godwin wanted to change opinion, he would have to write a new novel.

By the summer of 1798 he was again hard at work. He wrote steadily during the period of his disappointments with Maria Reveley and Harriet Lee until at the end of 1799 the manuscripts of four volumes of *St. Leon, A Tale of the Sixteenth Century*, were ready for the printer. The Preface, always the last section to be drafted, was handed over on 26 November and the same day Godwin set off for a few days' holiday. He called on Charles James Fox at St Anne's Hill and spent a day with Mrs Cotton at Cookham (where Mary Wollstonecraft had stayed in 1796 after her suicide attempt) before returning to London at the weekend. Publication

Crazy Tom, from *Lessons for Children*

was due the following Monday, 2 December, nicely in time for Christmas and the coming of the new century.

St. Leon is a novel of astonishing ambition. The last time Europe had suffered a convulsion to be compared with the French Revolution had been at the time of the Protestant Reformation, an event which even Tories, with the benefit of hindsight, were now inclined to perceive as a liberation. Hence the choice of that period as his setting. During the writing of the book Godwin read some fifty works of sixteenth-century history as well as dozens on the French Revolution. He would change the future by explaining the past.

But whereas *Caleb Williams* had been conceived as a unity from the start, *St. Leon* consists of connected episodes, each volume reflecting the preoccupations of the author at the time it was being composed. When he began in 1798, he could think of little but Mary Wollstonecraft and the picture of Marguerite de Damville has been seen by many as his tribute to her memory idealized by grief. 'Your Marguerite is inimitable,' Holcroft wrote from Germany in a generally unsympathetic criticism. 'Knowing the model after which you drew, as often as I recollected it, my heart ached while I read.'[2] As if in expiation of the impiety of the *Memoirs*, *St. Leon* is a celebration of the traditional feminine virtues. Marguerite is loyal, supportive, forgiving, long-suffering, domestic, motherly, religious, and lacking in any kind of overt sexuality. If she shares any authentic features of the real Mary Wollstonecraft they cannot now be detected. If Marguerite is the culmination of the perfecting policies recommended in *Political Justice*, few people of either sex would wish to accelerate the process.

But Godwin was less interested in individual personality than in ideas. The portrait of Marguerite was intended to signal an important recantation. In the Preface Godwin publicly withdrew his previous view that personal considerations should carry no weight in the impartial calculation of justice. For more than four years, he wrote, he had been looking for an opportunity to modify some aspects of *Political Justice*, and although he saw no reason to change the main argument, he admitted that his psychology had been faulty.

True virtue will sanction this recommendation; since it is the object of virtue to produce happiness, and since the man who lives in the midst of domestic relations will have many opportunities of conferring pleasure, minute in the detail, yet not trivial in the amount, without interfering with the purposes of general benevolence. Nay, by kindling his sensibility and harmonising his soul, they may be expected, if he is endowed with a liberal and manly spirit, to render him more prompt in the service of strangers and the public.[3]

With these tortuous words Godwin again addressed the ethical problem implicit in all utilitarian theories which he had so graphically illustrated in successive versions of the story of Fénelon and his valet. It was never made exactly clear how the extra weighting should be measured. Presumably an aggregate of small private beneficences could outweigh the occasional big public improvement but it would have been interesting to know how a mother, whether prostitute or not, could set about establishing a higher claim than Fénelon. Lacking an effective technical vocabulary, Godwin's efforts at 'moral arithmetic' – as he called it – were not taken much beyond the theoretical stage.

He took care to refer to 'domestic affections' so as to include all personal relationships whether of blood, of contract, or of choice. But everybody knew that what he really meant was marriage. *St. Leon* is a celebration of the most odious of all monopolies and the retraction in the Preface was the most important statement in all the four volumes. Within a few weeks, an anonymous hack writer had put on sale a whole book of parody entitled *St. Godwin, A Tale of the Sixteenth, Seventeenth and Eighteenth Centuries*, whose own Preface translated Godwin's words into common parlance.

For more than four years I have been anxious for opportunity and leisure to recant this and other vain and absurd doctrines which I have so studiously and perniciously inculcated.[4]

But Godwin would not have expected *St. Leon* to be a candidate for special attention if it had been simply a story of love and marriage, the standard fare of novels and romances. Like all his books it was intended as a new contribution towards raising the truth and virtue level in the whole intellectual and moral economy, and the boldness of his imagination matched the grandeur of his ambition. Godwin again develops the favourite themes which were to become the mark of the Godwinian school, curiosity turning to obsession, pursuit and counter pursuit, isolation and craving for friendship, the influence of early upbringing on behaviour, and the contrast between conferred honour and true virtue. But as he explained in the Preface, in hopes of shocking the minds of his readers out of familiar patterns of thinking, he also bursts through the conventions of the popular contemporary gothic novels to which *St. Leon* has some resemblance.

In former times, the narrator declares in the first paragraph of the story, a favourite topic of speculation was how to devise a perfect system of government. In more recent centuries the chief interest has been the search for the elixir of life and for the alchemy of turning base metals into gold. The puzzled reader soon realizes that, since the story is told in the first person, the Count de St. Leon is talking about the fifteenth century, and by this brilliant reversal of times, the main point is emphasized from the start. The modern search for the principles of justice can be compared with the quest for the philosopher's stone.

In the story the Count actually discovers the elixir of life, and is thus able to survive through the centuries untroubled by illness or by death. By his bold stroke, Godwin neatly turns the laugh against those who had derided his theory of perfectibility and of immortality. St. Leon also discovers how to make gold in unlimited quantities – fortunately these two discoveries invariably go together – and he is able to help his fellow men in any economic way he chooses without adverse effects on the money supply or the inflation rate.

In the late 1790s it was commonly believed that international Jacobinism had been masterminded by a secret society called the 'Illuminati' – neatly cognate with 'Enlightenment' – who originated in the mysterious heartland of Europe round the upper Danube. The Abbé Barruel's highly influential *Memoirs of Jacobinism* which Godwin read in 1798 gave currency to this theory in four large volumes and also connected the conspiracy with the Freemasons. Robison's *Proofs of a Conspiracy*, which he also read, linked the Illuminati and the Freemasons with the English reading societies who were also believed to perform secret mysteries behind closed doors. Others blamed Cabalists and Rosicrucians.[5] An English writer of 1800 suggested, as further candidates, alchemists, astrologers, mystics, magnetizers, prophets, projectors, sectaries, visionaries, enthusiastics, and rationalists.[6] As the end of the century approached, some people feared that God had chosen this moment in history to apply a heavy collective punishment. Others believed that Napoleon Bonaparte was Antichrist. It is no accident therefore that St. Leon's discovery of the philosopher's stone is made in south east Germany where Barruel had located the origin of illuminatism, a particularly inventive region which was soon to produce Byronic vampires, Frankenstein monsters, and other metaphors of the same terrifying political phenomenon.[7]

Philosopher's stone stories are usually intended to reassure the poor that wealth does not bring happiness. Godwin uses the myth to illustrate the difficulties faced by original thinkers in winning acceptance of their views. Ancient alchemists had not been much concerned with the social problems they might encounter after the stone had been discovered, understandably concentrating on securing the initial chemical breakthrough. But modern philosophers such as himself who actually had made discoveries of greater potential benefit now realized that the initial research is the easiest part of the process.

St. Leon's attempts to help his fellow men all rebound in disaster, and – a point whose importance Godwin and Wollstonecraft had at first underestimated and then tried to correct – they impose huge penalties on friends and associates who do not necessarily share their views. Whether he relieves famine in Turkey or promotes post-war reconstruction in Hungary, St. Leon is always seen as a social threat and after a few centuries of travels he understands that 'the whole is a chain, every link of which is indissolubly connected from one end to another'. Surrounded everywhere by fear and suspicion, which quickly turn to hostility, St. Leon is alienated from friends and family until he is at last left to wander the world totally alone.

By setting the main story in a remote period with which few of his readers were familiar, Godwin was able to set the issues of his own day in the broad sweep of the history of ideas. Since St. Leon brings to his problems the preconceptions of a French nobleman brought up in the age of chivalry, his moral values are necessarily different from those of an eighteenth-century narrator, but Godwin ensures that the contemporary parallels are plain. When an Italian mob burns down St. Leon's house, readers were reminded of the Birmingham riots of 1791 in which Priestley's library and laboratory were destroyed. In describing the advocate who smears his opponents without mentioning either their names or their alleged crimes, Godwin had Mackintosh in mind.

One of the best passages is the defence of the Spanish Inquisition put into the mouth of the Chief Inquisitor. All that is valuable to mankind, the Inquisitor declares, whether in this world or the next, depends upon maintaining the strength of the Church, and it is the duty of its leaders to be active and vigilant in its defence. Since God acts through the agency of men, it is presumptuous to believe that the end will necessarily be secured if the means are neglected, and truth unfortunately cannot be maintained solely on the basis of evidence. The people lack the education to judge for themselves, and there will always be arrogant upstart theorists to claim superiority over the inherited collective wisdom. The Inquisition, the Inquisitor argues, is the most benevolent institution in the history of the world, for by a judicious and selective use of anticipatory terror it prevents worse disasters and greater misery. 'The passions of mankind are on the side of falsehood,' he explains. 'Man, unrestrained by law, is a wild, ferocious, and most pernicious beast.' Those who demand a right to think for themselves are striking at the foundations of all ordered society. Because St. Leon is an outsider whose life nobody can explain, he must therefore be put away even if he has not committed any identifiable crime.

In 1800 it was mainly authoritarian governments who assumed a power to control their subjects' lives and opinions, and men like Godwin who insisted on their right to think for themselves. But events in France had shown that Jacobins too could suppress dissent, and they used many of the same arguments in justification. Man, if not quite the beast of the Inquisitor, had not shown himself in recent events to be so benevolent that institutions could be safely dismantled. If he was benevolent in the state of nature before the corruptions caused by institutions set in, then it would take time to re-educate him before he could be again set free, and meanwhile he would have to be restrained. Even the Church, the heaviest mind-forged manacle of them all, Godwin concluded sadly, might still be needed for a while in the current state of progress. Like the bright flimsy tape round the unguarded royal palace in Paris which for a while kept back the rioting mob at the time of the Revolution, organized religion might have to be temporarily tolerated as part of the cultural defences against chaos.[8]

On the day of publication Godwin began a special journal in addition to his normal journal, and during the following weeks he recorded the comments on his new book of fifty-six friends and acquaintances.[9] First results were encouraging. Robinson, who had printed an edition of a thousand copies, decided on the day after publication that a second edition should be prepared immediately, and Godwin was allowed four days for corrections. The booksellers reported a lively demand, especially from the circulating libraries; translations were set in hand into French and German; and pirate publishers in Ireland and the United States rushed to seize a share. A new work by the author of *Caleb Williams* was an important literary event, and during the winter of 1799–1800, *St. Leon* was the talk of London – 'quite the novel of the day' according to William Lane, owner of the Minerva Press circulating library, who was in a good position to judge.

After the heaped disappointments of recent months, Godwin was nervous about what his sincere friends would say. Marshall, who had advised the immediate burning of *Caleb Williams* at a comparable stage, expressed his disappointment as soon as he had read the first volume. Nicholson declared that 'it does not answer, is a clear failure'. Barry felt that the last two volumes were much inferior to the first two. Fuseli's comment to Marshall – 'very amusing, a well-chosen tale, will be a favourite, better than *Caleb Williams*' – carried a characteristically quashing hint that the book deserved only popular esteem. Two visiting German literary men whose names Godwin did not catch said that the first two volumes were cold and uninteresting.

He was hopeful that his new attitude to marriage would change his own prospects. Holcroft had remarried earlier in the year, and the subject was much on Godwin's mind. In September he reread the letters of Mary Wollstonecraft, surprised for a second time that love could cause such outrage. He had not yet given up all hopes of Harriet Lee, but her polite acknowledgement for sending an advance copy of the novel implied no change. A 'letter to MR' noted in his journal for 1 November may have been a similar overture to Maria Reveley but when he met her the day after publication, she was accompanied by John Gisborne to whom she was already engaged.

He also hoped that *St. Leon* would revive his friendship with Elizabeth Inchbald, which had been abruptly cut off at the time of Mary Wollstonecraft's death, and on this occasion he attempted the diplomatic arts which in theory he despised. A mutual acquaintance came back with the message that she was willing to end the quarrel. It was therefore with a certain jaunty confidence that in sending her an advance copy of *St. Leon* on 28 November he suggested in an accompanying letter that two years' banishment ought to be sufficient expiation:

I allow you ten days from the date of this, to say, if you please that you respect or despise, as the case may happen, my talents in the present book – but that you feel an invincible repugnance, if you can be so severe, to the renewal of our acquaintance. If I do not hear from you by that time, I shall then venture to come to your habitation.[10]

Mrs Inchbald, he knew, would remember how her excessive repetition of superlatives when *Caleb Williams* was first printed had earned her the name of Mrs Perfection. But again Godwin had misjudged. Mrs Inchbald wrote back guardedly that she would be pleased to see him in company but that she could never receive him at her own house. 'While I retain the memory of all your good qualities,' she wrote in a typical Godwinian rejoinder, 'I trust you will allow me not to forget your bad ones.' A woman in her circumstances, she indicated politely, could not be too careful and she feared what the world would say if she were to see him alone.[11]

Three weeks later she wrote a long letter of comment in which her numerous detailed compliments did not counterbalance her general conclusion that *St. Leon* was a failure. 'I detect the married man in the author,'* she wrote, 'and rejoiced to find how experience had endowed his bosom with a new crowd of passions.'[12] But she objected to his Preface, and she did not change her mind about seeing him. Like Mary Wollstonecraft in earlier years, whether unmarried or married William Godwin remained an intolerable threat to female virtue.

At the end of the first week Godwin was so depressed that he could scarcely move out of doors. As he wrote in his special journal in a passage subsequently deleted.

This day I was desirous of calling on someone, to learn more exactly the character of the book, but had not the courage . . . to look an acquaintance in the face: at length I ventured to call on Ritson: excellent, an hundred times better than Caleb Williams.[13]

Thereafter he noted lists of writers who offered 'applause' or 'full applause' including Mary Hays, Southey, the Fenwicks, and the novelist Charlotte Smith. Horne Tooke told Godwin that every book he wrote was better than the last. Charles Lamb said – it was their first meeting – that the book was grand but too austere for his own cast of mind. Coleridge, whose views Godwin especially respected, offered the thought that the book was 'of a better species than *Caleb Williams*, because, though less impressive in a first reading, more acceptable in a second', a compliment more acceptable at first hearing than after its implications are thought through.

Godwin asked Robinson to send a complimentary copy to Dr Parr with which he enclosed a long letter. A visitor from Warwickshire, he reported incredulously, had told him that Parr was spreading a tale that Godwin had been reconverted to Christianity by the death of Mary Wollstonecraft. He also mentioned his disappointment that Mackintosh had chosen to attack him in an underhand way.

Sheltering himself under, what I think, a frivolous apology of naming nobody, he loads indiscriminately the writers of the new philosophy with every epithet of contempt – absurdity, frenzy, idiotism, deceit, ambition, and every murderous propensity . . . and has contributed to raise a cry against them . . . to be torn in pieces by the mob, or hanged up by the government.[14]

* Mrs Inchbald was the author of a comedy called *The Married Man*.

Godwin had not seen Parr or corresponded since his visit in 1797, but he understandably assumed that his old opponent would welcome his public change of view on marriage even if, like his daughter, he would want to give him a good-humoured roasting. He was therefore surprised and hurt when no word of acknowledgement arrived from Hatton.

The puzzle was explained a few months later when at Easter 1800 Parr delivered the annual Spital Sermon before the Lord Mayor of London which was printed soon afterwards. Taking as his text 'let us do good unto all men, especially unto them who are of the household of faith', Parr delivered a fierce attack on the doctrine of the domestic affections, which Godwin had now publicly withdrawn and in terms which suggested that he had copied Mackintosh's method. Limping in after the race was over, Dr Parr unwittingly provided an example of one of the themes of *St. Leon*, and when Godwin wrote to ask what had happened to his gift, his coldly offensive letter of explanation supplied a few more.

A parcel came to my house in December last . . . together with a letter, which from the direction I knew to be from you . . . I read only the preface to your novel, and afterwards having heard from Mrs Parr some account of its contents, I felt no anxiety at the time to look into them. I happened to be then very busy upon subjects which were far more interesting to me . . . Your letter I laid aside, and as I did not expect to find the contents of it agreeable to me, I laid it aside unopened. With some uncertainty whether I should or should not venture to read it, I afterwards looked for it in my library and could not find it. But my search was not very diligent and I suppose that some day or other it will fall into my hands. I cannot however pledge myself either upon finding to read, or upon reading, to answer it.[15]

In plainer English, having read the Preface to *St. Leon*, Parr realized that his forthcoming anti-Godwinian sermon was rendered out of date before it was even delivered, and he had therefore averted his eyes. 'For the principles I defend in the pulpit,' he wrote in words that might have been taken from the Inquisitor's speech which he had not read, 'I am conscious of an awful responsibility not only to society but to Almighty God.' Not having read Godwin's letter, he defended Mackintosh on the grounds that, since he had not mentioned Godwin by name, Godwin had no right to complain. In search of other justifications he claimed that he had never wanted to know Godwin in the first place, that he had seen the effects of Godwin's opinions on the lives of the young, and that 'in common with all good and wise men' he had been shocked by the *Memoirs*. When Godwin's letter eventually turned up in his library, it was returned, still unopened nearly a year after it had been sent, along with the gift copy of *St. Leon* which, Parr explained, had been read by Mrs Parr, Mrs Wynne (the former Sarah Anne Parr), by his other daughter Catherine, but not by himself.

By the time Dr Parr delivered his last hypocritical blows against his former friend, the fever of anti-Jacobinism had already passed its peak, and although it was to burn for another twenty years, it never again reached the extremes of 1798 and 1799. By the end of 1800 it was certain that Britain was not destined to be revolutionized. The defeat of the French fleet at the Battle of the Nile removed the risk of a French invasion and the Irish rebellion was quickly put down. Attacks on the enemy within continued, but the English Jacobins were no longer regarded as a serious threat to security. The personal attacks on Godwin himself also abated. Having recanted on sex, it was expected that he would soon repent his other errors. The *Anti-Jacobin* noted approvingly that *St. Leon* contained less evil than it had feared, and other reviewers even recommended that it might be read, although in the case of women only with proper precautions.

It was however difficult for an outsider to follow the train of thought from the original *Political Justice* of 1793 through its various revisions to the *Memoirs* and then to *St. Leon*. In the spring of 1801 therefore Godwin decided to publish a pamphlet that would offer both a summary of his emerging opinions and a defence of his own conduct during the recent controversies. *Thoughts Occasioned by the Perusal of Dr Parr's Spital Sermon, preached at Christ Church April 15, 1800: being a reply to the attacks of Dr Parr, Mr Mackintosh, the author of An Essay on Population, and others* was an unfortunate if accurate title, but the whole work was written in the generous rancour-free spirit which is the mark of true philosophy.[16]

For some years, he began by noting, he had been a silent spectator of the flood of intolerant attacks which had been pouring out against him and his writings. *Political Justice*, which had stood admired and unchallenged for four years after its first publication, was, Godwin affirmed, a child of the French Revolution, and had been written, as everyone at the time acknowledged, in a spirit of honest inquiry. 'I have fallen', he wrote, '(if I have fallen) in one common grave with the cause and love of liberty.'

But although the Revolution had not, as matters had turned out, proved to be the decisive break into a new age which he and others had hoped for in 1789, substantial accomplishments had been consolidated – hereditary government was gone, feudal rights had been abolished, and the oppressive grip of the Church over the lives of the people had been loosened.

He had himself revised his own views on the French Revolution soon after the Jacobin terror of 1794, unlike the British revolutionaries and radicals who had continued to defend the indefensible long after it was clear what was really happening across the Channel. But now in 1801 opinion had swung so far in the opposite direction that it could see nothing but evil in the present Government of France.

'I wrote my Enquiry Concerning Political Justice in the innocence of my heart,' Godwin explained. He had condemned violence, he had belonged to no party, he had offered his ideas frankly without dogma, inviting discussion and contradiction. It was hard to accept that he should now be 'dragged to public odium and made an example to deter all future enquirers from the practice of unshackled speculation'. He went on to explain in detail the substantial change in his views on the domestic affections quoting at length from the Preface to *St. Leon*, and offering yet another exegesis of the story of Fénelon and his valet.[17] Nevertheless, when all allowance was made for the disappointments, delusions, deceptions, intolerances, misrepresentations, and injustices he had suffered and witnessed since 1793, Godwin was unrepentant:

The great doctrine of the treatise in question is what I have there called (adopting a term I found ready coined in the French language) the perfectibility, but what I would now wish to call, changing the term, without changing a particle of the meaning, the progressive nature of man, in knowledge, in virtuous propensities, and in social institutions.

The *Reply to Parr* is one of the best things that Godwin ever wrote. In a note for his literary executors written shortly afterwards he asked that in any future editions of *Political Justice* the pamphlet – to be retitled 'Defence of the Enquiry concerning Political Justice' – should be reprinted after the prefaces to the three formal editions.[18] Although it is readily understandable why this has never been done, the result has been that modern opponents of Godwin's philosophy, like the unadmirable Dr Parr, have usually been fighting the last war and attacking the wrong enemy.

CHAPTER 17

The Discovery of Poetry

In the summer of 1800 Godwin paid a visit to Dublin. *St. Leon* had brought him four hundred guineas and although most of the money had long since been advanced and spent, he was briefly comfortable. The invitation had come from the Irish barrister, John Philpot Curran, later Master of the Rolls in Ireland, whom Godwin had met in London the previous autumn and who had quickly become an admirer. Curran and Grattan (another eminent Irish lawyer whom he also got to know well) were, he told Coleridge, the Fox and the Sheridan of Ireland, and since he was a guest who would soon go home, they had no inhibitions in accepting him at once as a friend.

Mary Wollstonecraft's two sisters Eliza and Everina also lived in Dublin and he saw them once or twice, but they had never forgiven him for the *Memoirs* and although they kept in touch, it was mainly out of concern for their two motherless nieces. He also met the Countess of Mountcashell to whom Mary Wollstonecraft had been governess in the 1780s – she was the girl pupil in Mary's *Original Stories from Real Life* – and who had inherited her teacher's views both on the rights of women and on the upbringing and education of children. Daughter of an Irish peer and unhappily married to another, she proclaimed herself democrat and republican, and in her determination to break free of sexual and class stereotypes, she dressed so plainly that even Godwin was surprised.

Curran arranged for him to sit on the bench at an assize court where

An Evening Vision, from *Blossoms of Morality*

he heard a man sentenced to be hanged for theft, and he visited a village to see for himself the effects of the rebellion of 1798. The rebellion, which had begun with many of the slogans of the New Philosophy on the lips of its leaders, had quickly become a series of massacres and counter-massacres by Catholics and Protestants. The chief weapon had been the pike, which Godwin had suggested in 1793 was ideally suited for defensive operations against armed invasion, but which was equally effective for piercing defenceless neighbours. Godwin discussed Irish politics with many of the Irish leaders. He read a great deal of Irish history – unfailing corrective for anyone with too simple a belief in progress. *St. Leon*, which is concerned with the political and religious issues of the sixteenth century, was, he told Marshall, a great favourite in Ireland.

He was beginning to re-establish his self-confidence. In Ireland he had been everywhere treated as a celebrity. On his leisurely journey home, he had dinner at Shrewsbury with Erasmus Darwin whose works on the origin of life (which anticipated the discoveries of his more famous grandson) caused disquiet among believers in the literal truth of the Bible. He also again met Robert Bage whose two novels of the early 1790s *Man As He Is* and *Man As He Is Not* had influenced *Caleb Williams*. *Political Justice*, he now admitted freely, had contained blunders, and the faulty analysis was attributable to his own upbringing and to the development of his own character. For all his intrinsic intelligence, his immense reading, and his incessant conversations, he had been blind to obvious truths. His life had been a series of violent revolutions, and who could tell when the next change would occur? A philosopher sincerely interested in finding truth should be on the lookout and not resist.

As it happened, another was already under way. The year 1799 was, he wrote later, the beginning of a 'great epocha' in his life, for that was when he first discovered the old English writers.[1] Like most of his contemporaries, he had previously taken it for granted that his own century had outstripped the achievements of earlier generations in litera-ture as in science. In March 1799 however in order to try to improve his own literary technique he looked through the works of Beaumont and Fletcher, and his journal for the next few months records steady reading through all their surviving plays. After the Elizabethans he turned to the Jacobeans and from the dramatists to the poets and prose writers. He read the histories of the English Civil War and of the Commonwealth period, and became an acknowledged expert on the contemporaries of Milton. He was delighted to discover Sir Thomas Browne, and unusually for his time, he developed an admiration for John Donne whose poetry he would quote eagerly until it became something of a party piece. Within a few years Godwin had filled the long chronological gap in his reading and he started to look further back towards Chaucer.

The older English authors opened a new world. At a time of life when he might reasonably have expected some blunting of the senses, he was suddenly presented instead with new and unending pleasure. He was a poor man who suddenly became rich, a sick man given a new lease of life. It was, he said, 'as if a mighty river had changed its course to water the garden of my mind'. Characteristically in recalling those days he emphasized not only the pleasure but the 'field of improvement'. Old books opened his eyes to new truths. He had discovered a new source of wisdom. He had discovered poetry.

Many of the older authors had never been reprinted since the time of the original editions. He was obliged to spend hours at the British Museum, chafing at the rules which prevented him taking the books home, and to beg from noblemen the privilege of searching their private libraries. The wartime shortages caused thousands of books to be bought to be broken up for wrapping paper.[2] Those who, like Godwin, shared in the revival of interest felt themselves in a race against time. They were the humanists of a new renaissance, and they tended to spend more money than they could afford.

Charles Lamb, a noted book collector, was soon to become one of Godwin's firmest friends. 'Are you the frog or the toad?' Godwin is said to have asked when first introduced in one of his few recorded jokes. Gillray's anti-Jacobin cartoon with the pig holding *Political Justice* had also included two reptiles holding *Blank Verse by Toad and Frog*, a reference to the volume of poetry recently published by Charles Lamb and Charles Lloyd. (To write in the new 'natural' medium of blank verse was regarded by the *Anti-Jacobin* as a sign of revolutionary sympathies.)

Although a considerable writer and scholar in his own right, Lamb was unusual in having a salaried job at the East India Office which kept him more in touch with the affairs of the world – and more immunized from disasters – than those whose income depended solely on their pens. His habit of deflating a conversation by a well-placed pun made him the wittiest member of a circle more distinguished for earnestness than for fun. The *Essays of Elia* were later to be packed in Victorian suitcases and kitbags by exiles and travellers in search of English gentleness, but the examples of his conversation which contemporaries admiringly recorded for posterity only confirm that humour is a relative concept. One evening at Godwin's Holcroft and Coleridge were debating which was better, the original state of nature from which humanity had degenerated or the ultimate future after perfectibility had been attained, *Man as he was, or man as he is to be*. 'Give me', said Lamb, 'man as he is *not* to be.'[3]

Robert Southey, the pantisocrat of 1794, was another enthusiast for the older writers. He continued to visit regularly whenever he was in London, and Godwin called on him during the visit to Bath and Bristol in 1798 when he first met Harriet Lee. During that visit Godwin was probably more interested in meeting the established authors of the vicinity, including Christopher Anstey whose *New Bath Guide* of 1766 was still reckoned one of the wittiest books of the century, and Ann Yearsley, known as 'Lactilla' whose verses written while delivering milk had briefly raised hopes that England had produced a vernacular poet to match Robert Burns. Godwin accepted a copy of Southey's youthful epic *Joan of Arc* – which is replete with Godwinian sentiments – and devoted part of a day attempting to read it.

From the day in 1793 when he first 'read and almost worshipped' *Political Justice* in a library at Bristol, however, Southey had moved steadily away until he became one of the most rabid of the anti-Jacobins. There can have been few literary men to have occupied so many places along the philosophical spectrum. An intense admirer of Mary Wollstone-craft – he too had a picture hanging in his study – he could not forgive Godwin for 'stripping his dead wife naked'. Before long, although he continued to visit regularly, he was describing the theory to which he had once wished to dedicate his life as a 'cursed mingle-mangle of metaphysics and concubinism and atheism'.[4]

William Hazlitt was only sixteen when he accompanied his parents on a visit to Godwin's home in 1794. The Reverend William Hazlitt, his father, was, like Godwin's father, a dissenting minister of the independent tradition, and had held the living at Wisbech in the 1760s after the Godwins moved to Guestwick. The young Hazlitt at the time of his first meeting with Godwin was a student at Hackney Dissenting College where he was taught by Andrew Kippis, Abraham Rees, and some of Godwin's other former tutors from Hoxton. As in Godwin's day they still proudly encouraged free speculation about religion although when in Hazlitt's year all the students for the ministry abandoned their faith and the College had to be temporarily closed, there were immediate calls for the reintro-duction of the mind-forged manacles. Hazlitt himself was already preparing to write a first book on the question whether human nature is intrinsically vicious, as his religious teachers believed, or merely temporarily corrupted by political, economic and ecclesiastical institutions, as *Political Justice* had recently demonstrated.

One of a group of younger friends whose affectionate but not uncritical respect survived the tiresome provocations, the protracted disagreements, and the fearlessly frank recriminations that acquaintanceship with Godwin entailed, Hazlitt, who had shared so much of his earlier experience, understood him well. In 1799 he began to visit Godwin frequently as he was to do until the end of his life whenever he was in London. Occasionally he stayed overnight. For years he sat quietly at many gatherings observing Godwin and his friends in conversation, and his essays include many glimpses of him even when not mentioned directly by name.

It was however Samuel Taylor Coleridge who made the deepest impression. In an autobiographical fragment written many years later, Godwin noted sadly that it was not until he was aged forty-seven that he had known anyone with a profound sense of poetry. In another fragment he put the time a little earlier in 1799 when he was forty-three, but there is no contradiction, for Godwin was recalling two periods when Coleridge was in London. In the winter of 1799/1800 Godwin was seeing him every few days and Coleridge stayed at The Polygon for three days in March. In 1801 there was another long visit. Godwin listed Coleridge as one of 'the four principal oral instructors to whom I feel my mind indebted for improvement'[5] – the emphasis being on the word oral, for Coleridge took his place alongside Fawcett, Holcroft, and George Dyson as a man whose conversation was more influential than his writing.

As Hazlitt noted, the two men were very different in their character and in their talents:

Mr Godwin, with less natural capacity and with fewer acquired advantages, by concentrating his mind on some given object, and doing what he had to do with all his might, has accomplished much, and will leave more than one monument of a powerful intellect behind him; Mr Coleridge, by dissipating his, and dallying with every subject by turns, has done little or nothing to justify to the world or to posterity the high opinion which all who have ever heard him converse, or known him intimately, with one accord entertain of him. Mr Godwin's faculties have kept at home, and plied their task in the workshop of the brain, diligently and effectually: Mr Coleridge's have gossiped away their time, and gadded about from house to house, as if life's business were to melt the hours in listless talk.[6]

With the help of his younger friends Godwin read and saw Shakespeare with new eyes. In *The Enquirer* he had described Brutus's ineffectual speech after the assassination of Caesar as due to 'the contagion of a vilest taste', assuming in accordance with prevailing standards of criticism, that a heroic figure could not be permitted to utter unheroic words.[7] Shakespeare's plays, Coleridge pointed out, are constructed with extreme artistry. You can as soon remove a stone from the pyramids with your bare hands, he would say, as alter a single word of the poetry. Far from trying to tell an improving tale, as the eighteenth century tended to assume, fitting Shakespeare with difficulty into their preconceptions about the nature of the drama, his purpose was to expose the complexities and contradictions of his characters.

Coleridge and Hazlitt gave public lectures on Shakespeare which Godwin attended. He read Schlegel as soon as it became available in English. Lamb and others published selected reprints from the newly discovered old English dramatists, and many attempts were made at this time to recapture Shakespearian qualities in modern writing. Hazlitt tells the story of a friend who quoted some lines of poetry* which Godwin to his annoyance could not place. After searching in vain through the works of Beaumont and Fletcher, Ben Jonson, and other likely candidates, he asked Lamb for his help, only to discover that Lamb had written them himself in his tragedy *John Woodvil*.[8]

Godwin regarded Coleridge as one of the most innovative thinkers of the day, and since he knew that most of the books he intended to write would never be more than talk, he took care to learn what he could from the conversations. Coleridge, building on the grammatical and etymo-logical theories of Horne Tooke, urged him to soften the sharp distinction which his necessitarian theory had implied between facts and words, and consider whether the act of thinking is separable from the verbal symbols with which it is practised. The Godwinian model of intellectual discourse, striking out truth by the clash of mind on mind was, he suggested, unhelpful. The Aeolian harp metaphor exaggerated the passive quality of mind. Conversation should not be regarded as contradiction and criticism but as an opportunity for 'mutual propulsion' whereby a loving and imaginative sympathy can mysteriously coax out new insights.

Literary men, Hazlitt remarked (with people like Godwin and Coleridge in mind), treat their friends like books, searching them for ideas, laying them aside as soon as they cease to be useful, and picking them up again whenever they want to check a point.[9] And the opposite was also true.

---

* To see the sun to bed and to arise,
  Like some hot amourist with glowing eyes,
  Bursting the lazy bands of sleep that bound him,
  With all his fires and travelling glories round him.

Books are friends, to be consulted whenever their opinion would be helpful, to be argued with, contradicted and corrected, and the best friends are those who are always available. Lamb used to look sadly at the gaps in his shelves where once had stood *The Anatomy of Melancholy*, *Urn Burial*, and *The Compleat Angler*, and reflect on the borrowing habits of his friends. Do not lend books, he advised, but if you do so, lend them to Coleridge, for he would return them 'enriched with annotations, tripling their value', his own thoughts poured out on the margins as he conversed with the great men of the past.[10] Godwin himself had such respect for Coleridge's comments on Daniel's *Civil Wars* – in a letter to Lamb, the owner, written on the end papers – that he laboriously copied them out for his own use.[11]

For a time Godwin contemplated writing Coleridge's biography, an astonishing compliment to a man scarcely out of his twenties, but the egalitarian philosopher was as guiltless of ageism as of sexism. Driven by the unrelenting curiosity which was to be a persistent theme in his novels, he recognized at once the brilliance of Coleridge's gifts and there was never a hint of jealousy. Coleridge, he remarked in one of the notes for his projected biography, 'always longed to know some man whom he might look up to by that means to increase his sentiment of the importance of our common nature: every man knows himself to be little'.[12] For a while he had himself been that man but by 1799 Coleridge had come increasingly under the spell of Wordsworth. 'I have done a great deal with my *Political Justice*', Godwin recorded him as declaring, 'but also much harm. Oh; that it had been possible for such a man as Wordsworth to have taken your place.'[13]

Coleridge's decision to move to the English Lake District in order to be near Wordsworth pained Godwin as much as it did his other friends. On the day in April 1800 when he left London, Godwin went round to the Lambs and together they drank punch to drown their sorrow. Writing about a proposed visit to Keswick (which did not occur), he explained to Coleridge himself how much he missed him.

This is partly because we have thought a good deal on the same subjects, but not less because we have pursued dissimilar objects and contemplated the same objects in a dissimilar spirit. I longed for the opportunity of engrafting your quince upon my apple tree, and melting and combining several of your modes of feeling and deciding, into the substance of my mind. Perhaps too I mention something better than this when I say that I feel myself a purer, a simpler, a more unreserved and natural being in your company than in that of almost any creature.[14]

Coleridge suggested that Godwin also should take a house and settle near him in the Lake District where – with Wordworth – they could all continue their philosophizing. Besides the scenery, he urged, books were also available, but it was a residual pantisocratic fantasy more than a realistic plan. Wordsworth, who had been brought up in the area and had a secure network of family and friends, lived happily with his admiring sister, but Coleridge's attempts to endure the cold and damp for twelve months of the year were disastrous. Already dangerously dependent on opium (another symptom of his more general tendency towards dependency) he soon found that drink and drugs provided the only sure antidote to the rheumatism, the isolation, the lack of conversation, and the crushing rural boredom. Like his admirer, Thomas de Quincey, who in his turn later went to the Lakes from a similar sense of dependency, he spent many days lying on the hearth rug, dreaming horrifying and delicious dreams, and gradually disgusting family and friends to the edge of endurance.

Godwin was perplexed by the early deterioration in Coleridge's character, by the wilful laziness, the broken promises, the self-pity, and the extravagant waste of his talents. If at times Coleridge seemed possessed of brilliant insights, at others he was an insufferable and unstoppable bore. Endowed with the fatal gift of charm, he preferred talk to thought, and much of what sounded like profound wisdom on first hearing turned out on examination to be worthless. 'The solemn – the superemphatical – the man of immeasurable complacence in his own rare and unfinished conceptions, yet conceptions brought forth with throes indescribable', Godwin wrote in exasperation about this side of Coleridge's character. 'Look to his writings – the deeper he dives, the more absolutely beyond all comprehension.'[15]

Godwin was amazed that a man of Coleridge's knowledge and intelligence could believe in Christianity, openly avowing in one conversation, which Godwin recorded in detail, a belief in such notions as the Trinity, the Incarnation, and the Fall of Man.[16] The Christian party, he said, contained all the great men. The war was just and admirable and he wished it would last forty years. Under Coleridge's influence however, as he openly acknowledged,[17] Godwin moderated the positive atheism to which he had progressed after abandoning religion in 1788. Although never at risk of reverting to Christianity, an error which had caused untold damage and misery, he became a deist, prepared to acknowledge a Supreme Being in the spirit of nature which blows through the Hartleian medullary particles like the wind through an Aeolian harp. Never having been able to shed his dissenter's habits of speech which were full of expressions like 'God Bless You', he now told teasing friends that any mentions of God which inadvertently slipped out were to be taken as referring to the God of Coleridge and Spinoza.[18]. However he declined to be Spinozan godfather to Coleridge's infant son Hartley, named after the philosopher whose theories they both admired.

Much of the conversation was about the lessons to be drawn from the older authors. Godwin long continued to believe that without elevated language, poetry could not be poetry. 'The great and fundamental error in Coleridge's canons of criticism', he wrote in a memorandum for his planned biography, 'is the not perceiving that it is the onction, the ripeness, the finish, the roundness, the harmony, the quotableness that constitutes the principal beauty of poetry.'[19] The poets of his own day, he had written percipiently in *The Enquirer* with the metaphor which had shaped so much of his thought, are compelled by the fetters of versification to write in an artificial language far removed from contemporary speech.[20] Robert Merry, the only poet whom he knew well before meeting Coleridge, carried Augustan archaeizing to such mannered extremes that his Della Cruscan school is now chiefly recalled as an example of the absurdities against which later poets were reacting.

Here again however Godwin was in at the start of a revolution. While at Bath in 1798 Southey introduced him to Joseph Cottle, the Bristol bookseller who financed Wordsworth's and Coleridge's experiment in a new type of poetry, and we know from the journal that Godwin read *Lyrical Ballads* as early as April 1799 and on several other occasions over the next few years. It was a shock. Proudly English in contrast to the internationalism of Godwin's generation, unashamedly emotional, distrustful of theories and respectful of traditional wisdom, Coleridge and Wordsworth had already lost what little confidence they once had that modern philosophers had discovered Newtonian moral principles which would offer a complete theory of man. *Lyrical Ballads*, with its celebration of such anti-Godwinian qualities as gratitude, its emphasis on the humanity of simple people, and its respectful sense of wonder at unexplainable mysteries is as much a reply to *Political Justice* as the other more obviously philosophical books which mentioned Godwin on their combative title pages.[21]

When Coleridge wrote to ask for his opinion of the second edition of *Lyrical Ballads* and of the long Preface in which the two young poets explained their theory of poetry, Godwin advised him to try to be more eloquent. A man brought up to regard Cowley and Pomfret as among the greatest of the English poets could not be expected to change his notions overnight, and Godwin too was not as immediately impressed as he ought to have been.[22] However under Coleridge's influence Godwin's views on the nature of literature also gradually changed. Convinced that literature is one of the great shaping influences on human conduct he began to speculate that poetic imagination might be the essential further link in the complex psychological chain which (according to the theory of necessity) connects true perception with virtuous motive. No man was ever a great poet, Coleridge proclaimed, without being at the same time a profound philosopher, and Godwin began to believe that the reverse was also true. As the proud eighteenth century drew to its sombre close and the age of reason gave way to the age of romanticism it was a more modest and more thoughtful Godwin who offered his accumulating wisdom to a confused world.

Surrounded by poets of the younger generation, he liked to recall that he too was a poet, although none of his numerous published works was in verse. In particular his mind turned again to the possibility of writing a play. *The Iron Chest* was being regularly and profitably performed, and if such a pale derivative could command public attention, why not a verse play written direct by the master? Maybe the fantasy he had described in *Damon and Delia* could come true at last, with theatrical success bringing fame, riches, and the love of women?

Novels and plays, he still tended to believe, were primarily useful for conveying complex ideas down to the less well-educated classes and to women who could not be reached by philosophical treatises. He was confident that a man of his talents could do better than the new verse works which he saw at Covent Garden and Drury Lane. Before embarking on *St. Leon* he had started to write a play – provisionally called *Alonzo* – and in 1799 he obtained a guarded undertaking from Sheridan that if he were to complete it, Drury Lane would consider staging it.

As ever, he worked hard on the technical side of the craft. During the composition he attended dozens of performances (mainly of Shakespeare and of eighteenth-century works) and he read dozens more, including the best-known plays by Racine, Corneille, and Molière as well as those of the English dramatists. He studied several books on the theory of drama and of tragedy. He attended another performance of *The Iron Chest*, but, having seen it three times before, he could only bear to stay for a quarter of the performance. Among his papers is a scrap of advice addressed to himself of the kind which the former minister occasionally used to boost his courage:

I have been a metaphysician, a political theorist – I have been a writer of fictitious histories and adventures. Enough; let these be dismissed – be now another man – turn your whole thoughts to the buskin and the scene – be that the labour of your being . . . [23]

He received little encouragement from his friends. 'There is a defect in the tale which no power of genius can overcome,' Holcroft advised in an extensive note, 'and which I am surprised that genius should not at once have perceived.' Holcroft disliked the plot, the characterization, and the lack of literary skill, and offered his old friend the frank opinion that he should try something more worthy.

. . . With such domestic tales as these, you are liable at every moment to be lounging along Grub Street . . . I do not know by the by whether you have ever been in that street: but I know that I have often and that it is cursedly dirty and ill-paved. It is a short cut indeed which I like a hasty fool often have taken as you have at this moment a proof that you have never failed to remind me how bemired I have come back, for which I owe you ten thousand obligations. [24]

The three plays which Holcroft had written since 1795 were shouted down as 'Jacobin' by London audiences unable at that time to bear the lightest of social satire, and a fourth only escaped the same fate when Holcroft allowed it to be falsely ascribed to another author.

On 5 January 1800 the journal records Godwin's reading of *Osorio*, a verse tragedy by Coleridge which had recently been turned down by Drury Lane. *Antonio, or The Soldier's Return*, as Godwin's play was renamed, contains many similarities and may have been written in a spirit of friendly rivalry. Also set in fifteenth-century Spain, it is concerned with the familiar Godwinian contrast between artificial honour and real virtue, this time as regards duties towards women. Antonio, the embodiment of the chivalric military virtues, cannot forgive his sister for marrying a man without his approval, but when full weight is given to the necessitarian moral preconceptions which he brings to the situation, his decision to seize her by force from her husband and lock her up for life in a nunnery seems over-punctilious. Later in the play he kills her although only to suffer remorse.

It is difficult for modern taste to take *Osorio* and *Antonio* seriously but they are no worse than many in the seventeenth-century style which were acted with success at the time and a great deal better than some. Although classed as tragedies, they conventionally included episodes of melodrama, of self-parody and even of comedy, and provided there were a few good speeches and plenty of action, audiences did not expect profundity or poetry.

The first performance of *Antonio* was fixed for Saturday 13 December 1800 with John Philip Kemble in the title role and Mrs Siddons as Helena. Charlotte Smith wrote the Prologue and Charles Lamb provided a facetious Epilogue about the risks of not keeping marriage promises.[25] Although both Coleridge and Lamb cautioned against over-confidence, Godwin believed that acceptance by Drury Lane guaranteed success, and he wrote long scolding letters to Kemble in answer to his criticisms. According to Hazlitt, he assured Wordsworth in a letter that the play could not fail,[26] and Lamb recalled seeing lists on his desk of the rare books which he hoped to buy from the profits – Dodsley's collection of old plays, Malone's edition of Shakespeare, even that prize of Enlightenment philosophers, Diderot's Encyclopaedia. Preparations were made in advance for a celebratory party.

In the event *Antonio* was a disaster, and Godwin's most sympathetic friends could not claim that it was undeserved. Since the first night was the subject for one of Lamb's best Elia essays[27] (written and published twenty years later when time permitted some artistic stretching of the facts) *Antonio* enjoys the immortality reserved only for the best and the worst. As the audience took their places, Lamb recalled, Godwin was cheerful and confident, Marshall silent and frightened. The first act passed without a sign from the audience – exactly as he intended, Godwin assured his companions, the dramatic tension was building up. During the second act, however, when Marshall tried to start a round of clapping, nobody followed. Kemble had warned Godwin not to invite too many friends to applaud on the first night for fear that the audience might suspect, but this risk had been exaggerated. The audience at one point expected a display of sword play and when they received instead a philosophical debate on the absurdity of duelling, coughing gradually drowned the actors' words. After that there was uproar and the performance was only completed with difficulty. *Antonio* was remembered for having been coughed off stage at its first and only night.

The notices the next day confirmed the failure. 'We are damned,' Lamb told his friends, and the Epilogue he had written had been declared worthy of the play.[28] Mrs Inchbald, editor of a long series of reprints of British plays, grimly assured Godwin that standards were so low that he was better off among the unsuccessful. But Godwin needed no comfort. A man who during his ten-year literary apprenticeship had written a dozen failed books was not going to be cast down by a single poor showing.

Kemble, he knew disliked modern plays, and had previously botched the first night of *The Iron Chest* by his own coughing and poor acting. If *Antonio* was flawed, it too could be revised and shortened, and snatch a late success. Instead of slinking away he set to work, with Lamb's help, to prepare the text for publication, and it was put on sale, much revised, with Godwin's name on the title page, a week later. However the opportunity which he thus defiantly offered the public to judge for themselves ensured only that damning theatrical reviews in the dailies were followed by damning literary reviews in the monthlies.[29]

An immense vanity and confidence in his own abilities saved Godwin's self-respect, Lamb told his friends, not without admiration, but it was a calmness deliberately cultivated. If like one of his ancient Roman heroes he could detach himself from his problems and survey the world with the impartial eyes of a philosopher, he would not only preserve his dignity but reduce the risk of fits. He had recovered from setbacks before and would no doubt have to do so again. Indeed repeated practice was quickly making him more perfect.[30]

Coleridge was at Keswick when *Antonio* was performed and it took a day or two for the London newspapers to be delivered. 'I received the Newspaper with a beating heart and laid it down with a heavy one,' he wrote with his habitual charm. 'But cheerily, Friend! it is worth something to have learnt what will not please.' He went on to suggest that the review had been deliberately biased by the editor, a well-known anti-Jacobin. Having recently advised strongly against Godwin's suggestion of a life of Bolingbroke, Coleridge perhaps felt some obligation to make a better suggestion, and he had one ready:

If your Interest in the Theatre is not ruined by the fate of this, your first piece, take heart, set instantly about a new one . . . There is a paint, the first coating of which, put on paper, becomes a dingy black, but the second turns to a bright *gold* Color. – So I say – Put on a second Coating, Friend![31]

Coleridge even had a suitable topic to suggest, the story of the death of Mirza, son of the King of Persia, about whom he had recently been reading in an old travel book. It was a theme with crowds, character, passion, incident, and pageantry, he wrote, and since nobody would know the real history, a playwright could take whatever liberties he needed.

Coleridge's letter, which is dated 20 December 1800, probably did not reach London for a couple of days. The Preface to the printed version of *Antonio* marking the end of Godwin's revising of the text, is dated 22 December, and the play was published the following day. By Christmas

Eve Godwin had accepted Coleridge's advice, and as the 'Invent Mirza' in his journal for that day proves, he was already sketching out an outline in his mind. Within a week he was hard at work on the new play which would restore his reputation as a dramatist. Books on Persian and Turkish history were borrowed and scholars and friends who knew about Eastern customs sought out and questioned. In February 1801 we find him reading again the Shakespearian tragedies as well as going to the theatre several times a week in what was evidently a new effort to improve his dramatic technique. If Godwin's stubbornness was often irritating, his powers of resilience never ceased to astonish.

By the end of April 1801 he had completed *Abbas, an Historical Tragedy*, a verse drama in five acts, complete with suggestions for the actors and actresses considered suitable for the leading roles. A fair copy was dispatched to Coleridge in Keswick and Godwin eagerly awaited comments. Two months after he had received the manuscript, however, Coleridge still had not returned it. In a letter sent on Tuesday 23 June he promised to return it by the following Friday's post, but again it did not arrive. 'It would be needless to recount the pains and evils that prevented me from sending it on the day I meant to do,' he explained a fortnight later, after receiving a further hurt letter of reminder. Instead of sending the comments which he had first intended, he promised instead to use the time to prepare a more considered opinion.

My Criticisms Etc were written in a style and with a boyish freedom of censure and ridicule that would have given pain and perhaps, offence. I will rewrite them, abridge them, as rather extract from them their absolute meaning, and send them in the way of Letter.[32]

The copy of the manuscript of *Abbas* has recently come to light including Coleridge's spontaneous comments.[33] The curtain rises to reveal a mob of exulting Sunni Persians outside the smoking ruins of Medina where they have just destroyed the religious shrines of the Shiite Ottomans, and it is soon evident that Godwin had learned much from his visit to Ireland. In *Vaurien*, one of the earliest of the anti-Jacobin novels, d'Israeli mocked philosophical writers who, to avoid the censorship laws, wrote Constantinople when they meant London and Mahometanism when they meant Christianity. Shelley was still using the same convention in *The Revolt of Islam* twenty years later.

Coleridge advised that the first two acts should be entirely rewritten. He devised symbols to represent what he saw as the play's four main failings – false or intolerable English; passages which sounded flat or mean; vulgarities and clichés (such as 'bred in the lap of luxury'); and bad metre; and there is scarcely a page of manuscript which is not liberally spattered. One passage of five lines is condemned on all four counts. One single line of seven words, 'The furtive reverence due to silver age' scores three. The marks are sometimes reinforced by comments – 'Execrable metre', 'a solecism in manners', 'Too bad', 'a foul line', 'Whoo!!'. When a mute eunuch enters the Harem and, according to the stage direction, 'expresses his intelligence by signs', Coleridge writes in the margin 'Would not this be ludicrous on stage?'. When Godwin attributes to Abbas some trite sentiments on the heavy responsibilities of kingship – 'Horrors and darkness! who would be a King! Cut off from nature and her sweet content; Thrust out a gloomy, uncompanion'd monster' – Coleridge fearing the anti-Jacobin claque warns that 'These 3 lines would be enough to *damn* your play.' When a passage listing the disasters attending a failing King Abbas includes anarchy and impotence, Coleridge is quick to point out the dramatic dangers:

'*and impotence*'. The equivoque latent in this word would of itself damn your play. This speech is the first spirited passage, I had almost said the first tolerable passage I have met with.

In only two other places is there a word of commendation 'well written' to offset the 111 separate faults that Coleridge had noted before he began to tire somewhere in Act II.

A speech by Bulac, the Iago of the story, on the insomnia which afflicts the guilty, is a fair example of Godwinian Shakespearian at its best.

> Oh how I hate these tedious hours of darkness!
> How they subdue and quite unnerve the mind!
> Would it were day! – The poorest idlest thoughts,
> The shadows, that the glorious light of heaven
> Makes nothing of, seem to my slumbering sense
> Evils unconquerable, mountain mischiefs,
> Loftier than Taurus. Why do I call them shadows!
> Each night they haunt me, banish my repose,
> And change my vigorous frame to gaunt and ghostlike.
> Three times, since I forsook the lengthen'd banquet,
> I have sought a different couch, a different chamber,
> Impelled by some strange power, that seems to guide
> My steps, and lead me blindly to its purpose.

Coleridge's comment is probably a fair example of his celebrated after-dinner conversation.

This is a natural and affecting thought; and the first clause is well expressed. Loftier than Taurus is ridiculous. We never speak of an evil as *lofty* – it is a blunder for *Irishmen*, who, I presume, derive their peculiar Talent from the Muses that reside on Mount Taurus rather than those on the Mount Parnassus.

Many an established writer would have taken offence at such treatment from a younger man whose own reputation owed more to promise than to achievement. Apart from anything else the fair copy had been ruined and it would be time-consuming and expensive to have the whole play recopied. Godwin however, perhaps recalling the undiluted sincerity which he himself always inflicted on his own friends' manuscripts, thanked Coleridge politely. He could bear harsh words, he said – would despise himself if he did not. He then conscientiously went through Coleridge's criticisms, accepting some, rejecting others.

If he was known to be the author, the theatre management might ask for cuts in the political passages or turn the play down altogether for fear of a repetition of *Antonio*. Drury Lane employed two readers (whose identity was kept secret) to report on submitted manuscripts and to act as censors. In theatre parlance they were the 'buckram men' in commemoration of the non-existent 'four rogues in buckram' who attacked Sir John Falstaff in *Henry IV Part II*, and they were noted for the speed with which they did not read submitted manuscripts.

When Godwin sent *Abbas* to Kemble on 10 September he therefore asked that the buckram men should be told in confidence that he was the author, and the request was readily agreed. At the last minute he changed his mind, the arrangement was hurriedly altered, and *Abbas* was sent anonymously. When however, a few days later Godwin received a brief routine rejection addressed to 'The Author', he wished that he had allowed his name to be given. Nine months' hard work by one of England's most famous authors had been entirely wasted – probably not even read. As ever when he felt humiliated, Godwin relapsed into boastful self-assertion, crossing the narrow line between persistence and unreasonableness, and Kemble soon shed any sympathy which he may have felt for his disappointed author. In a series of robust replies to Godwin's complaints,[34] he would only offer the ambiguous reassurance that the play had been read with all the attention it deserved. Drury Lane, he said, did not receive fifty or a hundred manuscripts each year – the figure Godwin had guessed – but five or six hundred; the theatre's readers, buckram men or not, would form their own judgement on how much time to devote to each.

It was a hard message, but Godwin had his habitual answer. Before the final rejection was even received, he was already hard at work on a third play and had even persuaded Covent Garden to promise to pay for it, although without any promise to perform. This play too was to be a tragedy and in verse but after working hard at it for a number of months, he completed it in prose. Like its predecessors the main theme is the difference between honour and virtue, and as with the others, the modern reader needs more historical imagination than he can easily muster to sympathize with the moral dilemma round which the action turns. Faulkener, a military hero returning from the wars, is in search of his long lost mother whom he has not seen since he was four. The Countess Orsini, while delighted to see her son, cannot forget that – like many ladies of her generation – she once went to bed with King Charles II.

Faulkener was eventually produced at Covent Garden in December 1807 where it ran for three performances with no disaster beyond occasional outbreaks of laughing.[35] It was never again performed. But on one point at least the author was now prepared to accept the verdict of friends and of enemies. William Godwin might be an acute philosopher, a fine essayist, and a perceptive novelist, he might love poetry, he might have read a great deal of it, he might understand its power and talk about it regularly with some of the best poets of the day, but he could not write it. To the relief of friends who had followed his career as a dramatist with despairing admiration, Godwin decided that enough was enough.

CHAPTER 18

The Second Mrs Godwin

On 5 May 1801 Godwin noted among other events of a routine day 'Meet Mrs Clairmont'. On the 27th he took tea at her house with Fanny and Mary, and on the 30th he went alone. Soon he was seeing her there every few days although it was not until 27 June that Mrs Clairmont made a return social call. Her children, Charles Clairmont, then aged five, and Clara Mary Jane Clairmont aged three, made happy companions for Fanny and Mary who were then seven and three, and before long the two families were taking walks together. On 6 July they went to the panto-mime to see *Puss in Boots*.

According to stories put about after her death it was Mrs Clairmont who took the initiative. As Godwin sat on his balcony one evening, she is said to have introduced herself from her own balcony, with the words, 'Is it possible that I behold the immortal Godwin?' In another version she waited until Godwin took his regular evening walk in his garden before walking up and down in her own garden across the wall clasping her hands and audibly murmuring, 'You great Being how I adore you', and it was only when these more tactful approaches produced no response that she is said to have accosted him in the street with the words, 'Mr Godwin, I have compromised myself for I adore you.'[1]

Since none of these stories has any documentary authority before 1878, they should be regarded more as indications of the reputation which Mrs Clairmont eventually bequeathed than as orally transmitted historical

Poetry for a Lady, from Colman's *Broad Grins*

facts. But myths have a truth of their own. In May 1801 Mrs Clairmont was undoubtedly living at number 27 The Polygon, the next house to the Godwins at number 29 and presumably she had only recently moved in or there would surely have been mention of her before that time among the other less pushful Somers Town neighbours who make frequent or occasional appearances in the journal. The rate books which record 'Mary Jane Claremont' of The Polygon paying rates in May 1801 unfortunately do not go back any earlier,[2] nor can it be ascertained how far those who spread the stories had access to genuine information which is now lost.

Mrs Clairmont had no need to be shameless to attract Godwin at this time. After the humiliations at the hands of Harriet Lee, Maria Reveley, and others, he was an easy target, flattered to be found attractive by a woman who was some ten years his junior and eager to appreciate both his person and his genius. After three meetings in May, Godwin saw her eleven times in June, sixteen times in July, and fifteen times in August. He read to her both from *Antonio* and from *Abbas*, and no doubt she helped encourage the delusion that he was a poet and a dramatist.

On 16 September Charles Lamb reported in a disappointed letter to a friend that Godwin was behaving strangely. 'He bows when he is spoke to,' he wrote, 'and smiles without occasion, and wriggles as fantastically as Malvolio, and has more affectation than a canary bird pluming his feathers when he thinks somebody looks at him. He lays down his spectacles, as if in scorn, and takes 'em up again from necessity, and winks that she mayn't see he gets sleepy about eleven o'clock.'[3] Mrs Clairmont, who wore green spectacles, was also, he decided, unattractively artificial in her manners and not solely from the temporary exigencies of courtship.

In the summer of 1801 Godwin had good reason to feel pleased. *The Reply to Parr* was drawing much favourable comment – Coleridge was particularly impressed – and *Abbas* was still being considered by Drury Lane. He had just heard that Covent Garden had promised to pay money for his third play and he had recently concluded a well-paid contract for a life of Chaucer with the prosperous innovative publisher Richard Phillips. The characteristic Godwinian tenacity and resilience were, it seemed, again bringing promise of success, and to mark the turnabout in his fortunes, he started to sit for a new portrait by his friend James Northcote. Furthermore, in his journal for 13 July, after 'tea Clairmonts' there is an unenigmatic X – Mary Jane Clairmont, as he had said of Mary Wollstonecraft in the *Memoirs*, was evidently not a woman to await the sounding of a ceremonial trumpet before permitting the overflow of love.

As with Mary Wollstonecraft, the affair was kept highly secret. Only a handful of his friends – such as James Marshall and Louisa Jones – were invited to meet Mrs Clairmont. (Lamb's remarks were written after he had called unexpectedly for tea on 23 August and surprised Mrs Clairmont on one of her rare visits.) She in her turn did not introduce Godwin to any of her own friends with the exception of members of the Hodges family who were probably mutual neighbours. As far as outsiders were aware, Godwin's life was unchanged, writing, reading, conversation, dinners at Johnson's and visits to the theatre. But as the one surviving letter which he sent to Mrs Clairmont at this time makes clear, he was in love. Among a heavy programme of professional and historical reading we find the *Elegies* of Tibullus, the *Confessions* of Rousseau, Mary Wollstonecraft's *Letters from Sweden* and other books known to intensify sensibility.

On the day after he met Mrs Clairmont Godwin received a visit from Malthus and the two men met frequently in the following months. In 1800 Malthus had produced a second anonymous pamphlet, *An Investigation of the Cause of the Present Price of Provisions*, in which he set out for the first time the notion of effective demand. Godwin had recently read it, and Malthus had read Godwin's *Reply to Parr*, a large section of which was a reply to Malthus's earlier book. They had a great deal to talk about. By 1801 Malthus's theory had already been widely adopted. Two years of poor harvests had led to widespread distress. Prices were 300 per cent up on 1793 and although wages had also risen, there had been a drastic fall in the income of the poor. Relieving starvation by public expenditure, many taxpayers now believed, would make the situation worse, and the only answer was to reduce demand even further. In 1800 a law was passed to forbid bakers from selling bread for twenty-four hours after baking – it being well known that since new bread tastes better, the poor eat more of it.

Godwin's remedy was different. It would be better, he argued, to prevent overpopulation at the point of conception. We should remember, he proclaimed in his *Reply to Parr* in an unfortunate phrase to whose overtones he was characteristically deaf, 'the inventions and discoveries with which every period of literature and refinement is pregnant'.

In the South Seas a tribe had been found who considered it shameful to have sex before twenty – and the babies, it was said, were healthier as a result. The Ceylonese had discovered methods of abortion which, he had read, were entirely harmless. As the remoter areas of the world were explored by amazed Western travellers, such observations offered a rich source of wishful ideas about alternative models of social organization;

and Godwin, who had been urged by Coleridge to read more travel books, became an anthropologist. It was long believed that a happy land near Tahiti had perfected a successful birth control technique which depended solely on the partners adopting the correct state of mind. But the details of this useful piece of knowledge remained elusive.

It can only be a guess whether Godwin at the time of his conversations with Malthus in the summer of 1801 was himself exercising the prudence and restraint which he advocated. If however he and Mrs Clairmont were applying the 'chance medley' system of birth control which had failed with Mary Wollstonecraft, it failed again. At the end of October 1801 the journal records a flurry of consultations with doctors at which it was confirmed that Mrs Clairmont was pregnant.

Tantalizing abbreviations in his journal refer to discussions with members of his family, hurried journeys in central London and elsewhere, the writing of important letters, the raising of loans, and the working out of complex secret plans. As in 1797 there was a crisis and it was solved in the same way. According to the family tradition, Mrs Clairmont demanded that Godwin should marry her, and he replied, 'Well, if I must, I must.' On 21 December the couple were formally united at St Leonard's Church, Shoreditch. Both are described in the register as 'of this parish' and although The Polygon is a long way from Shoreditch, they had taken temporary lodgings in the parish in St Agnes Street in order to qualify, Godwin spending two nights there on 23 November and 19 December. Only Marshall was present as witness and they went to a great deal of trouble and expense to prevent anyone else from knowing. For honeymoon, the couple spent one night at an inn at Snaresbrook in Essex, and returned immediately to London.

A few days later Godwin wrote letters giving the news, and at a series of dinners early in the New Year the second Mrs Godwin was introduced to his family and friends. On 8 January Curran, Fuseli, Perry, Carlisle and the twenty-one-year-old Irish poet Tom Moore were among the guests, but the stars, Sheridan, Horne Tooke, Coleridge and Charlotte Smith were among *invités* who sent apologies for absence. Coleridge, Lamb, Humphrey Davy, Northcote and Charlotte Smith came with others on the 30th, regretting the absence of the *invités*, Johnson, Southey and Hoare. As was the custom, the wives and daughters of Godwin's friends felt that they had to take the first step in making calls unaccompanied by their men, but, by one means and another, before long Mary Jane had been made known to all of Godwin's huge circle.

The pregnancy which had precipitated the hurried marriage did not turn out well. The entry in Godwin's journal for 4 June 1802 'William I ½ after 11' apparently refers to the death of a baby, Godwin with his usual positive attitude already looking forward to a future William II. The earlier entry for 8 May 'Casualty chez Fell' may be read as a threatened premature birth at the house of his friend Fell or even as the birth itself which must have been due about this time. There was then much visiting by doctors until 4 June when Godwin fetched Mary Jane home from some unknown address, perhaps a maternity hospital. The records of St Leonard's Church, Shoreditch, where the Godwins had been married, note the baptism of William, son of William and Mary Goodwin [sic] on 24 May, the date of birth being given as 30 April, information which cannot be reconciled with the evidence of Godwin's journal.[4] Whatever the explanation of the first birth however Mary Jane became pregnant again almost immediately, and on 28 March 1803 she gave birth to another William, a healthy boy who grew up to be known as William Godwin Junior.

According to Thomas Robinson who met her in 1803, the second Mrs Godwin was an elegant and accomplished woman.[5] Although unmistakably English, she spoke perfect French, had travelled widely in Europe, and – for a woman – was well educated. She was a Roman Catholic – the *Anti-Jacobin Review* teased that she had converted Godwin to Catholicism – and had close connections with the French *émigré* community many of whom had settled in Somers Town.[6] On 18 May 1804 she was to persuade Godwin to accompany her to a Requiem Mass for the Duc d'Enghien who had recently been put to death in France. Like many of the women of Godwin's acquaintance, at the time of her marriage she was earning a meagre living in Grub Street, traditional fate of ladies fallen on hard times.

She is known to have been the translator of a number of books originally written in French, including Piccini's *Thoughts of Voltaire*, Golberry's *Travels in Africa*, von Struvel's *Travels in the Crimea*, and a book by Rousseau of unknown title.[7] Mrs Godwin also wrote numerous children's books, and presumably took whatever other commissions were available at the going rates. Ancillary workers in the literary industry invariably remained anonymous, or even, as in the case of Mrs Godwin's translation of Golberry, saw their efforts attributed to a better known editor, and Mrs Godwin's name never appeared on the title page of any book. The only work for adults of which she is known to be the sole author is *A Picture of the New Town of Herne Bay, its Beauties, History, and the Curiosities in its Vicinity . . . by a Lady*, which appeared in 1835 when she was nearly seventy.[8] Composed during a holiday in the town when she was recovering from an illness, *A Picture* is a guidebook which, besides much practical information, historical chat, and enthusiastic description, contains a number of spirited passages in verse which appear to be original.

But Mary Jane Godwin was no Mary Wollstonecraft, either in talent or in charm. If Mary was depressive, Mary Jane was neurotic. Within a few years, she started to complain that she had lost her good looks – and Charles Lamb made jokes about the size of her bottom – but Godwin himself remained genuinely fond of her. Letters over the years hint at a satisfactory sex life and whenever they were apart, they not only wrote nearly every day – complaining of the pains of deprivation – but they went to extraordinary lengths to keep separations to a minimum. On one occasion Godwin spoke of the animal magnetism which drew them together. They were both unusual and remarkable people, he would tell her, and like the heroes of Godwinian novels, their craving for love and friendship could not easily be met. Fear of isolation, he remarked, was part of the price which William Godwin had to pay for being a man of genius, and his wife could not escape a share of the difficulties. Sorely tried by her unpredictable moods, sudden flares of temper followed by huffiness and sulks – Charles Lamb called her the 'Bad Baby' – Godwin advised her on one occasion to 'suppress in part the excesses of that baby-sullenness to be brought out every day for every trifle' which he was sure she could control if she wanted.[9] Maintaining his right, as he put it, to act as monitor as well as lover, and exercising it more frequently than was perhaps wise, he always gave proper weight in his scoldings to her many redeeming qualities. With a tincture of philosophy, he told her, she would understand the absurdity of distressing herself over trifles.

Mary Jane in her turn regularly promised that she would try to do better. If she lived in the country, she told Godwin when on a visit to Charlotte Smith in Fareham, she could be a better wife and mother.

Here, my best beloved, I could make up the long arrears I owe for all the sweet patience of your temper and go hand in hand with all your wishes.[10]

Even at her most loving, however, Mary Jane struck a querulous note. As she wrote in September 1805 when Godwin suggested at short notice that she should meet him halfway on his return from Norfolk at Snares-brook where they had spent their honeymoon night or at nearby Ilford.

How cruel, how more than cruel you are to make me seem unkind!
If you could be a woman and a *managing* woman but for a single day you would

understand better what the most affectionate of wives could or could not do – I have had our bedroom nicely cleaned, the furniture put up, have fancied your arrival at seven, your stepping into more than half our bed, the kind embrace, the cup of coffee all ready, the refreshing slumber for an hour, the broken day, the fête of walking with you to town and idling all the day with you . . . My dearest love I have set our own sweet house a more kindred scene for blissful meeting than Ilford . . . [11]

Godwin acknowledged his sense of dependence as he had done to Mary Wollstonecraft, and he demanded comfort, consolation, and understanding as rights due from a wife to a husband. Unafraid of permitting her a motherly role, he frequently addressed her as 'Dearest Mamma' in his letters, and a few days after his own mother died in 1809 at the age of eighty-six he confided that his life was now transformed.

While my mother lived I always felt to a certain degree as if I had someone who was my superior and who exercised a mysterious protection over me. I belonged to something, I hung to something; there is nothing that has so much reverence and religion in it as affection to parents . . . You shall now be my mother; you have in many instances been my protector and my guide . . . [12]

Mary Jane for her part, like her famous predecessor, was genuinely grateful to be steadied by Godwin's strength and revived by his optimism. But when in 1805 she sent him a happy letter from Kingston his choice of compliment was scarcely tactful.

I hope you will understand me as I mean, when I say that the whole reminded me strongly of an epistolary style that never was written but by one person before, in the world [Mary Wollstonecraft]. You cannot misunderstand me, since, alas! the compositions which I allude to were not confined to me but before my turn were addressed with no less fervour to others. But yet, whether they were superscribed to a fusty old pedant of a painter [Fuseli], or to an imprudent and unprincipled debauchee [Imlay], the same sensibility irradiated them, the same warmth of feeling, the same agonising alarm, the same ardent hope, as I trace with such unspeakable delight in the letter before me.[13]

However literary she might be, the second Mrs Godwin was always aware that everyone who entered number 29 The Polygon was bound to compare her with the first Mrs Godwin whose portrait dominated the little parlour. She determined to assert her own claims from the start. James Marshall who had enjoyed family terms in Godwin's house since they had been boys together at Hoxton Dissenting Academy discovered that he was no longer welcome to drop in for dinner whenever he liked. He later described Mrs Godwin as a 'clever, bustling, second-rate woman, glib of tongue and pen, with a temper undisciplined and uncontrolled; not bad-hearted, but with a complete absence of all the finer sensibilities'.[14] Charles Lamb also disliked her. His letters are full of backbiting stories and spiteful comments – on one occasion he calls her a bitch – and some people have taken the description of the unattractive Mrs Pry in *The Lepus Papers* as his vengeful verdict.[15]

In a group which valued sincerity above friendship, Mary Jane's preference for the lesser virtues was deeply shocking. *Political Justice* had discussed the long chain of moral destruction which comes from asking your servant to tell an unwelcome caller that you are not at home, but Mary Jane followed a different tradition. One day when the Lambs called, they were given an elaborate explanation that Godwin had scalded his foot and could not possibly receive them. But when they called the next day to offer their sympathy, they met the philosopher hale and hearty in the street completely unaware of the accident. Having no high regard herself for literal truth, Mary Jane was genuinely surprised that people should take offence at her politeness, and never saw the slightest need to explain her inconsistencies, let alone to apologize. Sometimes she told lies for trivial reasons, and sometimes for no discoverable reason at all. Thirty years after their marriage her husband was still writing long patient complaining letters on the point, unscrambling her fibs and urging her to do better in the future.

At the beginning Godwin's friends took little trouble to make her welcome. Godwin recalled years later how Fuseli rose from his dinner table one evening telling Mrs Godwin as he left that he could not understand why he had been invited to meet such wretched company – an incident which must have occurred at the introductory party on 8 January 1802, one of the few occasions when Fuseli deigned to visit Godwin's house.[16] Coleridge, who happened to be in London at the time of the marriage, caused offence by not answering the invitation to the celebratory dinner – although it turned out later that he had not received the letter in time. When Holcroft betrayed some lack of enthusiasm on first introduction, Godwin accused him of always trying to sabotage his relationships with women from the time in 1796 when Amelia Alderson had courted their friendship.[17]

Godwin defended his new wife as best he could. Not infrequently after an evening out he would feel obliged to write to complain about some alleged disrespect, sounding on occasions unlike a philosopher who believed that dishonour could be earned but not conferred. It was hard to fit a new wife into the established life pattern of a forty-six-year-old man who had lived alone for most of his life. Dinners were often boisterous. Many of his friends shared his views on the usefulness of the clash of mind on mind; and the Godwinian duty to tell your neighbour that he is a fool (if you sincerely believe that he is) was often encouraged by drink. Coleridge behaved so badly on one occasion that he thought that Godwin would break with him altogether.

In October 1803 John Philpot Curran on a visit from Dublin, promised to dine at The Polygon on the 18th and then again on the 26th, but did not turn up on either occasion and the dinner was wasted. When the following day he did the same thing, for the third time within a fortnight, Mary Jane decided that she had had enough and told Godwin that she was leaving. It was a threat — or an offer — which she was often to repeat and there were several times when she actually left. The impartial analyses of her character which her husband offered on such occasions could easily have tipped the balance from exasperation to despair, but she always came back.

However it is easy to forget in reading of these crises how unrepresentative the references in surviving documents may be. It is easy too for a biographer to give undue weight to the opinions of the people who happen to have written things down. Charles Lamb and his sister, despite all their outbursts against Mrs Godwin, were to remain friends of the Godwins for the next thirty-three years — for long periods scarcely a week passed without some contact between the two families. Marshall too soon resumed his visits although less frequently than before. Godwin's journal, with its comprehensive notes of the comings and goings of ordinary life, is an excellent reminder that the commonest events are the least frequently recorded. For every stormy occasion described by Hazlitt, Coleridge, Lamb and others, there must have been thirty when Godwin and Mrs Godwin drank tea with the same friends, chatted quietly, or played a few rounds of whist.

The literary eye is selective in other ways. It is evident from the journal, for example, that one of the most important people in Godwin's life was Sarah Elwes. A lady of the same age as himself, she had married John Elwes, son of the meanest man in England,* after the death of her first husband but she seems to have lived separately at any rate for part of the time. Godwin first met her in 1799, and until the time of his second marriage he was often seeing her several times a week, calling in the

---

* While MP for Berkshire and worth £100,000, he is said to have eaten half a dead moorhen which he found at the side of his lake. Godwin read the amusing *Life of John Elwes* shortly after meeting Sarah.

afternoons, going to the theatre with her, dining or supping frequently at her house and she at his, often with other friends but more often just the two of them. Whenever he left London he called to say goodbye and she was always among the first to be visited when he returned. On at least two occasions she went with him to the country, including once on a visit to Charles James Fox. After Godwin's marriage, Mrs Elwes disappeared from his life for several years, but after occasional visits – and the death of her second husband – she was later fully accepted as a family friend. Godwin was with her the day before she died in 1817. He must have spent at least as many hours with Sarah Elwes as he ever did with Mary Wollstonecraft. Yet among the collections of letters, essays, records of conversations, and other documents which dozens of literary friends left in impressive quantities, she is never once mentioned, let alone described.[18]

The same is true of Godwin's family. His brothers, John, Joseph, and latterly Nat were often to be found at his fireside. In the years after Mary Wollstonecraft's death Joseph's wife Harriet was often in and out, perhaps helping to look after the children, and there were nephews and nieces. But since no literary writer chose to mention them it is as if they had never existed. It would be possible to compile a list of fifty other men and women whom Godwin met frequently – and who were presumably bound to him by varying ties of friendship – but about whom almost nothing is known but their names. The very richness of Godwin's personal records, which permits so many facts about his life to be reconstructed and explained, also vividly demonstrates the limitations of biography.

The second Mrs Godwin arrived out of the blue. No one knew who she was or where she came from. Godwin himself maintained from the time of the announcement of his marriage that Mrs Clairmont was a widow with two children by her previous husband, but no word was ever recorded about the mysterious Mr Clairmont. When shortly after the marriage, Godwin had to obtain a copy of a birth certificate for Charles Clairmont, Mrs Clairmont described herself as a daughter of Andrew Peter Devereux, but nothing was known about her life before the fateful 5 May 1801 when she first called to him from her balcony.[19] Eighteen years later, Henry Crabb Robinson, an indefatigable recorder of invaluable gossip noted:

It is said she was never married, but was kept and abandoned by her keeper, or rather, left destitute at his death. She was relieved by a charitable subscription, and taken out of a prison; on which she came up to town with her young children, met with Godwin at Somers Town, and became certainly towards him a meritorious wife, though towards others I doubt both her sincerity and her integrity.[20]

That was the nearest that anyone at the time came to uncovering Mrs Clairmont's past. In the late 1950s however the researches of Professor Herbert Huscher brought to light some astonishing facts from official archives and other documents, as a result of which all previous accounts of the second Mrs Godwin have had to be substantially modified. To those facts more can now be added, but as Huscher also found, each new revelation raises more questions, and many puzzles remain.

What is beyond doubt is that when the hurried decision to marry was taken at the end of October 1801, Godwin made himself party to an elaborate deception that he was to maintain for the rest of their lives. Mary Jane Clairmont, he knew before the marriage, was not a widow but an unmarried mother of two. If Godwin had not married her she would have been an unmarried mother of three. In addition to the quiet marriage at St Leonard's, Shoreditch on 21 December at which Marshall was present, it is now known from the parish records that the couple were married for a second time on the same day even more secretly at St Mary's, Whitechapel, with only church officials present. Godwin did not mention either marriage in his journal, noting only 'Shoreditch Church etc w[ith] C[lairmon]t & M[arshall]'. In the register of the first marriage at Shoreditch, Mary Jane describes herself as 'Mary Clairmont, widow of this parish: in the second she is 'Mary Vial of St Mary le Bone, spinster'. To obtain permission for the second marriage Godwin had made a further false declaration under oath before the Bishop of London's representative on 23 November that for the past four weeks his usual place of abode was in Whitechapel. The second marriage was no doubt intended as a precaution in case the first marriage – with its false statements – should ever be challenged and declared null and void.

Political Justice permits and encourages the setting aside of promises if greater good results from non-compliance than from compliance, but it offers no trade-off between utility and truth, even a utility heavily weighted by considerations of family ties. It was therefore presumably a difficult decision to become a party to a deliberate deception, even if the institutions being deceived had no call on his respect or his obedience. If Godwin calculated that greater good would result from insincerity, he was probably right, and if he was concerned about the implications for political justice, his theory could have been rescued by permitting a trade-off between large short-term welfare gains and small long-term revelations of truth. As it happens, it has taken over a century and a half to disentangle the network of falsehood, but with the help of modern progress truth has staged a belated triumph, and Godwin's theory is vindicated.

What is difficult to ascertain is how much of the truth about Mary Jane he himself was told. He knew from the beginning that she had strong French family connections, and their first plan was to be married in France where there would be less fuss about the expected baby. As it happened, the ceasefire which was to lead to the brief Peace of Amiens was declared on 1 October 1801 shortly before the pregnancy was confirmed, and on 1 November, two days after a medical consultation with Carlisle, Godwin wrote to Lord Pelham of the Aliens Office asking for a passport to go to Paris.[21] We do not know what reason he offered but a crisp refusal from Pelham's office arrived by return of post. The Government did not want to see England's foremost Jacobin writer visiting the enemy capital before a treaty had even been negotiated.

Godwin knew too that Mary Jane had lived in France while a girl. In one of his later letters he reminded her of how courageous she had been in emigrating to the Continent at the age of eleven (about 1777), implying that she had done so on her own initiative against the wishes of those about her. He believed that she had later 'fled from sights and sounds of inhumanity', a phrase which, taken with remarks elsewhere, suggests that she was in France at the time of the Revolution along with her sister Charlotte, and had fled to her brother at Cadiz in order to escape. All this seems reasonably well established even if based mainly on what Mary Jane herself told him.

What is more doubtful is whether she ever told him the truth about the children, Charles Gaulis Clairmont and Clara Mary Jane Clairmont (called Jane by the family but later known as Claire). In 1830, when she was about sixty-five, she prepared a letter for them in which she purported to pass on the secrets of their births. She had, she said, met Karl Gaulis, a member of a prominent Swiss family, in Cadiz when on a visit to her brother, and she then went with him to Bristol where Gaulis anglicized his name to Charles Clairmont. Their father, the children were told, had died on a visit to Hamburg in 1798 in a cholera epidemic.

Charles and Jane had evidently been told most of this when they were children. Both were aware of their Swiss family connections and of the fact – of which Mary Jane was proud – that their father's sister, Albertine Marianna Gaulis was married to Robert Trefusis, Lord Clinton, the biggest landowner in Devonshire, who lived in Trefusis Hall near Falmouth. But there is no evidence that Lady Clinton took any interest in her illegitimate nephew and niece or had any connection with the Godwin family.[22]

From the records it can be confirmed that Charles Clairmont, who was born on 4 June 1795, was almost certainly the son of Karl Gaulis. But it has also been established from contemporary records that Karl Gaulis did not die in Hamburg in 1798, but in Silesia in 1796. He cannot therefore have been the father of Jane Clairmont, if, as she herself believed, she was born at Bristol on 27 April 1798. It is possible that Jane – who shared her mother's distaste for literalism – was mistaken about her birthday or later pretended to be younger than she was. The birthday of 27 April – known only from her diary – happens to be the same as that of Mary Wollstonecraft and she may have adopted it. The probability remains however that Jane Clairmont's father was a man – about whom nothing is yet known – with whom Mary Jane took up after Gaulis had gone abroad.

It is not surprising therefore that Mary Jane was keen to marry Godwin. To be the unmarried mother of one could be passed off in the mid-1790s as a proper gesture of social defiance. To be the unmarried mother of two by different fathers was harder. To add a third by a third father in the middle of the anti-Jacobin anti-feminist reaction would have condemned her to be treated as a prostitute.

One speculative conjecture is worth a mention. Among the group of French *émigrés* who provided many of Mary Jane's friends after her marriage to Godwin there is regular mention in 1811–13 of a man called Weale, and it is conceivable that he was a member of the de Vial family who had anglicized his name.[23] Weale and MadameTopping often appear together in the journal at family occasions, such as the children's birthdays, and at other times (such as when Mary Jane threatened to leave) when her family might be expected to take an interest. If Weale is the same as Vial, particular interest attaches to a unique entry in Godwin's journal for New Year's Day 1801: 'Miss Weale breakfasts and dines.'

Godwin had gone the day before that meeting to Old Windsor to attend the funeral of his friend Mary Robinson, the famous actress whose rendering of Perdita in *The Winter's Tale* had started her on her career as the most famous courtesan of her day. Like Charlotte Smith and perhaps Mary Jane she had spent time in a debtors' prison, and when the Prince of Wales offered her a post-dated bond for £20,000 in return for becoming his mistress, she accepted. But when Perdita proved less interesting offstage, the Prince dishonoured both her and his bond, and she was obliged to turn elsewhere for support and protection. Godwin was one of the few friends who kept in touch.[24] Since the meeting with Miss Weale on 1 January took place at Windsor, the likelihood is that she was also a guest at Mrs Robinson's funeral and therefore perhaps also a lady lacking in respectability. Is it carrying imagination too far to suggest that a Miss Weale met in Old Windsor on 1 January could with the help of French friends have installed herself in the house next door in London as a pushful Mrs Clairmont by the following May?

At the end of 1807 Godwin was introduced to Mrs Pilcher, one of Mary Jane's sisters, and when he started to see her regularly in 1809 he must have learned something more of Mary Jane's past if he was not told everything in 1801. Sophia Elizabeth de Vial had married Edward Pilcher at Crediton in Devonshire in 1792 and a number of children were christened in a batch on one day at Barnstaple in 1796.[25] Edward Pilcher was obviously a man of some substance since the family were then living in 'The Vines', the biggest house in Rochester, Kent, now known as the Restoration House because Charles II stayed there after his return from exile.

The Godwins and the Pilchers were to visit one another often in following years and their children came to be friends although Godwin disliked 'the padrone' as he called Edward Pilcher. The Vines* had been the residence of monarchs, one of Godwin's nephews-in-law wrote to him in 1820, but it was now more honoured by the recent visit of the author of *Political Justice*.[26] Given Godwin's opinion of Charles II, that was not much of a compliment.

It was not however until the long wars with France came to an end that Mary Jane was able to visit her second sister Charlotte. Charlotte de Vial had returned to France in 1801 during the Peace of Amiens and married Pierre de Valette, an armaments merchant of St Etienne, and the renewal of the war meant that the two families were cut off for fifteen years. Mary Jane was too ill to make the journey to St Etienne in 1816 but she went there in the following year. After Mary Jane's visit, the Valettes came to England, their son Marc attending school in London along with Godwin's son William.[27] Another sister, Mrs Bicknall, whom Mary Jane mentioned in a number of later letters as living in Lynmouth in Devonshire, appears to be a fabrication.[28]

And what of Mary Jane herself? The municipal records of St Etienne which describe Charlotte de Vial as having been born in 'échetea ville

---

* The house was to be the model for Miss Havisham's residence in *Great Expectations* but it is unlikely that the Rochester schoolboy Charles Dickens ever saw William Godwin entering its forbidding gateway.

d'angleter, département de Vonshier' (the best the French clerk could manage for Exeter, Devonshire) daughter of Pierre Vialle, a merchant, and Catherine Okehe, have led to the discovery of records of Mary Jane's family in Exeter, the first independent evidence of her family background that has yet come to light. Unfortunately this evidence is incomplete and raises almost as many puzzles as it solves. Peter – or Pierre – de Vial is recorded in the Exeter parish records as having married Catherine Oak in 1782.[29] There can be little doubt that he was the father of the three sisters Mary Jane, Sophia and Charlotte. He is described as a merchant, and since he had close connections with St Etienne, he was perhaps also engaged in the armaments business for which that town is famous. An advertisement in the *Exeter Flying Post* of December 1791 implies that at that time he had recently died and that his business was bankrupt. All his goods were being sold to pay off his debts.

It emerges from the St Etienne records that his widow Catherine Oak emigrated there in 1801 with her daughter Charlotte during the brief Peace of Amiens. Godwin's journal makes occasional mentions of a man called Oak, who may have been a relative and on 7 August 1812, the whole family including the children were entertained to dinner by a Captain Oak on board his ship the *Abundance*. It is highly unlikely however that Catherine Oak could have been Mary Jane's mother. If Mary Jane was aged seventy-five when she died on 17 June 1841, as her tombstone records, then Catherine Oak was only about fourteen years old at most at the time of her birth, since she is recorded in the St Etienne records as having died in November 1833 at the age of eighty-one.[30]

There is an earlier record in Exeter of a Peter de Vial marrying a Mary Tremlett in 1764.[31] It is possible therefore that Mary Jane was a child of that earlier marriage, along with Sophia, the brother who settled in Cadiz and perhaps Charlotte as well, although de Vial – a Huguenot name – is not as uncommon in Devon as one would first expect. The signature in the register of the Peter de Vial who married Mary Tremlett is markedly different from that of the man who married Catherine Oak. It is therefore possible that Mary Jane was an illegitimate daughter of Peter de Vial before he married Catherine Oak. Charlotte was born five years before her parents' marriage – unless she was being untruthful in telling the French registrar that Catherine Oak was her mother – and her first son was born six weeks after her own wedding. The de Vials all had a lot to hide, especially in revolutionary and counter-revolutionary times, and concealment, lies, and illegitimacy were evidently all strong family traditions.

And what of the name Clairmont? The likelihood is that it was invented. The fashionable novels of the day, from which foreigners regularly derive misinformation about England, were almost exclusively stocked by aristo-crats of solid Anglo-Norman lineage. It would be impossible to count the Montforts, the Clairvilles, and the St Aubyns who caused flutters in the bosoms of the Miss Savilles, the Lady Beauforts and the Hon. Elizabeth Vernons. (St Clair was an especial favourite when Mrs Godwin was a girl as she herself recalls in the *Picture of Herne Bay*.) Godwin's journal records several walks with Mary Jane to Leadenhall Street, site of the Minerva Press Circulating Library which specialized in society romances and gothic thrillers. It should cause no surprise if the unhappy, impover-ished, and deracinated Mary Jane de Vial chose the names Devereux and Clairmont for her imaginary father and invented husband.

In time no doubt the power of truth will make further advances. Mean-while the following outline of Mary Jane's earlier life may be ventured. She was the daughter of a French merchant settled in Exeter. About the time when her father decided to marry Catherine Oak, she boldly set off by herself to find her French relations in St Etienne. With the coming of the Revolution, however, she and her family were plunged from riches to poverty, and she herself moved first to Cadiz and then back to England. As a Roman Catholic and a royalist, there was no place for her in revolutionary France. But fatherless in England she was equally out of place, and the coming of the war in 1793 cut her off completely from her family across the Channel. She was therefore an easy prey to a visiting French-speaking Swiss, who abandoned her after the birth of an illegit-imate son, and she soon took up with another man who in his turn gave her an illegitimate daughter before disappearing. She again quickly sank towards poverty and spent time in a debtors' prison from which she was released by charity money, and was barely able to maintain herself when Godwin presented himself.

To cope with the misfortunes and betrayals that had marked her life, Mary Jane had developed her own pragmatic style which verged on fantasy. While she remained grateful to Godwin for giving her a status, she never forgot that she had been used to better things and she resented being poor. As for Godwin, when he married her he scarcely knew her, and more than most wives she turned out to be entirely different from what he expected. But he was not disappointed and he was willing to adapt. In educating the philosopher in the complexities of human nature, the second Mrs Godwin was as influential as the first.

The change was huge. In 1797 he was a solitary bachelor. Mary Wollstonecraft had left him with two children, and two years after meeting Mary Jane he had three more. All five were under the age of eight. They were an unusual family. Charles Clairmont was the half-brother of Jane Clairmont who was the half-sister of William Godwin Junior who was the half-brother of Mary Godwin who was the half-sister of Fanny Imlay. Four of the five had either Godwin or Mary Jane as a natural parent, but no two of them had the same father and the same mother.

CHAPTER 19

Body and Mind

During his long years as a bachelor, Godwin was usually short of money.[1]
He started in London with no resources but his genius, and the early
years in Grub Street were a constant struggle. His afternoons frequently
included calls at the Fleet and Marshalsea prisons to bail out or visit
friends arrested for debt, and the entry in his journal for 13 September
1788 'Sleep in Cold Bath Fields' implies that he spent that night in prison
probably for the same offence.[2]

On the whole however he managed to remain reasonably comfortable.
His needs were modest, he worked long and hard, and since he was rising
rapidly in his profession he did not mind. After the publication of *Political
Justice* and *Caleb Williams* his finances improved. Although the money
for both books had been mostly advanced and spent before publication
day, by the mid-1790s Godwin believed reasonably enough that he could
make an adequate livelihood by his pen. He was able to afford a few
extras such as antiquarian books and visits to friends in the country. After
his first tour in 1793, he seems to have promised himself a holiday as a
reward whenever one of his books came out.

Dr Johnson – the dominating literary figure of Godwin's youth – was
one of the first writers to throw off the shackles of patronage and earn
his living from the market. In the early 1790s a few undiscerning people
had hailed Dr Parr as the 'Whig Dr Johnson', drawing a misleading
parallel between his pedantic quarrelsomeness and the robust learned

Birthday Gifts, from *Lessons for Children*

conversation of the great lexicographer. But after *Political Justice* and *Caleb Williams* it was William Godwin who looked set to be the Dr Johnson of the new age, a man who had risen by talent and persistence to fame and influence, a prolific writer who could turn his pen to every literary genre, whose door was open to any man or woman interested in good conversation on serious subjects.[3]

Godwin never doubted that writing for money was a compromise with things as they are. Selling manuscripts to publishers might be less objectionable than queueing in a rich man's parlour but he regarded both with distaste. In *Political Justice* he described the prevailing system of property – meaning the whole economic system – as the most damaging of all the institutions which enchain natural benevolence. As an individual his opportunities for changing the system were limited but if he were obliged to operate within it, there was no reason why he should give it active support. On the contrary it was his duty to practise political justice impartially.

Strangers in distress could rely on receiving money, although not having much to share, justice did not require him to give a great deal. Over the years he gave considerable amounts to help his brothers and their families. When the poet Robert Merry was in prison in Norwich in 1796 Godwin persuaded some of his richer acquaintances such as Dr Alderson to settle with the creditors and enable Merry to start a new life in America. But it was obvious that, on any view of political justice, the financial flows ought to run mainly in the other direction. A man of genius who – like Fénelon – had huge potential for accelerating the progress of perfectibility by his writings ought to be given the means to do so. Among the many admirers of *Political Justice* there were fortunately a number of rich men willing to put these principles into action. Tom Wedgwood in particular, who with his brother Josiah had conferred an unconditional annuity of £150 a year on Coleridge, was always ready to help if asked.

In accepting what was his due, Godwin was alert to any implication that he was incurring an obligation. When John King the moneylender asked him in 1796 to put in a word on his behalf with a certain nobleman, Godwin's scolding was severe. 'Did you imagine that your dinners were to be a bribe,' he demanded, 'seducing me to depart from the integrity of my judgment? That would be a character meaner than that of the poorest pensioner of the vilest court that ever existed.' He had been in two minds, he explained frankly, when King first started asking him to dinner, whether he ought to associate with a man of his reputation, but he did not 'believe that the right way to attempt to correct the errors of the vicious is that all honest men should desert them'.[4] King answered in good humour asking him to dine the following day.

Ever ready himself to offer a needed rebuke, Godwin expected his friends to treat him with the same frankness. When John Philpot Curran declined to lend him money in early 1801 despite having offered to do so during his visit to Dublin, Godwin was full of lofty regret.

I consider the question of any serious pecuniary assistance from one man to another as almost the most inviolable and sacred of all subjects; and no earthly consideration should have induced me to pollute our intercourse with such a question, had I not written under the full persuasion of your having made me an express offer of assistance.[5]

The conventions in such matters were very different from what they have since become. To borrow money from a friend or an acquaintance carried little or no stigma. In the absence of a national banking system there was no simple way for a holder of money to put it out at interest while keeping his investment easily realizable. Government stock was far from risk free and other financial investments such as mortgages carried their own difficulties. With inflation running high, and the rate of interest fixed by statute at 5 per cent maximum, it was a borrower's market. A reliable payer who borrowed on good security was doing the lender a favour.

It was two families of Norwich both known well to Godwin – the Taylors and the Gurneys – who were developing an effective method of employing the financial surpluses of the country areas to finance the growing capital needs of the towns. By buying post-dated bills from London at a discount for cash, they were able to pay interest to their depositors without moving the actual money, and when the bills became due for payment they could usually be rolled over for a further period. Several of Godwin's friends who owned property helped give him access to credit by guaranteeing his bills without themselves parting with money, and if he was in difficulty in rolling them over, he could usually turn to friends in Norwich.

The risks were high. Whenever there was a scare – and since the country was at war they were frequent – everybody wanted to withdraw money at once. Even in normal times, with the rate of interest fixed, there was usually some imbalance between demand and supply, and anyone wishing to discount a bill on a day when the bill brokers had already bought their quota might find it difficult to do so. If a bill was not settled or rolled over when the due date arrived, the credit of the borrower was destroyed and he could not expect to discount his bills again, and in Regency England there were few more pitiable men than insolvent debtors.

There were five debtor jails in central London and a number of private 'sponging houses'. The creditor employed bailiffs to make the arrest and the prison authorities would not allow the debtor to be released unless he either paid up in full or persuaded a creditworthy friend to stand bail. Imprisonment was permitted for any debt of £10 or more. Some finance houses made a business of buying bills, pouncing on debtors the moment they became due, and then offering to refinance at exorbitant illegal rates of interest. Settling with one creditor did not protect the debtor from immediate re-arrest by another: it made it more likely.[6]

For anyone who had money, arrest for debt was not onerous. The marshal of the prison could provide comfortable quarters and would let prisoners out for the day on parole. William Combe pursued his writing career for twelve years from prison rather than pay a disputed debt. We hear of gentlemen going off to the shires for a day's hunting and even crossing to France while technically in prison. But for those who had no money, there was no escape. Unable to settle or to obtain bail, they lost their livelihood, and the mounting costs and interest payments turned misfortune into catastrophe. In the wall of the Fleet Prison which Godwin passed every day was an open iron grated window where a succession of starving half-naked debtors took turns to beg alms from passers-by.[7] Many died of jail fever – a call by Godwin at the New Jail in 1793 was to see a friend called Munnings who was dying. A charity known as the Thatched House Society every year secured the release of thousands imprisoned for debts of a few pounds. Mary Jane Clairmont is said to have been one of their beneficiaries before she met Godwin. When a Select Committee reviewed the credit laws in 1813 they found debtors who had been in prison for twenty years or more.

By the late 1790s it was clear that Godwin was not destined to follow in Dr Johnson's path to success. He had a wife, five children and no savings – indeed, his net asset worth was heavily negative if account was taken of the 'advances' made to him by various admirers. Charles and Fanny were reaching the age when they needed to be sent to school – for which fees were required – and Jane and Mary were not far behind. The house in The Polygon – often described as a cottage – was far too small to accommodate a family of seven and it was urgent to find somewhere bigger.

At the same time just when he needed money most, Godwin's earning power fell rapidly away. By 1803 the price of remaindered copies of

Political Justice had fallen to two shillings.[8] *Caleb Williams* was out of print. *St. Leon*, while by no means a failure, was a financial disappointment. *Antonio*, which had been put on with the help of borrowed money, was a disaster. The long boom in the book market had been brought to an end by the war. Manuscripts were more difficult to place and publishers less willing to invest.

At the time of their marriage Godwin and Mary Jane gave a great deal of thought to how they could make ends meet. Godwin took her on a round of London publishers searching for work, but the results were meagre. She obtained a number of contracts for French translation at a guinea a sheet, and Godwin helped with the work.[9] She also continued preparing children's books for Benjamin Tabart of Bond Street, one of the lowest paid types of hack work, and here too Godwin read and revised her drafts.

Godwin approached the problem with his usual resilience. If his books were selling less well, he would have to write more of them, although it was difficult to find peace with young children romping round the overcrowded house and a baby crying in the next room. If philosophy and serious novels were out of fashion, he would write histories or biographies or whatever type of works the publishers suggested. Although it was his duty to continue serious writing – and he would never neglect that duty – he would also write lesser works to keep the pot on the boil. The only thing he would not do was literary journalism. He had already done too much of that in his youth, and he would never again compromise his independence. 'I swear by all the ancient Gods of Rome and Greece', he told Marshall, 'that (at least till I am provided with apartments in a certain College on the other side of the water) [i.e. Bedlam Lunatic Asylum] I will never Scribble essays for a Magazine or articles for a Review.'[10] In later life it was one of his proudest boasts that he had never been forced back between the stocks of a hackney carriage.

In 1801 came the death of George Robinson, his publisher and friend since *New Annual Register* days, and although the family continued the business for a time its reputation had gone. Joseph Johnson too was less active than in the past. It was therefore gratifying when Godwin found himself adopted as an author by Richard Phillips, rising sun of the publishing trade, who brought the skills of his successful hosiery business to the designing and marketing of books. Phillips had liberal sympathies – like many publishers he was proud to have been to jail for selling *The Rights of Man* – but he was primarily a businessman. Godwin found him dull, pompous, and slow,[11] severe words from a man himself more noted for persistence than for sparkle, but Phillips had energy and capital, and Godwin was pleased to accept his post-dated bills and turn them into cash. Phillips – soon to be Sir Richard – was the first member of the book trade to become Lord Mayor of London.

In 1802 and 1803 Godwin wrote two books for Phillips, a *Life of Chaucer* in two quarto volumes aimed at the topmost end of the market, and *Bible Stories*, a children's book, intended for sale in bulk to schools. The contract for the *Life of Chaucer* was finalized before the marriage, but work on the two books continued concurrently, and in the event *Bible Stories* was finished first. Since the Godwin children had to be properly educated, what could be more efficient than to write up the lessons which he was giving them into books which could be sold for money? As always, there was no gap between a decision taken and putting it into effect. Godwin started work on both books within days after his marriage.

Meanwhile the family had to live. On 1 January 1802 Godwin and Mary Jane walked to Lombard Street where they met John King who, despite the frank exchanges of 1796, still offered Godwin frequent dinners and ready credit. Shortly afterwards Godwin called on Lord Lauderdale the Whig politician who had admired his political writings in the mid-1790s. (The Prince of Wales happened also to be paying a call at the same time.) He also wrote to Fox and to Sheridan. If the market would not provide, he could revert to the older tradition of patronage. Meanwhile he would do what everyone else did in such circumstances, he would borrow. If the future looked uncertain, he still had numerous rich and powerful admirers who would ensure that England's foremost liberal writer suffered no disaster.

It was a bold plan and it deserved to succeed. But hard work needs good health. When William Godwin Junior was born in March 1803, William Godwin Senior was already forty-seven. His youth had come late, and he was now well into the second half of life. His hair was thin and his teeth loose. He suffered from piles – noted in his journal discreetly in Greek – and also from constipation, a painful combination.[12] But what was most worrying was what he called his delirium. In July 1803 he suffered a new attack of the fits which had begun in 1800. They lasted for three days and the fourth was taken up with vomiting. The disease was growing in intensity and the intervals between fits were shortening.

Anthony Carlisle and the other physicians whom he consulted could offer no cure. Bleeding and clysters which were at the time applied to virtually every illness made no difference – they probably did harm – and were soon abandoned. As a believer in the essential benevolence of nature,

Godwin then tried an alternative approach. Although he had never been a heavy drinker he now gave up the wine which he normally drank with his dinner. He also stopped eating meat apart from an occasional carefully selected bite. Enlightenment philosophers and political radicals from the time of Jean Jacques Rousseau had been attracted to vegetarianism. Just as powdered Church and King men flaunted their yeoman virtues by whipping their animals and eating large quantities of steak, their long-haired democratic opponents often affected a fastidious sensibility towards pets and food. But the natural diet which Godwin adopted in the mid-1800s was for reasons of his own health only. He still served meat to his guests and never scolded them for enjoying it. He also offered wine although not much. A letter to his vintner about one of his parties orders two bottles of wine and twenty glasses.[13]

One of his friends, John Frank Newton, believed that the asthma from which he had suffered had been cured by a strict water and vegetable diet, and *The Return to Nature; or, a Defence of the Vegetable Regimen*, a muddled pamphlet which he published in 1811, was based on three or four years of success.[14] Richard Phillips was also an aggressive vegetarian. But the evidence was not all in one direction. Rousseau's last years had been spent in something approaching madness. Joseph Ritson, Godwin's friend, who had helped him with historical points for *Caleb Williams* and *Cursory Strictures*, also wrote an influential pamphlet on natural diet. Ritson had lived on vegetables, biscuits, tea and lemonade devoting himself quietly to his historical and antiquarian studies. But by the time he was fifty – as Godwin noted in his obituary notice in the *Monthly Mirror*[15] – Ritson was subject to fits, his prodigious memory had gone, senility advanced rapidly, and he died comparatively young.

His own fits, Godwin knew, were related to his mental state. He usually had about a minute's notice of an attack. Sometimes when he was excited or irritated, he felt the sickening giddiness which was an early symptom, and fear was almost enough by itself to bring on an attack. The important thing was to keep calm, and to redirect his mind from worry. Mary Jane's answer to worry was to let her emotions be known, but as soon as her storms started, her husband would retire to his study and read the ancient philosophers. Godwin under stress reached for Seneca the way Coleridge reached for laudanum.

He was fascinated by the implications of his personal experience for his general psychological theory. In his day there was only one system of knowledge which purported to offer an explanation. Phrenology, which had been developed by Gall and Spurzheim on the Continent, had recently arrived in England and was arousing the same kind of initial interest that psychoanalysis was to cause a hundred years later. Here, maybe, was a possible contribution to the puzzle of the body/mind dichotomy. Mary Wollstonecraft and Holcroft had devoted many months to translating Lavater's *Essays in Physiognomy*, which scientifically related the expressions of the human face to the underlying emotions.* What phrenology tried to do, taking that idea further, was to use the outside shape of the skull as an indicator of the unseeable medullary particles inside. Gall and Spurzheim mapped the surface of the skull into thirty-one major and innumerable minor organs of mental qualities, and new ones were being discovered all the time.

To many contemporaries, the skull of William Godwin was living proof of the essential validity of the new science. His broad forehead was a fine example of the 'walls of reason'.[17] It was to become something of a joke that there was an indentation at the place in the head where phrenologists expected to find the protuberance marking veneration, and the mismatch of the right and left sides evidenced the personality split which had conceived *Caleb Williams*. Godwin would have been disappointed to read Dr Combe's comment in the *System of Phrenology* that a certain roundness indicated defective imagination,[18] but this was contradicted by a picture of dignified purposeful strength included in Sir George Mackenzie's *Illustrations of Phrenology*. Another phrenologist who was shown Godwin's portrait without being told who it was gave such an accurate analysis of his character that the experiment was quoted as certain proof of the truth of the phrenological method.[19]. But, to his credit, Godwin himself never succumbed. In an interesting essay written towards the end of his life he dismissed phrenology's claims as based on wishful thinking while looking forward to the day when valid techniques might be found to investigate the internal workings of the brain.[20]

The New Philosophy had always been prey for cranks. For a time in the 1790s Godwin and Holcroft were friends with John 'Walking' Stewart who after spending some years in India, walked across Persia to Arabia and Ethiopia before returning to Marseille and walking home. At the time Godwin first knew him he was pausing between a walk through North America and another to Constantinople, all intended to help gather philosophical information. He lived on bread and milk and enjoyed such good health that the financier who sold him a life annuity lost heavily on the

---

* Mary Wollstonecraft met Lavater on a visit to London in 1792. Shortly after her death William Nicholson wrote for Godwin a detailed analysis of the character of the three-week-old Mary Wollstonecraft Godwin from a Lavaterian study of her face.[16]

transaction. Latterly Stewart asked that copies of his privately printed books *Travels to discover the Source of Moral Motion* and *Apocalypse of Human Perfectibility* should be translated into Latin to ensure a wider European readership, and he invited his friends to bury them in secret places for the benefit of anyone who might survive the Apocalypse. *Political Justice*, he declared was a useful introduction to his own works which began where Godwin's ideas left off, but neither he nor anyone else has been able to understand them or even read them.[21]

In the 1800s it was the Newton and Boinville families and their friends who provided the eccentricity. The wives – who were sisters – were the initial link. Their father, a planter in the West Indies, had been involved in Godwin's and Marshall's plan to emigrate in 1784, when Marshall had made the trip to St Vincent and stayed with him. One sister married John Frank Newton, the vegetarian, the other married Chastel de Boinville, an aristocratic Frenchman who had been ADC to Lafayette. It was perhaps the French connection which drew them to Mary Jane. The Godwins saw both families frequently both at the Newtons' house in Chester Street and at the Boinville home in Bracknell.

The women adored Godwin and worshipped *Political Justice*, rolling their eyes in ecstasy, according to one witness, whenever his name was mentioned. But their imaginations were insufficiently under control. In *The Return to Nature* Newton suggested that Prometheus – who has been held responsible for many things – was suitably punished for bringing men the fire which permitted meat to be cooked and thus made more edible. Meat-eating, he believed, caused syphilis. Newton was convinced too that the signs of the zodiac represented an ancient symbol of vegetarianism, and that some mystical philosophy of number was secretly preserved in old tavern names. The publican of the Four Horseshoes to whom he put this idea suggested that the number was related to the number of legs of a typical horse.[22]

Mrs Boinville, who wore a red sash as a sign that she was a revolutionary, also practised 'nakedism' as she called it as part of her return to nature. One of their friends James Lawrence, known as the Chevalier Lawrence, took naturism a step further.[23] The liberation of women, he proclaimed, would only come about when they learned to practise 'Nairism', shedding not only their clothes but their inhibitions. Much interested in titles and genealogy, he was convinced that inheritance had once been on the female line, writing a poem *The Navel String* to illustrate the closeness of the physical bond. Godwin who knew him well, having first been introduced as early as September 1796, used to see him at the British Museum pursuing his unusual researches.

The Nairs, Lawrence explained in his long book *The Empire of the Nairs*, are a sophisticated people in India who have fortunately escaped the European system of marriage and are still living according to the system of nature. They have no restrictions on sex, and it is usually the woman who takes the initiative. This natural system produces no bad consequences either for individuals or for society. The Nairesses are the best of mothers. According to Lawrence, following the popular wisdom, frequent sex is a sufficient contraception in itself, so there is no problem about overpopulation. Nairism is also the answer to prostitution. Before the French Revolution, according to Lawrence, there were 20,000 professional whores in Paris, but freedom had reduced the figure to 8,000. In anti-Jacobin London, by contrast, the figure had risen from 50,000 to 70,000 over the same period. One of the stories in the book concerns the Countess Camilla, an English lady brought up among the Nairs who continues practising their customs on her return to England. To the surprise of friends, she hitches up her skirts and adjusts her garters in public; she takes off her clothes when she feels hot; and she delights the boys of Eton College by going swimming with them in the nude. She also 'makes happy' any man who takes her fancy. Lady Camilla's behaviour, she herself knows instinctively, is in accordance with the system of nature, but when she finds a copy of *A Vindication of the Rights of Woman* in a library, she realizes that she is acting on sound philosophical principles as well. In an earlier essay Lawrence had combined his ideas on Nairism with a plea for a reformed spelling. 'It is the privilege of Nair laides tu hav menny lovers,' he wrote. 'Can enny wun dout ov the miseries proceeding from the restraints under which love still labors.'

The Newton–Boinville circle were the kind of people who gave the New Philosophy a bad name. Living on high incomes from West Indian slave plantations they played at radicalism. The Aeolian strings of their minds could be made to vibrate by any passing breeze, and they could not tell a good argument from a bad one. Mrs Boinville's husband and her son were now officers in Napoleon's army fighting Britain and her allies, and during the war Mrs Boinville made repeated journeys across the Channel to enemy territory. Lawrence too – whose money also came from sugar – spent some years in France after 1803 having been detained there on the outbreak of war, and his French sounding title alerted suspicion. If the New Philosophy was not in fact a dangerous coalition of traitors, spies, and cranks, the Bracknell circle offered all the evidence that most anti-Jacobins required.

With a wife like Mary Jane and friends like these, it was difficult for Godwin to hold to essentials. But he never flirted with the more cranky notions. And he had his reward. Whether it was the water or the vegetables or the Seneca, his health improved. After the frightening fits of 1803, there was no recurrence until 1807 although he suffered from an outbreak of skin disease in April 1805 which may have had a psychological origin. His constipation, we may be confident, also benefited from the vegetables. At the age of fifty Godwin noted proudly that he walked the six miles to Wimbledon to see his old friend Horne Tooke in exactly ninety minutes.

CHAPTER 20

Imagination and Sensibility

It was probably Richard Phillips, his new publisher, who suggested that he might like to write a life of Chaucer. On a visit to Huntingdon in 1800 Phillips had been shown a full-length portrait painted on board on which the name Chaucer could be discerned. It came from the house where Oliver Cromwell was believed to have been born and Phillips bought it on the spot. At about the same time when the Chamber of the House of Commons was being enlarged to make room for the hundred new members from Ireland, a series of fourteenth-century frescos was discovered behind the wainscoting of St Stephen's Chapel. They were of a quality not previously associated with fifteenth-century England.

In the debates on the French Revolution, English conservatives longed to believe that the olden days of chivalry so worshipped by Burke had not been as barbarous as the philosophers of the Enlightenment tended to assume. In the middle of a desperate war with France they needed reassurance that England too was a nation with a long and admirable cultural history. A book on Chaucer seemed exactly what the public mood demanded. It was true that Tyrwhit's recent edition of the *Canterbury Tales* had summarized all the known biographical facts in eight pages, but, as Godwin told Phillips, a similar shortage had not prevented Middleton from writing his best-selling life of Cicero in two substantial quarto volumes.

In the three years which Godwin devoted to the book before Phillips

The Proof of Love, from *Lessons for Children*

insisted on bringing it to a halt, he did a great deal of original historical research. He read extensively at the British Museum going there nearly every day. He delved among the public records then preserved at the Tower of London and uncovered references to Chaucer that had not previously been known. He visited the sites connected with Chaucer and with the Chaucer family at Woodstock and Ewelme in order to get a feel for the places. He studied the surviving visual evidence, commissioning an engraving of the portrait of John of Gaunt which is preserved in stained glass at All Souls College, Oxford.

Godwin's general theory led him at once to a modern view of biography. By imaginative reconstruction from the fragmentary record, he would, he hoped, retrieve the characters of Chaucer and his contemporaries and offer his readers the illusion that they had known them personally. He worked, he said, 'to rescue for a moment the illustrious dead from the jaws of the grave, to make them pass in review before me, to question their spirits, and record their answers'. To understand the man it is necessary to understand the times. He therefore explained the effects of Chaucer's education, the likely influence of his reading, the presuppositions he brought to his work, and the long chains of necessity which determined his character.

Godwin pointed to differences in manners that modern readers should allow for in reading Chaucer's poetry – such as the tendency of medieval people to complain too much. He tried to give a sense of how the world might have appeared in Chaucer's day. He explained the workings of the law, the role of the church, the distribution of political power, the position of women, and how changes in the economic background affected his subject's finances and behaviour. The *Life of Chaucer* was not only a biography but a history of the cultural, social, and political background of Chaucer's England.

For Godwin the Middle Ages – as a later generation was to call them emphasizing an intermediate status which was not apparent at the time – were an episode in the progress from ancient to modern times and one that made a unique contribution to the advance of human perfectibility. His historical narrative abounds with comments on modern issues such as the ethics of violent revolution, the ambiguous benefits of martyrdom, and the distinction between just and unjust wars. He takes space to praise the wisdom of the Treason Act of 1351. Chaucer himself he sees as a great English poet who revived the English language* and the English spirit after its long submersion by the Normans.

---

* Godwin noticed that the Anglo-Saxon words cow, sheep, and pig survived among the

At times he writes like Burke himself, praising the great chain of subordination of the feudal law which binds neighbour to neighbour. If to the ancients we owe the concept that men belong to the state, he writes, it is to the feudal system that we should attribute the notion of family. From feudalism came chivalry, and from chivalry came honour, which in its turn led to the notions of disinterested generosity which marked the modern age before the recent reaction set in. In an essay on the name Marguerite – a beautiful but despised flower found in profusion in every field – he traces the civilizing of sexual love. Readers might have recognized the name of the heroine of *St. Leon*, the idealization of pre-Wollstonecraft woman. At one point he suggests that the upper classes should set an example to the lower orders by avoiding love affairs outside marriage.

The *Life of Chaucer* is a celebration of the imagination as a moral force. Coleridge, Godwin had come increasingly to believe, had correctly identified one of the missing links in the original theory of necessity as set out in the 1793 *Political Justice*. He himself had never doubted the power of imaginative artists and writers – poets as he called them in the Greek fashion – to change the perceptions of society and so to accelerate perfectibility. They were an essential instrument for turning minds from things as they are to things as they might be. What was less clear was where the poets themselves obtained their creativity. Like many of his friends of the new romantic school Godwin was now less sure that the mind could be explained by purely passive metaphors such as that of the Aeolian harp. Imagination, whatever it was, was an active ingredient.

The romances of the age of chivalry, he now suggested, by describing an imaginary world, had lifted men's eyes and altered their behaviour with the result that life had indeed approached a little nearer to the ideal.[1] The responsibility that rests on writers who promote this process is therefore a heavy one. It is the duty of a poet, Godwin advises, in describing how Chaucer nearly ruined his genius by becoming a lawyer, to keep his intellect and his emotions free to receive every external impression. The poet is 'the legislator of generations and the moral instructor of the world', a thought that Shelley was later to immortalize in his famous adaptation, 'Poets are the unacknowledged legislators of the world.' It was a romantic view of the role of the artist. It was also political justice.

In the autumn and winter of 1803, as he anxiously awaited the reception of *Chaucer*, Godwin irritated his friends to the edge of endurance. Coler-

subjected English peasantry who looked after the live animals; for the Norman lords who ate them, the same animals became veal, mutton, and pork, all words derived from French.

idge, he had hoped, would write a favourable review of the book of which he was an inspirer, but he was too far gone with drugs to keep the simplest of promises. When Charles Lamb also pleaded to be excused – on grounds that he was not well – Godwin was sure his friends were deserting him. His persistent demands for a full explanation eventually drew out some at least of the truth in a letter from Lamb of the kind that nobody likes to write.

You never made a more unlucky and perverse mistake than to suppose that the reason of my not writing that cursed thing was to be found in your book. I assure you most sincerely that I have been greatly delighted with Chaucer. I may be wrong, but I think there is one considerable error runs through it, which is a conjecturing spirit, a fondness for filling out the picture by supposing what Chaucer did and how he felt, where the materials are scanty. So far from meaning to withhold from you (out of mistaken tenderness) this opinion of mine, I plainly told Mrs Godwin that I did find a *fault* which I should reserve naming until I should see you and talk it over. This she may very well remember and also that I declined naming this fault until she drew it from me by asking if there was not too much fancy* in the work.[2]

Lamb was then obliged to explain at length how he did not normally talk about his friends before third parties, even – or perhaps especially – before their wives and to risk turning his apology into a complaint. Given Godwin's liking for sincerity and Mary Jane's preference for family loyalty, such embarrassments were common.

The reviewers agreed that the book showed too much imagination. Unable to decide whether Godwin was still a Jacobin writer or had apostatized to the other side, they criticized him for both. It was considered gross bad manners to ask for the names of reviewers – whose anonymity provided a protection against being challenged to duels – but Godwin had no patience with such a convention. More than once he affronted his hosts at a dinner party by asking the direct question across the table. A call on Walter Scott was probably to demand whether he was the author of the pronouncement in *The Edinburgh Review* that the heavy volumes of Godwin's *Chaucer* ought to be used by the Navy to block the enemy's ports.

Walter Scott featured in another incident which took place at Horne Tooke's home in Wimbledon. When Godwin arrived and his name was sent up, Tooke was talking to Scott but he sent word that he would be

---

* 'Fancy' in the idiom of the time was almost synonymous with 'imagination' although critics strove to establish a distinction.

down in a minute. Unfortunately the talk was so good that he forgot and Godwin was kept waiting outside. When he demanded an explanation, Horne Tooke gave him the sort of deserved scolding which his younger friends were seldom bold enough to attempt:

You have the whole history and ought to be ashamed of such womanish jealousy. You will consult your own happiness by driving such stuff from your thoughts . . . Your jealousy, like all other jealousy is its own punishment. I wish you punished a little for compelling me to write this letter which is a great punishment to me; but I do not wish you to be tormented so much as this fractious habit will torment you if you indulge it . . . Hang you and your weakness, or rather Hang your weakness for making me write this stuff to you upon such a foolish business. I am, with great compassion for your nerves, very truly yours

J. Horne Tooke[3]

On 2 February 1804 there was another quarrel at the Lambs'. When Coleridge suggested that authors should review their own books, Godwin declared that no honest man could possibly agree to such a plan. When Coleridge then mischievously suggested that Godwin already reviewed his own books in his explanatory Prefaces, the argument became heated, Coleridge who was drunk baited him further by declaring that Southey and Wordsworth – whom he referred to as 'Godwin's betters' – agreed with his own view. The argument then moved to the even more explosive topics of religion and the war. It was a deliberate provocation and, as with other such incidents, led to exchanges of long letters of explanation, accusation, apology, and recrimination.[4]

Not long afterwards Southey wrote an anonymous review of Godwin's *Chaucer* in the *Annual Review for 1804*, a recent venture aimed at providing a record of the previous year's publications in permanent book form. Before Godwin wrote a new book, Southey sneered, he should 'work off his fancy'. The author must have been eating raw pork or toasted cheese when stewed prunes would have been more suitable. Pursuing the same metaphor, he compared Godwin and his philosophy to the fashionable doctors of the day who sold 'Nervous Cordial' and 'Balm of Gilead' which were nothing more than strong laxatives. Godwin's literary reputation would, he went on, continue to 'stink'.[5] Southey who knew about Godwin's constipation problem may have thought he was being witty and he made other knowing comments on Godwin's bald head, his long nose, and his sleeping problem. When Godwin assured his friends that he would never be driven back to journalism, he had toadies like Southey in mind.[6]

Commercially too, the *Life of Chaucer* was not a success. Phillips had spared on the production costs and the volumes lacked the sense of authority which quartos normally commanded.[7] A second edition in four volumes octavo was produced almost immediately, but it did not sell well either. Phillips had advanced considerable sums during the writing, but when the book at last came out, Godwin was no better off than when he had started. On the contrary his financial problems were more pressing than ever. A friend who had advanced money at the time of *Antonio* was now himself in financial difficulties, and had a strong moral claim to have it back. Godwin therefore borrowed from friends such as Holcroft who had recently returned from his unsuccessful stay in Germany and France. He postponed payment of his rent and he accepted a further advance from Richard Phillips for a proposed history of England which was never written. He began paying the tradesmen's bills for food, candles, and other household items by post-dated bills.

By the spring of 1804 however he was obliged to turn once more to Tom Wedgwood, the source which had never failed him in the past.

I hope I could almost perish, sooner than apply to you for further assistance to myself, but in this case, to use the ordinary phraseology, I would move heaven and earth to acquit myself. If I had any other resource that I could imagine or invent, you should not be troubled by this ungracious intrusion. Yet, my dear friend, consult your own convenience in this case. I am sure you would assist me if that would permit. But this is no claim upon you whatever it is on me.[8]

Wedgwood was now very ill. The money would be paid at once, he wrote from his sickbed the following day. Furthermore, to save Godwin the possible embarrassment of calling at the bank with a note signed by himself, he was arranging for his banker to make ready a note which would keep the whole transaction confidential.[9] Since the Wedgwoods made numerous donations to societies and individuals, Godwin's credit rating on the money market might be damaged if it became known that he was in receipt of charity. 'I do therefore invite you to still consider me as your friend in every honourable sense of the word,' he remarked in evident hurt at the tone of Godwin's request. Godwin had sought help in spite of being his friend. Wedgwood wanted to give it precisely because he was a friend. But Godwin was no longer in a position to insist on philosophical scruples. He needed the money for himself and he accepted it with bad grace, feeling more gratitude than was proper.

Of all the topics considered in *Political Justice* the one which most needed to be revised was the discussion of feelings. In that book Godwin had assumed that emotion can normally be expected to reinforce clear perception and rationally determined motive. As Adam Smith had argued in his *Theory of Moral Sentiments*, feelings are essentially benevolent. Human beings feel a spontaneous natural sympathy for other people. Endowed with the unique gift to see themselves as others see them, they have developed an internal monitor which gives the moral advice they could expect to receive from an impartial outsider. By showing how emotions could be regarded as part of the mechanism of Hartley's medullary particles of the mind, Adam Smith both explained and legitimated the attitudes of his optimistic time. Godwin read the book – probably for a second time – in 1795.[10]

Enlightenment deists were inclined to attribute these arrangements to the wisdom of God's design, but atheists committed no self-contradiction if they merely saw them as part of the essential nature of things. The ethical implications were the same either way. It is the duty of human beings to cultivate their inborn sense of sympathy. Those people who try to stifle it, such as lawyers, not only inflict moral damage on themselves but act as a brake on the general advance of perfectibility. During Godwin's youth and young manhood when the cult of sensibility had swept Europe, the sensitive classes had given increasing freedom to their feelings of natural sympathy. The march of progress was the march of sentiment.

It was a view much favoured by Mary Wollstonecraft one of whose descriptions of the improving power of sensibility was anthologized:

Sensibility is the most exquisite feeling of which the human soul is susceptible: when it pervades us, we feel happy; and could it last unmixed, we might form some conjecture of the bliss of those paradisiacal days, when the obedient passions were under the dominion of reason, and the impulses of the heart did not need correction. It is this quickness, this delicacy of feeling, which enables us to relish the sublime touches of the poet, and the painter, it is this which expands the soul, gives an enthusiastic greatness, mixed with tenderness, when we view the magnificent objects of nature; or hear of a good action . . . Softened by tenderness, the soul is disposed to be virtuous.[11]

In accordance with such advice women had allowed their feelings to overflow. During the late eighteenth century the number of social occasions on which it was proper to shed tears rose steadily. For stronger emotions fainting was more appropriate – in one Minerva Press novel twenty-seven separate swoons have been counted.[12] Women supplied the sentiment which benevolently reinforced (or moderated) the decisions of men, feminine and masculine neatly matching the division of the mind into passion and reason.

The discoveries of travellers appeared to offer empirical confirmation of the theory of natural benevolence. The natives of Tahiti who, according to Diderot, had lived in a paradise before the Europeans arrived were much envied by those who favoured nature against institutions, simplicity against riches, and love against marriage. The Nairs too were an attractive model for anyone who wished to shed chains or clothes. More worrying were the Tououpanimpos whose moral monitor prescribed ritual revenge, tribal murder, torture, and cannibalism.[13] It was due to the urging of Coleridge that Godwin started to read travel books although he continued to dislike them. But he preferred to rely on his own personal experience. In boyhood he had believed in congenital evil; in manhood he had swung to the opposite extreme. Now, as he approached his fiftieth birthday, he moved back towards the middle ground.

In the Preface to *Fleetwood or the New Man of Feeling*, a novel which he completed in February 1805,[14] he explained that once more he was attempting something entirely new — a story of love and marriage, which readers would recognize at once as directly applicable to themselves. The original choice for the title was *Lambert*, the name of one of Cromwell's two most famous generals, but Lambert was also the name of one of Godwin's creditors. As a boy at Guestwick Godwin had heard much of the Fleetwood family whose country home stood nearby, and he knew that the Cromwell chair in the chapel came from the Fleetwood family home. His fictional Fleetwood lives in an ancestral mansion built in Cromwell's day, set among the Welsh mountains which were already a literary cliché for freedom and self-reliance. As so often Godwin's names helped to remind readers of periods of history when Englishmen had been in the moral forefront.[15]

But it was not necessary to know dissenting history to recognize the significance of the secondary title. Henry Mackenzie's *Man of Feeling* first published in 1770 was second only to *The Vicar of Wakefield* as the favourite of the sentimental school and was already firmly established — so it was commonly believed — as one of the greatest works of English literature. By calling *Fleetwood* the *New Man of Feeling* Godwin was inviting a comparison with the book which, above all others, represented the extreme of current sentimental conventions.

Casimir Fleetwood, like most Godwinian heroes and increasingly Godwin himself, is a man cut off from society, the Aeolian strings of his mind being so delicately strung, as he remarks early in the book, that he cannot respond without dissonance to any but the gentlest breezes. And the book teems with incidents drawn from Godwin's experience. He discusses the feelings of a widower who marries an attractive younger woman and is worried about what his friends will say. He also describes the difficulties to be experienced in marrying a dishonoured woman. If Marguerite de Damville in *St. Leon* is derived from Mary Wollstonecraft, the half-foreign Mrs MacNeil who has to be rescued from an Italian seducer owes much to Mary Jane Clairmont.

I have often remarked that this mixture and result of the manners and habits of different countries, particularly in the female sex, presents something exquisitely fascinating and delightful. She was never embarrassed, and never appeared to meditate how a thing was to be done, but did it with an ease, a simplicity, an unpretendingness, which threw every studied grace into contempt in the comparison. She had been humbled by the miscarriage of her early youth . . . There was a cast of the Magdalene in all she did . . . [16]

Godwin describes the changing relationship of a married couple as each partner tries unsuccessfully to adapt. He notes the tiny unintended insults, the humiliations swallowed to preserve the peace, the sacrifices unappreciated, and the accumulation of resentments which lead to bitterness, spite and eventually to hate. At the end a mild story of domestic manners erupts into uncontrollable violence and tragedy.

The eighteenth-century theorists of benevolence had preserved the integrity of their psychological model by treating destructive emotions as aberrations. 'The passions of men', says the hero of the *Man of Feeling* 'are temporary madnesses.' In a visit to the lunatic asylum at Bedlam where the metaphor is carried to pleasing literary extremes, he describes the various inmates, chained in body as well as in mind, who had succumbed to various forms of obsession – a mathematician, a financier, a scholar, a lover. Great achievers like Alexander the Great and Julius Caesar, it is noted, had been afflicted by madness. Jean Jacques Rousseau, the man who had done more than anyone to spread the cult of sentiment throughout Europe, had ended his life in a terrified delusion, a point made explicitly in *Fleetwood* by someone who is said to have known Rousseau personally.[17] Deeply immersed in the Elizabethan and Jacobean drama, Godwin and his young romantic contemporaries were now more aware of the irrational and the subconscious. Passions are not intrinsically benevolent or even neutral, but can be diabolic. *Fleetwood* grafts the psychology of *Othello* to the Newtonian models of Hartley and Adam Smith.

Godwin had another retraction to make, and as usual it was boldly volunteered in the Preface. In *St. Leon* he had publicly modified his earlier views on marriage. Now in *Fleetwood* he went further. There was no point, he said, in individuals making isolated attempts to defy the prevailing rules of society – the correct course was to try to raise the moral level of society as a whole by discussion and reasoning.* The thought was presented as a correction of a misunderstanding, and no doubt that was needed. But Gerrald and the other 1794 martyrs to the power of truth would have been surprised to see the theory for which they gave their lives so drastically modified. The Prefaces to Godwin's works which comment on *Political Justice* are milestones on a long slow retreat.

Fleetwood is full of interest but readers were puzzled and unenthusiastic. As in the *Life of Chaucer*, they disliked the mixing of conventions. The place for dark satanic passions was on the classic stage where the context was suitably remote. To bring the violence of the barbarous past into a sentimental tale of love and marriage in the present day was shocking. Like *Caleb Williams* and *St. Leon*, Godwin's book was highly original, reviewers conceded, but no second edition was called for.

But if others were reluctant to discard the comforting assumptions of a passing age, Godwin's own experience continued to confirm that he was right. The meaning of the strange letter which he received from his dearest friend a few days after publication of *Fleetwood* was not immediately apparent.

28 February 1785

Sir,

I write to inform you that instead of seeing you at dinner tomorrow I desire to never see you more, being determined never to have *any* further intercourse with you of any kind.

T. Holcroft

I shall behave as becomes an honest and honourable man who remembers not only what is due to others but himself. There are indelible irrevocable injuries that will not endure to be mentioned: such is the one you have committed on the man who would have *died* to serve you.[18]

Holcroft, it turned out, believed that one of the minor characters in

---

* The exact words are quoted on p. 322 below.

Fleetwood was intended as a description of himself and he was so morti-fied that he had misdated his letter by a full twenty years.

Godwin had not intended to represent Holcroft personally, as he hast-ened to explain. The remarks of the fictional Mr Scarborough were a comment on the belief, which Godwin had once shared, that the human mind at birth is a blank sheet on which experience then writes. Strong passions, Mr Scarborough explains, are not aberrations or temporary lapses into insanity but congenital.

I brought into the world with me the seeds of a stern and severe disposition; this has been the source of all my misfortunes. My temper is firm; my judgement, perhaps, is clear; and I have ever been somewhat too peremptory in enforcing it. My ordinary speech . . . is pithy and sententious. I have been prone to lay down the law, and too impatient of the perverseness, real or imaginary, that demurred to my dictates. I have always seen these faults of my character . . . and have endeavoured to correct them. But either they were so twisted with my nature, that they could not be separated and discarded, or I have found myself weak, and insufficient to the office.[19]

After Holcroft's return from Germany in 1802, he and Godwin had again started to dine together nearly every Sunday as they had done, with few interruptions, since 1786. In the autumn of 1804 they had exchanged merciless comments with the same freedom as they had applied a decade before. Even if Mr Scarborough had been intended to represent Holcroft, worse insults had been offered and accepted by the two friends many times in the past in the interests of striking out truth from the clash of minds. Holcroft, who had always prided himself on his fearless bluntness – and fully deserved his reputation as a disagreeable dinner guest – should have welcomed the new insights. He had himself written novels in which living people were portrayed and explained, and in the anti-Jacobin novels Thomas Holcroft appears almost as frequently as William Godwin.

But for all their determination to penetrate the secrets of the human mind the two men had much to learn about their own characters. Both men, for all their championing of the power of mind over body, were in the grip of slow illness. A few weeks before *Fleetwood* appeared, Godwin demanded to know why Holcroft had been heard to propose the health of Colonel Harwood (his son-in-law), Dr Buchan and Mr Carlisle as the three men who had been particularly attentive to him during his recent illness. 'I have neither so much money as the colonel nor so much medical skill as the other two gentlemen,' he wrote in a peremptory note, 'but in anxious and disinterested attention I far surpassed them all.'[20] Holcroft in his turn, although he remained patient and conciliatory was using up his reserves, and when the crisis came, there were none left.

As *Fleetwood* had sought to demonstrate, a quarrel is seldom related to the importance of the specific issue. The silly misunderstanding over 'Mr Scarborough' was the cumulation of twenty-nine years of mutual sincerity. The intensity of their relationship remained unabated, but for all the theorizing over imagination and sensibility, their own powers to change were no longer what they had once been. The reply sent to Holcroft on 3 March 1805 is unfortunately typical of Godwin under strain. There is little sign that the New Man of Feeling who had recently written with acute understanding of the build-up of quarrels knew how to resolve them.

Repetitious, self-righteous and replete with the double negatives to which he always resorted when agitated, Godwin's cruel letter is a cry of pain which only a lover could have uttered.

Thomas Holcroft

I write this on the supposition that after every explanation you still persist in the tenour of your last note.

I write on my birthday. This day I enter into the fiftieth year of my age. It is contrary to everything we know of human character, that if I deserved for forty eight years the exalted notions you have entertained of me, I should have forfeited my claim to that estimation in the forty ninth.

I will never think of you, but as a dear friend, who died on the 28th of February last. I will never recollect, that you then deserted me for no intelligible cause, and on a mistake which was, immediately after, fully explained and cleared up. I will think only of the friend I possessed for a period of nearly twenty years. I will dwell upon the 'man who would have died to serve me'; and will neither do you nor myself the injustice to call to mind the man who, in one unhappy moment of weakness, trampled that character underfoot. I will always think and speak of you with the tenderness due to a deceased friend, who, after twenty years of an attachment difficult to be paralleled, has expired.

William Godwin[21]

All efforts by others to bring about a reconciliation met with no response and the two men were not to exchange another word for four years. Opie's portrait of Holcroft continued to hang in Godwin's study accorded the same reverence as that of the dead Mary Wollstonecraft but no move was made by either man to break the deadlock. The most important friendship in their lives was at an end, smashed by the unremitting exercise of the qualities which had drawn them together in the first place and which they both regarded as the key to all progress.

CHAPTER 21

The Bookshop

The other book which Godwin wrote for Phillips, *Bible Stories*, first appeared in the summer of 1802. Phillips published it as the work of 'William Scolfield' and the secret of its true authorship was so carefully kept that it has not hitherto been attributed to Godwin's pen. The book must have brought the publisher some commercial success since it was still being advertised in a new edition as late as 1831. It was also pirated at least twice in the United States, a sure sign of ready sales. But school books are seldom loved and seldom kept. Only one copy of the English edition of *Bible Stories* (volume one only) and only one copy of each of the American editions have hitherto been located.[1]

The young men who came to Godwin for advice were referred to the Preface as his classic statement of the theory of education, and many years later, when he was drawing up instructions for his literary executors, he asked that it should be reprinted alongside his major works. But the only modern writer who has noticed the book at all – deriving his information from reviews – draws an enthusiastic contrast between the imaginative wisdom of Scolfield and the conventional stupidity of Godwin.[2]

With children of his own to educate, Godwin notes in the Preface, he had spent time reading some of the most popular children's books which were then for sale. But none was suitable. They were too full of facts and too full of moralizing.

Aesop telling his fables, from *Lessons for Children*

These modern improvers have left out of their system that most essential branch of human nature the imagination. Our youth, according to the most approved recent systems of education, will be excellent geographers, natural historians, and mechanics; they will be able to tell you from what part of the globe you receive every article of your furniture; and will explain the process in manufacturing a carpet, converting metals into the utensils of life, and clay into the cups of your tea-table, and the ornaments of your chimney: in a word, they are exactly informed about all those things, which if a man or a woman were to live or die without knowing, neither man nor woman would be an atom the worse.

Bible Stories, like the *Life of Chaucer*, is a celebration of the poetic imagination as the link between perception and virtue.

Imagination is the characteristic of man. The dexterities of logic or of mathematical deduction belong rather to a well regulated machine; they do not contain in them the living principle of our nature. It is the heart which most deserves to be cultivated; not the rules which may serve us in the nature of a compass to steer through the difficulties of life; but the pulses which beat with sympathy, and qualify us for the habits of charity, reverence, and attachment.

Education was a subject which had always interested him deeply. As *Political Justice* repeatedly emphasized, it is in childhood that people pick up the opinions and attitudes which determine conduct in later life. Although he had long since modified the belief that all children are born with equal potentialities, he remained convinced that the best time to try to redirect the necessitarian chain is when minds are young and flexible. Mary Wollstonecraft too had been much interested in education. During a visit to Eton she had been shocked at the brutality and the piggishness, but the methods used by her friend Hewlett at his aptly named boarding school at Shacklewell were little better. During their few months together Wollstonecraft and Godwin had talked a great deal about how they would bring up the children, much of which found its way into *The Enquirer*. They talked about the children as she lay dying and he was determined that baby Mary and three-year-old Fanny should both be educated in the way their mother would have wished.

Among the papers left at her death were notes for an intended book for children which Godwin published in 1798 among her posthumous works as *Lessons for Children*. Mary Wollstonecraft had also begun work on a book on child care of which he published an extensive fragment. Godwin also studied her early *Original Stories from Real Life* (to which William Blake contributed the plates) which had been based on her experiences as a governess in the Mountcashell home in Ireland. Good habits,

Wollstonecraft explains in the Preface, are more effective than lectures, but if you explain to children the reasons why some actions are preferable to others, they will quickly learn and quickly improve. In the stories, the wise Mrs Mason demonstrates to two spoiled children the importance of telling the truth, the folly of personal vanity, and the need to be kind to animals.

After his visit to Dublin in the summer of 1800 Godwin wrote to Lady Mountcashell asking her to confirm that he had understood Mary Wollstonecraft's views properly, and Lady Mountcashell, unoffended at being deprived of her final l, sent him a number of letters with advice from her own experiences as a spoiled child who had been successfully rehabilitated.[3] Children, Lady Mountcashell advised, should be treated with mildness, kindness, and respect. They should be shown plenty of affection – although parents should never turn them into toys. She rejected the idea that children need get used to harshness and disappointment as preparation for the injustices of later life. On the contrary, the overriding objective should be to make them happy and – therefore – virtuous. She herself was convinced, she wrote, 'that had it not been my peculiar good fortune to meet with the extraordinary woman to whose superior penetration and affectionate mildness of manner I trace the development of whatever virtues I possess, I should have become in consequence of the distortion of my best qualities, a most ferocious animal'. In the summer of 1801 shortly before Godwin's marriage to Mary Jane, Lady Mountcashell passed through London with her husband on their way to the Continent and was able to meet the children and give direct advice.

The methods favoured by Godwin, Wollstonecraft, and Mountcashell were still new and shocking. The traditional view that congenital sinfulness had to be crushed in early life remained widespread even if few people now took their duties as seriously as Godwin's own parents had done. Until the minds of children were formed, it was assumed, they were more or less interchangeable and their main function was to amuse grownups. When Southey's son died, Coleridge assured him that until God sent a replacement he could use his children as if they were his own.[4]

Others were worried about the effects of uncertainty. Before John Newbery started publishing in the 1760s, there had been virtually no books for children and the parents who worried about the effects of books on children in the 1790s and 1800s had seldom been allowed to read them during their own childhood. Children – like women and members of the lower classes – needed to be protected against the notion that they had choices. If their imaginations were inflamed at an early age, they might become discontented and find it difficult to accept the subordinate status to which society had assigned them.

Bible Stories consists largely of favourite extracts from the King James Bible which Godwin read to the children. At first sight, the subject is an astonishing one to have chosen, but Godwin recalled the delight the Bible had given him in his own early years – he had read it through by the age of eight – and he was determined that his own children should share in that heritage and understand the historical origins of the culture within which they lived. When he found young men sneering at Christianity, he surprised them by the sharpness of his reaction. Christianity was undoubtedly untrue and harmful, he would agree, but its errors should be confuted by argument and not by abuse.[5] Otherwise opponents would simply be confirmed in their attitudes. To Godwin the Bible was a collection of literary and historical documents of extraordinary interest, containing stories of people and ideas which had been as influential as those of the Greeks and Romans and the Englishmen of the seventeenth century. Godwin preferred to call his book 'Jewish Histories' or 'Scripture Histories'.

As a boy Godwin had also loved fairy tales, virtually the only non-religious stories he had been permitted, and we may guess that there is some element of rationalization in his spirited defence of traditional methods. But it was fully in line with his emerging philosophical views. The giants and dragons, he wrote, might be fantastical but they had real tempers and real feelings which a child could recognize. Since they stimulated the imagination they provided a better introduction to real life than the priggish children and smug parents who inhabited modern books (not excluding *Original Stories*).[6] As he now repeatedly affirmed, imagination is the great engine of morality, the quality which permits new insights to be acquired and political justice to be advanced. The way to make children good is to make them happy, and how better to do that than to sit with a laughing child on your lap turning over the pages of a jolly book?

John Harris of St Paul's Churchyard was the first to put on sale a cheap edition of *Old Mother Hubbard* in which comic pictures alternated with comic verses in large type. It was such a success that within months the other children's booksellers were pouring out nursery stories, plain and coloured, in the same format. Mary Jane was employed by Benjamin Tabart as editor of his own successful rival series which was one of the first to follow Harris's breakthrough, and under her direction some thirty traditional stories from France and Germany as well as from England were made available to British children. Some were written in simple prose; others were turned into verse for younger children. Mary Jane evidently wrote many of them, and from the journal, it is clear that Godwin also contributed since he notes the reading and revision of such works as *Robin Hood*, *The Pedlar*, and *The Little Woman and Her Dog* among his morning's tasks.

> There was a little woman
> As I have heard tell,
> She went to market,
> Her eggs for to sell.

Nursery rhymes and fairy stories had been repeated by parents to children from time immemorial, but by the late eighteenth century they had come to be regarded as shameful barbarisms which only survived among ignorant country people. And it was true that the unacknowledged legislators who composed them had not always been progressive in their thinking. *Blue Beard* and *Hansel and Gretel* were almost as frightening as the religious stories with which Godwin's early life had been filled. *Cinderella* and *The Sleeping Beauty* were hardly in line with the *Vindication of the Rights of Woman*. Few of the stories showed grown-ups in a good light and a number were highly improper. Nevertheless they were poetic. They rang true and children enjoyed them.

By deciding to join Mary Jane in writing children's books Godwin was continuing his life work. If the fury of the anti-Jacobin reaction ruled out serious debate on philosophical issues, he could work quietly away at influencing the next generation. He would have to be careful to avoid causing alarm or offence. Hence the pseudonym. In *Bible Stories* Godwin scrupulously avoided offering any explicit endorsement or condemnation of Christianity. Most readers could have easily assumed that the author was a traditional Christian parent – indeed in some places Godwin is so concerned not to appear deistical that he perhaps goes too far in the opposite direction for intellectual comfort.

But the anti-Jacobins were vigilant. In May 1802, a few weeks before the publication of *Bible Stories* a new monthly periodical, the *Guardian of Education*, was established under the editorship of the formidable Mrs Trimmer with the aim of upholding traditional values in education. If the *Anti-Jacobin Review* was successfully cleansing adult literature from the contamination of the New Philosophy, the *Guardian of Education* would do the same for children. For five years it offered guidance to parents on which books were sound and which were dangerous. In its long review of *Bible Stories*, the *Guardian of Education* saw at once that it was an 'engine of mischief'. The author's linking of the imagination with conduct was part of the torrent of irreligion which was engulfing the world. As Godwin had discovered years before at Stowmarket, a book which respectfully treated the Bible as a historical document and Jesus as an admirable historical figure was as repugnant as an outright attack. Mrs Trimmer was herself the editor of volumes of Scripture Histories, and if she and her colleagues had known that the rival book was produced by the man whose name was synonymous with atheism, sedition, and sexual immorality, their belief in an international Jacobin conspiracy would have been further confirmed.

Mary Jane pressed ahead but her contribution to the family income could never be substantial as long as she was selling her copyrights outright to publishers for a few pounds only. After the disappointments of *Chaucer* and *Fleetwood* it was clear too that Godwin would not be able to support the family by serious writing alone. They guessed however that they might do better if they started in business on their own so that they could themselves enjoy the profits from the books which they wrote. Godwin would take time off from serious writing to produce a few children's books which, to judge from the success of *Bible Stories*, might be expected to sell well. Mary Jane knew the trade, and as the market was growing, there was room for another successful shop in London.

On 25 March 1805, within a few days of the publication of *Fleetwood*, Godwin took up his pen once more to ask for money from Tom Wedgwood, making clear in the best traditions of political justice that although £100 was all he needed for the present he might well have to ask for more before long.[7] Wedgwood, who was now in the final stages of his long and painful illness, sent the money as usual by return.[8] A house was accordingly engaged in Hanway Street off Oxford Street for £40 a year of which £35 was to be offset by rent from letting the rooms upstairs to lodgers. For protection against the anti-Jacobins and the *Guardian of Education* the shop was established in the name of Thomas Hodgkins, a man whom Godwin employed to run the shop, and it opened for business in the summer of 1805 with a flourish of advertisements.

Besides books, the shop soon offered a wide range of stationery, paper, ink, pens, paints, cards, maps, games, puzzles, and toys. Although trading with France was legally forbidden in time of war, Mary Jane found ways of importing children's books using American and other friends as intermediaries and the list of French books on offer was almost as long as that of the English. The shop made a special effort to appeal to the

French *émigré* community among whom Mary Jane had many friends, and before long it was renamed the City French and English Juvenile Library. The main stock was however the books which Godwin composed specially for the purpose. The pseudonym 'William Scolfield' remained with Phillips and was not used again. Godwin, still subordinating sincerity to utility, chose two new names, 'Theophilus Marcliffe' and 'Edward Baldwin' and in the years after 1805, this unlikely pair produced nearly a dozen books.[9]

Theophilus Marcliffe, a parent would probably have guessed from the name alone, was likely to be a dissenting divine keen to inculcate the virtues of education, hard work, and self-help. His *Life of Lady Jane Grey* has more than one echo of Janeway's accounts of the joyful deaths of goodly children which had made Godwin's own childhood such misery. 'This young lady', Marcliffe noted on the title page, 'at twelve years of age understood eight languages, was for nine days Queen of England, and was beheaded in the Tower in the seventeenth year of her age, being at that time the most amiable and accomplished woman in Europe.'

Marcliffe's *Looking Glass*, also unashamedly intended to stimulate ambition, was described on the cover as a mirror 'in which every Good Little Boy and Girl may see what He or She is; and those who are not yet Quite Good may find what They ought to be'. The book describes the early career of the artist William Mulready, a friend of the Godwins, who had reached the Royal Academy by dint of hard work from an unpromising background, and who provided Godwin with his illustrations. Parents thinking of buying would have been reminded of the other *Looking Glass* published by Newbery, one of the best known children's books of the earlier generation, and of Newbery's best-selling *Goody Two Shoes* which is dedicated to 'All Young Gentlemen and Ladies who are good or intend to be good.'

Godwin's other persona, Edward Baldwin (who usually appeared on the title page as Edward Baldwin, Esquire), was very different. He might have been a country gentleman or the retired headmaster of a distinguished school. His solid, reliable, scholarly books on history, mythology, and grammar were of a type no browsing parent or schoolmaster would hesitate to give to children. In one of his early works Baldwin included a puff for Marcliffe, but the buying public left no doubt about which of the two they preferred. Marcliffe, the earnest advocate of persistence, gave up writing after two books and few people noticed when a new edition of *Lady Jane Grey* was published as the work of Edward

Baldwin, even although Godwin's advertisement brochures still carelessly ascribed it to Theophilus Marcliffe.

Baldwin's *Fables Ancient and Modern*, a collection of short stories, each one illustrated by a picture, appeared in 1805. Some are drawn from Aesop; others are original; a few are taken from his own childhood – the one aspect of parents' lives in which children maintain an inexhaustible interest; and he also slipped in a few of the themes from *Caleb Williams*. The 'my dear Charles' in one story indicates that it was told to Charles Clairmont. Godwin noted that children, while enjoying and appreciating the moral of such famous stories as the Fox and the Grapes were usually disappointed when it stopped abruptly after the punch line, and were liable to ask 'what happened then?' He accordingly supplied extra paragraphs to round them off. Sometimes he also provided a happy ending in defiance of the traditional story, although never at the expense of the lesson.

Edward Baldwin was also known for his three history school books, the *History of England*, 1806, the *History of Rome*, 1809, and the *History of Greece*, 1821, into which Godwin was able to incorporate many of the ideas he had wished to include in a full-scale historical work. The *History of Rome* quietly praises the republican virtues. The *History of England* devotes disproportionate space to the periods of the Civil War, Cromwel, and the Glorious Revolution. Baldwin's *Histories* were still being reprinted as late as the 1860s.

Baldwin's *Pantheon or Ancient History of the Gods of Greece and Rome*, which was first published in 1806, was also to become a standard school textbook and to be reprinted many times during the following decades. The books on Greek mythology which Godwin wanted to displace – notably the Jesuit-inspired *Pantheon* of 'Andrew Tooke' – had sneered at ancient religion and suppressed the sexuality. Godwin, while denying any wish to win converts from Christianity, accorded the ancient religions a delighted respect. His simple and unpretentious book shows deep understanding of the symbolic and psychological meaning of the ancient myths and of their poetic power, and although it was sufficiently discreet to be reviewed and advertised as 'proper' for both boys and girls, it caught something of the liberating joy of Ancient Greece. In 1810 in order to secure an order for *Pantheon* from Charles Burney, the headmaster of the school at Greenwich where young William was a pupil, Godwin agreed to the re-engraving of four of the pictures which were thought to be too suggestive, and in all later editions, Venus, Apollo, Mercury and Mars are modestly covered.[10]*

Godwin's formula worked. The works of Edward Baldwin were widely praised and soon in demand. The reviewers did not penetrate his pseudonyms. The *Critical Review*, which always had an anti-Jacobin bias, declared that it could recommend Mr Baldwin's *Fables* without reserve. The notice in the *Anti-Jacobin Review* provided a favourable quote which Godwin was able to use for years in his advertisements. One of the royal princesses gave the book to a grandson of the king. But lack of sincerity carries disadvantages. Thomas Hodgkins, the front man, whose name appeared as publisher and proprietor on the title pages, was discovered to be helping himself to the bookshop money. When challenged he declared that legally it was his business which was true. Godwin managed to have him removed before they lost everything.

In the light of what was to happen later, it was unfortunate for Godwin that his credit was so good and his integrity so unimpeachable. The decision to establish his own business made lightly and without advice in 1805 was to have profound and far-reaching results on every aspect of his life. An individual with his modest tastes did not need much money even if he did have five children to educate and a taste for buying old books. He would not have needed to borrow much to keep going. But a growing business has a limitless appetite for money. Of the £100 provided by Wedgwood, £60 was spent on the initial fitting out and purchase of stock, and the business had virtually no reserves or cash in hand. Since Godwin scrupulously avoided asking too much even at the risk of asking too little, from the beginning the bookshop was hopelessly undercapitalized.

The money crisis of 1806 was more severe than any that had been overcome in the past. From his previous borrowings Godwin had outstanding bills in the market which would become due at various dates in the immediate future, £50 on 10 February, £140 on 22 February, £160 on 3 March. He had himself guaranteed smaller debts for others whose needs were even more pressing than his own. Earlier emergencies had usually involved sums of £10 and £20. But each transaction was now equivalent to the expected earnings for literary work for a year or more.

Tom Wedgwood died in the summer of 1805 writing off all the money that he had advanced to Godwin over the years, but that relief was only temporary. When Godwin wrote to his brother Josiah, he received a

* For the influence of this book on John Keats see p. 426.

further advance of £50 – as a mark of respect to his brother's memory – but it was only a fraction of what was needed to keep the business afloat, and Josiah made clear that further requests would not be welcome. Godwin therefore wrote to Curran and to Lord Lauderdale. In approaching Sheridan he recalled the offer which he and the other Whig leaders had made eighteen years before when pressing him to become paid editor of the *Political Herald*. At a dinner at Lord Holland's he appealed directly to some of the other rich politicians who had admired him at the time of the treason trials.

It is a measure of the respect that Godwin had accumulated that he was able to call on some of the greatest names in the land, and that the response was satisfactory. But many of his friends now knew that their 'loans' or 'advances' were unlikely to be repaid or rolled over. Samuel Rogers was probably typical in offering to lend £50 for two months only, making clear that he could give nothing more in the future. Soon Godwin was forced to turn to comparative strangers. He borrowed to the limit from the shop's trading partners – with the result that they forced him to give generous discounts – and the Somers Town shopkeepers were asked to give credit for his smallest household bills.

As his needs became more pressing, the wording of his claims became more extravagant. In asking Sir Francis Burdett to roll over one of his loans for a further three months, he assured him that there could be no risk since the stock in the shop was worth £2,000. When Richard Sharp declined to renew, Godwin assured him of 'the absolute impossibility of failure'.[11] It was hard to be as impartial and sincere as political justice required. It was also hard not to feel gratitude, and to express it despite the moral dangers. With money, as with marriage, the difficulties of courageous non-conformism had been underestimated.

But if Godwin ever paused to reconsider the ethics of borrowing, it was soon too late to change course. Faced with the choice between immediate ruin and the longer-term problems of servicing increased debt, the utilitarian calculus could give only one result. If he failed to refinance any one of his debts within the three days' grace of the due date, he would be ruined, liable to be arrested and taken to a debtors' prison. His creditors might seize not only the assets of his bookshop but his house, his furniture, his books, and anything of value that he possessed, and Mary Jane and the five children would be reduced to unimaginable misery.

In the proud days of 1796 when he was in love with Mary Wollstonecraft and at the height of his fame, he had composed a spirited essay for *The Enquirer* in which he described the corruptions which assail the

1. Thomas Holcroft (left) and William Godwin at the Treason Trials, 1794. From a sketch made by Sir Thomas Lawrence in the courtroom. Private collection.

2. William Godwin. From a portrait attributed to Lawrence, but more probably by Thomas Kearsley, 1795. Private collection.

3. William Godwin. From an engraving said to be taken from a drawing by Lawrence.

4. Mary Wollstonecraft, the
fierce defender of the rights
of woman. A portrait by an
unknown artist about 1792.
Walker Art Gallery,
Liverpool.

5. Mary Wollstonecraft,
after her marriage to
Godwin, pregnant with her
second daughter. By John
Opie, 1797, National
Portrait Gallery.

1796   1796

6. Extract from Godwin's journal 4 September to 17 September 1796 showing the secret code marks which record his sexual relationship with Mary Wollstonecraft. Bodleian Library.

7. Percy Bysshe Shelley. From a portrait by Amelia Curran. National Portrait Gallery.

8. Mary Wollstonecraft Godwin, later Shelley. From a miniature made posthumously by Reginald Easton. Bodleian Library.

9. Claire Clairmont. From a portrait by Amelia Curran. Newstead Abbey.

10. Lord Byron. From an engraving used by John Murray to illustrate early editions of his collected works. This portrait shows Byron before the Byronic image was deeply established.

11. Skinner Street from Fleet Market, the house taken by Godwin as his bookshop on the left. From Tegg and Castleman's *New Picture of London*, 1805.

12. St Pancras Churchyard. The square pillar marking Mary Wollstonecraft's grave is to the right of the church between the trees. An engraving by L. Pye from a drawing by I. P. Neale, 1815. From volume 10, part 4 of J. Norris Brewer, *The Beauties of England and Wales*, 1816.

13. The first illustration of
Frankenstein. From
Bentley's Standard Novels
edition, 1831.
'*By the glimmer of the half-
extinguished light, I saw the
dull yellow eye of the
creature open; it breathed
hard, and a convulsive
motion agitated its limbs.*'

14. Godwin as an old man
in his shop. From *The
Maclise Portrait Gallery of
Illustrious Literary
Characters*, 1898.

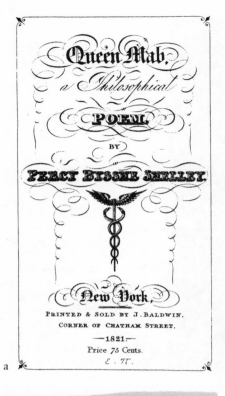

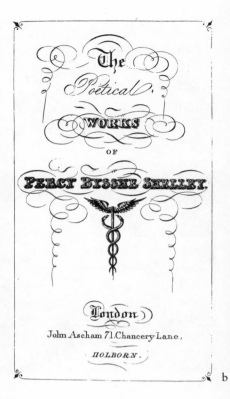

Printed and Published by W. Clark, 201, Strand.

T.

d

15. Secret marks of the book pirates. a) Title page of Benbow's 'New York' (actually London) edition of *Queen Mab*, 1821, showing the initials of Erasmus Perkins in Greek letters at the bottom. b) Title page of Asham's edition of 1834 with the H of Holborn shaped like a Greek P [Π]. c) A mark used by Erasmus Perkins in several books. From the Preface to the 'New York' edition. d) Imprint of Clark's edition of *Queen Mab*, 1821, with the initials of Thomas Moses.

16. Indicator hand in the 1813 *Queen Mab*.

the accursed book of God, ere man can read the inscription on his heart. How would morality, dressed up in stiff stays and finery, start from her own disgusting image, should she look in the mirror of nature!

☞

various professions, politicians, lawyers, clergymen, officers in the armed forces, and others. His sharpest contempt had been reserved for the shopkeeper.

Yet this being, this supple, fawning, cringing creature, this systematic, cold-hearted liar, this being, every moment of whose existence is centred in the sordid consideration of petty gains, has the audacity to call himself a man . . . 12

Now that he was himself a shopkeeper with a wife and five children Godwin saw the world with different eyes. His only choice was to press ahead, relying on whatever combination of commercial success, patronage, and political justice might see him through. There was a characteristic bold defiance in the decision in 1807 to move his family from The Polygon in Somers Town to a new house in a more central location which was more promising for business.

Five storeys high, 41 Skinner Street stood on a corner site with fine bow windows in two directions.* The ground floor was ready to be fitted out as a shop, and there was no entrance to the house except through the front door. Upstairs the main living quarters were on the first floor, with bedrooms further up. One room was set aside as Godwin's study. Over the door Godwin installed a statue group of Aesop and his children, probably made of artificial stone in the elegant custom of the day, and a picture of the group was reproduced in some of the books published by the firm as a trademark.13†

Although the building had been ready for occupation for six years, Godwin was the first tenant. When he moved in, he paid two quarters' rent to a Mr Rolfe, but it was not certain that he was the legal owner. In pleasing illustration of the essential arbitrariness of property ownership, the original developers of the Skinner Street properties had sold them by lottery, and Number 41, the eleventh prize, had passed into the possession of a firm of stockbrokers. When they in their turn went bankrupt, they had assigned the building to another party unknown from whom it was thought to have passed to a Mr Read. Since the question of legal title was so complex neither Rolfe nor Read was able to demand rent from Godwin with any certainty of being backed by the courts, with the result that after 1808 he declined to pay any rent at all, leaving it to his putative landlords to agree amongst themselves if they could and challenge if they dared. For once fortune seemed to have smiled. With those who were foolish enough to regulate their lives by the letter of an absurd system of

* See Plate 11 and p. 299.
† See p. 279.

unjust law he was ready to try his strength. But in political justice his title was secure. Who was more able or suitable to help Godwin than rich speculative capitalists who did not even know whether they owned the asset or not?

Skinner Street had been built as recently as 1801 as part of an ambitious redevelopment, but with the renewal of the war with France in 1803 the investors had run into financial difficulties and the project had been abandoned with many houses left unfinished. If peace had been restored, the original building scheme might have been successfully completed, but with every year the area became more run down. Since Smithfield was nearby, flocks of animals regularly passed through on their way to slaughter, and since the district had traditionally been a centre for the leather industry – hence the name Skinner Street – vacant sites were diverted to this foul-smelling activity. Over the years other houses were converted to warehouses for cheese, oranges, coffee, sugar, and oil, and if their exotic smells helped to disguise the animal stinks, they did not bring customers to the bookshop.

Skinner Street stood near three prisons, Newgate, the Fleet, and the Giltspur Compter. In 1806 Godwin bailed his old friend the scientist William Nicholson no less than fifteen times with money unlikely ever to be repaid.[14] On one occasion he received a despairing letter from Nicholson's assistant saying that he too had been arrested for failure of a bail in which Godwin had taken a half share, and he had had to hurry round to the prison to release them both with borrowed money.[15] Nicholson was soon to die in poverty leaving a widow and family unprovided for. John Fenwick, another friend who had helped in the composition of *Political Justice*, now lived full time in the Fleet Prison although allowed out on parole during the day. At one time worth £14,000, he had endorsed a large post-dated bill for a friend who was unable to honour it. He had been arrested, his goods seized, and Mrs Fenwick and his children were now living in poverty.[16] In the winter of 1807 Mrs Fenwick worked in Godwin's shop six days in the week, with Sundays devoted to writing hack work for another children's bookseller about the rewards of early rising and the penalties of sloth. Godwin paid more than the going rate, but Mrs Fenwick went without food all day and since there was no fire in the shop, she suffered badly from cold. At the same time Mary Hays was also reduced to writing children's books for Joseph Johnson – friends clubbed together to buy her a set of clothes.

But if the penalties of economic failure were severe, those for breaking the property laws were worse. To the east of Skinner Street, barely a hundred yards from 41, was the New Drop of the Old Bailey, where public executions took place every few weeks.* The shouts of the crowds could be heard from the Godwins' windows. In 1807 when two men were being hanged, panic broke out and twenty-eight people were trampled to death. In 1817 a sailor who broke into a shop in Skinner Street was hanged in the old style on a gallows erected at the scene of the crime.

The City Juvenile Library opened for business at its new address on 18 May 1807. The family made the move in August, while Godwin himself remained at The Polygon until November. Shortly before he was due to leave The Polygon for the last time, he was again seized by his illness, struck down successively over a longer period of days than in any previous attack. Once again he was gripped with the twin terrors of destitution and madness, and once again he turned to his friends.

In the spring of 1808 a second subscription was opened. Lord Lauderdale and Lord Holland took the lead and Joseph Johnson made the arrangements. A printed letter calling for public subscriptions was sent in the name of an impressive committee whose promised contributions totalled £1,220 before the lists were even formally opened. There is no record of the total that was collected but it was a huge sum. Some of it was 'advanced' to Godwin as loans on which he was expected to pay interest at the statutory maximum of 5 per cent; it was as much investment as charity although no date was set at which the money was to be paid back. Some of the other advances were consolidations and renewals of existing debt, and others were outright donations or the writing off of existing obligations. What happened to this huge amount of money cannot now be reconstructed in detail, but the vast bulk of it went towards paying off debt, paying the interest on other debt, and building up the business.

After the dishonesty of Thomas Hodgkins, Godwin decided to assume formal ownership, but the risks of being overtly identified with the Jacobin philosopher were still considerable. One of the earliest publications from Skinner Street contains the name of W. Godwin on the cover coyly buried in a long paragraph.[17] Others were printed 'for the Proprietors of the Juvenile Library'. Shortly afterwards the business was established in the name of Mary Jane as 'M. J. Godwin and Company'. There was already a long-established stationer called John Godwin (although of no family connection) in nearby Holborn. The name was a fairly common one, and since William Godwin seldom appeared downstairs in the shop, the secret

* Between 1800 and 1820 there were between seven and eight hundred executions a year in Great Britain, the highest ever recorded.

was surprisingly well kept. A number of people misread the name on the door post as 'Mr J. Godwin' and it is possible that some deliberate confusion was attempted.[18]

Within a few years M. J. Godwin and Company had one of the strongest lists any children's publisher could wish to advertise. Godwin and Mary Jane worked hard to write, to commission, to print, and to distribute according to a sensible general plan. The books covered the main categories of education, fable, romance, and moral tales. They were well illustrated by Mulready, Cruickshank, and other leading engravers and artists in wood-cut. All ages of children were catered for, and there was an adequate spread of price. Although the books were mostly of an improving tendency, they were not so modern as to put off the majority of parents and deliberate attempts were made to copy existing best-sellers. To rival the well-known *Parent's Assistant* Godwin published a *Parent's Offering*. In place of Fénelon's *Adventures of Telemachus* he provided an *Adventures of Ulysses*. A network of contracts was established with booksellers outside London, and the business grew rapidly. In the first few years it produced an average annual profit of about £800 after all costs had been met.

Godwin invited his friends to join him. William Hazlitt wrote an English grammar to which Edward Baldwin contributed an interesting long essay on etymology based on the theories of Horne Tooke and Coleridge. William Frederick Mylius, a headmaster, compiled a school dictionary whose sale of 100,000 copies may have softened his annoyance at having his name misspelled.[19] Eliza Fenwick drafted a number of books to which Godwin wrote the Prefaces. In *Lessons for Children* the words are di-vid-ed in-to syl-lab-les with hy-phens on the since ex-plod-ed the-o-ry that chil-dren learn to read by sounding the words. In *Rays from the Rainbow*, intended to teach grammar, boxes are provided under each word for children to colour in, blue for nouns, red for verbs, and seven others. The text consists of improving lessons – Go to the Ant, thou sluggard, consider her ways and be wise – so that the pupils could ingest sound morality while painting their rainbows.

Lady Mountcashell contributed a number of story books in the style of Mary Wollstonecraft's *Original Stories*, one of which, *Stories of Old Daniel*, was still being reprinted in Victorian times. On a visit to the Continent she parted from her disliked husband, and in a bold gesture of independence set up home with an exiled Irishman George Tighe. 'I wish to be a woman and to be like Mrs Mason,' the spoiled girl had announced in *Original Stories* when she was finally reformed, echoing, no doubt

something the real Lady Mountcashell had once said to Mary Wollstonecraft. In deciding to live her life according to Wollstonecraftian principles,
Lady Mountcashell asked henceforward to be known as 'Mrs Mason',
George Tighe with sincere respect for sexual equality obligingly becoming
'Mr Mason'. They settled at Pisa beyond the reach of British law, a
favoured place of exile for irregular couples on small incomes, not far
from Maria Reveley and her husband John Gisborne.

Charles Lamb's sister Mary Lamb wrote *Mrs Leicester's School* and
edited *Poetry for Children*, an anthology to which she herself contributed
a number of original pieces. Together they wrote the *Tales from Shake-
spear* which quickly became a favourite and has been in print ever since.
Originally the *Tales* were to be anonymous but Godwin persuaded the
unreluctant Charles to have his name printed on the title page. Mary
Lamb's did not appear for many years although she wrote most of the
stories. When Lamb followed up his success by writing *Adventures of
Ulysses* Godwin begged him to make a few alterations to the text before
the book was printed.

We live in squeamish days. Amid the beauties of your manuscript, of which no
man can think more highly than I do, what will the squeamish say to such
expressions as these: 'devoured their limbs, yet warm and trembling, lapping the
blood', p. 10. Or to the giant's vomit, p. 14; or to the minute and shocking
description of the extinguishing the giant's eye in the page following. You, I
daresay, have no formed plan of excluding the female sex from among your
readers, and I, as a bookseller, must consider that if you have you exclude one
half of the human species.[20]

Lamb made no comment on Godwin's discrimination between boys and
girls, but delivered a sharp lecture on the difference between the nauseous
and the shocking. The giant's vomit could go, but nothing else.

As an author I say, to you an author. Touch not my work. As a bookseller I say,
Take the work such as it is, or refuse it. You are as free to refuse it as when we
first talked of it. As a friend I say, Don't plague yourself and me with nonsensical
objections. I assure you I will not alter one more word.[21]

It was the kind of rebuff that Godwin had often delivered to cowardly
publishers in earlier years.

Mary Jane, besides taking a turn serving in the shop, herself undertook
a number of books and translations. Her *Dramas for Children* is a series
of plays on such themes as the dangers of excessive curiosity and gossiping
– in both of which she was personally well experienced. But if she herself
behaved like the parents in the stories, it is not surprising that her children

disliked her. In the first play a mother promises her daughter a treat, lays a trap for her, and then punishes her. Good children are rewarded by being taken to the Juvenile Library at 41 Skinner Street and allowed to choose another improving book.

When Godwin asked his friends to help he was unable to conceal his lack of enthusiasm for the whole distasteful business. In 1811, apologizing in advance for the insult, he invited William Wordsworth to write three hundred verses for a new edition of *Beauty and the Beast* of which the pictures were already prepared, offering a fee of ten guineas. 'I beg your pardon for intruding on you so humble and childish a project,' he wrote halfheartedly. 'If you feel that your mind refuses to stoop so low, I have only to receive your denial and your forgiveness.'[22] Even if Wordsworth had been inclined to accept, the tone of Godwin's request would have put him off, and he declined coldly.

The greatest of all children's books is *Robinson Crusoe*. Rousseau — whom anti-Jacobins hated more than any other writer — had made it the centre of his entire educational system, the first book to be given to a child and the only one he was to be permitted to see during his earliest years. The solitary man on his desert island provided incomparable opportunities for the teacher to describe the imagined state of nature and to prescribe practical lessons for improvement. Such a flood of imitations and improved versions appeared on the market in the late eighteenth century as rival educational theories competed to capture the prestige of the original that no children's bookshop could afford to be without a suitable stock of robinsonnades.

Among Godwin's papers is a fragment of a story about a sailor called Timothy Brown about to set sail for the Pacific, which was probably the beginning of his own intended contribution to the genre, but it was never completed.[23] When Coleridge heard of Wordsworth's refusal he offered Godwin a translation of Gessner's *First Mariner* but it too was never completed.[24]

Godwin did however have the distinction of introducing to England the only imitation of *Robinson Crusoe* which has come near to equalling the popularity of the original. Having obtained an early copy of *Der Schweizerische Robinson* in 1814, he published an immediate English translation under the title *The Family Robinson Crusoe*, changed in later editions to its more familiar name of *Swiss Family Robinson*, and it has probably been continuously in print ever since. Robinson is hardly a common name in Switzerland, but nobody has ever minded the lack of credibility, and a copy of *Robinson Crusoe* is happily discovered among the stores recovered from the wreck. The Swiss family's little island is crammed with tigers, kangeroos, ostriches, flamingoes and penguins in a concentration of wildlife unseen outside the world's major zoos. In later versions elephants also appear, and a snake big enough to swallow a donkey. All are happily slaughtered, the father explaining to his sons that God has provided wild beasts to make men brave and to stimulate the international fur trade. There is not a trace of sex.[25]

But if some of the publications of M. J. Godwin and Company resemble the moralistic tracts that Godwin had condemned in his Preface to *Bible Stories*, the five Godwin children were living proof of the general success of his educational methods. Unlike many would-be enlightened parents, he refused to push them forward. 'It is a miserable vanity', he wrote to a bookseller in explaining his theory, 'that would sacrifice the wholesome and gradual development of the mind to the desire of exhibiting little monsters of curiosity.' When a stranger wrote to ask whether the two daughters of Mary Wollstonecraft were being brought up in accordance with their mother's system, his reply betrayed some impatience with the question:

The present Mrs Godwin has great strength and activity of mind, but is not exclusively a follower of their mother; and indeed having formed a family establishment without having a previous provision for the support of a family, neither Mrs Godwin nor I have leisure enough for reducing novel theories of education to practice, while we both of us honestly endeavour, as far as our opportunities will permit, to improve the minds and characters of the younger branches of the family.[26]

The second Mrs Godwin, who must often have cursed the portrait of her predecessor above the fireplace and the dutiful walks to St Pancras Churchyard, was later to be accused of favouring her own three children at the expense of the other two, but the role of stepmother is never easy. Mary actively disliked her, but Jane wanted to be a Wollstonecraft and was also fiercely proud of her stepfather. The Godwin five, in pleasing vindication of his natural loving approach, always saw themselves as a privileged group. They never felt any inclination to rebel. Money might be short and food plain, but their home was full of life and visited by some of the most interesting and famous men and women of the day. In later life they used to tell how one evening they had crept downstairs to listen to Mr Coleridge reciting *The Ancient Mariner*. The beloved father who in his childless days had advocated that children should be brought up in common as in Ancient Sparta, was soon much respected for his failure to observe his principles.

The situation of the eldest, Fanny Imlay, was the most difficult. After the final meeting with Mary Wollstonecraft in 1796, her father Gilbert Imlay never reappeared, and nothing is known of his later life except that what may be surmised from the epitaph on a tombstone at St Brelade's, Jersey:

> Stranger Intelligent! should you pass this way
> Speak of the social advances of the day –
> Mention the greatly good, who've serenely shone
> Since the soul departed its mortal bourne;
> Say if statesmen wise have grown, and priests sincere
> Or if hypocrisy must disappear
> As phylosophy extends the beam of truth . . . [27]

If the Gilbert Imlay who died in Jersey in 1828 was the father of Fanny, he too had evidently tasted the disappointments as well as the joys of the New Philosophy.

Fanny was old enough to be aware of the odious campaigns waged against her mother's reputation in the early anti-Jacobin years. In 1805 Mary Wollstonecraft's sisters, aunt Everina and aunt Eliza, wanted to take her away from Godwin's care and send her to a boarding school, but he refused absolutely.[28] When she was eleven as the journal records, he gave her an explanation, perhaps the first time she discovered that Godwin was not her true father, and she was soon able to read the famous love letters that her mother had addressed to her absent father, including the references to herself as the 'barrier child'.[29] As the member of the family who did the shopping and negotiated credit with tradesmen, it was difficult for Fanny to maintain a philosophical detachment. She is said to have been plainer than Mary and Jane, but was much loved and admired for her warmth and her kindness. Godwin felt a special tenderness towards her. He had treated her as his daughter from the happy time in 1796 when she had carried books and messages from Judd Place to Chalton Street.[30] Nevertheless, Fanny was increasingly conscious that, unlike the other four children who had least one natural parent in the family, Papa was not her father and Mamma was not her mother.

Mary Godwin and Jane Clairmont, who were near in age, were always friends. Both were strikingly intelligent and brightly energetic from an early age. Christy Baxter, a friend of Mary's, recalled a discussion in which Mary and Jane championed the right of a woman to have a life outside the home while she and Fanny defended the traditional view. Visitors were amazed at the differences. Mary who had inherited her father's hazel eyes and fair complexion, was set to grow into a traditional English beauty. Jane was distinctly southern in appearance, with eyes so dark that the irises and pupils could scarcely be distinguished. Jane loved music – which Mary disliked – and played and sang well. Mary enjoyed writing stories and was both precocious and persevering.

At the age of ten, Mary prepared a version of the poem *Mounseer Nongtongpaw* that was so good that Godwin published it as one of the new comic picture books. The extended joke concerns a stupid John Bull visiting France who is given the same answer to so many of his questions that he believes that a man of that name must be the greatest man in France:

> A shepherd with his flock appears,
> The sheep were large and fat;
> Not understanding John, he hears,
> But humbly doffs his hat.

> For John with earnest looks began
> To ask whose flock he saw;
> At length he heard the poor old man
> Cry – 'Je vous n'entends pas'[31]

The boys of the family were also distinctive. Charles Clairmont, who was already nearly seven when his mother married Godwin, soon developed a respect and affection for his father-in-law* which he never lost. Soon after the marriage Godwin wrote a number of letters to influential friends trying unsuccessfully to have him educated without fees at Christ's Hospital, the school of Coleridge and Lamb, and a birth certificate which contains false information about his mother's parentage was obtained for the occasion.[32] A few years later Charles was sent to Charterhouse, having apparently been educated by private tutors in the meantime. As befitted a child from such an international background he showed an early talent for languages, speaking French and German as well as later learning Spanish and Italian.

The youngest of the family, William Godwin Junior, was something of a trial during his early years. He could learn quickly without effort, but like his mother he was unreliable, impatient, and unpredictable. He was sent first to a Roman Catholic school, no doubt at his mother's insistence,

---

* The term commonly used at the time for stepfather. Mary and Jane regarded themselves as sisters-in-law.

before going to Charterhouse as a day boy at the age of eight. After remaining there for a few unhappy years, much bullied by the boarders, Godwin moved him to the school kept by his friend Charles Burney at Greenwich, where, somewhat to his father's surprise, he revealed a marked talent for mathematics.[33]

Surveying the five extraordinary children of his family it was difficult for Godwin even in the early years to recollect that he had once shared the Enlightenment delusion that all children at birth are equal in their capabilities, and that he had once proposed opening his own school founded on that theory. Every month provided further confirmation that the main features of his children's characters had been essentially the same since birth, that some of their most marked chararcteristics were inherited, and that if environment and education could bring about improvement, the process was slow. In education, as elsewhere, it was increasingly obvious that the confident solutions of *Political Justice* needed to be modified. He had educated five children but their contribution to his own education was just as significant.

CHAPTER 22

Towards the End

The door of 41 Skinner Street was always open. If Godwin was poor in money he was rich in wisdom and he redistributed without stint. Letters continued to arrive from all parts of the country and from abroad. Authors and aspiring authors still sent their books and manuscripts for approval or – more often – for disapproval. Strangers who called personally during the afternoon were shown straight in; and if they came in the mornings when Godwin was 'not at home', they were advised when he would be back. With the failure to effect change by political action – methods which Godwin had in any case always distrusted – the only hope of resuming the advance lay in patient discussion among individuals. This was an aspect of his life's work which the philosopher never neglected.

It was pleasing to be reminded of how influential his book had been. *Political Justice* had been scattered like ten thousand sparks of truth some of which had lit fires in unlikely places. The Martin Smart who sent in a long commentary of detailed criticisms of the book was a serjeant in the militia.[1] The ominously named twenty-one-year-old H. M. Chatterton, who believed he had a unique Godwinian mission, wanted to know how he could make his living with the pen while he awaited the death of an elderly relative.[2] Henry Crabb Robinson, a lawyer whose life had been transformed by *Political Justice* at the Royston Literary Society in 1795, hung about Skinner Street out of respect for Godwin and in hopes of meeting other literary lions. A procession of American students equipped

41 Skinner Street, from *Lessons for Children*

with unnecessary letters of introduction demanded moral advice and reading lists.

Aaron Burr, former vice-president of the United States, had brought up his daughter Theodosia in accordance with the principles of *A Vindication of the Rights of Woman*. During his two visits to London in 1808 and 1812 when he visited Skinner Street nearly every day, he arranged for a copy of the Opie portrait to be made for his own house.[3] According to an American anti-feminist satire[4] his most shocking innovation was to teach Theodosia to vault astride into the saddle of her horse but actually he took Wollstonecraft's advice a good deal further, sending her frank man-to-man letters about his sexual conquests and encounters with prostitutes.[5] Burr, who had recently been acquitted on a charge of treason in the United States, believed he was also a follower of Godwin, but a few conversations soon put him right. 'I wish I could persuade you', Godwin wrote to him when he left London, '. . . that my method, the method I have laid down for doing good is – which I sincerely believe – the best.'[6]

As before people turned to Godwin when they were in trouble or depressed. The pattern was the same. A cry for help, conversations and visits, a period of adoration and dependence followed by painful quarrels and plain speaking, until gradually the association became a friendship of near-equals. Sometimes the young men drifted off. Usually they did not, but retained a deep sense of respect and gratitude for the rest of their lives. Occasionally they joined the *amis perdus*, but even they often came back.

A letter which Godwin received on 4 July 1803 was to have far-reaching consequences.

Mr Godwin

I am confident that you are a man of benevolence and therefore entreat your assistance. I totter on the brink of perdition and call on you to save me. Two years ago by reading your works I was incited to study. Assiduous and happy I advanced with rapidity in the road to Learning. Last September an intimacy took place between me and two young men whom I proudly designed to guide to knowledge and virtue. Instead of this they are dragging me to ignorance and vice. I see my danger, I lament and condemn my folly but I go on. A violent affection for one of these youths reduces me to the most abject slavery. I have absented myself from them, I have shut myself up in my study, I have had recourse to my books in which I once found felicity; my books are dumb, my study is a dungeon and absence encreases the fire that consumes my soul. I must fall or I must go mad should you in whom is my last hope deny me the support I am soliciting. Let me come to your house and enjoy your conversation once a week or once a month. Let me in your company regain my love of wisdom. There may be presumption in this request but do not I conjure you do not refuse to grant it. If you do the blossom which you have called forth in me will be destroyed I shall wither like a blasted tree.

Thomas Turner

At 8 o'clock this evening I shall call at your house.[7]

Godwin's journal duly records the call. Turner asked to come again for regular conversations, and before long he was so often to be found at Godwin's fireside that he became an embarrassment. He constantly complained of Godwin's high-handedness, his condescension, and his vanity, but the violent affection which he had felt for the unsuitable youth had been transferred and he also protested his admiration, his friendship, and his love. In 1809 Godwin decided to break off the acquaintanceship, but after an exchange of frank letters, he relented. He would be prepared to see Turner every second Sunday for dinner, he offered, and would invite him when there was special company. Turner could also call at other times if there was a reason, but no more.

Godwin never hesitated to impose rationing and the advice eagerly sought was not always so eagerly received. He had to wean some pupils from the intense involvement which is a feature of such relationships. The best political justice, Godwin believed, and the best psychotherapy, should be concentrated and regular but not unnecessarily prolonged. In Turner's case the recipe worked. Before long he was regarded as an honorary member of the Godwin family. Through his friendship with the Godwins he met the Boinvilles, whose daughter Cornelia Boinville was both a beauty and an heiress, and in 1812 he married her. He became a qualified lawyer, able to repay some of the practical advice which he had received from Godwin in earlier years, and his marriage confirmed the close connection between the Godwin and Boinville families which was to increase over the years. Tom Turner was a success, and for the rest of his life he was to regard Godwin as his rescuer and his adopted father.[8]

Godwin had similar difficulties with a young man called Patrickson who went to Cambridge University in 1810 to study mathematics. Patrickson who had been a pupil at Charterhouse – where Godwin's friend Matthew Raine was the headmaster – came from an unhappy family background and Godwin arranged for friends to provide money for his education. Patrickson was Turner's successor as Turner had been Montagu's and he received the same treatment. Godwin saw him regularly at Skinner Street for conversations and in a series of long thoughtful letters he invited him to explore the roots of his problems, to widen his reading, and to give more freedom to his imagination and to his natural sympathy. Without ever making light of Patrickson's difficulties, he maintained the attractive mixture of honesty and forthrightness which his predecessors had found sustaining.

'Your mother is a wrong-headed, not an abandoned woman,' he wrote when Patrickson threatened to break with her,

... We all of us endeavour to square our actions by our conscience, or our conscience by our actions ... You and I, who are of course among the enlightened, should pity those who are less fortunate than ourselves and not abhor them: even an erroneous conscience by which he who bears it in his bosom tries and examines his actions, is still a thing to be respected. I think that you should write to your mother as little as possible, and perhaps for the present ask no favours of her ...[9]

Patrickson was mocked at Cambridge. He was the 'Barber's Clerk' who was attempting to cross the fiercely defended social boundaries and his anti-Jacobin colleagues never let him forget it. Treat your enemies like buzzing night flies, Godwin advised,[10] and fortify your indifference by reading Seneca, but the remedies which Godwin found helpful did not always work for others and Patrickson continued to suffer from deep depressions.

It was hard to be optimistic. In February 1806, Charles James Fox became Prime Minister, a day which all progressives had been hoping for for a generation. Godwin recorded it in red letters in the journal but by September Fox was dead and the Tories were back, more repressive than ever. Godwin wrote an obituary under his own name for the *London Chronicle*. Reform itself was dead, and many who had once been liberal now favoured strong government. Trouble was brewing in Ireland for the third time since 1798. The long struggle with Napoleonic France showed no sign of being won or of coming to an end. War was becoming more normal than peace.

Each year the snows came earlier and departed later as Europe was struck by a mini ice age. In the Alps the glaciers advanced and in Scotland the sea froze. The severe weather brought poor harvests. In England wheat doubled in price between 1802 and 1808 and was to go even higher in 1812 when a loaf of bread cost one shilling and sixpence. Gangs of unemployed roamed the streets, their numbers swollen by immigrants. With estimates showing an increase in population in Great Britain over the first ten years of the century of one and a half million, or nearly 15 per cent, it was now normal to attribute the problem to high birth rates.

The rise in prices, the *Annual Register* noted in one of its reviews of the past year, was due to excessive public expenditure, and provision for the relief of poverty (which had quadrupled) kept numbers artificially high. The rioters and the roaming beggars were seen not only as symptoms of the imbalance between population and resources but as part of the correction mechanisms by which equilibrium was to be restored. Many people who repudiated the concepts which Enlightenment philosophers had devised to explain the workings of society felt no contradiction in stealing their vocabulary, proclaiming that immutable 'principles' or 'laws' of population had been 'discovered' by Malthus, and demanding stern measures to restore the 'natural' level of unemployment.

For years Godwin gave help to a man called Alexander Walker who often called at his house for meals and – presumably – for money. Whether the court case in which he was involved in May 1800 was for crime or for debt the result was destitution. Nothing is known of the circumstances of the following letter but it is evident that Godwin had withdrawn his support at least temporarily.

I know not what induces me to trouble you, whether reason madness or despair; my feelings are indescribable. But ever since the moment when you abandoned me, I have been the most wretched of beings; I have unceasingly exerted myself, but the fatal consequences of your displeasures have cruelly thwarted all my endeavours. I am indebted to the persons with whom I live, with tears in their eyes they beg from me a little money; but I and my poor family have wanted food for two days, my wife has no cloaths to cover her though afflicted with disease, and in a delirium she begs permission to put a period to her existence, or forcibly endeavours to effect it; but this is not wonderful, for we are surrounded by other numberless miseries from which we cannot escape unless you, at last, will alleviate them.[11]

A number of letters to Godwin survive from J. J. S. Lisle, a wounded former soldier, now aged sixty, sentenced to seven years' transportation for fraud.

The charge according to the evidence for the prosecution was a fraud *for food* to the amount of a few shillings!! . . . I leave this [country] on Monday pennyless and destitute, let me implore from your humanity some little mite and my heart will be grateful – let this console you, I cannot by any possible means have power *again to importune* you . . . The remains of an old shirt and a handkerchief will be a valuable present.[12]

In another letter Lisle wrote that he could take no more:

... fatigued to death and faint from privation, I venture a *last* appeal to your humanity – as a *farewell boon* accord to my distress but a little silver.[13]

It is not known what happened. The chances of surviving Botany Bay at Lisle's age were minimal. At the end of 1814 Godwin was to receive a visit from Maurice Margarot who had been among those found guilty of sedition in 1794 and was the only one of the transported reformers who returned. Margarot's health was broken, his sight was gone, and he was to die within a year. He was asking for charity.

At the time of Lisle's punishment the country was fascinated by the case of Benjamin Walsh, a Member of Parliament who was charged with stealing £22,200 from his employer Sir Thomas Plomer. Walsh had been arrested on his way to Falmouth to board a Portuguese ship, and since he had already changed much of the money into Portuguese currency, the crime was hard to deny. But unlike lesser offenders he was not executed or transported but was given a royal pardon. The criminal law, like the economic laws, it seemed, was deliberately weighted in favour of the privileged in order to preserve a properly structured society.[14]

Godwin continued his work. But it is difficult to be a tower of strength to others if one's own foundations are insecure. As he entered his fifties it was evident that the slowdown in the advance of his disease had only been temporary. When in May 1808 he went on a last visit to see his mother, he was again struck for three days. When she died and he went again to Norfolk for her funeral, the attacks were stronger and more prolonged than they had ever been before. For weeks afterwards he believed that he would never fully recover and his friends thought the same.

By the beginning of 1809 it became clear that Holcroft too was dying, and immediately with typical bravado he announced his intention of writing his autobiography. Racked by continuous spasms and spitting blood, the man who had never doubted that disease would eventually be overcome by the growing power of mind was determined that his own story would make its contribution to the progress of perfectibility.[15] The doctors were told that he did not care how severely they treated him provided that he could live six months longer, and by dictating a word at a time from his bed he succeeded in six weeks in composing seventeen marvellous chapters describing his boyhood and early life.

Godwin had not seen his former friend since the quarrel about *Fleet-wood* in 1805 despite all the efforts of others to bring about a reconciliation. On Sunday 19 March 1809, however, when Holcroft lay dying,

Godwin was told that Holcroft wished to see him and he hurried to the bedside. Holcroft took his hand, pressed it repeatedly to his bosom, and with tears in his eyes murmured the words, 'My dear, dear friend,' again and again. Nothing else was ever said. Godwin came on each of the next three days but Holcroft was too weak to speak and died on the Thursday. He had been the most important man in Godwin's life.

Only a few friends besides himself gathered round the graveside, ageing men from a past age, Thelwall the reformer, Shield the musician, and Nicholson the scientist temporarily out of debtors' prison. Godwin attended a dinner a few days later to raise money for the destitute widow and the six children all under the age of nine, but most of the people who ate the food were more in need of support than able to offer it. The passages of Holcroft's autobiography, which Godwin read shortly afterwards, were given to Hazlitt to work them up into a book in hopes of raising more money.

On 21 December of the same year a few of the same friends gathered at Fulham Churchyard for the funeral of another of Godwin's closest friends. He had first met Joseph Johnson in 1791 at the famous occasion when Wollstonecraft had spoiled his talk with Tom Paine. After her death Johnson, who had published the *Memoirs* and the *Posthumous Works*, acted as a kind of unofficial trustee for the orphan Fanny. From that time on Godwin had dined with him at St Paul's Churchyard once a week year in and year out for more than a decade along with Fuseli and Bonnycastle. The four men had been a miniature philomathic society, the publisher, the mathematician, the painter, and the philosopher, and Johnson often invited other authors and thinkers to join them for an evening's conversation. Fuseli provided a fine epitaph for Johnson's tomb, and Godwin wrote an obituary notice for the *Morning Chronicle*:

... He was on all occasions ready to apply his time and his thoughts for the benefit of others; and ... was the perpetual resort of all his connections in seasons of difficulty and embarrassment ... His table was frequented through successive years by a succession of persons of the greatest talents, learning, and genius; and the writer of these lines can cheerfully bear witness that all were delighted when he took his share in the conversation, and only regretted that the gentleness and modesty of his nature led him to do it so rarely.[16]

For a time Johnson's successor in St Paul's Churchyard, Rowland Hunter, continued to give dinners, but it was not the same, and they were soon discontinued. In his quiet way the older man had held the foursome together and after his death the other three only occasionally met. For

Godwin however Johnson's death was more than a tragedy, it was a disaster. In his will he left Godwin a bond for £200, but his heirs decided to call in loans for a further £800 which Johnson had 'advanced' at various times. A few months later Sir Richard Phillips went bankrupt. When his bankruptcy was declared, all his assets had to be called in, with the result that Godwin had to find another £500 cash. Other loans totalling £200 which he had received at the time of the subscription were also called in at about the same time.

In a few short months in the winter of 1809 Godwin's financial situation was catastrophically transformed. Five years of hard careful work in building up the business seemed certain to be swept away. Immediately there was only one thing he could do. He borrowed from new creditors to pay off the old. The loan capital of the business was replaced by new very short-term debt which had to be continuously rolled over as one debt after another came due for renewal. The journal bears witness to virtually continuous financial negotiations with his suppliers, his printers, and his distributors in the book trade, as well as with financiers and brokers. By the autumn of 1810 he was near to despair.

Death was much on his mind. So was the fame – or oblivion – which death brings. From childhood he had longed for fame and he had achieved his ambition. But now he was not even infamous: he was forgotten. A stranger whom he met at dinner assured him across the table that the author of *Political Justice* had died years ago.[17] He had been reading Sir Thomas Browne's *Urn Burial* and Blair's *The Grave* which his grandfather had helped to popularize and which had recently been republished with engravings by Blake. At Newbury when he had successfully researched his ancestry in the records he found the gravestones too worn to read. A man of feeling, he believed, was right to be moved by tombs, but the benefit was not simply emotional. A pilgrimage to the grave of a famous man could help carry his ideas to future generations. The churches knew that and exploited it, reinforcing superstition from one generation to the next. But the monuments which cluttered Westminster Abbey and St Paul's did not, with some exceptions, commemorate the men and women who had advanced the cause of progress but royalty, politicians, admirals and soldiers who seldom did more than act out predetermined chains of necessity. Even in death institutions corrupted the truth; those who controlled the present controlled the past, and those who controlled the past controlled the future.

At the beginning of 1809 Godwin had taken time off from his children's books to publish an *Essay on Sepulchres*. He proposed that a society should be formed by public subscription to erect plain wooden crosses over the graves of the deserving dead. Being of wood the crosses would be cheap and easily renewable, and there would be no distinctions of rank. Soon they would cover the earth with proofs that human progress had occurred and was occurring. They would be libraries for the uneducated. Godwin's proposal was seriously meant although nobody but himself has ever taken it seriously. The *Essay on Sepulchres* is a curiosity, a link between the old passive view of the mind and his new enthusiasm for stimulating the creative imagination. Like virtually every book that Godwin wrote, it is an extended footnote to *Political Justice*.

A page of comment in the handwriting of Charles Lamb draws attention to some of the more obvious weaknesses in the idea, appealing to arguments which the philosopher of individualism might have thought of by himself.

The feeling of Greatness is an individual feeling. A permanent body of enthusiasm cannot be kept up, even if the first Component parts had it. Charitable Bodies grow cold. A Body professing charity to the dead would cool still faster. A Body cannot prescribe to free minds who is to be venerated, who not. Individual freedom laughs at public prescription. Such Crosses might be respected in a poor country, as in Switzerland the Crosses are memorials of murders. Bankers, Stock jobbers, and Jews, who are the Soul of Subscriptions, would not subscribe to this. *I* would not, who am not a Jew.

I don't want the Public to prescribe me my admiration. There is too much Public Interference, too little of Individual Free Will. It would require an Army of Excisemen or as numerous to keep up the Institution . . . [18]

In September 1810 the disease struck again with four attacks in three days. On 6 October, when he felt temporarily recovered, he composed a long meditative fragment of autobiography.[19] All he had to look forward to, he now believed, was suffering, senility, and an early grave. For the whole of his life he had worked hard, but he had never gathered the fruits of his labour. Many of his contemporaries, he remarked, with people like Mackintosh and Southey in mind, had reached positions of power and of comfort by compromising. He could have done the same, but like a Roman philosopher, he had insisted on his independence – when Godwin drew the sword, Godwin threw away the scabbard. Now all that was left to him was death, the apotheosis of a great man – death which alone could confirm the fame for which he had so long striven, death which the poet and the philosopher should always regard as the culmination of a life's work.

Oh, amiable, lovely Death!
Thou odoriferous stench! sound rottenness
Arise forth from the couch of lasting night;
And I will kiss thy detestable bones!

Godwin had come full circle. Thirty years of enlightenment overlay slipped off to reveal the frightened puritan youth who had so long been covered. Godwin's hymn to death could have been written by his reverend grandfather in the seventeenth century, and as he sank back into misery the religion of misery renewed its grip. Once more Godwin was a frightened child struggling to rival the holy dying of the doomed children of Janeway.

But only for a moment. The tone of resignation is only a prelude to a more typical Godwin. As his pen traced the fatalistic incantations on the paper, he felt once more a resurgence of the pugnacity which had enabled him to throw off his upbringing more than once before. Looking back over the many disasters which had afflicted him, he reflected, breaking into the double negatives with which he habitually evinced his obstinacy, he still could not 'banish some emotions of triumph'. Applying to his own case the advice which he had prescribed to others over the years, he determined 'to put the force of my mind into the muscles of my animal frame'. He might be overwhelmed, as Holcroft had been, but like his friend he too would not give up. Like Seneca he would do his duty and his conscience would be clear.

If Godwin had helped others, he could be helped in his turn. All over London and beyond there were men whose lives had been redirected by reading Godwin's books. The urgent problem was to obtain new capital for the bookshop, and with the help of such friends a plan was devised. Francis Place, a successful businessman, was asked to advise. Born in a 'sponging house' – a privately run debtors' prison – where his father was a bailiff, Place had been apprenticed to the leather-breeches trade and took part in a disastrous strike in 1791 in which the leather workers were driven back to work by starvation and loss of customers to other types of breeches. It was as a result of reading *Political Justice*, Place used to explain, that he had overcome his ethical distaste for borrowing and soon afterwards he built his own thriving tailoring business. Although his logic was obscure he was happy to help the author of that great book and save him from the sponging house. Another rich friend, Elton Hammond, the son of a successful tea merchant, was also willing to help. He had been so impressed by reading the economic chapters of *Political Justice* that his life was to be an unending anxiety that he might be misusing the responsibilities of inherited wealth.

The assets of the bookshop business, Place estimated, were worth £7,770 and it had liabilities of £4,770, giving a clear net worth of £3,000. All the assets were however tied up as working capital, credit extended to customers, stocks of books, and copyrights. Although the business had been making profits it was certain to collapse if it could not obtain an immediate injection of longer-term capital to replace the money that had been withdrawn. Place advised that a sum of £3,000 was desirable and warned that anything less than £2,000 would not be enough. He himself was willing to lend £1,000 and he arranged for a professional financier called Lambert to put up another £1,000, normal interest to be paid quarterly and the principal repaid as soon as the business could afford it. All that was needed was a further £1,000 to be raised from other sources in the market. If this financing could be arranged, Place concluded, he would recommend it 'with more pleasure and greater certainty of success than for anyone in existence'.[20]

Any capital investment in Godwin's business had to be in the form of loan. As the law stood, there was unlimited liability both for sole traders and for partnerships and, short of an Act of Parliament or a Royal Charter, a company could not be established with limited liability or tradeable shares. There was no way therefore in which an investor could take a share of the equity of Godwin's business without putting at risk his whole fortune including his house, his chattels, and the clothes he wore. However friendly an investor might be, and however confident in Godwin's longer-term commercial success, all he could hope for was a rate of return marginally above the rate on Government stock and, in the event of difficulty, he would have no higher claim on Godwin's assets than any other creditor.

It was John Fairley, an Edinburgh businessman who had helped Godwin to establish a sales network for his books in Scotland, who suggested a solution to the problem. John Hepburn, a landowner who lived near Haddington, would, he had reason to expect, be willing to offer security for a loan. Hepburn, who had inherited the £30,000 Bearfoot estate in 1800, was another early admirer of *Political Justice*. He had visited France in the early 1790s where he met Marat, Danton, and Robespierre. He had been introduced to Godwin at a dinner at Horne Tooke's on 3 May 1795 after the treason trials when Godwin's fame was near its height, and his admiration remained undiminished.

Hepburn offered, if a loan was raised, to guarantee it against his own property, an excellent mixture or so it seemed, of political justice and imaginative use of financial markets. Hepburn would not have to part with any money: all he was accepting was a small contingent liability. It was a great pleasure, Godwin wrote in a letter of appreciation, for one who had written so extensively about human benevolence, to find such an example of actual practice. But the mail to Edinburgh took several days and it was rarely possible to get a reply to a letter within less than a week.

A month passed and nothing happened.[21] A heavy burden of debt was due to mature over the early weeks of 1811: 27 January (£200); 4 February, 16 February, and 6 March (£100 each); 27 March (£200), 19 April, 22 April (£100 each) and others beyond, each of which had to be replaced immediately on the due date. Godwin was in perpetual terror. He was now often refused by the professional discounters – 'the smooth men of the Exchange' – and was having to rely on personal friends and on colleagues in the book trade. When things became difficult, he sent his bills to Norwich to his old friend Taylor, but the day when his credit would collapse could not long be delayed.

Godwin wrote to Fairley every few days, imploring him to send the documents by the next post. The worry of waiting was a million times worse than bankruptcy, he told him, but he would not contemplate that alternative. It would not only reduce him and his family to beggary, but it would also involve 'treachery and moral dishonour'. It would mean damaging the friends who had backed him when the professional money lenders withdrew their support, and, in some cases, involving them in his ruin.

On the morning of Friday 17 May 1811 Mary Jane left for a holiday in Margate taking Mary and William with her. Mary was suffering from chicken pox or possibly smallpox. Charles left to join them a few days later and since Jane was also away, Godwin was left with Fanny. The end of the week was a busy time, but as Godwin told Mary Jane, this was more stressful than most.

I had less than £20 remaining in my drawer. I sent Joseph [his brother] to Lambert [financier] and Macmillan [printer of M. J. Godwin books]: no answer from either: Lambert not at home. Bradley [perhaps his shop assistant] then undertook the expedition to Mercer and Tabart [children's booksellers]; he preferred Friday to Saturday; I therefore desired him to take Lambert in his way. This time I was successful: the good creature sent me £100, and at six in the evening Macmillan sent me £50, having, as you remember, brought me the other £50 on Tuesday last. This was something; but, as there is no sweet without its sour, about the same time came a note from Hume [financier and politician] desiring he might have £40 on Monday . . .

I began to cast about how I was to comply with Hume's request. I was still £30 short for my bills. £30 and £40 are £70. I had however Place's bill in my possession, but how was I to discount it? I thought perhaps Toulmin [financier] would do it, I looked upon my list of discounters. By some oversight I had omitted to put the name of the discounter to the memorandum of one of Hume's bills. I thought by studying my journal I should be able to find it. I was unsuccessful. In the midst of this, however, my eye caught a bill for £140 of Place, that fell due next Friday. I had carefully put this out of my mind in the midst of the embarrassments of the present week, and I had wholly forgotten it. Perhaps I never felt a more terrible sensation in my life, than when it thus returned to me. Lambert's and Macmillan's money had made me cheerful. I walked erect in my little sally to the Temple: I flung about my arms with the air of a man that felt himself heart-whole. The moment I saw the £140, I felt a cold swelling in the inside of my throat – a sensation I am subject to in terrific situations – and my head ached in the most discomfiting manner . . . 22

Godwin was saved by Place agreeing to delay until the 30th and by the arrival of £100 from one of his customers. But the next crisis was due on 1 June. He had the temperament of a classical hero, he told Fairley, and when his creditors released him from one torture, he became young and gay again until the next borrowing was due. On 29 May Godwin was finally told that the London financiers were unwilling to lend money on the security of Hepburn's estate. The property was worth considerably less than they had expected and was already heavily mortgaged. Again however there was a reprieve. Place and others were persuaded yet again to postpone or renew, bills were discounted by Taylor of Norwich, and the business continued to trade. Six months of anxious negotiations had been wasted, and £100 spent on lawyers' fees.

June was to be another month of anxious waiting, every post a disappointment or a brief renewal of faint hope. But as always Godwin tried to continue his life as usual. On Sunday 9 June, he was approached by a young man called Barker who had just left university and was on his way to join the guerrillas in Spain. He had been intended for the Church, but had recently changed his mind. As Godwin told Mary Jane, he immediately invited him to dinner with Tom Turner:

He had lately met with my Political Justice in which he first found his own ideas of morals and the chief end of man developed; and he could not bear to quit a country, to which he knew not when he should return without attempting to see the author.23

In the middle of June Godwin tried another approach. He wrote to Josiah Wedgwood, Thomas Wedgwood's brother, explaining the situation and inviting him to lend money for the bookshop against the security of Hepburn's estate. Josiah Wedgwood had never been a believer in Godwin's principles as his brother had been, but he admired Godwin's energy, his resilience, and his determination to establish an independent business. In July 1811 to Godwin's intense relief he made an advance and offered to provide further loans provided that they were well secured.[24] When at about the same time Hepburn also provided a bill, Godwin wrote to Fairley that, like the Romans after Cannae, he offered thanks to the general for not having despaired of the republic.

But until the whole £3,000 was in place, all such advances were postponements of the day of ruin, not solutions. In his weekly financial letter to Fairley on 10 July Godwin said he feared that he was sinking. The next day the disease struck. It struck again two days later and again nearly every day for more than a week, including – a new development – two attacks during the night. Henry Crabb Robinson came to the conclusion after a visit on the 31st that Godwin's health was now totally and finally broken. Even if he did not die at once, he would certainly never again be capable of intellectual effort and would probably lose his faculties.

But after a week the attacks ceased, and gradually his health improved. As the weeks passed, it became evident that he was going to survive. The obstinate pride, so unattractive and destructive in many other situations, continued to provide new resources of strength. Few people knew that, besides his illness and his money problems, he was simultaneously confronting a third crisis.

Mary Jane and the children had returned on 16 June, and as far as outsiders could see, life at Skinner Street had reverted to normal. In fact Mary Jane had decided that she could take no more. She moved out and went to live with a French family, the Toppings, in Baker Street, although continuing to work at the bookshop and to see Godwin during the day. On 14 August she wrote a letter inviting him to a talk:

I know not what the state of *your* mind is at this moment, but mine will be that to which ten thousand daggers are mild till I hear you accept the reconciliation I now send to offer. Perhaps I was irrational – but it is not a trifling wound to my heart to see myself put by, and thought of as a burden that law will not let you be free from because in the hardest struggle that ever fell to the lot of woman, I have lost my youth and beauty before the natural time.[25]

It had been a bad day. In the afternoon Godwin heard that Henry Crabb Robinson was unwilling to provide a guarantee for Wedgwood – why should poor men underwrite the risks of rich men? Godwin went for a walk in the evening air to 'meet the great spirit of nature', as he told Robinson in a complaining letter, and was now more calm. If he and his family were to be ruined, he was resigned to it, but he could not condone Robinson's sloppy thinking. 'Sacrifice me to your nerves', he wrote, 'and I am contented. Whatever befals me, I will not repine. I will not utter a murmur. But to sacrifice me to false reasoning . . . that is too much.'[26] The journal notes his subsequent supper at Madame Topping's with Mary Jane and 'Wele' (who was perhaps a brother)* and there were other meetings with Mary Jane's friends and relatives over the next few days. On 25 August the terse entry 'M J sleeps' records Mrs Godwin's return to the matrimonial home.

Soon afterwards Godwin himself left Skinner Street for a week's holiday. He went to Chichester and the Isle of Wight visiting booksellers and sightseeing. In a series of chatty, cheering and loving letters he urged Mary Jane to gather her strength and fortitude until their problems could be overcome. 'Be assured', he wrote shortly before his return, 'that I admire you not less than I love you. We are both of us, depend upon it, persons of no common stamp.' There were signs, he told her, that the worst had passed and that the end of their troubles might soon be in sight. On his return they settled back into their previous precarious uncertainty, but as the autumn drew on, the problems remained as threatening as before. Their tenth wedding anniversary was not a happy occasion nor was Christmas. Godwin was now convinced that his life was over and it was a matter of relative indifference whether death or bankruptcy struck first.

In the first days of the New Year 1812, there arrived a letter from Keswick in the Lake District requesting an interview:

You will be surprised at hearing from a stranger. – No introduction has, nor in all probability ever will authorize that which common thinkers would call a liberty; it is however a liberty which altho' not sanctioned by custom is so far from being reprobated by reason that the dearest interests of mankind imperiously demand that a certain etiquette of fashion should no longer keep 'man at a distance from man' and impose its flimsy fancies between the free communication of intellect. The name of Godwin has been used to excite in me feelings of reverence and admiration, I have been accustomed to consider him a luminary too dazzling for the darkness which surrounds him, and from the earliest period

* See p. 250. The name is variously spelled.

of my knowledge of his principles I have ardently desired to share on the footing of intimacy that intellect which I have delighted to contemplate in its emanations.[27]

The name of the writer, Percy B. Shelley, was unknown, but every sentence suggested that he was another of those worried young men who wanted to hang about Skinner Street talking about their problems. Godwin took up his pen to reply politely – perhaps wearily – along the standard lines. He assured Shelley of his goodwill, but before agreeing to the investment of his time which the proposed conversations would require, he asked him to provide more information. The lack of personal details, he remarked tersely, rendered his first letter 'deficient in interest'.[28]

CHAPTER 23

Retractations

Shelley was only nineteen when he intoduced himself to Godwin and youth shone from every sentence. He was the eldest son of a landowner in Sussex, he explained in a long second letter sent by return of post. Before the age of seventeen he had published two novels, copies of which he was arranging to be sent for Godwin to read. He had been twice expelled from Eton but had been reinstated. At Oxford he had become an atheist and had printed an anonymous pamphlet to defend his point of view. Although assured by the College authorities that nothing more would be said if he would go through the formality of denying authorship, he had spurned the insincerity and accepted expulsion. He had quarrelled with his father. He was already married. Now, he declared, he was writing an inquiry into why the French Revolution had failed to benefit mankind. His life was to be devoted to the dissemination of truth and happiness in accordance with the principles of political justice, and he invited Godwin to become his adviser. 'To you,' he concluded, 'as the regulator and former of my mind, I must ever look with real respect and veneration.'

Godwin had received appeals like this before. Expressions of admiration for *Political Justice* and for its author were normal. To have come from a rich family and to have quarrelled with the father were frequent and a passion to reform the world not uncommon. But it was evident that this young man possessed a good deal more self confidence than his usual clientele of doubting law students and impatient would-be authors.

Every Man in his Station, from *Select Fables*

Shelley's first letter had politely contained no direct form of address; his second was prefixed 'Sir', but by the time of his third less than a fortnight later, Godwin was already being addressed as 'My dear Sir'. In asserting at once his right to be treated as an equal, Shelley's mixture of assertiveness and abasement matched the style which Godwin had adopted in approaching prominent strangers when he himself had been a young man in a hurry in the 1780s.

Shelley's first letter, Godwin may also have noticed, bore some resemblance to a fictional letter which he had included in *Fleetwood*, at the point in the story when Casimir Fleetwood seeks to make the acquaintance of the MacNeil family. The suspicion would have been reinforced when shortly afterwards Shelley invited Godwin to meet him among the mountains of Wales. 'I had pictured to my fancy', he wrote, 'that I should first meet you in a spot like that in which Fleetwood met Ruffigny.' In Godwin's novel the young Fleetwood had been taught wisdom by Ruffigny and MacNeil: Shelley was evidently already viewing his own relationship with Godwin in pre-set literary terms.

If however allusions to Godwin's works were intended to provide a pleasing dash of flattery, the effect was diluted by the young man's repeated expressions of surprise at finding Godwin alive at all. 'I had felt regret that the glory of your being had passed from this earth of ours,' he wrote in his first letter. 'It is not so – you still live, and I firmly believe are still planning the welfare of humankind.' Even after the receipt of a few crisp replies should have demonstrated that the famous philosopher was still in full possession of his faculties, Shelley persisted in referring sympathetically to 'the sunset of your evening days' – dubious comfort to a man who had not yet celebrated his fifty-sixth birthday. Given his own precarious state of health, he told the philosopher with a touch of implied reproach that the old man should have survived so long, he himself was looking for quicker results.

Godwin responded to Shelley's overtures with typical forthrightness. He was delighted that *Political Justice* had thrown a spark into the unpromising territory of rural Sussex, and was eager to keep it alight. But there was no condescension. He scolded the young man roundly for his anger towards his father – a regular theme of his advisory letters. Far from being impressed with the record of early literary achievement which Shelley paraded before him – and he had as yet made no mention of his poetry – he advised that Shelley was too young to be publishing books and was evidently motivated by a desire to show off. 'Being yet a scholar,' he suggested in a typically deflating phrase, he ought to feel 'no intolerable itch to become a teacher'.¹ As for the nonsense about dying young, he himself had suffered from poor health when he was Shelley's age. 'I think it not improbable', he remarked carefully, 'that at thirty or forty you will be a robust man.'²

Shelley was delighted. As he wrote to his friend Elizabeth Hitchener after he had received the first two replies:

Godwin has answered my letters, and he is now my friend, he shall be your's. – Share with me this acquisition more valuable than the gifts of Princes. – His letters are like his writings the mirror of a firm and elevated mind. They are the result of the experience of ages which he condenses for my instruction; it is with awe and veneration that I read the letters of this veteran in persecution and independence. He remains unchanged. I have no soul-chilling alteration to record of his character, the unmoderated enthusiasm of philanthropy still characterizes him. He preserves those principles of extensive and independent action which alone can give energy and vigor.

When *Political Justice* was published, Shelley was seven months old. To his generation the French Revolution was past history – and Shelley never liked history. Anti-Jacobinism had been the prevailing mood for as far back as his memory went. To rediscover Godwin was like rediscovering Rousseau or Voltaire. He had purchased his own copy of *Political Justice* in November 1810, but he was familiar with its ideas before that time. He knew the differences between the first edition and the third edition and he preferred the first.³ He was also deeply imbued with Godwin's other books, especially *The Enquirer* and the three novels, and he regarded them with the same veneration as the great work whose lessons they modified. In letters to friends he habitually underlined the name *Godwin* which, to his poet's ear, already carried a solemn incantatory power.

The word perfectibility was seldom far from his lips. He longed for the day, he told his friends, when Man would live in accordance with Nature and with Reason and in consequence with Virtue. He discussed ideas for establishing a new pantisocratic society whose members would live together without selfish preferences, and he told people of both sexes that he loved them after the briefest of acquaintanceship. The world's ills, he explained to Elizabeth Hitchener, could be explained by the misuse of monopoly. Generosity was a duty not a virtue. He despised the false values of gratitude, obligation, and modesty, chains all of them, he told her, which had been forged by institutions to constrain sincere judgement and natural feeling. Already he was using his own favourite term of contempt, 'Custom', as a convenient shorthand to describe the Godwinian

317

chains of necessity which fetter the minds of unthinking men. Even in arguments with his father about the need to give him more money, Shelley invoked the power of mind and the invincibility of truth.

With the confidence that Godwin had shown in his day, Shelley sought out famous men and offered to engage them in philosophical argument. From Oxford he wrote to Josiah Wedgwood and he sent his pamphlet on atheism to several of the bishops of the Church of England. He introduced himself to Leigh Hunt, editor of the radical newspaper, *The Examiner*, whom Godwin had met at Johnson's, and to Sir Francis Burdett, leader of the few reforming politicians who remained active. When someone mentioned in 1811 that William Godwin was still alive and running a bookshop, a friend was immediately dispatched to check out John Godwin's bookshop in Holborn, only to find that there was no connection. He had gone to the Lake District to introduce himself to Coleridge and more especially to Southey, whose poetry he admired. It was therefore disappointing on his arrival at Keswick to discover that Coleridge had not lived there for years and that Southey was out of town, but he had decided to wait, spending the evenings hanging about admiringly outside Southey's house.

When the meeting took place, Southey was amazed. Here on his doorstep was a perfect example of the spirit of 1793. The species had never been common, and after fourteen years of anti-Jacobinism, it was generally assumed to be extinct. But Shelley was genuine, pure, and uncompromised. Meeting him, Southey told a friend, was like meeting the ghost of his own past, but such a throwback could not survive in the current environment.[4] Before long, Southey predicted, Shelley would be following him in his long retreat. At some point the conversation evidently turned to Godwin, and Southey was able to tell him that his hero was still alive and running a children's bookshop. Shelley's first letter was sent immediately from Keswick.[5]

In a way Southey was right. The philosopher whom Shelley was so eager to meet was now himself far less Godwinian than his pupil. In essentials the theory of political justice still stood. The 1812 Godwin remained convinced that he had consolidated the discoveries of his predecessors and given a coherent account of the process of perfectibility. The way to accelerate progress, he still believed, was to free individuals from the fetters of the mind, the environmental and institutional factors which corrupted their natural benevolence. But after twenty years the modifications were significant. Godwin no longer wished to dismantle all institutions at once or even over time. Forms of government and social organization, he was now inclined to argue, might match the circumstances of different stages of history. Even marriage had major redeeming features which compensated for its tendency to promote insincerity. He was less sure than he had once been that his theory had correctly identified the crucial relationship between correct perception and virtuous motive. The imagination – which scarcely featured in his early philosophical writings – was, he now believed, part of the engine of improvement.

His early account of emotion was also, he now saw, inadequate. It had not been until he reached his forties that he had himself felt intense love, grief, anxiety, rejection, and terror. To regard emotion as a kind of auxiliary engine for the exercise of reason would clearly no longer do. Godwin at fifty-five regarded himself as a wiser man than the author of the clear-cut explanations and confident predictions of 1793. He was more experienced, more doubting, more patient. Perhaps his greatest single achievement had been to combine a political theory with a theory of individual psychology, but his description of how the two are linked was now, though more plausible, also more obscure. Further research would be needed before his general theory could be regarded as fully established. Meanwhile there was a case for pragmatism, making progess here and there as opportunity offered within the general framework. Godwin, as he now freely admitted, was in thought a radical, but in action only a Whig.

The debate between Shelley and Godwin which began in January 1812 was also a debate between the younger Godwin and the older Godwin. Godwin's theory of progress had always allowed for retreats as well as for advances. The difficulty was to know at any time which were the advances and which were the retreats. Just when Godwin felt old and tired and forgotten, he was suddenly challenged to defend himself by a man who was as passionately committed to the original theory as he himself had ever been. If to Godwin each modification was a new insight rationally derived from examined experience, the younger man was not so certain. Unlike Godwin's more biddable pupils Shelley had no intention of accepting everything the master told him without question or criticism: in the best Godwinian tradition he insisted on being convinced.

Why, Shelley demanded, should Godwin assume that the views of older men contain a higher proportion of truth than those of their younger successors? Why should younger men not publish? A thinking man should express his views and his feelings with caution and sincerity at every stage of his life, he suggested, so providing the research materials for the proper investigation of the development of individuals and of humanity as a whole. How otherwise could anyone judge whether old men's modifications are not merely successive accommodations to things-as-they-are, further illustrations of the destructive power of custom which enslaves each hopeful generation in necessitarian fetters. If men like Godwin who begin by urging boldness then devote their later years to dampening the enthusiasm of the next generation, where is the progress? When does compromise become cowardice? When does realism become hypocrisy?

Shelley wrote enthusiastically about Helvétius and about *Le Système de la Nature*, the two books which had most influenced Godwin when he had been a young minister at Stowmarket thirty years before. But he was no slavish follower. He disliked the history which Godwin urged him to study, especially the history of the age of chivalry from which Godwin had learned about the origins of modern notions of honour and of love. He also disagreed about the value of the classics. The benefits, he concluded, did not justify the intellectual investment required, and the few who succeeded in acquiring a knowledge of the classical authors then imposed a literary despotism on the excluded others. Furthermore Latin literature – with the possible exception of Lucretius – was mainly a tacit celebration of military virtues. When Godwin suggested in reply that moral feelings could not be corrupted by mere words, Shelley reminded him sharply that ideas and attitudes cannot exist without words which as *Politcal Justice* had itself emphasized, are among the most constricting necessitarian chains of the mind. The pronouncements of Godwin might not always coincide exactly with those of immutable truth, he insisted politely. Reason, he suggested on one occasion aparently without intended irony, was as superior to Godwin as Godwin was to Shelley.

But young and committed though he was, Shelley had himself already started on the retreat from the spirit of 1793. On Godwin's advice he promised not to publish any more provocative pamphlets on atheism for the time being. He did however spend time compiling a little book of extracts from the Bible, selecting 'all that was best' from the Jewish writers. The moral sayings of Jesus, he believed, if stripped of their ecclesiastical encrustations would be useful in tempting waverers from Christianity to deism, a more promising strategy than a full frontal attack. It is not known whether Shelley ever learned that Godwin had produced the same type of book with the same intention and almost exactly the same title ten years before.

Shelley's *Biblical Extracts*, unlike Godwin's *Bible Stories*, was not however printed. In 1812 the risks were simply disproportionate to the likely benefit. At the end of the year in a new clampdown on freedom of expression, Daniel Isaac Eaton was found guilty of publishing Tom Paine's anti-religious pamphlet *The Age of Reason*. It was Eaton who had printed Godwin's *Cursory Strictures* in October 1794 despite official intimidation and then his *Reply to an Answer to Cursory Strictures*. He had subsequently fled as a refugee to the United States but after his return in about 1801 his property was seized and he spent fifteen months in prison. Now in his late middle age, the brave publisher was sentenced to another eighteen months' imprisonment and forced to stand in the pillory one morning every month to be pelted by religious conformists. Godwin read – and presumably signed – a circular protest on his behalf, and was to meet him at the Lambs' after his release.[6]

Shelley was most embarrassed by his own retreat on one of the other great topics of the New Philosophy, marriage. In replying to Godwin's request for more information about his wife, he offered his justification.

... The reasons that operated to induce our submission to the ceremonies of the church, were the many advantages of benefiting society which the despotism of custom would cut us off from in case of our non-conformity. *My* peculiar reasons were considerations of the unequally weighty burden of disgrace and hatred which a resistance to this system would entail upon my companion.

In the spring of 1811 he had fallen in love with the sixteen-year-old Harriet Westbrook, a friend of one of his sisters, and he had had to decide urgently what to do. Until this moment he had never been in doubt that *Political Justice* had been right. The institution of marriage, he had told Elizabeth Hitchener a few weeks before, in discussing the recent marriage of one of her friends, was 'an evil of immense and extensive magnitude'. It was, he said, quoting a famous passage from *Political Justice* from memory, monopolizing, exclusive, and jealous. 'A kind of ineffable sickening disgust seizes my mind', he wrote on 8 May 1811 to a friend about the detestable institution, 'when I think of this most despotic, most unrequired fetter which prejudice has forged to confine it's energies.'

But when he was himself faced with the choice between conforming with society's conventions, accepting the consequences of ignoring them, or giving up Harriet, the philosophical arguments seemed less compelling. His friend Hogg spent time convincing him that, at the present stage of perfectibility, marriage was the solution that was most fair to Harriet, and with an honesty reminiscent of Godwin in 1796, Shelley submitted himself to compromise. In August he persuaded Harriet to elope. They went straight to Scotland where they were privately married. In order to have the ceremony performed at once, rather than waiting the six weeks required after the calling of banns, Shelley obtained a falsified certificate, and he and Harriet were later to follow Godwin's example by marrying a second time in order to legitimate the earlier ceremony. In the first major issue in which sincerity was patently in conflict with utility, Shelley, like Godwin, reluctantly chose hypocrisy.

Neither man knew it, but in the matter of his marriage, Shelley's experience was even more closely linked with that of Godwin. To help dissuade Shelley from what he called his antimatrimonialism, Hogg asked him to read *Adeline Mowbray*, the book written by Amelia Opie, formerly Amelia Alderson, as a deliberate warning against the irregular life. Recalling the real life cold-shouldering of Mary Wollstonecraft, both before and after her marriage to Godwin, she had described vividly the contempt to which a dishonoured woman is subjected. Before the book is half way through, Glenmurray, the Godwinian figure, confesses that the views on love and marriage which he had published at the age of twenty-four were not justifiable:

I will own that some of my opinions are changed; and that, though I believe those which are unchanged are right in theory, I think, as the mass of society could never at *once* adopt them, they had better remain unacted upon, than that a few lonely individuals should expose themselves to certain distress, by making them the rules of their conduct.[7]

Shelley's reading of *Adeline Mowbray* is one of the few documented examples of an anti-Jacobin novel actually achieving its intended effect. When Shelley explained his sudden change of opinion about marriage to Elizabeth Hitchener however he laid stress on another aspect of the argument:

. . . how useless to attempt by singular examples to renovate the face of society, until reasoning has made so comprehensive a change as to emancipate the experimentalist from the resulting evils.[8]

These words are so close to Godwin's own public defence of his own marriages in the Preface to *Fleetwood*, that Shelley must surely have had them in mind if he did not actually look them up.

The author of Political Justice . . . is the last man in the world to recommend a pitiful attempt, by scattered examples to renovate the face of society, instead of endeavouring by discussion and reasoning, to effect a grand and comprehensive improvement in the sentiments of its members.[9]

Having compromised on religion and on love, Shelley's eyes were now fastened on the third and greatest of the Jacobin trinity. In the spring of 1812 he decided to devote himself to politics. The coming year, he believed, would mark a turning-point of opinion, and he was determined to play his part. He intended to start a political campaign, he told Godwin in his next letter, and had decided that the best place from which to launch it would be Ireland. He then proposed to move to Wales for the summer before coming on to London in the autumn. With a speed and energy that astonished everyone who knew him, Shelley was soon in Dublin, holding public meetings and distributing his own privately printed political pamphlets.

Shelley's plan was not as unrealistic as it may at first appear. He was known to be the son and heir of Timothy Shelley, the Member of Parliament for Shoreham, himself the heir of the baronet Sir Bysshe Shelley, a close political ally of the Duke of Norfolk who was the leader of the English Roman Catholics. In the normal course of events a wealthy young man in Shelley's position could, even without merit, expect to follow his father into Parliament and eventually into power. Young though he was therefore – and his Irish servant pretended to think he was only fifteen – he could be sure of publicity. All the main Irish newspapers reported his activities in extensive detail.

When Godwin heard of Shelley's plans, he wrote at once to urge caution. Ireland was a subject about which he knew a great deal. He had met many Irishmen of all persuasions some of whom had been hanged. Curran, the senior judge in the country, was one of his closest friends. He had seen for himself what had happened after the rebellion of 1798 and had devoted a large part of St. Leon to explaining the consequences of religious rivalry. Before Shelley plunged into Irish politics, he suggested politely, he ought to be quite sure that his actions really would be helpful to the cause of progress and not simply 'widen the breach between the kingdoms'.[10]

Shelley's answer came straight from Political Justice. How could his pamphlets cause harm when their purpose was to mobilize the energy of truth? He enclosed a copy of An Address to the Irish People so that Godwin could see for himself. But as Godwin read his way laboriously through Shelley's rambling and repetitive pamphlet he must have been alternately amused and exasperated. Large parts read like a bad sermon, with earnest exhortations to the Irish to practise reasonableness, toleration, patience, thoughtfulness, coolness of temper, sobriety, and other virtues for which their nation has seldom been noted. A thin Godwinian philosophical basis could occasionally be discerned – reason and virtue, the Irish are repeatedly told, lead to liberty and happiness – but the general impression was very different. Although violence was firmly condemned, readers were also told that Acts of Parliament could not take away their rights. They were warned against being deceived by smooth-faced imposters, and urged to 'resist and conquer'. Any nation, Shelley proclaimed, can be free provided it has the will – a sentiment which Godwin had offered to readers of the *New Annual Register* but whose validity was even more questionable in the middle of the greatest war in history than it had been in the year of the Bastille. In a hurried postscript Shelley offered to establish a nationwide network of 'associations' to press for the moral and political regeneration of Ireland, promising a further pamphlet in which the details would be revealed. He was willing to spend money he noted, and the *Address* itself was being made available at a specially subsidized price.

The *Address* was not *Political Justice*: it was a partisan tract dressed up with a few feathers of philosophy. A lesser man might at this stage have broken off the correspondence with the impatient stranger who was deluging him with letters. Godwin had enough worries running the bookshop and in keeping the bailiffs from the door. Charles Clairmont, who had recently moved to Edinburgh to learn the bookselling trade, needed letters of advice and his other current protégé, Patrickson, also took up a great deal of his energies. Deciphering Shelley's handwriting was hard work in itself.

But that was not Godwin's way. In any theory of perfectibility the point at which wisdom is transferred between the generations is critical. The thoughtful letter which he sent in reply to Shelley is one of the longest he ever wrote. He took two mornings off from his normal work to draft it, and gave careful attention not only to its contents but to how it should be presented. Assuming the tone of voice of a concerned but loving guardian, he began by reassuring Shelley of his admiration and respect. 'My good friend,' he began:

I have read all your letters (the first perhaps excepted) with peculiar interest, and I wish it to be understood by you unequivocally, that, as far as I can yet penetrate into your character, I conceive it to exhibit an extraordinary assemblage of lovely qualities, not without considerable defects.

He reminded him of his youth and inexperience. He explained how difficult it can be to judge what the effects of any particular piece of writing will turn out to be, quoting from *The Enquirer* to illustrate the point. It was not enough, he suggested, just to put in routine disclaimers against violence as Paine and Thelwall had done. But, most serious of all, Shelley had misunderstood one of the central propositions of *Political Justice*.

Discussion, reading, enquiry, perpetual communication, these are my favourite methods for the improvement of mankind: but associations, organised societies, I firmly condemn. You may as well tell the adder not to sting.

> You may as well use question with the wolf
> You may as well forbid the mountain pines
> To wag their high tops, and to make no noise,
> When they are fretted with the gusts of heaven

as tell organised societies of men, associated to obtain their rights, and to extinguish oppression, prompted by a deep aversion to inequality, luxury, enormous taxes, and the evils of war, to be innocent, to employ no violence, and calmly to await the progress of truth. I never was at a public political dinner, a scene that I have not now witnessed for many years, that I did not see how the enthusiasm was lighted up, how the flame caught from man to man, how fast the dictates of sober reason were obliterated by the gusts of passion, and how near the assembly was, like Alexander's compotators at Persepolis, to go forth and fire the city . . .

By all means write, he advised, accepting Shelley's argument that truth might be honestly perceived in different ways at different stages of a man's life, but do not publish:

The life of a thinking man who does this, will be made up of a series of Retractations. It is beautiful to correct our errors, to make each day a comment on the last, and to grow perpetually wiser; but all this need not be done before the public . . . You have already begun your Retractations . . . I think the second chapter of your Retractations is not far distant.[11]

It was a powerful statement. Shelley having perhaps half-expected to be commended was taken aback by the sharpness of the reprimand, but he could not claim that it was unjust. He had begged the philosopher to advise him, and the philosopher had obliged him in full measure. Like a returning penitent Shelley confessed his youth, his inexperience, his ambition, his vanity, and his errors. In promising to allow himself to be guided in future the religious tone of his abasement was scarcely concealed:

Your letter affords me much food for thought; – guide thou and direct me. – In all the weakness of my inconsistencies bear with me; – the genuine respect I bear for your character, the love with which your virtues have inspired me is undiminished by any suspicion of externally constituted authority, when you reprove me, reason speaks. I acquiesce in her decisions.

With more than a touch of disappointment however, he queried whether Godwin was right to insist on a total prohibition of associations. *Political*

Justice envisaged a trickling down of enlightenment from the better-educated to the less-well-educated, but was there not a case for speaking direct to the people, as Paine had done?

The *Address to the Irish People*, he explained, had been designed to operate on the Irish mob whom he could now see, having been in Ireland for two weeks, had been dehumanized by hard labour and drunkenness, and were at the same level of enlightenment as the oysters on the shore. If *Political Justice* had set out the answers as long ago as 1793, why was there so little to show by way of results after twenty years? Had not the time come to modify the insistence on individual improvement – which was one of the few aspects of the theory still unmodified – and try direct political action instead? The long newspaper extract which he enclosed with this letter revealed that he had already gone ahead. At a packed meeting in Dublin he had again publicly promised to devote his wealth to establishing a national network of political groups.

It was a different Godwin who took up his pen to protest. This time there was no 'my good friend' or personal address or greeting of any kind, but the cold formality which Godwin reserved for his sternest pronouncements. He could see at once that Shelley's retractation was not sincere. 'I smile', he wrote, 'with a bitter smile, a smile of much pain, at the impotence of my expostulations.' As the author of *Political Justice* he had to accept a share of the responsibility, for if Shelley had not read the book, he would not have involved himself in politics. But he took comfort from the thought that even if Shelley had mangled his message and was intent on doing harm, there had been others who had not and the book might still produce a net benefit. Shelley's impatience was the same as that of the French revolutionaries. You are preparing a scene of blood, he declared, and when the calamities come, you will have to share the responsibility. At that stage it will be small comfort that you included a token warning against violence. It was a hard lesson, but it had to be learned: the only way to improve society was 'to put off self, and to contribute by a quiet, but incessant activity, like a rill of water, to irrigate and fertilise the intellectual soil'. Do not be restrained by false shame from retreating your steps, he implored, and he begged Shelley to come straight to London before he made any further mistakes.[12]

It was the most severe reprimand Godwin had delivered in thirty years of moralizing, and this time it achieved its purpose. If Godwin's first scolding caused Shelley to pause, his second redirected the chain of necessity. Shelley replied at once. Although still not convinced that his proposed associations would be harmful, he conceded that his method was wrong. The pamphlets would be withdrawn. 'Had *I* like you been witness to the French revolution it is probable that my caution would have been greater. – I have seen and heard enough to make me doubt the Omnipotence of Truth in a society so constituted as that wherein we live.' He promised to keep Godwin informed of his plans and requested him to continue to challenge whenever he was at risk of falling into error. Henceforth, he said, he was determined to devote his life to the Godwinian duty of changing opinion.

It was a handsome retractation and a permanent one. Never again was Shelley to attempt to change things by organized political activity: he would henceforth devote his life to improving the operation of the moral economy by changing the perceptions and opinions of individuals, an activity in which he turned out to be one of the supreme masters. The conversion of Shelley in 1812, before Godwin and he had met, was a triumph of political justice, greater in its longer-term effects even than the triumphs of 1794.

CHAPTER 24

Distress in the House

At Skinner Street, meanwhile, Godwin continued with his efforts to recapitalize the bookshop. At times prospects appeared hopeful. Place had stipulated that nothing less than the full recommended £3,000 would be sufficient to ensure survival and in the spring of 1812 Godwin had received promises of £2,500. By the time the last piece was ready to be put in position however one of the others had usually fallen out. Godwin continued to roll over his debts – £100 on 7 June, £100 on 11 June, £100 on 13 June, £100 on 28 June, £100 on 4 July. When summer arrived with still no solution, his friends were becoming weary. Place told him that he could do no more and was giving up the search. When Hammond advised him cryptically shortly afterwards to 'set down his contingency on the unfavourable side',[1] Godwin knew that he must prepare for disappointment.

Occasionally he would pen a letter to someone he knew from the past asking for an investment in his business. To the embarrassment of his hosts he would pounce on new acquaintances across the dinner table and explain the commercial – and political justice – benefits of advancing him funds. At some houses the servants were instructed to say the master was not at home. Henry Crabb Robinson told him frankly that when he recognized the handwriting, he would put Godwin's letters aside until the next day before opening them.[2] Place was later to accuse him of having given him misleading information about the prospects – an extreme case

The Caprice of Fortune, from *Blossoms of Morality*

of preferring utility to truth commonly known as fraud – and Godwin admitted to Hammond that, out of consideration for his family, he was inclined to present his affairs in an overfavourable light.

There was one man who might be willing to save him. Percy Bysshe Shelley whom he had not yet met evidently had money as well as expectations. Godwin had been shocked at Shelley's readiness to fritter away his fortune waging a political campaign in Ireland. Since he financed his own publications, he was able to cascade his youthful thoughts on many people who would never have dreamed of paying money to read them. Shelley was impatient of small obstacles and disdainful of small expenditures. By overweighting one of his letters, he made Godwin pay one pound one shilling and eightpence in excess postage, the equivalent of several weeks' grocery bills for the whole Skinner Street household. A man like this might be the successor to Tom Wedgwood. As soon as Shelley's letter of retraction was received from Ireland, Godwin wrote to offer his thanks and his congratulations. His young pupil, he now suggested, should become the chief instrument of conveying the ideas of *Political Justice* to the next generation. 'Now I can look on you', he wrote in a significant phrase, 'not as a meteor, ephemeral, but as a lasting friend, who according to nature, may contribute to the comforts of my closing days.'[3] It was a thought which Shelley had himself volunteered in one of his earlier letters.

But Godwin's letter was greeted with silence. After seven long letters in the first two months, Shelley suddenly stopped as unaccountably as he had begun. Like the meteor to which Godwin had perceptively compared him, his enthusiasm seemed to have already burned out. Perhaps, Godwin may have suspected, he had been offended at his continuing admonitory tone. Or maybe the phrase about being a comfort had put him on the alert. The rich have a keen nose for any hint of money creeping into a relationship. And who knew what terrible warnings Southey might have passed on?

The explanation was more straightforward. Shelley had left Ireland before Godwin's conciliatory letter of 30 March arrived and had understandably assumed that it was Godwin who had terminated the correspondence. A letter to Skinner Street at the end of April announced that he and his family were now settled in Wales, but it was not until June that Shelley received the letter of 30 March which had been forwarded from Ireland. The reply sent immediately on 11 June showed at once that he had picked up the implications of Godwin's hints.

I can return no other answer than that I will become all that you believe and wish me to be. I should regard it as my greatest glory should I be judged worthy to solace your declining years.

It was not much, but it was enough to revive Godwin's hopes. Shelley, who had consistently affirmed his wish to devote his talents and his resources to promoting Godwin's ideals, was likely to be responsive to the thought that Godwin – like Fénelon in the story – had a high claim to be rescued. Once more the long chains of 1793 had shown their power to promote good. Once again the stubborn Godwinian refusal to accept so-called facts – things as they are – was proving to be more than just a psychological defence against disappointment. At the beginning of July Robinson noted in his diary that there was a new atmosphere of hope at Skinner Street that the money problem might at last be over.

With the eagerness for friendship which was always one of his most engaging characteristics, Shelley urged Godwin to bring his family to stay with them in Wales. When Godwin explained that he could not get away, Harriet Shelley wrote to suggest that in that case Fanny might come on her own. They felt rather let down when Godwin said no. The reason offered, that he could not permit his daughter to stay with strangers whom he had never met, struck a discordant note. Surely Godwin, of all men, ought to have despised the absurd conventions which custom had erected to separate man from man?

The refusal came especially hard because Shelley was at that same moment himself experiencing their unfairness. When he invited Elizabeth Hitchener, he offered to pay her travel expenses in a mildly pantisocratic gesture, explaining that all the wealth of his little community was to be held in common. But his friends in Sussex felt bound to tell him that his generosity had been misconstrued. Shelley wanted Elizabeth for sex, it was being loudly whispered: now that he was married he had good cover. Shelley would have been surprised if he had known that in 1798 Godwin had urged an earlier unmarried schoolmistress Harriet Lee to stay with him in London.

When Shelley considered taking a large house near Chepstow, Godwin was asked to help with the financial negotiations with the owner who lived in London. To his astonishment, he discovered that Shelley thought the house would be too small to accommodate all the friends that he wanted to invite. Assuming once more therefore the duty to correct his pupil's errors, he wrote at once to offer his advice. 'You love *frankness*', he noted by way of pre-emptive apology, 'and you honour *me*, but when this frankness proceeds to unreserve and unceremoniousness in my person, who [how] will you hear that?'

Your family consists of yourself, a very young wife, and a sister – yourself as I conceived, a plain philosophical republican loving your species very much, and caring very little for the accumulation of personal indulgences. Tell me how much of truth there is in this picture?

The Enquiry concerning Political Justice may, unknown to me, be a mass of false principles and erronious conclusions. To me it appears otherwise. There is one principle that lies at the basis of that book. 'I am bound to employ my talents, my understanding, my strength, and my time, for the production of the greatest quantity of general good – I have no right to dispose of one shilling of my property at the suggestion of my caprice.'

There is no principle, as it appears to me that is more fundamental to a just morality than the last. Now my property and money are most essential for promoting the good of others; but he that misuses them undermines all the good qualities he might otherwise have ... The very act of having no conscience in the expenditure of his money and pampering all his whims will corrupt his understanding and taint his benevolence. It is in this point of view that the apostle says well – He that offends in one point is guilty in all.[4]

As yet Shelley knew nothing of Godwin's financial difficulties and of the potential claim on himself which every letter he wrote was making more likely. Far from being offended at the tone of Godwin's letter, he assured him that he loved and venerated him the more. Godwin was right to have reproved him like a wise and tender parent – even although in the matter of the house he was wrong. Although he invited Godwin to continue to look for faults in his character and to bring them to his attention, he had no intention of forgoing the advantages of an unearned income. If he and Harriet had been obliged to earn their living by working they would both be less useful to society. Shelley believed that it was wrong for people of the opposite sex to have to sleep in the same room unless they were married or closely related and it was so as to be able to entertain the numerous Godwins that he had stipulated a minimum size for the house. In the present state of society, he added tactlessly in a Malthusian observation, promiscuous sexual intercourse would inevitably lead to injurious consequences.

On 14 July Elizabeth Hitchener called at Skinner Street on her way to join the Shelleys and she stayed overnight. It was the first direct contact between the two families, and although Elizabeth had only met Shelley on a few occasions, Godwin no doubt learned more about his extraordinary new friend. But meanwhile his finances continued to deteriorate. In the week beginning 16 August he devoted three days to preparing accounts and they offered little encouragement. There was a frantic round of correspondence and visits to Place, Lambert, Hammond, and other potential backers, but – as Godwin might have said – with no favourable result.

On Tuesday 8 September, the day after Lisle sailed for Botany Bay, the event which Godwin had feared for so long at last arrived. He was unable to pay one of his debts and the creditor obtained an order of execution.[5] Three days' grace were usually allowed between the issuing of an order and the actual arrest, but if he were once to be arrested, other creditors would close in. Henry Crabb Robinson met him that afternoon at his brother's begging for money 'as a distress was in his house' but although he was refused there, he did manage to find some means of staving off disaster. The following day after receiving a call from his lawyer and twice visiting Bagley the banker, he set off on the afternoon coach on the long journey to Lynmouth in Devonshire where the Shelleys were staying. If he was out of London, he was more safe from bailiffs. The day before the execution order was given, he had written to Shelley to tell him that he was on his way, and it was evidently on the strength of his projected visit to his rich new friend that he was able to stay his creditor's hand.

He was alive and well, he told Mary Jane in a note penned while the horses were being changed at Bath, 'without pain and as strong as a lion'.[6] Mary Jane knew that worry and exertion were likely to bring on his fits. He had been depressed in August and had started to have sleeping attacks in the mornings, a development of his disease which had not occurred before. Travelling by coach was uncomfortable and dangerous. Accidents and robbers were frequent, and it was always cold – on 2 March two of the outside passengers were found to have died of exposure when the night coach arrived at Bath after a rainy journey.

Whenever Godwin was away from home, his letters were mainly devoted to assuring Mary Jane that he was safe and explaining why he could not write more often. This time when bailiffs were at the door she was especially worried and until Godwin told her to stop, she wrote her letters under an assumed name. Think what might happen if they fell into the hands of strangers, he pleaded with her, more fearful of being suspected of having taken a lover than of the risks to his financial secrets.[7]

He had hoped to find a ship to take him by sea from Bristol direct to Lynmouth, but none was due to sail until the following Monday. He therefore wrote a further letter to Shelley telling him of his new expected time of arrival and set off on a tour of the local sights including a visit to Chepstow Castle where Henry Martin had been imprisoned for twenty-

five years for signing the death sentence on King Charles. Already short
of money, on his return to Bristol he paid as many business and social
calls as he could to save the expense of dinner and tea, and Gutch and
Cottle, the two booksellers in that town were probably glad to see him
go.

The ship eventually set sail at one o'clock on Wednesday 16 September,
a full week after he had fled London, but there was hardly any wind and
virtually no progress was made on the first day. There were only four
berths for fourteen passengers. On the following day a storm blew up
and the captain decided to put in on the Welsh coast where he intended
that the passengers could sleep ashore overnight in a barn. However
when the storm passed, he decided instead to press on and Godwin was
eventually landed at Lynmouth at three o'clock on Friday. He had been
on the ship for fifty-one hours, seasick much of the time, and had not
eaten for two full days. While on board he suffered one of his fits. It was
the most uncomfortable journey he had ever undertaken and was to
confirm a horror of travelling which was to persist for the rest of his life.

There was no sign of the expected welcoming party on the quay, and
when he made inquiries, the disappointment was overwhelming. The
Shelleys, he learned, had left the district a full three weeks before and
were unlikely to have received any of his recent letters. Nobody even
knew where they had gone although they were believed to be heading for
London. That night in his rented room he was struck down by another
fit. The next day he hired a horse and rode to Barnstaple where he spent
the night. It was a town with which Mary Jane had had connections in
her youth. Three of her sister's children had been baptized there in one
batch in 1796, and maybe Mary Jane had lived there herself. As Godwin
walked along the Mall, as he told Mary Jane, he considered boldly
knocking on the door of Dr Wavil's fine house, and introducing himself,
but he decided not to for fear that she might not approve.[8] Mary Jane
later pretended that she had a sister in Lynmouth, which was untrue but
she was carefully coy about some of her real relations. Perhaps Wavil was
an anglicized version of de Vial?

The main worry now was what he would be able to say when he got
back. The creditors must somehow be persuaded that everything was still
going according to plan and this meant in the first place persuading Mary
Jane. 'Beware of spreading unfavourable ideas of Shelley to Place or any
of the persons concerned in our pecuniary affairs,' he wrote from
Barnstaple. The only ray of hope was that Shelley was expected shortly
in London, and 'this quite comforts my heart'.[9] By the time Godwin

reached Salisbury, he had run out of money. He was travelling as an outside passenger on the coaches and living on bread and cheese. On the 22nd the disease struck again, and then again on the 23rd, but Godwin eventually reached Skinner Street on the evening of Friday 25 September. He had been away for two and a half weeks, spent a great deal of money, damaged his health, and accomplished nothing.

One of his last duties before reaching home was to write a long letter preparing Mary Jane for the trials ahead. Her disappointment he knew would be worse than his own – there would be emotional scenes and recriminations and she might again walk out. His careful letter written with all the deliberation of an appeal to the power of truth gives a peep into an unusual marriage. He always found it difficult to speak about his true feelings, he began, and he was afraid that his remarks would be misconstrued. He disliked giving praise when people asked for it, yet he knew how deeply appreciated a few spontaneous words could sometimes be. He begged her to accept the disappointment in the same philosophical spirit as he himself had adopted and not to vent her temper on the minor failings of her husband.

You were perhaps destined by your intrinsic nature for something much better than my wife. Most deeply do I grieve that you should be involved in any straights of mine, or that you should experience any privations arising out of my circumstances. Yet in reality nothing can more crown your merits than the readiness with which you have submitted to this, the cheerfulness with which you have applied yourself to plans for the common benefit and support of our united family, and the courage with which you have stooped even to put yourself behind a counter, because you thought it led to those objects. Only remember that the highest honour in all this is that you should constantly honour yourself, and hold yourself on all occasions exalted and not degraded by the virtuous and heroic acts of your life.[10]

It was a Godwinian love letter, the genuineness of his emotions overflowing his cold precise sentences. Mary Jane's daughter preserved it carefully to rebut the story that Godwin was among the many people who disliked her mother.

Francis Place called at Skinner Street the day after Godwin's return, no doubt to talk about money, and the now continuous round of calls, explanations, and requests for more time began again. Two days of the following week were devoted to the accounts, but they yielded little comfort. Then on the following Monday, word arrived that Shelley was in London. He, his wife, and Elizabeth Hitchener dined that afternoon in

Skinner Street along with Hammond. After ten months of letters, the master and his pupil came face to face for the first time.

Shelley came the next day and on each of the following two days. 'Need I tell you that I love them all,' Harriet Shelley wrote to a friend in Dublin.[11] Godwin's manners were so soft that nobody could be offended at what he said. It was a pleasure just to see him and hear him talk. With his balding head he looked like a bust of Socrates – a comparison which many men would not have found flattering but which would have delighted the modern Seneca. Mrs Godwin, Harriet decided wishfully, was a woman of great fortitude, magnanimity, and independence of character. Despite her life of hardship, she was sweet-tempered and well known for her kindness. Fanny too was a delight, the beauty of her mind making up for the plainness of her face, and the nine-year-old William was extremely clever and certain to follow his father. Shelley and Harriet immediately decided to settle near London so as to be near their new friends.

CHAPTER 25

The Two Philosophers

Face to face at last, after ten months of letters, the two philosophers immediately plunged into conversation. They had a lot to talk about, religion, philosophy, politics, psychology, literature, women, money – everything of concern to the New Philosophy. At the first meeting they discussed 'matter and spirit' and 'atheism'; at the second 'utility and truth' and 'party'. They then moved on to questions of Church government, the war in Spain, ancient and modern literature, and the responsibilities of stewardship. For the first time for fifteen years Godwin took notes of his chief conversations. Shelley, it was already clear, was the best pupil he had ever had.

They made a strange pair. Godwin with his huge straight bald forehead was short, erect, and slightly overweight: Shelley with a mop of long hair, tall, stooping, and unhealthily slim. Godwin, precise in manner, neat in dress, careful in handwriting: Shelley exuberant, untidy, illegible. Sitting in his study surrounded by walls of embanked books – and his own writings already took up several feet on the shelves – Godwin was patient and persistent. Shelley liked walking up and down, swinging impetuously from one enthusiasm to another, picking ideas up and throwing them down: his first reaction to every new fancy was to write a book about it and he usually did.

At the first meetings Godwin explained again the implications of his theory of necessity. He scolded Shelley again for his atheism and for his

The Two Friends by Hone

misguided excursion into party politics. He told Shelley he was too young and inexperienced to be so dogmatic and self-confident, and quoted the saying of St Cyril that 'humility is truth'. Shelley laughed and said he would listen to Socrates and Plato, but not to a saint and that he could see no merit in past ages except in the pagan republic of Athens. A horrified Mary Jane blamed his conceitedness on his having been brought up in a Protestant country. Nobody understood quite what she meant, but even William Godwin, she may have reflected, was not noted for modesty.[1] On 7 October Shelley met Lady Mountcashell who was paying a visit to London, and we may be certain that the rights of woman came up either on that day or in subsequent conversations. During another visit to Skinner Street he met Patrickson, the Cambridge undergraduate who was also undergoing Godwinian tuition at the same time. In early November he was introduced at Skinner Street to John Frank Newton, the vegetarian, and he soon also met the Boinville family including his predecessor Tom Turner and his wife Cornelia.

Contrary to first impressions however Shelley and Harriet did not enjoy their visits to Skinner Street as much as they had expected. Godwin demanded a degree of deference which they did not feel he fully deserved. On the other side Mary Jane was exasperated by Shelley's habit of not keeping his appointments. In earlier years she had threatened to walk out when Curran and Coleridge were guilty of the same discourtesy, and in a household on the verge of bankruptcy, a wasted dinner was a serious matter. While Godwin and Shelley argued delightedly in the next room, the two wives found no such easy rapport. Harriet Shelley soon decided that the fussing Mrs Godwin was thoroughly disagreeable and after a time she refused to go to Skinner Street. As a couple they preferred the more open and comfortable way of life of the Newtons and the Boinvilles.

Shelley who always had been nearly a vegetarian now became a vegetarian fanatic, finding, he believed, in Newton's muddled little pamphlet, a philosophical justification for his own eating habits. He had long been inclined, like the dainty ladies described in the *Vindication*, to regard physical weakness as a sign of enhanced sensibility and, to Godwin's annoyance, took pride in his vulnerability to illness. With his mind on higher things, he went for days eating nothing but lumps of bread carried loose in his pockets, and he would then try to relieve the resulting stomach pains with opium-based medication. While the middle-aged Godwin struggled, with some success, to control a degenerative disease by the sheer power of mind over body, his twenty-year-old follower spluttered incessantly with unnecessary colds and coughs, not helped by his habit of plunging his head into a bucket of cold water several times a day and leaving nature to dry his long hair. He and Harriet talked constantly of death and of suicide and they carried poison in their baggage in case they were caught unprepared by a sudden irresistible wish to die.

Soon Shelley was also enthusing about Zoroastrianism, Nairism and the other -isms which the Newtons and the Boinvilles included in their return to nature. The Chevalier Lawrence to whom Shelley introduced himself by letter in the summer of 1812, was a regular visitor at the Boinvilles, and when Shelley called Mrs Boinville's home a paradise of love, he was alluding to a phrase in the Preface to *The Empire of the Nairs*. Mrs Boinville was not quite brave enough to practise her nudism in public, but the children were encouraged to romp about without clothes. As for free love, the women talked about it a great deal, although the icy bonds of custom kept their actual behaviour under restraint.

Shelley's conversation with Godwin about 'Germanism' on 9 October 1812 was probably a discussion of the gothic novel. Godwin was proud that he had adapted the genre to more serious purposes in *Caleb Williams* and *St. Leon*, and having read Shelley's *St. Irvynne* in the previous June, he probably felt a need here too to administer a scolding. They may also have talked about the romantic novels of Wieland which Shelley and Harriet were reading with admiration at this time: the Chevalier Lawrence had known the author in Germany and his *Nairs* had first appeared in Wieland's *Merkur*. The topic on 15 October, 'Rosa M', was style in poetry – Rosa Matilda was the heroine of his old friend Robert Merry's Della Cruscan style which Coleridge and Wordsworth had made the target of their scorn.

In literature it was evident to Godwin that Shelley's taste needed to be corrected. He should read Shakespeare, Milton, and Bacon, Godwin consistently urged, and he suggested a list of over twenty Elizabethan and Jacobean poets, dramatists, and prose writers whom Shelley ought to study. Most important of all, Shelley should read more factual history as an antidote to the poetry and metaphysics which were disturbing his judgement. But when Shelley reluctantly ordered a reading list of history books from his bookseller, he confessed that he found the subject hateful and disgusting to his very soul.

In literature, as in philosophy, Godwin had moved far from his eighteenth-century heritage. He continued to read the latest publications and to keep up with the latest theories. In the winter of 1811 he had attended the series of lectures on Shakespeare, Milton, and the nature of poetry which Coleridge gave twice a week at the London Philosophical Society. The start of the lectures had been delayed for Coleridge was suffering from the usual opium and constipation, and Godwin was asked to insert the advertisements in the newspapers. He also lent Coleridge money. He himself attended every lecture, sometimes accompanied by Mary Jane and whichever of the children were at home. Lamb, Robinson, and Hazlitt were also occasionally among the party.

On 23 January 1813 he also attended the first performance of Coleridge's verse tragedy *Remorse*, which played for several nights. Under its original title, *Osorio*, the play had been turned down in 1798 – when *Antonio* had been accepted – and the manuscript lay for several years in Godwin's study until Coleridge retrieved and revised it. If *Osorio* could be revived so perhaps could *Antonio*. At the time he was discussing poetry with Shelley in October 1812 Godwin was again negotiating with Drury Lane, but the play was dead beyond recall. When Shelley took tea at Skinner Street on 18 August 1813, Coleridge had called earlier in the day but that was the nearest the two poets ever came to a meeting.

It was at Coleridge's lecture on 20 January that Godwin first met Lord Byron, just returned from Greece, and in September he read the first two cantos of *Childe Harold's Pilgrimage*. He met him again at John Murray's on 4 August 1813, the only other occasion when they were to meet. Byron is said to have asked why he did not write another novel. 'It would kill me,' Godwin replied. 'And what matter,' said Byron, 'we should have another *St. Leon*.'[2]

Falkland in *Caleb Williams* is easily recognizable as a prototype of the Byronic hero, noble and good but seriously flawed, a role that Byron both popularized in his poetry and presented to the world as his own character. Byron deeply admired Godwin's novel and he loved to play-act it. After he quarrelled with his wife he used to tell her that he would haunt her as Falkland had haunted Caleb Williams. He terrified her by hinting that he too had committed a secret crime. Once, she records, when she let him know that she had picked up his meaning, he shouted some words from *Caleb Williams** and vowed he would persecute her for ever.[3] When he was fourteen, Byron had also read *Kruitzner or The German's Tale*, another story of pursuit, which Harriet Lee contributed to the *Canterbury Tales.*† Like *St. Leon* the story is set in Germany at the time of the thirty years war and is concerned with pursuer and pursued bound together by

---

* Probably from Falkland's outburst when he is disturbed with his iron chest in Chapter 1, 'Quit the room or I will trample you into atoms'.
† See p. 201.

powerful opposing passions. In a handsome acknowledgement of gratitude when Byron adapted the story for his own verse play *Werner*, he
declared that it contained the germ of much of his later writing.[4] He
probably never knew that the author had been pursued by the love-lorn
Godwin in 1798, but had not succumbed.

Godwin read Byron's poetic tales soon after they were published, and
his appreciation was fair. As he advised his son William:

Lord Byron is a writer of a very different sort [from Walter Scott]. His energy is
real energy; his language is truly felicitous; he is in the true sense of the word a
poet. All that I have to object against him, is the narrow range of his talent; that
he can do but one thing well. All his poems are the same poem with a different
title. All his heroes are misanthropes, and rogues, and ruffians, always daring, but
always wicked, used ill by the world but taking good care in this respect that they
will not die in the world's debt.[5]

It is not known when exactly Shelley told him that he too was a poet.
On 31 October, however, three weeks after their first meeting, he lent
him the manuscript of the long poem called *Queen Mab* on which he had
been working for several months, and Godwin read its forty-four pages
at a single sitting. If he expected his pupil to write in the superseded
eighteenth-century fashion which he preferred, he was quickly disillusioned. Like Southey, Shelley had written an epic in complex Spenserian
stanzas, but this poem was no fake medieval romance but a full scale
philosophical treatise. Its full title was *Queen Mab, A Philosophical Poem*.
As Shelley had told his publisher, in offering his manuscript from
Lynmouth, the themes he had chosen were the past, the present, and the
future, all of which offered plenty of scope.

Godwin ought to have been more impressed than he was. *Queen Mab*
is a scarcely believable achievement for one so young. Later generations,
astonished at its poetic power but shocked by its message, hid it amongst
the author's juvenilia, for *Queen Mab* cannot be misunderstood except
by the wilful. Following the example of Volney's *Ruins of Empires* – a
book which Shelley adored and Godwin despised – the poet takes the
reader on a fantasy ride into the heavens in the chariot of the fairy queen.
Only from a proper distance is it possible to see things as they are on
earth and to consider things as they might be. Queen Mab, who is the
narrator, begins with the theory of Necessity. She explains how some men
– the good and the sincere – can burst the chains of custom while
others remain the unwilling sport of circumstance and passion. All the
professions belong to the latter category, kings, priests, soldiers, lawyers,

bankers, merchants; and large parts of the poem are devoted to luscious and gorgeous descriptions of their seething corruption. Hypocrisy is institutionalized in their medullary particles, custom interposing between nature and virtue.

Queen Mab having described the problem also offers the solution. The seed of perfection remains in every heart, ready to be germinated by the Spirit of Nature. That impartial force once freed can make harmonies on the life-strings of the soul. The omnipotence of mind can reconcile reason and passion. Perfectibility can be advanced. The way forward is clear:

> Some eminent in virtue shall start up,
>   Even in perversest time:
> The truths of their pure lips, that never die,
> Shall bind the scorpion falsehood with a wreath
>   Of ever-living flame,
> Until the monster sting itself to death.

Shelley was determined to be one of those who would start up and his poem was itself the message.

The argument, spread through nine singing cantos and a huge addendum of explanatory prose notes, is almost identical with that of the first edition of *Political Justice*. The vocabulary and the images are also the same. Government is an upas tree which poisons everything that comes under its shadow. Sparks of truth are struck off throughout the poem. The drone of a metaphorical Aeolian harp can be heard fifteen times, and there are at least twenty direct references to chains in their double meaning of chains of events and fetters of the mind and body.

Shelley calculated that the Government would be less likely to prosecute poetry than prose and he could therefore be more forthright. He also however explained the verse with long prose notes including summaries and quotations from *Political Justice*, *The Enquirer*, and other sceptical philosophers from Lucretius to Voltaire. Although he began the poem before meeting Godwin and continued writing it during the conversations, by the time it was finished he added a long non-Godwinian section on the moral damage caused by meat. Under the influence of Lawrence and his *Nairs*, Shelley was also quickly relapsing – as yet only intellectually – from his previous retractions on love. There is therefore a long section, more Godwinian than Godwin had been even in 1793, in which marriage is described as an odious monopolistic usurpation of woman's natural appetites, a legalized prostitution.

The poem could not be published in the normal way, Harriet Shelley explained to one of her friends, 'on pain of death', and when Shelley distributed copies which he had privately printed, he cut out the title page and the imprint at the end which revealed the name of the author. One copy was sent to Lord Byron whom Shelley did not yet know personally but who at the age of twenty-four was the most famous poet of the age. Byron showed the copy to the poet William Sotheby, translator of Wieland's *Oberon*, presumably in the belief that the king of the fairies and the queen of the fairies should be brought together, and it is doubtful if Byron read it at this time. In 1821 when Shelley and he were friends, it was publicly suggested that Byron had supplied the prose notes to the poem, but nobody who knew the views of the two men could have taken that charge seriously.[6]

Godwin read his own copy of the printed version on the day after Christmas 1813, admitting in his journal that he skipped. Two weeks before, he had cautioned Shelley in a letter against his 'false taste' in poetry. He had warned him against the love of superficial sparkle and glitter which marred the poetry of modern poets such as Robert Southey, Sir Walter Scott, and Thomas Campbell – and, he might have added, Lord Byron. On 26 December 1813 he drafted his own critique of *Queen Mab* intended, we may guess, to be used as a memorandum for his next conversation with Shelley.

Is there method

What means the 🖑*

Versification

English

How excellent the philosophy of modern poetry; how unhappy the drunken, reeling, mystical, Pythia form in which it clothes itself

Oh, for a manly style, that tranquillity, that sobriety, that clearness of method, that pure simplicity of language, which deep feeling, when duly concocted and matured, always supplies.

With what a firm step does the true poet hear, seeing all, and planning all – the joints of his discourse are well knit – no word occurs in vain – nothing is wild, incoherent, and abrupt:

His words flow in the sweetest and richest stream – all is perspicuous – subjected to the severest laws, and therefore revelling in the most perfect and only liberty.

In the other poetry there is a gloomy rawness; the feelings of its author are not lovely and harmonious, and by fits and starts only, if ever, does he impart genuine joy and admiration to his reader.

---

* Shelley printed an indicator hand against eight of the Notes. See Appendix 3.

I would distinguish between a divine, sober, heart entertaining admiration, and that wild, uneasy, frantic, staring, wonder which modern poetry imparts.[7]

To use a Godwinian idiom, Godwin's verdict is not lacking in validity. In his desire to glamorize, Shelley had turned Godwin's theories into goddesses and demons, Necessity, Reason, Perfectibility, Custom. Unable in his chosen format to include the detailed steps in the philosophical argument, his concentration on lurid portrayals of the world's oppressive institutions detracted from the poem's persuasive power. As with *Political Justice* in its own day, many readers would prefer the descriptions to the philosophy. Like Godwin, Shelley had provided many quotable passages of use to a partisan politician. By including vegetarianism and water drinking amongst his prime remedies, *Queen Mab* offered comforting confirmation to anti-Jacobins who saw their opponents as a collection of cranks.

Thomas de Quincey, the opium eater, another admirer of the first edition of *Political Justice*, was to compare Shelley to Walking Stewart, the arch-eccentric of the previous generation who had turned Godwin's theory into nonsense.[8] Most serious of all for the future, *Queen Mab*, much of which was written before the discussion with Godwin about 'party' on 7 October 1813, blurs the vital difference between the individual liberalism of Godwin's theory of progress and the collectivist socialism by which impatient reformers have hoped to accelerate the process.

343

CHAPTER 26

Stewardship

The discussion about 'stewardship' which took place on 15 October gave Godwin an opportunity to expand on the advice in his letters. If by the operation of an absurd economic system a teacher lacks the modest resources necessary to do his duty, then it becomes the duty of others to divert some of their surplus towards him. Shelley needed no convincing. In every town that he visited the beggars had cause to thank him and he habitually gave sums of money to friends and acquaintances who required it. But direct relief of hardship, he knew, can only be a temporary expedient and – as Godwin himself had long ago accepted in *The Enquirer* – may even encourage a morally destructive attitude.[1] In Ireland Shelley had decided to use part of his available money to finance political pamphlets aimed at raising the enlightenment level. Later, with *Queen Mab*, he was concerned to make his impact further back along the chain by stimulating the imagination. But he hankered for more direct means of bringing about improvement. After leaving Lynmouth in August 1812, he and his entourage moved to North Wales after seeing an advertisement for a 'romantic residence' to rent, and they decided immediately that it was exactly what was wanted.

Tannyralt, perched on a steep hillside above the town of Tremadoc, with spectacular views over the sea, offered the exhilaration of a wild and mountainous setting forever associated in the literary mind with simplicity, frankness, and freedom. The house contained all the modern amenities

The Old Man and his Son, from *Select Fables*

that the finest Regency taste could devise, including a water closet, an invention destined to transform comfort more effectively than other more celebrated inventions. In 1805 Robert Southey, who was still Shelley's favourite poet, had published his huge epic *Madoc* about the legendary Welsh warrior who had sailed from this corner of Wales to discover and settle the New World. Just as exciting, a modern eponymous hero was now engaged on an enterprise of comparable magnificence.

Maddocks, the local landowner stood in the tradition of the great eighteenth-century improvers. Foreseeing a build-up of traffic on the road to Anglesey following the union with Ireland, he had built the town of Tremadoc as a staging post where travellers would delight to stay. It was a model of modern civilized life with fine buildings, picturesque gardens, landscaped belvederes, a library and a theatre. By building an earth embankment across a corner of the estuary sands he proved that it was profitable to reclaim agricultural land from the sea. Now he was engaged on the much more ambitious project of throwing a stone embankment across the estuary. This he hoped, would not only gain several thousand more acres of productive new land but cut many miles from the journey from London to Dublin.

Here was a project in which there was no conflict between short-term improvement and long-term damage, or between material welfare and moral enlightenment. The values of commerce and of political justice exactly coincided. Shelley at once subscribed £100 and promised more. At a local meeting on 28 September – just a week before his first meeting with Godwin in London – he publicly pledged himself to spend the last shilling of his fortune and devote the last breath of his life to the great and glorious cause.

The hurried trip to London in October 1812 was primarily intended to raise money for the embankment. Within three days of Godwin's first meeting with Shelley, Maddocks himself called at Skinner Street hoping to find Shelley there. Shortly afterwards Godwin met both him and his agent Williams at the Shelleys' lodgings where the plan was discussed.[2]

If unkind friends sometimes compared Godwin's own financial problem to a bottomless pit, Maddocks's business had no need of metaphors. For years, hundreds of men and horses were employed in cutting stones from quarries and dumping them into the sea. As the two ends of the embankment approached one another, the tide flowed ever more strongly through the narrowing gap and carried away most of each new deposit. Maddocks had run up debts in excess of £30,000. His credit was exhausted and another £20,000 was thought to be needed to complete the embankment. If Shelley was able to mobilize the finance for Maddocks's vast scheme, a contribution to solve Godwin's problem would hardly be noticed.

Shelley had very little money of his own. He was not due to reach the age of twenty-one until 4 August 1813 and having quarrelled so bitterly with his father there was no certainty that he would then be made independent. Meanwhile his sole income was a modest allowance conferred by his father mainly so that he could threaten to withdraw it. Shelley already had a string of debts, a growing entourage of dependants and a heavily pregnant wife. But his credit was good. As the eldest son of the eldest son of a wealthy landowner, he stood to inherit a huge fortune. A substantial part of the estate was entailed on the male heir which meant that, short of an Act of Parliament, Shelley was certain to inherit whatever steps his family might take to disown him in other ways. Shelley was able to buy most things he wanted on credit simply on the strength of being a gentleman, it being assumed that sooner or later he or the family would pay. He could also borrow by signing bonds. But the amounts being talked of for Maddocks – and even for Godwin – were of a different order of magnitude and different considerations applied.

Since time immemorial the Shelley family had been proud and undistinguished minor gentry. At the end of the eighteenth century however, Bysshe Shelley, the poet's grandfather had built up the family fortune by a series of judicious marriages and bold speculations, reinforced by lucky inheritances from unlucky relations. In 1806 during the brief Whig administration, he obtained a baronetcy, and soon afterwards Timothy Shelley, the poet's father, was installed as Member of Parliament for a local pocket borough. With their new wealth, the Shelley family could now expect to become ancient aristocracy. A thousand years of deferred hopes seemed at last to be on the point of realization.

Entails enabled the hereditary landed classes to maintain their monopoly of power. Originally intended to preserve concentrations of wealth so that certain families could afford the armoured horses needed for military knighthood, they were later justified on grounds of economic efficiency, broad acres being thought more productive than small holdings, and rich men more careful with their money than the middling and lower classes. In Burkean terms entails were part of a beautifully balanced system of political and economic privilege which strengthened the ancient bonds between the people and the land. They symbolized the continuity of the generations and the unwritten contracts between the living and the dead. They gave the nation its coherence, its identity, and its sense of shared purpose.

To Godwin and Shelley, such ideas were, of course, among the grossest of errors. The social bonds so admired by the traditionalists who benefited from them were servile chains to keep the poor in subjection. If, as Godwin had argued in *Political Justice*, property is the main corrupter of society, entails (which prevent even the unhealthy buying and selling of property among the rich) render it 'a thousand times more stagnant and putrescent than before'. Entails were a brake on progress, an affront to reason and an admission of despair. They were an attempt by the past to tie the future, a defeatist acceptance that the dead were more wise than the living, and the rich more deserving than the poor.

The bulk of the Shelley estate, worth about £120,000, was the personal property of Sir Bysshe, and he could dispose of it in whatever way he chose. The remainder, worth about £80,000, was entailed. Sir Bysshe Shelley could have chosen to will away the unentailed portion and dare his grandson to dismember the rest in due course when he inherited. But, as befitted a successful dealer in rotten boroughs, he preferred a bolder strategy. By a complex series of wills and codicils, he attempted instead to make Shelley an offer which would keep the property together.

His will stipulated that, after his death, his grandson would lose all financial interest in the unentailed part of the fortune if he did not agree, within a year, to hold the whole estate together. These arrangements were buttressed by a general provision to void the whole will if Shelley took any action which contravened its purpose, a standing invitation to other members of the family to try their luck in the courts. Much of Shelley's adult life was to be devoted to a negotiation with his family as the two concepts of stewardship battled for supremacy, the family desiring above everything to keep the estate together, Shelley equally determined to divert as much as he could lay hands on into schemes that would advance political justice. Sir Bysshe, who was wise in the ways of the world, was sure that by the time his grandson came to inherit he would have shed his disrespect for the laws of God and of property and himself be eager to prolong the dynasty.

In 1812 meanwhile, Shelley had no way of raising substantial sums except by borrowing on his expectations. In exchange for immediate cash he could sign a bond for a larger sum to be payable after he inherited. Sir Bysshe Shelley was eighty-one and his son Timothy was nearly sixty; neither man could be expected to survive for very many years and to help convince anyone who doubted the actuarial tables, Shelley added another seven years to his grandfather's age. Such post-obit bonds were, by their very nature, highly speculative. The financier was taking a bet on when two men would die. If he was lucky and they both died soon, he would make a financial killing. If not, a portion of his capital could be tied up for years without earning interest. Those who borrowed from such speculators felt no strong moral duty to treat them with scrupulous fairness. If for Maddocks's embankment and Godwin's shop, commerce and political justice, morality and legality all tended to coincide, that happy argument did not apply to the post-obit bonds by which they were to be financed.

For his first loan of £2,000, Shelley gave a bond for £6,000. The moneylenders were naturally concerned to ensure that their capital was safe, and there was much poring over wills and deeds. They knew that judges – who are often of the Burkean persuasion – tended to take the side of the heirs against the financiers, so every agreement had to be legally secure in the last detail. They were usually concerned too to offload some of the risks by insuring the heir's life. This took time and involved further costs especially as the insurers normally imposed conditions on foreign travel and demanded extra premiums for sea voyages and other potential hazards. Shelley, constantly on the move to and fro across the three kingdoms, ceaselessly complaining of illness, and frequently talking of suicide, was not an obviously good investment. But every risk has its price. In the autumn of 1813, when Shelley was especially pressed for cash he signed a post-obit for £2,000 for a mere £500 in cash. As Sir Bysshe and Timothy Shelley were painfully aware, it would not take many such contingent liabilities to be laid on the estate for their dynastic ambitions to be thwarted.

On 11 November 1812 Shelley with Harriet and her sister dined with the Godwins at Skinner Street. Two days later the Godwins were invited to dine with the Shelleys at their hotel where they would meet the solicitor dealing with Shelleys financial affairs, and they may have been expecting some arrangement to be proposed on that occasion. Godwin knew that an attempt was being made to restore a measure of order to Shelley's affairs, with his father paying off some of his debts and new money being raised with new borrowing. But that morning, without a word of explanation or apology, Shelley and his entourage suddenly left London to return to Wales as they had been secretly planning to do for some time. It was the third time in three weeks that Shelley had failed to keep an appointment, and this time the result was more serious than a wasted dinner.

December was when the year's accounts for the bookshop had to be finalized, and once more Godwin was obliged to go on a begging round of his creditors. It was only a few weeks since Shelley had announced his intention of settling in London for ever in order to be near his teacher and now he had vanished. Once again he had shown himself unpredictable. Not long before Godwin had witnessed the summary dismissal from his life of Elizabeth Hitchener to whom he had been declaring eternal love and friendship only a few weeks earlier. It seemed that it was now his turn to be dumped. When Godwin solemnly assured Francis Place for the umpteenth time that he would never again ask him for money, he knew by now that his own promise was unlikely to be kept.[3] And when Place, still banking on the Shelley connection, agreed to yet another deferment, Godwin again accepted his bills with the cool indifference of a man receiving no more than his due.

During the following months he read his way again through the sustaining writings of Zeno, Epictetus, Marcus Aurelius and Seneca. Once again it was demonstrated that Godwin's weaknesses were also his strengths. The stubbornness, the irrepressible persistence, the lofty disdain for commercial values, the proud air of certainty in his own genius, the arrogant presumption that he stood outside events and would be judged against higher standards all enabled him to withstand anxieties which would have overwhelmed others. And for anyone who might forget that other reactions were more normal there was Mary Jane, fussing, threatening, complaining, and nursing her wrath to keep it warm.

In January 1812 it had been the letter from Shelley that had proved that the spirit of 1793 was not extinct. In January 1813 it was Robert Owen, whom Godwin first met on 8 January at a dinner attended by Dugald Stewart, Coleridge, and Washington Alston. On 20 January Owen called at Skinner Street, and during the following weeks Godwin and he saw each other every few days. By the time Owen left London at the beginning of April they had met over twenty times, and when he returned in May their friendship was at once resumed, with meetings whenever opportunity permitted. Once more, the seeds which had been planted twenty years before turned out to have sprouted in an unusual and unexpected place.

Owen was already one of the most famous industrialists of the industrial revolution. When he took over the cotton mills at New Lanark, they were recruiting illiterate children from the orphanages of Edinburgh, and working them eighteen hours a day. The mills resembled the silk factory in Spitalfields that Godwin had visited in 1805 to add realism to his descriptions of child labour in *Fleetwood*.[4] Under Owen's management, the workers were now better housed, better educated, and better paid than anywhere in the county and the mills had been turned from loss to profit. Owen's factories stood as a spectacular refutation of the Malthusian orthodoxy that unemployment is caused by high wages, and his success was deeply worrying to those who believed that the correct economic answer to social misery is to make it worse.

When he met Godwin in 1813 Owen was composing his own series of essays *A New View of Society*, in which he sought to generalize the lessons of New Lanark. In his youth he had been a prominent member of the Manchester Philosophical and Literary Society, where, we may be sure, he felt the full blast of *Political Justice* in the years after 1793. On 24 January Godwin noted in his journal, he discussed with Owen 'property', 'free-will', and 'population.' Owen's book is permeated with Godwinian sentiments, the chain of necessity, the progress of perfectibility, the power of truth, and much else. As Hazlitt was to proclaim in 1816 when the *New View* was published, Owen's theories were not new, but old, old, old,

Does not Mr Owen know that the same scheme, the same principles, the same philosophy of motives and action . . . of virtue and happiness were rife in the year 1793, were noised abroad then, were spoken on the house-tops, were whispered in secret, were published in quarto and duodecimo, in political treatises, in plays, poems, songs, and romances, made their way to the bar, crept into the church, ascended the rostrum, thinned the classes of the universities . . . got into the hearts of poets and the brains of metaphysicians, took possession of the fancies of boys and women, and turned the heads of almost the whole kingdom.[5]

But a vital change was occurring unnoticed even by Hazlitt who knew both Godwin and Owen and who sat in on their conversations. Godwin and Owen both believed that environment, education, morality, and prosperity all progress together, or as Godwin might have put it, imagination leads to enlightenment which in its turn leads to virtue and on to social and economic justice. But whereas Godwin saw the constant exercise of political justice by individuals gradually pulling society along towards perfection, Owen's chain was drawn in the opposite direction. He believed that employers, governments, and others with stewardship responsibilities could devise and apply policies for the obedience of subordinates; and it was the Owenite version which was to become the future orthodoxy. Shelley had slurred over the point in *Queen Mab*, but Owen positively preferred the more authoritarian approach. The conversations which

Godwin conducted with Shelley and Owen were to be among the last struggles between the individual liberalism of Godwin and the newly emerging socialism in which it was soon to be submerged and drowned.

In April 1813 Shelley and his family suddenly arrived back in London. Since their abrupt departure in November they had not only gone back to Tremadoc but had made another unexplained visit to Ireland. Godwin had written eleven times in the meantime, but his disciple on his return to London made no attempt to see the man whom, a year before, he had been begging to grant him just one short interview. When Godwin eventually tracked him down on 8 June, Shelley explained frankly that the reason he had not made contact was that Harriet could not bear to visit Mrs Godwin, an understandable explanation. When Mary Jane, swallowing her insulted pride, made a call at the Shelleys' hotel to mark her forgiveness of the discourtesies of November, the philosophical conversations were resumed, and the two families again began to meet regularly.

Shelley had already lost interest in the Tremadoc plan, and although he was liable to take up other expensive enthusiasms – such as supporting Leigh Hunt in jail or relieving the families of men who had been executed after the bread riots, he now accepted that Godwin was a worthy cause. On 4 August he reached his twenty-first birthday, which made financial contracts a little easier. On 30 August Godwin was as a result able to write to Josiah Wedgwood offering him a new financial opportunity. If Wedgwood would advance the £3,000 needed to refinance the bookshop, he suggested, one of Godwin's friends would guarantee the regular payment of the interest and the capital sum would be secured against a baronet's estate.[6]

It was an attractive investment which, if it had been available when the need was first diagnosed, might have been accepted. But Wedgwood would not lend the money, unless the proffered security was in the actual ownership of the guarantor. There was no alternative therefore to further short-term borrowing while further attempts were made to put together a new long-term rescue package. Copies of the needed documents were obtained from lawyers, Mary Jane making a special journey to Horsham in the Shelley homeland for one of them.

Every month brought new evidence of Shelley's unpredictable nature. He refused to take butter on his muffins or to wear woolly socks. A chemical still to produce distilled water was installed in the kitchen. For a while he subsisted on a natural food of his own recipe which consisted largely of sugar buns, and soon he had printed his own pamphlet on the philosophy of diet. In July, Shelley and Harriet with their new baby moved from London to Bracknell mainly in order to be near the Boinvilles who had a house there. In October however they suddenly rushed off again with the baby on another long, expensive and apparently aimless journey to the Lake District and Scotland. Since their elopement, they had been to the Lakes twice, to Scotland twice, to Ireland twice, to Devon once, to Wales three or four times and several times to Sussex. The constant moving made it easier to escape creditors, one of the more pressing of whom was the supplier of Shelley's carriage in which the escapes were made.

The little extravagances of the Godwin family were trivial by comparison. Mary Jane insisted on a holiday every summer for the sake of her health, determined to escape both the smoke of London and her husband's unbearable calm. It was essential for her sanity, she would say, and she was probably right. Godwin enjoyed her absences – when he would dine with old friends whom she disliked – although every day she was away he wrote to say how much he missed her. When however at the beginning of September 1813 he himself took a Sunday off to visit Mary Jane and their ten-year-old William at Southend, he received a sharp letter of protest from Francis Place. A man in Godwin's financial position, Place suggested, should be hard at work at his desk. 'Should I be torn to pieces and destroyed merely because I am not a young man', Godwin wrote back, 'and because I employed my youth in endeavouring with my pen to promote the welfare of my species?'[7] Later in the month he defiantly went again to Southend travelling down on a barge on the Friday and returning on a fishcart the following Tuesday. Perhaps the paddling in the sea which he noted in his journal for Sunday the 19th refreshed him for the encounters with Place and the other indignant creditors who called on him immediately after his return.

Godwin wrote twenty-three letters to Shelley in the latter months of 1813 – all now lost – probably all about money, and he received few if any replies. Then on 10 December Shelley suddenly again appeared at Skinner Street for breakfast, having returned unexpectedly from Edinburgh. On 11 December he stayed overnight for the first time, and on the 12th he remained talking until three o'clock in the morning. But by the end of the week, he and Harriet had again left London in their crowded coach with the baby to settle this time at Windsor not far from the Boinvilles at Bracknell. The signs were growing that for all the talk, Shelley would never take Godwin's financial problems seriously. William Godwin was, it seemed to be just another of the long list of people and projects that Shelley picked up and threw down with such disconcerting consistency.

On the day after Christmas, Godwin was as depressed as he could ever remember. Six chapters of Seneca were unable to revive his spirits as he contemplated the start of another year of poverty and of worry. The letter which he wrote to himself on the subject of fortitude, at the same time as he wrote his critique of *Queen Mab*, was an attempt to recruit his strength from the self-disgust which he knew is the prelude to despair. It was a device which he had learned from his religious heritage, a meditation on misfortune, self-awareness, and courage, and he reserved it for situations when other remedies had failed, and when fits were expected. He began with a quotation from Seneca, 'Nobody is despised by other people unless he has first lost his respect for himself,' a thought which had governed his conduct ever since he was a precocious and unbiddable child at Guestwick. What did it matter where he lived, he asked himself, or how much money he had. Serenity of mind and freedom of thought should not depend on such externalities. Indeed, if he had not enjoyed the stimulus of poverty he might never have produced anything original.

It is uncertainty and suspense only that are perplexing. Place me in the lowest and most impoverished situation that is compatible with my faculties, and I shall live, and shall find the supply of my wants in my own contrivance and industry – or I shall die: that is the worst. But I shall not die. I have in myself effective powers, and I shall find friends to assist me in the application of them.[8]

On 2 January 1814, he noted in his journal, he was 'raised from great depression' by Francis Place, whose presence and advice normally tended in the other direction, and before long new financial negotiations were in progress. A few visits to John King may have pointed to the solution, for suddenly a firm plan was agreed. A money broker would auction a post-obit drawn on the Shelley inheritance. Meanwhile pressure would continue to be exerted on the Shelley family to come to a settlement which might obviate the need for the sale altogether.

The date of the auction was fixed for 3 March. It was prominently advertised in *The Times* on 4 February and twice a week during the intervening weeks. The sum offered was £8,000 and the bond was expected to fetch in excess of £3,000. Godwin later claimed that he had been led to expect £3,000, the original amount recommended by Place to put his shop back on a sound footing, and on the evening before the auction, following a visit to Skinner Street from his brother Nat, he noted in his journal the unexplained figure of £3,860. Whether that was an estimate of the amount expected to be realized, or of a new assessment of the amount which M. J. Godwin and Company required for financial recovery, or some other calculation entirely, the auction the following day did not match it. The bond was knocked down to the brothers Andrew and George Nash, glass manufacturers, for £2,593–10s of which they paid a deposit of £519.

Godwin at once wrote to Shelley telling him the news. Shelley came to dinner on 7 March and devoted the next day to business, but he was not much interested, and left London immediately, leaving Godwin and the lawyers to act for him in his absence. Shelley then wrote to his father telling him that he could no longer delay taking steps to raise substantial amounts, the excessively respectful tone of his letter providing only modest cover for what was in effect an ultimatum.

When that final overture brought no response, intensive negotiations were begun at once to complete the deal. Although the Nash brothers had signed a legal agreement to purchase the bond, they did not intend to hand over the balance of the money until all their doubts were satisfied. With professional advisers drawing fees on either side, there were still plenty of legitimate queries to be answered. Godwin made several visits to life insurance companies to arrange insurance on Shelley's life in case he should predecease his father. In order to make even more sure that their reversionary rights were secure, the purchasers also wanted the bond secured against the property of Shelley's heirs. But would the runaway marriage in Edinburgh be accepted as valid by an English court? On 22 March Godwin accompanied Shelley to obtain a licence for a second marriage, and Shelley and Harriet were duly remarried the following day according to the rites of the Church of England.

Another point of concern was the extent to which the Shelley estates were already encumbered by liabilities. Shelley's own contingent borrowings were difficult enough to disentangle, and he had been less than sincere. He gave his word of honour – which the creditors foolishly assumed had a value – to enter into no new contracts prejudicial to the interests of the purchasers, a commitment which opened up scope for numerous queries later. When it was discovered that Sir Bysshe Shelley himself had made a contingent agreement with a son of the Duke of Devonshire, as long ago as 1791 the only hope was to approach the Duke, but why should one of the greatest hereditary landowning families in England wish to promote Godwinian stewardship against Burkean? Godwin's letter of 31 March did not receive a satisfactory reply, if one was sent at all, and when he attempted to call on the Duke at Chiswick, he was not at home. Every day was a ceaseless round of such visits, letters, and negotiations, sometimes with Shelley, sometimes on his own. For a time Shelley virtually moved into Skinner Street, taking his meals there with Godwin's three now nearly grown-up daughters, Fanny, Mary, and Jane, who all shared in the excitement and in the anxiety.

In May the disease struck, the first time – apart from a minor attack in March – since the disappointments of Lynmouth. One fit came on the 7th – the day before £150 had to be paid to or borrowed from Davison the printer. It struck again on the 10th, twice on the 11th, and three times on the 12th. But before long Godwin was on his feet again, forcing himself into equanimity with large doses of Seneca. Two days after the attacks abated he also read his friend Isaac d'Israeli's *Calamities of Authors* with its descriptions of the disasters which await writers who cannot pay their bills. In the drive to redirect his medullary particles, deterrence had a place alongside encouragement.

Gradually, one by one, the obstacles were overcome or circumvented. On 2 July the Nashes made a further advance to Shelley of £1,000, and on 6 July, the final balance was paid over. That afternoon Shelley came to a celebratory dinner at Skinner Street but the proposals he put forward were very different from what Godwin had been led to expect. He had decided, Shelley said, to advance £1,120 for the bookshop, exactly half the proceeds of the bond after the various expenses had been met, keeping the remainder for himself. Instead of rescuing the Godwin family from the fear which had hung over Skinner Street for so many years, Shelley was merely offering a further stay of execution.

Godwin was bitterly disappointed. He felt deceived and betrayed, and no talk about the duty to set aside promises was ever to convince him that Shelley had dealt fairly with him. The raising of the money had been a massive exercise in which he and his friends had done most of the work. The difficulties had been immense and it was unlikely that the operation could be repeated: indeed part of the deal with the Nashes was that there could be no new post-obit borrowing if that put their own bond at risk. But worse was to follow. In the evening after dinner when Godwin took Shelley on a walk in Spa Fields, Shelley explained that he had fallen in love with Mary Godwin – who was then just short of her seventeenth birthday – and that he intended to end his marriage with Harriet and live with Mary. They proposed to leave England and settle in Switzerland. The money from the bond was needed to pay the costs of the travel and other expenses. Shelley asked Godwin's approval for these proposals.

355

CHAPTER 27

Five in the Morning

Shelley's proposal, it need hardly be said, was fully in accordance with the view of marriage set out in the first edition of *Political Justice*. That odious monopolizing institution, Godwin had argued, must never be permitted to override the free decisions of individuals, and if one partner in an arrangement wishes to bring it to an end, the other has no complaint. Had not Mary's mother, Mary Wollstonecraft, exercised her right to live with the man of her choice, first with Imlay and then with Godwin himself? The story and the arguments were there to be read in the *Memoirs* and in the love letters which Godwin had himself published.

It was true that when Shelley married Harriet, he had followed the advice of a slightly later Godwin, the Godwin of *Fleetwood* who had by then undergone three marriage ceremonies. But now Shelley had decided to exercise his right to retract his retractions. He had never been comfortable with arguments for compromise or conformity based on the reactions of other people. As a good Godwinian he knew the difference between conferred honour and real virtue. In any case since he and Mary intended to live abroad, far from the wagging tongues of English society, the relevance of such arguments fell away. The obligations of political justice and the urgings of love exactly coincided.

The couple's declared choice of Uri in Switzerland as the place to run away to was also a compliment. At the beginning of *Fleetwood*, Godwin had described the cottage at Uri of the wise Ruffigny which, though set

The Visitor, from *Religious Courtship*

among the mountains, was equipped with a garden of special interest to vegetarians.

> Though roses, woodbines, lilacs, and laburnums, with such other flowering shrubs as require little aid from the hand of the cultivator, were interspersed, the plots . . . were principally appropriated to pulse and other esculent vegetables, and were bordered with fruit-bearing plants and shrubs.[1]

Ruffigny's imaginary cottage also contained a library stocked with the works of the sixteenth- and seventeenth-century English writers whom Godwin had recently been urging Shelley to read. It was at Uri that William Tell had established the Swiss liberty which had gradually spread to the other cantons and was eventually going to reach the whole world. If Tremadoc in Wales had seemed a good place from which to spread enlightenment, Uri was even better.

Shelley sought Godwin's approval in all sincerity. Although, like Godwin, he frequently changed his mind, he was never in doubt. Whatever view he held at any time was pursued tirelessly until it was superseded. The catalogue of causes picked up and thrown down continued to grow. A few weeks earlier Maddocks's agent at Tremadoc had again been at Skinner Street but Shelley's interest in that great enterprise was as dead as his commitment to Ireland to whose emancipation he had also publicly promised his whole life and fortune. For a while in 1813 freedom of opinion absorbed his attention. In 1814 it was natural food and natural love. On the few occasions when Godwin had been able to see him during the previous months, Newton had usually been there and sometimes the Chevalier Lawrence as well. No doubt they and their causes would be dumped in due course as suddenly and as unregretfully as Elizabeth Hitchener and William Maddocks had been, and sure enough in March 1814 there was a quarrel with Newton. It was plain that Shelley for all his talents was also a spoiled young man of aristocratic tastes who treated people and ideas like an endless supply of colourful toys.

Godwin had all along been aware of the damage that Shelley could do, but his fears had been for society at large and not for himself or for his family. Now the New Philosophy in all its original brightness was shining directly at 41 Skinner Street. His beloved Mary had only recently returned from a long stay in Scotland, and although Shelley had probably seen her during his visits to Skinner Street in October 1812, their first real meeting had taken place as recently as 5 May just two months before. During the second half of June when the negotiations over the bond were at their most intensive Shelley had dined at Skinner Street virtually every day.

With Mary Jane busy with the bookshop and Fanny on a visit to relatives in Wales, the running of the household had been left to the younger daughters Mary and Jane.[2]

Mrs Godwin was later to claim that Shelley had been warm in his attentions to both girls, and indeed to Fanny too, and that all three were more or less in love with him. Shelley was later to explain that his manner to all women was the same. What is certain is that on Sunday 26 June, Mary took Shelley on a visit to her mother's grave in St Pancras Churchyard and on that sacred spot she declared that she loved him. Shelley immediately said that he loved her too, explaining in a poem which he sent shortly afterwards that his feelings had been fettered until that moment. Something special also happened on the following day which Shelley was later to say was his true birthday. There were kisses and promises of eternal love and secret arrangements to exchange letters.[3]

Shelley presented Mary with a copy of *Queen Mab*, cutting off the title page and imprint at the end in the usual way in case the book fell into the hands of the authorities. He inscribed it 'Mary Wollstonecraft Godwin' adding his illegible initials, and when later he wrote his name in full he did so in pencil presumably so that, if necessary, the evidence of authorship could be erased. *Queen Mab* is hardly a love poem although the long notes attacking marriage may have helped to sway Mary's mind if not her feelings. It was however on the end papers of the book that Mary – who shared her father's liking for keeping secret records – wrote down what Shelley had said.

This book is sacred to me and as no other creature shall ever look into it I may write in it what I please – yet what shall I write that I love the author beyond all powers of expression and that I am parted from him.

Dearest and only love by that love we have promised to each other although I may not be your[s] I can never be another's
But I am thine exclusively thine – by the kiss of love by

> The glance that none saw beside
> The smile none else might under[stand]
> The whispered thought of hearts allied
> The pressure of the thrilling hand

I have pledged myself to thee and sacred is the gift –
> I remember your words, you are now
> Mary going to mix with many and for a
> moment I shall depart but in the solitude of
> your chamber I shall be with you – yes you
> are ever with me sacred vision

But ah I feel in this was given
A blessing never meant for me
Thou art too like a dream from heaven
For earthly love to merit thee[4]

The long tail of the final d of 'pledged' was curled back into a tiny tell-tale x. The verses were not original. They were adapted from Lord Byron's love poems 'To Thyrza' which were published in 1812 in the volume that contained *Childe Harold's Pilgrimage*.

Shelley did not cut off the printed leaf of *Queen Mab* which dedicated the volume to Harriet. With the title page cut off, a poem to Harriet was therefore the first thing that the reader saw. Whatever view one might take of the revocability of love and marriage, it was a poetic pledge of another love, sincerely offered when it was written just a few months previously and it needed an explanation. At the foot of the page Shelley wrote 'Count Slobendorf was about to marry a woman, who attracted solely by his fortune, proved her selfishness by deserting him in prison', words presumably intended to imply that Harriet had only married him for his money. In fact, such aspersions were unfair both to Harriet and to the Count. The Graf von Schlabrendorf, who had lived in England before the French Revolution, had been a member of the 1794 Paris circle along with Mary Wollstonecraft. For a time he was engaged to marry Thomas Christie's sister, but the engagement was broken off after Schlabrendorf was imprisoned by the French authorities. Mary Wollstonecraft was one of those who visited him in prison, and in a note written later he declared that he loved her. Godwin was shortly to receive a visit from the French economist, J.-B. Say, described in his journal as 'from Slabrendorf' which suggests that, with the ending of the war, communications with the Count had recently been re-established and he was being talked about in Skinner Street. Whatever Shelley and Mary decided to do, there was, it seemed, ample precedent and justification in the actions of either Godwin or Mary Wollstonecraft.[5]

On the walk after the dinner on 6 July Godwin told Shelley categorically that he could not give his approval. But what should he do? Should he refuse to see him? It was particularly unfortunate that the crisis over the money and the crisis over Mary were occurring at exactly the same time. Godwin remained angry that Shelley would not give him the full £3,000 or at any rate the full proceeds of the sale. But even £1,120 was still a substantial sum and it would be a pity to forgo it for no useful result. Maybe he was in danger of making too much of an incident which was common enough amongst teenagers and might be expected to pass? As far as he knew – and he was probably correct – there had been only words, the young people's behaviour still remaining fettered by custom.

As often in the past Godwin put his trust in the written word. Shelley had been persuaded by this means before and he might be again. The drafting took several days and the letter eventually ran to ten pages and five thousand words.[6] At the same time he had a long talk with Mary which he also followed up with a letter. He also spoke to Jane and to Charles. All seemed to go well. Shelley and Mary agreed to give up their scheme. Although Shelley was told that he was no longer welcome at Skinner Street, the financial negotiations were allowed to go ahead, and Godwin continued to see him nearly every day. On 19 July Godwin was able to note in his journal, with great relief, that the transaction was finally completed and his share of the money was paid over.

A few days earlier news came that Shelley's wife Harriet had arrived in London. When Shelley called with her at Skinner Street on 15 July, Godwin was 'not at home', since he refused to allow him into his house, but later in the day he returned the call. He was received by Harriet and was able to hear from her a great deal more of what had been going on. When staying at Mrs Boinville's house in Bracknell in the spring, Shelley had, it was now said, also shown a warm interest in Mrs Boinville's daughter Cornelia. Harriet had been on a visit to Bath with her father and Cornelia's husband was in London. Shelley and Cornelia had spent much time together, reading novels, learning Italian, and talking deep into the night. In a poem, Shelley left little doubt where his inclinations lay:

> Subdued to Duty's hard control,
> I could have borne my wayward lot;
> The chains that bind this ruined soul
> Had cankered then – but crushed it not.[7]

In another poem he had spoken of his difficulties in coping with 'another's wealth'. Anyone who knew Shelley knew that in his philosophy the only thing to do with chains is to shed them, and that other people's wealth is there to be redistributed to the more deserving.

Among Godwin's papers is a copy in the handwriting of Thomas Turner, Cornelia's husband, of an unsigned letter. Turner presumably gave it to Godwin. The distraught writer, whose identity has not been established, accuses Turner of having destroyed his religious faith by Godwinian sophistry, and begs for forgiveness and guidance. It is clear that he too – although not as good a poet as Shelley – had found difficulty in resisting the beautiful Mrs Turner.

The verses which the fair Cornelia a little while ago received you said I could not write. Fear not! Seducing novelty which subdues us all has now subdued me. I wrote not from love (pardon me lady) but because the name suited the verse. Liar, restrain your false tongue you cannot keep under your burning flame. But Thomas I resign the lady.[8]

When Cornelia Turner herself called at Skinner Street on 16 July followed by her mother on the 18th, Godwin wrote immediately to Tom Turner. He acted at once, took his wife to Devon and never allowed her to see Shelley again. Neither he nor Godwin acted like believers in the rights of woman, but they apparently solved – or at any rate put an end to – the problem.

Within a few days it was also clear that Shelley had set aside his promise to Godwin and was still secretly embracing his principles. Jane Clairmont was part of a plan whereby letters were secretly passed to Mary at the shop. All three also continued to visit St Pancras Churchyard. While Shelley and Mary spent time among the willows which surrounded the grave Jane walked up and down waiting for them to reappear. Mrs Godwin was to claim later that one day Shelley burst into the shop at Skinner Street and rushed upstairs. Pushing her aside, he went over to Mary. 'They wish to separate us, my beloved,' he is said to have exclaimed, 'but Death shall unite us.'[9] After Marshall was sent for, he was persuaded to leave. A few days later, again according to Mary Jane, a messenger arrived at Skinner Street at midnight to say that Shelley had taken an overdose. The Godwins hastened to his lodgings where they found a doctor who was making him walk up and down. They themselves then arranged for him to be looked after until Mrs Boinville arrived. Since however there is no trace of these events in Godwin's journal, it is possible that Mrs Godwin gave a dramatic poetic enhancement to the excitements more lurid than the plain facts warranted.

What is certain is that on 25 July Godwin wrote again to Shelley accusing him of having broken his promise. The full text is lost, but a substantial extract has survived.

You entered my home on June 19th. You dined with me and my family every day in the following that was a week of virtue . . . I trusted to your principles. I could not entertain the idea of suspecting a man of so much virtue, honor, generosity, and philosophy, nor did I fear more for the principles of my child. If you had been a young man unentered in the engagement of a previous marriage,

I should have reflected severely and strictly on the subject. But I could not fear that the existence of your wife and child could be overlooked by either of you. I would not have believed that you would set up caprice and a momentary impulse over every impulse that is dear to the honest heart – I could not believe that you wd. sacrifice your own character and usefulness, the happiness of an innocent and meritorious wife, and the fair and spotless fame of my young child to fierce impulse of passion – I could not believe that you wd. enter my house under the name of benefactor, to leave behind an endless poison to corrode my soul. I would as soon have credited that the stars would fall from Heav'n for my destruction . . . [10]

The concept of seduction is a difficult one for those who sincerely believe in the equality of the sexes. Godwin was accusing Shelley of seducing his daughter.

At dawn on 28 July Mary met Shelley at the end of Skinner Street where he was waiting with a hired carriage. Jane Clairmont went with her and all three were driven straight to Dover where they hired a boat for Calais. In his journal Godwin noted simply, 'Five in the Morning.' A few hours later Mary Jane set off immediately in pursuit, Godwin himself perhaps being afraid that he would bring on an attack of fits if he himself attempted the journey, and she caught up with them in a hotel in Calais where they were resting before the next stage of the journey. Godwin had told her to have no direct dealings with Shelley, fearful that in his frenzied state he might resort to violence. She had a talk with Jane but made no impression. The three runaways continued their journey to Paris and Mary Jane returned empty-handed to London. In their efforts to save one daughter, they had now lost two.

When Mary Jane was away, a letter arrived at Skinner Street from Patrickson, Godwin's other protégé at this time. Patrickson had just returned to Cambridge after a visit to Godwin and was again short of money and plunged in gloom. 'I am so exceedingly pressed at the moment', Godwin wrote to him dutifully, 'that I must request you to be contented with £2, and must endeavour to send you a further supply on this day week.' Pay no attention to the people whom you dignify with the name of enemies, he advised. Their ignorant taunts will not make any difference to your ultimate career, and before long you will be surprised that you ever allowed yourself to be upset. 'I am sure', he added, 'that a little reading in Seneca, the philosopher, would set you right in this pitiable wrong.'[11] The following weekend Patrickson came back to London and dined at Skinner Street on two successive days. But Godwin no longer had the resources to sustain more than himself. On 8 August Patrickson returned to Cambridge. He wrote his teacher a long despairing letter and then shot himself dead.

That day the ten-year-old William Godwin Junior ran away from home and was lost for two nights.

Soon the joke was going round the money markets that Godwin had sold his daughters to Shelley, one for £800, the other for £700.

CHAPTER 28

The Runaways

The journey across Europe was less pleasant than the runaways had hoped. In the days before they left, London had been preparing to welcome the victorious allied sovereigns and the restored Bourbon King of France. In St James's Park, where Godwin took walks as he wondered what to do, a celebratory Castle of Despair was transformed by clever lighting every evening into a Temple of Concord. In France itself, however, after years of war, it was unrealistic to expect a welcome even for travellers who professed themselves, without insincerity, to have been on the French side all along. In Paris they sought out Mary Wollstonecraft's friend, Helen Maria Williams, who had lived there through most of the war, but she was not in town. The weather was hot. The inns were dirty and so were the beds.

In Paris, they also bought a donkey, intending to travel the remaining distance to Switzerland on foot with the girls taking turns to ride. The innkeeper and his wife shook their heads at the plan, but Shelley, who was used to walking forty miles a day, believed in the equality of the sexes, and it seemed a good way to see the country. A few hours later when the donkey was unable to carry the luggage, let alone a girl as well, they sold it and bought a mule instead. But by the time they reached Troyes, Shelley and Jane were both too lame to walk, and they were obliged to sell the mule and hire a private vehicle to take them to Switzerland.

Mary and Jane's Room, from *Lessons for Children*

Mary had been sick on the journey to Dover, on the boat to Calais, and intermittently thereafter. At the time her illness was attributed to the heat and to the excitement, but Mary was also suffering from what her mother had called the inelegant complaint of morning sickness. On 22 February 1815 she was to give birth to a premature baby described as a seven-months child, but the arithmetic need not be taken exactly. Mary may have conceived in St Pancras Churchyard.

When two are lovers, three is an awkward unit. Jane Clairmont was at the same time indispensable and unwanted. As the only one who could speak French, she was needed to help make the arrangements with the innkeepers. She had been told by her mother that she was the daughter of Karl Gaulis of Lausanne and was eager to see what she believed was the homeland of her ancestors. But when Shelley and Mary decided to keep a journal, in the Godwinian manner, Jane had to be given one of Shelley's notebooks so that she could keep hers separately. When Shelley and Mary went to bed, Jane was left alone in another room although on one occasion when rats got in the others let her sleep in theirs. When at one of the inns an opportunistic Frenchman offered to even up the numbers in bed, he was necessarily refused. All three were also aware that a young man who spends every day with two attractive young women can alternate.

Uri, by the Lake of Lucerne, which they reached in August, although beautiful, was not as they had hoped from their reading of *Fleetwood*. With difficulty they found a house which they took on an expensive lease of six months. Later described by Shelley as a ruined château, it lacked the amenities which had made life at Tremadoc so pleasant, and the magnificent views were insufficient by themselves to sustain a waning sense of romance. The weather, which had been unendurably hot a few weeks before, suddenly turned cold. They could not get the stove to work, and when they did, it filled the rooms with smoke. On the day they moved in, they received a visit from the local priest and the local doctor, curious about the circumstances and intentions of the strange ménage. Their other neighbours they found petty-minded, inquisitive and dull, contradicting as the Welsh had done earlier, the literary reputation of mountain peoples.

Having reached journey's end, hope ebbed like water from a bath. Mary, whose pregnancy was now beyond doubt, feared the winter. Jane, who a few weeks before had happily waved goodbye for ever to the white cliffs, now decided that England was 'the most reasonable and the most enlightened' country in the world.[1] In the various journals each tried to offload responsibility, but sense triumphed over pride, and on the second day after they moved into what was to be their new home the runaways decided to return. They took a boat down the Rhine, crossed to England, and reached London seven weeks after they had left. They rented a home in Margaret Street, St Marylebone on the other side of town from Skinner Street.

All three had set out heavy with preconceptions. They would probably never have run away in the first place if they had not believed that they were doing what Godwin and Wollstonecraft had done or would have done, and they needed constantly to convince themselves that they were in the right. One of the duties of the overloaded mule was to carry the books which sustained their illusions. They read to one another from Mary Wollstonecraft's early autobiographical novel *Mary*, and from her *Letters from Sweden*, so influential in prescribing correct sentiments for travellers among moutains. They had Shakespeare, Tacitus, Rousseau's *Emile* and the four heavy volumes of Barruel's *History of Jacobinism*, read not only as a history of why things had gone wrong but in order to learn the mind of the enemy.

After the return to England they all continued the same intensive study. In 1814 they read or reread *Political Justice*, *Caleb Williams*, *St. Leon*, and the *Posthumous Works* which contained Mary Wollstonecraft's letters to Imlay and the *Wrongs of Woman*. After the major, they turned to the minor, the *Life of Chaucer*, Mary Wollstonecraft's *Historical and Moral View of the French Revolution*, and her adaptation of Salzmann's *Elements of Morality*. Shelley had read the *Vindication* the previous summer and presumably the girls knew it so well that rereading was unnecessary. The same may have been true of the *Memoirs*, but if they lacked a copy of the family's own defence of sexual freedom, they now had *The Empire of the Nairs*.[2]

It scarcely mattered that the books had been written at different times, in different circumstances, and to teach different lessons: it was enough that they had been written by Mary Wollstonecraft and William Godwin. If the books offered encouragement, the runaways were strengthened in their resolution. If they warned of suffering, they were comforted to know that their own lives were conforming to pattern. When in France the three tried unsuccessfully to adopt an orphan girl, they knew how Mary Wollstonecraft's sensibility in Scandinavia had been enhanced by the presence of baby Fanny. Reading together can add excitement to the dullest book and it was the only entertainment. When the three were curled up together in front of the fire, the revered books took on new and warm assocations. One of Mary's favourites was the *Essay on*

Sepulchres which she would take with her to St Pancras Churchyard and read alone as she lay on the grass by her mother's grave.[3] Jane caught up by reading *Queen Mab*.

Godwin was heartbroken. But his reaction to the crisis was characteristically to become even more imperturbable. He continued with his writing, his reading, his conversations with friends, his visits to the theatre, his work in the bookshop, and his financial tergiversations. Seneca was put aside in favour of Shakespeare, the only author who was a match for such events, and Godwin read a sonnet a day during the period of cruellest grief. As he told John Taylor, when rolling over a debt on 27 August, a month after the elopement, he had lost his daughters and the money in circumstances which would have caused the strongest minds to give way to despair.

I felt it however still to be my duty, not to desert myself, or so much of my family as was yet left to me, and even to provide, if possible, for the hour of distress (which, I believe, is not far distant) when these unworthy children shall again seek the protection and aid of their father.[4]

He never seriously considered that Mary and Shelley could be right. If Jane had committed an 'indiscretion', Mary was guilty of a 'crime'.[5] The stories that he had condoned Shelley's seduction in exchange for money were too plausible to be shrugged off, for the girls had indeed run away with Shelley within days of the completion of the deal. But which was better – to suffer the slander in silence or to tell the whole story? He could only make things better for himself by making them worse for the girls.

Godwin had foreseen the worst before it happened and had taken precautions. The two long letters of protest which he had written to Shelley on 10 July and 25 July had been served on him like a writ. Charles Clairmont was asked to take a copy of one and Jane Clairmont of the other, perhaps to invite them to share the responsibility. These copies were the vindication he would need if he were ever forced to defend his conduct and they were too precious to be entrusted to an iron chest in Skinner Street. At Mary Jane's suggestion he sent them to Taylor of Norwich, his discounter, the equivalent of depositing them under seal in a bank.[6]

Seduction was not uncommon in Regency England – it had become more common, many anti-Jacobins believed, since the publication of the *Vindication* and of the *Memoirs* – and the conventions were well established. If Mary and Shelley stayed together, she would have a recognizable place in the scheme of things, understood if not approved by anyone who had ever been in love. She and Shelley had done right to lead their irregular life abroad which was the right place for it, beyond the range of English law and English manners. The cities of Europe were already full of happily unmarried couples including Godwin's friends Helen Maria Williams and John Hurford Stone in Paris and Lady Mountcashell and 'Mr Mason' in Italy. If, however, as seemed more likely, Mary was abandoned by Shelley in favour of some new enthusiasm, she would join the ranks of dishonoured women whom the monied classes created in great profusion: if that were to happen the outlook was grim indeed.

Paradoxically the situation of Jane Clairmont was less conventional and even more worrying. There was no place either in morality or in political justice for a girl to run away with a man and live in his house just because she preferred his lifestyle to that of her family. Jane was at risk of being dishonoured from the first, even although, unlike her stepsister, she had not strayed far across the boundary between a non-sexual and a sexual friendship.

Mrs Godwin erected her own psychological defences. She was never much of a philosopher and cared little for literature or literalism. Shelley, she concluded, was a monster of depravity who shamelessly tried to seduce every young woman he met. If her beloved daughter Jane had run away, and then at Calais resisted her pleas to return, the fault must lie with Mary. It was she who had beguiled her from her natural mother to worship the dead saint in St Pancras Churchyard whose birthday she just happened to share. In a series of letters to Lady Mountcashell, who had witnessed the preamble in London but was too far away to check facts, Mary Jane offered a version which showed her imaginative powers. Determined to tell a story that would exonerate herself, she ran together events which were widely separated and added incidents which are demonstrably untrue. She said that it was James Marshall who went to Dover and Calais in pursuit of the runaways, unwilling, it would seem, to admit that Jane had withstood her own mother's entreaties. She also asserted that Marshall had followed the fugitives to Paris, presumably to rebut the thought that insufficient persistence had been shown at Calais.[7]

Whether Godwin was aware of these insincerities is not known. After thirteen years he knew his wife and did not interfere. For himself the most urgent problem was, as before, money. Of the £1,120 received from the sale of Shelley's bond he paid £500 immediately to one creditor who had obtained a court order against him, but the remaining money gave him a new chance to climb out of his difficulties. Suddenly in July it looked as if a lasting solution was in sight. Two brothers, John and William Stone, offered to make a capital injection in return for a partnership. Exactly who they were has not been ascertained, but they may have been relatives of the brothers John Hurford Stone and William Stone who had been amongst the most hated Jacobins of the 1790s.[8] After three weeks of daily negotiations in late August and early September, it was agreed that the Stone brothers would buy a half share in the business for about £3,000. The exact figure was to be determined by two valuers who would make a professional valuation of the stock and of the other assets. Contracts were exchanged on 15 September with Godwin nominating as his valuer a Mr Miles, who had taken over Johnson's business in St Paul's Church-yard, and the Stones choosing a Mr Saunders, a book auctioneer.

At the end of August Godwin again took up his pen to explain to Francis Place and others that unexpected events had again supervened and that he was still unable to repay the money which had been promised from the sale of the Shelley bond. But he now had hopes from the Stone brothers. Godwin had always in the past been able to overbear Place's objections by invoking the responsibilities of the rich towards men of genius. But Place, who had financed him for two years longer than he had intended on the strength of the connection with Shelley, had now had enough. He had only met Shelley once – he had disliked him – and he probably guessed, despite Godwin's attempts to keep silence, that the proceeds of the bond sale was the last money Godwin was likely to receive from that quarter.

Place was now irritated by Godwin's repeated appeals to his family responsibilities – why had the philosopher taken on a widow and three of other people's children if he was not able to provide for them? Like his complaint about Godwin's weekend's paddling at Southend, the charge came badly from a man who purportedly believed in Godwinian prin-ciples. Place had enjoyed little success himself in practising late marriage and moral restraint. His years of celibacy until the age of nineteen had been a torment, and he had been obliged to employ some of the 10 per cent of the female population who were in business to relieve this problem. After his marriage he fathered fifteen children. But with sex, as with paddling, Place took the view that success as a businessman gave him authority to moralize.

The more that Place complained, the more haughty Godwin became. In a series of acerbic exchanges, the two men debated the meaning of a sentence in *Political Justice* as if they were discussing a critical crux in an ancient author. It was not a usual way for a potential bankrupt to discuss his affairs with his principal creditor, but the prestige of his book was Godwin's last negotiating asset. He sent a defiant letter to Place on 11 September. The contract with the Stone brothers which would at last have cut him free was sent for signature on 15 September. Then suddenly there were complications.

Miles, Godwin's nominee, objected to working with Saunders who he said, as a book auctioneer, had no expertise in the valuation of the copyrights. Godwin's colleagues in the book trade agreed that Saunders was unsuitable, but when he asked for this point of the agreement to be reconsidered, the brothers stood firm. Godwin had not intended to make the matter a sticking point, and he wrote again to the Stone brothers to say that he accepted the nomination of Saunders. But it was now too late. Although the two brothers were still keen, a third brother – who had not hitherto been involved – advised against it, and the whole deal collapsed.

Without the money from the Stone brothers, Godwin could not pay Place, and Place made it clear that this time he would take legal steps. If Place moved, the other creditors would do the same. Place was later to tell a Commission investigating the insolvency laws that he favoured imprisonment for debt, with close confinement for the rich, and he was known to be a man who carried out his threats. As he had advised from the beginning, anything less than a full recapitalization of the business would be to send good money after bad, and so it was proving. It would only be a matter of time – perhaps a few weeks or months at most – before the Godwin family were again facing the forced sale of their possessions, possible imprisonment of the head of the family, ejection from their home, and a life of destitution.

Godwin made his unsuccessful concession to the Stone brothers on 15 September. On 22 September he made a further despairing appeal to save the deal, having spent the 18th going over the stock of the business once more with Mary Jane and Charles Clairmont. It was on the 16th that a letter arrived at Skinner Street in the now familiar untidy scrawl of Percy Bysshe Shelley. The runaways were back in London. But was this good news or bad?

CHAPTER 29

The Very Great Evil that Book has Done

While the Shelleys could see all the similarities, the Godwins could only see the differences. The philosopher had always been cautious, even furtive, in his social defiance. Even at his bravest in 1793 and 1794, he had never favoured the flaunting of breaches of law or convention, arguing like Sir Thomas More, that the powers-that-be should be given every opportunity to avert their eyes and escape a confrontation. He and Mary Wollstonecraft had been well into their thirties when they slipped into each other's beds, and they kept their love a well-guarded secret. In 1796 there was still widespread respect for the New Philosophy, and they were financially independent. As soon as Wollstonecraft became pregnant they hurried into marriage.

By contrast Mary and Jane were only seventeen. Neither Shelley nor they were making any attempt to conceal what they were doing, and the social disapproval was far more severe than it had been in the 1790s. Shelley, for all his great expectations, had no money and was on the run from creditors. Mary had become pregnant as quickly as her mother, but this time there was Harriet to be considered who had a daughter, Ianthe, and another baby on the way. In 1796 William Godwin and Mary Wollstonecraft had made a calculated attempt to practise their principles with minimum shock to an imperfect world. In 1814 Mary Wollstonecraft Godwin, Jane Clairmont, and Percy Bysshe Shelley were behaving with flagrant irresponsibility.

Goodwill, from *Lessons for Children*

On the day Shelley's letter was received, Mary Jane and Fanny hurried round to Margaret Street, but when Shelley went out to meet them, they refused to speak, so that they had only a brief conversation with the girls through an open window. That night after everyone was asleep Charles Clairmont went round, and to the delight of the girls he stayed until three o'clock to hear and tell the whole story. But at Skinner Street there was to be no welcome for the return of the prodigal daughters. On 22 September Godwin wrote to Shelley that he would have no further dealings with him.[1]

Godwin and Shelley with their respective supporters faced each other like two hostile camps. For a month all contact was broken off, and then in October messages again began to pass across the lines. James Marshall who as Godwin's oldest friend had been a virtual uncle to the girls brought a message from Jane, and she and her mother walked round the streets of Holborn together. Fanny paid a visit to the Shelley camp. Charles crossed with a letter from Fanny to Jane which led to a meeting at Marshall's house. Mary wrote to Fanny, and Mary Jane wrote to Mary. But when Shelley, accompanied by Mary and Jane, tried to visit Skinner Street they were all refused admission, and when Shelley sent Thomas Love Peacock as his emissary, he too was turned away.

The flurry of diplomacy produced no solution and only small growth in trust. Godwin felt most deeply about Mary. Mary Jane could not conceal that for her the important thing was to persuade Jane to leave the others. Fanny, whom everybody loved, just wanted everybody to be friends again and could not understand why this was impossible. Charles was inclined to think that he had been accidentally caught on the wrong side of the battle lines.

The Godwins suggested to Jane that, if she would leave Shelley, she could be established in a family in the country – perhaps as a governess – where there would be some chance of covering over her indiscretion and re-establishing her respectability. But Jane rejected the proposal indignantly: she was not going to be shut away like a fallen woman in a convent. Precautions were taken against a possible kidnap attempt by the Godwins, and the Shelley camp made plans to spring Shelley's own sisters from his father's house so that they too could join them in the unfettered life. In early November when Mrs Godwin was ill, word was passed to Jane that her mother was dying. It was a *ruse de guerre* from the other side. Jane came round at once and stayed at Skinner Street for two nights. She was, she said, willing to stay longer but only if she could come and go as she wished and continue friendly with Shelley and Mary. When

Godwin and Mary Jane said no, she moved out again and this time took her clothes.

Godwin's policy was a complex balancing of competing considerations and confusing emotions. He wanted to rescue the girls from the wrongs of woman which he was sure soon awaited them. Whatever else happened, he was determined that they should never have to endure the miseries that had assailed Mary Wollstonecraft, Mary Jane Clairmont, Charlotte Smith, Mary Robinson, Mary Hays, and most of the women friends who had taken part in the 1790s campaign for greater freedom and equality. But if he was to help them, he must continue to disapprove. It was not enough that documentary proof of his efforts to stop Shelley was deposited at Norwich: teenage girls had been unlucky before and had been able to live down their foolishness, but girls who lived with married men with the condonation of their fathers were ruined irretrievably. *Queen Mab* and *The Empire of the Nairs* compared legal marriage with prostitution. But that was one of the notions which had been neatly reversed. What else could a woman be, the anti-Wollstonecraftians sneered, if she was not widow, wife, or maid?

To the young people in the Shelley camp, Godwin's attitude was puzzling and deeply disappointing. Surely he, of all men, should not now start bowing to propriety? Had the author of *Caleb Williams* forgotten the difference between virtue and honour? Why could Mamma and Papa not welcome them all back? They were very happy to help in the house and in the shop; 41 Skinner Street was their home. The girls could not believe that their beloved and admired father could have adopted such an unnatural attitude. Left to himself, they were sure he would rush to be reconciled with them, and if he foolishly held out against his natural feelings it must be as a result of pressure from Mary Jane.

During the period of coldest confrontation in the autumn of 1814 all three members of the Shelley camp read *Political Justice*, sometimes together, sometimes alone. Godwin had, they decided, reneged on the principles which he himself had discovered and codified. The Shelley camp were now the true inheritors of the New Philosophy: Godwin and his supporters were the revisionists and backsliders. 'I confess to you', Shelley wrote to Mary on 24 October, 'that I have been shocked and staggered by Godwin's cold injustice.' It was their severest term of condemnation.

After the first few days in London the Shelley ménage moved to Somers Town which was cheaper and safer from bailiffs. The house was near Chalton Street and The Polygon where Godwin and Mary Wollstonecraft had lived and loved and within sight of St Pancras Churchyard. They considered moving out of London altogether, but until the money problems were resolved, that was impossible. Shelley's plan was to raise a large new loan but when his agent offered a post-obit bond for sale on 21 September on the same terms as had been agreed for the Nash brothers, there was not a single bidder. For a time it looked as if the Shelleys would narrowly pip the Godwins in a close-run race towards disaster. Destitution was averted by pawning Shelley's microscope, which brought in £5, while he went the rounds of the brokers, the insurance men, and the discount houses to try to interest them in his expectations.

A man on the run from creditors is not able to negotiate fine terms. Shelley was offered only £400 for a £2,400 bond. One financier offered £300 a year for a bond of £15,000. Another suggested £15,000 in exchange for the reversion of Goring Castle which his grandfather had recently completed at a cost of £80,000. Feckless and irresponsible though he was by the standards of commercial morality Shelley jibbed at redistributing his family's wealth to speculators whose contribution to the advance of perfectibility was unlikely to be positive. Besides, given the scale of his urgent debts, sums of the magnitude he was now able to raise could give only a temporary relief and would effectively rule out other more substantial flotations later. It was clear that Shelley, like Godwin, would never be able to restore his financial affairs to a tolerable footing without a full-scale capital reconstruction. For that he would have to negotiate with his father when the terms of his grandfather's will came into effect: his grandfather was eighty-two and he decided to wait.

For half a year in late 1814 and early 1815 Shelley was constantly on the run, borrowing small amounts here and there to pay the household bills but leaving his major creditors unsatisfied. If his tall stooping figure was recognized in the streets of London, the bailiffs would be on to him. Even when he was with friends there was the fear of betrayal. At times when danger was closest, Shelley moved out entirely, slinking from hotel to hotel while the girls stayed at their lodgings and worried. Since the law did not permit arrest for debt on Sundays, there was one day in the week when Shelley and Mary could safely be together. But on other days, their meetings had to be carefully conspired. Mary hated public parks or the streets where young women walking up and down were normally understood to be seeking clients. Their favourite rendezvous was St Paul's Cathedral where Mary's purpose could be more satisfactorily misunderstood.

If the Shelley circle had few friends, the relationships were compensatingly intense. Shelley was now a convinced believer in unrestricted love, far along the road to full-scale Nairism. As he was to proclaim in one of his best poems in 1821, pretending that he had never changed his views:

> I never was attached to that great sect,
> Whose doctrine is, that each one should select
> Out of the crowd a mistress or a friend,
> And all the rest, though fair and wise, commend
> To cold oblivion, though it is the code
> Of modern morals, and the beaten road
> Which those poor slaves with weary footsteps tread,
> Who travel to their home among the dead
> By the broad highway of the world, and so
> With one chained friend, perhaps a jealous foe,
> The dreariest and the longest journey go.[2]

Hogg, Shelley's friend from Oxford days with whom a coolness had developed in 1812 when he had shown too warm an interest in Harriet, now repeated the experiment with Mary, visiting her alone when Shelley was away. This time Shelley actively encouraged the affair. Love should be shared. If there was to be sincerity in personal relationships – political justice in emotions as well as in intellect – then sex should be as free as sensibility.

Mary, pregnant at the time, was content to accept both Shelley's philosophy of love and Hogg's embraces, although – like Cornelia Turner and other apparent converts – she probably never threw off the constraints entirely. On 22 February 1815 she gave birth to the child who had been conceived at the time of the elopement the previous summer. The following day Fanny and Charles Clairmont were out all night from Skinner Street, no doubt visiting their sister. When the baby died a few weeks later in what would today be described as a cot death, Mary was thrown into depression and before she was fully recovered, she was again suffering morning sickness from a second pregnancy.

Jane meanwhile, among all the talk of love and babies, began to feel increasingly *de trop*. The strongest link between the Shelley and the Godwin camps, she had no role in either. Peacock offered to marry her which would have been a betrayal: on the other hand she did not wish to go back to Skinner Street. It was not enough for a Wollstonecraftian to live at second hand as a dependant: she too must have a life of her own although what it could be she had not yet decided. The Godwins suggested to Mrs Knapp, who had been Godwin's landlady when he lived in Somers Town, that she might take her in, but Mrs Knapp refused: already her undeserved reputation was becoming a liability. Disliking her real names, which related her too closely to her mother, she decided that henceforth she would be known as Claire Clairmont, and after some hesitations, the other members of the Shelley circle agreed to indulge her. In referring to Claire in her journal, Mary now sometimes drew the symbol of a moon in case her stepsister should chance to pry and discover quite how redundant she had become.

Then there was Harriet. On the first day back in London from Switzerland Shelley had gone to see her, and he was surprised when she refused to sympathize. The correct outcome for Harriet had been obvious to him from the first and he had written to suggest it from France. Harriet should join him and the two girls as a second non-sexual partner with Jane. Or, if she preferred, she could go her own way with money from Shelley which he would provide as soon as he had any, but remaining on terms of perfect friendship and trust. He begged her, as he put it, 'to return to philosophy and reason', and was genuinely shocked that after their years together, Harriet should also now betray the Godwinian principles which she had earlier professed. When, as he put it, 'an occasion of the sublimist virtue' occurred, Harriet had reverted to the old superseded values. She too was being unjust.

Harriet had had her own explanation. As she told a friend in Dublin in confirming that Shelley had left her:

Your fears are verified. Mr Shelley has become profligate and sensual, owing entirely to Godwin's *Political Justice*. The very great evil that book has done is not to be told.[3]

Not long afterwards, her two babies now consigned to the care of her sister, Harriet moved out of her father's house to live with another man and within a few months she was pregnant for a third time. Whatever view society took of her as a deserted wife, she now joined the others as a dishonoured woman.[4]

Those who protested that she was innocent or that she had been seduced were being equally unfair. Harriet, disillusioned although she was with *Political Justice* and inclined to relapse into conventional morality, remained a confused Godwinian and Wollstonecraftian, and Shelley who always hoped that she would be restored to his pantisocracy, never ceased to appeal to her nobler feelings in those terms.

CHAPTER 30

Pursuits

Since the first revolutionary scares of the early 1790s the country had teemed with spies and informers, some directly employed by the Government, others financed by private associations. Most political organizations were infiltrated. *Agents provocateurs* were common and in the absence of a regular police force, the local supporters of the Government were encouraged to use whatever methods seemed best without too keen a regard for propriety. Coleridge and Thelwall had enjoyed addressing one another ostentatiously as 'citizen' and talking in a loud voice about 'Spy Nozy' to the puzzlement of a suspicious shadow who hung about listening to their conversation.[1] Robert Merry interlarded his letters with ostentatious expressions of loyalty for the benefit of the post office interceptors.[2] The trials of 1794 showed that the dangers were real enough. Godwin, who had taken part in the unmasking of Charles Sinclair's attempts to incriminate Horne Tooke, always took care to avoid offering hostages to a hostile Government. As long as the Two Acts of 1796 stood on the Statute Book it was unwise to test the power of truth too flagrantly even in private.

When it was noticed in the summer of 1812 that Shelley was posting packages from Lynmouth to addresses all over the country, he immediately came under suspicion. One was dispatched to William Godwin. Another went to that other figure from the 1790s Lord 'Citizen' Stanhope, the man who congratulated William Godwin when he was the rising

The Good Family, from *Lessons for Children*

political journalist from the *New Annual Register* at the first Bastille Day celebration dinner on 14 July 1790. Another was sent to Sir Francis Burdett. When Shelley was observed on the shore playing his favourite game of launching toy boats, they were discovered to contain copies of a printed *Declaration of Rights*.

At other times the authorities might have ignored the activities of the absurd propagandist but now they took no risks. Shelley was evidently in pursuit of some plan which took him on frantic journeys all over the country. When his Irish servant Dan Healey was sent into Barnstaple to hand out his pamphlets and stick posters on walls, he was promptly arrested on the charge of circulating printed matter which did not carry the printer's name. He was sentenced by the magistrate to a huge fine of £200 with six months' imprisonment in the event of default. Once more the uncomfortable lesson was being learned that reformers bring trouble on other people besides themselves or, in Shelley's case, other than themselves for it was Healey who had to serve the sentence. It was because of his experience at Lynmouth that Shelley printed his name as the author and publisher of *Queen Mab* although he always cut off the pages which said so.

On the day that Godwin set off from London on his fruitless journey to Lynmouth, the town clerk of Barnstaple was writing a full report to the Home Secretary in London. Although the authorities decided against prosecuting Shelley on this occasion, they asked for the surveillance to be stepped up. But Shelley had already left for Wales leaving his books as security for arrears of rent. He may have been in the Chepstow area when Godwin was passing through in the opposite direction.

Not long afterwards Godwin was also the subject of a report to the Home Office.[3] The anonymous informer who sent a description of the bookshop in June 1813 made the affairs of M. J. Godwin and Company sound deeply sinister. William Godwin, he reported, after twenty years was still, under the cover of 'Edward Baldwin', infiltrating his Jacobin principles into the country's unsuspecting youth. By offering discounts on his books, Godwin 'allured' the schools which taught the lower classes, and was secretly spreading atheism, republicanism, and sedition. In his book on Greek mythology, he was deliberately encouraging sexual immorality. His *History of Rome* implied that only republican government was worth studying. Even his school dictionaries played their part in the plan of subversion. The word 'revolution', the spy claimed, was defined as 'things returning to their just state' although that appears to have been his own invention.[4] With increasing success, he warned, seeing evidence of conspiracy both in Godwin's secretiveness and in his openness, he was growing more bold. When the shop started there had been no name: now at Skinner Street 'Godwin' was blatantly painted in large letters above the entrance.

With surveillance went intimidation and terror. On 26 February 1813 when Shelley was at Tremadoc, he was the victim of what he believed was an assassination attempt. According to his own account, Shelley was half expecting an attack and had armed himself with pistols. When a man broke in during the night, there was a scuffle, shots were exchanged, and the man escaped, but Shelley decided immediately to leave the district and he was never to return. Shelley believed that the attacker was Robert Leeson, a member of a prominent 'loyalist' Anglo-Irish family who was mounting his own anti-Jacobin terror.[5] Others, however, including some of the people who knew Shelley best, were inclined to suspect that the whole incident occurred mainly or exclusively in Shelley's imagination. Whatever the facts, Shelley was henceforth convinced that Leeson intended to track him down and kill him. He thought he saw him in Dublin and again in Dover. As late as 1821 he believed he caught a glimpse of him lurking in Pisa.

In the oppressive atmosphere of anti-Jacobinism it was easy to see enemies at every street corner. Shelley enjoyed the notion that he was being followed which helped to justify his impulsive travelling. 'Go on until you are stopped' was the advice he consistently gave himself until friends recognized the words as a kind of Shelleyan catch-phrase. He feared that, like Kotzebue, he would be officially assassinated as the quickest way of shutting him up. But, in this as in other matters, his character was a product as much of literature as of life. The book which, above all others, caught the psychology of the pursuit was *Caleb Williams* which though written in 1793 and 1794 rang as true twenty years later. The aristocratic Falkland, the embodiment of the false values of conferred honour, could have been Shelley's father. Caleb Williams, innocent of everything except a desire to discover the truth, was, like Shelley himself, a martyr to the cause of progress. Falkland's agent, Gines, like the putative Leeson, was both extraordinarily resourceful in pursuing his victim and extraordinarily inefficient at actually catching him.

Shelley reread *Caleb Williams* in 1815 along with *St. Leon* and *Fleetwood*, the novel of Godwin's which he liked best. He also turned to the other Jacobin novelists who had attempted in the previous generation to disseminate the lessons of the New Philosophy. He read Holcroft's *Hugh*

Trevor to be followed in later years by *Anna St. Ives* and *Bryan Perdue*. He read Robert Bage's *Man As He Is* and *Man As He Is Not*.

The American, Charles Brockden Brown wrote five such novels in quick succession in 1798 to 1801 and another later. Like many of his generation, he had been so overwhelmed by his reading of *Caleb Williams* that, in the best Godwinian tradition, he abandoned the morally corrupting profession of the law for the life of improving writer. He was living in the household of William Dunlap, his future biographer, when Dunlap sent Godwin and Holcroft his long admiring missives in 1795.[6] His plots too are concerned with innocents overendowed with curiosity who fall foul of misanthropic rich patrons. There are papers hidden in chests and unexplained murders. The themes are pursuit and counterpursuit, transfiguration and reconciliation. In Pennsylvania as in Transylvania, the atmosphere is heavy with gothic menace. One of the characters is transformed by reading *Political Justice* 'which changed in a moment the whole course of his life'. There are disquisitions on the rights of women taken from Mary Wollstonecraft. As readers at the time and since have recognized, Brockden Brown is more Godwinian than Godwin.

In 1814 and 1815 Shelley and Mary obtained and read five of Brown's novels, *Philip Stanley*, *Edgar Huntley*, *Jane Talbot*, *Ormond*, and *Wieland*. The last named made an especially strong impression although the title has nothing to do with Shelley's favourite German poet. Godwin looked through *Caleb Williams* and *St. Leon* in 1815. He also read the same five novels by Brockden Brown in one gulp in 1816; *Wieland* 23–24 May, *Edgar Huntley* 4–5 June, *Ormond* 14–15 June, *Philip Stanley* 23–26 June, *Jane Talbot* 28 June, being like Shelley, especially impressed by *Wieland*. As the Godwins and Shelleys faced one another in 1815 and 1816 the two leaders were steeped in the literary genre which Godwin had made peculiarly his own.

In the Godwinian novel the pursuer and the pursued alternate their roles. At a sudden twist of events, the action reverses and the pursued sets off in pursuit of the pursuer. The characteristics which the two heroes share are more important than those that divide them. Both are admirable but each is flawed. Their fates are inextricably linked, and without a resolution they are doomed to mutual destruction. The relationship of Godwin and Shelley was now assuming the same pattern. During most of 1812 it was Shelley who had bombarded Godwin with letters begging for his friendship. After the first meetings it had been Godwin's turn to pursue his pupil with requests. Now, after the events of July 1814, it was again Shelley who was the suppliant. Without a reconciliation both were doomed to misery, but how could the circle of mutual distrust be broken?

At the end of 1814, an opportunity occurred. On 3 November Godwin failed to meet an obligation of £150 due to Lambert, being allowed the usual three days' grace. Since his credit was at an end, the money could only be found by the sale of assets and the next day he called in a book auctioneer to help to dispose of the stock. It looked again as if the final demise of M. J. Godwin and Company had at last arrived, but when Mary Jane became very ill – she was said to be dying – Lambert evidently granted some extension. At this point Shelley suddenly came to the rescue. Hearing from Charles Clairmont and Fanny about the desperate situation at Skinner Street, he called on the financier personally on 22 November and offered a post-obit on the Shelley estate in settlement of Godwin's debt. The offer was accepted.

It was a neat arrangement. Shelley had no money of his own to pay Godwin's debts, nor could he borrow money directly by post-obit. But from Lambert's point of view, a post-obit on the Shelley estate was a more valuable asset than a claim on Godwin's collapsing business. From Godwin's point of view too, the solution was a good one. Since there was no need for him to be personally involved in any of the meetings or financial negotiations with Lambert, he could maintain the breach with Shelley which he had proclaimed in September.

In December 1814 Shelley settled at least two other of Godwin's debts by the same method. In cancellation of Godwin's debt of £365 to Place, Shelley promised to pay £1,095 within three months of inheriting, with the further proviso that if the money was not paid within three months, the value of the bond rose to £2,190.[7] A similar arrangement was made with Hume. Although the debts settled by Shelley in this way totalled only about £700, he signed over £2,000 of post-obit with a full contingent liability of perhaps £5,000.

By any standard but that of political justice it was a generous act. Mary Jane and Fanny were full of misplaced gratitude. But was such a response tolerable? Shelley was after all only belatedly – and partially – discharging a financial obligation, and for Godwin to be seen to be enthusiastic would help confirm the rumours that he had sold his daughters. In the end it was decided that the philosopher would not personally write to thank Shelley, but that he would not object if Mary Jane did. The message was duly conveyed, and other letters passed between Shelley and Charles and Fanny. It was a compromise, a dereliction (though in different directions) from moral principle and from ordinary good manners. It was also a break in the deadlock.

As the winter drew on everyone at Skinner Street knew that it was only because of Shelley that they still had a roof over their heads. But there were plenty of other bills outstanding. December, when the book trade accounts had to be paid, was always a time of crisis. Henry Crabb Robinson, who called occasionally for a round of whist, was again touched – in more than one sense – by a family enduring more than their share of wretchedness. On the last day of the year Godwin noted in his journal a visit from a man called Merry 'to distrain'. The 'auction mart' of 6 January 1815 was presumably the sale at knock-down prices of goods seized from Skinner Street. Godwin's journal for February also notes two visits to court as other creditors proceeded against him.

But if Shelley's help had been accepted once it could be accepted again. On the same day as the sale, the eighty-three-year-old Sir Bysshe Shelley at last gave up his long struggle for life. With his death Shelley's father inherited the title and the estates, and Shelley was now the direct heir. After years of skirmishing the way was now open for a negotiation between Shelley and his father for a full-scale reconstruction of his finances under the terms of his grandfather's will. Any deal struck now would be the last occasion for many years – perhaps the last occasion ever – when Shelley could expect substantial sums from the family fortune. It had been money which started the rapprochement with Godwin: now it gave it another push. Early in the New Year, Godwin sent a message to Shelley through Charles Clairmont, warning him against making too hasty a settlement with his father. The roles were again reversing: if Godwin was not yet the pursuer, he had started to move towards his antagonist.

Sir Bysshe's death did not affect Shelley's ambition. He had no wish to inherit the title and the lands. He needed money at once – to pay off his most pressing debts, and to make provision for Harriet, Mary, Claire, and his various children. Reforming the world, he knew, could not be done cheaply. He also remained convinced that he had not long to live, and when he was attacked by a heavy cold in the spring of 1815, his physician was inclined to agree. Shelley was in a hurry.

Sir Timothy Shelley was prepared to offer a reconstruction of his son's finances in exchange for an agreement not to dismember the estates further. He was willing to pay off Shelley's debts and provide him with a comfortable income for the future. The contingent liabilities could then be discharged, the existing post-obits bought in, and the Shelley dynasty's fortune could resume its growth unencumbered until the young man saw sense. Although two concepts of stewardship were in direct conflict, there was plenty of money and therefore plenty of room for compromise.

Negotiations advanced quickly. An outline agreement was reached on 13 May 1815 and the way seemed clear for a final settlement. Among the debts for which Sir Timothy agreed to accept responsibility was £1,200 to be paid to Godwin, said to be the difference between what Shelley had promised in 1814 and what he had handed over from the Nash bond. The sum of £1,000 was paid to Godwin by Shelley's bankers some time in the second half of the month. For the first time in nearly five years he could enjoy an interval of relief and he was able to resume his literary career. In April 1815 Mary Jane had staged one of her periodical walk-outs, staying away overnight to demonstrate that she had an alternative. The arrival of Shelley's £1,000 saved the marriage as well as the matrimonial home.

To Sir Timothy's legal advisers, the claim on behalf of Godwin must have seemed tenuous to the point of invisibility, but Shelley was determined to help Godwin not only as a matter of duty but to enable him to get back on personal terms. Besides, as he told Godwin frankly in a message passed through Charles Clairmont, he himself benefited from the arrangement. Since his father was prepared to settle existing debts but not to advance his son any capital, Shelley wanted to exaggerate his liabilities. Of the £1,200 paid by Sir Timothy for Godwin, Shelley siphoned off £200 for his own use. In the language of political justice he was diverting resources to more deserving causes: in the language of law he was inviting Godwin to conspire with him to defraud his father.

It would by now have required a skilled moral casuist to disentangle the legal obligations, considerations of political justice, personal claims and straightforward self-interest with which the two philosophers had entwined their financial relationship. It was a moot point which of the two men had the greater claim under the utilitarian criteria. Was it the twenty-two-year-old heir to a vast fortune with all debts now paid, an assured income of £1,000 a year and a huge potential for changing the future? Or was it the fifty-nine-year-old former benefactor of mankind who faced the imminent prospect of ejection into the street? Which was Fénelon and which was the chambermaid? Despite the £1,000 from Shelley, Godwin was still facing a lawsuit for £200, which happened to be the figure which Shelley had withheld. If Shelley had provided the full £3,000 at the original time stipulated then Godwin would not have had to renege on his promise to his other creditor. *Ergo*, according to the tortuous logic which Godwin now applied, Shelley was still directly responsible for Godwin's present plight.

In any case, if political justice was to be the criterion, why was Shelley's duty limited to £3,000? Surely the events of July 1814 increased his obligation? But the more Godwin accepted Shelley's money, the more he laid himself open to the charge of selling the girls into prostitution. Both men needed secrecy. Shelley could scarcely hope to complete a successful negotiation with his father's lawyers if he was piling up new contingent liabilities as quickly as the existing ones were being bought out. On Godwin's side, if it became known that the Shelley fortune stood behind him, he would encourage every creditor active or inactive to sue for the repayment of every 'advance' ever made.

It was difficult to resolve the subtleties when the two men were not on speaking terms. On one occasion when Godwin happened to meet Shelley in the street, he told Charles Clairmont that it was a pity that one so beautiful should be so wicked – a remark which Falkland might have made of Caleb Williams.[8] According to Mary Jane, when the £1,000 was received Godwin was induced to write a letter of acknowledgement but it was couched 'in a style of freezing coldness'.[9]*

Once again money was succeeding where philosophy had failed. Sir Bysshe Shelley's will gave Shelley a year in which to decide whether to accept the conditions he had stipulated for holding the estate together† and the anniversary of his death fell on 5 January 1816. On 11 November 1815 Godwin took up his pen to ask for the money which he felt was still due to him, and when Shelley replied politely by return, Godwin wrote again. Before the end of 1815 he had written no less than eight letters direct to Shelley, including three on successive days, and by March 1816 the total had reached thirty-three.

He suggested various ways in which more money could be extracted from the Shelley estate – direct payments, post-obit, borrowing against guarantee – and he employed Tom Turner to give legal advice. His letters were cold and formal. They contained no greeting – not even the 'Sir' which he reserved for his most crushing rebukes – and each letter was left unsigned. Godwin adopted a high moral tone. If he had to cringe to help his family he would do so with insolence.

Shelley for his part did his best to co-operate, suggesting possible ways in which they could conspire. In January 1816 however he registered a polite protest.

* There is however no note of such a letter in his journal.
† See p. 347.

Perhaps it is well that you should be informed that I consider your last letter to be written in a certain style of haughtiness and incroachment which neither awes nor imposes on me: But I have no desire to transgress the limits which you place to our intercourse.[10]

The text of Godwin's reply has not survived, but its tone can be readily perceived from Shelley's next letter, which should be read as genuinely contrite and conciliatory, without irony.

If you really think me vicious such haughtiness as I imputed to you is perhaps to be excused. But I who do not agree with you in that opinion cannot be expected to endure it without remonstrance. I can easily imagine how difficult it must be, in addressing a person whom we despise or dislike to abstain from phrases, the turn of which is peculiar to the sentiments with which we cannot avoid regarding such a person. Perhaps I did wrong to feel so deeply or notice so readily a spirit of which you seem to have been unconscious.[11]

For a time the two men consented tacitly to confine themselves to financial business, the only matter on which they needed to agree. But that unrealistic fiction could not be maintained for long. On 24 January 1816 Mary gave birth to a second child who was named William in a gesture of goodwill. On another occasion at the New Year arrangements were made for Claire to spend a few days at Skinner Street before crossing the lines back to the Shelley camp. When Shelley suggested the need for a meeting he admitted that having to suffer Godwin's contempt face to face would be deeply hurtful. However, he pleaded, he would not shrink from the encounter if it was necessary to benefit 'a man whom in spite of his wrongs to me I respect and love'.[12]

The prospects sometimes appeared hopeful, sometimes not. In Turner's considered opinion as a lawyer Shelley could easily make a deal and was stringing Godwin along, and although he was probably wrong both on the law and on Shelley's motives, his advice coloured Godwin's attitude. In February 1816 however - just over a year after Sir Bysshe's death – Shelley suddenly wrote to say that he was giving up his efforts. Sir Timothy had decided to go to court to clarify a number of legal matters connected with the will. He was also suing the Nash brothers in hopes of obliging them to sell back Shelley's post-obit – they were refusing £4,500 for the bond which they had bought for £2,593–10s a few months before. 'I shall certainly not delay to depart from the haunts of men,' Shelley declared in a phrase which could have come straight from *Caleb Williams*, *St. Leon*, or *Fleetwood*.[13] His intention, he explained in another Godwinian passage, was to hide himself and Mary 'from that contempt which we so unjustly endure'.[14] If a certain event were to happen, he wrote darkly, hinting at his own imminent death, Godwin's prospects would be even more calamitous; he was therefore thinking of going to Italy which was both warmer in climate and more tolerant of love.

It was a new crisis. A horrified Godwin hurriedly dispatched Tom Turner to urge him to change his mind. At the same time Godwin wrote a letter direct to Shelley which in his terms was the most conciliatory he had ever sent. Only part survives, but the change of tone was clear. He addressed Shelley as 'Sir' and explained at patient length that he felt obliged to deal through an intermediary.

What has been most wanting hitherto is, that, under the state of estrangement between you and me (which, and the cause of it, no one can more deeply lament than I do) we should have an able and adequate medium of communication.[15]

He went on to commend Tom Turner's legal knowledge and clarity of mind, making no reference either to the fact that Turner was Shelley's predecessor as a pupil or that Shelley had been in love with his wife. In the portion of the letter now lost, he went on to speak of the possibility of some ultimate forgiveness.

But if the novelist believed that the moment had now arrived for a transfiguring psychological catalysis to occur, he had not sufficiently studied his own books. It was now Shelley's turn to reverse. His reply was unsigned, the first time he had ever turned this weapon against his pursuer. And for the first time he gave vent to his own indignation, not hesitating to use the ugly word which had hung round the reputation of Mary's mother and which now threatened Mary and Claire.

In my judgment neither I, nor your daughter, nor her offspring, ought to receive the treatment which we encounter on every side. It has perpetually appeared to me to have been your especial duty to see that, so far as mankind value your good opinion, we were dealt justly by, and that a young family, innocent and benevolent and united, should not be confounded with prostitutes and seducers.

He protested at Godwin's 'harshness and cruelty'. He expressed his disappointment in the man and in 'all that your genius once taught me to expect from your virtue'. Godwin, he declared flatly, was only interested in the money. Having refused to help Shelley and Mary when they were in most need, he was only moved to offer reconciliation by the prospect of losing it. Shelley was angry, and like the misanthropic hero of a Godwinian novel he now felt contempt and pity for the whole human race:

Do not talk of *forgiveness* again to me, for my blood boils in my veins, and my gall rises against all that bears the human form, when I think of what I, their benefactor and ardent lover, have endured of enmity and contempt from you and from all mankind.[16]

Shelley's letter crossed with a further letter (now lost) in which Godwin renewed his overtures, offering, it would seem, greater personal kindness towards Shelley provided that it was not misinterpreted as approval for what he had done. This caused a further angry outburst from Shelley:

The hopes which I had conceived of receiving from you the treatment and consideration which I esteem to be justly due to me were destroyed by your letter dated the 5th. – The feelings occasioned by this discovery were so bitter and so excruciating that I am resolved for the future to stifle all those expectations which my sanguine temper too readily erects on the slightest relaxation of the contempt and the neglect in the midst of which I live.[17]

Godwin's reply, if softer in tone, conceded nothing on substance.

I am sorry to say that your letter this moment received is written in a style the very opposite of conciliation, and that, if I were to answer it in the same style, we should be involved in a controversy of inextinguishable bitterness. As long as understanding and sentiment shall exist in this frame, I shall never cease from my disapprobation of that act of yours, which I regard as the great calamity of my life. But the deed being passed, and incapable of being recalled, it may become a reasonable man to consider, how far he can mitigate that anguish which he has felt towards the actor in the affair under which he suffers.

In a postscript, after he had explained his financial business, he repeated his own exasperated complaint.

The sense of the first paragraph in my letter, which you profess not to understand, is to be found in every book of sound morality and the principles of moral conduct, that ever were written.[18]

It was a fair point as Shelley, to his credit, was obliged to admit. If Godwin's words were not the invincible power of truth, they were a calm, reasonable and sincere statement of his opinions and of his feelings. Shelley accepted the rebuke. His anger subsided as quickly as it had inflated, and he was ready to relent. If he appeared hard and haughty, he explained in his next letter, it was only a disguise put on in self-protection. In the following sentence he was apologizing for the violence of his words. The two men would continue to deal with one another, but only on money. Godwin's triumphant reply, penned the same day, is a fine example of his style and of his character.

The kindness I spoke of in my letter of the 5th must certainly under all the circumstances have been a very little thing and might not be worth your acceptance. If I understand you, you will accept no kindness without approbation; and torture cannot wring from me an approbation of the act that separated us. To business then . . . [19]

Godwin had resumed the initiative and was soon in full pursuit. For the next two weeks the financial negotiations continued. Letters were exchanged, some unsigned by both men, and oral messages were carried to and fro by Turner and by Fanny. At the end of March matters were moving to a climax as the date of Sir Timothy's lawsuit approached. Shelley's father was – with good reason – deeply suspicious of his son's good faith and it was increasingly urgent that the conspirators should meet and agree tactics. When however Shelley called at Skinner Street on the 23rd he was told that Godwin was not at home. The next day the journal records three more rebuffs 'PBS calls three times na.' It is not certain whether 'na' means the polite fiction 'not at home' or the more sincere 'not admitted'. On 7 April Godwin left on a visit to Edinburgh, reasonably hopeful that sooner or later a satisfactory financial deal would be struck.

CHAPTER 31

An Author Again

In early March 1815 Napoleon Bonaparte escaped from Elba where he had gone into exile after the Peace of 1814. When he raised his standard his former troops rushed to join him, deserting their loyalty to the restored Bourbons without regret. After the false calm of 1814 Europe was once more thrown into crisis and at the end of the month the British Parliament met to consider whether it was to be peace or war.

The issue ought to have split the country more than it did. When Napoleon's armies had been marching aggressively all over Europe, many people had supported the war. But now that the French had been militarily defeated and forced to withdraw within their own frontiers, what right had the European powers to intervene in the country's internal form of government? It was not necessary to be a flaming Jacobin to doubt the wisdom of restoring all former kings, aristocrats, and priests to their previous privileges and powers.

Shortly before Parliament met, Godwin composed a number of open political letters under the name of Verax. They were published first in the *Morning Chronicle* and then as a pamphlet under his own name.[1] Shelley's money having temporarily relieved the pressure of his debts, he was able to rejoin the larger world. This was his first substantial piece of writing since 1809.

During thirty-six years of his life, he noted in his Preface, his country had been at war. Many younger people had never known peace. The

The Disasters of Impatience, from *Lessons for Children*

allied powers, having behaved with commendable generosity to defeated France in 1814, were now in the grip of passion, ready to embark on a war of aggression which, he predicted, would be more violent and more prolonged than anything that had gone before. But he was too late. Parliament met and voted for war before the pamphlet even appeared. As with the other pamphlet which he composed before the outbreak of war in 1793, his proposals were overtaken by events before they could even be read.

Godwin was one of the few Englishmen who hoped to the last hour that Napoleon would win, and – what was even more unusual – continued to say so after the completeness of the victory became known. Although the original aims of the French Revolution had been diluted and disgraced, Napoleon had to the end represented the forces of progress. At the end of 1815 Godwin prepared proposals to write Verax Part II, a Dirge of Waterloo as he called it, describing the 'miserable consequences of that accursed field'.[2] He made notes for a life of Napoleon, a lament for the liberator who – like Cromwell in an earlier century – had thrown away an opportunity to effect a lasting benefit.

Godwin believed that his *Letters of Verax* would be his last book, a final imploring cry from the edge of the grave: 1814 had been the worst year of his life, with attacks of fits on three separate occasions and it was reasonable to expect that the acceleration would continue. In the week of Waterloo however he also published another substantial work, *The Lives of Edward and John Philips, Nephews of Milton*, for which he had been reading – mainly as a distraction from contemporary worries – for several years. A decade had passed since the publication of *Fleetwood*, with only pseudonymous children's books and the brief *Essay on Sepulchres* of 1809 to mark his long middle age. Obsessed now with the imminence of his own death he rushed out *The Lives of the Philipses* as another final offering before the end.

The unengaging title disguised a work of considerable novelty and originality. As with *Chaucer* Godwin searched out primary sources which had not previously been looked at. He studied manuscript notes on Milton at Oxford and he checked detailed points in parish registers. Instead of the four or five printed works which had previously been attributed to the Philips brothers, Godwin identified forty or fifty and he made numerous other discoveries, his lifelong interest in old books producing a rich harvest of knowledge. But his work was more than a collection of antiquarian jottings. By writing about the Philips brothers Godwin was, in effect, offering an innovative biography of Milton seen from an unusual angle.

The book was also an illustration and a reaffirmation of Godwin's philosophical and political opinions. In the year of Waterloo to praise an author as a 'patriot of the world' was to flaunt lack of commitment to a narrow nationalism. In explaining why Milton clung unenthusiastically to Cromwell despite his drift towards authoritarianism, Godwin implied that a flawed Napoleon was preferable to the irremediable Bourbons. Describing in detail the events which marked the restoration of the Stuart kings, the solemn amnesties cynically ignored, the repressive legislation, the treacheries and the tortures with which reformers were crushed, Godwin was commenting on anti-Jacobin England as much as on the nation's last great political reaction. Reviewers were quick to denounce it as an attempt to justify the regicides of King Louis by linking them with the regicides of King Charles.

The English however enjoy honouring men they have hated as soon as they cease to be dangerous. It was a pity, literary voices now regularly remarked, with the forgiving condescension that comes easily to the victorious, that Godwin had been diverted into controversial writing when his prime talent was as a novelist. When the former vice-president of the United States came to Skinner Street, he could only be given the remains of the previous day's dinner. 'We starve at four,' Godwin noted in an invitation to one of his rare dinner parties, and the guests had to be content with one marrow bone and good conversation.[3] When former enemies saw the old man defiantly holding his outsize head aloft, they now mixed a reluctant respect with their pity. Rich men, Godwin remarked in describing Milton's last days, are disadvantaged as writers: a man oppressed by poverty on the other hand may 'perhaps retain the pride and independence of his spirit but not in so clear and sparkling a hue as if the world had not frowned upon him'.

Godwin firmly rebuffed all attempts to turn him into a harmless eccentric or grand old man. He had modified his beliefs since 1793, he would explain proudly, but he had not truckled to threats and he was not going to truckle to implied flattery or proffered forgiveness. If he was a Seneca he was also a Commonwealthsman who had survived into the Restoration. The seventeenth-century education which he had rejected in the eighteenth was proving a useful support in the nineteenth.

Sir James Mackintosh was one of several former friends who were now ashamed of the part they had played in stirring up anti-Jacobin fear and hatred in 1799. As early as 1804 while enjoying a judgeship in India, his reward for turning against his friends, Mackintosh wrote a letter to a friend of which Godwin obtained a copy.

If I committed any fault which approaches to immorality I think it was towards Mr Godwin. I condemn myself for contributing to any clamour against philosophical speculation, and I allow that both for his talents and character he was entitled to be treated with respect.[4]

The man whose *Vindiciae Gallicae* of 1791 had been one of the best replies to Burke, and who had been present at the decisive meeting between Godwin and Wollstonecraft in 1796, was now eager to give practical help. Only a few courageous men had stood by Godwin in the 1790s, Mackintosh remarked in two reviews of the *Philips* book published in the *Monthly* and in the *Edinburgh*, with the disingenuous implication that he himself had been one of them. In the tradition of reviewers who are determined to write favourably about an author even when they dislike his book, Mackintosh then proceeded to write a long eulogy on Godwin's earlier writings, characterizing *Caleb Williams* as the finest novel to be produced in England since *The Vicar of Wakefield*.

At the end of 1815 Godwin was as a result able to arrange for the re-publication of both *Caleb Williams* and *St. Leon* neither of which had been available for many years. They too were rushed out quickly to catch the interest which had been generated by the reviews of the *Philips* book and which, he believed, would shortly be further stimulated by obituary notices. Using some of the Shelley money, he financed the printing costs himself and then sold the stock to a publisher. He did not read the books through again. In a brief Preface explaining why he was not offering a revision, he included a third person double negative which takes the prize for defiant Godwinian understatement.

. . . various avocations and demands upon his thoughts and attention, some of them not altogether pleasant, have indisposed him from allowing himself in that degree of luxury which might have been his seducer in a more commodious fortune.

In reality, all the talk about Godwin's forthcoming death was – not for the last time – to prove seriously premature. The next cataplectic fit did not strike until near the end of 1815: the attacks of the previous year had been a bunching not a major departure from trend. Godwin was destined to write seven substantial works and one book for children – twenty entire volumes in all – before the long delayed end, and his heirs found the manuscript of a completed eighth on his desk.

In the years after Waterloo, the outlook for the moral economy was worse than at any time since he started to study it in the 1780s, and the world had more need of philosophers than ever. If the advocates of the French Revolution had exaggerated the invincible power of truth to change men's minds and turn back the wrath of armies, the new orthodoxy believed that unwelcome ideas could be indefinitely held down by censorship, by religion, and by the police.

If they could defeat atheism and free thinking, the Government seemed to believe, demands for political reform and rights for women would fall away. At a time when many of their countrymen were hungry, they spent huge sums on church building, hoping to transplant the values of a rural deferential society into the new urban areas. In 1816, they started a new clamp-down on the press. By imposing anticipatory fines which the defendants could not possibly pay as security for good conduct the courts sent many men and women to prison for long periods without even the need for a conviction. When on 28 January 1817 the window of the Prince Regent's carriage was broken on his way to the Opening of Parliament the Government exploited the incident – as they had done in 1795 – to obtain fierce new powers. In 1817 there were forty-two prosecutions of publishers and by 1819 the number had risen to ninety-six.

Godwin's disgust was shared by a few members of the younger generation, notably Lord Byron, but of his immediate circle only Hazlitt was willing to agree that the wrong side had won the war. The anti-Jacobins were now supported by many people who had previously taken the liberal side. Southey was now a rabid church and king man. While it was reasonable and right for a man to change his opinions in the light of changing perceptions, he had made a successful career of flattering the prevailing orthodoxy and had been rewarded by appointment as Poet Laureate. True to the spirit of the new age, he rushed out a commemorative poem *The Poet's Pilgrimage to Waterloo* in which the battle is described as a straightforward struggle between the forces of good and evil. Napoleon is Satan; Waterloo is the triumph of True Religion. Adopting the device of a visionary conversation which Shelley had copied from Volney, he attributed all the world's sufferings from the year 1789 to the false philosophy of reason, justice, and equality.

Coleridge too was a disappointment. For several years after 1812 Godwin seldom saw the man he had once admired as the most instructive conversationalist he had ever met. Destroyed by drink and drugs, Coleridge produced scarcely any work for years and when it came it was rambling, confused, and self-justificatory. In 1817 Coleridge proclaimed his belief in nationalism, imposed religion, and state authoritarianism.

Any individual, he said, who decides to join a society not sanctioned by the government of his country forfeits his rights as a citizen.[5] This was a far cry from the proposed pantisocracy of 1794 when he and Southey had intended to establish a new society on Godwinian principles. Shelley considered that Coleridge had changed his beliefs by an act of will rather than from conviction – a politer accusation than hypocrisy.[6] As for William Wordsworth, an argument with Godwin about Waterloo one evening led to such frank speaking that the two men could thereafter scarcely bear to be together in the same room.[7] Only wealth could guarantee political integrity, Wordsworth argued publicly in 1818. According to Peacock he believed that the House of Commons should be selected by the House of Lords.[8]

In January 1815 Godwin's diary records two visits from a man called George Cannon. Later in the month he called several times on Shelley and Mary, and it may have been at Skinner Street that he discovered their secret address. Cannon was a friend of Daniel Isaac Eaton and he too operated in the murky dangerous world of illegal publishing. He was responsible for a series of open letters on religious persecution under the pseudonym Erasmus Perkins, and he was evidently making plans to go into business on his own account. One of his projects was to publish cheap reprints of the philosophers in a series of 'Sceptical Classics', and he may have hoped to include *Political Justice*. In 1815 however it was the pupil who caught his attention. For several months in 1815 'Erasmus Perkins' edited a magazine in London which contains so many references to Shelley's works that it is difficult to avoid the conclusion that Shelley was one of the sponsors.*

Godwin's hopes for changing the world were now more modest and more patient than those of his pupil. From time to time he had considered writing a fourth novel and at one stage he had started to draft it. It was to be a story of a man waking after a long sleep, the supernatural context giving scope – as in *St. Leon* – to make some general philosophical and psychological points. The overwhelming need, if one generation was to avoid replaying the mistakes of its predecessors, was to harness imaginations to take a long-term view. On 18 December 1815 having laid aside his earlier plans, Godwin put a new plan to the Edinburgh publisher Archibald Constable. It was couched in his usual style of defiant modesty:

Several of my literary friends and persons of eminence among whom I may mention Madame de Staël, Lord Byron, and Mr Curran have importuned me to

---

* See Appendix 3.

write another novel. I have generally answered that I was afraid I could not do better than I had done in Caleb Williams and St. Leon, and that therefore I had no motive of fame to undertake it. Sir James Mackintosh, in particular, replied to this argument that if by such a work I did not add to my fame, I might at least add to its vigour and freshness. I am the least in the world an obstinate man in refusing to do that which my conscience does not forbid me to do, and I must own that the multiplied remonstrances I have received have somewhat moved me.[9]

Since 1809 Archibald Constable had been the distributor within Scotland for the publications of M. J. Godwin and Company. More recently he had provided an expensive apprenticeship for Charles Clairmont in the bookselling business. He was both a friend and a bold and successful publisher. Eighteen-fifteen was the year when the anonymous *Waverley* ushered in a long succession of best-selling historical romances, a genre in which Godwin regarded himself as an earlier master. Constable's files were, however, already full of Godwinian letters about money. He was interested in having Godwin's novel but he knew his man and jibbed at the financial terms. As soon as spring arrived therefore Godwin decided to accept his long-standing invitation and to make a personal visit to Edinburgh.

The journey was further proof of his returning confidence and returning vigour. His last comparable expedition had been the visit to Dublin in 1800 when his fits first started. The long ineffectual chase after Shelley to Lynmouth in 1812 had also been extremely disagreeable and he had decided then never to travel more than was absolutely necessary. There was something about the lurching motion of a coach which disturbed him and brought on his fits: on more than one occasion he had collapsed open-mouthed and wide-eyed into the lap of a surprised lady sitting opposite. The journey to Edinburgh by land took four full days.

In the event the visit to Scotland was a resounding success. The money question was quickly resolved and Godwin was able to send Mary Jane a cheque which he had obtained from Constable. He was treated everywhere as a celebrity, was introduced to everyone of literary or artistic importance in Edinburgh. He spent time with Dugald Stewart the philosopher, with Francis Jeffrey, the editor of the *Edinburgh Review*, and with Raeburn the portraitist. At one dinner party he met Henry Mackenzie whose *Man of Feeling* published in 1770 had prompted Godwin's *Fleetwood*.[10] Fairley, the umbrella manufacturer who had worked so hard in 1811 to raise funds on his behalf, took him to meet Hepburn at his Bearfoot estate near Haddington. The Earl of Buchan, to whom one of the Mucius letters had been addressed, invited him to dinner and provided him with a carriage.

After nearly two weeks in Edinburgh, he spent a day and a night with Walter Scott at Abbotsford. Godwin almost certainly knew that Scott was the author of *Waverley*, which he read before his visit to Scotland, although with the caution which he brought to all secrets, he always took care to refer to him as 'the poet'. Leaving Constable at the Scottish border he went on to the Lake District, where he spent two disagreeable evenings with William Wordsworth.

On the journey back, as he told Mary Jane, he was already 'all on fire' to get to his desk. Shelley's and now Constable's money had given him the chance of a further few months' uninterrupted writing. On 23 May he noted in his journal 'invenio' – which he mistakenly believed meant 'I invent'. In a few days he had sketched out the main features of a new three-volume novel. On the 31st he began drafting and was soon hard at work every morning. To feed his imagination he read Scott and Byron. The fourth Godwinian novel would be the most ambitious of them all, linking the old truths of the Enlightenment with the new truths of the age of romanticism and repression. John Milton – he liked to point out as he neared his sixtieth birthday – had been past sixty when he wrote *Paradise Lost*.

On the day he got back to London he learned that Shelley and Mary with Claire had left the previous day for the Continent. A long letter from Shelley, sent from Dover on 3 May before the boat sailed, was mainly devoted to financial affairs. The valedictory paragraph however could have come straight from *Caleb Williams*.

I leave England – I know not, perhaps forever. I return, alone, to see no friend, to do no office of friendship, to engage in nothing that can soothe the sentiments of regret almost like remorse which under such circumstances every one feels who quits his native land. I respect you, I think well of you, better perhaps than of any other person whom England contains, you were the philosopher who first awakened and who still as a philosopher to a very great degree regulate my understanding. It is unfortunate for me that the part of your character which is least excellent should have been met by my convictions of what was right to do. But I have been too indignant, I have been unjust to you. – forgive me. – burn those letters which contain the records of my violence, and believe that however what you erroneously call fame and honour separate us, I shall always feel towards you as the most affectionate of friends.[11]

Shelley had now assumed the role of the misunderstood Godwinian hero, cut off from his fellow men, tempted to bitterness, but keeping misanthropy at bay by a forgiving remorse. Even the charge that his flawed hero puts his honour before his virtue was a cry of regretful pain not a taunt. But there was to be no transfiguration. Godwin wrote back immediately, but his letter was confined to financial matters and complaints at Shelley's thoughtlessness in disappearing at such an important moment in the financial negotiations. Other events, more important even than money, were now at the same time bringing them closer together and dividing them further.

CHAPTER 32

The Sins of the Mothers

On 27 June 1815 Godwin wrote one of his infrequent letters to Everina Wollstonecraft in Dublin. He always tried to keep the Wollstonecraft aunts up to date with the family news, and although the text of this particular letter has not survived, the main points can be readily surmised. No doubt he told her – in his usual guarded terms – of the return of the runaways in the autumn of 1814 and of his decision to have no direct dealings with Shelley. He may not have told her of Mary's baby who had died shortly after birth and of the recent – temporary – improvement in his financial prospects brought about by the £1,000 received from Shelley in May.

The letter was mainly about Fanny. Everina Wollstonecraft and Eliza Bishop were virtually the only blood relatives that Fanny knew. They kept a small school in Dublin, Miss Wollstonecraft teaching the boys and Mrs. Bishop the girls. Although their feelings for Godwin were lukewarm – and for his principles decidedly cold – they took a close interest in Fanny and visited London from time to time to see her. In the summer of 1814 Fanny had spent part of the summer with her aunts on holiday in Wales; it was from there that she had been hurriedly summoned back when Shelley ran off with Mary and Jane – or Claire as she was now known.

An adopted orphan with nothing to commend her but a lively intelligence, a good education, and a loving personality, Fanny was not well suited for a world which judged women by their faces and their fortunes.

Which is Humane? from *Lessons for Children*

Like her mother, she had always been liable to moods of depression. Even as a child, Godwin's housekeeper had complained, Fanny had been impossible to make happy. Godwin had long been worried about what would happen after he was gone. Now, when he believed that his own death could not be long delayed, he was increasingly anxious to see her settled. On 14 May 1815 Fanny reached her twenty-first birthday and it was time to make plans.

For years it had been tacitly expected that she would become a teacher, and where better to begin than in her aunts' school in Dublin? But the response to Godwin's letter was not as expected. Sixteen years earlier Godwin had damaged the aunts' reputations – and their incomes – by publishing his revelations about Fanny's mother. They had moved to Ireland in order to escape the Wollstonecraft scandal. Now, it was soon apparent, Everina was unwilling to risk a second disgrace. In August 1815 Eliza visited Skinner Street to say that the aunts were no longer willing to accept Fanny at their school.

The difficulty, they claimed, was money: they could not afford to keep her now that the money left by Mary Wollstonecraft had run out. But the real reason was Claire. Mary Godwin's ruin was complete, but as long as she remained with Shelley she was not a danger. Claire was a different matter. If, as Godwin and Mary Jane hoped, she could be persuaded to leave Shelley and Mary and return to Skinner Street, she would pass her taint to Fanny. Here was another consequence which Shelley had not considered when he and Mary had thoughtfully or thoughtlessly decided to take Claire with them on their elopement to France because she happened to speak French. They had not only ruined Claire but had deprived Fanny of a future.

In the *Memoirs* Godwin had described the puzzling social conventions which had caused some of Mary Wollstonecraft's women friends to shun her as an unmarried mother and then others to shun her later after she had married. Now the situation was being repeated in the next generation. The sins of the mothers were being visited on the daughters and the sins of the daughters were being visited on the sisters. Aunt Eliza's letter in which she explained her attitude to Fanny was sent to Shelley by Mary Jane as proof of the damage he was doing. But the young man was still disinclined to compromise. According to Mary Jane's account, Shelley replied that 'he would never regret having withdrawn one victim from the tyranny of prejudice',[1] but he offered to leave Fanny an independent income in his will. Mary Jane was surprised that 'such a harum scarum man could have been so thoughtful'.

There was only one solution that would give a hope of limiting the damage both for Fanny and for Claire. If Claire could be detached from Shelley and Mary and resettled away from Skinner Street for a time, then her own reputation might be gradually resuscitated, and the threat which she posed to Fanny might be contained. A few meetings with E. Oak, noted in the journal, may imply that Mary Jane was in touch with her own relatives. But how could Claire live away from Skinner Street without money, and who else could provide money but Shelley? As so often, Shelley was both the problem and the solution, and the Godwins had no alternative but to seek and take his help and his money.

On 13 May 1815 Claire left Shelley to live in Lynmouth. She left without warning and as soon as she was settled she wrote to Fanny to apologize. 'Pray be cheerful,' she urged in a passage which speaks loud for Fanny's state of mind at this time. 'Do not be melancholy, so young in life and so melancholy.' Mary Jane, in giving the news to Lady Mountcashell, explained imaginatively that she had arranged for Claire to stay with Mrs Bicknell, the widow of an army officer in the Indian army whom she had met while on a visit to her sister three years before. Her own family came from Devonshire – Mrs Pilcher lived in Exeter – and since the whole point of Claire's resettlement was to break the link with Shelley, there was little point in proclaiming – even to Mary Wollstonecraft's protégée – that Shelley himself had arranged it. For once Mary Jane's lie was both plausible and utilitarian. Shelley's advice to Claire as he said goodbye, as recorded by Mary Jane, was 'not to let her mind get corrupted by the world and above all not to eat any meat'.[2]

Claire was no home-loving old-fashioned girl like Fanny. More than either of Mary Wollstonecraft's two real daughters, she regarded herself as the successor of the famous feminist whose birthday she shared. After the continuous crises of recent months, life at Lynmouth was at first a relief. No longer needed for her French, there had been no obvious role in the ménage for a highly attractive sexually pulsating maiden sister with no income and nothing to do all day. At Lynmouth, however, the endless walks along the same seaside paths soon lost their appeal. Reading has its charms but at seventeen is no substitute for life. Claire knew that she had been sent into exile as a social quarantine and she hated it. As a Godwinian she knew too that she was being sacrificed to a false sense of honour for her own true virtue was undamaged. When therefore it was suggested that she might like to come back to London in the spring of 1816 to keep her mother company while Godwin was on his visit to

Edinburgh, she was delighted at the reprieve. It was now her turn to make a fateful decision.

From her reading of Godwin and Wollstonecraft Claire knew that in an unequal world women who wait to be helped wait a long time. If she was to break out of the humiliating role to which she was consigned she would have to take the initiative. Since her talent as a writer was limited – although she was trying hard – she decided she would enter the only other profession which traditionally enabled women to shake off their silken social fetters. Like Elizabeth Inchbald, Amelia Opie, Mrs Siddons, and several of Mary Wollstonecraft's other friends and contemporaries she decided to seek a career in the theatre.

Claire's first letter to Lord Byron began with the convention employed by a hundred petitioners:

An utter stranger takes the liberty of addressing you. It is earnestly requested that for one moment you pardon the intrusion and, laying aside every circumstance of who and what you are, listen with a friendly ear.[3]

Since Lord Byron was a member of the board of Drury Lane Theatre he might help launch her on a career on the stage. The initial aim being simply to secure an interview, Claire gave away little in her letter except to say that she stood on the edge of a precipice. She signed it 'E. Trefusis'.

The name would have rung a bell with Byron. While waiting for his ship to sail from Falmouth in 1809 he and Hobhouse had gone shooting in Lord Clinton's grounds. Byron knew Lord Clinton, and since Trefusis Hall was obliged by its position to maintain open house to noble travellers, it is highly likely that he had met Claire's putative aunt. Byron might also have known that Lord Clinton's sister, Ella Trefusis, was a poetess of some note whose name had been in the news for causing noblemen to fight duels.[4]

Claire had set eyes on Lord Byron once before. In the winter of 1811–12 Godwin had taken her – with Fanny and sometimes Mary also – to hear Coleridge's lectures on Shakespeare, and on 20 January 1812 Lord Byron had been in the audience. But, as Claire probably knew, the link had recently almost become a much closer one. When at the end of 1815 Murray sent Byron a cheque for £1,000 as payment for his two latest best-selling verse tales, Byron returned the money. As a nobleman with old chivalric values surviving amongst his liberalism, he declined to write for money. It was therefore an entirely appropriate suggestion made by Sir James Mackintosh through Samuel Rogers that if Byron did not want it, he might like to give some of it to Godwin whose novels he was known to admire, and he readily agreed to give £600. As he himself wrote:

I shall feel very glad if it can be of any use to Godwin – only don't let him be plagued – nor think himself obliged and all that – which makes people hate one another etc.[5]

The money was never paid. Murray while not exactly refusing to do what Byron asked, was reluctant to see ideas of political justice enter into commercial publishing. From an entry in Godwin's journal for 27 January 1816, 'Write to Mackintosh on Byron and Murray', it is evident that he knew of his bad luck. His letter, we may guess, probably maintained the tone of gracelessness on which his pride depended.

Byron's desk was already full of letters from admiring women. Some were from society ladies, others from servant girls. Several professed a deep interest in literature or asked for an opinion on their own poems. Lady Caroline Lamb, who had tried slashing her wrists and was still bombarding him with letters, had just published a three volume novel, *Glenarvon*, of which her affair with Byron was the main theme and embarrassment her main aim. Prostitutes, who in Regency England suffered from a chronic excess of supply over demand, regularly offered Byron their services. Not many months before, Harriet Wilson, the most desired courtesan of the day, had introduced herself to Byron in terms not dissimilar to Claire's. Claire's initial letter, knowing that she would be suspected of the same purpose, asked Byron to give her credit for a higher motive.

In the spring of 1816 Byron's name was the scandal of London. His marriage had recently ended abruptly amidst a torrent of public rumour, innuendo, and outrage. He was said to be having an affair with an actress called Mrs Mardyn, a story put about by his housekeeper called Mrs Clermont, a woman unconnected with her near namesake.[6] It was whispered by those close to the truth that he was more interested in boys than in women. Byron had also boasted to a few friends that he was having an affair with his half-sister Augusta, and Claire was to be amongst those who were shown letters which were said to provide corroboration. The man who a few months earlier was the darling of society was hissed at in the House of Lords. He was about to go into exile, ready to journey across Europe – by way of the cursed battlefield of Waterloo – in a replica of Napoleon's huge travelling carriage.

Claire's approach to Byron succeeded more through persistence than novelty. She wrote several long letters before she was given a personal earing. But when he agreed reluctantly to her request for an introduction to Drury Lane Claire immediately changed her tack. She was not so much interested in a career in the theatre, she protested, as in becoming an author, and she begged his opinion of a novel she was writing of which she included a long summary. It was to be a Godwinian – or Byronic – tale, but instead of the usual noble – but flawed – hero, the main character would be a woman. Brought up amongst the mountains and deserts the lady would obey no impulse but that of her own natural self. To most readers, according to Claire's literary plan, the story would be a normal anti-Jacobin warning against a free life, but atheists would know better and take the true message.

Claire told him her real name and of her connection with the author of *Queen Mab*. She said she believed in nature and detested marriage and she reminded Byron of her Godwinian upbringing. References to her 'theory' in one of her letters suggest that she urged on him the philosophy of perfectibility. She introduced him secretly to Mary Godwin and to Shelley who were amazed that she should have made the acquaintance of the most famous man in London. Claire wanted love and demanded sex. In a letter to Byron written shortly before her eighteenth birthday she begged to be allowed to 'offer you that which it has long been the passionate wish of my heart to offer you'. She suggested that they should go secretly to the country for a night, and although they probably did not go, Byron without much enthusiasm allowed himself to be seduced. Some time in the month of April Claire became pregnant.

Shelley, Mary, and Claire, the 'whole tribe of Otaheite philosophers'* as Byron called them picking up a phrase that Claire herself had used, left England on the day before Godwin got back to Skinner Street from Scotland. As far as he was aware it was just the latest example of Shelley's frantic unexplainable urge for journeying which had proved so disconcerting in the past. The next that he heard was that the three were again in Switzerland, attempting for a second time to capture the spirit of *Fleetwood* which had drawn them there in 1814. They settled in a villa outside Geneva, a few yards from the large house where Byron was staying, and the two poets quickly became friends.

---

* The common spelling at the time for Tahiti in the South Seas where sex was allegedly guiltless.

CHAPTER 33

The Wrongs of Woman

Things were very different from the last visit to Switzerland. Then they had been frightened and furtive: this time, because of the association with Byron, the Otaheite philosophers were famous. With the reopening of the Continent after the end of the war, Switzerland teemed with tourists. Stories of the poets and their women were soon the talk of every Alpine dinner table.

Geneva had been the home of Rousseau, of Voltaire, of Gibbon, the refuge of the Enlightenment ideas which the allies had fought for twenty years to destroy. With typical impulsiveness Shelley made a contract with a local publisher to prepare a French edition of *Political Justice* which was never started. In the registers of the hotels he proclaimed defiantly that he too was a democrat, a philanthropist and an atheist. At Chamonix he added the initials of his companions 'Mad. M. W. G.' and 'Mad. C. C.' and gave their destination as 'L'Enfer'.[1] A contemporary diarist called Smith meeting Sir John and Lady Shelley at dinner there – they were a family with no connection – noted that they 'were anxious not to be confounded with a Mr Percy Bysshe Shelley of Sussex and his lady whose names we had seen in every Inn's Register since we left Cluse, with the horrid avowal of *atheism* industriously subjoined'.[2]

Democrat meant political revolutionary – the word had been adopted in the 1790s by those opposed to the aristocrats. Philanthropist meant a follower of Thomas Spence who advocated the nationalization of land,

Which is Humane? from *Lessons for Children*

then the basis of most political and economic power.[3] Atheism was especially blasphemous amongst the grandeur of the mountains where according to long convention the correct feeling was an overpowering sense of religious awe. But when Shelley saw the effects of the glaciers of Mont Blanc which in recent years had advanced deep into the valleys and reduced whole communities to starvation, he was even more sure he was right.[4]

In politics and philosophy Byron only partly agreed with Shelley. Like Godwin he was more deist than atheist. And although he too was a lover of his fellow men, he was more famous as a lover of his fellow women. At Geneva it was customary for visitors to shudder at the sight of his Villa Diodati across the Bay. It stood on the hill well shrouded in trees not far from the Villa Chappuis near the lakeside where Shelley lived with Mary and Claire. Godwin had mentioned the house in his recent book as a place where John Milton had stayed: now it was reputed to offer free love and orgies.

From hired boats sightseers would strain with telescopes for a distant glimpse of the evil seducer. 'We passed the house in which Lord Byron lives in a sullen and disgraceful seclusion,' Smith noted. 'Besides his servants, his only companions are two wicked women.' The tablecloths hanging out to dry were, Byron said, taken to be their petticoats, and as if Claire Clairmont did not provide enough, he was said to venture out nightly to ravish the virgins of the city of Calvin.

Byron and Shelley enjoyed being shocking. As Regency men of fashion they thought it amusing to spin tall tales. The game was to see how far their listeners could be induced to gape. Bamming and humming it was called, slang for bamboozling and humbugging.[5] Mary Godwin and Claire Clairmont being young, female, naïve and literal-minded were prime targets, often failing to detect Byron's irony even when he was not trying to mislead. When Mary asked Byron about the Thyrza poems, which she had copied into her copy of *Queen Mab*, he told her that Thyrza was a real woman – now dead – whom he had loved before his journey to Greece. Thyrza, he said, had produced him two children; she had wanted marriage, but – a cruel hint – he would never marry a woman of mean birth and when he went to Greece she committed suicide; it was because she was buried at a crossroads that there was no memorial on her grave.

Shelley – although more openly serious than Byron – was also not averse to the same kind of fun. He told his cousin Medwin that the night before he left England he had been approached by a beautiful young married lady who offered to renounce her husband, her fortune, and her reputation for the author of *Queen Mab* – in Shelley's stories women usually wanted to embrace his principles as well as his body. The lady is said to have followed him to Switzerland, and gazed at him from afar through her spy glass. Later – with the indefatigable inefficiency of a pursuit story hero – she followed him to Italy and died of a broken heart.

Stories of the goings on in Switzerland soon found their way back to England. Already by the summer Fanny was aware of some of them, but with gossip the best bits are seldom written down. Elizabeth Inchbald, one of the ladies who had behaved with crushing correctness to Mary Wollstonecraft in 1797, wrote quizzically to Godwin in December that she 'had some curiosity to know whether you have a daughter or an adopted daughter or neither the one or the other in Switzerland at present'.[6] Later Byron's doctor Polidori published *The Vampyre* first in the *New Monthly Magazine* and then as a separate book which was prefaced by an 'Extract from a Letter from Geneva'. It included the following passage:

I must however free him [Lord Byron] from one imputation attached to him – of having in his house two sisters as the partakers of his revels. This is, like many other charges which have been brought against his lordship, entirely destitute of truth ... Mr Percy Bysshe Shelly, a gentleman well known for extravagance of doctrine, and for his daring, in their profession, even to sign himself with the title of [Atheist]* in the Album at Chamouny, having taken a house below in which he resided with Miss M. W. Godwin and Miss Clermont (the daughters of the celebrated Mr Godwin) they were frequently visitors at Diodati, and were often seen upon the lake with his Lordship, which gave rise to the report, the truth of which is here positively denied.

Godwin knew Polidori's father, a serious scholar who had helped him with his *Life of Chaucer*. He also knew the publishers. By writing letters he was able to have the passage withdrawn, but scandal thrives on denials.[7] Others hopefully put about a story that when Byron's and Shelley's boat was struck by a storm, Shelley threw himself on the deck, recanted his atheism, and in tears begged forgiveness from his Creator.[8] Similar stories had been circulated about Godwin in 1800.

The new scandals coincided with old scandals. In 1817 there was published and quickly reprinted the two volumes of *Memoirs of a Sexagenarian* by William Beloe, a regular diner-out at literary tables whom Godwin first met in 1794. His book consists of a series of sketches of his contemporaries written in style of blunt, heavy, and earnest anti-Jacobin

* Printed in Greek.

humour. Many of Godwin's friends of the 1790s came in for ridicule especially the ladies, Helen Maria Williams, Amelia Opie, 'Perdita' Robinson, Mary Hays, and others. The main target was Mary Wollstonecraft whose immoral life was sneeringly summarized from the account in Godwin's own book.

... She united herself to a man whose peculiarities of opinion were as strange and as preposterous as her own. Mark, reader, she did not marry him ... Her new lover had, on the subject of marriage, already and solemnly declared, that 'so long as he should seek to engross one woman to himself, and to prohibit his neighbour from proving his superior desert, and reaping the fruits of it, he would be guilty of the most odious of all monopolies'. The mind sickens at the continuation of a narrative, so replete with folly, and so offensive to everything which piety, delicacy, and human obligations render sacred.[9]

At Skinner Street there was little of the fun or the love which made flagrant liberalism so delightful to Byron and Claire, Shelley and Mary. When Godwin returned from his expedition to Scotland in May 1816 firm reality soon began to press. The money he had received the previous summer was already all gone. By the summer he was again being hounded by printers and other trade creditors of the unprofitable M. J. Godwin and Company. He had now only one bankable asset left: in his farewell letter from Dover in May, Shelley, while discouraging all hope of a substantial sum, did give a firm promise that £300 would be available later in the summer. On the strength of this promise Godwin was able to borrow £300 from a professional moneylender called Kingdon[10] but only on terms that were particularly unfavourable: he was required to give an on-demand bond which after the end of June could be called in at any time, but the expiry date passed and there was still no sign of Shelley's money.

The worry was unceasing. Godwin could not settle to write the novel he had begun so confidently after his holiday. Without money he could not write and without writing there was no money. He found himself unable to sleep, an unusual experience for one whose problem was normally in the other direction, but for a narcoleptic sleeplessness is a serious disturbance. He knew that any deviation from stoical calm would throw Mary Jane into panic, and on 3 July after failing to sleep for twenty-four hours he became ill with virtually continuous headaches.

On 7 July came the death of Sheridan who with Burke and Fox had been Godwin's boyhood hero and who had become his friend. Sheridan had lived his life with eighteenth-century extravagance, generosity, and style both as a politician and as a dramatist, but his last months were a warning to anyone tempted to admire or to emulate. Old and ill, all his possessions, even his books, were in the hands of a pawnbroker. His pictures were sold including the portrait of his wife by Reynolds. In the freezing March of 1816 one of the greatest geniuses of the age spent three days in a debtors' prison followed by as many days weeping when he was released.

Sheridan's funeral was attended by an array of royal dukes, Whig aristocracy, politicians, writers and dramatists, but none grieved as sincerely as Godwin. In the week that followed he visited the grave several times. His own end would be much the same, he guessed. A few days later the journal records an unexplained visit to Aylesbury jail, perhaps to say goodbye to a friend dying of debt.

When life is intolerable the mind can be relieved by thoughts of death. It was one lesson his own parents and grandparents had never neglected. On 17 July we find him reading Fox's *Book of Martyrs*, a Janeway for grown-ups, one of the books by which his ancestors had sought to explain the cruel and unfair world. Simpkin and Marshall who were promoting the 1816 editions of *Caleb Williams* and *St. Leon* also republished Janeway's book. In the conditions of post-Waterloo England, seventeenth-century comforts were all that many people could expect. Godwin withdrew ever deeper into a spiritual hibernation, torpid and subdued, which offered some analgesic protection to himself if not to others.

In the middle of August Aunt Everina and Aunt Eliza arrived in London. At family conferences on 19 August and 30 August the future of Fanny was discussed. Mary Wollstonecraft's brother Edward was present at one of them. Everina was stern, inflexible, and disagreeable, and although Eliza was gentler, she normally submitted to her sister. Fanny, who was now alone at Skinner Street with Godwin and Mary Jane, knew that she was regarded as a problem, but to a person of her character and upbringing the solution was almost as unattractive. In a letter to Switzerland she told Mary and Shelley that she would prefer their way of life, but if the hint was noticed it was not taken up. Fanny, it seemed, could neither leave nor remain. She was not to be permitted to earn her own living but must continue as an extra mouth to share the cold poverty of Skinner Street. By 23 September when Godwin called on the aunts after nearly a month's gap it had been decided that Fanny should visit them for a holiday – or a probation – after which their decision would be reconsidered. They left London the next day.

Earlier in the month, Shelley, Mary, and Claire returned to England, summoned back much against their wishes by Sir Timothy's lawyer. Claire who was now heavily pregnant with Byron's child was settled at Bath as 'Mrs Clairmont' with Mary and her baby and a Swiss nurse. Shelley himself restlessly journeyed to and from London. During his absence he had continued to correspond with Godwin about money and there seemed to be some hope that after all a large sum might be raised. On a visit to London on 10 September Fanny went to his lodgings to give him the news from Skinner Street and explain the worry over Kingdon's bond. It therefore came as a complete surprise when on 3 October a letter arrived from Shelley which had an air of finality.

I am exceedingly sorry to dissappoint you again. I cannot send you £300 because I have not £300 to send. I enclose within a few pounds the wrecks of my late negotiation with my father. In truth, I see no hope of my attaining speedily to such a situation of affairs as should enable me to discharge my engagements towards you . . .

There followed a detailed explanation of what Shelley had tried to do and why he had not succeeded. The letter concluded:

Shall I conclude this unwelcome letter by assuring you of the continuance of those dispositions concerning your welfare which I have so often expressed? Shall I say that I am ready to cooperate in whatever plan may be devised for your benefit?[11]

Enclosed was a cheque for £200 made payable to William Godwin.

'Shelley's letter came like a thunderclap,' Fanny wrote in a letter to Mary sent on the day of its arrival. 'I watched Papa's countenance while he read it (not knowing the contents), and I perceived that Shelley had written in his most desponding manner.' Needlessly accepting the blame for any misunderstanding on her own inadequate shoulders, she explained again the seriousness of Kingdon's threats. She also felt that she may have given a wrong impression about Mary Jane's attitude.

I either related my story very ill to Shelley, or he, paying little regard to what I might say, chose to invent a story out of his own imagination for your amusement, which you too have coloured to your own mind and made what was *purely accidental*, and which only occurred *once* a story after the manner of 'Caleb Williams' viz. of 'Mamma pursuing you like a hound after foxes'.

Fanny went on to give news of Harriet Shelley which Mary Jane had learned during a recent visit to Bracknell.

These things I thought it right to mention to Shelley when he said you thought of settling in that neighbourhood. I told him these, and I still think they originated with your servants and Harriet, who, I know, has been very industrious in spreading false reports against you. I, at the same time advised Shelley always to keep French servants, and he then seemed to think it a good plan. You are very careless, and are forever leaving your letters about.[12]

There is no mention of what the stories actually were, but they can be easily guessed – that Godwin had encouraged Mary to set her cap at Shelley and that he had accepted money as his price for condoning their running off together. It was the old joke that he had sold his daughters.

Fanny's letter is long and loving, concerned to offer explanations and to avoid being unfair to anyone. As ever she is the peacemaker drawing on to herself the anxiety, the guilt, and the frustrations of both sides. Godwin knew the letter was being sent and that it would be read by Shelley as well as by Mary. Indeed the formal letter which he sent to Shelley by the same post is otherwise scarcely understandable. It needs to be quoted in full.

I return your cheque because no consideration can induce me to utter a cheque drawn by you and containing my name. To what purpose makes a disclosure of this sort to your banker? I hope you will send a duplicate of it by the post which will reach me on Saturday [or] Monday. You may make it payable to Joseph Hume or Jas. Martin or any other name in the whole Directory. I should prefer its being payable to Mr Hume. He and Kingdon will of course be greatly disappointed at the reduction in the amount. I will negotiate myself out of the danger of a prison if I can.

You know so well my general situation that it is almost superfluous to remind you of it. I am making the greatest efforts in writing a novel which (*when finished*) will I hope be considerably advantageous to me. But the great point for that purpose is to keep my mind free and disengaged and to defend myself from those disasters which forever threaten me from the side of Hume's acceptances and the discounters (Taylor of Norwich in particular) who had those acceptances; and from these disasters you only can relieve me.

It is of course a thing most deeply pressing on my mind to understand your motions and locality. If I could depend upon your not suddenly leaving Eng. with that abruptness and unexpected rapidity which I have twice experienced, I think I could attain to temporary tranquility on everything else. But you say not a syllable on this subject, nor does Mary (as Fanny informs me) in a letter from her this day: and alas, if you did, you know so little of your own motions![13]

Godwin is condescending, sardonic, and exasperated. He addresses Shelley like a spoiled child beyond correction and beyond redemption. Characteristically his first concern is now about appearances rather than substance – a far cry from the fearless avowal of truth which the author of *Political Justice* had once advocated as the only way to advance perfectibility. After twenty years of misinterpretation and misrepresentation his moral calculus may now have given too heavy a weighting to other people's reactions. He may have too often preferred utility to truth. But he defended the remnants of political justice with the same asserting pugnaciousness.

Shelley was not put out. Although more inclined to flaunt and exaggerate his opinions than to conceal them, he had always deferred to Godwin's susceptibilities. If the older man wished to maintain a fiction that their relationship was formal and financial only, he had no choice but to accept. If the philosopher had slid back – or been driven back – from his original principles, that was a matter for sadness and regret. It was not a reason to deny him the money or slide back himself. Shelley obediently made out a new cheque in the name of the financier Joseph Hume. It is dated 7 October and probably reached Skinner Street by return of post either on the 8th or the 9th.[14]

But this time the strain on Skinner Street was too much. On the 7th (or perhaps the 6th) but certainly before the new cheque arrived, Fanny Godwin left Skinner Street. She took the coach which connected London with Bath and Bristol. Although the point is not confirmed, it seems likely that she was on her way to Ireland to her aunts. Two days later a letter from Fanny arrived at Skinner Street which had been sent on the 8th from Bristol. Its message was so alarming that Godwin at once set out on the Bristol coach. On 9 October Shelley and Mary who were at Bath also received a similar letter from Fanny addressed from Bristol. Shelley went there immediately but returned at two in the morning having been unable to find out anything. He went again the next day and both Godwin and he were in Bristol on the 10th making separate inquiries, although they did not meet.

They were too late. On the night of 9 October Fanny arrived at Swansea and checked into a hotel. When she did not reappear the next morning, the door of her room was forced and she was found dead. She had taken an overdose of laudanum. A farewell note was found.

I have long determined that the best thing I could do was to put an end to the existence of a being whose birth was unfortunate and whose life has only been a series of pain to those persons who have hurt their health in endeavouring to promote her welfare. Perhaps to hear of my death will give you pain, but you will soon have the blessing of forgetting that such a creature ever existed as

The signature was torn off, probably by a member of the hotel staff who knew the indignities which the law commanded for suicides. One of the identification clues was that her stays were marked MW.[15] It was appropriate that the home-loving Fanny should have assumed the female fetters which her mother had thrown off. Claire Clairmont caused some scandal by never wearing them.[16] As one of the notes to *Queen Mab* declared, 'How would morality, dressed up in stiff stays and finery, start from her own disgusting image should she look in the mirror of nature!' Godwin simply noted 'Swansea' in his journal.

In the desperate days before the truth was known Godwin and Shelley had shared in the anxiety, they had shared in the search, and now they shared the anguish. Both men were ill with grief. However, by removing herself from the scene Fanny helped to bring about the long hoped for reconciliation. In a letter to Shelley written as soon as he got back to London, Godwin offered no recriminations:

I did indeed expect it.
I cannot but thank you for your strong expressions of sympathy. I do not see, however, that that sympathy can be of any service to me; but it is best. My advice and earnest prayer is that you would avoid anything that leads to publicity. Go not to Swansea; disturb not the silent dead; do nothing to destroy the obscurity she so much desired that now rests upon the event. It was, as I said, her last wish; it was the motive that led her from London to Bristol and from Bristol to Swansea.

I said that your sympathy could be of no service to me, but I retract the assertion; by observing what I have just recommended to you, it may be of infinite service. Think what is the situation of my wife and myself, now deprived of all our children but the youngest; so do not expose us to those idle questions, which to a mind in anguish is one of the severest of all trials. We are at this moment in doubt whether, during the first shock, we shall not say that she is gone to Ireland to her aunt, a thing that had been in contemplation. Do not take from us the power to exercise our own discretion. You shall hear again to-morrow.

What I have most of all in horror is the public papers, and I thank you for your caution, as it might act on this.

We have so conducted ourselves that not one person in our home has the smallest apprehension of the truth. Our feelings are less tumultuous than deep. God only knows what they may become. The following is one expression in her letter to us, written from Bristol on Tuesday: 'I depart immediately to the spot from which I hope never to remove'.[17]

The circumstances of Fanny's death were hushed up. Henry Crabb Robinson, who heard about the suicide a few years later from Mary Hays, commented that it was only one of the many catastrophes that could be blamed on the errors in Godwin's early writings.[18] Soon afterwards another suicide occurred where the comment was more appropriate. On

10 December the body of Harriet Shelley was taken from the Serpentine: she was heavily pregnant and had been dead for three weeks.

For the last few months of her life she had been living away from her father's house in Chapel Street, where she had moved after Shelley left her. According to an account which Godwin believed, she had lived first with a Major Ryan then with a Major Maxwell, officers in a regiment stationed at Knightsbridge. Others including Shelley were to say that she lived with a man called Smith who was a stable groom. In the harsh language of the day she had become a 'prostitute', not somebody who plied her body for hire but a 'fallen woman' forced into economic dependence on a man to whom she was not legally married. She too left a suicide note – addressed to her sister Eliza and to Shelley – and the circumstances of her death were hushed up, her family arranging for her to be buried under the false name of Harriet Smith.[19]

Shelley had married her reluctantly in accordance with the principles of *Fleetwood* and he had left her eagerly in accordance with the principles of *Political Justice*. When married to her he had included a note in *Queen Mab* declaring that marriage is a form of legalized prostitution, but in talking of her last months he too now used the ugly word in its conventional sense. Of all the victims of Godwin's ideas Harriet's case was the most pathetic. But this tragedy, like Fanny's, also had its place in the emerging reconcilation. In the long struggle between Shelley and Godwin, between the young and the old, between the freedom of nature and the constraints of institutions, pragmatism was about to win another notable victory over philosophy.

CHAPTER 34

Magic

On 16 December Godwin received a letter from Shelley telling him of Harriet's death. He replied the next day and on the 18th Shelley called at Skinner Street and spent two hours with Mary Jane. It was the first time he had been allowed across the threshold since July 1814, and Godwin himself still refused to receive him, leaving the talking to Mary Jane.

The talk – negotiation would be a better word – made progress. On Christmas Eve Godwin wrote to Mary, the first time he had allowed himself any direct dealings with his daughter since she ran away. The letter was about marriage. As it happened Mary Jane had been sounding out some of Godwin's lawyer friends on the possibility of a divorce and remarriage only a few days before the news of Harriet's death arrived.[1] As it happened too, four members of the Oak family and Mrs Elwes were having their Christmas dinner at Skinner Street on the day the decisions were made. Although none of them had enjoyed their own marriages they all knew the alternatives. On the day after Christmas Godwin wrote again to Shelley suggesting a second meeting. On the next day Shelley called again and this time Godwin allowed himself to be at home. On the following day Godwin, Mary Jane, and Shelley all went to see Mary together. Father and daughter met for the first time since the elopement and everything was settled.

Shelley had been rereading *Political Justice* and he remained deeply

The Way to be Happy, from *Lessons for Children*

opposed to marriage in principle. But he had already made up his mind to marry Mary if this would help him gain legal custody of his children. He had been advised that if Harriet's family contested his claim, the court would award him custody in such circumstances, but he still hoped to avoid a contest. His contingent and half-hearted proposal of marriage to Mary, buried in a letter about other matters, recalls Godwin's shamefaced justification of his marriage to her mother and outgodwins Godwin in its combination of double negative and unfortunate metaphor.

At least it is consoling to know that if the contest should arise it would have its termination in your nominal union with me. – that after having blessed me with a life a world of real happiness, a mere form appertaining to you will not be barren of good.[2]

Shelley acknowledged to Godwin that he had contracted to marry his daughter, but asked for a year's delay out of respect for Harriet. According to Mary Jane, who was always more reliable at remembering attitudes than at recording facts, negotiations were deadlocked until Mary rose from her corner and put her hand on Shelley's shoulder. 'Of course you are free to do what you please', she said, 'and I am free to act as I like and I have to tell you, dear Shelley, if you do not marry me, I will not live – I will destroy myself and my child with me.' It was a neat playback of the threat Shelley is said to have made at the time of the first elopement, but after the suicides of Patrickson, Fanny, and Harriet, it no longer sounded like a literary pose taken from a gothic novel.[3] Mary had been rereading *The Rights of Woman*. She knew she was again pregnant – for the third time since St Pancras Churchyard although only one child was still alive. Like her mother she too knew that the difficulties of an unmarried mother of two were more than double those of an unmarried mother of one.

On 30 December 1816, Percy Bysshe Shelley and Mary Wollstonecraft Godwin were married in accordance with the rites of the Church of England. Godwin and Mary Jane were in attendance. The date was a few days after the anniversary of Godwin's marriage to Mary Jane Clairmont fifteen years before, and as then false declarations had to be made about residence as well as on the greater matters. Both Godwin and Shelley had now been married twice. With the booster ceremonies that both men had undergone in order to remove legal doubts they had now submitted to hypocritical social validation three times each. Three of their four brides had been pregnant at the time.

The effects of the ritual were, in Shelley's word, magical.[4] They were also instantaneous. Mr and Mrs Shelley – as Godwin now styled them according to custom – dined and supped at Skinner Street on their wedding day and spent the whole of the next day there. On 2 January Godwin recorded uniquely in his journal, 'vehemently impassioned dream; imprecation'. Earlier in the day there had been a 'slight access of disease' but there was no attack. In one disturbed night Godwin shed two and a half years of hostility, anger, fear and guilt.

In January the couple stayed overnight at Skinner Street for two successive nights in a matrimonial bed, the final symbol of family acceptance. Soon Shelley was popping in and out every few days as he had before July 1814. His letters were addressed to 'My dear Godwin' and dotted with references to 'my dear friend'. They were replied to with equal warmth. Henry Crabb Robinson noted that Godwin was in high spirits although with a touch of the manic excitement that accompanies relief. There was no more talk of suicide.

Love between man and woman, Shelley was now inclined to argue, was the key to progress which Godwin's system had overlooked, the missing link between reason and sensibility, the creative force that could redirect the necessitarian chain. Early in 1817 he took a house in Marlow where at last he and Mary could find some peace together. It was far enough away from London to be rural, but not too remote to prevent regular meetings with financiers. Shelley installed two statues in the garden which were made by Leigh Hunt's wife. Apollo, the god of poetry, and Venus, the goddess of sex, they represented his preoccupations.

On his frequent visits to London Shelley sometimes stayed at Skinner Street, sometimes at Leigh Hunt's house in Hampstead. On 24 January Godwin made the long walk there to discuss some piece of business, but his son-in-law was not at home. Not for the first or last time Shelley had carelessly failed to keep an appointment and he had to be given a scolding. Soon Mary Jane was taking offence at not being given her proper respect. Within two months of the death of Harriet Shelley, things were back to normal.

It was Mary Jane who gave the news to Constable who was pressing for delivery of Godwin's promised novel.

I have now the pleasure to announce that Mr Godwin's daughter Mary has entered the married state with Mr Percy Bysshe Shelley, eldest son of Sir Timothy Shelley, Baronet, of Field Place, Horsham, Sussex. We are endeavouring to forget preceding sorrows and to enjoy the flattering prospects which seem to present themselves. The young couple have been in town in several weeks, principally under our roof, and my poor nerves begin to cry quarter from the bustle and feasting occasioned by the event.[5]

Hull Godwin, Godwin's brother in Norfolk, who supplied the turkey and the ham for the feasting, was told the outcome but not the background. As Godwin wrote in one of his infrequent letters:

... Her husband is the eldest son of Sir Timothy Shelley, of Field Place, in the County of Sussex, Baronet. So that, according to the vulgar ideas of the world, she is well married, and I have great hopes the young man will make her a good husband. You will wonder, I daresay, how a girl without a penny of fortune should meet with so good a match. But such are the ups and downs of the world. For my part, I care but little, comparatively, about wealth, so that it should be her destiny in life to be respectable, virtuous, and contented.[6]

A tone of self-satisfaction is also audible in his letter to William Baxter of Dundee, one of the men who had sought his acquaintanceship in the 1790s. Mary had been staying with Baxter's daughter Isabel in 1814 before she met Shelley, and after the elopement Baxter refused to allow his daughter to remain her friend. Now Godwin invited him to reconsider.

Time has of late been very pregnant of events in my family. My first information you will be very glad to hear. Mrs Shelley died in November last and on the 30th December Shelley led my daughter to the altar. I shall always look with poignant regret upon the preceding events but you can scarcely imagine how great a relief this has brought to mine and Mrs Godwin's mind. Mary has now (most unexpectedly) acquired a status and character in society. Shelley is not without faults, but he is also not without many good and even noble qualities; and if he had come into my family as a bachelor I should unquestionably have regarded his choice of my daughter as a subject of congratulation.[7]

Godwin's choice of the pregnancy metaphor was, as often, unfortunate. It was also unnecessarily sincere to rejoice so openly in Harriet Shelley's death. In a new spirit of solidarity he went on to accuse her of 'levity' and 'unfaithfulness' perhaps hoping by so doing to exonerate the same behaviour in Shelley. But the Baxter family were not assuaged. All contact between Isabel and Mary Shelley remained forbidden by Isabel's husband David Booth. Like Mary Wollstonecraft Godwin, Shelley was a threat to virtue even after social legitimation.

Shelley did not share in the general sense of satisfaction. He disliked Godwin's new unctuous tone and he was ashamed of his own retreat from principle. On 17 January 1817 he wrote to Lord Byron to tell him that Claire Clairmont had given birth to his daughter on the 12th. He told of the death of Harriet and of the 'severe anguish' he had felt in the autumn at the death of someone whom he did not name – Fanny Godwin. But he said nothing about Mary Godwin or about his remarriage. It was left to Mary who sent a letter in the same package full of the same news to note coyly at the end:

Another incident has also occurred which will surprise you, perhaps; It is a little piece of egotism in me to mention it – but it allows me to sign myself – in assuring you of my esteem and sincere friendship Mary W. Shelley.[8]

Shelley himself slipped the news into a second letter sent to Lord Byron on 23 April which explained that Byron's new daughter had been sent into the country and that Claire had 'resumed her maiden character'.

. . . Indeed all these precautions have now become more necessary than before, on account of our renewed intimacy with Godwin, which has taken place in consequence of my marriage with Mary, a change (if it be a change) which had principally her feelings in respect to Godwin for its object. I need not inform you that this is simply with us a measure of convenience, and that our opinions as to the importance of this pretended sanction, and all the prejudices connected with it, remain the same.[9]

In letting out his shameful secret in April 1817 Shelley was as dilatory and defensive as Godwin himself had been when he married Mary's mother twenty years before.

The magic of the marriage ritual also relieved the money crisis. Shelley suggested that, with patience, the successful post-obit operation of 1814 could be repeated. Creditors stayed their hand in deference both to Godwin's bereavement and to his improved financial prospects, and Shelley arranged enough advances of money to keep him afloat. In February Shelley made a new will naming Byron and Peacock as his executors in an elaborate arrangement by which he left £6,000 to Claire and the bulk of the unentailed estates to Mary. Marriage, it was explained in *Political Justice*, is primarily an economic institution.

The magic of the marriage ritual did not however solve everything. The Westbrooks, Harriet's family, refused to hand over custody of Shelley's two children and when the case was taken to court, they argued that Shelley was an unsuitable father. In a deposition their lawyers noted that he had left Harriet and unlawfully cohabited with Mary Godwin, 'daughter of a Mr Godwin the author of a work called Political Justice'. They also drew attention to the avowals of atheism and the condemnation of marriage in *Queen Mab*. Consultations about Shelley's reply took place at Skinner Street with Basil Montagu among those giving legal advice.

Shelley's own lawyer advised that the best approach was to shrug off the charges. The poem had been written when he was nineteen. Only about twenty copies had been distributed other than to friends. The court should be invited 'not to think very seriously of this boyish and silly, but certainly unjustifiable publication of Queen Mab'. The best defence was to turn it all into a joke. Shelley, the philosophical opponent of marriage, had at the age of twenty-five just been married for the second time – 'he is no sooner liberated from the despotick chains which he speaks of with so much horror and contempt than he willingly forges a new set'.

But the young man who had been advised by the priests to tell a lie as the neatest way of avoiding expulsion from Oxford was not disposed to take similar advice from lawyers. His deposition to the court admitted openly that he disagreed with marriage in principle and had broken the established rules in practice. It was a traditional liberty that people who did not agree with the law were free to say so, and divorce had a long and respectable history. He had not been out to flout authority for the sake of doing so: in the circumstances (including a hint that he could say a great deal about Harriet) he had done his best.

There survives a fragment of the draft of the document in the handwriting of Mary Shelley with a number of comments and amendments written in by Godwin.[10] Godwin and Shelley had both always insisted that it was the contemporary European institution of marriage they objected to not marriage itself. They both believed that an unsuccessful marriage should be terminable by either the man or the woman. In the document Shelley proposed to say frankly that it was because he was legally married to Harriet that he had been unable to make Mary his legal wife – in another Godwinian phrase he explained that his preference for Mary 'arose from no light or frivolous attachment, but such as in their sense of the word as well as mine I wish to express by the word wife'. But the more worldly-wise Godwin suggested deleting nearly all the implied references to theory. With the help of a few other deft amendments he swung round the whole approach. Shelley's version started from his principles: Godwin's version started with the marriage laws. Shelley's version tried to explain to the court why he had done what he had done: Godwin was content to seek mitigation.

Whatever the final version the court were not impressed. There was a suggestion that a criminal prosecution for blasphemous libel might be ordered against the author of Queen Mab. In deciding against Shelley, the court ordered that his two children should be brought up at his expense by a provincial clergyman in accordance with the doctrines of the Church of England. Charles – who was three – was to be given a classical education and in due course sent to university and fitted for a profession. Ianthe – who was five – was also to be educated, although without neglecting feminine accomplishments such as music and the 'homely employments' of fancy work and sewing. Her reading was to carefully controlled, with novels largely forbidden and Shakespeare to be read only in Dr Bowdler's bowdlerized edition. There was to be no wearing of fashionable clothes which revealed 'an apparent abandonment of all feelings of feminine delicacy and decency.' Ianthe, it was decided, was to spend her life in stays.

Godwin who in 1793 proclaimed his contempt for the family as yet another corrupting institution was in practice the most careful, considerate, and loving of fathers. Shelley who was forever proclaiming his love of family and offering to adopt other people's children was, like Godwin's parents, more interested in children's beliefs than in their lives. He never attempted to exercise the rights of monthly access to Ianthe and Charles which the court allowed, and he never saw them again.

Nor could the magic of the marriage ceremony solve the problem of Claire Clairmont. Even if Byron had been legally free to marry, there could never be social validation for Claire or for her baby as she and Byron had each conscientiously explained to the other before they first tumbled together on his sitting room sofa in London. A huge fortune was due to revert to Byron as a result of his marriage even though he was parted from his wife. In any case peers of the realm – however strong their admiration for liberal writers – did not marry their penniless step-daughters. If there had ever been love it had gone. Byron refused to have any further dealings with the woman who had seduced him, and was now living a wildly promiscuous life in Italy. In letters read aloud to the literary men at John Murray's he boasted week after week of his ladies and his whores.

A fiction was maintained that Claire was looking after a baby on behalf of friends. She made a few visits to Skinner Street although without the baby, and Godwin met them both when on a visit to Marlow. After one visit he wrote approvingly to Mary Jane that her daughter was again accepting proper feminine restraints.

... she wears stays, and dresses herself every day becomingly and with care: this at the entreaty of Shelley and Mary.[11]

It is not known when Godwin first knew that Allegra was Claire's baby. If he suspected, he probably believed that Shelley was the father. Shelley had certainly had opportunities and – at certain times at least – had believed in unfettered free love for both sexes. David Booth, Isabel Baxter's husband, who met Shelley at Skinner Street in the autumn of 1817, once with Mary and once with Claire, believed that he alternated between the two. When he met Shelley and Claire at Skinner Street he noticed that she left with him at the end of the evening. She disliked sleeping in a room by herself, she explained, because of the ghosts.[12] She refused absolutely to spend a single night at Skinner Street.

Leigh Hunt, with whom she was at this time lodging with her baby, was also known to be as strongly attached to his wife's sister as to his wife. Like Shelley he was seen sometimes with one, sometimes with the other, and sometimes with both. His house in Hampstead teemed with legitimate children – the latest was christened Percy Bysshe Shelley Leigh Hunt and there were eventually to be eleven – but Hunt made little secret that the desire he felt for the sister-in-law was only kept in place with difficulty. At least one friend, bored with his interminable agonizings, told him bluntly to follow Shelley's example and take her to bed. But although Hunt fawned and flirted, he never got further than assuring Bessie that he would marry her the moment Mary Anne died.[13]

Shelley, Leigh Hunt, and Byron were all suspected of breaking one of the most powerful of European marriage and kinship customs. Incest was not at the time a criminal offence, but it remained a deeply dreaded taboo punishable by the church courts. Byron was believed to have had a sexual affair with his half-sister Augusta – whom he hardly knew until they were both grown up. But the forbidden degrees were not confined to blood relatives. In 1816 a church court punished a man for marrying the daughter of his deceased wife by a previous marriage, Leigh Hunt's interest in Bessie was almost as shocking as Shelley's alleged alternating between Mary and Claire.

Whatever Godwin knew or suspected about Claire, he let matters ride. Having unexpectedly rescued the reputation of one daughter, he did not inquire too diligently about the other. If Shelley was indeed the father of her child at least he had the sense not to flaunt it, and Godwin was content to avert his eyes in a new silent conspiracy. If patience had rescued Mary, discretion might still save Claire. It was not a heroic stance for a philosopher of sincerity. But after two generations of the wrongs of woman so densely concentrated in one family, his attitude was kind and it was useful. It may even have been right.

Of all the enthusiasms which Shelley had taken up in his brief career, free love was the most dangerous. As Hazlitt wrote, none of Shelley's absurdities was more absurd than his belief that society could be reformed by 'introducing the domestic government of the Nayrs'.[14] European marriage might be in need of liberalization, but could it ever be replaced by the freedom of nature? At the end of 1819 Godwin's journal records a number of visits to Sir Joseph Banks, the great naturalist and explorer who had sailed with Captain Cook on the voyages of discovery to the South Seas. Banks, who was now an old man, may have been able to tell him something about the real Tahiti and the customs of its happy beautiful people. But it is clear from the journal that Godwin went in order to meet someone he called 'Nairman'. It seems likely that a real live member of the tribe was in London and Godwin was doing his own anthropology.[15]

If so, he would not have found his research easy. A traveller who visited the area in the early eighteenth century had reported that each Nair lady had up to twelve husbands who lived with her by turns, in strict order of seniority, for ten days at a time. A more recent traveller put the matter a different way. Members of the higher castes did not marry but enjoyed all the Nairesses in common – a privilege which visiting Europeans also laid claim to by reason of their superiority to Brahmins. According to one report, if a peasant had the misfortune to touch a lady of the warrior class, he would immediately be put to death along with all his relatives and the lady herself. According to others, virginity was regarded as a bar to Paradise so that – as with Christian baptism – a rite sometimes had to be hurriedly performed by a priest before it was too late. Two facts alone seemed to be established with reasonable certainty: no Nair was much interested in who his or her biological father was provided that his mother had a secure social status, and all property was held and inherited on the female side. In Malabar as in Sussex marriage was primarily an institution for passing family wealth undivided to the next generation.

CHAPTER 35

Renaissance

The reconciliation transformed Godwin's life. By the summer of 1817 he was happier and more active than he had been for years. As he repeatedly told Mary, he hoped to become young again and it seemed to be happening. Old friends were looked up and new friends welcomed. Invitations to dinner were accepted and the Godwins occasionally offered modest dinners of their own. Soon Skinner Street was again full of visitors and conversation. There were no attacks of cataplexy.

Sometimes Shelley and Mary were to be found at Skinner Street but although older friends were eager to meet the young man who had caused such trouble, it was Godwin that they came to see. Charles and Mary Lamb called more frequently for chat and whist. Hazlitt and Robinson were again to be found at the fireside. Robert Owen of Lanark called when he was in London although he did not meet Shelley. Coleridge, now a closely supervised drug addict, very occasionally made the journey from Highgate, although the friends who looked after him were always fearful of what he might do if he strayed too far. Even the disdainful Wordsworth paid a few calls in 1818. Of the friends of pre-1814 days only Mrs Boinville and Tom Turner kept their distance, fearing perhaps a renewed outbreak of free love if Shelley again met Cornelia.

As ever Godwin attracted Americans – a senator called Hunter, a university professor called Verplank. The eccentric Godwinian of the 1790s, James Ogilvie, who strode around the United States in a Roman

The Eagle and the Snake, from Bewick's *British Birds*

toga was often accompanied by the young poet John Howard Payne – author of 'Home, sweet home'. In 1819 it was the turn of Washington Irving, a young writer whom Godwin greatly admired. In later years after Shelley's death John Howard Payne was to offer love – and perhaps marriage – to Mary Shelley, and Mary was to offer the same to Washington Irving.

Once more Godwin was doing what he was best at, talking, educating, clashing mind on mind, coaxing truth from her hiding place. He now had worthy opponents with whom to debate the issues of the age and the problems of eternity. He had successors ready to carry the message to the next generation. A young American visitor George Ticknor, who was invited to dinner at Skinner Street noted Lamb's gentle humour, Leigh Hunt's passion, Curran's volubility, Hazlitt's sharpness, and Godwin's 'great head full of cold brains'.[1] Like others he was surprised to find the author of *Caleb Williams* so apparently lacking in emotion. Godwin's cool and dogged conversation, Ticknor wrote in his diary, was 'as far removed from everything feverish and exciting as if his head had never been filled with anything but geometry'. It was a good thing, he noted in an illuminating aside, that he had a strong-willed wife to give his obstinacy a shake from time to time.

In the autum of 1817, another sign of renaissance, Godwin took on a new pupil, the seventeen-year-old Henry Blanch Rosser. He was the first – apart from Shelley – since the death of Patrickson in 1814, and he was to receive moral conversation and instructive letters for several years. Rosser came from a familiar mould. As he wrote from Cambridge:

When I review my past life, and look for the causes that have operated to mould me into what I am, I always recur to the time when I first read 'Political Justice', September 1815. I should not now be in Cambridge had I not read it. How doubly fortunate then am I in the friendship of the man to whose book I – the world – owe so much.[2]

Godwin by now had a sizeable collection of such letters, each one a proof of the validity of his method and of the wide – although scattered – range of his influence. An American student, Joseph Beavan also came for regular lessons, and Godwin's letters of advice to him were extensively reprinted in the United States.

Godwin again started to haunt the bookshops, centres of political and literary chat. A new friend in the trade, Thomas Rodd of Fleet Street held open house; Godwin started to visit him at least once a week as with Joseph Johnson in the old days. On a visit to Perry, editor of the *Morning*

Chronicle, he met William Blake after a long absence. The talk was probably of Mary Wollstonecraft for the next day Godwin took down her *Original Stories* from the shelf to look at Blake's illustrations.[3]

Eighteen-seventeen was the year of the three trials of the bookseller William Hone charged with blasphemous libel for publishing anti-Christian parodies. As a young man Hone had been much influenced by the New Philosophy, and it was a Godwinian gesture to decide to conduct his own defence. A public subscription was raised to help meet the costs, and a list of the main subscribers was later printed. It reads like a roll call of Godwin's friends including Shelley, Leigh Hunt, and 'the ghost of Horne Tooke'. Godwin himself paid something although his contribution was too small to be recorded in the printed list.[4] Hone's test of the power of truth was more successful than Gerrald's had been. His acquittal was a victory for freedom comparable to those in the treason trials of 1794. Godwin called on him personally to offer congratulations, and although he was out the call was returned and Hone came to Skinner Street. According to a later story Hone told the philosopher that he deeply admired his essay on truth, but Godwin was so afraid of being teased by the famous humorist that he did not realize that the compliment was genuinely meant.[5]

The younger men, whether friends of Godwin or friends of Shelley, had all read *Political Justice* and *Caleb Williams*. Most of them also knew *St. Leon* and Godwin's other works and were aware that he was working on a new novel. *The Iron Chest* still played regularly in London. Godwin took parties of young friends to see it several times no doubt to the usual murmurs that *Caleb Williams* had been both plagiarized and mutilated. He wrote to Drury Lane asking them to consider a revival of his own play *Faulkener*. Even *Antonio* was again taken from the shelf and Rosser and Beavan had to listen as he read it aloud.

But the compliment from the young was fully returned. Political justice is a two-way process, with the old expected to learn from the perceptions of the young as well as the other way round. In 1817 Godwin read all the recently published books by Shelley's friends – Peacock's novels *Melincourt* and *Headlong Hall*, Hogg's romance *Memoirs of Prince Alexy Haimatoff*, Leigh Hunt's poem *The Story of Rimini*. He read *Manfred* and other poems of Lord Byron as soon as they came out. He read pamphlets which Hazlitt and Rosser wrote on the Malthusian controversy and many other books both old and new. On 15 May 1817 more shelves had to be fitted at Skinner Street.

On one of his visits to Marlow Godwin's journal notes that he discussed 'novels and perfectibility' with Shelley and Peacock. Both the novels of Peacock which he had just read contain comic arguments between perfectibilians and deteriorationists in which the voices of Godwin and Shelley can be heard alongside those of Southey, Wordsworth, Coleridge, Byron, Malthus, and other would-be opinion formers. One conversation occurs at Tremadoc where the philosophers had gone to inspect the dam. But Godwin, we may guess, would not have enjoyed Peacock's humour. Perfectibility was too important a subject to be made fun of and novels were too powerful an engine of improvement to be used to spread confusion and doubt.

It was at Shelley's lodgings on 18 November 1817 that he was introduced to the twenty-two-year-old John Keats. He and Mary Jane were having dinner there when Keats and Leigh Hunt paid a call.[6] Earlier in the year when Godwin was dining at Leigh Hunt's in Hampstead with Shelley, Hazlitt, Basil Montagu and others, Leigh Hunt had showed them examples of Keats's poetry and they were all said to have been much struck with its beauty.[7] Keats's first book of poems was published shortly afterwards – Leigh Hunt probably had an advance copy – but Keats was as yet unknown. Godwin met him again on 18 December when they were both at the theatre to see a play called *Riches*, an adaptation of Massinger's *City Madam* in which Edmund Kean gave a wonderfully good performance as the servile dependant. He saw Keats again on Christmas day, apparently meeting him in the street and stopping for a chat.[8]

To Keats Godwin was a literary giant. Both *Political Justice* and *Caleb Williams*, which he knew well, had been published before he was born. His friend Charles Dilke, whose Hampstead house is now the Keats Museum, was an ardent disciple believing in Godwin's theory so literally and single-mindedly that Keats called him a Godwin-methodist. When Hazlitt gave his lecture on the English novelists Keats borrowed a copy of the manuscript and laboriously transcribed Hazlitt's remarks on Godwin in a long letter to his brother. But Godwin also had a more direct influence.

While a schoolboy Keats was taught about the Ancient Greeks with the help of the *Pantheon* by 'Edward Baldwin'. It was one of his favourite books and he knew it from cover to cover. It was among the volumes he took with him to Rome which were found after his death.[9] To the young romantic who knew no Greek Godwin helped open a vision of another world. If – as his friends used to say – Keats could not look out on Hampstead Heath without seeing a Dryad, Godwin's unpretentious little textbook is partly responsible. At the time when Godwin knew him,

Keats was composing *Endymion* which was to be published with much trepidation in May 1818. Since we know from Godwin's journal that he read *Endymion* on 13 and 14 March,[10] a day or so after Keats finished fair-copying the manuscript for the printers, it seems likely that he was asked to read it – perhaps by the publisher John Taylor whom he was seeing frequently at this time. If so, it is to be hoped that he was asked to do more than check the mythology and that he gave a favourable report.

Later, after Keats had gone to Italy in a vain attempt to fight his tuberculosis, Godwin's journal for 27 December 1820 records that he read *The Pot of Basil*.[11] Keats's third and last book of poems had been published in July of that year and was probably given to Godwin as a Christmas present. If he also read *Lamia* and *Hyperion* printed in the same volume he would have noticed how helpful his *Pantheon* had proved. Keats had not only revived and revitalized some little-known myths, which he would probably not have known about if he had undergone the usual classical education, but the reconciliation theme in the wars between the Titans and Olympians described in *Hyperion* was drawn directly from one of Godwin's own suggestions in the *Pantheon*.[12]

Meanwhile Shelley too was hard at work. In early 1817 he began an autobiographical poem. The Shelleyan figure Athanase – whose name means immortal – is an outcast and a wanderer, old beyond his years, although not, as the poet hastens to explain to anyone mistakenly picking up Byronic echoes, loaded with secret guilt. He is, like Shelley, born to be privileged but he does not succumb to:

> Those false opinions which the harsh rich use
> To blind* the world they famish for their pride;
> Nor did he hold from any man his dues,
>
> But, like a steward in honest dealings tried,
> With those who toiled and wept, the poor and wise,
> His riches and his cares he did divide.
>
> Fearless he was, and scorning all disguise,
> What he dared do or think, though men might start,
> He spoke with mild yet unaverted eyes;

Athanase learns his wisdom from an old man, the Godwinian figure in the poem. Zonaras – whose name means flowing with life – is wan and withered 'yet calm and gentle and majestical'. He is the last survivor of

---

* In one manuscript Shelley wrote 'bind' but the final version was less of a cliché.

a civilization engulfed by wars, repression, and resurgent superstition. The fountains from which he refreshes his pupil are now overgrown with weeds and almost lost from sight but his philosophy and his wisdom remain clear and pure. *Athanase* was a pleasing compliment from the young Godwinian to the old Godwinian although the author insists that the young man's version of the theory is to be preferred. The poem was however soon laid aside, and by the end of the year Shelley had completed a much more ambitious work, twelve cantos of Spenserian stanzas, the longest poem he ever attempted.

Shelley's *Laon and Cythna* was named after the two lovers who are the principal characters in the poem. As the reviewer of the *Quarterly Review* at once pointed out, it too was autobiographical.[13] The name 'Laon' – the Shelleyan figure in the poem – reminded the educated reader vaguely of Laos the Greek word for the People, and 'Cythna' – the Mary figure – recalled the Cynthia who was the lover of the Roman poet Propertius as well as the Cytheran Aphrodite goddess of sexual love. As with Athanase and Zonaras Shelley's classical cognates were immediately recognizable as such but the names themselves were free of the misleading associations of accuracy. If Shelley's elegy on the death of Keats had been called *Adonis* instead of *Adonais*, it would instantly have recalled the fat Adonis the Prince Regent. A letter to Godwin of 1796 teases him for spending his Sundays with 'Fair Cynthia' meaning Mary Wollstonecraft and there were discordant modern overtones in that name too which Shelley wished to elide.[14]

Shelley's poem was dedicated to Mary — —[15] but readers and reviewers had no difficulty in supplying the missing 'Wollstonecraft' and 'Godwin' for she is praised not only for gloriously breaking the chains of custom by living with him in love but for following the glorious tradition of her famous parents

> They say that thou wert lovely from thy birth,
>> Of glorious parents, thou aspiring Child.
> I wonder not – for One then left this earth
>> Whose life was like a setting planet mild,
>> Which clothed thee in the radiance undefiled
> Of its departing glory, still her fame
>> Shines on thee, through the tempests dark and wild
> Which shake these latter days; and thou canst claim
> The shelter, from thy Sire, of an immortal name.

The next stanza, as originally drafted, was a direct reference to Godwin's huge, but short-lived, influence on the previous generation.

> A voice went forth from that unshaken Spirit,
>   Which was the echo of three thousand years;
> And the tumultuous world stood mute to hear it,
>   As some lone man who on a sudden hears
>   The music of his home: – unwonted fears
> Fell on the pale oppressors of our race,
>   And Faith, and Custom, and low-thoughted cares,
> Like thunder-stricken dragons, for a space
> Left the deep human heart which is their dwelling place.

For anyone too young to catch the reference, a footnote referred readers to *An Enquiry concerning Political Justice.* In the final version Shelley altered the 'unshaken Spirit' to 'many a mighty Spirit'. It was a concession to accuracy rather than a falling-off of respect. Godwin, even in the most messianic moments of 1792 and 1793 had never claimed to have reversed three thousand years of institutionalized false thinking by himself.

Like Zonaras, the old man in *Laon and Cythna* is a hermit who has hidden himself during a time of troubles, he is mild and wise, an ancient Greek who has survived into modern times. His writings, the result of a lifetime's converse with men and with books, are secretly read and gradually making converts. But although the old man knows what is needed for a peaceful revolution he is not able to persuade:

> But I alas! am both unknown and old,
> And though the woof of wisdom I know well
> To dye in hues of language, I am cold
> In seeming, and the hopes which inly dwell,
> My manners note that I did long repel.

To complete his work another approach is needed, and he is ready to hand over responsibility to the younger man.

Shelley's poem was written at Marlow in the summer of 1817 during a period of intensive excitement mostly in the open air. Shelley was seeing Godwin frequently and the notebook in which he did the main drafting has 'William Godwin' doodled over it in several places.[16] Since Godwin was writing every few days, his letters were sometimes the only writing material to hand when poetic inspiration struck. In an unused space at the end of Godwin's letter of 27 June, Shelley wrote a couplet for *Laon and Cythna* – to judge from the writing he used his left hand as a desk.

> Turned his wide eyes to the lightning's rift
> And neighed with a loud threnode.[17]*

* An unused version for Canto VI, 45.

Godwin's letter of 29 April is about a scheme whereby Shelley would buy a property with post-obit bonds in order to provide his father-in-law with an income.

> ... The rental of these chambers is about £950 per annum, the ground-rent and other outgoings £250, leaving a clear income of £700 per annum. This property is offered to us at the price of £2,500 in money, or £5000 in Post obit ... I heard to my surprise yesterday ... that you are raising £1000 for Mr Leigh Hunt ... [18]

The grudging envious proprietorial tone would surely not have been lost on the son-in-law who was now tied to him by sacred ties of property.

Shelley's mind was high above such mundane matters. On a blank space of the letter he wrote

> Mighty eagle, thou that soarest
> Oer the misty mountain forest
> And amid the light of morning
> Like a cloud of glory liest
> And when night descends defiest
> The embattled tempests warning[19]

Shelley had recently been writing a full translation of Plato's *Ion* in which the wise old Socrates explains to the confident young poet Ion that skill in poetry is quite unlike other skills. The image of the eagle and the snake which he was to employ in *Laon and Cythna* is taken direct from the *Iliad* Book 12 which is quoted in the dialogue* and Shelley may have momentarily pictured his own contest with Godwin in these terms, with Godwin as the eagle and himself as the snake. But he was more interested in the theory of poetry discussed in the dialogue. Poetry, Socrates explains after confuting Ion's commonsense rationalist arguments, is a divine power. It is an unexplained force like magnetism which can transmit itself along the iron rings of a chain from generation to generation. In order to be a poet, Socrates insists, a man must shed reason and allow inspiration to be the interpreter.

The words had struck Shelley like a shaft of truth. Here in one of the neglected books of antiquity was a new meaning to the metaphor of the chain which had dominated thinking about the mind during the age of unsuccessful revolutions. Since boyhood he had been fascinated by magnetism and electricity. In 1816 he had taken Mary to see the experi-

---

* In this passage Homer uses the actual word 'laon' meaning the people operating as an army – what old translators of the Bible and the classics called 'the host' – and it may be that Shelley intended to imply a slight menace.

ments performed at a public performance by the French scientist Garnerin in which an electric current was made to flow from person to person as they held hands. The thought was also adopted by Lord Byron who in *Childe Harold's Pilgrimage* spoke of nature 'striking the electric chain wherewith we are darkly bound'.

On 13 November 1817 when David Booth called at Shelley's London lodgings, Shelley read aloud from the Preface to *Laon and Cythna*, waiting until after Godwin had gone home before beginning.[20] The poem, that Preface explained, was presented to the world 'in the cause of a liberal and comprehensive morality' − a striking phrase − picked out by the reviewers − not only for the ambitiousness of its aim but because 'liberal' was still synonymous to many ears with 'Jacobin'. Godwin would have remembered it from the 1793 Preface to the first edition of *Political Justice*, which was offered as 'the proper vehicle of a liberal morality' embracing both politics and ethics. There were other similarities. Godwin wished *Political Justice* to be a book 'from the perusal of which no man should rise without being strengthened in habits of sincerity, fortitude and justice'. Shelley intended to kindle in the bosoms of his readers 'a virtuous enthusiasm for . . . liberty and justice'. Godwin, who believed he faced criminal prosecution, wrote proudly that 'it is the property of truth to be fearless'. Shelley, whose concern was more with hostile reviewers, declared that 'in this as in every other respect I have written fearlessly'. Both Prefaces deny that they have copied other writers and both apologize for flaws uncorrected because of urgency. Godwin, in referring to his sixteen months of writing, noted that 'this period was devoted to the purpose with unremitted ardour'. Shelley wrote of his six months: 'That period has been devoted to the task with unremitting ardour.'

As elsewhere in Shelley's writings, Godwin's words had penetrated so deep that it is almost as if he had looked them up. And his purpose was equally ambitious. *Laon and Cythna* is the successor to *Political Justice*, an attempt to adapt the truths of the old Enlightenment to the new post-revolutionary generation. If Godwin's book − described as 'unanswerable' − was appropriate for the beginning of the French Revolution, a different approach was needed when its achievements had been swept away in terror, war, and repression. Reason was for a time of hope: in a world gripped by despair what was needed was Feeling. Prose was for the spring with the summer still ahead: in the deepening autumn only Poetry could effect a change.

Godwin was given one of the first copies to be printed. His journal for 5 December 1817 records curtly 'Laon and Cythna II, III'. Evidently he skipped Canto I which Shelley's Preface warned was introductory and optional. But the philosopher who had been teased by Coleridge for reviewing his own books in his prefaces would never have skipped the Preface, and whatever he may have thought of the rest of the argument, the last paragraph must have horrified him. Adopting Godwin's device in *St. Leon* Shelley explained that he wanted to startle his readers from the trance of ordinary life – in order to emphasize that some so-called crimes are merely matters of convention he was revealing the lovers as brother and sister!

It was only a few weeks earlier that Godwin had been reading Byron's *Manfred*, which has an incest theme. Soon afterwards he ploughed through Leigh Hunt's *Story of Rimini* on the same subject. And, as if the flagrance was not enough in itself, Shelley printed a footnote which stands out on the printed page like a defiant proclamation of guilt and approval:

The sentiments connected with and characteristic of this circumstance have no personal reference to the Writer.

Stories of the 'incestuous' relationship between Shelley, Mary and Claire were now common. Byron believed that the odious Southey was helping to spread them. A direct denial by Shelley, following the direct denial in Polidori's *Vampyre* published earlier in the year, could only reinforce them. No smoke without fire.

The point occurred to others who were given advance copies, and Shelley was reluctantly persuaded to make changes. The lovers were recast as childhood friends, not brother and sister. References to God which might cause offence were altered to Divine Power, and Jesus was changed in one place to Joshua. The political message was also diluted. As Godwin had been taught at his theology class, a war to drive the Turks out of Europe was a universally accepted paradigm of a just revolution.[21] Under another old convention writers could more safely attack organized religion if they called it Mohammedanism. Before the French Revolution philosophers teased the censors by pretending that their books were printed in Constantinople. The title of Shelley's poem was accordingly changed to *The Revolt of Islam.**

Godwin read the whole of *Laon and Cythna* for within a few days he had sent two long letters of criticism to Shelley. His reaction was the same as it had been to *Queen Mab*. Shelley had amazing powers, but they were

---

* Not everybody saw through the disguise. Shelley's cousin Medwin, a professional soldier, was surprised to find a copy on sale in Bombay – the Indian booksellers had thought the book was intended for imperialists worried about the loyalty of their Moslem subjects.

undisciplined and therefore ineffectual. And it was true. Poetic ideas poured from Shelley's mind like an Alpine torrent. Old metaphors of chains and harps were swept along through the winding rivers and hidden caverns to which Shelley increasingly compared his imagination. Sparks of truth light new fires of enlightenment. Seeds of renewal are scattered by autumn winds. Proud eagles soaring on high struggle with slavish crawling earth-bound snakes. In an excellent phrase Godwin advised the young poet to conserve 'the economy of intellectual force'.[22]

For a poem purportedly intended to promote the power of love, *Laon and Cythna* is full of hate. Henry Crabb Robinson a Godwinian of the old school disliked its extremism. In the eyes of David Booth, Shelley was certainly insane. But it was Hazlitt, the man who had sat through every act of the Godwin drama since 1795, who offered the best picture of the Shelley of this time. He only met him a few times – twice at Leigh Hunt's when Godwin was also present – but it was enough to make an emphatic judgement. Shelley, he wrote:

... has a fire in his eye, a fever in his blood, a maggot in his brain, a hectic flutter in his speech, which mark out the philosophic fanatic.[23]

He went on to describe Shelley's red face, his shrill voice, his thin bending figure, characteristics often associated with the self-righteous priests whom he both hated and resembled.

In 1817 Shelley was intoxicated by ideas. Like his poetry, he imparted a 'wild, uneasy, frantic, staring, wonder'.[24] Believing he was dying he was in a hurry both to change the world and to leave a monument to himself. Despite the reconciliation with Godwin he felt a deep sense of having been personally wronged, and his behaviour remained highly unpredictable. In the debates on the French Revolution, Hazlitt noted, it had been the poets Wordsworth, Coleridge and Southey who had swung from one extreme to the other. The prose writers Godwin and Bentham – and Hazlitt might have included himself – had proved more sound, more steady, and more resilient. Poets, with their seething brains, made bad philosophers. Prose writers who took matters step by step testing ideas against experience were more effective.

In fact Shelley was never at risk of turning anti-Jacobin. It was one of his many attractive characteristics that he listened carefully to criticism. His appreciation of the 'most kind and wise admonitions' which Godwin made in his long letters about his poem was sincere as well as polite. In his eagerness to throw in all the insights which tumbled from his racing brain Shelley knew that he had sacrificed unity and form. However,

Godwin's suggestion that he should stick to prose writing showed that the older man had not only mistaken his purpose but misunderstood the needs of the post-war world.

Two years later Shelley was to rework some of the ideas of *The Revolt of Islam* into one of his most flawless compositions. In the *Ode to the West Wind*, written during a real storm in the autumn of 1819, Shelley proudly accepted the charge of wildness of which he had so often been accused, seeing the wild west wind as the perfect metaphor for the storms of life. The final verses, reviving and reanimating the three commonest metaphors of the New Philosophy – chains, Aeolian harps, and sparks of truth – mark the triumphant handing over of responsibility to the next generation.

> A heavy weight of hours has chained and bowed
> One too like thee: tameless, and swift, and proud.
>
> Make me thy lyre, even as the forest is:
> What if my leaves are falling like its own!
> The tumult of thy mighty harmonies
>
> Will take from both a deep, autumnal tone,
> Sweet though in sadness. Be thou, Spirit fierce,
> My spirit! Be thou me impetuous one!
>
> Drive my dead thoughts over the universe
> Like withered leaves to quicken a new birth!
> And, by the incantation of this verse,
>
> Scatter, as from an unextinguished hearth
> Ashes and sparks, my words among mankind!
> Be through my lips to unawakened earth
>
> The trumpet of a prophecy! O Wind,
> If Winter comes, can Spring be far behind?

The transforming power of literature in which Shelley and Godwin so passionately believed was never more conclusively demonstrated. Forcing its way – by sheer poetic power – into the anthologies and school books of those who detested his message – the *Ode to the West Wind* has led innumerable readers back to Shelley's longer works. The ideas of Godwin and Shelley might be unacceptable but henceforth they could never be ignored. The *Ode to the West Wind* established them for ever among the unacknowledged legislators of the English-speaking world.

Meanwhile if *Laon and Cythna* was the new *Political Justice*, a new *Caleb Williams* was also ready. On 24 November 1817 only a fortnight before Godwin read Shelley's poem, he finished reading the three volumes of *Frankenstein or The Modern Prometheus* by his daughter Mary. It had been begun when she and Shelley were with Byron in 1816 and completed with Shelley's help at Marlow. There had been difficulty in finding a publisher, with several rejections, but Godwin's friend Lackington was eventually persuaded to print an edition of 500 to be published anonymously. Godwin read the book from the first proofs or from the manuscript. At that time the Preface – which was written by Shelley not by Mary – was not yet printed.[25] Godwin therefore probably did not read the explanation – reminiscent of the Preface to *St. Leon* – that the author, in a search for a new approach, was deliberately mixing human emotions in a superhuman situation. He did not read the claimed comparisons with the *Iliad*, with Shakespeare, and with Milton. Nor did he read the Dedication:

To

WILLIAM GODWIN

Author of Political Justice, Caleb Williams, Etc

These Volumes

Are respectfully inscribed

By

The Author

As the first reviewers at once noticed, amazingly original though *Frankenstein* is, the book is also the work of her father's daughter. Like Caleb Williams, Frankenstein is a man driven by an excessive and obsessive curiosity. Like St. Leon, he quickly discovers that the effects of scientific discovery are not all beneficial. As in *Fleetwood* much of the story takes place in Switzerland where the human story can be set against the immensity of nature and where the open honesty of the free mountaineers can be contrasted with the urban oversophistication of the main character. *Frankenstein* is a story of pursuit in which pursuer and pursued reverse their roles – to the extent that many people now think that Frankenstein is the name of the Monster – and when at the end the Monster eventually succeeds in his quest he feels no sense of triumph but only an overwhelming regret.

The story teems with lesser Godwinisms, admiration for seventeenth-century English republicans, invocations of the calming effect of Seneca, chains of the mind, the power of truth. The Monster's promise to live in benevolence and peace if only Frankenstein will create a female companion resembles the passage in *St. Leon* in which Godwin extolled

435

the improving effects of married love. Like the other pursuers of Godwin's and Shelley's imagination, Frankenstein and the Monster slip effortlessly and relentlessly over land and ocean, never short of forward intelligence about their victim's next hiding place. When the German Frankenstein visits Oxford he immediately thinks of Falkland, King Charles's secretary of state who had provided a name for the chivalrous Godwinian hero.

In Switzerland Shelley and Byron had discussed the potential of the Prometheus myth for modern purposes. Byron's *Prometheus* was being written at the time and Shelley was to choose the story for his most ambitious work *Prometheus Unbound*. It was the chained Prometheus of the Caucasus who fascinated the poets – the unconquerable demi-god who struggled defiantly against gods and men was a powerful image of hope in an age of reaction. The detail that Prometheus's sufferings included perpetual liver pains had been quoted in *Queen Mab* as proof that man had originally been vegetarian. Mary's *Modern Prometheus*, the secondary title of *Frankenstein*, referred to the story that it was Prometheus who created the first man and later the first woman. It was this aspect of the Prometheus myth that Godwin had emphasized in Baldwin's *Pantheon*, a book with which Mary is certain to have been familiar. As Godwin had explained in his commonsense style:

The fable of Prometheus's man, and Pandora the first woman, was intended to convey an allegorical sense; the ancients saw to how many evils the human race is exposed; how many years of misery many of them endure, with what a variety of diseases they are afflicted, how the great majority is condemned to perpetual labour, poverty, and ignorance, and how many vices are contracted by men, in consequence of which they afflict each other with a thousand additional evils, perfidy, tyranny, cruel tortures, murder, and war.

It was a stroke of genius – although not an original idea – for Mary to suggest electricity as the principle of life which reanimated pieces of dead body. The electricity came direct from lightning, the most vivid metaphor of the deistic life force of nature. The Being created by Frankenstein is an archetypal man in the state of nature, spontaneously virtuous until corrupted by the treatment he receives from other people. The handful of books he reads in order to educate himself are a crash course in Western civilization – Plutarch for the Greeks, Milton for the Judaeo-Christian tradition and for seventeenth-century England, and Goethe's *Sorrows of Young Werther* for sensibility. For Modern Philosophy he reads Volney's *Ruins of Empire*, a surrogate for *Political Justice* which might have been thought too difficult. Although Mary was less interested in her mother's writings than in her father's, there is also an echo of the *Vindication of the Rights of Woman* in the story of the constricted upbringing of Safie where the reader was expected, as in Shelley's poem, to see the references to Turks and to Mohammedanism as criticisms of contemporary England.

Like Shelley, Mary drew on the Platonic dialogues, which they translated at Marlow, especially the notion of the accompanying 'daemon' to whom Socrates attributed his own actions. The creature created by Frankenstein is called Daemon more frequently than Being or Monster, although several incidents in the story leave no doubt that he is real and physical not just imaginary or psychological.

Frankenstein's discovery of the principle of life takes place at Ingolstadt on the upper Danube not far from the place where St. Leon was given the philosopher's stone and the elixir of immortality. Robison's *Proofs of a Conspiracy* and Barruel's *History of Jacobinism* had each traced the founding of the Illuminati 'The Enlightened' to Ingolstadt, and purported to demonstrate how their conspiracy had led directly to the French Revolution. In 1816 Henry Crabb Robinson had gone there to meet the founder, a former Jesuit. Like her father Mary Shelley not only told a fascinating story in the gothic genre but provided a metaphor for the upheavals of the age. The phrase 'to create a Frankenstein monster' was to become a nineteenth-century political cliché.[26]

Caleb Williams had been written in order to carry the philosophical message of *Political Justice* to those whose reading never rose above novels. *Frankenstein* shared the same aim, as Shelley himself proclaimed in the Preface. The author, he wrote, was 'by no means indifferent to the manner in which whatever moral tendencies exist in the sentiments or characters . . . shall affect the reader'. And its underlying moral purpose was immediately detected. The Tory *Quarterly Review* noted contemptuously that the book was 'piously dedicated to Mr Godwin and . . . written in the spirit of his school'. The *Edinburgh Magazine* perceived that it was 'formed in the Godwinian manner and has all the faults but likewise the beauties of that model'. Sir Walter Scott, reviewing the book in *Blackwood's*, conjectured from the Godwinian parallels that the author must be Percy Bysshe Shelley.

Shelley himself prepared a review which was not published until the fragments of his prose works were collected after his death. As he pointed out, the first experiences of the Being are an illustration of Godwin's explanation of the origins of evil:

Nor are the crimes and malevolence of the single Being, though indeed withering and tremendous, the offspring of any unaccountable propensity to evil, but flow irresistibly from certain causes fully adequate to their production. They are the children, as it were, of Necessity and Human Nature. In this the direct moral of the book consists; and it is perhaps the most important, and of the most universal application, of any moral that can be enforced by example. Treat a person ill, and he will become wicked. Requite affection with scorn; – let one being be selected, for whatever cause, as the refuse of his kind – divide him, a social being, from society, and you impose upon him the irresistible obligations – malevolence and selfishness.

'The encounter and argument between Frankenstein and the Being on the sea of ice', Shelley wrote of the last paragraph of the novel, 'almost approaches, in effect, to the expostulation of Caleb Williams with Falkland. It reminds us, indeed, somewhat of the style and character of that admirable writer, to whom the author has dedicated his work, and whose productions he seems to have studied.'[27] The 'almost' resonates with respect for *Frankenstein*'s predecessor, but it is also a touch of modesty. As no reader of the printed book could know, Shelley himself had written the passage he refers to, transforming Mary's draft into a fitting poetic culmination of a great book.[28]

Godwin was delighted with *Frankenstein*. It was, he told his daughter later, 'the most wonderful work to have been written at twenty years of age that I have ever heard of'. (It was in fact completed when she was only nineteen.) Her talents, Godwin told her – and he was never one to flatter – were 'truly extraordinary'. In one remark alone was he proved wrong – the book, he believed, was too good ever to be popular.

Frankenstein was to be another magnetic electric chain which links the generations, another vindication of the power of the written word. In 1823 when the story was adapted for the stage it was an immediate success. Godwin was present at the first night on 27 July and a month later he saw the play again accompanied by Mary herself.[29] The actor Cooke who took the title role in Richard Brinsley Peake's version was to play in nearly four hundred performances. In the 1820s there were at least two other adaptations. *Frankenstein* was to be staged many times in Victorian times – an actors' edition for amateur dramatic societies being available price one penny. By the time the story was adapted for the cinema, it had become one of the most pervasive and enduring of modern myths, much of its essential message preserved even in the crudest versions.

Godwin had been unfortunate with *The Iron Chest* which preserves little of the spirit of the original. *Frankenstein* demonstrated that the electric current could flow in both directions. The stage adaptation of 1823 renewed demand for the novel and Godwin was able to arrange a reprint. Thereafter the book was seldom out of print, usually read as a simple thriller but no doubt in its turn it has hauled at least some of its readers a few points higher up the intellectual and moral economy. *Frankenstein* has joined the canon of classic works of English literature. Mary Shelley is an unacknowledged legislator as influential as her father, her mother, and her husband.

Meanwhile William Godwin himself had at last completed his own latest attempt to change the world. On 25 November 1817, the day after he finished reading *Frankenstein*, he composed the Preface to the novel on which he had been working for many months. On the 30th he started to read the proofs and by 3 December he had reread the three volumes. The advance copy which he sent to Shelley and Mary must have reached Marlow almost simultaneously with his own receipt of *Laon and Cythna*.[30] The three books produced by the three members of the family were all read by one another within a few days.

Godwin believed that *Mandeville* would be his last work, a thought that had already influenced his previous two books and was to influence half a dozen more. At the end of 1817 he was nearly sixty-two and his imagination was slower. *Caleb Williams*, *St. Leon* and even *Fleetwood* had been dashed off in a few months. *Mandeville* was started and laid aside several times and it showed. His original intention was to adapt the theme of the Seven Sleepers. If the hero could fall asleep and wake up thirty years later, Godwin would be able to explore the changes in outlook between one generation and the next. It was a wonderful idea, as Washington Irving – perhaps encouraged by Godwin – was soon to demonstrate in 'Rip Van Winkle', another story with a modern mythic quality. In the event however Godwin found himself unable to rise to the imaginative challenge and settled for a lesser ambition. *Mandeville* also spans the generations but it traces the chains through the fortunes of one family.

The first two volumes are competent but pedestrian, more history than novel, and already Godwin reveals an old man's tendency to quote from other people's books rather than write his own. The familiar Godwinian themes are worked over yet again, the influence of early impressions on the mature man, conferred honour and true virtue, obsession and pursuit, loneliness. Only in the third volume, which was composed after the reconciliation with Shelley and Mary, did he attempt something new, and his creative burst was not fully sustained. *Mandeville* comes to a stop rather than to an end, and when an enterprising imitator produced a spurious fourth volume, some buyers added it to the other three without noticing the break.

Written like all his novels in the first person the book attempts to show how obsession leads to madness. Godwin sought to trace the breakdown of personality from within. By setting his story in the seventeenth century he was able to draw on his deep understanding of his puritan heritage. He was able to relate the political and religious hatreds to the personal psychology of the individuals on either side. But he too, like Shelley and Mary, now used nineteenth-century metaphors such as the animating 'electrical fluid'. If Mandeville could be freed from his irrational involvement with his rival, he remarks at one point, he would have felt 'like Prometheus upon the supposition that the adamantine chains that Vulcan forged for him could have been dashed to the earth'. Godwin's novel is an openly avowed exploration of the subconscious mind which gradually overrides and destroys conscious rationality and objective judgement. The old theory of necessity is stated again in the clearest terms, but juxtaposed against more modern notions of the diabolic. Passions, he declares, laugh at philosophy. *Mandeville* – with its echo of Man Devil – is an essay in one of the great themes of romanticism.

Shelley was delighted. A few days before he received Godwin's criticisms of *Laon and Cythna* he poured out his enthusiasm in a long letter which was immediately adapted as a review. Since he was depressed at the time, lying for hours in a torpor and seeing things with the keen exactness which makes depressives believe that they have a unique access to truth, Shelley could appreciate the pervasive blackness of Godwin's vision. The insights in the debate between Mandeville and his sister, he declared, were only matched by Plato's Socratic dialogue on love – if indeed they were not superior. Most of all he was impressed by the sheer power of Godwin's conception which he compared to his own wild west wind.

For the interest is of that irresistible and overwhelming kind, that the mind in it's influence is like a cloud borne on by an impetuous wind, like one breathlessly carried forward who has no time to pause, or observe the causes of his career. I think the *power* of Mandeville is inferior to nothing that you have done, and were it not for the character of Falkland, no instance in which you have exerted that power of *creation* which you possess beyond all contemporary writers might compare with it. Falkland is still alone: power is in Falkland not as in Mandeville. Tumult hurried onward by the tempest, but Tranquillity standing unshaken amid its fiercest rage! But Caleb Williams never shakes the deepest soul like Mandeville.[31]

Another of the first copies of *Mandeville* was sent to Elizabeth Inchbald who was now in her sixties and living in deep retirement. She had been sent copies of each of Godwin's previous three novels as they came out and had never restrained her sincerity. In his letter Godwin recalled how in 1794 her detailed comments on the first printing of *Caleb Williams* had turned the novel into the perfection of the second. If she would return the three volumes of *Mandeville* with her comments in the margins, Godwin promised, he would immediately send her a clean copy.[32] He did not mention that his Preface to the second edition was already drafted. As a woman of the theatre it had always been difficult for Mrs Inchbald to maintain either her virtue or her honour. Recently – in a throwback to her religious youth – she had become so terrified of what would happen after death that life had become a burden. It was also said by her biographer that she ruined her health by lacing her stays too tightly. Godwin had tried to persuade Constable to publish the memoirs she had been writing to try to raise money, but when he delayed she asked for the manuscript back and consigned it to the flames. If she ever did send Godwin her comments on *Mandeville*, there is no record, and the book has never been reprinted.

There was however another younger friend who could also be expected to understand. William Hazlitt, another product of seventeenth-century dissenting gloom, shared Godwin's intensity, the shyness sliding easily into truculence, the feeling of helplessness in the face of passion. In 1823, as a result of an unsatisfactory love for his landlord's daughter, he was to write the joyless *Liber Amoris*, a book near in spirit to *Mandeville*. When however Godwin wrote to the editor of the *Edinburgh* suggesting that William Hazlitt was the best man to review *Mandeville*, he received a pained complaint at the implied affront to editorial independence.[33]

Hazlitt did however have his say. In 1818 he offered two courses of lectures in London, first on the English poets, then on the English comic writers, sixteen evenings in all. On 22 December 1818 Godwin attended the sixth lecture of the second series, on the English novelists. He heard Hazlitt trace the history of the novel in England from translations of *Don Quixote* and *Gil Blas* through Fielding, Richardson, Smollett, and Sterne to the novelists of the present day. Hazlitt mentioned the women writers, Fanny Burney, Mrs Edgeworth, and Elizabeth Inchbald. The absurd fashion for gothic ruins, he suggested, reflected nostalgia for the tottering of the old regime. He preferred the older style. 'I could be in love with Mrs Inchbald.' The two best novelists of the age were undoubtedly the author of *Waverley* and the author of *Caleb Williams*; and the climax of the lecture was a long critique of *Caleb Williams* and *St. Leon* with a few sympathetic remarks about *Mandeville*.

Unlike Scott, Hazlitt remarked, Godwin did not adorn his novels with antiquarian learning but wrote from pure imagination. The interplay of Falkland and Caleb Williams, he declared with the authority of the foremost interpreter of Shakespeare, was like that of Othello and Iago 'inimitably well-managed and on a par with any thing in the dramatic art'. The novel as a whole was 'utterly unlike anything else that ever was written, and is one of the most original as well as powerful productions in the English language'. If *Mandeville* showed some falling away, that was only because the people had come to expect too much. The lectures were published in book form shortly afterwards. Hazlitt returned to the same theme in *The Spirit of the Age* and enlarged on it. The story of Godwin's life was, he said, the story of changing attitudes between the generations. In the 1790s Godwin was known everywhere; now he was scarcely known. Nobody pointed him out in the street; nobody bothered to attack him; most people assumed he was long since dead. His books were as remote as if they had been written 150 years before. In fact, Hazlitt went on, Godwin's immortality was already secure. The author of *Political Justice* and *Caleb Williams* could never die. His works were already standard works in the history of thought, and would be read as classics in 150 years' time.

For the old man it was a pleasing vindication. Godwin had achieved his ambition. Like an ancient Roman he had deserved well of his country – or rather of the world. But the valedictory tone was less acceptable. Was William Godwin, whose direct knowledge stretched back to the previous century and indirectly to the century before, content to leave perfectibility to men and women who had not even been born in 1793? Was the investment of sixty years of serious reading and serious conversations to be so lightly discarded? What use the creativity of youth without the wisdom of experience? The teenage Shelley, when scolded for publishing too young, had protested that the experiences of the young deserved to be written down if only for the purpose of allowing biographical research into individual whole human lives. Was the same not true of those whose best years were behind them? On 30 December 1817, before the ink was properly dry on the three great Godwinian works of that year, the journal records that William Godwin had already started to write his next book.

CHAPTER 36

Defiance

The literary triumphs of 1817 were however soon overshadowed. At the end of the year Shelley and Mary began to hint that they intended to go abroad again. The English cold and wet was, they believed, ruining Shelley's health and drawing Mary ever deeper into a Wollstonecraftian depression. They were afraid that the courts might still order their two children to be removed from the care of an avowed atheist, and they worried that if they did not take Claire's baby to Lord Byron they would be stuck with her for life. Italy, where Lord Byron had settled, was sunny, easy-going, cheap, and beyond the reach of English property laws.

It was scarcely more than a year since the magical ceremony which had purportedly made living abroad unnecessary. Shelley's plan was, to Godwin's mind, only the latest example of his reckless unpredictability and his wilful shirking of responsibility. No one could remember how often he had disappeared to announce by letter weeks later that he was in Scotland or Wales or the Lake District or Ireland. The need to avoid Leeson, who he believed had been on his trail since Tremadoc, seldom seemed a convincing excuse. On two vital occasions Shelley had left the country altogether, as Godwin had pointed out in the letter in 1816 which precipitated Fanny Godwin's suicide. This time the young people, while at least aware that there was a problem and giving some notice, were, to Godwin's mind, again intent on running away from their duty.

The long dispute between Godwin and Shelley which broke out again

The Tortoise, from Bewick's *Select Fables*

in early 1818 was principally about money. But it also reflected deepening differences in temperament and in approach. Shelley liked to see himself as quick and flexible: he was – as Byron described him – a snake, ready to slip into any opportunity which the unreformed world left unclosed. Godwin was direct but slow. Having decided on his destination he would proceed towards it in a straight line. If he was obstructed he would stop and retire defensively into his shell to await a more favourable opportunity to advance. The more he was prodded at such times, the more stubbornly he refused to budge. It was not a subtle method but, as the author of *Fables Ancient and Modern* was well aware, tortoises often win races.

The reconciliation had revived him like the returning warmth of spring: 1817 was one of his best years since the harsh anti-Jacobin winter began to set in nearly twenty years before. He had become more open, more friendly, more adventurous, more creative. He was back in the world and again on the advance. But it only needed one sharp frost to drive him into another sullen torpid hibernation.

On 30 January 1818 in preparation for Shelley's departure he and Shelley called on a professional moneylender called Willats from whom Shelley obtained £2,000 in exchange for a post-obit bond of £4,500. In a letter sent to Godwin immediately afterwards – now lost – Shelley explained that he needed most of the money himself, but he enclosed a cheque, perhaps for £150. The situation was a replay of at least two previous episodes in 1814 and in 1816 when Shelley had refused to hand over money which Godwin believed was intended for him. Once more Godwin felt betrayed and deceived and once more he reacted as before. His reply sent on the 31st was in his most formal style. Gone was the 'My dear Shelley' and the 'yours very affectionately' of recent exchanges: his letter was an attempt to deliver a sharp moral shock. It was unaddressed and unsigned. Never again, he told Shelley, would he try to deal with a matter so important by letter – a method which allowed such scope for misunderstanding and – he implied – for deception. He did not go so far as to demand the presence of a third person as witness when they next met, but he was determined to alter his whole approach.

Since our last conversation at Marlow I have reflected much on the subject. I am ashamed of the tone I have taken with you in all our late conversations. I have played the part of a suppliant and deserted that of a philosopher. It was not thus I talked with you when I first knew you; and I will talk so no more. I will talk Political Justice; whether it makes for me or against me, no matter. I am fully capable of this. I desire not to dictate; I know that every man's conduct ought to be regulated by his own judgement such as it may happen to be. But I hold it to be my duty once to state to you the *principles* which belong to the case. Having done that, it is my duty to forbear: I would enlighten your understanding if I could; but I would not, if I could, carry things by importunity. I have nothing to say to you of a passionate nature; least of all, do I wish to move your feelings; less than the least to wound you. All that I have to say is in the calmness of philosophy and moves far above the atmosphere of vulgar sensations. If you have the courage to hear me, come: if you have not, be it so. What I have to say, I *must* say, if I ever stand in your presence again, but I were rather it were without a witness.[1]

Shelley did not come. Godwin wrote another ten letters in rapid succession, all now lost but all presumably in the same vein, until he eventually met Shelley on 6 March. He was calling on Mary at her request when Shelley arrived. The deadlock was broken and the two men saw each other frequently over the next few days. We may be sure that Godwin delivered another moral scolding, although he now had so many complaints against Shelley that it is difficult to guess which one he had in mind. But Shelley, conscious of the duty to set aside promises in certain circumstances, made no change. When he and his ménage moved to London in preparation for their departure, they therefore encountered nothing but icy disapproval from Skinner Street. The two families scarcely met. Mary Jane, who had always blamed Mary for taking Claire with her in 1814, was bitterly resentful that her daughter had successfully resisted all efforts to separate her from the Shelleys. Claire only paid two brief visits home and she did not bring her baby. On 9 March 1818 when the three grandchildren were taken to church for baptism – in order to preserve their legal status if that should be called into question later – neither Godwin nor Mrs Godwin was present. The following day Shelley brought Claire to Skinner Street to say goodbye. That evening Godwin visited Shelley's lodgings to say goodbye to Mary.

On 11 March, Shelley, Mary, and Claire set out for Dover. It was the third time they had made the journey together but now they were accompanied by three babies and two nursemaids. Shelley was twenty-four, Mary twenty and Claire still only nineteen. Unpredictable and restless though they were, no one had much doubt that this time they would not be coming back. They were going into exile, silently conceding victory to the powers of tyranny, custom, and superstition, but also silently rejecting the father figure who had hitherto determined their lives.

After their departure the outlook from Skinner Street was more dismal than it had ever been. Wherever he looked Godwin saw only death, poverty, and despair. In October 1817 John Philpot Curran had died in

445

London after a long illness. During the summer Godwin visited him regularly and he was at his home on the day he died. On the day after Christmas had come the death of Sarah Elwes, possibly the woman he knew best apart from Mary Wollstonecraft and Mary Jane, to be followed next day by that of his sister Hannah who had been his main support during his early years in London.

James Marshall was also now desperate, sinking under an insupportable load of debt and unable to work. After Holcroft's death in 1809 he had arranged the subscription for the widow and six children, going from door to door round all his fellow workers in the literary industry. Now it was his turn to be destitute. When Shelley declined to help – he was already supporting Leigh Hunt, Peacock, and several others besides Godwin himself – Godwin wrote to Josiah Wedgwood in a style which might have sounded smug if it were not also sincere. Marshall, he explained, was:

a person nearly of the same age as myself whom I first became acquainted with when I was seventeen and whom from that time I have never lost sight of. His career in this world has been similar to my own except that he wanted that originality of talent that the world has been good-natured enough to impute to me.[2]

His friend, Godwin explained, was now unemployed and quickly 'going down the descent of life'. It is not known if Wedgwood gave money.

In January 1817 there had been another warning. A letter from John Fairley in Edinburgh told of the ruin of John Hepburn of Bearfoot, although he carefully omitted naming him:

If you are accustomed to read the Gazette you have by this time seen there a notice that would give you infinite pain – if you are not, pause!!! Prepare yourself to hear that this world is not made for the worthy!!! The good the generous the noble minded – has sunk beneath the pressure – He that has so often and so liberally relieved others – He that has kept many a name from the Gazette and who more than any man I ever knew delighted in doing good is himself irretrievably ruined.[3]

This time the moral lesson was for lenders as much as for borrowers. Hepburn had kept open house at Bearfoot and he was never known to refuse a request for money. But what finally broke him was the initially costless habit of guaranteeing other people's credit. He himself remained true to political justice to the end. When bankruptcy threatened he destroyed all his bonds so that his creditors had no proof that he had claims on other people. Godwin was one of the beneficiaries, his debt neatly converted into a gift.

Elton Hammond, another of the rich men who had helped Godwin in the past took his own life on the last day of 1819. As a depressive he had been drawn to Godwin the man as well as to his ideas. He was one of the investors who with Place had intended to refinance the bookshop in 1812 and it was his withdrawal which led to Godwin's rushed visit to Lynmouth in search of Shelley. His admiration survived, but his sense of political justice was never quite strong enough to tolerate the lack of appreciation which Godwin proclaimed at each successive favour. Not long after his death Godwin composed an essay on the ethics of suicide: a justifiable solution in some situations, he believed, but certainly not for somebody with his own heavy family responsibilities.

For years Godwin and Mary Jane had lived in fear, clinging to the hope that sooner or later Shelley would give them some financial security in their old age. The chances of his fulfilling that promise were now minimal. Godwin remained convinced that Shelley could raise the needed money without difficulty if he wanted to. Whenever he took up a new enthusiasm of his own he never lacked the means of pursuing it. For all his pro-testations, Shelley was refusing to take the problem seriously – perhaps even deliberately exploiting Godwin's economic dependence to keep him on the moral defensive.

After Shelley was settled in Italy he wrote to confirm his decision. The letter is lost but its tenor can be guessed from Godwin's reply addressed to 'my dear Shelley'.

I read your letter . . . with great pain. Let us therefore correspond no more on such decisions. If ever we meet again, perhaps something satisfactory may be arranged. But since a certain period, you seem never to take up a pen on these matters without being converted, as by a sort of spell, into a kind of being at which my nature revolts. If any great calamity suddenly overtakes me, I shall not fail to communicate that by letter either to you or Mary.[4]

To be fair to him – as many biographers have not been – Shelley accepted Godwin's claim. Occasionally he lapsed into impatience and behaved as if the wealth fortune had given him was indeed his own to spend. But in his steadier moments he fully acknowledged that under the criteria of political justice his duty was to dispose of it for the greatest good. He never ceased to proclaim his deep respect for Godwin and for his philo-sophy, and Godwin's revised utilitarian calculus gave a heavy weighting to 'domestic affections' over other claims. Shelley practised the philosophy himself with less discrimination than his mentor, repudiating debts, delaying payment on tradesmen's bills, keeping books borrowed from rich men's libraries, and weakening the bonds of property whenever he saw an opportunity.

But Shelley also suspected, probably rightly, that however much money he provided for Godwin it would go the way of the rest, to pay off professional moneylenders. M. J. Godwin and Company remained in business, apparently a source of continuing income but in reality an unplugged drain which sucked away any cash that Godwin either earned or borrowed. Money had not solved Godwin's problems in the past, but neither had withholding it brought on catastrophe. Godwin's actual level of welfare had remained static, plus or minus a few bottles of wine and a few more old books, for ten years or more. It was easy to assume that somehow or other he would continue to muddle through. Maybe that was the correct outcome in justice. But Godwin, who had cried wolf so often, had more wolves at the door than ever.

Surprisingly the bereavements of 1818 did not bring on the expected cataplexy. In 1819 however came unmistakable signs that the advance of the disease was continuing. In March he lost the use of the little finger of his right hand. In November he suffered a slight stroke and in December he lost the use of his whole left hand. Although he seemed to recover, there were worrying sudden attacks of giddiness. On one occasion he fell downstairs and there are alarming references in his journal to 'scald' and to 'red hot pipe'. With the trepidation of one less steady on his feet he began to note the changes in the weather, the fogs, the frosts, and the lingering snows which had made London life increasingly difficult and expensive for most of the decade. As he advanced into his sixties Godwin's journal is more frequently dotted with references to illness, 'indisposed', 'headache', 'fever', 'depression' and with remedies, 'leeches, linseed poultice 9 days', 'lax'. Despite a vegetable diet he suffered badly from constipation, which can shake the equanimity of the sternest philosopher, and as Coleridge could have told him, the opium-based 'panegoric' which he bought on 4 March 1818 would worsen the problem even if it temporarily relieved the pain. The 'rhubarb' was probably more efficacious but the main remedy continued to be Seneca.

He found himself drawn back towards the past. He resumed writing passages for his autobiography, renewing the times when the future still held promise for himself and for the world. He took William Godwin Junior to visit Hoxton where he had studied for the ministry. He read the Bible again. He drafted more than one essay on religion, tracing again the doctrinal differences which had once seemed important, although he was never at risk of reverting to Christianity. When a boy at Guestwick, he had learned to escape from anxiety by imagining himself alone on a desert island: during the last weeks before the Shelleys left London he again read *Robinson Crusoe* right through.

There were worries too about William, the last of the five children. He had always been difficult, talented but unstable like his mother. Godwin moved him from school to school and encouraged his talent for mathematics. He arranged for him to be examined by his old friend Bonnycastle with whom he had shared the weekly dinners at Johnson's years before. The first steam engines for ships were being built in yards along the Thames and William wanted to join in the exciting new technology. Godwin sought advice from Rennie, Maudslay and other prominent engineers and William started training as an engineer. But when he damaged his hand in an accident, he had to give up hopes of that profession. He next thought of architecture, but before long it was clear that, like his father and mother and most of their family, William Godwin Junior too would have to settle for the uncertain future of a writer.

In 1818 the family was extended by the arrival of Marc Valette, Mary Jane's nephew from St Etienne, who was being sent to school in London and who stayed frequently at Skinner Street. His mother, Mary Jane's sister Charlotte, paid a long visit. The Pilchers, Mary Jane's other sister's family from Rochester, were also frequently to be found at Skinner Street. His own brothers, Nat Godwin and Joseph Godwin, who had resumed contact at the time of Hannah's funeral, each became frequent callers thereafter. As old age approached the bonds of family began again to tighten. Lives which had diverged thirty or forty years previously now turned slowly back towards one another.

The worst threat of all now looked set to become a reality. On 23 June 1818 Godwin received a notice to quit Skinner Street. From the time he first moved from The Polygon he had paid no rent. The ownership dispute had dragged on, but the law was now ready to take its course. Godwin shut the door on calls from the claimants and their representatives, but when they took the matter to court there could only be one outcome. His claim in law was tenuous; even by the elastic standards of political justice it stretched credibility. Since there was no question of his finding ten years' arrears of rent the owners would sooner or later be given a court order for repossession, and the family would be turned into the street.

In 1821 the journal notes calls by Wake and by Walker, men who had appealed to him for money before going into prison either for debt or for crime. They had presumably served their sentences and been released. On 19 June 1821 Joseph Godwin went to trial – on what charge has not been discovered – and he too was sent to prison.[5] Frantic discussions with Hudson Gurney may have been an attempt to stave off ruin by refinancing Joseph's debts, but if so they were unsuccessful. Over the following months Godwin's round of calls included a visit to his brother at least once a week – it is likely that he was in a debtors' prison. He was to die in the Fleet three years later, Godwin arranging the funeral with the prison authorities.

Most men would have acknowledged long ago that the position was hopeless and tried to make an arrangement with creditors for bankruptcy. That would be a disaster, but at least something might be salvaged if only hope for the future. If Godwin could make an agreement he might be able to sell out or move out with consent. But having fought successfully against impossible odds in the past Godwin was incapable of changing. He exploited every legal quibble that the imagination of his expensive lawyers could conjure up. If to some eyes he was a pitiable relic of former greatness, so long habituated to hardship, disappointment and dependence that he now resembled the crabbed complaining misanthropes of his own novels, his own view was different. Like Fénelon he deserved to be rescued, not for his own sake, but for the unique contribution he could still make to human progress as a philosopher and as an educator.

Godwin would now admit openly that he disliked Shelley. For the most part he refused even to write to him direct although he kept up a regular correspondence with Mary. It was a reversal of his practice during the earlier confrontations when he had written to Shelley but never to Mary, and emphasized his continuing distrust and disapproval. Shelley regularly sent money, but never enough to discharge the enormous obligation which Godwin felt that he owed. On each occasion when Shelley had let him down, his troubles had accelerated. It was an easy step to believe that Shelley was responsible for the whole accumulated mess. A scrap of a business letter to Shelley survives in which Godwin evidently compared himself to a marble block. On the back there is a comment by Lord Byron

Instead of 'Marble block' read 'Barbers' i.e. a head without a heart. Oh Caleb William!!![6]

In 1821 'Edward Baldwin' at last completed the History of Greece which had been started and laid aside many years before. In the past, he admitted in the Preface, he had preferred the Romans, but now he had learned to appreciate the Greeks.[7] Above all he admired Socrates who had not only made philosophical discoveries but transmitted them by Socratic conversations to his pupils. When Shelley and Harriet first met Godwin in 1812, his large head had reminded them of Socrates, but Shelley had turned out to be not a Plato but an Alcibiades. 'What master', Godwin noted in his *History*, 'can always be responsible for the future character of his pupil?'

A psychologist might say that Godwin vented his dislike of Shelley by trying to make him feel guilty about money. But he was also providing an example of the essential truth of his own theory. Godwin's medullary particles had become so accustomed to assertiveness and defiance that he could no longer react to disappointment or anxiety in any other way. As each year advanced Godwin became more deliberate, more precise, more dogmatic, less tolerant, more ungracious, more unfair. As much as any king, courtier, or priest, he was slowly being deprived of his freedom to think impartially. He was chained.

In 1820 King George III died after sixty years on the throne. Godwin could remember as a boy being taken by his father to see the firework display to celebrate his accession. For decades the King had been intermittently mad, an embarrassment and a warning to others destined for a similar fate. One consequence of his death was the founding by the new King of the Royal Literary Fund to give money to authors – although the trustees took care to confine their charity to church-and-king men like Coleridge and anti-Jacobin writers like Mathias. Malthus, who did not need money, was also given a grant. Another consequence of the King's death was that performances of *King Lear* were again permitted on the English stage. On 27 April 1820 Godwin saw Edmund Kean perform the title role in the play which most perfectly expressed the thoughts and fears he had tried unsuccessfully to bring to his own times in *Mandeville*. His own beloved Cordelia was far away in Italy, but he too in his old age would defy the storms of disappointment until he was overcome.

Meanwhile Shelley, Mary, and Claire were moving restlessly from city to city with their unfortunate children, before coming to comparative rest in Pisa, a town well known to English exiles on investment incomes with something to hide. As a last favour before they left England Godwin wrote a letter of introduction to Mrs Gisborne who had lived in nearby Livorno since 1801.[8] The former Maria Reveley, who had offered him love when they were both married and refused him marriage when they were both legally free, had been at The Polygon when Mary was born in 1797 and had helped look after her when Mary Wollstonecraft died. The Shelleys also renewed acquaintance with 'Mrs Mason', the name by which

Lady Mountcashell liked to be known, whom they had met on her occasional visits to England. Even in Italy Shelley and Mary were under the continued influence of her distant father and her dead mother.

In 1820 when Maria Gisborne accompanied her husband on a visit back to England, she kept a diary to show to the Shelleys on her return.[9] Shelley wrote her a long poem, *Letter to Maria Gisborne*, listing one by one the friends in London whom she would meet and the diary was a prose reply. First and foremost was of course William Godwin and she visited Skinner Street several times to see him. Her former admirer, she found, was more corpulent than when she had last seen him twenty years before when he had been slim and sharp-featured. The radical dandy with his bright waistcoats was now dressed in shabby, old-fashioned clothes, much patched. He was also less sincere. On the first visit her son met Mary Jane working busily in the shop. Mrs Gisborne was therefore surprised to receive a note from Godwin saying that she was 'extremely ill' and could not therefore receive her. It was later explained that Mary Jane refused to meet any friend of Mary Wollstonecraft Shelley but Godwin's excuse had been genuinely intended to deceive.

Mary Jane later relented and the first love of Godwin's life and his last met on a few occasions. The second Mrs Godwin was pretty, Mrs Gisborne noted, forcing herself to be fair, but her 'physiognomy' was distinctly bad – she too was fat. Her own second husband, she may have reflected, might be one of the dullest men in the world, but his money had kept them in reasonable comfort. Most of the conversation was about Shelley and his affairs, both sexual and financial, and how he had proved both disappointing and deceitful. Mary Jane confided that Shelley would be the death of Godwin, and Godwin himself gave her a full account of the money quarrel when they were alone. Since her diary was intended to be read by Shelley and Mary, few details of what he actually said are given, but she went away fully convinced that the faults were not all on the Godwin side. Godwin questioned her closely about Claire and whether she was still involved with Lord Byron. He still found it difficult to credit that Byron was the father of her child. He talked of Tom Turner – Shelley's predecessor – and of Cornelia. Turner's conversation, he said, was more interesting and varied than that of any person he knew. As for Cornelia, she was agreeable but nothing more – he might meet twenty such forgettable women every day. Neither Fanny, Mary, nor Claire had liked Turner but they had all been in love with the unsuitable Shelley.

Shelley's poems, Godwin complained to his old friend, were written in a tone of anger, bitterness and violence. They were also 'full of obscurities and puzzles' which he hated. As criticism of *Queen Mab* and *The Revolt of Islam*, the only two long works that he had read hitherto, nobody could say that he was unjust. *The Cenci*, which Godwin read on 26 March 1820, was little better but at least it had a story and was concerned with individuals not abstractions. As Godwin told Mary,[10] he was pleased to see Shelley coming down from his airy-fairy speculations and trying to delineate real people, but it was a restrained compliment.

Godwin doubted whether Shelley had the knowledge, the judgement or the experience to be a philosopher, and Shelley was inclined to agree. As he wrote in the Preface to *Prometheus Unbound*, he had in mind to produce 'a systematical history of the genuine elements of human society'. It would be a prose work, an updating of existing moral and intellectual science, but like the author of *Political Justice*, whose example he was following, Shelley distrusted his ability to make new discoveries. Until he was able to do so he would reform the world with poetry. Poets, Shelley wrote, are the creators of their age as well as the creations. His previous poems had been merely intended to display 'idealisms of moral excellence', not to set out a reasoned theory of life. Now he had a more ambitious purpose. The Greeks had started the liberation of the human mind. The writers of the Elizabethan age had helped break the grip of Christianity in its most oppressive form. Milton, a staunch republican and fearless inquirer, had carried forward the same spirit. The great writers of his own age, among whom he included Godwin, were also forerunners of future improvement.

Godwin told Maria Gisborne that he was eager to read *Prometheus Unbound*, but like others he found the poetry harder going than the Preface. The journal for 19 September 1820 records his reading Act I only, and when he lent his copy to Henry Crabb Robinson he confessed that he had been unable to read it through.[11] Godwin therefore missed the magnificent ringing speeches in which the philosophy that he had taught to Shelley was given one of its most vivid and most enduring expressions. But even a cursory glance would have given the main message. *Prometheus Unbound* is a celebration of defiance. The chained but unsubmitting Titan represents suffering humanity at its most noble and at its most effective. It is the Promethean spirit which has brought about every worthwhile human advance. The moral corruption that keeps humanity down among the writhing worms is the institutionalized servility which accustoms them to accept their fate, to perpetuate it, and even to enjoy it.

Aeschylus in his lost drama of *Prometheus Unbound* envisaged an eventual reconciliation between Prometheus and Jupiter, the Champion and the Oppressor – but this was a feeble conclusion, as Shelley could see. Compromise with a cruel and unjust God would be tantamount to submission. Godwin's novels turn on remorse, but as his miseries mounted it was the robust Prometheus of Shelley's myth which increasingly underlay his own life. In his own drama there was going to be no reversal, no triumph, only a long forced retreat until he was overwhelmed. He would however continue to withhold the knee worship, the whining prayers, and the fawning praise which Jupiter demands from the despised slaves who crouch in gratitude round his throne. After two decades of compromise and humiliation, he held hard to the little that was left. Defiance was Godwin's last dignity.

CHAPTER 37

Misery, Vice, and Moral Restraint

The book which Godwin began on 30 December 1817 within hours of finishing *Mandeville* was, as he usually believed, likely to be his last but also his most important. It was necessary to make another effort to change opinion by direct argument. All he needed was time, which he did not expect to have, and he laid plans for the book to be completed by others if he should die before it was finished. If Shelley persisted in denying him financial security – and therefore peace to write – Shelley was not only abusing the duties of wealth and kinship but helping to prolong the current supremacy of anti-Jacobinism.

It was a contorted argument and it could only have occurred to a man untroubled by excessive modesty. But Godwin felt that he carried a share of personal responsibility for the present sad state of opinion. In 1812 a misunderstanding of *Political Justice* had nearly led Shelley to stir up further violence in Ireland: if Godwin had never written his book he would never have had to blame himself for Shelley's mistakes. In the years after Waterloo the prevailing error was more serious and more pervasive, but the chain led back directly to *Political Justice*. As Malthus declared from the start, his *Essay on the Principle of Population* had been written as a reply to Godwin's theory of perfectibility and Malthusianism was now the political orthodoxy. If Godwin was to go out of the world as a net benefactor, he would have to defeat this modern version of an old fallacy.

The Proof of Love, from *Lessons for Children*

In the early years Godwin and his critic had exchanged thoughts and theories in a spirit of friendly inquiry. Malthus was attracted to Godwin's theory even if he could not believe it. Godwin too was happy to acknowledge that the younger man had made a contribution to the understanding of how the economy works even if his explanation was not valid. Now the balance and the courtesies had gone. Whereas *Political Justice* had not been reprinted since 1798, Malthus's book exploded like one of his geometrical ratios. The original concise little essay gave way to a heavy quarto. The third edition was in two volumes and the fifth, which appeared in 1817, was in three. Godwin read it through with an increasing sense of despair soon after its publication. After twenty-five years, it seemed, his own most enduring contribution to the advance of ideas was that he had provoked a successful counter-movement. The theory of perfectibility had brought forth a theory of reaction. The anti-Jacobins whose intellectual platform had been their dislike of philosophy now had a philosopher of their own eager to defend things as they are.

Malthus now made scarcely any attempt at analysis. He simply asserted that unemployment and poverty were due to 'overpopulation'. Mitigating the misery of the poor, he and his followers now argued, was not only burdensome to the rest of the community: it made the situation worse. Blunting the effects of 'natural' checks on population growth encouraged laziness, sex, and large families. Poor relief should therefore be cut back, and the churchmen and officials who administered the funds encouraged to take a tough line. The penalties of bastardy should be stepped up in accordance with the Biblical injunction to visit on the children the results of their parents' sins. Charitable lying-in hospitals which accepted unmarried mothers should be discouraged. So should the foundling hospitals which took in the abandoned babies to be found every morning on the doorsteps of London and the orphanages which gave a roof to the street urchins and child prostitutes who ran wild in some parts of the city.

The so-called principle of population, Godwin could see, was not a scientific or philosophical theory at all but a throwback to the days when the world was believed to be ruled by forces beyond the reach of human control. The worship of economic 'law' was a slightly secularized attempt to return to the time when every misery could be ascribed either to sin or to the mysterious benevolence of God. Malthus's apparently inexorable ratios relieved governments of responsibility. They were a justification of selfishness, of greed, of competitiveness, of contempt for the unfortunate, and of every sophistry by which the privileged maintained their privileges. But what caused Godwin to take up his pen again was a more personal sense of irritation. In the fifth edition Malthus had dropped the references to the ideas which had been the occasion for the book in the first place. Not only was Malthus carrying opinion before him, Godwin was being denied his share of the blame.

As always, having decided what he wanted to do, he turned to his new task with impressive conscientiousness and he worked hard on it for more than two years. David Booth, the husband of Mary's friend Isabel, who had good mathematical knowledge, agreed to work with him on what was to be in effect a collaborative project. Hazlitt who had written his own reply to Malthus helped in the conversations. Other friends were also asked to contribute, and Godwin used his extensive circle of contacts to obtain information from many parts of the world. He scrutinized the British census figures and talked to John Rickman who had compiled them.

There was little evidence of unsustainable proliferation – indeed, as he remembered from his work on the *English Peerage*, families frequently died out. Malthus claimed that in the only historical example where resources were unlimited – the settlement of North America – the population doubled every twenty-five years. But the Indians who previously inhabited the vast continent had not teemed. Godwin wrote to Boston and consulted emigrant dealers to discover how much of the increase was due to immigration. He read travel books about China where the population really had teemed and talked to explorers such as Lamb's friend Manning who had been there. He studied the ethnology of India – Malthus saw the curious conventions of the Nairs as an attempt to restrict population growth.

Godwin remembered Adam Smith's estimate that if national income were more fairly distributed, nobody would be poor and nobody need work more than a few hours a day. He calculated how much land was kept deliberately unproductive as private parks and as woodlands for shooting. The conclusion was straightforward. If there was a potential imbalance between population and resources, between demand and supply, all that was needed was more thought, more care, and more justice. But, on the whole, Godwin concluded that there was no problem except possibly in Ireland where such remedies were more difficult to apply.

Godwin's *Population*, which was completed in 1820, is a very different book from *Political Justice*. If Malthus had become an old-fashioned sin-and-doom moralist, Godwin was now a modern economist. But Godwin would have done better to forget his tables of figures and resume the argument on the grounds on which he was strongest. For although he weakened Malthus's empirical arguments, he did not destroy them. It was not enough to have scaled down the figures – even a smaller divergence between population and resources would produce disaster. Godwin missed the target which he had hit directly as early as 1801.

Malthus had originally argued that the only choice was between misery and vice. By misery he meant famine, disease, and the other results of overcrowding and undernourishment: vice included the murders likely to break out among the survivors as they fought for a share of inadequate resources. It was in response to criticisms in Godwin's *Reply to Parr* and elsewhere that he later added a third possibility, 'moral restraint', by which he meant a conscious decision to limit family size. As he prescribed it – no sex during the sexually most active years or outside marriage with late marriage for those who could afford children – moral restraint did not sound like a realistic social policy. It was however not necessary to be an uncritical perfectibilian to see that Malthus's late addition to the theory – this 'snivelling interpolation' as Hazlitt called it – destroyed the determinist inexorability of his mathematical ratios. By admitting that people could prevent overpopulation if they chose to, Malthus effectively acknowledged that there was nothing inevitable about his 'principle'.

While preparing his reply Godwin exchanged frosty letters with his opponent on points of fact. Regretting the public compliments he had once paid to Malthus's honest search for truth, he was now sure he was a hypocrite who hung to his refuted theory for the sake of personal fame and party advantage. Malthus in his turn treated Godwin with disdain. When on 6 June 1821 Godwin called on Rowland Hunter, Johnson's successor at St Paul's Churchyard, and Malthus happened to be there, they shook hands frigidly as Godwin noted in his journal in embarrassed Latin.[1] In an anonymous review in the *Edinburgh* which Godwin had not yet seen, Malthus had dismissed Godwin's book superciliously as 'a poor old-womanish performance'. Godwin's true contribution was now under-rated, he remarked patronizingly, just as previously it had been exaggerated. When the two men again found themselves in the same room on 12 December 1822, there was no handshake or greeting but a studied silence on both sides, the cut direct as Regency men said.[2]

As an economist Godwin knew that he must deal in aggregates not in anecdotes. But neither man was unaware of the situation of the other. Malthus drew a secure income of £500 a year as professor at Haileybury, a training college recently founded to supply recruits to the East India Company. Nominations for places were strictly limited by family patronage, and the college had a formal monopoly in supplying monopolists to the monopoly Company. In addition he drew an unearned income of £400 a year from a parish in Lincolnshire, which was in his family's gift. (The work was done by a curate who cost only £80 and Malthus scarcely visited the place.) Malthus had not married until he was forty, and he had since produced three children, just enough but not too many to maintain his share of the population balance. His leisure hours were devoted to Bible societies and to schemes for encouraging the poor to increase their savings. For those who accepted the system, his life was a model of moral restraint.

Godwin, on the other hand, had been imprudent. He had produced two children — and adopted a collection of other people's orphans and hemi-orphans — without having the money to support them. The fact that he had worked hard all his life was neither here nor there: even Adam Smith had numbered writers among the unproductive sectors of the economy. Besides, he had led an immoral life. Most of Godwin's family, it was well known, owed their birth to sexual behaviour which had not been sanctioned in advance by the Church of England, and as Godwin remarked in one of his unintentionally witty phrases, in Malthus's mind vice and misery were perpetually coupled.[3] Mary Wollstonecraft had died, not inappropriately, in childbirth. Mary Jane Clairmont had been forced into prison for debt when she was an abandoned mother of two children under the age of five. And now the next generation of Godwins were proving to be equally vicious and equally miserable. The daughter and the stepdaughter were leading a life of debauchery and incest with the atheists Shelley and Byron. Two suicides in one winter must mean something.

To a modern reader the debate between Godwin and Malthus has an air of unreality. His mother's late marriage and moral restraint, Godwin may have recalled, had not prevented her from bearing thirteen children. Mary Wollstonecraft had been thirty-seven and Mary Jane thirty-five when Godwin first slipped into their beds but this had not stopped them from becoming pregnant almost at once. Even Malthus's wife gave birth to their first baby eight months after their marriage when he was forty and she was twenty-nine. Advancing years were not as limiting on human fecundity as studies of cows and racehorses might suggest.

Both Godwin and Malthus seem to have accepted that a woman could not conceive when she was breast-feeding. They also believed the old masculinist myth that sex with more than one partner prevents conception. What is more puzzling is the almost total absence of any reference to artificial contraception in which Godwin should have been interested.

Since according to his theory the advance of medical science would continue to improve the life expectancy of children, his answer to Malthus implied a corresponding advance in wisdom to forestall the consequences. In 1801 he had offered some speculations on what form such moral progress might take. In his 1820 book however he is entirely silent.

It had been Condorcet, the inventor of the term 'perfectibility' and one of the French philosophers whom Godwin most admired, who first mentioned artificial contraception in a serious book. Bentham, whom Godwin scarcely knew, was the first writer in English to follow him. In the 1817 edition Malthus curtly dismissed Condorcet's solution in a few phrases. It would, he remarked, 'remove a tendency to industry'. Believing sexual emissions to be weakening, Malthus feared that if workers were enabled to indulge without fear of children, their useful outputs would decline and the national economy would suffer.

It is tempting to speculate that Godwin's meeting with Booth and Bentham on 27 February 1820 might have brought the subject to Godwin's attention if he did not know of it already. But if Godwin knew what methods were available, he did not recommend them. He probably shared beliefs about the weakening effects of sex, and as an optimist about human progress he preferred a moral to an artificial solution. Godwin probably favoured a deliberate limiting of family size by avoiding sex at the most fertile times of the menstrual cycle, the fallacious 'chance-medley' system he practised unsuccessfully with Mary Wollstonecraft.

Godwin was also less perturbed than many by the other side of the population balance. His own childhood had been regularly punctuated with the deaths of brothers and sisters which his parents accepted without much feeling as dues payable to a wrathful God, inescapable as taxes. Very young children, he occasionally remarked, did not carry much moral worth. Godwin's enemies accused him of advocating or condoning infanticide which was a mischievous lie. But to a man with his upbringing the death of a child in the months after birth was as normal as a miscarriage before birth and to be accepted in the same spirit.

Meanwhile the Shelley family in Italy were making their own contribution to restoring moral and economic equilibrium. When Clara Shelley died in 1818 at the age of two, Godwin offered his comfort to his daughter in a letter of 27 October.

I sincerely sympathize with you in the affliction which forms the subject of your letter, and which I may consider as the first severe trial of your constancy and the firmness of your temper that has occurred to you in the course of your life.

You should, however, recollect that it is only persons of a very ordinary sort, and of a pusillanimous disposition, that sink long under a calamity of this nature.[4]

Godwin offered the same philosophy to his depressed daughter as he had to her depressed mother twenty-two years before when she threw herself off Putney Bridge. A sense of one's own sufferings, he suggested, could easily become morbid and self-indulgent, encouraged by the current excessive admiration for sensibility. Until scientific progress could find better ways of coping with population imbalance, premature deaths had to be accepted and the struggle continued. The main thing was not to give in, nor to give up. It was a view shared by Shelley. It was the spirit of Prometheus.

Shelley had however a more practical response. If one child died then another could be obtained to fill the gap. On 27 February 1819 he officially registered the birth of a daughter Elena Adelaide Shelley as having been lawfully born to himself and Mary on 27 December 1818 at Naples. It is certain that neither Mary nor Claire was the mother nor is it likely that Shelley was the father. Shelley, who like Godwin tended to think that very young children are of small moral worth, if not interchangeable, may have impulsively arranged a replacement for Clara, perhaps buying the baby from a foundling hospital. It is a method still used by some grown-ups to comfort children who have lost a favourite pet. Shelley was well known for offering to adopt other people's children – he had done it at Oxford, in France in 1814, twice in Marlow in 1817, and no doubt on other occasions. Elena Adelaide Shelley died just over a year later, never having been visited again by her putative parents.

Much of Clara's brief life had been spent in a carriage rumbling over Europe and she had died in a dirty inn waiting for the doctor. William Shelley, who was a year older than Clara was even more widely travelled. Having been on the expedition to Switzerland in 1816 when he was three months old, he had already crossed Europe three times in a carriage. At the age of three he had a personality of his own and his parents allowed themselves to love him as an individual. On 7 June 1819, however, he too died after a few days' illness. Mary was again thrown into distraction not made easier by the knowledge that the next child which she knew was on the way was unlikely to do any better.

Shelley, who was himself almost as ill and depressed, broke a long silence and wrote to Godwin direct asking him to do what he could by way of encouragement. It is probably this letter whose receipt is mentioned in Godwin's journal for 26 June 1819. The next day Godwin noted

461

'depression', a confession he reserved for days of the blackest gloom. The comforting letter he wrote to Mary on 9 September was a reinforced version of the other.

You must . . . allow me the privilege of a father, and a philosopher, in expostulating with you on this depression. I cannot but consider it as lowering your character in a memorable degree, and putting you quite among the commonality and mob of your sex, when I had thought I saw in you symptoms entitling you to be ranked among those noble spirits that do honour to our nature. What a falling off is here! How bitterly is so inglorious a change to be deplored![5]

A child had died, but this was a small thing when compared with the other blessings Mary still enjoyed – married to a rich husband; 'a man of high intellectual attainments whatever I and some other persons may think of his morality'. Some people confronted with misfortune, he went on, sit with their arms crossed, a prey to languor and apathy. Others, among whom he included his daughter, pick themselves up and use their talents as best they could 'to advance their whole species one or more degrees in the scale of perfectibility'.

On 12 November 1819 Mary gave birth to her fourth child, Percy Florence Shelley. She decided to breast-feed him, but it was a struggle, and she continued to be depressed and worried about her father. Every post which told of mounting disasters at Skinner Street exacerbated her guilt. Every Godwinian remark about Shelley made her wonder again if she had been right to run away with him. Leaving England had lengthened the chain that bound her to Godwin but it was stronger and tighter than ever.

Worry during pregnancy, it was commonly believed, could damage an unborn child and worry during breast-feeding was almost as dangerous. 'A woman should never suckle her child', Mrs Mason wrote in her book on child care, 'immediately after any violent agitation of mind . . . Children . . . are very liable to derangements of the stomach and bowels . . . I have known a child in perfect health attacked suddenly by convulsions, in consequence of the mother having imprudently put it to her breast just after seeing a person fall down dead.'[6] When in the summer Percy Florence Shelley was ill with the same raging diarrhoea that had carried off Clara and then William, Shelley believed that Godwin's letters were to blame. On 7 August 1820 in exasperation he broke a long silence and wrote Godwin a long letter of complaint. His main point was about Godwin's effect on Mary's milk.

Mary is now giving suck to her infant, in whose life, after the frightful events of the last two years, her own seems wholly to be bound up. Your letters from their style and spirit (such is your erroneous notion of taste) never fail to produce an apalling effect on her frame; on one occasion agitation of mind produced through her a disorder in the child similar to that which destroyed our little girl two years ago . . . Mary at my request authorized me to intercept such letters or information as I might judge likely to disturb her mind.[7]

In the first draft of this letter Shelley inserted the phrase 'united to other circumstances' after 'on one occasion'. But in the version which was sent it was omitted. Shelley put all the blame for the baby's diarrhoea on Godwin's letters.

Meanwhile Shelley and Mary were also doing their best to cope with the problem of that other effect of Godwinian theory, Claire's daughter Allegra. Lord Byron, who had even less regard for babies as individuals than Shelley, originally proposed that the bastard – as he habitually called her – should be dispatched to Italy with the courier who brought his newspapers, his books, and his medicines from London. When Shelley, on his arrival in Italy, suggested a meeting during which the father could get used to the child and the mother could get used to sharing her, Byron feared a trap. Shelley, he suspected, was hoping to revive by Lake Como the Shelley-Mary-Byron-Claire foursome which had caused such scandal at Lake Geneva two years before. He refused categorically to have any direct dealings with Claire. As the father his rights were absolute and he insisted on taking custody.

The frightened child was torn from her frantic mother to be brought up among the stinking hounds, the gibbering monkeys, the polluting peacocks, and the scented whores who frequented Byron's palace at Venice. Byron was kind to her, but as he openly admitted, he treated her like a toy. He liked to play with her in the afternoons, to show her off to his visitors, and to take her for rides in his carriage. Allegra lacked nothing except her dishonoured mother's love. Claire believed that she had been given promises of regular access, as the child's putative 'aunt', but she found herself excluded. When Shelley, in response to her distress, offered to take Allegra back, Byron declared that he was not going to have his daughter brought up on atheism and green vegetables, and indeed the chances of her thriving as part of the Shelley ménage must have seemed minimal. When Allegra was five, too big to be a toy but still not credited with having feelings of her own, she was sent in the Italian style to be educated by nuns in a convent near Ravenna. She died there in 1822.

Percy Florence Shelley, Shelley's and Mary's only surviving child, overcame his illness. During the whole of 1820 while he was being breast-fed and weaned Mary did not become pregnant. Nor was she pregnant in 1821. At the beginning of 1822 however when she was a little healthier both in mind and in body she became pregnant for the fifth time. The gap – the first since they ran away in 1814 – may not have been accidental. For if Godwin was ignorant of contraception Shelley was not. In the late eighteenth century condoms made from animal membranes were sold discreetly in London by various ladies who were – it seems – always called 'Mrs Phillips'. Costing about four shillings each, and not reusable, they were only for the rich, and – as their slang name of 'armour' implied – they were regarded primarily as a masculine preventive against diseases carried by women. Byron imported them discreetly from England, as can be proved from newly available evidence,[8] and they were successful in their purpose. In his youth he had fathered children by servant girls who were immediately bundled off and pensioned off. He also caught gonorrhoea. But in Italy, despite heavy bouts of promiscuity and whoring in Venice and elsewhere, neither problem occurred again.

But if Byron's attitude to women was coarse and exploitative, Shelley genuinely believed in the equality of the sexes. There was another method which was cheap, easily obtainable and altogether preferable for both parties in all cases where there was no risk of disease. A piece of sponge attached to a cotton and dipped in wine or vinegar was an effective contraceptive, especially as the sponges then came from the Far East and were not as pervious as the Mediterranean varieties which later replaced them. The method was said to have been devised for the French aristocracy during the dreary years of the *ancien régime* when they had nothing much to do, and it had won an established place in the etiquette of gallantry. Among the results of the French Revolution which twenty years of war had been unable to reverse was that knowledge of the technique was disseminated – as Godwin might have said – more widely in France and had soon crossed the Channel. It was however still a secret especially guarded from those who could make best use of it.

To Shelley – as to Godwin – Malthus was only the latest manifestation of the institutionalized conspiracy of priests, wealth owners, and governments to keep men ignorant, miserable and subservient, and women even more so. Not content with driving down the standard of living of the poor and blaming them for their own poverty Malthusians with their talk of 'late marriage' were now seeking to deny them even the comfort of sexual love. In one of Shelley's notebooks are a few jottings, much corrected, perhaps intended to make good the omissions in Godwin's book.

Malthus principle

As to this system being stated as an objection to a more civilized system of society, I wonder – It is remarkable that the comprehensive and penetrating intellect of Godwin [breaks off]

The sexual intercourse by no means presents, as has been supposed, the [?] horrendous alternative of a being to be invested with existence for whom there is no subsistence, or the revolting expedients of infanticide and abortion. Any student of anatomy must be aware of an innocent, small and almost imperceptible precaution by which all consequences of this kind are prevented, and the ends of an union of two persons of the opposite sexes in every other respect fulfilled

As nothing but evil could result from its partial and unauthorized use, I refrain from explaining myself, on a subject with which so much false delicacy is connected

It is curious to remark how few medical men of any considerable science have more children than they can comfortably maintain.[9]

It may be that contraception would have featured in the philosophical book which Shelley had in mind to write as his updating of *Political Justice*. With remarkable perspicuity he had foreseen the next great issue in the struggle for individual liberty which was to range friends of freedom against the forces of church and state for another hundred years and more. But the uncharacteristic references to 'partial and unauthorized use' suggest that even Shelley, lover of equality and freedom though he was, feared the social consequences if the secret were to be let out too quickly. He had now retracted far from the Nairism he had once found so attractive and which only needed safe female contraception to make practical.

Among the Godwins and the Shelleys it was not the preventive check but the direct check which restored the balance. On 16 April 1822 Godwin's case to be allowed to stay in Skinner Street came before the court and a verdict was given against him. He wrote to Mary that day to give the news (in a letter now lost) and three days later wrote again.

My dearest Mary

The die, so far as I am concerned, seems now to be cast, and all that remains is that I should entreat you to forget that you have a Father in existence. Why should your prime of youthful vigour be tarnished and made wretched by what relates to me? I have lived to the full age of man in as much comfort as can reasonably be expected to fall to the lot of a human being. What signifies what becomes of the few wretched years that remain?

For the same reason, I think I ought for the future to drop writing to you. It is impossible that my letters can give you anything but unmingled pain. A few weeks more, and the formalities which still restrain the successful claimant will be over, and my prospects for tranquillity must, as I believe, be eternally closed. Farewell.

William Godwin[10]

It was a moment of despair such as he seldom permitted himself. The hint of blackmail apparent in earlier letters was now unhidden. On 1 May his lawyers moved for a new trial in a higher court, but the petition was peremptorily refused. That evening a writ was served and two men put into the house. Told on the Thursday that if the family did not leave voluntarily by Saturday they would be thrown into the street, the Godwins finally moved out on the Saturday to stay with friends at Pemberton Row. On the Saturday shortly before they left they received a further writ for the arrears of rent.

Godwin was broken. His handwriting deteriorated overnight into the uncontrolled scrawl of a very old man. The 'saevitia' and 'castor oil' noted in his journal marked a savage attack of constipation and an equally savage remedy. It was left to Mary Jane and young William to write the letters passing the news to Italy. On 10 July his young pupil Henry Blanch Rosser died at Cambridge in circumstances reminiscent of the death of Patrickson in 1814. Towards the end of the month there was a new crisis at the Fleet Prison involving numerous calls on his brother Joseph and on the Warden: shortly afterwards it was confirmed that Joseph was suffering from the fatal 'dropsy' commonly brought on by conditions in the prison.

Godwin still had friends old and new including Lady Caroline Lamb whose affair with Byron had been the talk of London society in 1814 and whom Godwin was helping with the drafting of her latest novel.[11] On 20 March he took tea with the Boinvilles meeting again the Chevalier Lawrence. If Shelley genuinely wished to save him there was still time. On the day the eviction order was confirmed Willats, the moneylender who had accepted Shelley's post-obit in 1818, called to offer more money on the same terms – a fact instantly conveyed to Italy. A visit to Richard Taylor his printer to ask for time produced an abrupt refusal – 'Coarse and vulgar,' Godwin noted probably recording Taylor's words. But others were more indulgent. Tom Turner sent £50: so did Charles Lamb. By 4 July 1822 M. J. Godwin and Company was open for business as usual at 195 Strand.

In the event Mary did not read any of Godwin's letters to Italy, Shelley having kept them from her. She continued deeply depressed, irritable and languorous, and easily disturbed. In April Allegra died of typhus in the convent and Claire, maddened with grief, came to live in the Shelley household for a few distressing weeks. On 9 June Mary started to bleed and after a week she miscarried with a massive haemorrhage that lasted for seven hours. The efforts of the doctor were mainly devoted to reducing the pain of her death which he was sure was certain. Between fainting fits she was plied with brandy and rubbed down with vinegar and eau de cologne, and it was only when Shelley made her sit in a bath filled with ice that the bleeding stopped.

Mary was still very ill and depressed when Shelley left in his boat to meet Leigh Hunt on his way from England. Lying in bed she listened in terror to the storm which suddenly swept up the coast on the day he was due to return, and there were to be many other days of anguish before the news was confirmed. Shelley was dead, his drowned body thrown up by the sea on the beach at Viareggio. He was not yet thirty years of age.

The news reached London on 4 August when John Hunt's *Examiner* published a few details drawn from a letter from Leigh Hunt. Shelley was not a specially famous man but the newspapers saw an opportunity to make moral points. As with Mary Wollstonecraft's death in 1797 it was gratifying that divine justice could be so direct. 'Shelley the writer of some infidel, poetry is dead,' noted the *Courier* next day, ' . . . now he knows if there is a God or no.' *John Bull* suggested with satisfaction that God had deliberately arranged the drowning as an awful warning.

Godwin was told when someone from Hunt's office came round on 4 August. The letter of sympathy which he sent to his daughter two days later complained that he should have had to hear of the tragedy from strangers. Shelley was scarcely mentioned – to have eulogized him would have been intolerably insincere. All his earlier talk about ceasing to write to her was, however, he declared, a thing of the past. Shelley's death brought Mary back down to his own level. All he could offer was a sharing of troubles, and they each had more than enough to give to the other.

Her own letters to her father have, with unimportant exceptions, all been lost, perhaps deliberately destroyed later by members of the family embarrassed by the strength of love they revealed. A few phrases from the letter she sent him immediately on Shelley's death have, however, recently come to light.

I have some of his friends about me who worship him – they all agree with me that he was an elementary being and that death does not apply to him . . . I am not however so desolate as you might think. He is ever with me, encouraging me to become wise and good, that I may be worthy to join him.[12]

Mary, like her mother, although not a Christian, had never quite lost belief in a personal God and in an afterlife.

Mrs Gisborne was soon back in London with first-hand news, followed soon afterwards by Jane Williams whose unofficial husband Edward had been drowned with Shelley. Letters to the aunts had to be written, Shelley's friends seen, lawyers visited, certificates obtained. Moneylenders worried about their post-obits had to be shooed away. As always in moments of crisis Godwin cultivated an intensive normality, writing, reading, talking and going to the theatre. On 17 July he started writing his next book, a full-scale history of England during the Commonwealth, a project he had been contemplating since he sat in Cromwell's chair in the meeting house at Guestwick.

In a frantic effort to raise money he worked harder than ever. Mary's novel *Valperga* was edited and published. His own *Enquirer* of 1797 was revised and reprinted.[13] His play *Faulkener* was offered to Drury Lane yet again. Young William helped the family finances by writing a number of articles for the *Literary Examiner*. Plans to raise yet another subscription were encouraged with appropriate ungraciousness, he himself writing round remaining friends to ask for money, stretching deep into his memory to find rich men who had once crossed his path.

It is a thousand to one whether you recollect a little boy to whom you did a kind action between 50 and 60 years ago, and who has never seen you since . . . We met at Dr Christian's dancing school at Norwich. You were almost a man grown, and I was perhaps about twelve years of age . . .[14]

It is not known if he made a contribution, but others did not need to be reminded. James Ballantyne sent money without being asked, on the strength of having been introduced to Godwin at Thomas Holcroft's thirty years before.[15] To Malthusians private charity was the best way to relieve the burden which the imprudent poor imposed on public expenditure. To Godwin it was minimal political justice.

But as always the studied outward calmness concealed storms below. On 25 August 1822 Godwin felt the warning giddiness to be followed on the 28th by nausea and headaches. On 28 September he suffered a cataplectic fit. On 1 September when he was a little better he took a walk to the newly opened Waterloo Bridge near his shop, and on his return he composed a long meditation on misery and death.[16] In October he confided in Latin to his journal that he feared that he would never again be well. At the end of November he composed another long autobiographical meditation on the brevity of human life and the longevity of true worth. At the beginning of 1823 the giddiness started to strike nearly every month interspersed with almost continuous headaches, lack of sleep, and painful constipation. Instead of recording his illnesses he now noted the good days, 'sleep 15 days', 'well 5 days'. Seneca was laid aside in favour of the equally strong Cicero *On Old Age*. There was only one bright spot. Mary had decided to come home.

CHAPTER 38

Handing Over

Mary Shelley arrived in London at the end of August 1823 just in time to attend one of the first stage performances of *Presumption or the Fate of Frankenstein*. Her second novel had recently been published and *Frankenstein* itself was soon back in print. She stayed for a time in the Godwins' cramped lodgings above the shop at 195 Strand before finding accommodation of her own in Kentish Town not far from Somers Town where she had been born.

It was more than five years since Mary had last seen England or her father. When she left she had not reached her twenty-first birthday and life lay ahead: now the widow had to find a new start. For a time Godwin started again to refer to her in his journal as MWG, 'Mary Wollstonecraft Godwin', instead of MWS as he had called her since the marriage of 1816. Perhaps he hoped that the whole Shelley nightmare could somehow be put into the past. But if so his hopes were soon disappointed.

Her name would always be Shelley, Mary told more than one admirer, and the words carried a hint of defiance. By the time of her return the name Shelley was as notorious as Wollstonecraft and Godwin had been at the time of her birth. In 1821, when the poet was still alive, a pirated edition of Shelley's *Queen Mab* was put on sale in London, purporting to have been published in New York. The name of the publisher was given as 'J. Baldwin', perhaps a joke at the expense of 'Edward Baldwin', but it was in fact William Benbow. The initiative came from 'Erasmus

Moving House, from *Lessons for Children*

Perkins', the man who had arranged for the first public printing of the poem in the *Theological Inquirer* in 1815. When another pirate bookseller called Clark produced a fine octavo edition he was immediately prosecuted by the Society for the Suppression of Vice. Richard Carlile, another pirate publisher, obtained the stock, pasted over Clark's imprint, tipped in a new title page, and put the books on sale as if they were a new publication. By the middle of 1822 *Queen Mab* was available in four or more different versions. The trials of the pirates, coinciding with news of the author's death, ensured that it was to be by far Shelley's most famous and influential poem, indeed the only one easily available. Since 1821 Shelley's most Godwinian poem has never been out of print.*

As with Godwin and Wollstonecraft a generation before, opponents could not decide which was worse, the ideas or the attempts to live them. The influential *Literary Gazette* accused Shelley of robbing a confiding father of his daughters, incestuously debauching them, encouraging Harriet to support herself by 'prostitution', and laughing at her suicide 'while in the arms of associate strumpets'.[1] Coleridge's friend Cottle, whom Godwin had visited at Bristol, published a long poem warning Lord Byron to repent before he too should follow the fate of the author of *Queen Mab* and find himself standing unprepared before the Deity 'whose terrors now he knows'.[2] Nair Lawrence released a copy of the letter which Shelley had written to him in 1812 agreeing with his description of marriage as legalized prostitution, and it was frequently reprinted as a statement of his views.[3]

Mary Wollstonecraft Shelley, who arrived back in England after the brunt of the publicity was over, was a Shelley only in law as the poet's father was well aware. She had also, as he pointed out more than once, formed an unlawful connection with his son while his lawful wife was still living. The same was not however true of her son Percy Florence Shelley who had been born years after Harriet was safely dead and Mary legitimately married, and who at the end of 1823 reached the age of four. He stood second in line to succeed to the fortune and to the title after his half brother Charles, the son by Harriet whom the poet had scarcely seen. Sir Timothy Shelley, conscious of blood and honour, offered Percy Florence the same opportunities as had been conferred on Ianthe and Charles by the court decision of 1817. If Mary would hand over custody, he suggested, his grandson could be farmed out to a provincial clergyman. Lord Byron, who was executor of Shelley's will, advised acceptance – Sir

---

* See Appendix 3 for a fuller account.

Timothy was doing what he thought was in the best interests of the child as Byron had done when he tore Allegra from Claire to send her to a convent. But Mary refused indignantly and there was never a chance that she would change her mind.

Furthermore Percy Florence was her link to the Shelley money. Shelley's will of 1817 made Mary his residuary legatee. Since he had died before inheriting that will could not be executed. Godwin had meetings with Peacock – the other executor – and with Hanson, a lawyer acting for Lord Byron, but they could only confirm that there was no claim. Sir Timothy, who detested Mary as much as he detested his dead son, did however reluctantly agree to pay her a small allowance to help with the boy's education. As a Shelley, Percy Florence was entitled to the charity accorded to distant cousins and acknowledged bastards. The dependence was used without shame as an instrument of control. When Mary published an edition of Shelley's *Posthumous Poems* in 1824 Sir Timothy's lawyers forced her to withdraw the book by stopping payment of her allowance, and the threat was renewed whenever she looked like contradicting his wishes. It was a blatant exercise of economic power against the ideas that threatened it and Mary, with her young child and ageing father to consider, had little choice but to submit.

But those who live by the property laws perish by the property laws. In 1826, with the death at the age of eleven of Charles Shelley, Percy Florence unexpectedly became Sir Timothy's direct heir. (Ianthe, as a girl, had no claim.) It was now only a matter of time and of keeping the boy alive for the Shelley wealth to revert to the family who had done more than any other to subvert the values on which it had been built. Since Sir Timothy was now an old man – he was almost exactly the same age as Godwin – there could not be long to wait.

There were others who felt that Mary needed to be reminded of her past. Mrs Barbauld was among the literary contemporaries of Mary Wollstonecraft who had never risked her reputation. 'The ladies of my family,' wrote her niece Mrs Herbert Martin, 'though great admirers of Mrs Godwin's writings, were too correct in their conduct to visit her, and the same objection was felt to Mrs Shelley. When, many years after this time, my Aunt Lucy was at a large party at Mrs Daniel Gaskell's . . . and she brought up Mrs Shelley to introduce her to my aunt, hoping no doubt to give a mutual pleasure, my aunt resolutely turned her back on the fair widow.'[4] In the world of the 1820s women – even of the reforming kind – not only took their husbands' surnames and Christian names but embraced the whole masculine social system.

Mary Jane could scarcely bear the interminable expressions of sympathy which Mary Shelley attracted. The hated stepdaughter who had lured Claire and Charles Clairmont from their mother was now established in London as a beautiful literary lady with an interesting past and interesting financial expectations. Mary Shelley was turning out novels, tales, reference books, and journalism in profusion, although still as 'the author of Frankenstein' for fear of losing Sir Timothy Shelley's allowance, and if she was shunned by ladies, she was much sought after by men. Godwin implored his wife to control her jealousy – as he called it with his usual explicitness – but Mamma seldom accompanied the pair on their evenings out. Even when she went to visit her sister in Rochester and elsewhere, she complained that Godwin was seeing his daughter too often. And Mary Jane had a point. With Shelley's death Godwin's daughter could come home but her own daughter needed to go even further away. Without Shelley, Claire Clairmont had no money. Byron was now immensely rich, having recently inherited a new fortune from his former wife's mother – the fact that his marriage had broken up in bitterness within months of the ceremony was irrelevant to the property aspects. But when Mrs Mason asked him to give money to Claire, he refused angrily. He had grown to hate the girl who – in her innocence – had seduced him without taking contraceptive precautions.

Claire went first to Vienna where Charles was working as an English language teacher, but the secret police quickly identified the pair as children of the infamous revolutionaries Godwin and Wollstonecraft and associates of the atheistical Byron and Shelley. She then moved to Moscow and it was there that she heard of the death of Byron in 1824. Now even in the remotest city in Europe she could not be safe. As the obituaries and biographies poured from the presses she knew that somebody would sooner or later reveal that she was the Miss C. who had borne Allegra: on that day she would become not only unemployable but unvisitable, except by relatives, by immoral women, and by men.

Godwin himself had long since changed his views on biographical sincerity. The *Memoirs of the Author of a Vindication of the Rights of Woman* had done untold damage to two generations of his family without as yet bringing about any noticeable benefit. It was a hard lesson for a believer in intellectual and moral progress to accept. If those who are in a position to know the truth do not record it when it is available, how can accurate biography be written? If the describing of individual lives is constrained by taboo, how can new generations learn from the experience of their predecessors? Since all moral philosophy must ultimately rest on an understanding of the atomic unit, i.e. the individual human being, partial or insincere biography promotes false opinions, misdirected motives, and unjust conduct. As Voltaire had said, one owes respect to the living but to the dead one owes only the truth.

However Godwin now accepted that for biographies which mentioned the living some dilution was required. Holcroft had devoted his dying months to composing parts of a fearless autobiography, but when Hazlitt was given the task of completing it into a full-scale memoir, Godwin argued successfully for the deletion of all references to Mary Wollstonecraft's involvement with Gilbert Imlay, and there is no mention of Holcroft's proposal to marry her. He also protested at derogatory remarks about himself. It took more than ten years after Holcroft's death before Holcroft's contesting friends permitted the biography to appear.

In 1825 with the death of Fuseli the same question arose again in more acute form. Fuseli's friend and prospective biographer John Knowles, who inherited the painter's papers, found amongst them the love letters which Mary Wollstonecraft had sent during the intensive episode when she was composing the *Vindication*.[15] These were the letters to which Godwin had been refused access when he was composing the *Memoirs* and if he had had the opportunity, he would probably at that time have printed extracts from them alongside the letters to Imlay as further examples of romantic sensibility at its finest. Now Godwin took a different view. He begged Knowles that the name of Mary Wollstonecraft should be 'very slightly mentioned or not at all' and in the event only a few unsurprising and biographically misleading extracts from her letters were printed.

It was less risky to improve the future by writing about the remoter past. For six years after Shelley's death Godwin was far away in his beloved seventeenth century writing a four-volume *History of the Commonwealth of England*, although a defence of the English republican revolutionaries of the Commonwealth was the last thing that post-war England wanted to hear. The main reason why England's great experiment had failed, Godwin suggested, was that 'the intellect and moral feeling' of the country were not yet ripe.[6] They had still not been ripe when the next attempt was made at the time of the French Revolution despite a century of resumed progress. Perhaps, they never would be ripe. Only in the climate were there as yet any signs of improvement. All over Europe the snows retreated, the summers lengthened, and the harvests improved.

In the spring of 1826 it was reported that the frozen body of a man had been recovered in the Alps, and when he was defrosted he revived, none the worse for his ordeal except for some stiffness in the joints. He had, he explained, been caught in an avalanche in 1660. His name was Roger Dodsworth and he was the son of the famous antiquary who was a prominent figure in Cromwell's England. Godwin stopped work on his history in hopes of being able to arrange a personal interview. To the author of *St. Leon*, the father of the author of *Frankenstein* and the friend of the author of 'Rip Van Winkle', the notion of survival and reanimation was not incredible. The hoaxers took their fun. One of Dodsworth's quaint olde Englishe letters to the newspapers spoke of his puzzlement at hearing of something called the 'New Philosophy'.[7]

There was now plenty of time for writing. The daily round of borrowing, discounting and visits to lawyers was over. After long negotiations, he made an agreement with the owners of 41 Skinner Street to pay off some of his arrears of rent in instalments. In 1825 however Godwin and M. J. Godwin were at last declared bankrupt. The national financial crisis of that year began with that default of several overseas countries and the chain of repercussions ruined numerous British businesses and over seventy British banks. The proud house of Constable collapsed bringing down their printers, their London associates, and Sir Walter Scott. Sir Richard Phillips whose bankruptcy in 1809 had precipitated an earlier Godwin crisis went under again, and there was scarcely a firm in the book industry that did not have a struggle merely to survive. In the welter of forced sales and mergers that followed, the disappearance of the Juvenile Library was hardly noticed. The stock was sold at a knockdown price and the Godwins moved to a small house in Gower Place at the northern edge of Bloomsbury just across the road from Somers Town. It was an event dreaded for years, but when it came it gave relief to the point of delight. With so many others in similar difficulties Godwin was spared the usual condescending lectures on his irresponsibility, and his creditors were spared his charmless rebuttals. The crisis, it was generally admitted, had been caused ultimately by the system of unrestricted bill-discounting which allowed financiers to create their own credit.

Godwin, most people decided, ought to have chosen bankruptcy years ago. Obstinacy had cost him years of excruciating anxiety and it had damaged his writing career and his health. But he himself never admitted to any regrets. He had never felt a strong claim in political justice to owners of the house who for many years did not even know that they owned it. Nor did he feel any sense of obligation to the professional financiers who by their ingenuity had found ways of redirecting some of the Shelley family fortune to Shelley and to himself. Indeed it was pleasing to learn that many of them lost their speculation. By dying before his father Shelley had annulled their claims for post-obit, and even those who had insured Shelley's life against that risk had sometimes forgotten to pay the premium required to cover sea voyages.[8] Godwin and Shelley had diverted some of the rents and profits of the hereditary landowners to finance the books which would weaken their power. In the Promethean struggle they had emerged not quite victorious but more than undefeated.

Slowly the scandals subsided, calmness returned, and with it Godwin's defiant self-confidence. On 21 Ocrtober 1824 he read Hazlitt's *Spirit of the Age*, probably from the manuscript since it was not published until the following year. Unlike some of Hazlitt's other works, this book 'was written with admirable temper and fairness', as he told the publisher, 'except perhaps the article on Gifford'.[9] It was a restrained response to a book that contains the most perceptive and appreciative remarks on Godwin which had ever been written. The *Spirit of the Age*, which sets Godwin amongst the immortals, is as much part of his monument as *Political Justice* and *Caleb Williams* and much more frequently read.

There were now few opportunities to meet the other biographees of that remarkable collection of portraits. As he passed through his seventies Godwin was more prickly and truculent than ever, his outsize head more prominent as baldness advanced, and his stoop lower. On 16 May 1828 he breakfasted with Walter Scott, William Wordsworth, and other literary figures more famous then than now. On 12 June at the same house the guests included Coleridge whom he had not seen for several years. Dinners with Charles Lamb were less frequent than in the past, and when he moved to Edmonton they only met very occasionally. The men who had been young when he was middle-aged were now as frail and elderly and as testy and opinionated as himself.

Freed by the bankruptcy from the incessant worry about debt, he no longer suffered fits of cataplexy but only days of giddiness and nausea. More unpleasant was the incessant constipation which began to feature in his diary nearly every week and which did not improve his amiability. In 1830 a cataract obscured the left eye and in 1832 his right was also affected, but he was able to go on reading and writing. Occasionally he was languid and very occasionally he was confused for brief intervals. 'Unhinged twelve days' may however refer to the door of his house not to his mind.

Godwin felt his frailty, but for an old man he was in good health, and he was obstinately proud to be alive when so many others were dead. On 25 May 1831, when he was seventy-five, his journal was able to claim victory over the rival whose career he both despised and envied – 'Age of S. Johnson equalled'. He may have had a bet on his own longevity for his journal for 24 May 1833 notes a visit to the Tontine office.

In 1828 Claire Clairmont left Moscow and returned to England. Charles Clairmont also came home from Vienna with his Viennese wife. He had hoped to be appointed professor of German in the newly founded non-religious University College of London. He had also drafted a history of Germany which Godwin tried to have published, but again without success.[10] On 13 January 1829 Mary, Claire, Charles and William Godwin Junior were all together at the Godwins', the last time they were ever to meet as a family. It was decided that, if Percy Florence did inherit the Shelley fortune, the poet's will would be executed as he had wished, and Claire would be paid her £6,000. Meanwhile she must wait and the news from Sussex was not good: Sir Timothy Shelley was in as excellent health as William Godwin. Charles soon returned to Vienna and Claire, who had scarcely lived in England since she was a girl, found a position in Dresden.

And there was now another literary successor in the family. William Godwin Junior, the last of the five, combined the earnestness and persistence of his father with the emotional volatility and unpredictability of his mother. But after several false starts, he was engaged in 1823 as a reporter for the *Morning Chronicle*, a post once held by William Hazlitt, and he wrote regularly for the *Mirror of Parliament*; it was work similar to Godwin's apprenticeship on the *New Annual Register*. He wrote plays, short stories, an opera, and a full-scale novel. One of his comedies was called 'The Sleeping Philosopher'. Like his father he helped to found a literary debating club which met once a week.

Godwin was proud of his son. William and Mary Shelley came nearly every week to dine and to talk. But life in Grub Street remained as hard and as uncertain as in his father's day. William's output of journalism was huge, but none of his literary works was accepted for publication. In February 1826 he spent at least two weeks in the King's Bench Prison probably for debt although perhaps for crime. After he was liberated, he stayed with his parents for a few days to recover. In December there is evidence that he was arrested again.[11]

On 5 February 1830 William was married at a ceremony in St Anne's Church, Soho. Neither of his parents was present and William's wife seems to have made them only one visit before the marriage and none after. She was always called Emily, but her name is entered in the register as 'Mary Louisa Eldred'.[12] Like the earlier Mrs Godwins, William Godwin Junior's wife may have had something to hide.

William's friends became Godwin's friends, and the flow of new acquaintances never ceased. Some of the young men who visited simply came to stare at the survivor – and Godwin had to shoo away autograph collectors – but as ever he was on the look out for disciples. Edward John Trelawny who had been with Shelley during the last six months of his life and who shared his fierce liberalism was an attentive caller. Edward Bulwer – later Lord Lytton – wrote several Godwinian novels under Godwin's influence, one of which, *Eugene Aram*, achieved popularity. James Fenimore Cooper made several visits during his time in London, and Washington Irving was a friend. The young Thomas Carlyle, recently down from Scotland, paid a call on the man whose memory went back to the days of the French Revolution. Godwin was introduced to the promising journalist Thomas Babbington Macaulay and to Peacock's colleague at the India House, John Stuart Mill. He continued to go regularly to the theatre and to attend the major art exhibitions. He attended Faraday's lectures on electricity at the Royal Institution and met Charles Babbage, inventor of a mechanical computer.

When he was seventy-four he took tea with the painter John Martin and struck up a remarkable friendship. Martin invited him to dinner nearly every week and was to introduce him to most of the artists of the day including Turner, Wilkie, and Landseer. For a few years Godwin was a member of a social circle as settled as that of Joseph Johnson twenty-five years before. Martin's son tells of Godwin going with his father to visit the grave of Thomas Hardy of 1794 treason trials fame. On another occasion during the long debate on the Reform Bill, they were playing cards:

'But', said Martin, 'we have had the march on intellect, progress of education, intellectual development, throwing off prejudices, and how the Nation, the People, thinks'.

Old Godwin, now beginning to lead in trumps and transparently annoyed at the interruption, yet still as calm and cool as a cucumber, said 'I don't think a whole *People* can think'. 'Then' said Martin, 'you throw up the whole democratic principle?' 'People I do', said Godwin, making a trick.[13]

At the end of a long life the philosopher was still hovering as near the centre of literary and artistic London as he had done fifty years before.

It was gratifying to find that his ideas held their power, spread now as much by Shelley's poems as by his own prose. In October 1828 he received a letter from Frances Wright which might have come from one of the pantisocratists of 1794.

... But if you will pass *tomorrow evening* with me here, it is then that I will sollicit your attention to a short account of the experiment to which I have pledged my life and fortune in the forests of America; and which as being based on the principles of the Political Justice may possess some interest for its author. I need not say with how high an interest I venture to anticipate an interview with you, Sir – you from whom I first imbibed those views of human liberty and moral justice to which I now stand pledged you whose philosophy will I trust ever guide the practice of Nashoba and in the progress of time of the world – you whose name has so long commanded my respect and veneration ... [14]

In 1824 Frances Wright while still in her twenties had established a new community at Nashoba in Tennessee, then on the edge of the settled world. Hers was a more realistic experiment than Coleridge and his friends had ever had in mind – purchased slaves were to buy their freedom from the profits of their labour, the money being advanced and recycled like a mortgage fund – but it proved harder to work the land than had been hoped. Miss Wright was back in England hoping to recruit more colonists.

Godwin replied politely and a few days later Frances Wright called along with Robert Dale Owen, son of Robert Owen of Lanark, to be followed by tea the next day at Miss Wright's at which Robert Owen himself and Mary Shelley were also present. Frances Wright was keen to persuade Mary Shelley to join her in America. Robert Dale Owen, recalling the meeting many years later in his autobiography, implied that it would not have taken much for him to have offered to marry her.[15] As events turned out, although Godwin and Mary each saw Owen and Frances Wright on a few occasions later, the tea party on 1 November 1827 was to be the last meeting of the leaders of the two progressive traditions, the radical liberalism of Godwin and Shelley and the emerging socialism of Owen father and son.

In 1831 Wright and Owen were to publish the first American edition of *Queen Mab*, the book linking the two. In the same year Owen was to publish the essay on the Malthusian question that Shelley might have written had he lived. The first unambiguous information about contraceptive methods was published by Richard Carlile in 1828, in a pamphlet said to have sold 10,000 copies. The contraceptive sponge, Carlile proclaimed, was 'the most important discovery ever made'. It was already in use by the privileged – an English duchess never went out to dinner without one – and it would soon eradicate prostitution, onanism, pederasty and other substitutes for love. One reason why *Queen Mab* caused such deep hatred was that it was published by the author of this book and sold in his shop.

It was however Robert Dale Owen who presented the case for contraception in a more reasoned, calm and therefore – Godwinians believed – more persuasive form. *Moral Physiology* is a direct allusion to the 'moral restraint' which had featured in the debate between Godwin and Malthus. Although the physical details are frankly described – and Owen went to France to check them – the book is mainly devoted to the moral question whether or not artificial methods are justifiable. On the criteria of Utility and on the basis that the only foundation for Virtue is Knowledge, there could be no doubt. The book was illustrated by a frontispiece showing a woman leaving an unwanted child on the doorstep of a foundling hospital.

Owen was to see Godwin and Mary Shelley on a subsequent visit to London. He also saw Carlile in prison. *Moral Physiology* was soon to be followed by Knowlton's *Fruits of Philosophy*, another pamphlet whose title flaunts its links with the New Philosophy of the 1790s and which, when it was prosecuted in a famous case, helped to bring about one of the biggest advances in the status of women which occurred during the entire century.

CHAPTER 39

Waiting

And all the time the old man continued with his own writing. Over the decades he had four times written a novel in the intervals between his more substantial works. *Political Justice* had been followed by *Caleb Williams*; *The Enquirer* by *St. Leon*; *Chaucer* by *Fleetwood*; the *Lives of the Philipses* by *Mandeville*. This pattern allowed him to address different levels of the intellectual and moral population as well as giving his brain a rest. After the *History of the Commonwealth* he therefore again turned to fiction.

Publishers knew that a novel by the author of *Caleb Williams* would command a market in the circulating libraries if only for old times' sake, and they were not unduly worried about quality provided the story fitted the conventional three-volume format. *Cloudesley*, which appeared in 1830, is as Godwinian in its themes and purpose as its predecessors. The story of the honest servant who turns out to be the true heir to a rich nobleman provided opportunities to describe the temptations to crime encouraged by the property system. It also offered a pleasing fantasy for the old man hoping to outlive Sir Timothy Shelley. But Godwin, who was always better at describing his hoped-for literary effects than at achieving them, was losing his control. His narratives were now submerged among general comments which did not grow naturally out of the story.

Godwin demanded praise and money commensurate with the status he claimed. Publishers put up with his complaints, all delivered in a tone of

The Old Man, from *Lessons for Children*

exasperated affront.[1] After *Cloudesley* Colburn would have taken another novel, but Godwin was determined to return to philosophy. The collection of essays called *Thoughts on Man* was intended as an update of the influential *Enquirer* of 1797 and was likely, he claimed, to be his most enduring contribution to the history of progress.[2] The book is not uninteresting, but many of Godwin's observations although true are not original or even controversial. The manuscript was rejected by no less than eleven publishers before Godwin found a buyer.

But Godwin was never discouraged by discouragement. As he said when proposing his next book to a prospective publisher:

... The paper I propose will contain a totally new vein of thinking, never committed to publication in any age or nation, nor, as I suspect, having entered into the mind of any man; and at the same time that it will probably be admitted by all to be true and must, I think prove universally interesting.[3]

It was to be a series of studies of the religious leaders, cranks, and charlatans who at different times of history had claimed supernatural powers and had helped to spread belief in miracles. The older he became, the less atheistical Godwin felt, but he was more than ever convinced that organized religion was the grossest of superstitions and that the human mind could never be liberated until its falsity was exposed and its power broken.

It was not a subject which conventional publishers wanted to touch. Free thinking, like free love, was the preserve of pirates. But eventually a bolder newcomer was found. The resulting *Lives of the Necromancers* is an unusual book, and unlike the other books of his old age it was reprinted. Within days Godwin was hard at work on his next three-volume novel *Deloraine* which was to be completed even more quickly than *Cloudesley* and is more disappointing. It was then on to another series of essays, *The Genius of Christianity Unveiled*, which in a calm, reflective, and respectful tone explained how religion prevents men from seeing things as they are. It is a book which Shelley would have admired, a work which might have provided some of the footnotes to a revised *Queen Mab*. Godwin's last book, which took him full circle to the studies of his youth, is among his best.

Freed from outside strain and increasingly free from self-criticism he dutifully wrote his few pages every morning, and they quickly grew into volumes. If one publisher declined a manuscript or gave up negotiations in exasperation another could be found. By the early 1830s he was dealing with his twentieth, and there were to be a twenty-first and a twenty-second. By begging, bullying, and moral blackmail, Godwin eventually saw everything he wrote in print, except for the *Genius of Christianity Unveiled* which was not quite complete at his death. In his seventies Godwin published more books than most authors produce in a lifetime. It is alarming to speculate how many more he might have written in his tormented fifties and sixties if Wedgwood or Shelley had solved the money problem earlier.

But the long catalogue of tragedy was not yet at an end. On 31 October 1831 the journal notes as an item of the public news 'Cholera at Sunderland'. It was the subject of conversation when Tom Turner supped on 4 November. The epidemic which had spread over most of Europe had now reached London where the stinking Thames provided ideal conditions. On 1 September 1832 William Godwin Junior called on his father and mother for supper. Three days later he was still apparently in perfect health but overnight he became ill. Godwin and Mary Jane were sent for and they paid several visits to his bedside during the following two days. The next day he died and his body was hurriedly buried within a few hours.[4] He was twenty-nine and there were no children. Laying aside his own work, Godwin took over the manuscript of a novel on which his son had been working and edited it for publication. It appeared a few months later under the title *Transfusion* prefixed by a memoir whose honest, fair, and sympathetic character sketch of his dead son is amongst the best pieces of biographical writing that Godwin ever composed.

Slowly the old man was regaining the respect he had lost during the years of cringing and bluster. As he approached his eightieth year it was hard even for the unsympathetic to withhold a grudging admiration. Besides, public opinion was again swinging his way. After the repressions and reactions of the first decade of the post-war era, things were undoubtedly getting better. Malthusianism was in retreat. Prosecutions of writers and publishers stopped. In 1828 the Test and Corporation Acts were at last repealed to be followed the following year by Catholic Emancipation. The General Election of July 1830 brought to power a Whig government committed as its first priority to the reform of Parliament. In the same month a second French Revolution broke out in Paris, not as dramatic as the first but more lasting in its beneficial effects, and there were other more or less bloodless revolutions in Belgium and Italy. Maybe the long night of anti-Jacobinism was at last over? Maybe political and intellectual liberty could be regained and extended? Maybe the institutions of the old corruption could indeed be reformed or dismantled without violence? If perfectibility was again on the move, then surely the writings of the

Godwins and the Shelleys over half a century had contributed to the result.

In 1824 a pirate publisher produced a reprint of *Caleb Williams* in instalments selling at fivepence each and was said to have sold a great number before Godwin threatened him with the law. In 1831 however Godwin was able to arrange a more substantial reprint in exchange for selling the copyright outright for £50. It was an occasion for some self-congratulation. The book, he wrote in a signed Advertisement which followed the title page, had first been published in May 1794, the month when the Government plotted to put his friends to death. 'Every friend of the true interests of mankind will rejoice with the author that the prospects of the cause of liberty and sound thinking have so greatly improved since that period.'

Richard Bentley's 'Standard Novels' offered reprints of recent fiction closely printed in single volumes and already bound at six shillings a volume. The price was a dramatic reduction from the normal cartelized price of thirty-one shillings and sixpence, and Bentley was so successful that he was soon able to reduce his price until it reached two and sixpence. The honour of being number one in the new series goes to J. F. Cooper's *The Pilot*, but number two was *Caleb Williams*, number five was *St. Leon*, and number nine *Frankenstein*. Even *Fleetwood*, which had never been reprinted since its first publication in 1805, was accepted as number twenty-two. All four remained in print and in demand for the next twenty or thirty years. As the price of knowledge fell the moral level rose, as Godwin had predicted. The publishing revolution did as much to bring about the great social advances of early Victorian times as the Reform Bill.

At the beginning of the Standard Novels' *Caleb Williams* is a long memoir which traces Godwin's career from the time of his birth. Although written by Mary Shelley the misspelling of 'Thelwal' shows that her father had a hand in miscorrecting the proofs. Each of Godwin's major works from *Political Justice* to *Cloudesley* and *Thoughts on Man* is praised in extravagant terms, and he himself is compared both with the ancient Greek philosophers and with the author of the Sermon on the Mount. *Caleb Williams* is described as the novel which 'has been frequently, and we are apt to believe irrevocably, pronounced the best in the language'.[5]

Mary's Introduction is however as revealing in its omissions as in its assertions. Shelley is not given a mention. Thirteen books by Godwin are singled out for individual praise, but there is no word on the *Memoirs of the Author of a Vindication of the Rights of Woman*. On the contrary, in talking about Godwin's involvement with Mary Wollstonecraft, Mary slips in several ambiguous but in total misleading phrases which imply that she was the legitimate daughter of a conventional family. Her parents' marriage, for example, which took place on 29 March 1797 is described as occurring 'at the beginning of the year' and the date of her mother's death is noted with precision as 10 September 'having given birth to a daughter'. In her introduction to *Frankenstein* published later in the year, she uses the same sleight of drafting to imply that Shelley was her husband when they went to Switzerland in 1816.

If *Caleb Williams* was now irreversibly established as a classic, what of *Political Justice* of which it was merely a derivative? Godwin occasionally took the volumes from the shelf to check on particular passages. Sometimes members of the family were invited to listen as he read aloud as if from the family Bible. Every rereading confirmed him in the view that he had not been wrong. In essentials his theory still stood. Proposals were put to publishers to issue a new edition, and a prospectus was written, but there were no takers.[6] Godwin therefore prepared instructions on how the next edition should be presented after his death. If posterity was not yet ready, posterity would have to wait, but he would do what he could to make things easier.

In a note dated 2 January 1828 he asked that five of the works of Edward Baldwin should be printed amongst his Miscellaneous Works in the collected edition which he assumed would soon be demanded.[7] In an afterthought he added the Preface to *Bible Stories*, which had set out his views on children's education. He made no mention either of the two books by Theophilus Marcliffe or of the mass of the anonymous writing which he had produced before 1793. He had few material possessions to dispose of -- his books, his papers, and the portraits of himself, of Holcroft, and of Mary Wollstonecraft — but he made a careful will. When Dr Spurzheim the phrenologist visited London, a cast was made of one of the most interesting skulls of recent decades.[8]

The Whig Government which took office in 1830 contained men whom Godwin had known in the 1780s when they were at the outset of their careers. In 1833 after the Reform Bill was on the Statute Book they appointed him to the post of Office Keeper and Yeoman Usher of the Receipt of the Exchequer. It carried a salary of £200 a year, lodgings in New Palace Yard adjoining the Houses of Parliament, and minimal duties. At the end of his life Godwin became a pensioner, a placeman of government, and he accepted the indignity with relief.

He enjoyed the irony, and at his advanced age he was willing to risk the moral corruption. He delighted in showing visitors round the Star Chamber, scene of many cruelties and injustices described in his books, carrying the immense key which unlocked the chests of the Exchequer where the public money used to be kept. With a little of it in his own pocket he was able to have people to dinner, and to relieve the distress of friends who needed money more than he did. When shortly afterwards the reforming Government decided to clean up the abuses of patronage, he was thrown into a panic that the post would be abolished and he and Mary Jane would again be homeless. To his intense relief it was decided that reform could wait till after his death.

On the evening of 16 October 1833 fire broke out in the House of Commons. Mary Jane hurriedly started to move Godwin's books to safety. Artists including J. M. W. Turner rushed to the riverside to sketch the historic scene, but the Usher (among whose nominal duties was care of the fire appliances) was at the theatre that evening and did not return till the play was over. The next day he was back at his desk, writing, reading, and talking.[9]

A young man called Cooke was one of the latest of Godwin's pupils to attend for regular conversations. He begged Mary Jane to let him know at once if Godwin were to be taken ill. He wanted to offer help, but he also had hopes of being present to see how his hero would face his final test. Unfortunately he was himself taken severely ill before he had the chance to learn and before he died he relapsed into Christianity.[10] But the old man, maintaining the psychological detachment towards himself which had always been among his strengths, was now as interested in the forthcoming event as his friends.

On 21 August 1834, when he was seventy-eight, he looked through the journal which he had kept continuously since 1788. There were now thirty-two volumes, the entry for each day beautifully written and meticulously punctuated with scarcely a smudge or a correction. Every phrase and every name could reconnect his mind to a long chain of memory. To read them through was to relive his life. The journal told the public history of Europe, week by week from the Fall of the Bastille and the Treason Trials through the long years of war and repression to the recent renewal of reform. He read about his early liberation from religion, his period of rational confidence, of the rights of woman, the discovery of feeling, of love, and of poetry, the struggles to conserve his diminishing integrity, the years with Shelley and their aftermath, the deaths of friends and of family, and a final tranquillity. Godwin's life was the cultural history of his times. Indeed it was more, for his eighty years had begun in the rearguard of the seventeenth century and were ending in the vanguard of the nineteenth. A late survival from the puritan revolution, he had passed through his own accelerated age of enlightenment, taking it to new heights. He had been in at the start of romanticism and had outlived its end. Now he was already on the threshold of the Victorian era.

The journal told of his careers, as a journalist, writer, non-partisan politician, and children's bookseller. When his own tempestuous career was over, he had lived it again with Shelley and through his children. His life had risen and fallen not once but twice, but it was again on the way up. It was not what he had expected when he wrote *Political Justice*, but having since learned to take a longer view it was an outcome of which he need not be dissatisfied. Godwin tried to describe the rush of sensations that crowded in upon him as he read.[11] But although he made an interesting attempt to link the effect of the words on the paper with the real life he had lived, the valedictory message in which he hoped to sum up the spirit of his lifetime failed to rise to the challenge. He continued to fill in his entries day by day. The last, for 26 March 1836, not long after his eightieth birthday, is as typical as most:

Constip. Malfy, fin. Call on Hudson:
Trelawny calls.[n] Cough. Snow.

Malfy is the *Duchess of Malfi* by Webster, one of the old English plays which he believed had contributed as much to his wisdom as all his readings in philosophy and in history. Hudson is John Hudson, an official at the Legacy Office whom he had appointed as his executor and who needed to be urgently warned that the time for his services was now imminent.

The man who shocked his readers with the clinical details of Mary Wollstonecraft's death would have wanted the facts to be recorded. From the almost daily mentions of constipation in previous weeks, it seems likely that Godwin may have been suffering from a cancer. But it was the cough that carried him off. After five days of catarrhal fever he took to his bed. Mary Jane and Mary sat at his bedside in turns for the next five nights. 'His thoughts wandered a great deal', Mary noted, 'but not painfully.' Godwin knew he was dangerously ill but he never ruled out the possibility of recovery. He was dozing quietly when a slight rattle called Mary Jane and Mary to his side. It was a little after 7 o'clock on the evening of 7 April 1836.[12]

The funeral took place a few days later with only a few friends in attendance including Percy Florence Shelley, Trelawny and Thomas Campbell. In his will Godwin had asked that he should be buried in St Pancras Churchyard 'unless any substantial reason should be offered for a different destination'.[13] Perhaps he still had hopes of Westminster Abbey or St Paul's or at least of some official recognition for the last Yeoman Usher of the Receipt of Exchequer – but if so, no word came. Godwin's body was laid in the same grave with the author of *A Vindication of the Rights of Woman*, under the little square pillar where Shelley and Mary had declared their love.

CHAPTER 40

Afterwards

Despite a plea to be allowed to stay, Mary Jane was obliged to leave the official lodgings in New Palace Yard. The Royal Literary Fund made a grant of £50[1] but there was no other money and Godwin's few disposable assets had to be sold. The library was auctioned off, without sentimentality, including Godwin's own copies and manuscripts of *Political Justice*, *Caleb Williams* and other published works, his collections of seventeenth-century authors, and Shelley's presentation copies of his poems. The sale fetched £260.[2] Soon afterwards the Government conferred on Mary Jane a bounty of £300 and the contract for Godwin's biography promised 350 guineas.[3] Far from being left destitute by Godwin's death Mary Jane now found herself richer than she had been for years.

Within weeks a contract was signed for a biography. It was to be prepared in the name of the widow but actually compiled by Mary Shelley. Work began at once. Apart from the journal, Godwin had written numerous autobiographical pieces at various times of his life. He had accumulated letters, drafts, and other documents relating not only to himself but to friends and acquaintances over half a century or more. He had inherited the papers of Mary Wollstonecraft including the love letters, and kept copies of some of his own important outgoing letters on a letter-press machine given him by Tom Wedgwood. Although Mary returned letters from friends of her father who requested them, he had outlived

The Young Heir, from *Lessons for Children*

most of them and there was nowhere for them to go. Mary was also now the possessor of the papers Shelley had left at the time of his death as well as having her own detailed journals and other documents.

Mary had at her disposal one of the richest literary and biographical archives ever seen, spanning two generations and more of a family that wrote everything down and covering both sides of many fascinating exchanges of correspondence with some of the leading thinkers of the age. It not only documented the development of the public ideas but threw light on aspects of private life which are usually well hidden. If it is ever possible to understand and explain lives as they were, the materials were there. And with the Godwins and the Shelleys writing lives was as important as living them.

To edit the posthumous works for publication was a tribute Godwin had paid to Mary Wollstonecraft and to his son William and which Mary had paid to Shelley and hoped to pay again. It was the family tradition. Godwin had left ambiguous instructions on whether to burn or keep.

With respect to these papers I know not how to decide what should be printed and what destroyed. Let all that are not presently printed be consigned to the flames. But for the consideration of profit to be made, I should pass sentence of condemnation on nearly the whole . . . Let not a line of these papers be printed that should stand a chance of being justly deemed tedious or insipid.[4]

On the one book which had been completed however, and which he unequivocally wished to see published, Mary felt unable to carry out her father's wishes. Among the topics discussed in the *Genius of Christianity Unveiled* is the exploitation by church and state of people's hopes and fears for what might happen after death. It was a point which had fascinated Godwin ever since Dr Rees first explained the social purposes of heaven and hell to his shocked pupil at Hoxton. It had fascinated Mary Wollstonecraft who had never been able to shake off a lingering belief in the afterlife, and it had fascinated Shelley who was now – critics of *Queen Mab* delighted to point out – facing a long eternity regretting his error. Mary Shelley was a Wollstonecraft more than a Godwin. The main consolation which she had found from the moment of Shelley's death was the hope of being with him again. She proclaimed it to her friends and she proclaimed it to her father and she had no wish to change. To publish another anti-religious book was more than she could bear. The manuscript of Godwin's last book was accordingly laid aside.[5]

As for the biography, it was decided that it should be a life and letters of the type which was soon to become standard obituary. Mary arranged for the most important documents to be transcribed and she pinned up others for the printer. She drafted a few link passages with her special blend of truth and reticence. She had conversations with Mary Jane about identifying handwritings, and checked stories against memories. When Godwin was alive they had been rivals. Now that he was dead they could share him. To the surprise of both, the two widows found that they had become friends.

Mary Shelley found the research hard work and she was disturbed by some of the things she discovered about her father. In 1835, before Godwin died, she had been offered £600 to prepare a full edition of Shelley's poems, but had declined for fear of losing the allowance. In 1838 however when Shelley's poems were being extensively pirated and all hope of obscurity had passed, Sir Timothy's lawyers agreed that she should be given permission to prepare a proper edition provided there was only a minimum of biographical information. The life of Godwin was accordingly laid aside with relief and Mary devoted herself to the task which she had seen as a sacred duty long postponed.

In 1841 Mary Jane died taking her many secrets with her, and for lack of anywhere more fitting, she was buried alongside Mary Wollstonecraft and William Godwin in St Pancras Churchyard. She was just too soon to see the biggest revival of her husband's works that had occurred since the turn of the century. *Caleb Williams* was reprinted several times including a cheap edition in double columns. The *Rights of Woman* also reappeared in a cheap edition, its first reprinting in the nineteenth century.[6] Most gratifying of all, *Political Justice* itself was at last reprinted in full in two closely printed volumes, also for the first time in the nineteenth century. It was still being advertised into the 1850s at five shillings for the two volumes, eleven parts at sixpence or thirty-three at twopence, alongside other hated radical classics incluidng Volney's *Ruins*, Tom Paine's *Rights of Man*, Shelley's *Queen Mab* and Robert Owen's *Moral Physiology*.[7]

When Karl Marx's daughter recalled how her father and Engels used to speak of the influence of Shelley on the Chartist movement ('Oh we all knew Shelley then by heart,' Engels is said to have declared) and when an old Chartist proclaimed that *Queen Mab* was their bible, they mistakenly believed that Shelley shared their views. But if Godwin and Wollstonecraft entered the radical tradition, Mary Shelley had meanwhile ensured that most of Shelley went in another direction. *The Poetical Works of Percy Bysshe Shelley* in four volumes edited by Mrs Shelley which appeared in 1839 established Shelley finally and irreversibly amongst the great poets of the English language, his genius undisputed even by those who most detested his message. Mary Shelley brought Shelley into the mainstream of the national culture. He was no longer the author of a notorious banned poem only obtainable from shops specializing in blasphemy, sedition, and advice on birth control. He was the prophet of *Prometheus Unbound*, one of the most ambitious attempts ever made to uplift life by literature, and of other works such as the *Ode to the West Wind*, which if less ambitious were more often read. The notes that Mary attached are masterpieces of editing, adding so immeasurably to the reader's understanding that nobody would now consider printing Shelley's poems without them.

Mary Shelley made Shelley acceptable by diluting the message. Just as important, she broke the link between the ideas and the lives. In 1831 she had written a memoir of Godwin without mentioning Shelley: in 1839 she wrote her notes on Shelley without mentioning Godwin — let alone Claire or Harriet. By careful choice of words she contrived to give the impression that she had not been with Shelley until after their marriage at the end of 1816. (Until 1817 Shelley is invariably referred to in the singular — 'he' goes to Switzerland in 1814 and again in 1816, but at Marlow 'he' slides into 'we'.)[8] She started the story that the model for the wise old man in *Prince Athanase* and *The Revolt of Islam* was Shelley's schoolmaster at Eton, which may have been true for the silver hair but not for the opinions. Mary told no lies but she took no risks.

If she ever had doubts, she stilled them by remembering that she was protecting her son. Percy Florence Shelley had visited Godwin regularly with his mother, and the grandfather had watched his grandson grow up, measuring him proudly against the wall until he overtook him. When the boy reached his teens he was sent to be educated at Harrow School as preparation for the leisured life that awaited him if he survived. Shelley had wanted his children to be taught to think for themselves, but Mary, in a joke more true than she intended, said she preferred him to learn to think like other people.

In 1844 on the death of Sir Timothy at the age of ninety, Percy Florence was able to assume the title and take control of the Shelley fortune. He was married to a widow rather older than himself who outstripped him in energy, ability, and ambition, and there were no children. Rich at last, Mary Shelley was able to live a life of some comfort and she stopped writing. The £6,000 from Shelley's will was paid to Claire Clairmont but she lost it almost as soon as she received it and she never escaped from the furtive shabby-genteel wandering life that was the fate of dishonoured ladies, eventually sinking into an eccentric old age as a recluse. Claire, who became a Roman Catholic and suffered from attacks of madness, remained a distant embarrassment silently blamed not only for her own misfortunes but for those of Mary and Shelley.

Sir Percy Florence Shelley, the sole descendant of William Godwin, Mary Wollstonecraft, Percy Bysshe Shelley and Mary Wollstonecraft Shelley, shared few of the characteristics of any of them. Likeable and ineffectual, he was content to go along with whatever orthodoxy those around him recommended, and he never had the least inclination to reform the world. He was a perfect English gentleman. For forty years he and Lady Shelley continued the campaign to redirect the public perceptions of his amazing family. Serious efforts were made to suggest that Shelley would have become a Christian if he had lived a little longer.[9] But Victorians feared sex more than God. In another attempt to justify the poet's involvement with Mary against moral criteria which Shelley rejected and despised, Harriet's name was systematically blackened, her failings growing in fearsomeness through only being hinted at. Before long it was said that in 1814 Shelley had been obliged to 'take refuge' from her at Skinner Street and that it was therefore understandable that he had fallen in love with Mary Godwin.[10] It was whispered that Harriet had been 'unfaithful' to Shelley even before July 1814, that she had been extravagant with money – running up a hotel bill of £500 – and overfond of the bottle – 'rosy' in the slang of the day.[11]

Harriet's daughter Ianthe, Sir Percy's half sister, now the wife of a banker, was pressed to visit the Shelley home, and she eventually agreed on the understanding that certain matters would not be mentioned. On her first morning the hosts had to go out and her husband too decided on a long diplomatic country walk. Ianthe was left alone in the house with the key to the cabinets and an invitation to look at any of the Shelley papers except those in a certain drawer. On the family's return, she was found weeping, having proved as incapable as Caleb Williams of resisting the temptations of peeping, but she told Lady Shelley next day that she now saw how her father had been justified in leaving her mother.[12] The Shelley inheritance had passed into the hands of usurpers who were as skilled in legitimation as the Sussex gentry whom they had displaced.

Since it was impossible to mythologize Shelley and Mary without acknowledging Godwin and Wollstonecraft, they too were accorded a place in the legend. In 1851 when Mary Shelley died and was buried near the family home at Boscombe, the bodies of her father and mother were exhumed from St Pancras Churchyard and reburied alongside that of their daughter with the heart of their son-in-law in its silver casket. Mary Jane was left behind.

It was hard for a family who now had no wish to disturb the existing property system to see Godwin as other than an unscrupulous scrounger. Edward Dowden, the best of the early biographers of Shelley, could see that the poet had added little to Godwinism[13] but this was not something they wanted to hear. Mary Wollstonecraft's opinions were even more intolerable. An apologetic biography of Godwin and a new edition of Wollstonecraft's letters were commissioned from C. Kegan Paul, a respectful family friend. The books were written in a regretful tone of condescension, contrasting the literary genius of the dead with the errors of their opinions. Mary Wollstonecraft's life was excused away on the grounds that she had been unlucky in her youth in seeing only the wrong sides of the great English institutions.

Falkland may have preferred reputation to truth, but at least he kept the evidence of the facts in an iron chest. Sir Percy Shelley – encouraged by his wife – systematically weeded the family archive of embarrassing documents. Pages of journals were torn out, passages of letters were scratched over in ink or cut away with scissors. The letters which Mary Shelley wrote to her father disappeared with the volume of her journal which covers her adventures in Nairism. The family bought as many documents relating to Shelley as the market would supply – with the incidental effect of encouraging an active forgery business. Richard Garnett, keeper of manuscripts at the British Museum, whose preference for reputation over virtue was excessive even by Victorian standards, gave professional advice on which documents should be destroyed.[14]

When towards the end of her life Claire Clairmont offered to sell some letters, Sir Percy declined on the grounds that she was 'no relation of mine'. He did however give money in exchange for a gift of the love letters of Mary Wollstonecraft to Fuseli. 'They would do no good to her reputation,' Sir Percy wrote to Garnett, '– in fact they seem rather in the style of the Minerva press.' Since they have disappeared it is to be presumed that they were destroyed.[15] Godwin never denied the right of a person to destroy documents relating to his or her own life. But, as even his last book continued to proclaim, to falsify the past to defend the convenience of the present strikes at the roots of all hope of progress. To manipulate an archive is to manipulate access to truth.

Between the misunderstandings and misrepresentations the essentials of Godwin's theory slipped from view. Political justice had implied the dismantling of institutions in line with a rising intellectual and moral level, but the thinkers and politicians who claimed Godwin amongst their intellectual ancestors preferred to seek control of existing institutions and to build new ones. Attempts to provide the theory with a less misleading vocabulary – such as 'philosophical anarchism' – did little to relieve the confusion. With the rise of economics as a method of explaining and controlling the workings of society, interest in the intellectual and moral economies which the New Philosophy always regarded as prior, gradually lapsed. Socialists continued to try to push the chain of necessity which Godwin said that they should have been pulling.

As part of the Victorian programme of reform the hanging of criminals in chains was abolished along with chain gangs and fettering in irons for prisoners. At about the same time every household in the land threw away the Aeolian harps which had whistled under their open windows for the previous half century. The two most vivid metaphors for the Godwinian and Shelleyan theory of mind disappeared from sight and from hearing, leaving only the sparks of truth and the wild west wind to fill their place. But they had played their part. In the great political and social advances of the nineteenth century many of the ideas and causes for which Godwin and Shelley had argued were accepted and carried into effect. The importance of environment and education on character and conduct, the notion that true propositions can eventually prevail over false in fair debate, the implied analogy between the methods of science and those of political and social inquiry, belief in the possibility of progress – the liberal tradition grew strongly and entered the received wisdom of those who earlier would have been anti-Jacobins. If Godwin had lived another fifty years he would surely have agreed that the nineteenth century by the end provided even more proofs of the empirical foundation of his theory than the eighteenth had done.

The advance did not however occur across the whole front. The silken fetters and the stays of custom were not unbound. Victorian liberals were not much interested in the rights of women and the women provided no successor to Mary Wollstonecraft. At the end of the nineteenth century when the campaign for the vote began and when the first timid biography of Mary Wollstonecraft since the *Memoirs* was published, women were in a state of intellectual, moral, and economic subjection more constricting than they had been a hundred years before, and it was to be many years before they reattained the freedom of the 1790s. Women, like biography, had to wait until deep into the twentieth century for the advance towards openness and sincerity to be resumed.

Godwin's sexual relationship with Mary Wollstonecraft

Godwin maintained a secret record in his journal of his sexual relationship with Mary Wollstonecraft. It runs from August 1796 when they first became lovers until 29 March 1797 when they were officially married. Its existence has not previously been recognized.

Reliable biographical information about such matters is extremely rare for any time in the past, and in the case of Godwin and Wollstonecraft it has more than personal interest. In the *Memoirs* Godwin was scornful of what he called the 'factitious rules of decorum' which lead biographers to withhold truth and so delay the progress of knowledge about human behaviour. Wollstonecraft, too, made greater openness a major theme of her campaign for equality between men and women. Although both authors were cautious where the reputations of living persons were concerned, they set no limits on the study of long-dead historical figures. I therefore make no apology for intruding or for offering a detailed account of the implications.

The code is simple. Whereas Godwin in his journal normally divides the events of the day by means of neat stops or colons, concluding each day's entry with a full stop, his references to Wollstonecraft during the relevant months are sometimes followed by a dash and a dot. A typical entry, noting his writing, reading and visits is that for 23 September 1796

Essays, p. 110–113. Terence, Andria, Acts 3, 4 and 5: D'Orleans, p. 166. Meet Butler Odon & Sharp: Stoddart calls. chez elle, –.

Ancient Advice, from the frontispiece to *The Whole of Aristotle's Works Complete*, 1782.

On several occasions he has had to put the dash and dot on a new line when he has run out of space on the line before,* and on one occasion (11 November) he has inserted it neatly with a caret as a remembered afterthought. These marks do not occur anywhere else in the whole journal. For the weeks in question we are also fortunate in possessing numerous intimate letters exchanged between Godwin and Wollstonecraft. At some point Godwin put them in order, numbered and dated them and tied them together with a thread. Although some letters have been removed and others have had pieces cut off, enough remain to give ample confirmation of the meaning of the marks and to explain several other matters. The table (on pp. 502–3) shows the marks extracted from among the numerous other information in the journal plus a few notes by myself in square brackets to set the context.

The main conclusions are reasonably clear. Godwin and Mary became lovers on 21 August 1796 and were frequent sexual partners until the end of the first week in October. For a fortnight or so after that Godwin was ill, being visited by doctors nearly every day and confined to bed upstairs at Chalton Street for the first week. There are no dashes during this time. Immediately afterwards Mrs Cotton came to stay at Judd Place and there were still no opportunities for the lovers to be alone together until Mrs Cotton left on about 12 November after which the dashes start again. By 20 December, Wollstonecraft is worried that she is pregnant and by the end of the year she is sure that she is. The call on Godwin by Lady Lanesborough on 7 January concerns the seeking of professional advice from the St Marylebone Dispensary, a maternity hospital.[1] In early January, Wollstonecroft is suffering from an 'inelegant complaint' which is presumably morning sickness. Her baby was to be born on 30 August 1797, and since there is no suggestion that it was premature, it is likely to have been conceived towards the end of November 1796. The dashes are consistent with this timing.

Throughout the journal Godwin includes occasional words and abbreviations in French. Twice in September 1796 and once in November he notes 'fievre' apparently with reference to Wollstonecraft. The word does not occur elsewhere, but we know from references in Wollstonecraft's letters that she described herself as feverish during her menstrual period as well as at other times. The 'humour' and 'bonne' in early October appear to refer to one of the depressions from which she suffered regularly through her life. The 'frieze' for 19 November however may refer to a heavy cold which we know from other remarks began on that day. It may be significant that a few of the dashes are not followed by a dot. The plain dashes between 26 August and 6 September may imply no more than that Godwin had not yet perfected his code, but read with these for 28 September, 11 October, and 23 November (of which more later) they may be indications that something less than full sexual intercourse occurred on these occasions.

To judge from the pattern of abstinences, Wollstonecraft's menstrual cycle at

* An example, for 13 September 1796, can be seen on Plate 6.

this time was three and a half to four weeks. There was evidently a period at the end of September and another in mid November. Another is indicated at the end of August. When on 20 December Wollstonecraft is anxious but still hoping for good news, she would, according to this reckoning, be a week and a half late. A cryptic note probably written on 2 September is consistent with this pattern.

'This evening, dear Godwin, we must alter our plan – I am not actuated by anything like caprice – I mean to see you, and to tell you wh [The rest is cut away]'

Godwin and Wollstonecraft kept up a joke that they were not only lovers but philosophers, combining passion and reason. In inviting Godwin to 'philosophize' with her in late September Wollstonecraft twice makes it clear that it is only philosophy that she has in mind. In her note of Thursday 29 September, for example, she adds in French at the end

'Mais, à notre retour, rien que philosophie. Mon cher ami. Etes-vous bien faché? Mon Bien-aimé – Moi aussi, cependant la semaine approchant, do you understand me –'

The previous day shows only a plain dash. Her letter of 30 September praises Godwin for his tender considerate 'self-government' the previous night when there is no dash.

The pregnancy was both unexpected and unwelcome. Wollstonecraft's undated letter to Godwin written about the end of January 1797 when her condition was beyond doubt implies that, if she sat down with pencil and paper, she could work out where they went wrong:

'Women are certainly great fools; but nature made them so. I have not time, or paper, else I could drawn an inference, not very illustrative of your chance-medley system – But I spare the moth-like opinion, there is room enough in the world etc'

'Chance-medley' properly means a misfortune that is not wholly accidental, although in Wollstonecraft's day the word was already losing its precision and was commonly used to mean pure chance. But it seems likely that Wollstonecraft in this letter is accusing Godwin of not taking sufficient care to avoid making her pregnant or of having adopted an unreliable method.[2] The very fact that he kept a careful record may imply that he was applying some system.

In the *Vindication of the Rights of Woman* there are a number of remarks that throw light on Wollstonecraft's attitudes at the time she wrote that book. A husband, she writes in a passage describing the world she would like to see, will not forget, 'in obeying the call of appetite, the purpose for which it was implanted'. Godwin in *Political Justice* also emphasizes the 'natural' link between sex and its rational purpose of procreation. Both writers, who were probably virgins when they wrote their most famous works in 1792, combined the traditional dissenter disapproval of sex with the Enlightenment belief in natural laws and the power of reason.

By 1796 however both Wollstonecraft and Godwin had changed. In describing Wollstonecraft's love for Fuseli in the *Memoirs*, Godwin explained frankly how she had been unable to bear the frustration of a purely platonic friendship. Sexual attraction intensified by celibacy was also, he noted, a decisive factor in her love for Imlay. By the time Godwin and Wollstonecraft became friends in early 1796 neither believed that the only purpose of sex was to have children nor that desire could be easily controlled. Sex is the 'overflowing of the soul' which intensifies sensibility.

A remark in the *Vindication* appears to condemn contraception:

'Surely nature never intended that women, by satisfying an appetite, should frustrate the very purpose for which it was implanted.'

By 1796 however Wollstonecraft's view too may have been modified just as Godwin's views were modified in his debate with Malthus. In one of her last letters to Imlay in November 1795 she proclaimed:

'My child may have to blush for her mother's want of prudence – and may lament that the rectitude of my heart made me above vulgar precautions.'

But it may be anachronistic to read this passage as a reference to birth control. The vulgar precaution which Wollstonecraft disdained was to bind Imlay to her in a financial marriage contract. Godwin allowed the sentence to be printed in the *Posthumous Works* although he cut out six or seven other lines from the same letter: he would probably not have done so if he had seen a reference to contraception in the wording.

Godwin was deeply interested in the physical aspects of reproduction. During November 1796 he was attending medical lectures given by his friend Anthony Carlisle, the foremost surgeon of the time. In discussing methods of limiting family size in the *Reply to Parr* he referred readers to the medical books although unfortunately without giving names. There was however one book on the subject which everybody knew and which described popular beliefs – and popular errors.

Aristotle's *Problems*, one of the most enduring works ever written, gives answers to all the questions about women, sex, childbirth, and midwifery which convention insisted should never be asked. In origin it is a genuinely ancient Greek text although not by Aristotle. In the Middle Ages it was adapted to fit a Christian framework but not radically altered. It was amongst the first books to be printed at the Renaissance and the first English translation is dated 1583. In its modern English form, when it was combined with Aristotle's *Compleat Masterpiece* and other works, it dates from 1684 and there have probably been a hundred editions since. It was still being printed in the 1930s. A historian of medicine writing in 1977 says that in parts of Scotland it was still being offered to couples who announced the birth of a baby in the newspapers.

The book is so full of nonsense that it has been usual to regard it as an example of superseded beliefs surviving amongst the badly educated long after they have been abandoned elsewhere. In fact the book could not have been produced in such large numbers if it were merely a kind of chapbook for the semi-literate. Most editions are well printed and illustrated and are usually bound in plain sheepskin without any indication of the contents on the outside.

In Godwin and Wollstonecraft's time the Aristotle book still pervaded the culture. Much of the early part of Sterne's *Tristram Shandy*, which deals with Tristram's conception and birth, is not comprehensible without understanding the Aristotelian talk of humours and dispositions, animal spirits, wind and water, and other references: the book is actually named at one point.[3] Wollstonecraft, we know from her letters, regarded Sterne as a favourite and was reading *Tristram Shandy* during the months when she became pregnant. The letter about 'chance-medley' even contains a direct reference – Uncle Toby, the former soldier who can talk about nothing but battles and killings, opens a window specially to let out a buzzing fly with the words, 'This world surely is wide enough to hold both thee and me.'[4]

The early pamphlets on birth control protested that the Aristotle book gives advice on how to conceive babies not on how to prevent them. But it is easy to make the adjustment, and some passages – such as advice against letting in the cold by too rapid withdrawal if babies are desired – seem to have been drafted with the opposite in mind. Women are particularly fertile, Aristotle misadvises his readers, during the two or three days after their monthly terms are stayed. Infrequent sex gives the best chance of pregnancy. Frequent sex outside the dangerous days is safe. The reason why whores do not have children is that grass seldom grows on a path that is well trodden.

Readers do not have to believe everything a book says to find it useful and Aristotle had a virtual monopoly. There are numerous indications scattered through the writings of Godwin and Wollstonecraft that they shared the common belief that frequent sex reduces fertility. The evidence of Godwin's code now gives some support to the view that they may have been applying the false rhythm-method which the Aristotle book recommends. The menstrual period, which seems to have begun on 15 November, was followed by sex on the fourth day – and then nothing but a plain dash for six days. The period which occurred at about the beginning of September was followed by an interval of comparative restraint. Wollstonecraft probably expected her December period to begin about the end of the first week, and since Aristotle makes no recommendation other than for the days immediately after, it was reasonable to carry on until it started. But the evidence is by no means conclusive.

In the months that followed confirmation of pregnancy, the dashes drop to a fairly regular pattern of two or three a week, opportunities permitting. Apart from the trip to Ilford, Godwin and Wollstonecraft do not appear to have spent a whole night together until the day of their official marriage.

AUGUST
18 chez elle.

19

20 chez elle.

s21 chez moi, toute.

22

23 chez elle.

24 chez elle.

25

26 chez moi –

27 [calls on Mary Robinson with W]
s28

29 chez moi, –

30 chez elle, –

31 chez moi, –
SEPTEMBER
1 chez elle, –

2 dines.

3 [At *Iron Chest* with W]
s4 [meets Newton with W]

5 dines, –

6 chez elle –

7

8 chez elle, –.

9 chez moi, –.

10 chez elle, –.

s11 chez moi, –.

12 chez elle, –.

13 [W dines] –.

14 chez elle, –.

15 tea at Ilford; sleep, –. s16

16 chez moi, –.

17 chez elle, –.

s18

19

20 dines, –.

21 chez elle, –.

22 chez moi, –.

23 chez elle, –.

24 chez moi, –.

s25

26 chez elle, –.

27 dines; fievre

28 chez elle, –

29 chez moi

30 chez moi; fievre
OCTOBER
1 chez elle, dine.

s2

3 dines, –.

4 chez elle, –.

5 chez elle, –.

6 chez moi, –.

7 –.

8 dine. humour.

s9 chez moi, bonne.

10 chez moi. bonne.

11 [Godwin ill and in bed until 18th. Does not
12 see Wollstonecraft]

13

14

15

s16

17

18 [Godwin comes downstairs]
19

20

21

22

s23 [Godwin goes out for first time]
24 chez moi.

25 chez moi.

26

27

28

29 chez elle.

s30 sup at Wt's, w. Montagu.

31 sup at Wt's, w. Mrs Cotton.
NOVEMBER
1 [Mrs Cotton staying with W until 12 November]
2 sup at Wt's, w. Mrs Cotton.

3 sup at Wt's, w. Mrs Cotton.

4

5

s6

7 chez moi, Mrs Cotton.

8

9 dine at Wt's, w. Cotton.

10

11 dines –: chez elle, Cotton.

12 chez moi; –.

s13

14 dines –.

15 chez moi; fievre.

16

17

18 chez moi –.

19 chez elle, frieze.

s20 chez elle, m.

21 chez elle.

22 chez elle.

23 chez moi; – elle.

24

25 chez elle; –.

26 chez elle.

s27

28 chez elle; –. [Baby conceived about now]

29 chez moi, –.

30 chez elle; –.
DECEMBER
1 chez elle.

2 chez elle; –.

3 chez elle.

s4

5 dines; –.

6

7 chez elle; –.

8 chez moi, –.

9 dine; –.

10 chez moi.

11 [sups at Mrs Robinson's with W]
12 [sups at Mrs Robinson's with W]
13 chez moi; –.

14

15 chez elle; –.

6 chez elle.

7 dine; –.

8 chez elle; –.

9

o chez elle; –. [W suspects she is pregnant]

1 chez elle; –.

2 chez moi.

3 chez elle, –.

4 dines; –.

5 chez elle.

6 chez elle.

7 chez elle, –.

8 chez moi. [W depressed]

9

o chez moi; –. [W says she wishes they had never met]

1 chez elle.

NUARY

1

2 chez elle.

3 chez elle; –.

4

5 chez elle.

6 chez moi.

7 chez elle; –.

8

9 chez elle.

o [theatre with W]

1 chez moi.

2

3 chez elle; –.

4

---

s15

16 chez elle; –.

17 chez moi.

18 chez elle.

19 chez moi; –.

20

21 dine; –.

s22 [tea at Mrs Robinson's with W]

23 chez elle.

24

25 chez elle.

26 chez moi; –.

27

28 chez elle.

s29

30 chez elle; –.

31 chez elle.

FEBRUARY

1 chez moi; –.

2

3 chez elle; –.

4

s5 chez elle.

6 [Visits Bedlam with W and Johnson]

7 dine.

8 chez elle, –.

9 [sees W]

10 chez elle; Everina.

11 [W's sister staying until early March]

12 chez elle, E.

13

---

14 chez elle, E.

15

16 chez moi; –.

17

18 dine, E.

s19

20 chez elle; E.

21

22 chez elle, E.

23 chez moi; –.

24

25 [sups with W and EW]

s26

27

28

MARCH

1 Porson & Wt dine.

2 chez elle:

3 dines; –.

4 [Theatre with W and EW]

s5

6

7 chez elle; –.

8 chez elle.

9 chez elle; –.

10

11 chez elle.

s12 [sees W]

13 chez elle; –.

14

15

---

16 dine; –.

17 chez elle.

18

s19

20 chez elle.

21

22 chez elle.

23 chez elle; –.

24 [Tea with W]

25 chez elle.

s26

27 chez elle; –.

28 [tea with W and others]

29 sleeps; –. [Marriage] [The dashes cease after this date].

s = Sunday

Women: the evidence of the advice books

In the thirty-five years between 1785 and 1820 a large number of books were printed giving advice on the education and conduct of ladies. They include Hester Chapone, *Letters on the improvement of the mind addressed to a Young Lady*; Revd James Fordyce, *Sermons to Young Women*; Sarah Lady Pennington, *An Unfortunate Mother's Advice to her Absent Daughters*; John Gregory, *A Father's Legacy to his Daughters*; Ann Murray, *Mentoria* and *Sequel to Mentoria*; Hannah More, *Essays on various subjects principally designed for young ladies* and *Strictures on the Modern System of Female Education*; Revd Thomas Gisborne, *An Enquiry into the Duties of the Female Sex*; Jane West, *Letters to a Young Lady*; Revd John Bennett, *Letters to a Young Lady*; Revd Thomas Broadhurst, *Advice to Young Ladies*; Ann Taylor, *Practical Hints to Young Females*; M.H., *Affection's Gift to a Beloved God-child*, and the following anonymous works: *Maternal Letters to a Young Lady on her entrance into Life*; *Advice from a Lady to her granddaughters*; *Sermons particularly addressed to Young Women in the higher ranks of life*, by a Lady; and *Letters of advice from a Lady of Distinction to her Niece the Duchess of* **********, reissued as *Letters on Matrimonial Happiness by a Lady of Distinction*. No doubt there were others and it is not always easy to choose the border with such works as the anonymous *Address to a Young Lady on her Entrance into the World* and Elizabeth Hamilton, *Letters addressed to the Daughter of a Nobleman* which give moral advice which is not especially specific to women's roles.

Female Courage Properly Considered, from *Blossoms of Morality*

Although some were newly written, others were revivals, hastily reprinted to catch the new public mood. Gregory was reprinted most often followed by Chapone, Fordyce, and Gisborne. Sometimes extracts from several authors were printed together to form titles such as *The Young Lady's Pocket Library and Parental Monitor*. Gregory and Chapone were often bound in one book, sometimes abridged. Some of the anonymous works follow their predecessors so closely that I suspect them of being publishers' compilations, not genuinely original. Drawing mainly on the British Library and National Union catalogues and on my own black museum, I have noted 119 separate editions of these books published in Great Britain or in Dublin between 1785 and 1820, with others on either side. There were also numerous reprints in the United States.

There was a tradition before the eighteenth century. *The Ladies Calling* attributed to Richard Allestree went through at least seven editions between 1673 and 1700. The Marquis of Hastings's *Advice to a Daughter*, first printed in 1688, reached a fifteenth edition in 1765. There were also advice books for young men, most notably Lord Chesterfield's *Letters of advice to his son*, successors to the courtesy books on the arts of being a gentleman which were such a feature of the early seventeenth century. But nothing which went before approached the huge flood of didactic books for ladies that started to build up in the 1780s. There were even a few reprints of Allestree and Hastings which had been extinct for half a century or more. The sheer numbers of these books establish them as a cultural phenomenon unique to the revolutionary age and its aftermath.

The advice books were designed to be bought by parents, teachers, clergymen and others in authority to be given to young ladies of the upper- and middle-income groups while their opinions were still malleable. Wollstonecraft mentions that Fordyce's sermons 'have long made a part of a young woman's library, nay girls at school are allowed to read them'.[1] Many were sold in fine bindings, an unusual form of publishing at this time, an indication that they were meant to be kept and consulted. If the average edition size was in the range 500 to 1,000 copies, production totalled 59,500 to 119,000 copies. The income tax returns of 1801 record 320,000 families in Great Britain with incomes of £65 a year or more and only 70,000 with incomes above £200.[2] Although these figures certainly understate true incomes, it is evident that a high proportion of the upper and middle classes must have owned copies of at least one advice book.

Although designed for ladies, some books claim that their views are also applicable to women lower down the social scale who would not have been able to afford them. Family life and domestic duties, says Gisborne, are much the same in castle or cottage. We can be reasonably sure that their main lessons were promulgated in sermons, and those books published as sermons may have been intended to be drawn on for this purpose. There is also some direct evidence of attempts to reach deeper into society through the circulation of cheap tracts such as Bishop George Horne's *Picture of the Female Character as it ought to appear when formed*, 1799, although tract publishing was still unusual at this time.

In discussing Ancient Greek attitudes to sexuality, Michel Foucault remarked:

'Since there is an important and large literature about loving boys in Greek culture, some historians say "Well, that is the proof that they loved boys." But I say that it proves that loving boys was a problem.'[3]

If Foucault is right – as he surely is – then women were evidently a problem in Britain throughout the revolutionary and romantic period.

On the essentials of their approach the advice books show little disagreement. Nearly all commend the traditional feminine virtues and reinforce traditional gender roles. It is asserted or assumed that women are in body and in mind weaker than men. The prime female virtues are modesty, faithfulness, prudence, delicacy, and humility. The prime role is in the home, to give support and comfort to families and husbands. Ladies are told to be charitable to the poor and to be kind to servants.

A double standard is accepted and commended without the need for justification. Wit is an asset to a man but a liability in a woman. So is knowledge. 'Be cautious in displaying your good sense,' advises Gregory, 'But if you happen to have any learning, keep it a profound secret, especially from the men.' Men can pass through the world's dangers untainted or shrug off irregularities and misdemeanours, but women must keep themselves far from temptation. 'A bad man is terrible,' says Bennett, 'but an unprincipled woman is a monster.' A wife should thank God if her husband has faults, says Hastings. If he is drunken, foul-tempered, greedy, mean, weak, or incompetent, these faults will help to veil her own failings, and she can feel that her husband's natural superiority is to some extent offset. 'The greatest slavery is that of being obliged to serve those who are unworthy to command us,' says M.H., 'but it is a kind of agreeable servitude to be obliged to those whom we esteem.'

Women need to exercise restraint in virtually every aspect of life, in society, in the home, in dealings with tradesmen and servants, in conversations with friends, while dancing or playing at cards. Reading needs to be closely controlled by parents and husbands. Some subjects are too difficult for women's weak intellects. The advice books are particularly fearful of novels which are believed to inflame emotions and cause discontent. 'Avoid such works, as enervate the mind, soften the heart, or awaken the passions,' says the author of *Maternal Letters*. 'The indiscriminate reading of such books', declares Mrs Chapone, 'corrupts more female hearts than any other cause whatsoever.' 'There are very few novels, that can be read with safety,' advises Fordyce – a woman who reads the others 'must in her soul be a prostitute'.

One of the activities at which women are acknowledged to be superior to men is letter writing. Composing them requires no great ability or concentration and they can be about trivial subjects. Writing letters to friends is an innocuous way for women to fill in their time, but only provided it is done in moderation. Pouring out the secrets of the heart in letters is almost as dangerous as reading novels.

Advice books were presumably published as collections of letters on the assumption that advice which was packaged as a letter from a friend or a passage from an epistolary novel might stand more chance of being listened to.

There is much emphasis on religion, not so much because it is true but because it is useful. Here, as elsewhere, unequal gender roles are both accepted and reinforced. Praying is commended as a useful steadying activity for bored women, especially as religion can help to combat the womanly vices of volatility, vanity, and curiosity. Church is a substitute for literature and art, a compensation for lack of education. Whereas men under emotional strain can throw themselves into business, games, and outdoor sports, – even drink and other women although they are only hinted at – women only have religion when they are lonely or bereaved or when, as frequently happens, they find they have married a brutal husband. Chapter 31 of the Book of Proverbs is regularly invoked: 'Who can find a virtuous Woman? For her price is far above rubies.' In some books there is also a menacing hint of religion as sanction, with references to the all-seeing eye of the patriarchal God and the penalties He may exact in the afterlife if the advice is ignored.

The authors use every other opportunity to assert the legitimacy of their own authority and to exploit any sense of dependency. Gregory's *Father's Legacy* consists of letters written by a dying father to his orphan daughters. Mrs West is discharging a promise to a dying mother. Lady Pennington warns her daughters against repeating her own mistakes which have led to disaster. Nearly all claim to have the women's best interests at heart and say that following their advice will bring happiness.

A nationalist note can frequently be heard. Several of the books are dedicated to female members of the Royal Family, respected for long-suffering patience with unadmirable husbands. British ladies, suggests Fordyce, will support plain local fashions, not expensive fripperies from abroad. Pestilential publications from France and the Danube are swarming over Europe, says Mrs More, like the Huns and the Vandals of old. The fall of France to the revolutionaries, says Mrs West, was due to the indelicate behaviour of its women.

Many of the books complain of falling moral standards. Most acknowledge that women's education has advanced in the recent past, but they are dubious about the benefits and warn against going too far. The main difference is between those who concentrate on 'accomplishments' – which include conversation and manners, as well as needlework, music, drawing, and dancing – and those who want to build up understanding in order to give the accomplishments a more secure base. Some give practical guidance on how to wheedle, cajole and humour men. There is however nothing of the sentimentality about Motherhood which pervades Victorian attitudes. Nor are women yet seen as Angels in the House tending a shrine for men who are resting from their labours in the wicked world outside. For the most part the books maintain an impressive solidarity, quoting their predecessors and one another with approval. As Gisborne notes, any appearance of controversy would detract from effectiveness.

In cultural terms the books reflect the views of dominant groups who feel that their society's values are threatened. They long for the old days when order reigned, when the structures went unchallenged, when the agricultural economy was matched by a religious moral economy, and mutual respect marked relations between the privileged and their subordinates. They fear loss of authority and they fear change. They fear town life which corrupts country values. They fear women's emotions, women's friendships, women's education, and women's sexuality. In some of the books published when it must have seemed that the battle was being lost, a note of panic can be heard among increasing bitterness.

Of the sixteen authors, eleven were women and four were clergymen. The sixteenth, Gregory, was a medical doctor. It could be of course that the purchasers of the books – who were the determinants of the demand – were men. They might even have calculated that books written by quisling women would carry more conviction. However the presentation inscriptions which are often to be found written in such books tend to confirm that many of the donors were older women or clergymen. With many husbands and brothers away in the armed forces, they were the guardians of the home front.

It is not surprising that the views of opponents were seldom printed. Wollstonecraft was unusual in being able to publish. She had few predecessors and only a handful of successors, none of whose books attracted a wide sale.[4] However contrary views were evidently often heard even if they were not written down. In order to rebut them, the advice books had to mention them, although they were careful not to enhance their legitimacy by treating them with respect. Such opinions were evidently current well before the *Vindication*, indeed well before the French Revolution. Fordyce, defining the province of men as 'war, commerce, politics, exercises of strength and dexterity, abstract philosophy and all the abstruser sciences', warns as early as 1766 against 'those masculine women that would plead for your sharing any part of their province with us'. Mrs More, 1777, pours contempt on the 'soaring spirits' who reject traditional advice as 'unfit for ladies of their great refinement, sense and reading.'

The speed with which Wollstonecraft was able to write her book implies that her ideas were already organized in her mind. Since the *Vindication* was only printed three times before the 1840s (in 1792 twice and 1796), its influence must have spread, if at all, mainly by word of mouth. The attention which the advice books give to the dangers of acquiring unsuitable women friends reflects the fear that they were a source of subversive ideas, less easily controlled than reading. The advice books contain scarcely a single explicit reference either to Wollstonecraft or to her book, and the almost universal misspelling of her name in all discussions for or against suggests that many people who thought they knew her ideas did not have access to her book. The fear her name inspired can be detected most clearly in indignant outbursts, as when Mrs More writes, 'the imposing term of *rights* has been produced to sanctify the claim of our female pretenders . . . [to]

an impious discontent with the post which God has assigned them in this world', or when Mrs West complains about 'the petticoat philosophist'.

Wollstonecraft's achievement may therefore have been to unify and reinforce a protest that was already widely asserted and widely accepted, rather than to devise a new philosophy. Her ideas had probably featured in innumerable conversations up and down the country. In fact, those who did read the *Vindication* would have found that Wollstonecraft accepted a great many of the assumptions on which the advice books were built and she comments favourably on some of them. In the Preface to the *Female Reader*, 1790, she even commends the 'aimiable' Dr Gregory's prescription of religion as solace. The fear her name inspired arose as much from accounts of her life deriving from the *Memoirs* as from the *Vindication*.

In the following table I show the time curve of publication of the advice books, counting each identified British edition as a separate unit. To take account of the lags between demand and production and to smooth the curve I have aggregated the numbers in five-year periods.[5] Although obviously this methodology must be subject to all kinds of caveats and qualifications, the resulting pattern does show the correlation with larger events which might have been expected from the way in which the problem of women was perceived. For example the biggest rush comes after 1793 with the outbreak of war, the Terror in France, the treason trials, and the anti-Jacobin panic. There is a dip in the early 1800s when the short-lived Peace of Amiens (1801–1803) seemed to imply a return to normality, but numbers pick up again with the resumption of war. After Waterloo they fall rapidly back to pre-war levels. By the 1830s, although a few continued to be published or reprinted, they had become obsolete.

There is of course no sharp distinction between the advice books and other means of influence such as political and polemical pamphlets, anthologies, religious works, curiosities such as Hannah More's *Coelebs in Search of a Wife*, and discussions in the literary journals. However, although quantitative evaluation is less easy, the other literature seems to follow the same pattern. For example the thirty-six editions of anti-Jacobin novels which were published between 1796 and 1822 include a sharp peak in 1799 and 1800, accounting for nearly half the total.

Below the curve for advice books I have charted the changing price of 3 per cent consols.[6] For the revolutionary age, as now, the price of British government gilt-edged stocks is a useful index of the level of general worry among the proper-tied classes. The comparison suggests some further conclusions. In the years before 1791 women were already becoming an increasing source of anxiety, even though general confidence was still rising. The increasing concern goes back at least to the 1760s when Rousseau's ideas began to gain currency. After the early 1790s there is a change. The advice book curve rises as the gilts curve falls, worry about women recognizably correlating with wider worries even reflecting the interregnum of the Peace of Amiens. Gender privilege, during the years of the advice books, was only one of many ancient institutions which were shaking and toppling all over Europe, at least as fertile a source of anxiety as political discontent and threats to property at home and news of wars and revolutions far away.

Who can tell if these books were read, let alone if they ever changed anyone's mind?[7] If you are a girl at school or a lady isolated in the country you will read anything, and at a time when women's reading was controlled, we can probably assume some degree of monopoly forcing. There is no way of determining impact on opinion by looking at inputs alone. However we can be reasonably sure that many of the girls who received these books grew up to be the Victorian ladies whose commitment to traditional female values and gender roles was genuine, strong, and scarcely challenged. In the Victorian period advice books on conduct gave way to books on etiquette, cookery, and needlework. In the battle of ideas, women were defeated as decisively as the French and they ceased to be more than an occasional rumbling worry. Furthermore their subjection was to continue long after the post-war political settlements had been swept away by repeated resurgences of the other ideas which the wars had been fought to destroy. If it was the advice books which compelled women back into their previous unprotesting subordination, they proved more effective than the bayonets of the allied armies.

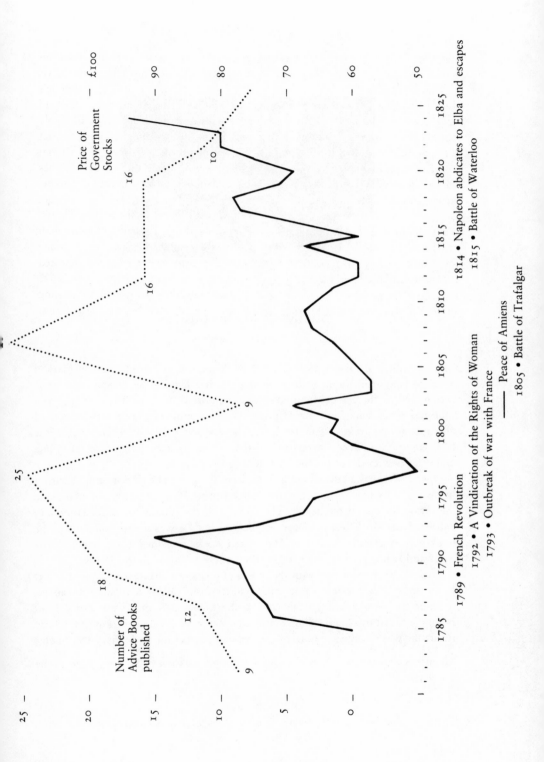

Shelley and the pirates

The reprinting of *Queen Mab* in 1821 by William Clark of Fleet Street marked a decisive point in the growth of Shelley's fame. The hostile reviews and court actions led to further prosecutions which helped to publicize the book. *Queen Mab* has never since been out of print. As an example of the perverse effects of attempts to suppress dissent by force, the episode is highly reassuring. In the following note I suggest a revision of the previously accepted version of events and offer new evidence on Shelley's debt to the pirates.

Queen Mab was an illegal publication from the start. The first printing occurred in early 1813 when Shelley sent the manuscript to Thomas Hookham who made the arrangements on his behalf. The identity of the printer to whom Hookham entrusted the work has not been established but he was a professional for the book was excellently produced. The unsold stocks remained in the hands of the trade and reappeared on the market when interest revived in the 1820s.

Shelley's next encounter with the world of illegal publishing occurred in 1815. In the spring of that year substantial extracts from *Queen Mab* were reprinted, without the author being named, in a short-lived periodical, the *Theological Inquirer*, edited by a man calling himself the Reverend Erasmus Perkins but whose real name was George Cannon. Mary Shelley's journal for 29 January 1815 notes

'Cannon calls but we do not see him – talk and look over Cannon's papers – he is a very foolish man'.[1]

The Printing Shop, from *A Cabinet of Useful Arts and Manufactures*

On 7 February Shelley takes up the story:

'Cannon the most miserable wretch alive καταριπτει υπνον ευδαιμονεστατον [katariptei hupnon eudaimonestaton – meaning discussed below]. He stays the evening. Vulgar brute – it is disgusting to hear such a beast speak of philosophy and republicanism. – Let refinement and benevolence convey these ideas.'

The journal has had pages removed at this point but there is another remark in Shelley's handwriting which appears to bear on the incident, although the tone is very different.

'after a conversation of uncommon wit and genius Erasmus exclaimed *aut Morus aut diabolus* [either More or the Devil] – More replied *aut Erasmus aut nemo* [either Erasmus or nobody]. This interview was the foundation of a long and firm friendship.'

The coincidence of names looks too unusual to be accidental. Shelley's anecdote seems to refer in some way to Erasmus Perkins and he is of course himself the Devil, the author of an atheist book. Godwin also may have been involved, although he was not on speaking terms with Shelley at this time. His journal for 24 January notes that 'Cannon calls'. There are also references at this time to Benbow, the pirate publisher with whom Perkins is known to have been associated. On 1 February Godwin notes 'Benbow calls' to be followed by other calls on the 16th and the 21st. On the last date Godwin returned the call on Benbow. There are no references to Benbow for long periods on either side of these meetings.

The Greek phrase in Shelley's journal for 7 February has been taken to mean that Cannon 'disturbs the happiest sleep', but why Shelley should bother to write this remark in Greek is not obvious. It is not a quotation from a Greek author. Again the coincidence – this time of the word *daimon* – looks too unusual to be accidental, and Shelley enjoyed the subterfuges of conspiracy. A more literal translation would be: 'he throws down the sleep blessed by the daimon.' Perhaps Shelley means that Perkins declines to print the opening passage of *Queen Mab*, the description of the sleeping Ianthe being wakened by the Fairy Queen. It was this passage which Shelley was shortly to publish in a reworked form as *The Daemon of the World*.

Research among the spy reports and criminal records has recently added immeasurably to our knowledge of London underground politics and publishing at this time. George Cannon (1789–1854) turns out to be a more considerable figure than had previously been suspected.[2] Unlike most of the other publishers of illegal books he was an educated man, familiar with Latin and Greek and several modern languages. He was admitted as a solicitor by one of the inns of court, and took out a preacher's licence. There is evidence that he was connected with Oxford University and he knew details of Shelley's expulsion and referred to them in a public letter as early as September 1813.[3] The alias of the Reverend Erasmus Perkins was not a joke: it was as believable a disguise as Theophilus

Marcliffe was for Godwin, radiating the same air of solid dissenting respectability, although sometimes, as when Perkins claimed to be a Jesuit, he was teasing.

Cannon was a close associate of Daniel Isaac Eaton, the boldest publisher of the previous generation.* He had been a founder member of a group calling itself the Union for Parliamentary Reform, which included some of Horne Tooke's former associates. Like William Clark, he was also a member of a number of radical clubs, known as the Philanthropists, illegal successors to the debating societies of the 1790s. Shelley's boast in the Swiss hotel register (also in Greek) that he was a philanthropist may imply that he too had been a member although if so his enthusiasm did not last long.†

One of the Cannon's favoured styles was heavy irony, appearing, for example, to defend religion when his aim was to undermine it – this made it harder for the authorities to mount a prosecution. But nothing ever appeared under his own name. He either used his alias of Erasmus Perkins or operated through front men, several of whom went to prison. The extracts from *Queen Mab* in the *Theological Inquirer* were edited by his friend R. C. Fair. Like Eaton before him, Cannon also published pornography – perhaps as a traditional way of financing his other activities, perhaps as a subversive weapon in its own right. His influence has been uncovered behind many of the illegal publishers of the 1820s and 1830s.

In some of his books which were published under the imprint of Benbow, the Preface is initialled G. C. with the addition of an identifying mark ¶.⁴ The device may have been chosen as resembling a reversed P or as the nearest thing a printer's font could provide to a monogram of the initials of Erasmus Perkins in the Greek alphabet. It is not known what this mark connoted or why the partners felt it had to be printed in the book instead of relying on a silent agreement between themselves. The existence of the mark may imply that whereas the printer – who had to be named by law – was taking the legal risks, books with these marks were in fact published by Cannon who took the financial risks.

Whatever may have been intended in 1815 *Queen Mab* aroused no public interest until Clark reprinted it in 1821, a piracy which Shelley publicly disavowed in an open letter to the *Examiner*. Clark was prosecuted by the Society for the Suppression of Vice and served four months in prison. Although he agreed to the handing over for burning of the unsold stocks, large numbers of copies or sheets were somehow transferred to the ownership of another pirate publisher, Richard Carlile, who was in prison for publishing the works of Tom Paine, and Carlile then produced a new piracy under his own imprint, using the same types.

It has been assumed that Clark's fine octavo was the first pirate, to be pirated in its turn later in the year by a much cheaper duodecimo version purporting to be published in New York by 'William Baldwin' but actually produced by Benbow in London with the co-operation of Erasmus Perkins. In fact neither piracy was

* See pages 131 and 320.
† See page 404.

taken wholly from the other.[5] Both have features which could have come only from Shelley's original, and the *Literary Gazette* for 19 May 1821, reviewing the Clark edition, mentions that *Queen Mab* 'has long been in limited and private circulation as a duodecimo'.[6] Again there are tantalizing references to the possible involvement of Godwin. On 25 October 1820 Godwin met 'Perkins' when he called on Miller, the bookseller, the first time he had had any contact with him since the single meeting in 1815. On 18 December 1820 he called on Perkins, but for what purpose is not known.

Some copies of the 'New York' edition carry a Preface signed by 'A Pantheist' with Perkins's identifying monogram printed alongside.* Since this mentions the Clark edition and quotes Shelley's public disavowal, copies with this Preface cannot predate Clark. However the make-up of the book reveals that originally it consisted only of title page and text, and copies of the book exist in this state, wrongly assumed to be incomplete.[7] The original title page, which is engraved, has the Greek letters ∈π engraved at the foot. Learned readers were perhaps expected to pick up an allusion to ἔπεα πτερόεντα, Homer's winged words, but they are obviously the initials of Erasmus Perkins.† When the Preface was added a new printed title page was prepared, and some copies have both title pages. These disguises were more effective than the one which Perkins put on for the piracy of Thomas Moore's *Melodies*. That book claims on the title page to have been printed in Pisa, that well-known hotbed of atheists, revolutionaries and seducers, at the 'Presso Erasmo Perchino.'[8]

If the 'New York' *Queen Mab* came before Clark's edition then Erasmus Perkins was clearly the instigator of the whole 1821 episode, resuming the campaign to publicize the admired book which he had started in 1815. A reordering of the dates would also help to explain another puzzle. Why should William Clark, as his first publishing venture, choose an extremely dangerous title and print a large and expensive edition? And how could he have found the capital? The answer may be that Clark was only a front man for a publisher who knew of the success of the 'New York' edition. On the last page of his edition after the colophon are the letters T.M. in gothic.‡ These are the initials of Thomas Moses, the printer to Richard Carlile who is known to have provided Carlile with credit and helped Carlile's wife to run the business while her husband was in prison.[9] He was the real investor in the Clark *Queen Mab*.

Could Shelley have been involved with Erasmus Perkins in arranging a reissue of *Queen Mab* in 1821 as he was in 1815? Although public denials were regularly used as camouflage, his denial shows all the signs of being genuine. However the piracy did not come entirely out of the blue as Shelley implied. Carlile claimed after Shelley's death that he had suggested bringing out a new edition of *Queen*

---

* See Plate 15 (c).
† See Plate 15 (a).
‡ See Plate 15 (d).

Mab in 1819 but had been refused[10] and although there is no surviving record on the Shelley side of such an approach (unless it is one of Godwin's calls) there is no reason to disbelieve him. There are other curiosities. Although Carlile and Perkins appear as rivals they may have been co-operating – Carlile published one of Perkins's books in 1820[11] William Clark too was evidently closely linked to both of them.[12] Whatever the details, it would appear that the pirate publishers and their political and financial backers were operating a sophisticated system of risk-limitation and risk-sharing.

The next decisive step in the growth of Shelley's influence occurred in 1834 when a pirate publisher called John Ascham put on sale a full edition in two volumes of all Shelley's published poems. Godwin, acting on Mary Shelley's behalf, tried to stop publication but failed, and it was the commercial success of this book which finally persuaded Sir Timothy Shelley to withdraw his veto and permit Mary Shelley to produce her authorized edition. If, as was now clear, the battle to suppress Shelley's ideas had been irretrievably lost, then the profits might as well go to his family as to the pirates.

The Ascham edition was a work of considerable care. It was reprinted from the original editions which by that time were hard to obtain and the text was so authoritative that Mary Shelley, in preparing her own edition shortly afterwards, used it as her copy text.[13] But again the question arises: why should Ascham have undertaken such a work? He is known otherwise only as a minor pornographer. Was he too just a front man? It is remarkable that copies of the book sometimes contain two title pages, one printed and the other engraved, almost identical to those of the 1821 *Queen Mab*. Should we therefore be looking for possible indications that Erasmus Perkins was again involved, attempting once more to promote the work of the poet he so fervently admired? He was still active, although now mainly as a pornographer, and had been sent to prison for eighteen months in 1830. Godwin met him at Rickman's on 29 May 1833. The long informative Preface is written in the style typical of Erasmus Perkins, commending *Queen Mab* while appearing to condemn it. And there is another tell-tale sign. Although the engraving is executed with the perfection of a banknote, the first letter of the word 'Holborn' at the foot of the page is not an H but a capital of the Greek letter P [Π].*

Erasmus Perkins was the unlikely spark which lit the fire of Shelley's reputation in 1821. The *Theological Inquirer* was the unextinguished hearth where it lay hidden between 1815 and 1821. If he was responsible for the Ascham edition, he was also the wild west wind which scattered Shelley's words among mankind. Admirers of Shelley and of freedom owe him a great deal.

One last puzzle. The notes to *Queen Mab* were as important as the poem – the verse was for moral feeling, the prose for intellectual persuasion. In the privately printed version of 1813 an indicator hand is printed against eight of the notes,

---

* See Plate 15 (b).

(To employ murder; There is no real wealth; Even love is sold; The north pole star; Necessity .... incongruity; There is no God; The consistent Newtonian; A book is put ... with itself).* Nowhere is it explained what, if anything, these hands signify.

The device was used by others as a sign of authorship. Leigh Hunt told readers of the *Examiner* that he would use an indicator hand to sign the articles for which he was personally responsible. Erasmus Perkins spattered the *Theological Inquirer* with hands – a printed letter from 'Varro' of Warwickshire asks that his contributions should 'be marked with an index or hand that I may know them again'. Perkins dutifully reproduced Shelley's hands in the 'New York' edition, and his example was followed by all the other early pirates, Clark, Carlile, Brooks, Stephen Hunt, Ascham, Hetherington and Watson, as well as by Mary Shelley in 1839. Carlile even printed the hands when quoting from *Queen Mab* in his newspaper.[14] In the dangerous world of illegal printing the pirates knew that such marks might have special significance.

'What means the ☞' was among the first questions which occurred to Godwin in 1813.† The 1821 reviewers were also interested. One suggested – absurdly – that the hands indicated notes which were written by Lord Byron.[15] Another said confidently:

'The Notes, which have a hand appended to them, partly original, but for the greater part extracted from other infidels, are not written by the author of the poem. They have been attributed to [Lord Byron]. . . but they are the production of a much less able and obscurer man. We saw him once some years, but whether he is still to be seen or is no more, we know not.'[16]

Maybe the hands were included simply for decoration or to give emphasis, although if the latter they were curiously chosen and they point out to the margin of the page instead of inwards. But it is also possible that Shelley, who was not yet fully familiar with the works of his philosophical predecessors, did employ an assistant from the radical underworld to compile these learned notes on his behalf. The writer of the first note introduces the then unpublished poem by Shelley 'Falsehood and Vice' in terms which may imply that he is not himself the author and which recall similar words used to introduce *Queen Mab* in the *Theological Inquirer*.

'I will here subjoin a little poem, so strongly expressive of my abhorrence of despotism and falsehood, that I fear lest it never again may be depicted so vividly. This opportunity is perhaps the only one that ever will occur of rescuing it from oblivion.'

If we are to look for such an assistant, Erasmus Perkins is an obvious candidate,

* See Plate 16.
† See page 342.

along with his friend R. C. Fair. In 1812 Perkins was publishing similar material in the wake of the trial of Daniel Isaac Eaton[17] – and may have learned about Shelley's *Letter to Lord Ellenborough* and sought out this unusual and unexpected ally. The truth may now be irrecoverable although, if someone were able to recognize the unusual font from which the hand is taken, this could help identify the printer.

When the right to freedom of thought was eventually conceded, the importance of such marks ceased to be recognized. The Victorians stopped reproducing them and I know of no twentieth-century edition which even mentions their existence. They ought to be restored to the text, not only in justice to Shelley's wishes, but as a reminder of the mysterious men whose heavy sacrifices helped to win the battle.

Bibliography of Works by William Godwin

* Not previously attributed.

1770
A story for *Town and Country Magazine*, 1770. Not further identified.

1783
History of the Life of William Pitt, Earl of Chatham printed for the Author and sold by G. Kearsley at No. 46 in Fleet Street, 1783. Anonymous.

A Defence of the Rockingham Party, in their late coalition with . . . Lord North, Stockdale, 1783. Anonymous. Reprinted in *Four Early Pamphlets*.

?*The Thespiad*, 1783. Listed by Godwin among his published works but no copy or review known. See notes to Chapter 3.

An Account of the Seminary that will be opened on Monday the Fourth Day of August at Epsom in Surrey, Cadell, 1783. Anonymous. Reprinted in *Four Early Pamphlets*.

1784
Sketches of History in Six Sermons, Cadell, 1784. Some copies anonymous, others with Godwin's name.

Italian Letters, or The History of Count de St. Julian, Robinson, 1784. Anonymous. Reprinted by University of Nebraska Press, 1965.

Damon and Delia, A Tale, Hookham, 1784. Anonymous. Only known copy British Library.

Imogen, a Pastoral Romance, from the Ancient British, Lane, 1784. Reprinted New York, 1963.

The Herald of Literature, as a Review of the most considerable publications that will be made in the course of the ensuing Winter, Murray, 1784. Anonymous. Reprinted in *Four Early Pamphlets*.

New Annual Register, 'British and Foreign History' in volumes for 1784–90. Possibly also part of volume for 1791. Godwin is known to have written 'Public Occurrences' and

The Resources of Happiness, from *Blossoms of Morality*

edited 'Public Papers' in volume for 1784 and it is likely that he contributed to these sections in later volumes also. All anonymous.

Instructions to a Statesman ... George Earl Temple, Murray, 1784. Reprinted in *Four Early Pamphlets.*

1785

*Review of 'The History of Ayder Ali Khan', Political Herald, 1785. Anonymous

* *Dr Priestley's Letters to Dr Horsley.* A series of reviews of books and articles written in reply to Priestley's *History of the Corruptions of Christianity, English Review*, 1785, unfinished. Anonymous.

* *Political and Historical Speculations: Critique of the Administration of Mr Pitt.* A series of articles in *Political Herald*, beginning 1785. Anonymous.

* *The Grounds of a Constitutional Opposition Stated, Political Herald*, 1785. Anonymous.

*Review of 'Criticisms on the Rolliad', *Political Herald*, 1785. Anonymous.

*Review of Boswell's 'Letter to the People of Scotland', *Political Herald*, 1785. Anonymous.

*Review of Burke's speech on the Nabob of Arcot's debts, *Political Herald*, 1785. Anonymous.

1786

* *Genuine Idea of a King of England, Political Herald*, 1786. Anonymous.

* *To the Earl of Buchan, on the Character of Dr Gilbert Stuart*, in *Political Herald*, 1786. Anonymous.

Letters and articles signed 'Mucius' in *Political Herald*, 1785 and 1786. Anonymous. Reprinted in *Uncollected Writings.*

1787

History of the Internal Affairs of the United Provinces from the year 1780, to the commencement of hostilities in June 1787, Robinson, 1787. Anonymous. Adapted from *New Annual Register.*

?Review of *Sympathy* by Samuel Pratt. Mentioned by Hazlitt in *Thoughts on Taste*, not further identified.

1790

* *The English Peerage; or a View of the Ancient and Present State of the English Nobility*, 3 volumes, Robinson, 1790. Anonymous.

1791

Review of Holcroft's translation of the *Posthumous Works of Frederic II. Monthly Review*, November 1791. Anonymous.

1793

Review of Mrs Inchbald's 'Everyone has his Fault', *European Magazine*, February 1793. Anonymous.

An Enquiry concerning Political Justice, and its Influence on General Virtue and Happiness, 2 volumes, Robinson, 1793; 2nd edition 1796; 3rd edition 1798.

1794

Things As They Are; or The Adventures of Caleb Williams, 3 volumes, Crosby, 1794.

* *An Impartial History of the Late Revolution in France*, Robinson, 1794. Anonymous. Godwin contributed to Chapter 1 and possibly to some of the later chapters taken from *New Annual Register* for 1790 and subsequent volumes. Another version published 'For the authors'. Principal author Gregory, Godwin's successor at the *New Annual Register.*

Cursory Strictures on the Charge delivered by Lord Chief Justice Eyre ... October 2, 1794, first published in the Morning Chronicle October 21. Anonymous. Reprinted in *Uncollected Writings.*

A Reply to an Answer to Cursory Strictures ... by the Author of Cursory Strictures, 1794. Anonymous. Reprinted in *Uncollected Writings*.

1795

Considerations on Lord Grenville's and Mr Pitt's Bills, concerning Treasonable and Seditious Practices, and Unlawful Assemblies. By a Lover of Order, Johnson, 1795. Anonymous. Reprinted in *Uncollected Writings*.

1796

Letter of ? 23 October 1795 to Thelwall, *The Tribune*, vol. 3, 1796.

1797

The Enquirer, Reflections on Education, Manners and Literature, Robinson 1797; revised edition 1823.

Memoirs of the Life of Simon Lord Lovat. Written by Himself in the French Language and now first translated from the original manuscript, George Nicol, 1797. Anonymous. Godwin edited and translated the manuscript in 1784.

1798

Memoirs of the Author of a Vindication of the Rights of Woman, Johnson and Robinson, 1798; 2nd edition revised 1798.

Posthumous Works of the Author of a Vindication of the Rights of Woman, 4 volumes, Johnson, 1798.

1799

St. Leon, A Tale of the Sixteenth Century, 4 volumes, Robinson, 1799.

1801

Thoughts occasioned by the Perusal of Dr Parr's Spital Sermon ..., Robinson, 1801. Reprinted in *Uncollected Writings*.

1803

*[William Scolfield] *Bible Stories. Memorable Acts of the Ancient Patriarchs, Judges, and Kings ... for the use of children*, 2 volumes, printed for R. Phillips and sold by Benj. Tabart, 1803. See note 1 to Chapter 21.

Life of Geoffrey Chaucer ... including Memoirs of John of Gaunt ... with sketches of ... England in the fourteenth century, 2 volumes, Phillips, 1803.

1805

Fleetwood: or The New Man of Feeling, 3 volumes, Phillips, 1805.

[Edward Baldwin] *Fables, Ancient and Modern*, 2 volumes, 1805.

[Theophilus Marcliffe] *The Looking Glass: A True History of the Early Years of an Artist*, 1805.

Obituary Notice of Joseph Ritson, *Monthly Mirror*, 1805. Anonymous. Reprinted in *Uncollected Writings*.

1806

[Edward Baldwin] *The Pantheon*, 1806.

[Edward Baldwin] *The History of England*, 1806.

Obituary Notice of Charles James Fox, *London Chronicle*, 1806. Reprinted in *Uncollected Writings*.

[Theophilus Marcliffe] *The Life of Lady Jane Grey*, 1806. Later reprinted under Godwin's other pseudonym, Edward Baldwin.

?*Rural Walks*, 1806. Listed by Godwin among his published works. See notes to Chapter 21.

1807
Faulkener, a Tragedy, 1807.

1809
[Edward Baldwin] *History of Rome*, 1809.
Essay on Sepulchres, Miller, 1809.
[Edward Baldwin] *Mylius's School Dictionary . . . to which is prefixed a New Guide to the English Tongue* by Edward Baldwin, 1809.
On Kemble's acting, *Morning Chronicle*, 5 April 1809. Reprinted in *Uncollected Writings*.
Obituary notice of Joseph Johnson, *Morning Chronicle*, 21 December 1809. Anonymous.

1810
[Edward Baldwin] *Outlines of English Grammar*, 1810.

1812
*Mrs Fenwick, *Rays of the Rainbow*, 1812. Preface by Godwin.

1814
[Edward Baldwin] *Outlines of English History . . . For the Use of Children from Four to Eight Years of Age*, 1814.

1815
Letters of Verax to the Editor of the Morning Chronicle, 1815. Reprint of letters originally published under pseudonym Verax in *Morning Chronicle*.
The Lives of Edward and John Philips, Longmans, 1815.

1817
Mandeville, a Tale of the Seventeenth Century in England, 3 volumes, Constable, 1817.
Obituary Notice of J. P. Curran, *Morning Chronicle*, 16 October 1817. Reprinted in *Uncollected Writings*.

1818
Letter of Advice to a Young American, M. J. Godwin, 1818.
Further Letters of Advice to Joseph Beavan, printed *Analectic Magazine*, 1818. Reprinted in *Uncollected Writings*.

1820
Of Population, Longmans, 1820.

1821
On Ireland, *Morning Chronicle*, 25 December 1821. Reprinted in *Uncollected Writings*.
Three letters on the population question 1821, 1822. Reprinted in *Uncollected Writings*.

1822
[Edward Baldwin] *History of Greece*, 1822.

1824–8
History of the Commonwealth of England, 4 volumes, Colburn, 1824–8.

1830
Cloudesley: a novel, 3 volumes, Colburn, 1830.

1831
Thoughts on Man, his Nature, Productions, and Discoveries. Interspersed with some particulars respecting the Author, Effingham Wilson, 1831.

1833
Fragment of a Romance, *New Monthly Magazine*, January 1833.
Deloraine, 3 volumes, Bentley, 1833.

1834
Lives of the Necromancers, Mason, 1834.

1835
[William Godwin Jnr] *Transfusion* with a memoir of his life and writings by his father, Macrone, 1835.

1873
Essays, never before published, by the late William Godwin, King, 1873.

Abbreviations

Beloe, *The Sexagenarian, or the Recollections of a Literary Life* [by William Beloe], 1817
Bentley, *Copyright Documents in the George Robinson Archive: William Godwin and others 1713–1820*, by G. E. Bentley Jr. *Studies in Bibliography*, 1982
BL, British Library
Bodleian, Bodleian Library, Oxford
Boucé, *Sexuality in Eighteenth Century Britain*, ed. Paul-Gabriel Boucé, 1982
Brightwell, *Memorials of the Life of Amelia Opie*, by Cecilia Lucy Brightwell, 1854
Clairmont's Journal, The Journals of Claire Clairmont, ed. Marion Kingston Stocking, 1968
Coleridge's Letters, Collected Letters of Samuel Taylor Coleridge, ed. Earl Leslie Griggs, 1956–1971
Cowden Clarke, *Recollections of Writers*, by Charles and Mary Cowden Clarke, n.d., [1878]
Critical Heritage, Shelley, The Critical Heritage, ed. James E. Barcus, 1975
CW, Caleb Williams, by William Godwin, ed. David McCracken, Oxford, 1970
DNB, Dictionary of National Biography
Dove Cottage, Wordsworth Museum, Dove Cottage, Grasmere, Cumbria
Dowden, *The Life of Percy Bysshe Shelley*, by Edward Dowden, 1886
Elopement, The Elopement of Shelley and Mary as Related by William Godwin, ed. H. B. Forman, 1911
Fenwick, The Fate of the Fenwicks: Letters to Mary Hays, ed. A. F. Wedd, 1927
Flexner, *Mary Wollstonecraft*, by Eleanor Flexner, 1972
Four Early Pamphlets, Four Early Pamphlets (1783–84) by William Godwin, ed. Burton R. Pollin, 1977
Godwin and Mary, Letters of William Godwin and Mary Wollstonecraft, ed. Ralph M. Wardle, 1966
Goodwin, *The Friends of Liberty: The English democratic movement in the age of the French Revolution*, by Albert Goodwin, 1979

The Industrious Scholar, from *Lessons for Children*

Grylls, *Claire Clairmont*, by R. Glynn Grylls (Lady Mander), 1939

Hays, *The Love Letters of Mary Hays*, ed. A. F. Wedd, 1925

HCR, *Henry Crabb Robinson on Books and Their Writers*, ed. Edith J. Morley, 1938

Hogg's *Shelley, The Life of Percy Bysshe Shelley*, by Thomas Jefferson Hogg, ed. Edward Dowden, 1906

Holcroft, *The Life of Thomas Holcroft* . . ., ed. Elbridge Colby, 1925

Holmes, *Shelley, The Pursuit*, by Richard Holmes, 1974

Huntington, Henry E. Huntington Library, San Marino, California

Ingpen, *Shelley in England*, by Roger Ingpen, 1917

J, Godwin's manuscript journal, Bodleian

Keele, Papers of Josiah and Thomas Wedgwood with some letters from Godwin, Keele University Library

Kelly, *The English Jacobin Novel*, by Gary Kelly, 1976

KP, *William Godwin: His Friends and Contemporaries*, by C. Kegan Paul, 2 volumes, 1876

KSMB, *Keats Shelley Memorial Bulletin*, since renamed *Keats Shelley Review*

Lamb's *Letters, The Letters of Charles Lamb*, ed. E. V. Lucas, 1935

Letters about Shelley, Letters about Shelley interchanged by three friends, Edward Dowden, Richard Garnett and William Michael Rossetti, 1917

Locke, *A Fantasy of Reason: The Life and Thought of William Godwin*, by Don Locke, 1980

Marshall, *William Godwin*, by Peter H. Marshall, 1984

Mary Shelley's Journals, The Journals of Mary Shelley 1814–1844, ed. Paula R. Feldman and Diana Scott-Kilvert, 1987

Mary Shelley's Letters, The Letters of Mary Wollstonecraft Shelley, ed. Betty T. Bennett, 1980–88

Memoirs, Mary Wollstonecraft and William Godwin. *A Short Residence in Sweden* and *Memoirs of the Author of a Vindication of the Rights of Woman*, ed. Richard Holmes, Penguin Classics, 1987

Morgan, J. Pierpont Morgan Library, New York

MS, Manuscript

MS Film, Microfilm of Abinger archive, Bodleian Library.

n.d., no date

New Southey Letters, New Letters of Robert Southey, ed. Kenneth Curry, 2 volumes, New York, 1965

NYPL, New York Public Library

Peck, *Shelley, his life and work*, by Walter Edwin Peck, 1927

Pf, Carl H. Pforzheimer Collection, New York Public Library

Philp, *Godwin's Political Justice*, by Mark Philp, 1986

PJ, *Political Justice*, first edition 1793

Pollin, *Godwin Criticism, A Synoptic Bibliography*, by Burton R. Pollin, Toronto, 1967

Reply to Parr, Thoughts occasioned by the Perusal of Dr Parr's Spital Sermon . . ., by William Godwin, 1801

Sale Catalogue, Catalogue of the Curious Library of . . . *William Godwin* . . ., 1836, reprinted in *Sale Catalogues of Libraries of Eminent Persons*, ed. A. N. L. Munby, vol. 8, 1973

SC, *Shelley and His Circle*: Documents in the Carl H. Pforzheimer Library, ed. Kenneth Neill Cameron and later Donald H. Reiman, 1961–

Shelley's Letters, The Letters of Percy Bysshe Shelley, ed. Frederick L. Jones, 1964

Sunstein, *A Different Face, The Life of Mary Wollstonecraft*, by Emily Sunstein, 1975

Thurman, *Letters about Shelley from the Richard Garnett Papers*, ed. William Richard Thurman, Ph.D. Dissertation, University of Texas, Austin, 1972

ABBREVIATIONS

Tomalin, *The Life and Death of Mary Wollstonecraft*, by Claire Tomalin, 1974

UL, University of London

UW, Uncollected Writings . . ., by William Godwin, ed. Jack M. Marken and Burton R. Pollin, Gainsville, Florida, 1968

V and A, Victoria and Albert Museum Library

Wardle, *Mary Wollstonecraft*, by Ralph Wardle, 1951

White, *Shelley*, by Newman Ivey White, 1947

Wollstonecraft's Letters, Collected Letters of Mary Wollstonecraft, ed. Ralph M. Wardle, Cornell, 1979

Notes

CHAPTER I

The chief sources for Godwin's early life are autobiographical fragments and drafts written at various times including b226/1–2, b227/5, b228/9, and c604/1–3; a note of dates until 1785 b229/2; a long piece about his ancestry MS Film 73; notes on Newbury baptisms b227/5. The family tombstone at Guestwick, still just legible, provides confirmation that John Godwin died 12 November 1772 in his fiftieth year; that Ann died 19 August 1809 aged eighty-seven; and that Richard died in infancy. For the other members of Godwin's family see note 5 to Chapter 4. Other sources include a brief history of the parish drawn from official records *Guestwick–Briston 1652–1952* with information about Cromwell's chair; on Godwin's early reading, b229/4 and a note dated 3 May 1818, b227/5; Mary Shelley's notes and transcripts which include materials not otherwise known scattered through the archive, e.g. in c606 and c532/8 (many quoted KP); a list of poems, plays and stories written in his teens and twenties c606/1–5. For the religious background, R. W. Dale, *History of English Congregationalism*, 1907; R. Tudur Jones, *Congregationalism in England 1662–1962*, 1962; John Browne, *History of Congregationalism in Norfolk and Suffolk*, 1877. Marshall is especially useful on Godwin's education.

1 He was detected bribing a Norwich hotel maid to go to bed with him. See Michael R. Watts, *The Dissenters*, 1978, p. 343.
2 References to Brother Edward Godwin in *Two Calvinistic Methodist Chapels 1743–1811*, London Record Society, 1975.
3 Revd Edward Godwin, *The Death Bed*, 1744, BL.
4 Revd Edward Godwin [senior], *A sermon preached to a Society of Young Men in Silver Street on 20 October 1721*, BL.
5 Noted in *Public Characters of 1799–1800*. The author was Godwin's friend John Fenwick. Godwin declined to write the article himself but agreed to answer questions, b227/5.

The Eldest Son of the Good Family, from *Lessons for Children*

6 Godwin's *Fables*, p. 198.
7 Minutes of the Trustees, Archives of the Coward Trust, United Reformed Church, London.
8 c532/9. Other sermons, *Sketches of History*.
9 From a poem of 1775 quoted by Mary Shelley c606/1–5.
10 *SC*, I, 22.
11 *Diary of William Dunlap*, 1930, I, 229.

CHAPTER 2

For the expulsion from Stowmarket *SC*, I, 22. For the development of opinions on religion, *Essay on Religion*, b227/1 and *Historical Deduction of My Creed*, c 663/4. *Essays* contains useful biographical material.

1 *SC*, I, 26. I have restored the full wording from the draft which is replete with unusual abbreviations.
2 Mrs Marshall to Godwin, 4 September 1784, and Godwin's reply, 6 September, b214/5. See also *SC*, III, 255. Godwin and Marshall were probably responding to Government incentives to encourage settlement in St Vincent.
3 William Langford, *A Sermon occasioned by the death of the late Reverend Mr Edward Godwin ... April 8 1764*, 1764.
4 Quoted KP, I, 28.

CHAPTER 3

Godwin's early works mentioned in this and the following chapter are listed in the Bibliography. Several have not previously been attributed. Note in his early handwriting which puts *The Thespiad* between *Defence of the Coalition* and *Account of the Seminary*, i.e. May/June 1783, b229/4. J, 1 December 1789: 'Dine with Robinson seul. Undertake Rousseau's Confessions' probably refers to *The Confessions of J. J. Rousseau ... to which is added a New Collection of Letters* published by Robinson in 1790. J also mentions agreements with Robinson to translate Livy and to write a naval history, but there is no evidence that these were proceeded with. J contains plentiful evidence of Godwin acting as editor, ghost-writer and proofreader.

For Johnson's publishing career, Gerald P. Tyson, *Joseph Johnson*, Iowa UP, 1979. Details of Godwin's work on the *New Annual Register* and his arrangements with Robinson for other works emerge from his letter of 12 May 1789, Columbia University Library, New York, which supplements the autobiographical note in c606. Further points from two undated drafts to Robinson in b227/2 and from references in the autobiographical fragments. See also Bentley. The document which mentions Godwin receiving money for 'a book to be written on the Revolution in France' may refer to a proposed successor volume to *An Impartial History of the Late Revolution in France*, 2 volumes, Robinson, 1794, which only took the story to the fall of the Girondins. This book is a compilation from the material written by Godwin and Gregory which had already appeared in the *New Annual Register*. Another edition appeared in 1794 'Printed for the Authors'. Godwin read the book on 10 October 1795. More probably it is the payment in advance to Godwin, as a research assistant, for a book planned to appear under the name of Lord Lauderdale. See Bentley and Lauderdale to Godwin, 4 February 1796, c514. Some notes, b229/7.

1 Copy of a letter from Marshall n.d., c607.
2 16 January 1783. *Correspondence of Edmund Burke*, edited by Alfred Cobban and Robert A. Smith, V, 63. It appears from a letter of 7 January 1783 from Marshall, b214/

5, that Godwin wrote similar letters to the other prospective patrons including Dr Johnson.

3 CW, p. 208.

4 Watson suggested that it would have been more politic to have called the book *Sketches of Sacred History*, letter to Godwin, 5 July 1784, b214/6. Some copies of the book anonymous. Those with Godwin's name appear to be later.

5 For example, Ford K. Brown, *The Life of William Godwin*, 1926, p. 22, 'Godwin's criticism . . . very youthful . . . in all such matters he had at all times very little taste.' George Woodcock, *William Godwin, A Biographical Study*, 1946, p. 25, 'Its judgments are unreliable and valueless.'

6 *Memoir and Correspondence of John Murray*, ed. Samuel Smiles, 1891, I, 24.

7 See Chapter 19, note 2.

8 T. Trotter, *A View of the Nervous Temperament*, 1806, p. 93. Trotter was also worried by the effects of drinking tea and the risks to children of imbibing the passions of wet nurses through their milk. Shelley was among those who took this book seriously, quoting from it in the Notes to *Queen Mab*.

9 *A Letter from the Lord Bishop of London to the clergy*, 1750.

10 Quoted KP, I, 22.

11 Now in BL. Mary Shelley had access to a copy. Extract quoted in c606/5.

12 T. Harris to ? Godwin, 19 October 1784, b215/1.

13 *English Review* IV, 133.

CHAPTER 4

1 Marshall to Godwin, 23 July 1784, b229/2.

2 Bodleian copy contains a number of inserted words written in Godwin's unmistakable handwriting and other markings in ink and in pencil. The three volumes, each with the book plate of Samuel Parr, are evidently those described in *Sale Catalogue*, p. 306, as having belonged to Parr. Articles marked with a cross include the Mucius letters known from other sources to be by Godwin and it is a reasonable inference that he wrote the others. The letter on Stuart (III, 278) is marked WG [William Godwin]. Some of the other articles are attributed to GS [Gilbert Stuart] and to WT [William Thompson]. One, a profile of Charles James Fox, reprinted from an Edinburgh publication, is attributed to Adam Smith. A few letters from this period c529.

3 From a draft, b227/2. Priestley's reply dated 9 February 1785, c514.

4 Godwin to Spencer, Wednesday 24 January [1787], b227/2. Another letter seeking support BL.

5 Information about Godwin's relatives has to be pieced together from scattered references, many in the letters from his mother in c516 and from a letter by Hull Godwin of 1 January 1829, c508. The account in SC, I, 444 needs to be modified by the prime evidence quoted in *Notes and Queries*, 1862, p. 503. There has also been confusion between nephews and uncles with the same names. Main dates are noted in the Family Tree. For Joseph Godwin's imprisonment see Chapter 36.

6 Godwin's journal notes his reading of Volney's *Ruins* on 26 October 1797. That Marshall was the translator emerges from Godwin's letter to Holcroft of 31 December 1799 – quoted KP, I, 349. According to Carlile's *The Lion*, II, 111, Volney disapproved of Marshall's version which he believed softened his message out of deference to Church and state. Another translation commissioned from an Englishman living in Philadelphia was also unsatisfactory. The version published in Paris which begins 'Hail solitary ruins . . .' was prepared by Volney himself with the help of Joel Barlow. In a letter to Smart, 10 February 1801, b227/2, Godwin said he had tried to read the book but found it bombastic and inflated and had given up in despair.

7 b229/2. The list runs from 1773 to 1794 on several sheets.
8 b229/2. A few other names crossed out. Godwin's underlinings in the first list seem to imply that he knew the people well. In the second list he underlined the names as he got to know them.
9 No modern biography. *Holcroft* includes documents and information not included in earlier editions.
10 *Decline and Fall*, Chapter 38.
11 Quoted *CW*, p. 335.
12 Godwin's authorship proved by his letter to Robinson of 12 May 1789, Columbia University Library, and Godwin to Robinson, n.d., from a draft, b229/1. See also Bentley.
13 For example, Godwin's *Population*, p. 97.

CHAPTER 5

Details of the historical background are mainly taken from Goodwin and from Godwin's contributions to the *New Annual Register*. Quotations from Burke from Penguin edition edited by Conor Cruise O'Brien. For the fears aroused by the excessive influence of the dissenters in politics and the media, see Revd David Rivers, *Observations on the Political Conduct of the Protestant Dissenters, c.*1799.

1 J, 14 July 1790.
2 *New Annual Register* for 1789, p. 15.
3 Helen Maria Williams, *Letters Written in France in the Summer 1790*, p. 14. Williams wrote further volumes under the general title of *Letters from France*.
4 Godwin's *Chaucer*, p. 120.
5 *Memories of Seventy Years, by one of a literary family*, edited by Mrs Herbert Martin, 1883, p. 19.
6 Details of the exact events surrounding the publication have remained obscure and disputed. There can be little doubt that the documents I quote refer to the incident and provide confirmation of the main features of my account. The date of formal publication was chosen as Washington's birthday. A letter from 'JF' [John Fenwick] dated 'Monday 4 o'clock', b229/6, asks Godwin to read the manuscript of an unidentified pamphlet that evening and not to mark it in case he finds himself shut up in the Bastille. This too may refer to the *Rights of Man*.
7 c511.
8 b227/6. Probably to Paine but possibly to Holcroft or Fenwick.
9 b215/6. Printed in KP, 1, 69 with some alterations.
10 b227/6.
11 The key can still be seen at Mount Vernon.
12 Notes of conversations, b227/5.
13 b227/2.
14 Drafts of letters to Fox and Sheridan, April 1791, b227/2, b215/6. A longer extract of the letter to Fox is printed in KP, 1, 75.
15 Quoted KP, 1, 67, from c606.
16 *New Annual Register* for 1790, p. 74.

CHAPTER 6

1 e196–227. Mary Shelley believed that her father did not record his marriage to her mother, having failed to notice 'Panc', which notes his visit to St Pancras Church to be

married. Philp, using social science techniques, attempts some interesting quantification of Godwin's social milieu during the 1790s.

2 Hogg's *Shelley*, p. 456.

3 *Diary of William Dunlap*, 1930, I, 229.

4 Amelia Alderson. From a letter, probably of September 1794, quoted Brightwell, p. 43. A note in b229/2 records a payment of 12s 9d for 1½ yards of neckcloth plus 9s for making. This compares with £1.1s for breeches, 16s for a hat, and £2.10s for a coat.

5 Story in *Holcroft*.

6 Essay on religion, 7 May 1818, b227/1.

7 Ann Godwin's letters, c516, extensively quoted KP.

8 R. W. Dale in his *History of English Congregationalism*, 1907, p. 544, gives a vivid description of the method of arguing to which Godwin was the heir.

9 *PJ*, I, 180.

10 *PJ*, I, 115. A. E. Newton, *The Amenities of Book-Collecting*, 1920, owned a copy that had belonged to Paine.

11 *Enquirer*, p. 27.

12 b229/2.

13 *CW*, p. 338. A meditative sermon addressed to himself 'Be not silent lest thou shouldest stumble' in b229/2 can be dated from J to 21 February 1792.

14 Godwin's *Thoughts on Man*, p. 143.

15 Hogg's *Shelley*, p. 523.

16 *PJ*, I, 21.

17 The manuscript of *PJ* which shows the alterations is in the V and A. A contract document dated 5 February 1793, b227/2. See Bentley.

18 Godwin to Paine, 7 November 1791, from a draft, b227/6. The other b227/2. The date supplied from J, 'Write to Paine'. The introduction by Hollis probably occurred on 4 November and the reference to yesterday in the draft was probably altered in the final version. The second draft was much worked over to try to get the tone just right. That it was addressed to Paine is proved by the second 'your' having been originally written 'Paine's'.

19 *Memoirs*, p. 236. Mrs was a courtesy title applied to women believed to be beyond marriageable age. See also *SC*, I, 145.

20 Godwin's *Thoughts on Man*, p. 311.

21 *Holcroft* gives some vivid examples drawn from 1798. Godwin objected to its publication. Hazlitt makes interesting remarks in *The Spirit of the Age* and elsewhere. See also Cowden Clarke, p. 37.

22 In *The Round Table*. Among the examples which Hazlitt mentions is the argument about the merits of Voltaire. This was one of the topics discussed at Godwin's meeting with Paine and Wollstonecraft. Godwin supped with 'Haslets' at Holcroft's on 20 February 1794. The first explicit mention of 'Hazlit Jr' is on 17 September 1794.

23 Godwin wrote to Erskine suggesting that Paine might have been acquitted if Erskine himself had not implied that his client was guilty. b227/2.

24 Meetings with Chauvelin noted in J. An extract from *World* of 14 May 1793 reporting Godwin's gift, c607.

CHAPTER 7

Quotations from first edition. Third edition edited by Isaac Kramnick, Penguin Classics. The secondary literature on Godwin's philosophical ideas is vast. Philp serves as a useful guide. Philp also discusses in detail Godwin's changes in the later editions.

1 *PJ*, p. 1.

2 *Reply to Parr*, p. 46 in *UW*.
3 *PJ*, p. 239.
4 *PJ*, p. 83.
5 *PJ*, p. 262.
6 *PJ*, p. 605.
7 *PJ*, p. 412.
8 *PJ*, p. 444.
9 *PJ*, p. 9.
10 *PJ*, p. 813.
11 *PJ*, p. 174.
12 *PJ*, p. 849.

CHAPTER 8

The main editions and reprints are listed in Burton R. Pollin, *Education and Enlightenment in the Works of William Godwin*, New York, 1962, although his list now needs to be augmented and corrected. Robinson's London first edition in octavo, author's collection. Watson's 4th edition of 1842 is also found with later dates on the title page.

1 c606/2. Compare the Attorney General's warning to Cooper 1793 that he would permit publications in octavo but would prosecute any version 'published for dissemination among the populace'. Tyson, *Johnson* (cited in Chapter 3), p. 124.
2 Goodwin, p. 475, quoting a document in the Public Record Office.
3 *The Life of Reginald Heber*, 1830, I, 13.
4 Advertised on the cover of Watson's reprint of Shelley's *Masque of Anarchy*, 1852. The parts were probably made from sheets of the 1842 edition. See also Chapter 40.
5 *Public Characters*, p. 374. See note 5 to Chapter 1.
6 In *The Spirit of the Age*, 1825.
7 Pollin.
8 *New Southey Letters*, I, 79.
9 The references to William Blake in Godwin's journal are discussed by David V. Erdman in *Notes and Queries*, August 1953. A note in b229/2 lists 'Blake' among prominent people met in 1794, but Holcroft's friend Arthur Blake could be intended. See also the story about borrowing reprinted in *Blake Records*, ed. G. E. Bentley Jr, 1969, p. 523, from Malkin, which I believe must refer to Godwin although the story itself may be apocryphal.
10 Sir Henry Taylor to Lady Shelley, 11 September 1871, Shelley adds. c8.
11 John Arnot, KP, I, 313.
12 Prospectus for a Select Club c532/4. Jardine was the author of *Letters from Barbary, France, Spain, Portugal etc.* by an English Officer, 1788.
13 H. C. Robinson to his brother, 12 December 1796, MS Dr Williams Library, UL.
14 *Enquirer*, p. vii.
15 *Recollections of the Life of John Binns*, Philadelphia, 1854, p. 43.
16 W. H. Reid, *Rise and Dissolution of the Infidel Societies of the Metropolis*, 1800.
17 Documented although not comprehensively by Philp.
18 For example, Dunlap to Godwin, 1 October 1795, b227/2, the replies to which, from Godwin and Holcroft, are printed in *Notes and Queries*, 1956, and Godwin's long letter of advice to an Oxford student, b227/8, quoted in KP, I, 141.
19 In *The Spirit of the Age*.
20 *The Prelude*, XI, 225, For a study of the effect of *Political Justice* on Wordsworth see Nicholas Roe, *Wordsworth and Coleridge, the Radical Years*, 1988.
21 Lovell to Holcroft, 11 December 1794, quoted *Holcroft*, II, 83.

22 *Coleridge's Letters*, I, 115. Godwin's chameleon metaphor, *Enquirer*, p. 33.
23 *Coleridge's Letters*, I, 138.
24 The story is included in Shelley's play *Charles the First* where the Fool describes the plan as 'gynaecocoenic and pantisocratic'.
25 Wedgwood to Godwin, 31 July 1797, c507.
26 Godwin to Wedgwood, 10 January 1798, b215/5.

CHAPTER 9

1 Joseph Fawcett, 'An Ode on the 14th of July 1792', in *Poems*, 1798.
2 *Procès verbal . . . Convention Nationale, 1793*, 28 April 1793.
3 *SC*, I, 116.
4 *Henry Crabb Robinson in Germany*, ed. by Edith J. Morley, 1929, p. 135.
5 Draft of letter to Jardine, b227/2.
6 Draft of letter to Fox, 29 September 1793, b227/2.
7 *Shelley's Letters*, I, 267. The point is discussed more fully in Chapter 23.
8 b227/1.
9 In *The Grounds of Constitutional Opposition Stated*.
10 Printed in *UW*.
11 Christina Bewley, *Muir of Huntershill*, 1981, p. 95. A copy of Godwin's letter dated 23 January 1794, c532/2.
12 A copy of Godwin's letter to the editor of the *Morning Chronicle* dated 3 March [1794] asking for his letter to be inserted, b229/6, but despite KP I cannot find that it was printed. The main letter and note, b227/2.
13 *Revolt of Islam*, XI, 20. For other close links with *PJ* see Chapter 35.
14 KP, I, 125.
15 Quoted in *The Trial of Joseph Gerrald*, 1794 and elsewhere.

CHAPTER 10

For the Jacobin novel see especially Kelly and the first part of Marilyn Butler, *Jane Austen and the War of Ideas*, 1975.

1 Godwin to Robinson, 29 March 1793, b227/2.
2 c663/1.
3 b227/6.
4 Review of the *Iron Chest* in *A View of the English Stage*.
5 Preface to 1832 edition of *Fleetwood* quoted *CW*, p. 338.
6 *CW*, p. 181.
7 *PJ*, p. 487.
8 The manuscript of *Caleb Williams*, V and A. Variations discussed in *CW*. A detailed note on the composition f66. Marshall's advice to burn b227/5. A note signed J.R. [Joseph Ritson] on the Black Act, b227/2. Interpretations of the novel are discussed in B. J. Tysdahl, *William Godwin as Novelist*, 1981. J. Middleton Murry regarded it as an allegory of Protestant history and one of his successors has perceived a symbolic picture in which Caleb Williams is Godwin, Falkland is the admired *ancien régime*, and the act of opening the chest the writing of *Political Justice* which will destroy that regime. A mythologist perceives Falkland as a worried deity in an innocent Eden in which the opening of the chest represents Adam's eating of the apple of knowledge; the same writer goes on to build an elaborate parallel between the pursuit scenes and the relentlessness of God described in Psalm 139. A critic whose love of partial techniques has fettered his understanding of historical evidence has concluded that *Caleb Williams*

is not political but a symbolic overthrowing of God. A Freudian has argued that Falkland and Caleb are aspects of Godwin's own personality, their divided feelings towards each other expressing the ego's split attitudes to the superego and the libido. No Kleinian, as far as is known, has yet postulated a satisfactory connection with Godwin's wet nurse, but the portraits of the two main characters have been convincingly compared to the rabbit and the duck with which gestalt psychologists illustrate the ambiguities of perception so that 'two entire *Weltanschauungen* vie in catching our attention'.

9 The name had topical associations. After the storming of the Tuileries in 1793, the revolutionary Government was said to have discovered an iron chest concealed in a wall of the palace in which the king had kept incriminating documents. *New Annual Register* for 1793, p. 135.

CHAPTER 11

1 Godwin to Thelwall, 18 September 1794, copy c511, quoted *Life of John Thelwall* by his widow, 1838, 1, 206.
2 b227/2.
3 c531.
4 Holcroft to Godwin, 10 October 1794, c515.
5 An undated fragment of a letter from Bland Burges (probably October 1794) records that 'The Attorney General [Scott] said the other day – I don't know whether the Grand Jury will find the Bill against Horne Tooke, tho' I think they ought; but if they do, I will undertake to hang him.' MS Bodleian. See Goodwin, p. 354.
6 Reprinted with other prime documents *UW*.
7 See note 5 above. For the planned round-up of suspects, I know of no primary source. However the story was circulating very early and was not denied. See, for example Francis Plowden, *A Short History of the British Empire during the year 1794*, 1795, p. 333.
8 Draft of a letter to Lord Chief Justice Eyre, b227/2.
9 Holcroft to Godwin, 24 November 1794, from Newgate Prison, MS V and A.
10 Brightwell, p. 45.
11 Draft of a letter to Charles Sinclair, 15 December 1794, b228/1. See also Chapter 30.
12 Gerrald to Godwin, 'Newgate Water-side', n.d., b214/8.
13 Alderson to Godwin, 5 February 1796, b210/6.
14 Fenwick to Godwin, 29 December 1795, b214/3.
15 Copy of his letter published in *The Tribune*, b227/7.
16 Preface to *Enquirer*.
17 Parr to Godwin, received 25 November 1795, and Godwin's reply, 4 December 1795, c512.
18 Projected works 1798, b229/9.
19 b229/8.
20 b227/5.

CHAPTER 12

1 *PJ*, p. 851.
2 See G. Talbot Griffith, *Population Problems in the Age of Malthus*, 1967.
3 See *The Travels of Lord Charlemont*, ed. by W. B. Stanford and E. J. Finopoulos, 1984, and a remark in *The Letters of John B. S. Morritt*, 1914, p. 137. Charlemont's account of survivals in Lesbos, *Transactions of the Royal Irish Academy*, 1794.
4 *Holcroft*, 11, 124.
5 [Joseph Fawcett], *A Humble Attempt to form a system of Conjugal Morality*, 1787.

6 Supplement to J, e273.
7 Hogg's *Shelley*, p. 436.
8 Quoted by Tomalin from *Letters from Barbary*, 1788, 1, 321.
9 Two letters from R. A. C. Prescott of Blackburn, 10 March 1799, 12 April 1799, c526, with Godwin's reply, 17 April 1799, b228/6.
10 Letter from R.M., Liverpool, 'Miss Lexington', 3 November 1800, b227/2.
11 *Hays*, p. 227.
12 *Memoirs of Emma Courtney* has been reprinted, 1987, in the Pandora Mothers of the Novel series.
13 Quoted Brightwell, p. 43. The letter can be dated to early September 1794.
14 Godwin to Alderson, 8 September 1794. MS private collection.
15 Alderson to Godwin, 12 February 1796, b210/6.
16 Godwin to Alderson, n.d. [February 1796] MS Huntington, quoted *Amelia* by Jacobine Menzies-Wilson and Helen Lloyd, 1937, p. 30.
17 Inchbald to Godwin, n.d., quoted KP, 1, 139.
18 KP, 1, 73.
19 For eighteenth-century misunderstandings of such matters see Boucé.
20 c513, identified from handwriting. A letter, n.d., signed 'Anne Parr', c512. One dated 25 March 1796, b227/2, signed 'Anne'.
21 Godwin's letters to Wollstonecraft in June and July 1797 in *Godwin and Mary*.
22 b227/2.
23 Godwin to ? Mrs Taylor 16 June 1791 [probably a mistake for 1795]. Pf.
24 Quoted Brightwell, p. 59.
25 Inchbald to Godwin, 22 December 1794, c509, dated from postmark.
26 b229/2.
27 b227/2.
28 c607.
29 *Hays*, p. 35 and see p. 28.
30 Quoted KP, 1, 337.

CHAPTER 13

The main biographies of Wollstonecraft are Flexner, Sunstein, Tomalin, and Wardle. Main primary sources for her involvement with Godwin are J, *Memoirs*, and *Godwin and Mary*. Much of interest in *Hays* of which the originals and others not printed on which I have been able to draw are in Pf. Note of important dates and events relating to Wollstonecraft c604/2. See Appendix 1.

1 Godwin to Hays, 7 January 1796, MS Pf. *Hays*, p. 232. Misspelling restored.
2 Hays to Godwin, 11 January 1796, MS Pf.
3 Mary Wollstonecraft, *An Historical and Moral View of the French Revolution*, 1794, p. vii.
4 Thomas Christie, *Letters on the Revolution in France*, 1791, p. 59.
5 Edition by Richard Holmes published with *Memoirs*, Penguin Classics, 1987.
6 *Memoirs*, p. 249.
7 Reported in the letter from Marshall to Hazlitt, 21 July 1821, quoted W. Clark Durant's edition of *Memoirs*, 1927, p. 332.
8 In *Poems*, 1797.
9 b214/3. Addressed to 'Mrs Imlay' at 'Finsbury Place No. 16'. The handwriting of the letter closely resembles other examples of Holcroft's writing especially the k. There are a number of minor misspellings characteristic of the self-educated man and the references to the millennium are typically Holcroftian. In a conversation, 1821, Godwin remarked

that there were two others besides himself who had courted Wollstonecraft in 1795–6, W. Clark Durant's edition of *Memoirs*, p. 332. One was presumably Opie. Godwin did not include Stoddart, and Southey is unlikely for the other candidate. Wollstonecraft later avoided Holcroft and Godwin blamed his friend for sabotaging his relationships with women. Handwriting experts at the Bodleian favour the identification with Holcroft, but the evidence, even taken with the other indications, is not quite decisive. The text of the letter is printed by Chris Jones in *Keats Shelley Review*, 1986. It is certainly not by Godwin as suggested there.

10 A tantalizing note in the Heal local history scrap books, Swiss Cottage Public Library, Biii, 84, may refer to Wollstonecraft – 'Mary Wolsoncroft was admitted a Monthly Pensioner June 1796 for a bastard child aged 5 years allowed 6 shillings per month. Waugh's MS Account Book.' Waugh was presumably the official of some parish charity, but is untraced. Fanny was only two at this time and it is possible that someone other than Mary Wollstonecraft is referred to.

11 Merry was arrested for debt on 8 July, the day before Godwin's proposal to Dr Alderson. The circumstances of his release are noted in an autobiographical fragment quoted KP, I, 154. Amelia Alderson was in London at the time of the proposal as is clear from a reference in J to Godwin calling on AA on his return. Merry's letter to Godwin dated 19 September 1796 tells of his decision to go to America and to pay back some money to Dr Alderson. Godwin replied the following day, c514. Dale Spender, *Mothers of the Novel*, 1986, p. 317, having seen my brief unfootnoted reference in *Dictionary of British and American Writers*, ed. Janet Todd, 1984, still prefers to believe that Godwin's proposal was one of marriage, but the evidence against this interpretation seems to me to be decisive.

12 Alderson to Wollstonecraft, 28 August 1796, b210/6.

13 See *Wollstonecraft's Letters* numbers 206–208. Wardle dates the incident to late 1795 but December 1796/January 1797 is more consistent with other evidence, including Wollstonecraft's sickness, the money crisis, and Godwin's solution. Both of these conjectures imply that Godwin printed the letters out of their chronological sequence in *Posthumous Works* and it may be that the incident occurred as early as February 1792 when it is known that Wollstonecraft received a proposal of marriage from a rich man.

14 Godwin to Wedgwood, 28 February 1797, c511, copy c528. That the £50 was for Wollstonecraft is proved by Godwin's letter to Wedgwood of 19 April 1797, quoted KP, I, 235.

15 On 6 December 1796 at a play called *The Voice of Ridicule*.

16 Inchbald to Godwin, 11 April 1797, c509, printed KP, I, 278.

17 Godwin to Inchbald, 13 September 1797, b227/8, quoted KP, I, 278.

18 Godwin to Hays, 10 April 1797, *Hays*, p. 241.

19 Holcroft to Godwin, 6 April 1797, b214/6, quoted KP, I, 240.

20 Godwin to an unknown correspondent, 9 May 1797, b229/1.

21 Godwin to Wedgwood, 19 April 1797, quoted in KP, I, 235.

22 The Heal Collection, Bii, 47, includes a woodcut of The Polygon as it appeared in 1850. It consisted of a circle of semi-detached three-storey houses each with outside balcony. The porches and front doors were in the gaps between. The gardens at the back must have been shaped like wedges of a cut cake.

23 Elizabeth Robins Pennell, *Mary Wollstonecraft Godwin*, 1885, p. 204.

24 Cecilia Lucy Brightwell, *Memoir of Amelia Opie*, Religious Tract Society, 1855.

25 *Godwin and Mary*, p. 79.

26 *Godwin and Mary*, p. 103.

27 b228/9.

28 *Advice to Young Mothers on the Physical Education of Children*, By A Grandmother,

1823. An edition 'revised and augmented by the author' published in 1835, with the author's name given as 'M.J., Countess Dowager of Mountcashell'.

29 In *My First Acquaintance with Poets*. The date derived from J.

30 For Wollstonecraft's pregnancy see Appendix 1 and the full discussion in *SC*, 1, 185. One puzzle is that the name of the midwife is given in all the accounts as Mrs Blenkinsop but Godwin's registration document is signed by 'Mary Holby' as having been present at the birth. Public Record Office RG 5/20, copy in Shelley adds c9.

31 *St. Leon*, Chapter 4.

32 *Advice*, p. 6.

33 e.g. Reverend Richard Polwhele, *The Unsex'd Females*, 1798.

CHAPTER 14

Letter press copies of many of the letters Godwin sent after Wollstonecraft's death, b227/8.

1 Quoted KP, 1, 284.

2 Hewlett to Godwin, 13 September 1797, b214/3.

3 Inchbald to Godwin, 14 September 1797, c509 quoted KP, 1, 279.

4 Obituary in *Monthly Magazine*, September 1797. Letter to editor acknowledging authorship from Mary Hays, October issue. Godwin objected to her remark that 'a far abler hand' intended to write a full memoir. He told her in a letter of 27 October 1797 that she could no longer have long and confidential conversations with him since she had poisoned the springs of confidence, b227/8.

5 Godwin to an unknown correspondent, 19 September 1797, b227/8. Quoted Kelly, p. 226.

6 'Explanation w Fanny', J, 8 February 1806. It seems a fair guess that this was when Godwin told her about her origins. A copy of *Posthumous Works* inscribed 'Fanny daughter of the author from William Godwin May 14th 1813' [her nineteenth birthday], private collection. The idea started by KP that her suicide in 1816 was precipitated by discovering that she was illegitimate speaks loud on Victorian attitudes to such matters.

7 A few letters from Louisa Jones, c508. She is also said to have attracted Dyson and Arnot.

8 e.g. Godwin to Holcroft, 10 September 1797, b227/8

9 c604/2.

10 A letter from I. B. Johnson of Derby, 13 November 1797, b214/3, is evidently one of Godwin's main sources for Wollstonecraft's life in France.

11 Printed in *Godwin and Mary*. Not all the letters in the series as numbered by Godwin are now present.

12 *Wollstonecraft's Letters*, p. 236.

13 In the first edition Godwin spoke of 'cruelty', softened in the second edition to 'severity'. According to his letter of 11 January 1798 to Johnson, b227/8, Godwin believed Wollstonecraft's father hit her but did not whip her. Johnson's notes b210, quoted KP.

14 The letters remained in the Knowles family. In 1870 when interest in Wollstonecraft's ideas was reviving, E. H. Knowles wrote in *Notes and Queries* (4th series, vol. 6) that the autograph letters to Fuseli were in his possession. They later passed into the hands of the Shelley family. A letter from Sir Percy Shelley to Knowles, 8 December 1884 (private collection) thanks him for being allowed to retain his grandmother's letters and encloses £50. A few documents that evidently come from the Knowles papers survive in the Abinger archive, e.g. a note from JJ (Joseph Johnson, wrongly attributed to Lord Jeffrey) of 11 September 1797 telling Fuseli of Wollstonecraft's death, b210, but the

letters themselves were probably deliberately destroyed. Sir Percy's opinion, given in a letter of 13 December 1884, quoted in Thurman is the only remaining record.

15 Godwin to Johnson, 11 January 1798, b227/8. Mary had a slight paralysis of the right eyelid which gave her a sinister look, but few people found her cynical.

16 *Memoirs*, p. 258.

17 Everina had protested to Godwin at his intention to write a memoir in a letter of 24 November 1797, c523.

18 Summarized in Pollin.

19 *Anti-Jacobin Review* for July 1798. Godwin read it on 30 August. Index entries under Godwin and Wollstonecraft.

20 Changes described in Holmes's edition of *Memoirs*.

21 See also biographies of Wollstonecraft, Janet M. Todd, *Mary Wollstonecraft: An Annotated Bibliography*, 1976, and Barbara Taylor, *Eve and the New Jerusalem*, 1983.

22 John Corry, *A Satirical View of London*, 1803, p. 229.

23 Revd Richard Polwhele, *The Unsex'd Females*, 1798. The reference is in Wollstonecraft's Introduction to *Elements of Morality*, 1790–91, which she freely adapted from the German of C. G. Salzmann.

24 Isaac d'Israeli, *Vaurien or Sketches of the Times*, 1797, Pollin, 1564. A manuscript of a review of *Vaurien* in c532/5 could be the version which Wollstonecraft asked Godwin to write for the *Analytical Review* but another version was printed.

25 e.g. Jane West, *A Tale of the Times*, 1799, Pollin, 1754; *Dorothea*, 1801, Pollin, 1565; and Sophia King's *Waldorf*, 1798, Pollin, 1625.

26 George Walker, *The Vagabond*, 1799. Pollin, 1730. Godwin read it 22–24 January 1799, J.

27 Elizabeth Hamilton, *Memoirs of Modern Philosophers*, 1800, Pollin, 1602.

28 Examples of anti-Jacobin novels, Pollin, 1509, 1513, 1563, 1564, 1565, 1601, 1602, 1624, 1625, 1629, 1632, 1658, 1687, 1730, 1734. Some went through several editions.

29 *Adeline Mowbray, or The Mother and Daughter, a Tale in Three Volumes*, by Mrs Opie, 1804. Pollin, 1658. See Locke, p. 137. Attractive though his view is it cannot be sustained unless we locate the contradiction deep in Opie's subconscious. The book represented her later views on marriage. It is fully in line with the conventions of such works and with her other novels. Neither Brightwell, p. 120, nor the *Edinburgh Review*, 1806, which described volume two as 'perhaps the most pathetic and the most natural in its pathos . . . in the language', perceived the slightest hint of irony. Even Shelley saw the book as a useful presentation of the arguments and was persuaded into marriage after reading it. See Chapter 23.

30 Mrs Mary Anne Burges, *The Progress of the Pilgrim Good-Intent in Jacobinical Times*, 1801, 9th ed., 1814, Pollin, 1531. The later editions have a preface by Sir James Bland Burges, evidently a relative, the under secretary at the Foreign Office. See Goodwin, p. 204 and note 5 to Chapter 11.

CHAPTER 15

1 Godwin to Knowles, 28 September 1826, c527, quoted KP, II, 298.

2 Godwin to Ash, 31 August 1807, c532/2; 21 May 1808, b215/6; Godwin to Lofft, 14 June 1808, b215/6. The first mention of faintness 31 August 1791 after a row. The fits usually described as 'deliquium'.

3 In *Public Characters*.

4 e.g. *Substance of the Bishop of Rochester's Speech*, 1800, pp. 8, 19.

5 *New Annual Register for 1793*, Public Papers, p. 78.

6 The full title is a good example of attempts to invoke authority to convince the sceptical. *Proofs of a Conspiracy against All the Religions and Governments of Europe, carried*

on in the Secret Meetings of Free Masons, Illuminati, and Reading Societies. Collected from Good Authorities by John Robison A.M., Professor of Natural Philosophy, and Secretary to the Royal Society of Edinburgh, 1797. See also [Hon. Robert Clifford] *Application of Barruel's Memoirs of Jacobinism to the Secret Societies of Ireland and Great Britain,* 1798.

7 In the list of famous people met in 1799 at the end of vol. 7 of J, Godwin noted 'Morris (Secret)'. See Goodwin, p. 436. Godwin met him on 27 October while dining at Kemble's with Sheridan, Curran and others, and on other occasions.

8 For example, Chapter 28 of *St. Leon.*

9 Godwin to Reveley, July 1799. Printed KP, I, 333. Letter press copies of originals c513.

10 Godwin to Reveley, 25 July 1799, b227/8.

11 Quoted KP, I, 335.

12 Godwin to Lee, April 1798. Printed KP, I, 298 from b228/4.

13 Holmes's edition of *Memoirs,* p. 256. This passage was defiantly added in second edition, published in the summer of 1798.

14 Godwin's drafts and Lee's replies, b228/4. Others c507. Extracts printed KP.

15 Quoted KP, I, 301 from b228/4. Author says Godwin's letter was returned with Lee's comments 'after the final cessation of their correspondence', but more probably it was returned at the time.

16 b228/4.

17 Notes for a letter or a conversation, n.d., c512.

18 Letter signed 'A Lancashire woman' from Warrington, 26 January 1799, b214/3.

19 Godwin to Miss Kinsman, 26 September 1798, b227/2.

20 Godwin to Mackintosh, 27 January 1799, printed *Reply to Parr,* p. 13.

21 Mackintosh to Godwin, 30 January 1799, quoted KP, I, 328. Godwin did not print the letter in his *Reply to Parr* because he knew Mackintosh had not kept his promise.

22 *Reply to Parr,* p. 17.

23 Godwin to Montagu, 28 June 1799, b227/8.

24 Godwin to Wedgwood, 24 April 1800, b227/8.

25 Sophia Lee to Godwin, 2 June 1799, c507. The phrase occurs in *The Clergyman's Tale,* II, 101 of the Standard Novels edition of 1832.

26 Pollin, 1624, 1625. Godwin read part of *Cordelia* on 5 June 1800. From a letter from Sophia King of 11 June, b227/2, it is evident that she regretted asking his opinion.

27 b228/9, quoted KP, I, 358.

28 William Austin, *Letters from London,* Boston, 1804, p. 203. Austin's visit was in May 1802. A letter of self introduction 15 December 1802, b215/2.

29 Journal of Joseph Carrington Cabell, MS, Universty of Virginia. Cabell met Godwin in September 1804. His description *Keats Shelley Journal,* XX, 1791, p. 19.

CHAPTER 16

1 Productions planned, b228/9. Printed in full KP, I, 294. He began writing 'First Principles of Morals' 7 September 1798. For *St. Leon* see especially Kelly.

2 Holcroft to Godwin, 9 September 1800, quoted KP, II, 25.

3 Preface to *St. Leon.* The passage is a direct quotation from the second edition of the *Memoirs* introduced in response to hostile criticism. Text *Memoirs,* p. 274. In the 1831 edition of *St. Leon,* the version most commonly read, the passage is fully incorporated into the text without mention of the *Memoirs.*

4 Pollin, 1569. The author Edward Dubois an anti-Jacobin hack.

5 Several anti-Jacobin novels, e.g. Charles Lloyd, *The Infernal Quixote,* 1800, Pollin, 1632, and Rigshaw Cincinnatus [pseud.], *Sans Culotides,* 1800, Pollin, 1687, specifically link Godwin with the Illuminati.

6 W. H. Reid, *The Rise and Dissolution of Infidel Societies*, 1800. Pollin, 1681.
7 *St. Leon*, Chapter 13. In a wolf-infested forest between Lake Constance and Lindau. See Chapter 35.
8 Essay on Religion, 1818, b227/1.
9 Judgements on *St. Leon*, c604/2.
10 Godwin to Inchbald, *SC*, I, 210.
11 Inchbald to Godwin, 4 December 1799, quoted KP, I, 350.
12 Inchbald to Godwin, 24 December 1799, c509.
13 c604/2.
14 Godwin to Parr, 3 January 1800, c512, quoted KP, I, 375.
15 Parr to Godwin, 29 April 1800, c512, quoted KP, I, 378.
16 The MS of the *Reply to Parr* is in the Huntington.
17 Including the passage which was a quotation from the *Memoirs*. See note 3 above.
18 Note dated 8 June 1801, b227/2.

CHAPTER 17

1 Autobiographical note dated 3 May 1818, b227/5, quoted KP, I, 354. Godwin drafted an essay on the style of the English prose writers on 24 March 1814, b227/3. He preferred the Elizabethans and Jacobeans but by no means all of them.
2 See for example *Memoirs of . . . the Life of James Lackington*, end of letter 39; Beloe, II, 272.
3 Hazlitt in *My First Acquaintance with Poets*.
4 *New Southey Letters*, I, 389.
5 c605, quoted KP, I, 17.
6 In 'Mr Coleridge' in *The Spirit of the Age*.
7 *Enquirer*, p. 392. In the autobiographical fragment begun 26 September 1798, b228/9, Godwin says that his first passion was for poetry but he did not know what it was for the first thirty years of his life. Hazlitt is also interesting on Godwin's changing attitude to poetry in *The Spirit of the Age*.
8 In the essay 'Elia' in *The Spirit of the Age*.
9 In 'On the Literary Character' in *The Round Table*.
10 'The Two Races of Men' in *Elia*.
11 b229/4. Original marginalia printed in *Harvard Library Bulletin*, 1953.
12 c604/3. Although brief, these unpublished notes report facts about Coleridge's early life which are not known from other sources, e.g. that in 1793 he led a sexually loose life and had spent the night before he enlisted in a brothel; that in 1794 Southey was still a virgin. Other unpublished notes on Coleridge, b229/2 and b229/4, some of which are quoted below.
13 b229/2. Godwin has slipped from reported speech to direct quotation, hence the confusing change from 'my' to 'you' But the sense is clear.
14 Godwin to Coleridge, 5 September 1800, MS Morgan.
15 b229/4.
16 b229/2. *Coleridge's Letters*, II, 1056. The conversation occurred on 2 February 1804.
17 Explictly acknowledged in, for example, c663/4.
18 Godwin to unknown correspondent, 4 September 1800, b227/8. During the argument on 2 February 1804 Coleridge accused him of not understanding Spinoza – he had 'perhaps looked at the outside of the book'. b229/2.
19 b229/4.
20 *Enquirer*, p. 370.
21 J records reading *Lyrical Ballads* on 11 April 1799, 11 December 1800, 1 March 1801 and 8 March 1801. He discussed the book with Northcote on 9 May 1801, J.

22 *Coleridge's Letters*, II, 714 and 738.
23 b229/6.
24 b214/3, n.d. Identified from handwriting.
25 Manuscript of *Antonio* with Lamb's comments and amendments, Morgan. There is also an interesting spiteful letter from Stoddart to Coleridge, 7 January 1801.
26 Hazlitt, *Collected Works*, XVII, 319.
27 'Artificial Comedy of the Last Century' in *Elia*.
28 *Lamb's Letters*, I, 230.
29 Summarized in Pollin. See also Charlotte Smith's sad farewell, 19 December 1800, b227/2, identified from handwriting.
30 *Lamb's Letters*, I, 237.
31 *Coleridge's Letters*, I, 656.
32 *Coleridge's Letters*, II, 742.
33 Not previously known, now deposited as c663/2. Coleridge's authorship of the comments identified from the handwriting. A few others are in another hand.
34 Mostly quoted in KP.
35 The lengths to which the Government were driven in trying to uphold popular respect for King and Church are well illustrated by the changes required by the Lord Chamberlain in the plays submitted to his censorship. Godwin's reference to the 'Seraglio of Charles Stuart' in *Faulkener* was altered to 'Gallery of Charles the Second'. MS Huntington.

CHAPTER 18

Neither the complexity of the Clairmont problem nor the extent of the deception was appreciated until the publication of two articles by Herbert Huscher in *KSMB*. 'Charles Gaulis Clairmont' in VIII, 1957 and 'The Clairmont Enigma', which partially supersedes it, in XI, 1960. By following the de Vial and Pilcher connections, I have been able to add further facts from parish and other official records in England and in France.

I have only noted points which modify or add to Huscher. See also note 32 to Chapter 21. Godwin's surviving correspondence with Mary Jane, c523. Large extracts are quoted in KP.

1 For family traditions about Mrs Clairmont see Maude Rolleston, *Talks with Lady Shelley*, 1925, and remarks in KP which derive from the same source. Lady Shelley may have drawn information from documents later destroyed.
2 Holborn Rate Books, Polygon, May 1801, mention 'Mary Jane Claremont' as paying £4-4-0 and 'William Godwin' paying £3-9-3. Archives of London Borough of Camden. For The Polygon, see Chapter 13, note 22.
3 *Lamb's Letters*, I, 273.
4 The events surrounding the birth and death of William I cannot be reconstructed with confidence. The St Leonard's record may refer to another family altogether, although the names Godwin and Goodwin are frequently confused. No burial record found, but curious entry in J for 21 June 1802, 'Call on White, FTC, incog[n]'. FTC usually means Fellow of Trinity College. On 12 June Godwin met 'Lanesborough SMLBD' probably St Marylebone General Dispensary, a charitable institution giving free medicine and advice including help for lying-in mothers. Lady Lanesborough was the wife of John King, the financier.
5 Thomas Robinson to his brother, 8 November 1803. MS, Dr Williams Library, UL.
6 Somers Town was greatly expanded by the influx of French refugees. They were thought to have been attracted to the area by the belief that St Pancras Church would give them Roman Catholic burial and that their souls would be prayed for in the church dedicated to the same saint in Rome. By the turn of the century the Abbé Carron had established

charity schools, an infirmary for the old, soup kitchens and other measures for the relief of *émigrés*. J. Norris Brewer, *Beauties of England*, vol. 10, part 4, 1816, p. 184.

7 Examples in Bentley.

8 Copy in Bodleian. Mary Jane's authorship proved by Godwin's letter to Leigh Hunt, 24 July 1835, Bodleian MS Eng. lett. c461. Not previously attributed.

9 Godwin to Mary Jane, 28 October 1803.

10 Mary Jane to Godwin, 3 June 1806.

11 Mary Jane to Godwin, September 1805.

12 Godwin to Mary Jane, 21 August 1809.

13 Godwin to Mary Jane, 5 April 1805.

14 Quoted Locke, p. 206.

15 The incident described near the end of *A Bachelor's Complaint* also almost certainly refers to Mrs Godwin.

16 Godwin to Knowles, 28 September 1826, quoted KP, II, 298.

17 Godwin to Holcroft, 9 September 1803, c511.

18 *Gentleman's Magazine* 1817 reports death at age of sixty-two of Sarah, widow of John Elwes of Portman Square. *Court Guide* of 1814 notes John Elwes living at Portman Square and Colesbourne, Glos. He was the second son of miser Elwes. He may be the same John Elwes who is noted in *Gent. Mag.* of 1789 as marrying Mrs Haynes, relict of Captain Haynes of the navy.

19 'two children by a former husband'. Godwin to Harwood, 28 February 1803, *SC*, I, 308. Same phrase used in another letter undated quoted KP, II, 129. For Devereux see also note 32 to Chapter 21.

20 *HCR*, I, 235.

21 'Write to L Pelham' J, 1 November 1801. The reply KP, II, 88. Records of the Aliens Office no longer exist.

22 Godwin met 'Trefusis', probably the poetess Ella on 9 February 1790, J. See also Beloe, I, 225 and 367. For Claire Clairmont's link with 'Trefusis' see Chapter 32.

23 According to Boyle's *Court Guide* James Weale was an official of the Inland Revenue.

24 From the J entry for 29 December 1800 'Character of MRⁿ' it seems likely that Godwin wrote an obituary of Mary Robinson but it has not been identified.

25 Edward Paul Pilcher married Sophia Elizabeth de Vial, Crediton, 25 January 1792. Edward Pilcher, Peter Pilcher, Sophia Pilcher, each baptized Barnstaple, 22 July 1796. Mormon Genealogical Index.

26 H. Incledon Pilcher to Godwin, 10 October 1820, from 'The Vines', b214/2.

27 Archives Départementales de la Loire, St Etienne, note marriage, 25 Nivôse, An 12 [i.e. 16 January 1804], of Pierre Valette and Charlotte Vialle said to be aged twenty-six and a half and born at Exeter 4 August 1777, 'fille majeure' of Pierre Vialle deceased and his widow 'viante' Catherine Okehe. Charlotte said to have lived about three years at an address in St Etienne. A record of 12 Nivôse, i.e. shortly before the marriage, which registers the birth of Leonard Valette, describes Pierre Valette and Charlotte Vial as married. Obviously some regularization was occurring. I am most grateful to Paula Feldman for going to St Etienne at my suggestion and for discovering and transcribing these records. A letter of H. M. Williams to Mary Jane, 24 April [1817], c526, refers to Charlotte as 'your sister'.

28 In one of her later doubtful letters to Lady Mountcashell (see notes to Chapter 27), Mary Jane said that 'three years ago I visited my sister at a little village called Lynmouth ... and have made acquaintance with Mrs Bicknell ...'. When Godwin visited Lynmouth in 1812 he made no reference to meeting a sister. Shelley had stayed with a Mrs Hooper whom Godwin called on. He also saw a Mrs Sandford. Possibly Mary Jane's sister was only on holiday in Lynmouth. More probably Mary Jane was telling a

deliberate lie to conceal the fact that it was Shelley who arranged for Claire to go to Lynmouth.

29 Parish records, St Thomas, Exeter, Devon Record Office. Peter de Vial Merchant of this parish and Catherine Oak of the same married 25 April 1782.

30 Huscher gives her age at death as seventy-three, probably drawing on a document. The tombstone in St Pancras gives seventy-five. Although parts of the stone have been recarved, this side appears to be original. A writer for the *Lady's Newspaper* of 12 April 1851 also read seventy-five as did others such as Ingpen. The St Etienne registers 26 November 1833 record that Catherine Oka, aged eighty-one, born Exeter, widow of Pierre Vial, was found dead at the Charité. Whether she was Mary Jane's mother or stepmother, there is no record that Mary Jane saw her when she visited St Etienne in 1817.

31 Exeter, St Paul's, 20 June 1764.

CHAPTER 19

1 Notes on early income and conversation with Caunter when he described his ambition to earn £100, rising by £10 a year, d474.

2 It seems from this and other references in J, and from his letter of 12 May 1789, MS Columbia University Library, that Holcroft persuaded Robinson to bail him.

3 See also Godwin to Wedgwood, 10 January 1798, quoted KP, I, 312. 'I love him less than most other men of equal talents and intentions, because I cannot reasonably doubt that when he drew so odious a picture of man he found some of the traits in his own bosom.' Wollstonecraft had been introduced to Johnson when she was young and the doctor's reputation was among the topics discussed at the unsatisfactory first meeting in 1791.

4 Godwin to King, 24 January 1796, b227/8, qoted KP, I, 155. King's reply, b214/3, partly quoted KP, I, 157.

5 Godwin to Curran, 3 February 1801, b227/2.

6 Information on the law on imprisonment for debt in Godwin's time is difficult to find, on the actual practice even more so. Best general account *Fourth Report . . . by the Commissioners appointed to inquire into the Practice and Proceedings of the Superior Courts of Common Law*, 1832. Also useful *Report of the Select Committee on Acts respecting Insolvent Debtors*, 1813.

7 S. C. Hall, *Retrospect of a Long Life*, 1883, I, 51.

8 Thomas Robinson to his brother, 16 August 1802, MS Dr Williams Library, UL.

9 Examples of contracts, Bentley.

10 Godwin to Marshall, 2 December 1806, b227/3. *Thoughts on Man*, III.

11 Godwin to Mrs Clairmont, 9 October 1801, c523, quoted KP, II, 75.

12 First reference to piles in Greek, 20 September 1792, J. Occasional references to evacuating 'cocu imaginaire'. See also suggestion in Chapter 39 that Godwin latterly suffered from rectal cancer.

13 b229/2.

14 The most readily accessible references to Newton's pamphlet are in the Notes to Shelley's *Queen Mab*.

15 *Monthly Mirror*, May 1805, reprinted in UW.

16 Nicholson to Godwin, 18 September 1797. Printed KP, I, 289.

17 Cowden Clarke, Chapter 3.

18 Godwin consulted a doctor called Combe almost as frequently as he consulted Carlisle, sometimes calling them both in for the same illness. Maybe he turned to one for the mind and the other for the body, but Godwin's William Combe was not the phrenologist although a member of the same family.

19 Sir G. S. Mackenzie, *Illustrations of Phrenology*, 1820. The portrait is reproduced in *UW* and Locke.
20 In *Thoughts on Man*.
21 *DNB*. A copy of the first edition of *Political Justice* with a few of his comments and Godwin's reply is in the Folger Shakespeare Library, Washington. Godwin told Hogg that Stewart was worth knowing for only then would a man know what a bore really was.
22 Stories in Hogg's *Shelley*. Godwin met Newton as early as 1795. On 14 January 1796 Godwin dined at Newton's with Wollstonecraft. Chester Street in J means Newton's house.
23 *DNB*, article by Richard Garnett. Godwin met him as early as 13 September 1796 and his name appears infrequently in J until near the end of Godwin's life. *The Empire of the Nairs* reprinted by Scholar in 1976 with introduction by Janet Todd. Godwin read it January 1810.

CHAPTER 20

1 For an interesting discussion about possible mottoes for the title page designed to emphasize these points, see the correspondence with an unknown friend (probably Marshall) in b229/3.
2 *Lamb's Letters*, I, 361.
3 Horne Tooke to Godwin, 6 December 1803, quoted KP, II, 105.
4 b229/2. See notes 16ff to Chapter 17.
5 Godwin's copied Southey's remarks in b229/9. See also the anti-Jacobin John Corry, *The Detector of Quackery*, 1802, which has interesting remarks on nervous cordial and balm of Gilead as well as on new philosophers, literary ladies, mesmerists and other targets.
6 See Chapter 19, note 10. Godwin wrote Southey a reasoned complaint, b227/8.
7 H. C. Robinson to his brother, MS, Dr Williams Library. Godwin did not mind. In a letter to Phillips, 19 July 1802, b227/8, he said he had no objection to making *Chaucer* 'the most inelegant book that was printed'. In another letter probably to Phillips, 6 February 1803, b229/1, he said that anyone who worried about such matters was 'the most egregious ass I ever heard of'.
8 Godwin to Wedgwood, 14 April 1804, c511, quoted KP, II, 124.
9 Quoted KP, II, 125.
10 Godwin read the *Theory of Moral Sentiments* on 20 December 1797 and 2 October 1798 and *The Vicar of Wakefield* on 6 October 1798.
11 From *Mary a Fiction*, Chapter 24. Piece included in *The Young Gentleman and Lady's Instructor*, 1809.
12 Quoted Amy Cruse, *The Englishman and his books in the Early Nineteenth Century*, 1930, p. 101.
13 Example quoted Leslie Stephen, *History of English Thought in the Eighteenth Century*, Chapter 9.
14 For *Fleetwood* see Kelly.
15 MS of *Fleetwood*, Pf., shows how Godwin toned down angry and combative tone of first draft of Preface. *SC*, I, 334.
16 *Fleetwood*, II, Chapter 13.
17 Ibid.
18 c511. Quoted KP, I, 49. This letter has usually been taken at face value as referring to 1785 but the quotation from it in Godwin's reply removes any remaining doubt.
19 *Fleetwood*, III, Chapter 17.
20 Godwin to Holcroft, 1 January 1805, c511.

21 Godwin to Holcroft, 3 March 1805, c511.

CHAPTER 21

Well covered in secondary sources. Some interesting remarks in *Hays* and *Fenwick*. Plans and financing described in letters to Tom Wedgwood, Josiah Wedgwood (MSs at Keele) and elsewhere. For the development of picture books see *A Nursery Companion* ed. by Peter and Iona Opie, 1980. See also *Children and their Books* ed. Gillian Avery and Julia Briggs, 1989, which contains an essay by myself on Godwin as children's bookseller. Godwin refers among his list of printed works to a children's book *Rural Walks*, 1806, of which no copy has been found. Possibly anonymous *Rustic Excursions* published by Phillips which proclaims (p. 81), 'You, my children, will, I trust, one day recal with rapture these rural walks.' Only known from copy in author's collection, dated 1811. That carries an advertisement among 'Elementary Books Recently Published' for *Scripture Histories or Bible Stories*, evidently Godwin's *Bible Stories* although without mention of Scolfield. Godwin may have been referring to 'Juvenile Accomplishments of Salt Hill', c532/9, the manuscript of a book for children not known to have been printed but written in 1806.

1 For full title see Bibliography. Godwin was proud of the little book which set out his views on the education of children. In *Letter of Advice to a Young American*, 1818, p. 4, *UW*, he recommends Beavan to read *The Enquirer* and 'more to the same purpose in the Preface to a small book for children, entitled "Scripture Histories, given in the words of the original" in two volumes 18mo'. In a manuscript note dated 2 January 1828, c604/2, he asks that works of Edward Baldwin, which he names, should be printed 'among my Miscellaneous Works from editions printed before 1825'. As an afterthought he adds, 'also the Preface to a book entitled Bible Stories'. J shows Godwin working on *Jewish Histories* during 1801 and 1802. By 25 April he is revising, normally a sign that publication is imminent. *English Catalogue of Books* reports publication in August 1802 of 'Bible Stories: Scolfield W 2 vols 4s'. No copy of the original edition found. Library of Smith College, Massachusetts, contains volume one of *Bible Stories, Memorable Acts of the Ancient Patriarchs, Judges, and Kings: extracted from their original historians for the use of children*, by William Scolfield, 2 volumes. A New edition. London. Printed for R. Phillips . . . 1803. Price 4s Half-bound. Copy of *Stories of Old Daniel*, author's collection, includes advertisement by Baldwin Craddock and Joy dated 1 January 1828 offering '*Sacred Histories . . . in the words of the original*, by William Scolfield'. *London Catalogue of Books*, 1831, lists 'Scholefield's *Sacred Histories*, 2 vol, Baldwin'. Andover-Harvard Theological Library contains a copy of an American reprint 'London, Printed: Albany. Reprinted by Charles R. and George Webster at their Bookstore, 1803'. Huntington contains a copy of another American edition, slightly different title, imprinted 'Wilmington, Printed for Matthew & Lockerman. Robert Porter, *Printer*. 1812'.

2 Geoffrey Summerfield, *Fantasy and Reason*, 1984.

3 Letters from Lady Mountcashell, 1800 and 1801, c507.

4 *Coleridge's Letters*, II, 982. Fuseli was among those who believed that children should be deliberately thwarted in order to develop inner strengths. *Thoughts on Man*, p. 48. Neither his character nor his paintings are a good advertisement for the theory.

5 A theme of letters to Turner and Patrickson. A fragmentary letter of Charles Clairmont, c530, refers to Godwin's disapproval of his reading the anti-religious works of Tom Paine.

6 See also Godwin to Cole, quoted KP, II, 118.

7 Godwin to Wedgwood, 25 March 1805, c511.

8 Wedgwood to Godwin, 28 March 1805, quoted KP, II, 141.

9 Godwin's known contributions to M. J. Godwin and Company, Bibliography.

10 *SC*, II, 563. Notes to *Pantheon* written by Dr Raine, c604/1.

11 Godwin to Sharp, 16 April 1806, b227/3.

12 *Enquirer*, p. 219.

13 See Ford K. Brown, *Notes on 41 Skinner Street*, *Modern Language Notes*, May 1939.

14 Godwin to Nicholson, 28 January 1810, b227/3.

15 Springsguth to Godwin, 1 July 1807, c507.

16 Fenwick's misfortunes described by Henry Crabb Robinson in letter to his brother, 21 December 1807. MS Dr Williams Library.

17 *Looking Glass*.

18 Contemporary directories confirm that 'John Godwin pocket book maker' had a shop in High Holborn. The spy report of 1813 read 'Mr J. Godwin' as the name on the shop in Skinner Street – see Chapter 30, note 3. Shelley's first letters to Godwin were addressed to him at 'Mr J. Godwin's Juvenile Library' perhaps implying that Southey had also misread the shop sign – see Chapter 23. Mrs Fenwick's *Rays of the Rainbow*, 1812, is described on the cover as published by 'J. M. Godwin'.

19 William Frederick [or –ic] Mylius, described as a schoolmaster of Red Lion Square, sounds like a pseudonym, but he appears in J.

20 Godwin to Lamb, 10 March 1808, quoted *Lamb's Letters*, II, 54.

21 *Lamb's Letters*, II, 53.

22 Godwin to Wordsworth, 5 March 1811. MS Dove Cottage.

23 b229/3.

24 Godwin to Coleridge, 27 March 1811. MS Film 74.

25 It is puzzling that M. J. Godwin and Company should have been the first to publish this book in England. Lady Mountcashell's eldest son married a Maria Wyss of Berne and there may be a connection. It is not certain, despite claims in the first edition, that Godwin's version was taken from the German original and not from the French translation.

26 Godwin to Mrs Fordham, 13 November 1811, b214/3, quoted by Mrs Julian Marshall, *Life and Letters of Mary Wollstonecraft Shelley*, 1889, I, 35.

27 Quoted Durant's edition of *Memoirs*, op. cit., p. 246.

28 A. Hamilton to Everina Wollstonecraft, 8 March 1805, b214/3.

29 See note 6 to Chapter 14. Fanny would also have read Mary Wollstonecraft's prediction that her child would blush for her mother's want of prudence – quoted in Appendix 1.

30 Mrs Julian Marshall, op. cit., I, 34.

31 Reprinted in *A Nursery Companion*. Attribution to Mary Godwin rests on Godwin's letter of 2 January 1808 to ? Burdett, known only from extract in a bookseller's catalogue. In her forthcoming biography *Mary Shelley: Romance and Reality*, Little, Brown and Company, Boston, 1989, Emily Sunstein conjectures, mainly from internal evidence, that the books published later by M. J. Godwin and Company under the name of Mrs Caroline Barnard may have been written by Mary. There are references to a 'Barnard' in J but not at the times when the books were being produced.

32 As a dissenter Godwin made his registrations at Dr Williams Library. Original in Public Record Office, Chancery Lane. Charles Clairmont was registered 9 February 1802. 'Charles Gaulis son of Charles Clairmont and Mary Jane his wife who was Daughter of Andrew Peter Devereux was born in Bridge Street Bristol in the Parish of St Nicholas the fourth day of June 1795 at whose birth we were present [signed] John Newman surgeon, [?] Cudlett Healett.' No record found at Bristol. Registration of William Godwin Junior's birth 8 November 1803, Godwin's handwriting, also describes Mary Jane as 'daughter of Peter Andrew Devereux'.

33 Godwin's memoir in *Transfusion*. Bibliography.

CHAPTER 22

1 Godwin to Smart, 12 January 1801, b227/2. He became a regular visitor.
2 Chatterton to Godwin, 27 September 1803, b215/1.
3 Now on public exhibition in NYPL.
4 Benjamin Silliman [not a pseudonym], *Letters of Shahcoolen*, 1802.
5 *Private Journal of Aaron Burr*, 1838. Burr was interesting to Godwin not only for having killed a man in a duel but as the grandson of Jonathan Edwards.
6 Godwin to Burr, 26 April 1809, quoted in *Private Journal.*
7 Turner to Godwin, 4 July 1803, c528.
8 Turner to Godwin, 19 May 1822, c525.
9 Correspondence with Patrickson, b228/8. Extensively quoted KP. It may be Patrickson that Godwin mentions as having written six comedies, *Thoughts on Man*, p. 54. Godwin met a Patrickson, perhaps the father, on 8 April 1796, J.
10 Godwin to Patrickson, 28 January 1812, b228/8.
11 Alexander Walker to Godwin, n.d., c526.
12 Lisle to Godwin, n.d., b215/6.
13 Lisle to Godwin, 3 September 1812, c530.
14 *New Annual Register for 1812*, p. 17. Godwin quoted the case to Shelley in his letter of 4 March 1812 on the duties of wealth, copy c524.

> When Mr Walsh resolved to purloin to his own use a few thousand pounds with which to settle himself, and his family and children in America, he tells us that he was for some time anxious that the effects of his fraud should fall upon Mr Oldham, rather than upon Sir Thomas Plomer because in his opinion Sir Thomas was the better man. And I have no doubt that he was fully persuaded that a greater sum of happiness would result from these thousand pounds being employed in settling his innocent and lovely family in America than in securing to his employer the possession of a large landed estate.

15 *Holcroft*, I, 38.
16 21 December 1809.
17 Godwin to Millar, n.d., b215/1.
18 b227/2. Identified only from handwriting and attribution not certain. From Lamb's letters it appears that he admired everything in the book except the actual proposal.
19 *Essay on Death*, 6 October 1810, b227/1.
20 c607/2. Place's papers BL. See also Graham Wallas, *Life of Francis Place*, 1898. Place's estimate that Godwin muddled away £1,500 a year during the ten years 1804–14 need not be taken as authoritative. Most of Godwin's borrowings were to repay or roll over other debts, not for spending.
21 Extensive correspondence with Fairley, b228/7. Hepburn's interesting life described in *East Lothian Biographies* by W. Forbes Gray and J. H. Jamieson, Haddington, 1940. Article of 1796 said to be in the *London Review* which describes meetings with Danton, Marat, and Robespierre not found.
22 Godwin to Mary Jane, 18 May 1811, c523, quoted KP, II, 182.
23 Godwin to Mary Jane, 10 June 1811, c523.
24 MS Keele.
25 Mary Jane to Godwin, 14 August 1811, c523.
26 HCR, I, 43. Godwin to Robinson, 15 August b227/3. Addressee identified from J.
27 *Shelley's Letters*, I, 219.
28 *Shelley's Letters*, I, 227.

CHAPTER 23

Shelley's early letters to Godwin are carefully printed from originals in *Shelley's Letters*, and need not be noted in detail. Godwin's replies are only available in print in highly edited and selective nineteenth-century extracts. Some originals and copies of originals, c524. Quotations from others come from Shelley's replies.

1 *Shelley's Letters*, I, 230 quoting a lost letter from Godwin of 13 January.
2 Godwin to Shelley, copy dated by Godwin, 4 March 1812.
3 Shelley's letter of 26 December 1812, *Shelley's Letters*, I, 214, makes clear that he was aware of the differences in the editions. Quotations and source references in *Queen Mab* and *Refutation of Deism* are to the third edition. A copy of the first edition with comments and sidelinings by Shelley in the margins of volume one is described in *SC*, VII: these were however probably made in 1820.
4 Quoted *Shelley's Letters*, I, 219.
5 See also Chapter 21, note 18.
6 J notes 'Circular 2 pp' on 27 May 1812, the day after Eaton stood in the pillory.
7 *Adeline Mowbray*, II, 193. See Chapter 14, note 29.
8 Shelley to Hitchener, 8 October 1811, *Shelley's Letters*, I, 144.
9 Preface to *Fleetwood*. For Godwin's draft SC, I, 345.
10 Shelley to Godwin, 26 January 1812, *Shelley's Letters*, I, 243, quoting Godwin's lost letter of 20 January.
11 Godwin to Shelley, copy dated by Godwin, 4 March 1812.
12 Godwin to Shelley, 14 March 1812, copy.

CHAPTER 24

1 Godwin to Hammond, 13 July 1812, b227/3.
2 e.g. *HCR*, I, 61, 109. Thomas Poole was amongst those approached, MS V and A. Jokes about Godwin 'picking pockets' refer to the same habit.
3 Godwin to Shelley, copy dated by Godwin, 30 March 1812, c524.
4 Godwin to Shelley, copy n.d., c524.
5 'Execution' J.
6 Godwin to Mary Jane, 11 September 1812, c523.
7 Godwin to Mary Jane, 19 September 1812, c523.
8 Godwin to Mary Jane, n.d., from Barnstaple, c523.
9 Godwin to Mary Jane, 19 September 1812, c523.
10 Godwin to Mary Jane, 26 September 1812, BL Ashley MS, reprinted *Ashley Library*.
11 Quoted *Shelley's Letters*, I, 327.

CHAPTER 25

Notes of the conversations J. Other indications in their exchanges of letters and anecdotes quoted in Dowden, Hogg's *Shelley* and elsewhere.

1 Quoted Grylls, p. 280. Also in MS Shelley, c1. See introductory note to Chapter 27.
2 MacGinn in *Maclise Portrait Gallery*, 'William Godwin'. The joke does not quite work.
3 Lady Byron's statements quoted Malcolm Elwin, *Lord Byron's Wife*, 1962, pp. 258, 340, 456. This book also provides the most direct evidence of Byron's admiration for *Caleb Williams*, p. 110, and of its influence on the Byronic hero, p. 364.
4 Preface to *Werner* written in February 1822.
5 Godwin to William Godwin Junior, incomplete probably late 1816, b227/3.

6 See Appendix 3.

7 b229/4. Evidently the piece referred to in J for 26 December 1813 'On Poetry 1 page' the day he read 'Queen Mab, passim'. Confirmation is provided by the significant hand for which see Appendix 3.

8 In the second article on Walking Stewart in *London Reminiscences*.

CHAPTER 26

1 'On Beggars', recast in 1823 edition.

2 Godwin had met Maddocks once before at a dinner at Johnson's in 1810.

3 Godwin to Place, 29 November 1811, MS BL.

4 SC, 1, 365.

5 'Mr Owen's "New View of Society" Etc.' in *Political Essays*.

6 Godwin to Josiah Wedgwood, 30 August 1813, MS Keele.

7 Godwin to Place, 5 September 1813, MS BL.

8 b227/3. This is essay *On Fortitude* 1 page noted in J for 26 December 1813. On same day he wrote 'On Poetry 1 page' [the remarks on *Queen Mab*]. He also read six chapters of Seneca, *Ad Helviam*.

CHAPTER 27

For events of July 1814 and later we are offered many vivid details in letters from Mary Jane to Mountcashell which were put on sale by Claire Clairmont late in the nineteenth century. The originals were not bought by the Shelley family, but Dowden kept copies, used them to inform his text, and quoted abstracts. Another set of abstracts which varies considerably is at MS Shelley, c1. The originals were later in the possession of Maurice Buxton Forman who permitted Rosalie Glynn Grylls (Lady Mander) to transcribe other sections in her *Claire Clairmont*. Their present whereabouts is unknown. Claire introduced substantial distortions in her copying, and the letters were not very truthful to begin with, but they undoubtedly contain genuine material. See also *Letters about Shelley*.

1 *Fleetwood*, 1, Chapter 8.

2 On 14 May Godwin presented Mary with a copy of *Essay on Sepulchres*. The occasion was Fanny's birthday and also the day he recovered from his latest attack of fits. Inscribed 'Mary Wollstonecraft Godwin' it may have been intended to prepare her for the day when he too would lie in St Pancras Churchyard. NYPL.

3 The square monumental stone erected over the grave of Mary Wollstonecraft can still be seen in the churchyard of Old St Pancras Church, although the stonework has been renewed. The grave was not where the stone now stands but in the north east of the churchyard in the area which was converted to railway use after 1851. The stone can be seen in Plate 12 at the right of the church between the trees. That picture was made in 1815 at about the time when Shelley and Mary spent time there, and the tall hunched young man on the bank even has a Shelleyan appearance. The stone can be seen more clearly in the engraving by George Cooke dated 1827 in Cooke's *Views in London and its Vicinity*. The opening of the extension to the churchyard, where Wollstonecraft was buried, had made St Pancras a more pleasant place than most London churchyards which were overcrowded and – in Godwin's phrase – odoriferous at this time. But the old churchyard nearby was no lawned garden. C. F. Webb, writing in the *New Monthly Magazine* in May 1815 reported that many tombs were dilapidated, coffins were broken open, and bones scattered everywhere. J. Norris Brewer in *Beauties of England*, 1816, volume 10, part 4, p. 173, noted that willow trees had been planted on either side of Wollstonecraft's monument, but 'the soil is not genial and the trees do not flourish'. A

correspondent for the *Lady's Newspaper* of 12 April 1851, who witnessed the clearances being made for the railway contractors, noticed that Wollstonecraft's monument was scattered in many places about the burial ground. Thomas Hardy was the assistant architect who supervised – often at night – the digging up and removal of hundreds of corpses, an experience he was often to draw on in his novels.

4 Copied from original. Huntington.

5 For Wollstonecraft's relationship with Schlabrendorf, Flexner with source references. Original papers destroyed during the Second World War.

6 Godwin to Shelley, 10 July 1814. Copy sold by Sotherans 1923, Catalogue 784, no. 841, described as 9½ pages folio. J notes 'Write to Shelley' on 8 and 9 July, 'PBS p$\frac{10}{2}$' 10 July, and 'PBS p 10' on the 11th. This and the copy of the letter of 25 July are presumably the copies, made by Charles and Jane Clairmont, which Godwin describes in his letter to Taylor of 27 August 1814, *Elopement*. Sotherans have no record of who bought the manuscripts – I hope this footnote will help bring them to light.

7 *Stanza, written at Bracknell*.

8 Copy of a letter in the handwriting of Tom Turner, n.d., watermark 1807, c529.

9 Dowden, II, 544.

10 Godwin to Shelley, 25 July 1814. Copy quoted in Sotherans Catalogue, op. cit.

11 Godwin to Patrickson, 30 July 1814, quoted KP, II, 198.

CHAPTER 28

1 *Clairmont's Journal*, p. 31.

2 It is possible that Godwin deliberately kept the *Memoirs* from his children. Alone of Godwin's books it is not mentioned in the letters or journals of Shelley or of Mary until 1820. A later MS list of Godwin's major works in his handwriting, NYPL, omits it. No copy in *Sale Catalogue*. By 1814 it had been long out of print. 'Read Memoirs' in *Clairmont's Journal* for 3 September 1814 has been taken to show that the runaways had a copy with them, but Claire is probably referring to Barruel's *Memoirs of Jacobinism*.

3 See note 2 to Chapter 27.

4 Godwin to Taylor, 27 August 1814, *Elopement*.

5 Ibid.

6 See note 6 to Chapter 27.

7 See introduction to notes to Chapter 27.

8 Godwin had met Stone on 15 June 1792. The deal offered by the two brothers would have been very unfavourable and risky to them. By taking a partnership, they would have made themselves responsible for all Godwin's debts.

CHAPTER 29

Main sources *Shelley's Letters*, *Mary Shelley's Letters*, *Mary Shelley's Journals*, *Clairmont's Journal*, and other original documents printed in Dowden and elsewhere.

1 'Write to PBS' J. Text lost but quoted by Shelley, *Shelley's Letters*, I, 398.

2 *Epipsychidion*, 149.

3 Quoted *Shelley's Letters*, I, 421.

4 See note 18 to Chapter 33.

CHAPTER 30

1 The story, in *Biographia Literaria*, need not be taken entirely seriously.

2 See P. W. Clayden, *The Early Life of Samuel Rogers*, 1887, p. 283.

3 Quoted Denis Florence MacCarthy, *Shelley's Early Life*, 1872, p. 161, from TS 11/951/ 3494 in the Public Record Office.

4 Not found in any of the copies I have examined.

5 *KSMB*, 1961. Godwin met a Leeson at a dinner attended by prominent Irishmen on 7 February 1796.

6 See note 18 to Chapter 8. Brockden Brown's ancestor, Charles Brockden, had emigrated after taking part in a conspiracy against Charles II.

7 Shelley adds c7.

8 *Mary Shelley's Journals*, 23 March 1815.

9 Mary Jane to Mountcashell, 28 July 1815. Dowden, II, 549. It is this remark which has caused commentators to call Godwin's undated letter to Shelley 'I return your cheque . . .' the 'freezing letter', but in fact it refers to October 1816. See note 13 to Chapter 33.

10 *Shelley's Letters*, I, 442.

11 Ibid., 443.

12 Ibid., 450.

13 Ibid. See e.g., *CW*, p. 6, 'He avoided the busy haunts of men.'

14 Ibid., 453.

15 Godwin to Shelley, 23 February 1816. Misquoted *Shelley's Letters*, I, 454. See Peck, I, 437 and *SC*, IV, 615.

16 *Shelley's Letters*, I, 459.

17 Ibid., 460.

18 Godwin to Shelley, 6 March 1816. MS Huntington. A draft kept as a copy: Godwin did not keep a copy of the passage about money.

19 Godwin to Shelley, 7 March 1816, *Shelley's Letters*, I, 461, corrected from the original draft, Huntington.

CHAPTER 31

1 *Letters of Verax*, Bibliography.

2 b229/8, 8 December 1816.

3 Godwin to ? Poole, 24 May [1815], MS V and A.

4 Mackintosh to Sharp from Bombay, 9 December 1804. Godwin had his own copy presumably supplied by Sharp.

5 *Biographia Literaria*, Chapter 10.

6 Mary Shelley's Note on Shelley's Early Poems, published with most editions since 1839.

7 *HCR*, I, 183.

8 In his *Address to the Freeholders* . . . Peacock's letter quoted *Shelley's Letters*, II, 24.

9 Godwin to Constable, 18 December 1815, MS National Library of Scotland.

10 Or may have been George Mackenzie the phrenologist.

11 *Shelley's Letters*, I, 472.

CHAPTER 32

1 Dowden, II, 549. Although Mary Jane's letters are unreliable this phrase has a genuine Shelleyan ring. A slightly different version Grylls, p. 278.

2 From the version of the same letter in MS Shelley c1. This too rings true.

3 Claire's letters to Byron not yet published in full. Extensive extracts quoted in Prothero's edition of *Byron's Works*, III, 429ff, Grylls, *To Lord Byron* ed. George Paston and Peter Quennell, 1939; and Marchand, *Byron*, II, 604.

4 Hobhouse to Byron, 10 December 1810, *Byron's Bulldog, The Letters of John Cam*

Hobhouse to Lord Byron, ed. Peter W. Graham, Ohio, 1984, p. 57. See also note 22 to Chapter 18.

5 *Byron's Letters and Journals*, ed. Leslie A. Marchand, v, p. 16.

6 Or at any rate not a close relative. In old age Claire told William Graham that she was 'a connection by marriage with an uncle of mine', *Last Links with Byron, Shelley and Keats*, 1898, p. 79.

CHAPTER 33

1 'The Atheist: an incident at Chamonix' by Gavin de Beer in *On Shelley*, 1938. The letter to the *Christian Observer* from 'S' is probably by John Pye Smith, see note 2.

2 John Pye Smith, *Journal of a Tour on the Continent*, MS Bodleian.

3 For the Philanthropists and others who kept radicalism alive between the 1790s and the Chartists see Iain McCalman, *Radical Underworld*, 1988. Shelley may have been flaunting his connection with campaigners such as Erasmus Perkins. See also Appendix 3.

4 *Mont Blanc*, 77.

5 William St Clair, 'Bamming and Humming' in *Byron Journal*, 1979.

6 Inchbald to Godwin, 11 November 1816, c509.

7 Godwin's letters on the incident, MSs Huntington. For details SC, vi, 777ff.

8 Published in the spurious *Narrative of Lord Byron's Voyage to Corsica and Sardinia*, 1824.

9 Beloe, Chapter 50.

10 Usually mistranscribed 'Kingdom'. Contemporary directories list William Kingdon a stockbroker. He lent Godwin £75 at the time of his marriage in December 1801.

11 *Shelley's Letters*, I, 509.

12 Dowden, II, 53. Begins as a letter to Mary but ends as a plea to Shelley.

13 Copy in Fanny's handwriting, Bodleian MS Eng. Lett. c461. Another MS Shelley c1 and others. None dated. The so-called 'freezing letter' (see note 9 to Chapter 30). Usually misdated either to 1814 or to early 1816, but there can be little doubt that it is the letter mentioned in J for 3 October 1816, 'Write to PBS' and sent on the following day.

14 Peck, II, 437, lists a Shelley cheque for £200 dated 7 October made out to 'Joseph Hume Esq. or bearer'. A cheque for £200 made out in the same terms to Hume on 26 December 1815 can be shown to be intended for Godwin (Peck, II, 436 and I, 433). Another cheque for Godwin of June 1816 was made out to Martin the banker. 'I have put this name', Shelley wrote, 'supposing you would not like your own to be stated', *Shelley's Letters*, I, 478. Evidently it made no difference to Shelley how he addressed his cheques; in the vital matter of the October cheque he had simply been careless and as soon as his slip was pointed out he corrected it.

15 Quoted from *The Cambrian*, KP, II, 242.

16 See Chapter 34, note 11.

17 Godwin to Shelley, 13 October 1816, c524. Owing to a mistake by a nineteenth-century transcriber this remarkable letter has always been understood to be addressed to 'Mrs Shelley'. The original leaves no doubt that it was for 'Mr Shelley'. Godwin was still refusing to have direct dealings with Mary and, despite the custom of nineteenth-century biographers of calling her Mrs Shelley from the time of her elopement, Mary was still Miss Godwin.

18 HCR, I, 234.

19 Full account of the suicide with documents SC, IV, 769. All accounts that Harriet had been 'unfaithful' to Shelley before July 1814 appear to derive from Godwin quoting stories originating at Bracknell (i.e. from the Boinvilles). In addition to previously known sources on this point, see Dowden to Garnett, 8 July 1884, Thurman, p. 230, 'Miss Stuart of Cambridge has 400 letters of Godwin in one of which he most definitely states

Harriet was faithless to Shelley before Shelley left England in 1814.' Perhaps the letter of 12 May 1817 to Baxter quoted *Shelley's Letters*, I, 528. The Shelley family took such remarks as conclusive despite the scholarly caution of Dowden. For the agonizings of nineteenth-century biographers about whether to use the word 'prostitution' see *Letters about Shelley*. See also Chapter 40.

CHAPTER 34

1 *HCR*, I, 199.
2 *Shelley's Letters*, I, 521.
3 Grylls, p. 272. Doubtful but *ben trovato*.
4 *Shelley's Letters*, I, 525.
5 Mary Jane to Constable, 3 February 1817, MS National Library of Scotland.
6 Godwin to Hull Godwin, 21 February 1817, *Elopement*, quoted KP, II, 246.
7 Godwin to Baxter, 12 May 1817, MS NYPL.
8 *Mary Shelley's Letters*, I, 26.
9 *Shelley's Letters*, I, 539.
10 Shelley adds c5. Quoted Dowden, II, 86. Dowden misjudged the handwriting and did not appreciate the purport of the amendments.
11 Godwin to Mary Jane, 2 June 1817, quoted KP, II, 250.
12 *SC*, v, 391.
13 Well discussed, quoting Haydon, in Ann Blainey, *Immortal Boy, A Portrait of Leigh Hunt*, 1985.
14 In 'On Paradox and Commonplace' in *Table-Talk*.
15 A speculation. No confirmation found in the records of the Royal Society or the papers of Sir Joseph Banks. For travellers' stories about the Nayar, current in Godwin's day and earlier, *Castes and Tribes of Southern India*, Madras, 1909.

CHAPTER 35

1 *Life, Letters and Journals of George Ticknor*, 1876, I, 294.
2 Rosser's letters c532/1.
3 J, 10 January 1819.
4 'Subscription', J, 29 November 1817.
5 Benjamin Robert Haydon, *Diary*, v, 39.
6 'dine at Shelley's w MJ adv. L. Hunt and Keates' J.
7 'An unnoticed early biographical sketch of Keats by Forbes Benjamin Winslow', *Modern Language Notes*, 1981, 'Hunt showed some of Keats's poetry to Godwin, Hazlitt, and Basil Montagu who were very much struck with its beauty.' This occasion noted in J for 16 February 1817, 'Dine at L. Hunts w. Shelleys, Hazlits, and B. Montagu adv. Colson, Gatty, and Clarke.'
8 These, with previous reference, are the only occasions when Godwin met Keats which are noted in J. Reference for 26 December 1817 a corrected error.
9 Keats's copy of Baldwin's *Pantheon, Keats Circle: Letters and Papers*, ed. Hyder Edward Rollins, 1948, I, 258. Cowden Clarke, p. 124 refers to his reading Tooke's *Pantheon* but either this is an error or Keats possessed both.
10 '. . . ½ Endymion . . .' and 'Endymion, fin:'.
11 Possibly not Keats's 'Isabella or the Pot of Basil'.
12 Noted also by Aileen Ward, *John Keats*, 1963, p. 429.
13 Quoted *Critical Heritage*, p. 131. Mary Shelley and Medwin later suggested that the old men in *Athanase* and *Laon and Cythna* were drawn from Dr Lind. Following SC, VII, 110, I no longer call the poem *Prince Athanase*.

14 Unidentified friend to Godwin, 22 January 1796, c607. 'You urge that on Sunday you will have an interview with your fair mistress Cynthia.'

15 MS Shelley d3. Manuscripts of *Laon and Cythna* which reveal Shelley's first thoughts not yet satisfactorily edited. The name in the Dedication was to have been given in full.

16 e.g. MS Shelley d3, among drafts of the passage about the eagle and the snake.

17 Godwin to Shelley, 27 June 1817, c524. Verses in Shelley's handwriting, difficult to decipher. Previously unpublished. 'Threnode' a variation on threnody not previously recorded in English as far as I know.

18 Godwin to Shelley, 29 April 1817, *SC*, v, 200.

19 *SC*, v, 206.

20 Booth to Isabel Booth, 9 January 1818. Cited *SC*, v, 390. Date from J 'dine at Shelleys adv. Curry, Baxter & Booth'.

21 b229/7.

22 Quoted in Shelley to Godwin, 11 December 1817, *Shelley's Letters*, I, 578.

23 In 'On Paradox and Commonplace' in *Table-Talk*.

24 See p. 343.

25 The dating of the Preface emerges from Shelley to Lackingtons, 28 November 1817:

> Mr Shelley presents his compt.ˢ to Mess.ˢ Lackington & begs to inform them that he has, as yet, recieved no proof of the preface or the title of frankenstein.
>
> Mr. S. suggests the advantage of announcing it by advertisement once before publication; as much expectation of its success has been excited in a particular circle, which such an announce might improve into a demand.
>
> Marlow, Nov. 28th 1817

This letter has not been printed hitherto other than in my inaccessible essay for the Pennyroyal Private Press, *Frankenstein*, 1984.

26 See *The Endurance of Frankenstein*, ed. George Levine, 1979, p. 168. The earliest reference I know of is in 1837 by de Quincey in 'Mr Godwin' in *London Reminiscences*.

27 *Shelley: Prose Works*, ed. Harry Buxton Forman, 1880, III, 9. Purpose and dating not certain. Claire Clairmont notes 17 January 1818, *SC*, v, 451, that she was writing part of a criticism of *Frankenstein* which could be a contributory draft or possibly a fair copy.

28 Shelley's part emerges from a comparison of two drafts in c524. One version, in Mary's hand, includes a few suggestions inserted in Shelley's hand. In the other, the final version which was printed, he rewrote the whole passage. The changes have the effect of elevating the language. Phrases that could appear trite are removed or worked up; some sentences are lengthened to give greater dignity; a few striking words are introduced, e.g. 'strangled', 'abortion'. As an example, Mary's version of the last sentence – 'Pushing himself off I soon lost sight of him in the darkness and distance' – is altered to 'He was soon borne away by the waves and lost in darkness and distance.'

29 Godwin to George Bartlay, 21 July 1823, asking about *Presumption or the Fate of Frankenstein*, MS Pf. proves that the adaptation like the *Iron Chest* was staged without permission from the original author.

30 *Shelley's Letters*, I, 573. Copy inscribed 'From the author to Percy and Mary Shelley Nov. 30 1817', NYPL. Medwin says that it was generally believed that the character of Mandeville was based on that of Shelley but no other evidence. Story in any case not credible.

31 Ibid.

32 Godwin to Mrs Inchbald, 1 December 1817, MS V and A. Second edition was to be called 'A Dream of the Seventeenth Century'.

33 KP, II, 252.

CHAPTER 36

1 Godwin to Shelley, 31 January 1818, c524.
2 Godwin to Josiah Wedgwood, 5 March 1817, MS Keele.
3 Fairley to Mary Jane, 17 January 1817, b228/7. See also Chapter 22, note 21.
4 Godwin to Shelley, 8 June 1818, c524.
5 That Joseph went to prison is noted by Hull Godwin (note 5 to Chapter 4). Details and dates from J.
6 Shelley adds c12. Previously unpublished. Godwin's letter probably much earlier than Byron's date. In writing to Lady Mountcashell in France in time of war Godwin signed at least one letter 'Caleb William', perhaps as a joke, more probably to confuse the interceptors of the mail.
7 Two versions dated November 1821 in editions of 1822. Only the long version discusses the value of Greek history.
8 Godwin to Gisborne, 10 March 1818, d475.
9 *Maria Gisborne and Edward E. Williams, Their Journals and Letters.* ed. F. L. Jones, 1951.
10 Godwin to Mary, 30 March 1819, c524. 'Cenci pp 104' in J shows that Godwin read the complete play.
11 HCR, I, 279.

CHAPTER 37

1 'Call . . . Hunter (adv Malthus dextrae conjunctio)' J.
2 'meet Malthus, silent' J.
3 *Population*, p. 298.
4 c524. Quoted Dowden, II, 232 and elsewhere.
5 c524. Quoted KP, II, 269.
6 *Advice*, p. 19. See note 28 to Chapter 13.
7 *Shelley's Letters*, II, 224.
8 *The Letters of John Cam Hobhouse to Lord Byron*, ed. Peter W. Graham, Ohio, 1984, p. 228, 'muniments for the mind or body . . . cundums'.
9 MS Morgan. A substantial extract quoted P. M. S. Dawson, *Unacknowledged Legislators*, 1980, p. 49. Full publication and commentary by Eugene Murray forthcoming. A phrase in Mary Shelley's letter to Marianne Hunt of 24 March 1829 (*Mary Shelley's Letters*, I, 136), 'I could say a great many things to prove to you that a woman is not a field to be continually employed either in bringing forth or enlarging grain', has been taken as a reference to artificial birth control but I doubt if it can be so read.
10 Godwin to Mary, 19 April 1822, quoted *Shelley's Letters*, II, 423.
11 According to a letter of Lady Holland, 25 March 1823, Lady Caroline Lamb's *Ada Reis* 'was chiefly compounded by Godwin', *Elizabeth Lady Holland to her son 1821–1845*, ed. Earl of Ilchester, 1946, p. 18. If so there is little evidence in J although Godwin saw Lady Caroline a few times in 1822 and 1823. Nor is there much evidence of his influence on the style, which is almost unreadable. The book was written during one of the author's quieter intervals when she was limited to one bottle of sherry a day. J records Godwin reading *Ada Reis* right through on 10 April 1823, presumably from the printed version.
12 Quoted in a letter from Godwin to Taylor, 16 August 1822, from an extract MS copy in Library of Duke University, North Carolina.
13 1823 *Enquirer* has significant modifications from 1797 edition. Another edition, c.1835, made from sheets of 1823 entitled *Book of Knowledge*, author's collection.
14 Godwin to Lens, 24 September 1823, quoted KP, II, 286.

15 Ballantyne to Mrs Godwin, 16 December 1823, b211.
16 Thoughts on Waterloo Bridge, 1 September 1822, b227/5.

CHAPTER 38

1 Quoted *Critical Heritage*, p. 79.
2 Joseph Cottle, 'An Expostulatory Epistle to Lord Byron', first published 1823 in *Dartmoor and other Poems*.
3 *The Lion*, 5 December 1828. Referred to in Cyrus Redding's memoir of Shelley in the Galignani edition 1829, and frequently thereafter.
4 *Memories of Seventy Years, by one of a literary family*, ed. Mrs Herbert Martin, 1883, p. 81. See also Eliza Fenwick's letter of 10 December 1821, 'I abhor its author [*Queen Mab*] but infinitely more his wife who of all human beings is the object of my sincerest detestation', *Fenwick*, p. 215.
5 See note 14 to Chapter 14.
6 *Commonwealth*, I, 6.
7 Charles E. Robinson, 'Mary Shelley and the Roger Dodsworth Hoax', *Keats Shelley Journal*, 1975.
8 Through the kindness of Royal Assurance, successors to the Pelican Company, I have been permitted to examine certain papers relating to Shelley. A meeting of the Board on 2 December 1823 rejected claims under two policies of £2,000 each on the grounds that Shelley had 'perished at sea within the meaning of the clause exempting the Company for sea risk'. On an application of Messrs English of Bath who had an interest of £1,200 in one of the policies, the Company decided on 15 April 1824 to refund the premium on that policy. The Company's records also include a resolution of 28 November 1816 permitting Lord Byron 'to go anywhere he pleases except the East and West Indies at 2 guineas per cent in addition to the Table rates'.
9 Godwin to Colburn, 22 November 1824, MS V and A.
10 MSs University College London.
11 Surmised from Godwin's journal entries of 16 February 'Call on W. KB' [King's Bench] and 3 March 'W calls, liberated'. In the intervening days Godwin wrote him several letters. In J for December 1826 there are two mysterious entries 'W X', the second of which is followed by letters to him from his father on successive days.
12 Godwin's typically unrevealing entry in J for 5 February 1830 'St Anne's Soho' has led to the discovery of the parish marriage record of 'William Godwin of St George the Martyr Queen Square bachelor and Mary Louisa Eldred of this parish spinster'. Neither of William's parents signed the register.
13 Charles MacFarlane, *Reminiscences of a Literary Life*, 1917, p. 99. See also Morton D. Paley, *Apocalyptic Sublime*, 1986, p. 126.
14 Frances Wright to Godwin, 17 October 1827, c527.
15 *Threading My Way*, 1874.

CHAPTER 39

1 e.g. Godwin to Ollier, 1 March 1830, MS Pf.
2 Godwin to Blackwood, 1 June 1830, MS Pf.
3 Godwin to F. Reynolds, November 1831, MS Pf.
4 His tombstone now set in the East Wall, St John's, Waterloo Road, is still just legible. 'In / Memory of / William Godwin / Who died 8th September 1832 / Aged 29 years / I shall go to him but he / shall not return to me.'
5 See *Mary Shelley's Letters*, II, 128. Mary was probably referring to Hazlitt's comment – see Chapter 10 note 4. The 'Criticism on the Novels of Godwin' dated 1816, which

is included in the Bentley edition, is puzzling. Since there was no occasion for a review that year Mary is printing an old MS, perhaps a blurb like Shelley's note on *Frankenstein*. But who wrote it? Admiration for *Fleetwood*, interest in the pursuit theme, use of 'miscalled' are all highly Shelleyan but the piece as a whole is perhaps not quite strong enough to be attributable to his pen even allowing for editing.

6 b226/1, 9 October 1832.

7 c604.

8 I take this to be the meaning of 'ceris mal', '?moulded with wax' in J for 10 February 1831. Godwin looked through Spurzheim's book on 22 December 1830 before drafting the section on phrenology in *Thoughts*. He met him on 16 February 1831 and attended the lecture on 24 February. The phrase may however refer to an illness or a remedy.

9 For the ironies of this episode, Locke.

10 KP, II, 323. Cooke may have been a relative of the actor who played the Frankenstein Monster.

11 Quoted from J in KP, II, 331.

12 Mary Shelley to Hays, 20 April 1836. *Mary Shelley's Letters*, II, 269.

13 12 March 1827, copy, MS Pf.

CHAPTER 40

1 Application on behalf of Mrs Godwin, 10 May 1836, and her letter of thanks for £50, 16 May. Archives of Royal Literary Fund, London.

2 *Sale Catalogue*. A list of his books in Godwin's hand, MS Keats House, Rome.

3 Bodleian MS Eng. Lett. c461.

4 Note dated 30 June 1834, b227/1.

5 Later apologetically published, as an intellectual curiosity, under the less provoking title of *Essays never before printed*. Bibliography.

6 Editions of CW by Smith, 1836 (author's collection), Allman, 1838, Chambers 1839, and Cunningham, 1841, in addition to foreign reprintings. *Rights of Woman*, Cleave, 1841 (author's collection), and Strange, 1844.

7 See note 4 to Chapter 8.

8 The same punctiliousness can be seen in the Preface to Mary's *History of a Six Weeks Tour* which, written shortly after the marriage, talks of the travels of the author 'with her husband and sister', implying that she and Shelley were married at the time. In the 1840 reissue, remembering the scandal that had attached to Claire, Mary substituted 'friend' for 'sister'.

9 This was the published view of Robert Browning.

10 Thurman, p. 36. See also note 19 to Chapter 33.

11 *Letters about Shelley*, p. 191 discussing a remark in Hogg's *Shelley*.

12 C. Kegan Paul, *Memories*, 1899, p. 253. Sylva Norman, *Flight of the Skylark*, p. 215.

13 *Letters of Edward Dowden*, 1914, pp. 242, 261.

14 The documents themselves show plentiful traces of the weeding. See *Letters about Shelley*, p. 36 and elsewhere. A letter from Garnett to Lady Shelley, 3 August 1898, proves that he actively advised destruction of documents.

15 See note 14 to Chapter 14.

APPENDIX I

The main sources are J, *Wollstonecraft's Letters*, and *Godwin and Mary*. For the presuppositions of the time, including an interesting discussion of the Aristotle books, see Boucé. Wollstonecraft uses plentiful dashes in her letters, but that was part of her normal style and they have no significance.

1 For the identification of Lanesborough, see Chapter 18, note 4.
2 The suggestion that 'chance-medley' might imply a method of contraception was made by Tomalin.
3 *Tristram Shandy*, Book II, Chapter 7. The book was still sufficiently well known in 1858 for Hogg to be able to make a joke about it, Hogg's *Shelley*, p. 422.
4 *Tristram Shandy*, Book II, Chapter 12.

APPENDIX 2

1 *Vindication*, Chapter 5, section 2.
2 J. Marshall, *A Digest of All the Accounts*, 1833, table 28.
3 From *On the Genealogy of Ethics*, quoted in *The Foucault Reader* edited by Paul Rabinow, Penguin, 1984, p. 344.
4 See the *Wollstonecraft Bibliography* by Janet M. Todd. An interesting precursor, not least in view of the title, is *Female Rights Vindicated: or the Equality of the Sexes Morally and Physically Proved*, By a Lady, 1752.
5 The figures for the years before 1785 and after 1820, are for twenty-one other editions of the fifteen named authors plus *Essays addressed to Young Married Women* by Mrs Griffith of which there were three editions in 1782.
6 Extracted from Sir John Sinclair, *History of the Public Revenue*, 1803, and Marshall, op. cit.
7 In 1784, after persuading her sister Eliza to leave her husband, Wollstonecraft lost the friendship of a certain Mrs Brook who was said to be following an advice book, *Wollstonecraft's Letters*, p. 86. The book was probably Griffith (see note 5) p. 93.

APPENDIX 3

For earlier discussions of the Erasmus Perkins problem, see White and the sources he quotes, and Louise Schutz Boas, *Harriet Shelley*, 1962, and her article in *Modern Language Notes*, 1955.

1 *Mary Shelley's Journals*, I, 62. Greek corrected.
2 Iain McCalman, *Radical Underworld, Prophets Revolutionaries and Pornographers in London 1795–1840*, 1988.
3 *Cobbett's Political Register*, 4 September 1813. Attributed to Cannon by McCalman, p. 257, note 46.
4 e.g. *The Adventures of Lazarillo de Tormes*, Benbow, 1821; Louvet de Couvray, *The Amours of the Chevalier de Faublas*, Benbow, 1822.
5 e.g. Benbow has the title *Queen Mab, A Philosophical Poem* in full. Clark follows the original's abbreviation of 'Disc' in the note to VI, 198. But whichever of the two was first, his successor consulted him on the translations of the foreign language quotations in the Notes: both mistranslate '*ceteris paribus*'.
6 Quoted *Critical Heritage*, p. 74.
7 One copy BL, rebound, another in original boards, author's collection. The last leaf advertises three other books obtainable from the same publisher – Moore's *Melodies* which must be the 'Pisa' edition, and two anti-religious works, Tom Paine's *Age of Reason* 'for the use of schools' and *The Three Impostors* 'printed uniformly with Watts's *Hymns*'. No copy of either of the latter two has been traced.
8 Copies BL, author's collection. Charles H. Taylor, *The Early Collected Editions of Shelley's Poems*, 1958, p. 11 notes the prosecution of Benbow for omitting his name as printer.

9 Joel H. Wiener, *Radicalism and Free Thought in Nineteenth Century Britain, The Life of Richard Carlile*, 1983, p. 30.

10 The Republican, v, p. 146.

11 'Erasmus Perkins', *The Trial of Reverend Robert Wedderburn*, 1820.

12 See McCalman. Clark and Clarke are probably the same person. Certainly Clark's name appears without the e both in *Queen Mab* and in his later edition of *Don Juan*.

13 Demonstrated by Taylor, op. cit.

14 e.g. *The Republican*, 6 May 1825.

15 *Critical Heritage*, p. 80.

16 *Critical Heritage*, p. 91.

17 See McCalman, p. 74.

Index